DONALD CREIGHTON
A LIFE IN HISTORY

A member of the same intellectual generation as Harold Innis, Northrop Frye, and George Grant, Donald Creighton (1902–1979) was English Canada's first great historian. The author of eleven books, including *The Commercial Empire of the St Lawrence* and a two-volume biography of John A. Macdonald, Creighton wrote history as if it "had happened," he said, "the day before yesterday." And as a public intellectual, he advised the prime minister of Canada, the premier of Ontario, and – at least on one occasion – the British government.

Yet he was, as Donald Wright shows, also profoundly out of step with his times. As the nation was re-imagined along bilingual and later multicultural lines in the 1960s and 1970s, Creighton defended a British definition of Canada at the same time as he began to fear that he would be remembered only "as a pessimist, a bigot, and a violent Tory partisan."

Through his virtuoso research into Creighton's own voluminous papers, Wright paints a sensitive portrait of a brilliant but difficult man. Ultimately, *Donald Creighton* captures the twentieth-century transformation of English Canada through the life and times of one of its leading intellectuals.

DONALD WRIGHT is an associate professor in the Department of Political Science at the University of New Brunswick.

DONALD CREIGHTON
A LIFE IN HISTORY

Donald Wright

UNIVERSITY OF TORONTO PRESS
Toronto Buffalo London

ISBN 978-1-4426-4947-7 (cloth)
ISBN 978-1-4426-2682-9 (paper)

Printed on acid-free, 100% post-consumer recycled paper with vegetable-based inks

Library and Archives Canada Cataloguing in Publication

Wright, Donald A., 1965–, author
Donald Creighton : a life in history / Donald Wright.

Includes bibliographical references and index.
ISBN 978-1-4426-4947-7 (bound)   ISBN 978-1-4426-2682-9 (pbk.)

1. Creighton, Donald, 1902-1979.   2. Historians – Canada – Biography.   I. Title.

FC151.C74W75 2015   971.0072'02   C2015-901757-2

This book has been published with the help of a grant from the Federation for
the Humanities and Social Sciences, through the Awards to Scholarly Publications
Program, using funds provided by the Social Sciences and Humanities Research
Council of Canada.

University of Toronto Press acknowledges the financial assistance to its publishing
program of the Canada Council for the Arts and the Ontario Arts Council, an agency
of the Government of Ontario.

Canada Council   Conseil des Arts
for the Arts   du Canada

ONTARIO ARTS COUNCIL
CONSEIL DES ARTS DE L'ONTARIO
an Ontario government agency
un organisme du gouvernement de l'Ontario

Funded by the   Financé par le
Government   gouvernement
of Canada   du Canada

For Frances, Harriet, and a black Lab named Holly

Contents

List of Illustrations   ix

Preface   xi

Creighton Family Tree   xvi

Introduction   3

SPRING

1 Family Tree   15
2 Childhood and Adolescence   40
3 Vic   62
4 Oxford and Paris   85

SUMMER

5 Historian   111
6 Professor   135
7 Mid-Career   152
8 Macdonald   173

FALL

9 Chairman   207
10 Decolonization   238
11 Confederation   266

Contents

WINTER

12 Despair 295

13 Endings 329

Appendix 1: Donald Creighton, Selected Bibliography 351

Appendix 2: Donald Creighton's Doctoral Students 355

Appendix 3: Luella Creighton, Selected Bibliography 357

Notes 359

Bibliography 445

Illustration Credits 457

Index 461

Illustrations

Donald Creighton's desk   xii

Map showing the Creighton family farm   19

Donald Creighton's great-grandfather on his mother's side and
his great-uncle on his father's side, Kennedy Creighton (1814–1892)   24

Donald Creighton's maternal grandmother, Eliza (Lizzie)
Jane Creighton Harvie (1840–1929)   27

Hillside, built by James and Ann Creighton, photographed ca. 1905   30

Donald Creighton's father, William Black Creighton (1864–1946)   34

Donald Creighton's mother, Laura Creighton Harvie (1869–1946)   36

Donald Creighton and his older brother, John (Jack) Creighton, 1902   39

Donald Creighton and his younger sister, Mary Isabel Creighton, ca. 1909   48

A young Donald Creighton's "Canadian Nature Journal"   53

Jack Creighton (centre) returning to Canada in 1918 for home service   60

Donald Creighton, graduate, 1925   73

Sarah Luella Sanders (1875–1901)   79

Luella Sanders Bruce with her father, James Walter Bruce (1860–1923),
ca. 1906   79

Luella Bruce working as a counsellor at a Canadian Girls in Training
summer camp   84

Luella Bruce, graduate, 1926   96

Honeymoon, Somerset cottage   98

Donald in Somerset   99

William and Laura Creighton in Muskoka, ca. 1930s   122

Donald Creighton's writing hut on Lake Muskoka   123

Donald Creighton, writer   153

Horse and buggy hired by Jack McClelland to promote *High Bright
Buggy Wheels*   181

Illustrations

Donald, Luella, and Cynthia on the *Empress of France* returning
  to Canada in 1953   194
Donald Creighton sitting on the veranda of his Muskoka cottage   196
Donald Creighton and Claude Bissell, president of the University
  of Toronto   234
Donald Creighton, teacher   236
1960 map of Northern Rhodesia, Southern Rhodesia, and Nyasaland   240
Political cartoon appearing in *Punch* during the Monckton Commission 244
Members of the Monckton Commission, Victoria Falls Hotel,
  Livingstone, February 1960   248
Donald Creighton travelling across the Central African Federation
  as a Monckton commissioner   249
Donald Creighton chatting with fellow commissioner, the writer
  Elspeth Huxley   252
Lionel Groulx with a copy of *The Road to Confederation*, University
  of Montreal, November 1965   273
Donald Creighton with members of the Ontario Advisory Committee
  on Confederation   277
John Diefenbaker attending the opening of the E.J. Pratt Library
  at Victoria College, 1961   289
Luella Creighton holding a tabby kitten   299
Donald Creighton, author, and John Gray, publisher   302
Donald Creighton depicted as Sir John A. Macdonald by artist
  Isaac Bickerstaff   307
Donald Creighton and fillmmaker George Robertson, working
  on *Canada's Heroic Beginnings*, 1972   317
Donald Creighton at his home in Brooklin, Ontario   331
Donald Creighton in his study in Brooklin   337
One of Donald Creighton's early heroes, his brother, Jack   338
Donald Creighton at his home in Brooklin, Ontario, in 1977,
  photographed by Arnaud Maggs   347
Gravestones of Donald and Luella Creighton, St Paul's Anglican
  Cemetery, Brooklin, Ontario   349

Preface

My God, how does one write a Biography?
Virginia Woolf

I am writing these acknowledgments at Donald Creighton's desk, given to me by his son Philip. Built from leftover lumber by a handyman in the early 1930s, it isn't ornamental. It doesn't even have a drawer. But it met Creighton's needs. In the summer months, he would escape to the family cottage, where he had a small writing hut that looked west across the lake, past the pine, spruce, and fir trees, and into the distant blue horizon. It was a view that inspired some of his best writing. Located on the lower reaches of the Canadian Shield, that "huge triangle of rocky upland" marked by "great, crude, sweeping lines," Lake Muskoka was one of his favourite places in the world because of its association with his childhood and adolescence and because of its connection to "the dominion of the north" and "the river system which seamed and which encircled it." To the very end, Creighton clung to the belief that it was on the Precambrian rock, the Great Lakes, and the St Lawrence River – "the bone and bloodtide of the northern economy" – that Canada was founded, and it was at this desk that the Laurentian thesis was born and eventually ran its course.

I often wonder what Creighton would think of my biography. Certainly he would appreciate my attempt to write a book that is no less academic for being readable. History, he always said, is a branch of literature. But he wouldn't care for some of my assessments which have been sharp at times. Where he let Sir John A. Macdonald off the hook, I have kept him on the hook: biography isn't a courtroom and biographers aren't barristers arguing on behalf of their subject. They are conjurers tasked with bringing someone back from the valley of the shadow of death. Of course, I will let others decide if I have been successful. Yet

Once an everyday object, Donald Creighton's desk is now an artefact embedded with multiple narratives of history, memory, people, and place: the biography of one man, the writer's life, the importance of time and place to historical interpretation, and changing definitions of Canada and what it means to be Canadian.

others will wonder why I even tried. Indeed, I have been asked more than once if I like the guy. That too is a difficult question to answer. Certainly there were occasions when I wished I could travel back in time and give his head a shake. But yes, I like him. He had the courage of his convictions; he was dedicated to his art; he had a remarkable work ethic and a deep sense of obligation; he was intellectually curious; and he was devoted to his wife. Because Luella was so important to him and to his success and because she was such an accomplished person in her own right, she is a key figure in this book.

If a book is "a portable volume consisting of a series of written, printed, or illustrated pages bound together for ease of reading," it is also an accumulation of debts incurred along the way, in this case to the Social Sciences and Humanities Research Council of Canada; to my employers, Brock University and the University of New Brunswick; to Clare Hall, University of Cambridge; and to the literally dozens of people who performed favours both large and small. To everyone who gave me a place to crash, shared their research, loaned me old letters and photographs, read draft chapters, or wrote me last-minute letters of reference, I say thank you.

I especially want to thank Creighton's children, Philip Creighton and Cynthia Flood, and his nephew, Denis Creighton. It must have been difficult having a complete stranger ask intimate questions about their family, its private dynamics and its public fault lines, but they could not have been more gracious. As a writer, Cynthia took an active interest in this project from the beginning, pushing me to remember that I was writing a book, not a monograph, and encouraging me to finish when I didn't think I ever would. Creighton's literary executor, Ramsay Derry, went above and beyond the call of duty. On more than one occasion he welcomed me into his Toronto home to read the Creighton papers in his possession, including a book manuscript that was never published. John Cairns, one of Creighton's University of Toronto colleagues, was enormously generous with his time. In our first of many conversations, he said, "You know, it couldn't have been easy being Donald Creighton." That observation stayed with me, giving me the empathy necessary to write Creighton's biography. Empathy is essential to biography because biographies, at least good biographies, are never hatchet jobs. I also want to thank Ramsay Cook. As Creighton's doctoral student, colleague, and friend, he shared his memories and his many insights into the man and what made him tick. At one point I asked him to read a section dealing specifically with him. He agreed, returning it a few days later with a handful of minor corrections and a generous note. Coming when it did, it meant a lot. Finally, to the two anonymous readers and to Len Husband, Frances Mundy, James Leahy, Val Cooke, and the folks at UTP, a huge thank you! Your comments, encouragement, and commitment to this project are much appreciated.

My family has lived with the biographer's obsession for longer than I dare to recall. For their part, Harriet and Frances have endured many absences, no doubt too many, and that is why I let them write the dedication. For her part, Joanne has accommodated my requests for time and put up with my occasional foul mood. In the last desperate months of writing when I was nothing less than a bear, she laid it on the line: it's either me or Creighton, so you better finish the damn book because this marriage isn't big enough for the three of us. I promise, your book is next.

November 2014

Creighton Famiy Tree

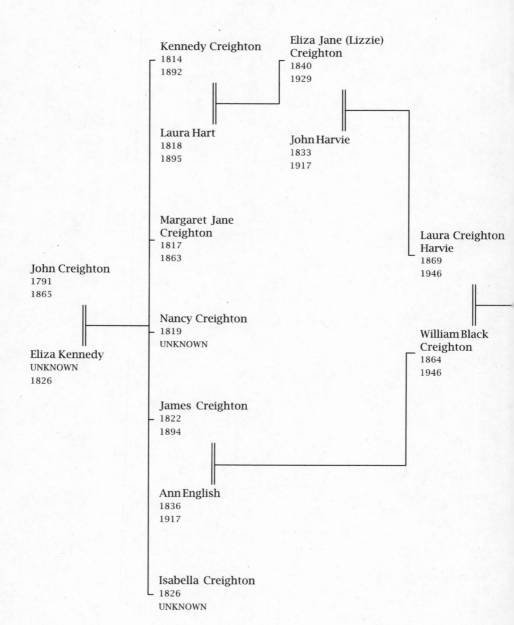

Kennedy Creighton
1814
1892

Eliza Jane (Lizzie)
Creighton
1840
1929

Laura Hart
1818
1895

John Harvie
1833
1917

Margaret Jane
Creighton
1817
1863

Laura Creighton
Harvie
1869
1946

John Creighton
1791
1865

Nancy Creighton
1819
UNKNOWN

Eliza Kennedy
UNKNOWN
1826

William Black
Creighton
1864
1946

James Creighton
1822
1894

Ann English
1836
1917

Isabella Creighton
1826
UNKNOWN

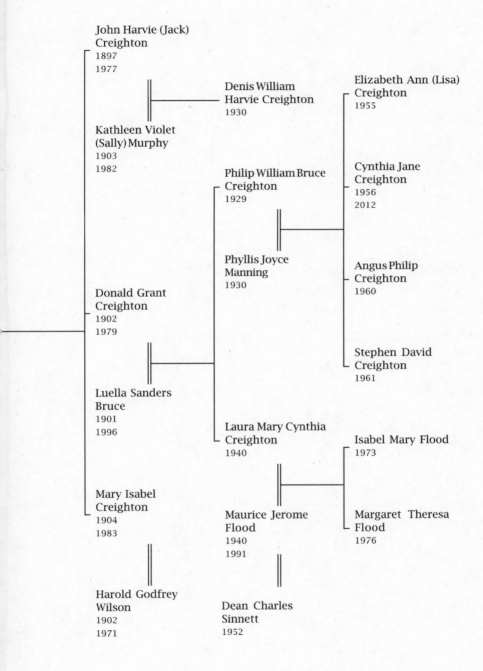

John Harvie (Jack)
Creighton
1897
1977

Kathleen Violet
(Sally) Murphy
1903
1982

Denis William
Harvie Creighton
1930

Elizabeth Ann (Lisa)
Creighton
1955

Philip William Bruce
Creighton
1929

Cynthia Jane
Creighton
1956
2012

Phyllis Joyce
Manning
1930

Angus Philip
Creighton
1960

Donald Grant
Creighton
1902
1979

Luella Sanders
Bruce
1901
1996

Stephen David
Creighton
1961

Laura Mary Cynthia
Creighton
1940

Isabel Mary Flood
1973

Mary Isabel
Creighton
1904
1983

Maurice Jerome
Flood
1940
1991

Margaret Theresa
Flood
1976

Harold Godfrey
Wilson
1902
1971

Dean Charles
Sinnett
1952

DONALD CREIGHTON
A LIFE IN HISTORY

Introduction

In 1917 Sir Joseph Pope transferred the entire collection to the Public Archives of Canada. Since that time – thirty-five years ago now – the Macdonald Papers have certainly not been left unused. Historians have searched them – or, at least, parts of them – in pursuit of evidence on a variety of special topics. But, somewhat curiously, the principal subject of the collection, Macdonald himself, has never been made the main theme of an extended study.

John A. Macdonald, vol. 1

At first, he said no, finding it "pretentious" even to describe his correspondence as papers. Important people have papers, he said.

But that wasn't the real reason. After all, he had deliberately saved his correspondence, research notes, and manuscripts; he had even saved his undergraduate essays because he sensed that, one day, they might be important. As a young man, he had had the temerity to believe that he could fashion a literature out of his country's history, that he could make it into something more than a private conversation between professional historians in unread journals. History wasn't an institutionalized string of footnotes. It was a form of memory, and as the author of English Canada's story he had become a national sage. When he was awarded the first Molson Prize for outstanding achievement in the humanities in 1964, the selection committee cited "the permanent place" his books had achieved "in the history and literature of Canada."

Clearly his papers were valuable, but he had no intention of selling them. He didn't have what he called "a Rousseau-like urge to reveal his soul" and he didn't relish the prospect of "utter strangers reading freely the confidences I have exchanged with my friends." The thought of graduate students "pouring over the intimacies" of his correspondence was, he said, a "painful" one: "I have no desire to become the subject of a doctoral thesis – or what is more likely – a Master's thesis at some Canadian university."

But that wasn't the real reason either. The real reason was his agonizing conviction of failure, his sense that, like King Lear, he had become "a poor, infirm, weak, and despised old man": "Nobody would want to write a proper biography of me."[1]

Five years later, he changed his mind. Perhaps it was his duty to history; perhaps it was vanity; perhaps it was the money; perhaps it was as simple as wanting to get rid of the damn stuff: whatever the case, he agreed to sell his papers to the Public Archives in 1977 for $10,000. Although he thought they were worth more, he wasn't about to "haggle." In fact, he felt "an enormous sense of relief" watching the large station wagon stuffed with boxes, files, note cards, and manuscripts pull out of his driveway.[2]

Since that time – forty years ago now – historians have consulted his papers, but the principal subject of the collection has never been made the theme of an extended study.[3] He was too outspoken, too controversial, too intolerant, too conservative, and too English Canadian at a time when English Canada was shedding its old British skin and growing a new, bilingual, and multicultural one. He was, in short, "a man who ruthlessly spoke his mind," and this, more than anything else, got him into trouble and made him a convenient target.[4] But even if he had been more tolerant and less difficult, the historical profession had changed. Now interested in social history, it didn't have much time for the biography of a single professor at the University of Toronto.

But that professor was a gifted scholar who had interesting things to say about Canadian history and the writing of Canadian history. No one else wrote as beautifully as he did. No one else evoked an emotional response in their readers, and if they tried, the results were often embarrassing. That professor was also a wonderful teacher who supervised a generation of graduate students. One likened him to "a sorcerer around a campfire telling the story of a great adventure"; another recalled a teacher "driven by a desire to create a Canadian past that was both exact and memorable"; and yet another remarked that it had been "a great privilege" to have been his student.[5]

Although he built his career inside the university, he was also a public intellectual who cared deeply about contemporary events, who advised prime ministers and premiers, and who, in 1959, was appointed by the British prime minister to the Monckton Commission on the future of Rhodesia and Nyasaland, an assignment that took him to southern central Africa in the difficult context of decolonization and the end of empire. Seven months later, he returned to a country experiencing its own decolonization. The Quiet Revolution and the Other Quiet Revolution were remaking Canada and what it meant to be Canadian. In short, his Canada was disappearing, and by 1970 he had become a man without a country. Haunted by the ghost of what had been, he became, in the last ten years of his life, something of a prophet. In books, articles, op-ed pieces, interviews, and convocation addresses, he called on his people to separate themselves from the United States, to renounce North American conformity, to resist the easy temptations of material progress, to declare their independence, and to defend their British inheritance. In all of this, he told Canadians, history could be a valuable compass. It "can give you a sense of courage in a difficult and dark world," he said. "You can say to yourself: I at least know something about this world, I know how it got the way it is, I know where it's possibly going, not certainly but possibly. I can stand up against the world."[6]

II

Donald Grant Creighton was born on 15 July 1902. His father, William Black Creighton, edited the *Christian Guardian*, the newspaper of the Methodist Church of Canada; his mother, Laura Harvie, looked after him, his older brother, Jack, and his younger sister, Isabel; and together William and Laura created a home that valued hard work and learning. Anxious to make the *Christian Guardian* a family newspaper, William Creighton instructed parents to get their children reading: "To train a child to like books," he said, "is to do more for him than to leave him a fortune."[7] A precocious boy, Donald developed an early interest in books and an early appreciation for words, for what made books possible in the first place. "I love words," he told one interviewer.[8] Indeed, he loved everything about them: their different sounds, their many meanings, and their infinite combinations; their shapes, their sizes, their colours, and their moods; their rhythm, their metre, and their movement across the page; and their power to remake lost worlds, to build new countries of the mind, and to fashion alternative ways of seeing.

After finishing high school at Humberside Collegiate in Toronto's west end, he entered Victoria College in the University of Toronto. His early ambition was to be a writer, but over the course of his undergraduate degree his interests changed and he set himself a different goal: he would still be a writer, but of history, not fiction. In his final year at Vic, he received a scholarship to study modern history at Balliol College, Oxford. Then, suddenly, events unfolded that were out of his control when he fell in love with Luella Bruce. Smart, energetic, and determined to escape the emotional and intellectual confinement of small-town Ontario, Luella gave as good as she got and she too wanted to be a writer. What she called her "obsessive urge to put words on paper" started when she was seven years old as a way of protecting herself from an unhappy child-hood.[9] Meanwhile, plans were quickly made: he would go to Oxford, she would finish her final year at Vic, and they would be married in the spring. To Creighton, Luella would always be the most beautiful woman in the world. There were never any trysts with pretty co-eds or lost weekends with brilliant grad-uate students. It was always "Miss Hughes" or "Miss Prang."[10] When a friend brought a much younger woman, a girl really, to a party, he announced, for everyone to hear, that women became more attractive as they got older.[11]

In 1927, Creighton joined Toronto's Department of History as a junior lec-turer. Initially, he set his sights on French history and, a year later, began a doctorate at the Sorbonne on one of the key figures of the French Revolution. But when he ran out of money, he turned to Canadian history. Although he later complained that it was "a poor second," that it filled him with "a real sense of deprivation," he was genuinely excited by his research at the Public Archives.[12] Beneath the petitions, the minutes of the Legislative Council, and the corre-spondence of the Montreal merchants was a story more compelling and more fundamental than Canada's dry-as-dust constitutional history.

Published in 1937, *The Commercial Empire of the St. Lawrence* present-ed an original and ambitious interpretation of Canadian history. Out of the St Lawrence River Valley and the Great Lakes basin, out of the Laurentian Shield, or what François-Xavier Garneau called that "immense couch of granite," came Canada.[13] The river had made Canada possible. It had allowed the Montreal merchants in the late eighteenth and early nineteenth centuries to build a trans-continental commercial empire based first on the fur trade and later on the trade in timber, minerals, and wheat. "The river meant mobility and distance; it invited journeyings; it promised immense expanses, unfolding, flowing away into the remote and changing horizons. The whole west, with all its riches, was the dominion of the river."[14] Reviewers, almost to an individual, were effusive, and Creighton's reputation as his generation's leading historian was established. He did for the St Lawrence River what Tom Thomson and the Group of Seven did for the Laurentian Shield: he mythologized it. In the same way that they turned, in his words, to "the rock, scrub, and pine" of northern Canada "to ex-press the rugged spirit of the country," he turned to the River of Canada to express both the country's origins and its destiny. Stretching some 3,800 kilometres from the Atlantic Ocean to the western reaches of Lake Superior, it was "the one great river which led from the eastern shore into the heart of the conti-nent," and the Laurentian thesis "was the only genuinely arresting paradigm ever to emerge from Canadian historical scholarship."[15] As a "meta-narrative of nation-building and collective identity," it carried "the idea of Canada."[16]

There would be more books, of course, including a short study on British North America at Confederation prepared for the Royal Commission on Dominion-Provincial Relations and a general history of Canada. But it was Creighton's two-volume biography of Sir John A. Macdonald published in 1952 and 1955 that confirmed his reputation. He was in his early fifties and at his peak. What he said of Macdonald as a politcian applied equally to him as a writer: "Every device, every ruse, every conceivable subtlety was instantly at his command." Writing in *The Spectator*, a British magazine of culture and politics, the Oxford historian Max Beloff described Creighton as "one of the half-dozen best historians now writing anywhere in the English-speaking world." Even his harshest critic had to concede that *Macdonald* was "an artistic triumph."[17] From the opening lines of volume one to the concluding sentences of volume two, it was a heroic Macdonald who understood the logic of Canadian history, who extended the empire of the St Lawrence across the entire northern half of North America by the Canadian Pacific Railway, who understood that the greatest threat to Canada was the United States, and who fought to preserve Canada's imperial connection.

When John Diefenbaker first met his British counterpart, Harold Macmillan, he presented him with a boxed set of *The Young Politician* and *The Old Chieftain*. Two years later, in 1959, the Royal Library at Windsor Castle requested copies of both *The Commercial Empire of the St. Lawrence* and *Macdonald*. An honoured Creighton duly complied, inscribing "this biography of the first Prime Minister of Canada" with "homage and loyal good wishes."[18]

Then came the 1960s, and the man who for so long had articulated English Canada's identity as a British country found himself on the outside looking in. "He wasn't part of the whole Quebec thing, or the new flag, or Expo, or Trudeau-mania," an acquaintance recalled. "He wasn't part of the re-invention of Canada. And, not only was he not a part of it, he couldn't understand it either."[19] Quebec's assertive nationalism – especially its Québécois and separatist variation – forced English Canada – already going through its own transformation from a British to a civic nation – to construct a bilingual and eventually multicultural identity. But, according to Donald Creighton, Canada was a British country with a French-speaking province and the imperial connection was not some antiquated piece of mid-Victorian plumbing. It was essential to Canada's survival on a continent dominated by the United States. Angry and confused, Creighton lashed out against Quebec nationalists. "I've nearly come to the conclusion that the best thing to do would be to boot them out, on our terms, not theirs, and, if I had anything to do with it, they would be harsh terms too," he told Eugene Forsey. "They have succeeded in wrecking my nation."[20]

Because of his outspoken opposition to Quebec nationalism and to official bilingualism, Creighton became a lightning rod, attracting charged opinion which he described as a "torrent of abuse."[21] Alternating between rage, impotence, and grief, he did the only thing he could do: he wrote. It wasn't a choice. It was an imperative. It was how he made sense of the world and negotiated his place in it. Published in 1970, *Canada's First Century* would be his last great book. Surveying the rise and inevitable fall of the empire of the St Lawrence, it struck a resonant chord with readers and, for a few weeks, even outsold the Bible. As the historical version of *Lament for a Nation*, it was an indictment of the Liberal Party and of Liberal prime ministers for betraying Canada's birthright as a British nation and for literally selling Canada to the United States. There would be a handful of other books – including an unfortunate contribution to the Canadian Centenary Series and a novel set in Toronto – as well as a series of essays and reviews for *Maclean's, Saturday Night*, and the *Globe and Mail* – but nothing matched the sweep of *Canada's First Century.*

III

"I begin to feel," Creighton once said, "that I will be remembered, if I am remembered at all, as a pessimist, a bigot, and a violent Tory partisan." He wasn't far off the mark. Séraphin Marion charged him with commiting "sins of omission" when it came to the history of French Canada. Arthur Lower acknowledged that he had written a number of important books, but felt that he was "un peu francophobe." Hugh Keenleyside called him a "Tory pamphleteer." C.P. Stacey remembered a difficult colleague who "frequently insulted me; but, then, I think, he insulted practically everybody." Stephen Clarkson and Christina McCall branded him a "notorious francophobic curmudgeon." Desmond Morton said that he was "a bitter old man"; George Fetherling claimed that he was "proudly racist"; and Veronica Strong-Boag cited his "blinkered vision" of the past. Because it depicted the Conquest as epiphenomenal and because it was "avidly read by the schoolchildren who now run English Canada," Ray Conlogue blamed *The Commercial Empire of the St. Lawrence* for English Canada's inability to imagine the Conquest as Quebec's founding trauma and its refusal to give up its role as conqueror. And in *La partition Du Québec: De Lord Durham à Stéphane Dion*, Claude Charron argued that English Canada's leading historian had made it impossible for subsequent generations of Canadians to recognize Quebec as a nation and that he had legitimated the movement to partition Quebec in the event of its separation.[22]

But Donald Creighton was more than a pamphleteer and his books were never anti-Quebec pamphlets. The image of schoolchildren – not high school students, not university students, but schoolchildren – avidly reading *The Commercial Empire of the St. Lawrence*, an academic monograph published in the 1930s, and taking from it their natural right to step on Quebec is laughable. And it is both a misreading of his scholarship and a silly exaggeration to claim that Creighton led subsequent generations of English Canadians to deny Quebec's right to self-determination. *The Commercial Empire of the St. Lawrence, Macdonald, The Road to Confederation*, and *Canada's First Century* remain in print because they are brilliant contributions to Canadian historical writing and English-Canadian self-understanding, not because they contain the seeds of Quebec's oppression and ultimate partition.

Of course, he could be difficult, or as one colleague put it, he could be "hell to get along with."[23] His friends at Balliol called him Ira, or Anger. Robert Finch – perhaps his closest friend at Varsity – called him Thunder Cloud. And John Gray, his friend and publisher, called him the Terrible-Tempered Mr. Bang after a character in the popular newspaper comic strip, Toonerville Folks. His fuse was famously short and he could explode without warning, meaning his family, friends, and colleagues learned to walk on eggshells in his presence.

But he wasn't only difficult. He was thoughtful, engaging, generous, and, when he wanted to be, a lot of fun. And his interests ranged widely, from literature to politics, from the French Revolution to American foreign policy, and from music to art history. He studied the great French writers – Flaubert, Maupassant, Proust, and especially Émile Zola – and he read the great British writers – Charles Dickens, Thomas Hardy, D.H. Lawrence, and Arnold Bennett. "If there is one thing I know, it's the novel," he said.[24] He adored classical music, especially the operas of Verdi, Puccini, Strauss, and Richard Wagner. The Ring Cycle not only fascinated him, it inspired his interpretation of Canadian history, and for years he talked about making a pilgrimage to the German city of Bayreuth and its famous opera house. And he loved to spend lazy afternoons in the great art galleries of Europe admiring the masters. He especially liked the paintings of Jacques-Louis David – the French painter famous for his depiction of revolutionary moments – because they spoke to his own instincts as an artist and to his passion for great events, dramatic moments, and heightened feelings.

"Look," Ramsay Cook said, "you don't have to like the guy. But he was an exceedingly important figure"; he was "the most important historian in English-speaking Canada and surely one of the best in the English-speaking world."[25] A towering figure in the intellectual and cultural life of twentieth-century English Canada, Creighton belonged to that "generation of giants" – that generation of intellectuals born in the closing years of the nineteenth century and the opening years of the twentieth – who "decisively altered our sense of ourselves and of our country."[26] An impressive group of visionaries, thinkers, and writers, its members included Frank Underhill, Harold Innis, Marshall McLuhan, C.B. Macpherson, Northrop Frye, and George Grant. Like all of these men, Donald Creighton lived a big and interesting life. He lived a life in history in both senses of the phrase. History was his profession, and, like all historians, his work cannot be fully understood without also understanding him and the time in which he lived. But what can be said of him cannot be said of all historians: the time in which he lived can be fully understood only if we understand his life and his work.

That work, Carl Berger concluded, "was a monument to the belief that history was akin to drama, that it moved in accordance with the deeper truths contained in the very forms of literature and music – that history, in short, imitated art. And it is with this proposition that any comprehensive assessment of his achievement must begin." Creighton later admitted that Berger had come closer "to the sources of my historical inspiration than any other Canadian critic is likely to do."[27]

Although history was something that he did for a living, it was always more than that. It was his passion. Totally committed, at times even tormented, he worked constantly – on Christmas Eve, on New Year's Eve, on Dominion Day, on his birthday, before class, after class, in his study, in his living room, at the office, and at the cottage – to realize in words what he saw in his mind, to represent not a thing's outer appearance but its inner significance. "The writer's only responsibility," William Faulkner said, "is to his art." "Everything goes by the board: honor, pride, decency, security, happiness, all, to get the book written. If a writer has to rob his mother, he will not hesitate; the 'Ode on a Grecian Urn' is worth any number of old ladies."[28] Creighton may not have sacrificed his mother, but the awful pace he set for himself in his twenties was sustainable only at the expense of his physical and emotional health. Back pain, stomach problems, psoriasis, irritability, moodiness, emotional outbursts, broken friendships, and strained relationships: in short, he suffered for his art because, in his mind at least, *Macdonald* was worth any number of friends and family members. His inextinguishable urge to create was like breathing. If he stopped writing, he would cease to exist. Left unfinished on his desk was his second novel.

Art, Émile Zola famously said, "is a corner of nature seen through temperament."[29] Creighton's art was *The Commercial Empire of the St. Lawrence*, *Macdonald*, *The Road to Confederation*, and *Canada's First Century*; his corner of nature was Canada's past; and his temperament was, at its most basic, romantic, or what Northrop Frye defined as "a diffused, resigned, melancholy sense of the passing of time, of the old order changing and yielding to a new one."[30] Accepting the limits of science and reason to apprehend reality and seeking the ideal over the actual, Creighton valued imagination and intuition. Truth, he believed, came through feelings and flashes of insight, not through experiments and measurement. His instinct for epic events and sweeping movements, his sense of historical destiny, and his respect for death's inevitability were all aspects of his romantic temperament.

By his own admission, he took his inspiration not from other historians, but from novelists, musicians, and painters. Their invented worlds were more real, their insights into the human condition more penetrating, and their abilities to tell a story more inspiring. Amazingly, he never once quoted or even mentioned another historian in any of his books. He didn't like academic clutter, but, more than that, he didn't want to obscure the individuality of his own voice. Like the romantic hero who transcends his social conventions and expectations, he stood outside the conventions of his profession in his noble and lonely quest for that elusive, unattainable ideal known as historical truth.

As a young man, he read Oswald Spengler's *The Decline of the West*. So did his contemporaries. Northrop Frye described it as "one of the world's great Romantic poems"; George Woodcock called it a "powerful and gloomy achievement"; Creighton relished its pessimism and fatalism, its promise that "each culture is an organism, endowed like any other organism with life and doomed to a history which is the exact counterpart of that of an animal, a tree, or a flower."[31] According to Spengler, the world-as-history exists over and above the world-as-nature and, like the world-as-nature, it unfolds according to an organic rhythm of birth, growth, maturity, decline, and death, of spring, summer, fall, and winter. But unlike the world-as-nature, the world-as-history is to be apprehended by imagination, intuition, and especially symbolism, not by science. It demands, Spengler said, "the power of seeing and not that of calculating"; it will be captured through art and "never through notions and proofs."[32]

Spengler didn't call his book a philosophy of history. He called it a philosophy of the future because history unfolded according to the inescapable laws of nature: civilizations are born; they mature; they decline; and, eventually, they die. That relentless and pitiless passage of time, Spengler believed, "can be imparted only by the artist."[33]

Creighton always maintained that biographies should never be written by "debunkers."[34] Because they demand love and equanimity, good biographies should be written by writers capable of walking a mile in someone else's shoes and by writers willing to temper criticism with empathy and understanding. Good biographies also demand an appreciation for time and its unforgiving passage. "Time is the essence of history; and any young student who wants to be an historian and hasn't a sensitive feeling for time – for growth and change and decay – had better alter his plans." Whatever is will cease to be, Creighton said, and if students cannot handle this essential fact then they should "take up a timeless and lifeless study such as political science or economic theory." Narrative, moreover, was the only way to capture time. Sharing G.M. Trevelyan's conviction that Clio was first and foremost a muse and that, in whoring after the false god of science, historians had betrayed their craft, Creighton understood that, whatever else it is, history "is essentially a story."[35] It is a beginning, middle, decline, and end, or a spring, summer, fall, and winter.

This story, therefore, starts at the beginning with the decision of one man to leave Northern Ireland in the spring of 1832.

SPRING

The character of Canada as British North America was in their flesh and bones.

George Grant, *Lament for a Nation*

chapter one

Family Tree

*In those days they came usually by boat. A few immigrants may have made the
long journey from Montreal by land, taking several weeks and stopping at a
score of friendly farm-houses as they pushed their way through the green forest.
But most people travelled westward by the river.*

John A. Macdonald, vol. 1

Everyone wanted to leave Ireland. From the end of the Napoleonic Wars to the
mid-1860s, Irish emigrants easily outnumbered English and Scottish emi-
grants. In the main, they were Protestant, although a sizeable minority were
Catholic. Most were from Northern Ireland, although certainly not all of them
were. And while in "reduced circumstances," they were not impoverished.[1]
Driven "by the vague hope of better things," the Irish settled in parts of Nova
Scotia, found work in the woods of New Brunswick, became tenant farmers in
Prince Edward Island, and tried their luck in the nascent industrial economy of
Montreal's Griffintown. But most set their sights on what Donald Creighton
once described as the "the lush, green, unoccupied lands of southern Upper
Canada."[2] In the 1830s alone some one hundred books were published extolling
the many virtues of British North America's largest English-speaking colony. Its
climate, growing season, soil conditions, forests, transportation networks, and
markets promised rich returns to any man who, in the words of one emigrant
guidebook, wanted "to get forward in the world," who wanted to be "the lord and
master of his own estate."[3]

Born in 1791, John Creighton lived in Tamlaght O'Crilly Parish in the valley
of the River Bann, County Derry, Northern Ireland.[4] As a boy, he had learned
its many glens, hills, and fields; later, he memorized the footpaths of the Sperrin
Mountains that stretch like a great spine up the middle of the county; but now,
he faced a much greater challenge. If he stayed, he would remain one more Irish

farmer struggling to raise a family on a shrinking plot of land. The staggering increase in the rural population of Ireland between 1780 and the Great Famine had led to smaller and smaller farms, each generation poorer than the last.[5] A family could live on a couple of acres and somehow manage with a small potato patch and a cow or two, but it meant periodic famines when the potato crop failed.[6] One of the key survival strategies for small farmers in Ulster had been weaving linen – linen meant cash – but the reorganization of weaving from a domestic enterprise to one operated by manufacturers after 1815 precipitated a steady and irreversible drop in economic opportunity.[7]

The tectonic plates of history – demographic pressure, agricultural decline, and market forces – were conspiring to push Donald Creighton's great-great-grandfather on his mother's side, who was also his great-grandfather on his father's side, out of Ireland. Also conspiring against him were personal circumstances. John Creighton's wife, Eliza Kennedy, had died in 1826, leaving him with five children. Kennedy, the eldest, was twelve; the youngest, Isabella, was an infant. Many years later, Kennedy would remember Tamlaght O'Crilly as a degenerate site of "profligacy, gambling, drunkenness, and all kinds of vice." "Very few," he said, "made pretense of religion because any who did were severely persecuted."[8] Perhaps, then, Creighton felt that it was no place for a man to raise a young family on his own. He wasn't unaware of British North America. No one in Ireland was. Advertisements appeared in every shop, guidebooks were passed from farm to farm, and stories about families in the neighbouring parish who had left circulated up and down the countryside. Leaving the familiar geography of Ireland for the unknown landscape of North America, its cathedral-like forests and its impossible enormity, wouldn't be easy. Northrop Frye famously likened entering the Gulf of St Lawrence to being "silently swallowed by an alien continent."[9] But Creighton knew that if he was going to provide a better future for his children, and for his children's children, he would have to act sooner rather than later. After all, he wasn't getting any younger. The majority of emigrants from County Derry were in their twenties. In 1826, he was thirty-five. When he left in 1832 he was forty-one.

According to one estimate, 50,305 emigrants left Ireland for British North America that year.[10] Such massive emigration was made possible by the expanding transatlantic trade in timber, coal, and slate. As cargo was brought to Derry, Belfast, and Cork, people were taken to Newcastle, Saint John, and Quebec, making "emigration a trade like any other." For £4 an emigrant could secure a berth in steerage. Men, women, and children were put in the dank and fetid hold, where seasickness was normal and disease not uncommon. A clever captain could pack as many as eighty or ninety people into an eight-square-metre space. In effect, the Irish were ballast. "Jammed together in narrow, unventilated quarters, ill-prepared for their journey, badly fed and inadequately cared for, they endured a voyage which was at best a stern discipline and which at worst became a savage test of survival."[11] The voyage itself – undertaken in the spring and summer months – took about forty-five days, although it could take as long as sixty days if the weather didn't cooperate. Death rates on board in the era before the Great Famine were about eight per one thousand passengers.[12] Cholera, of course, was the great fear. Spreading quickly and violently, it was a matter of hours from the initial onset of symptoms – diarrhea, vomiting, and hypotension – to collapse and almost certain death. In 1832 cholera was reported in every county in Ireland. In Lower Canada alone 5,800 people died, many of them emigrants.

And yet, despite the obvious risks and the many dangers, the Irish continued to leave Ireland. But they were never the bastard children of Eire. Actors in their own destiny, they left "because of a calculation that life would be better elsewhere."[13]

For Creighton, elsewhere was Middlesex County. Presumably he knew someone there. Or maybe an emigration agent in Quebec City – anxious to keep the tens of thousands of immigrants moving to points inland – told him to go there. Travelling west by the river, Creighton was surely filled with "a mixture of hope and regret and wonder and fatigue." Everything was unfamiliar but strangely intoxicating. "The stops and disembarkations, the jolting rides over the narrow bush roads, the nights spent in the hot, close rooms of crowded taverns and the days of interminable passage up the lake – all these passed rapidly like the unreal and disconnected episodes of an exciting dream."[14] And then came the final push through the green forest, already marked by clearings here and there, by log cabins, fields, split rail fences, and other signs of improvement.

A few years later, Lord Durham would describe the "great peninsula between Lakes Erie and Huron" as "the best grain country" in North America, its rolling hills, rich alluvial flats, and many rivers, streams, and creeks already supporting a diverse agricultural economy.[15] Life wouldn't be easy, but at least Creighton wouldn't have to wring a subsistence existence from a recalcitrant couple of acres. And, as the guidebooks promised, he wouldn't have to live "in dread of the agent coming to distrain him for *the rent,* or the collector of the *county cess,* or the tithe proctor, with many others, which are the daily visitors of the farmer in England and Ireland."[16]

II

In those days London was "a small hamlet built amongst the cedar and pine stumps at the forks of the north and east branches of the Thames" but it, and the surrounding area, offered work to any man who wanted it.[17] Within Middlesex County as a whole, there were grist mills, sawmills, tanneries, asheries, distilleries, and breweries. There was at least one foundry and one brickyard.[18] Initially, John Creighton worked on someone else's farm, making him a farmer without a farm. After all, land was not free in Upper Canada. In anticipation of settlement, and in orderly fashion, surveyors had divided the colony into districts, counties, townships, concessions, and lots. A lot was usually 200 acres, although 100-acre lots were not uncommon. Prices varied. And speculation was a problem. In 1834, it was reported that farms were selling for as much as £500, although one could be purchased for £200.[19] And if a lot had not been cleared it could be purchased for even less. The usual practice was to pay in equal instalments over a set period of time, say £40 per year for five years. But all of this lay in the future. Right now, Creighton needed to learn how to clear the land and then how to farm it. He also needed to pay for his children's passage. Earning that money would take a year or two, but, curiously enough, getting that money to Ireland would be relatively easy. Meeting a need, the banks readily facilitated the movement of money to Ireland and the return movement of emigrants to British North America.

In 1834 Creighton was joined by his two sons, Kennedy and James, and one of his daughters, Nancy. Two daughters remained in Ireland. Margaret was seventeen and, perhaps, already married; Isabella, the baby of the family, was no doubt her responsibility. (They would come later, however. In 1847, against the backdrop of the Great Famine, they made the same calculation that their father had made.) Shortly after arriving in Upper Canada, Kennedy got married and became a Methodist minister while James and Nancy, because they were still teenagers, remained with their father. The 1842 census listed John Creighton as a non-proprietary yeoman, or tenant, living with two other people – almost certainly James and Nancy – on an uncleared lot of 100 acres. He owned one cow.[20] The Canada Company – a land and colonization company chartered in 1825 – owned the lot. Although it preferred to sell lots, the Canada Company also rented them and in 1842 implemented a leasing system in an effort to expedite settlement. Presumably, then, Creighton rented and later leased with the option to buy. Tenancy was not uncommon in Upper Canada; actually, it "was an economically rational strategy for settlers of limited means" because it allowed them quick access to a farm.[21] But six years later, in 1848, it would be James, not John, who bought lot four on concession two in the Township of North Dorchester. James was now twenty-six and had his whole life ahead of him. John was fifty-seven and no longer a young man. The first house on the Creighton farm may have been a one-storey log cabin, but it was better than a stone cottage in Tamlaght O'Crilly because, at long last, the Creightons owned the land beneath it.

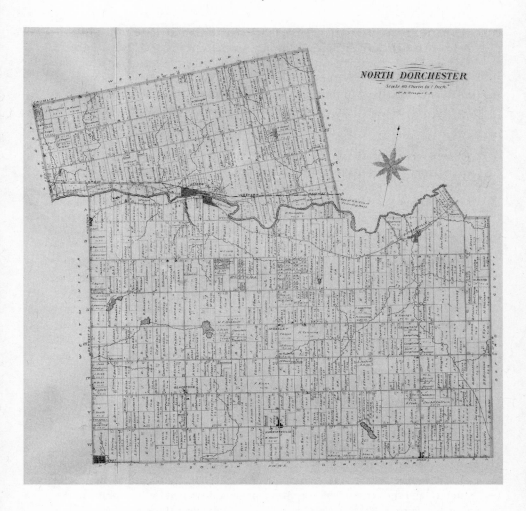

Located in the upper left corner (look for the word "Great" in Great Western Railway), the Creighton family farm had a generous water supply and an ample woodlot. Because the GWR and a rural road intersected on his property, James Creighton's farm would have been a whistle-stop, giving him convenient access to markets in London, Dorchester, and Woodstock, and to information about seeds, crops, livestock, markets, and prices from other farmers. In British North America, Donald Creighton wrote, "the family farm became at once the main unit of economic activity and the principal agency of social security and welfare" while the railway became the principal "tool of national expansion and integration."

The 1851 census enumerated James Creighton as the head of the household. Although born in Upper Canada, his wife, Mary English, was also Irish. Living with James and Mary were Eliza Creighton, their one-year old daughter, and Ann English, Mary's fifteen-year-old sister. John Creighton, identified as a labourer, also lived in the house. According to the agricultural schedule attached to the census, the Creighton farm was further ahead in terms of land cleared and of yield than its neighbouring farms. In 1851, it had 50 acres cleared: 25.5 acres were enumerated under pasture and 24.5 acres under cultivation.[22] Its crops included wheat, hay, peas, and potatoes, although oats were its primary crop. To be sure, oats were common in Upper Canada because of their hardiness – they survived where other crops failed – and because of their versatility – they could be fed to man, woman, and beast. As well, it was a common crop in the hard-scrabble areas of Northern Ireland and Scotland. Perhaps familiarity bred appreciation. Meanwhile, the farm's livestock consisted of five milk cows, seven calves, three horses, seven pigs, and thirteen sheep. That James Creighton had three horses and no oxen – oxen almost always being a sign of pioneer agriculture – is yet one more indicator of his early success. That year, his farm produced 16 tons of hay, 42 pounds of wool, 150 pounds of butter, five barrels of pork, and, from its woods, 100 pounds of maple sugar.[23] All told, it was a remarkable achievement: they had cut down trees, removed stumps, cleared brush, and moved stones as big as a man; they had pushed back the forest in one tiny part of Britain's commercial empire; and they had linked their farm to a market economy.

By the decisions they made and by the risks they took, the Creightons were participants in both "the great transformation" – or the relentless expansion of market liberalism across the globe – and "the great land rush" – or the taking of land from the world's Indigenous peoples and the making of British settlement societies in North America, Australia, New Zealand, and southern Africa. The growth of self-regulating markets, the substitution of the motive of subsistence for the motive of gain, the development of an economic order based on self-interest, and the doctrine of improvement all contributed to the making of the modern world.[24] It was John Locke who most clearly articulated the doctrine of improvement, perhaps the most persuasive idea in early modern political thought, when he argued that the value of land is not intrinsic but is derived from the labour that human beings put into it. God gave to the "industrious and rational" a mandate to improve the land, to cultivate it and lay claim to it. In Locke's analysis, therefore, private property trumps common possession. Underpinning the great transformation and the great land rush were Locke's theory of value and his doctrine of improvement, which also paved the way for the guarantee of property rights by the liberal state. Indeed, land ownership was the "absolute requisite" for economic and political development in British North America.[25] It created the legal context for, and provided the economic incentive to, settlement; settlement, in turn, was the necessary first step in railway construction; and railway construction – the most "successful tool of national expansion and integration" – led to the political union of the entire northern half of North America.[26]

But the making of modern Canada should not be romanticized. To be sure, the pioneers, including the Creighton family, displayed remarkable courage as emigrants, as tenants, and as farmers. But individual courage is not national romance. Rather, the narrative of emigration, settlement, railway construction, and the political integration of British North America from sea to sea must be problematized. After all, Donald Creighton's Dominion of the North came at a tremendous cost, one paid disproportionately by Native people. The "unoccupied land" of Upper Canada was unoccupied only insofar as its original inhabitants had been dispossessed. The rhetoric of unoccupied and empty land and of Locke's doctrine of improvement blinded participants – from English kings to Irish emigrants – to the human and moral cost of colonization.

That cost was also environmental. By turning the natural world into property to be measured, allocated, traded, bought, and sold, the great transformation remade, or "disjointed," our relationship to the natural world. Ultimately, it threatened "man's natural habitat with annihilation."[27] In other words, the same project to dispossess Native people of their land also sought to "improve" that land in violent and often catastrophic ways. By the First World War some 90 per cent of the eastern woodland that covered Ontario below the Laurentian Shield was gone. It was more than a forest. It was an entire ecosystem. It was an "awesome complex" of soils, plants, trees, animals, birds, and fish.[28] Like the language of unoccupied and empty land, the language of progress – of growth, expansion, and improvement – and the economic logic of progress – a tree has value only once it has been cut down – continues to haunt us today.

That the eastern woodland was there to be cut down was not only rooted in the logic of an economy based on self-interest and improvement; it was a notion deeply embedded in the Christian tradition: man was chosen by the Creator to subdue and rule His creation. "Thou madest him to have dominion over the works of thy hands: thou hast put all things under his feet" (Psalm 8:6). But the Christian tradition was always more noble and inspiring than its promise of man's dominion over nature. The making of modern Canada and its extension from sea to sea was not only a material vision, it was also a spiritual vision. In the Protestant culture of nineteenth-century Upper Canada/Ontario, there were two worlds: the material and the moral, the secular and the sacred, the world of railways and the world of God. Victorian Canadians envisioned a nation that was more than a collection of tables, graphs, and statistics measuring the length of the railways, the tons of coal mined, the population growth of major cities, and the average size of a farm in this or that county. They also envisioned a Christian nation, one that would be the Lord's dominion. After all, it was not any king who "shall have dominion also from sea to sea, and from the river unto the ends of the earth" (Psalm 72:8). It was the just king.[29]

Against this backdrop, the 1851 census holds an important piece of information. At some point in the 1830s or 1840s – it is not clear why, or under what conditions, or even when – the Creightons became Methodists. Perhaps they attended a camp meeting where they were reborn in the joy of Christian fellowship. Perhaps they were saved by the promise of God's grace from an itinerant preacher. Or perhaps, like John Wesley himself, they felt their hearts "strangely warmed."

III

Although part of a larger evangelical awakening that swept across much of Europe and North America in the eighteenth and nineteenth centuries, Methodism – as a method of finding God – was ideally suited to the frontier conditions of British North America. Its structure of connections, conferences, circuits, congregations, and classes; its use of mass evangelism, camp meetings, and revivals; its emphasis on individual and community salvation; and its promise that salvation was universal and therefore open to everyone regardless of race, class, and sex, all contributed to its astonishing growth. Unlike Anglicanism, which tended to be closed and even ethnocentrically English, Methodism was open, expansive, dynamic, joyful, social, and inspirational. Through conversion, it offered a personal relationship – unmediated by any church hierarchy – with an active, immanent God. Ultimately, the genius of Methodism "lay in its preaching a vital religion to the scattered communities of British North America."[30] Indeed, "vital" became something of a catchword for Methodists to describe their religion and themselves. Emphasizing religious feeling over intellectual abstraction, Methodism delivered, in John Wesley's words, "plain truth for plain people."

For their part, the clergy were not above their congregants, they were of their congregants. They had been converted themselves, and "their fervour offered an emotional release from the stultifying toil and empty silence of the bush; their camp meetings provided the occasion for a lengthy and exhilarating social gathering."[31] By 1871 Methodism was the largest Protestant denomination in Canada. Related to its rapid growth was Methodism's early decision to break first with the Methodist Episcopal Church of the United States and then with the Wesleyan Methodist Church of Great Britain in an effort to define itself as a Canadian church, as the church that would build the Lord's dominion in Canada and build Canada into the Lord's dominion. Representing "the growing nationalism of the Canadian frontier,"[32] the Methodist Church became "the most Canadian of all the churches."[33]

It was in this context that Kennedy Creighton – Donald Creighton's great-grandfather on his mother's side and his great-uncle on his father's side – became a Methodist minister. Although his parents, John and Eliza Creighton, were members of the Presbyterian Church, Synod of Ulster, and although this was the church in which he had been baptized, his grandmother – who had been "deprived of her sight" – was a Covenanter, at some point having joined the Reformed Presbyterian Church. At the core of Covenant doctrine and practice was the belief in the supremacy of Christ over the nation and the lordship of Christ in every sphere of an individual's life. Intemperance, fornication, and insolvency were offences against the glory of Christ, making Covenant doctrine and practice similar to the doctrine and practice of all evangelical denominations.[34] As the eldest child in the family, it had fallen to Kennedy to take his blind grandmother to church. Inspired perhaps by his grandmother's religious vision, he became a Covenanter when he was fifteen.[35] Because the Covenanters, or the Reformed Presbyterian Church, had a tiny presence in Upper Canada, and because he needed active, vital fellowship, Kennedy turned to the Methodists. A few months after his marriage to Laura Hart on Christmas Day in 1835, he was received on trial as a Methodist minister. Three years later, in 1839, he was ordained, beginning a long career as an itinerant preacher in, among other places, Bytown, Owen Sound, Dundas, London, Collingwood, and Bruce Mines. Over one twenty-year stretch, he and his family moved twenty times.

And, like so many of his Methodist brethren, Creighton carried the Gospel of Jesus Christ to Native people, the land's original owners, serving as a missionary to the Mississauga first at Rice Lake near Peterborough and then, in the 1880s, at Rama on the shores of Lake Couchiching.[36] At Rama, Creighton reported "the customary difficulties" associated with ministering to men who were frequently absent on extended hunting trips at the same time as he reported "marked signs of improvement" in the attendance of children at both Sunday school and day school.[37] It was through the Methodist Church that Creighton formed a friendship with Peter Jones, or Sacred Feathers, the Mississauga chief, Methodist convert, and minister who proved instrumental in navigating his people through the difficult terrain of accommodation, resistance, settlement, and, ultimately, survival in the face of an insatiable European hunger for land on the north shore of Lake Ontario. In 1838 he was granted a short audience

Donald Creighton's great-grandfather on his mother's side and his great-uncle on his father's side, Kennedy Creighton (1814–1892) was a dedicated witness, carrying the Gospel of Christ across Upper Canada/Ontario as an itinerant Methodist minister.

with a young Queen Victoria to petition his people's land claims. When Jones was gravely ill, Creighton opened his St Catharines parsonage to him and his wife in April 1856 so that he could consult doctors and try the town's much-talked-about mineral baths. But the diagnosis was bleak, the baths were ineffective, and, a few months later, Peter Jones died in Toronto.[38]

IV

Moving as often as Kennedy and Laura Creighton did placed an enormous strain on their family.[39] And, as a minister's wife, Laura faced exceedingly high expectations, her private obligation to her family matched by her public obligation to the church. As an 1831 article in the *Christian Guardian* explained, a minister's wife, by "her habits, her conversation, [and] her whole deportment," should be "the holiest, most spiritual woman in the church" and she should be "willing to live in any situation, however self-denying its circumstances may prove."[40]

Despite the physical challenges of moving so often and the self-denial she was expected to exhibit, Laura managed to raise five children, ensuring that her sons and her daughters received the best education possible.[41] The Methodists were early and optimistic supporters of women's higher education, though within gendered assumptions about appropriate roles for women. Still, they believed that women could contribute to the Lord's dominion not only as wives and mothers, but as teachers, nurses, missionaries, and temperance workers. But first, their innate talents had to be unleashed, their unique natures refined, and their peculiar strengths marshalled, and, to this end, a number of ladies' colleges were founded in southern Ontario. Eliza Jane, or Lizzie, attended the Wesleyan Female College in Dundas, where she would have taken courses in math, logic, modern languages, natural sciences, and philosophy and where, in a Christian environment, she would have been reminded of her natural, moral, and maternal obligations to her family and to her community. For Methodists in Victorian Canada, women's higher education was not about upsetting the gendered order of things. It was about preparing women to play a lead role in reclaiming "the earth as the Lord's."[42]

In 1860 her father was chairing the Barrie district of the Wesleyan Methodist Church when Lizzie Creighton met her husband. She was twenty years old, had finished her education, and, as her granddaughter later put it, was now "old enough to be thinking of marriage."[43] John Harvie, meanwhile, was born in 1833 in Campbeltown, Scotland, but emigrated to the United States when he was eighteen for the usual reasons a man emigrates: to better his chances. Family tradition also says that he left because Campbeltown – a city known for its many whisky distilleries – had been overrun by inebriates and degenerates. A letter of recommendation that he carried from his Campbeltown employer described him as "sober, attentive & well qualified."[44] In Toledo, Ohio, the abstemious Presbyterian Scot and former Sunday school teacher found work in the traffic department of the Michigan Southern Railroad. Shortly afterwards, in 1852, he visited Toronto, where a chance encounter with an old friend from Campbeltown led to a yet another move when his friend asked him what, exactly, he was doing in that republic to the south. Everyone knows, he is reputed to have said, that Americans are a godless people. Then and there, John Harvie decided to move to Upper Canada, where he worked as a freight conductor with the Ontario, Simcoe, and Huron Union Railway, later the Northern Railway.

A few months later, in May 1853, he was pressed into service as the railway's first passenger conductor on a train connecting Toronto to Aurora. In fact, "he issued the first ticket, collected the first fare, and accompanied the first passenger train in Upper Canada."[45] It was in Aurora that he met Lizzie. Actually, she noticed him at a community dance: he was dancing in the main room and she was sitting modestly in the mezzanine – as the daughter of a Methodist minister was expected to do – when she was hit by his auburn hair and fine moves. Apparently she "liked the way he danced" and they were married a year later, in

1861.[46] Kennedy Creighton performed the marriage service but, because John
was a staunch Presbyterian, it was Lizzie who converted, although it wasn't a
great leap of faith. The theological differences between Methodism and Presbyterianism were minuscule compared to the deep Protestant consensus emerging in Ontario in the second half of the nineteenth century, a consensus that
emphasized the union of the sacred and the secular, the spiritual and the material, and the dominion of God and the Dominion of Canada.[47]

By any definition, Lizzie Harvie was a powerful force. Donald Creighton
once described his maternal grandmother as the only woman he ever feared.[48]
Unyielding, tireless, and driven by a granite faith in God, she was an early
pioneer in the Christian reform movement. "Take everything, no matter how
trivial, to [Him]," she wrote, "and light will come, even out of great darkness."[49]
When her seven-year-old daughter died in 1874, she decided that health care
for children had to be improved, and so, with other like-minded women –
including Lady Macdonald, the second wife of Sir John A. Macdonald – she
founded the Hospital for Sick Children in 1875. Out of the darkness of a
child's death came the light of a children's hospital. Later, and again with other
like-minded women, she founded the Women's Medical College – the first
medical school in Toronto to admit women students – and served as its trea-
surer for several years. And as one of the founders of the Ontario Women's
Christian Temperance Union, she became the first corresponding secretary of
the Toronto chapter.[50]

Harvie was also part of "the feminization of the foreign missionary enterprise." Seeking a role in "the life and work of the church," women found it in
missionary work.[51] With a group of laywomen, Harvie founded the Women's
Foreign Missionary Society in 1876 to assist "female missionaries, Bible readers, and teachers, who shall labour among heathen women and children"[52] and,
for the next two decades, served as its foreign secretary. It was in her capacity as
foreign secretary that, in 1894, Harvie visited every Presbyterian mission and
reserve school in Manitoba and the northwest, "from Portage La Prairie on the
east to Prince Albert and Mistawasis on the west." It took six weeks and involved 5,000 miles of hard, "tedious" travel by railway, steamboat, and horse-
back.[53] But she soldiered on, delivering, like her father before her, Christ's
promise of salvation. Afterwards, Harvie recorded both her "satisfaction" with
the work being done and her "sorrow" with the work yet to be done: the sight
of "Christian Indians living an agricultural life, contented, industrious, happy,
and more or less prosperous, meeting together regularly to worship God in
comfortable little churches," must be juxtaposed, she said, with the sight of "pa-
gan Indians living a wild and careless life, ignorant, indolent, superstitious, and
abjectly poor without God and without hope in the world."[54] In 1894 alone the

Small in stature, Eliza (Lizzie) Jane Creighton Harvie (1840–1929) was a giant in Christian reform circles. Donald Creighton once described his maternal grandmother as the only woman he ever feared. Like her father, Kennedy Creighton, Lizzie Creighton was a tireless servant. "Take everything, no matter how trivial, to [Him] and light will come, even out of great darkness." In 1894 she "rescued" a prostitute named Edna with Mackenzie King, then a University of Toronto student and later Canada's longest-serving prime minister.

WFMS had gathered eleven tons of clothing items and blankets for its missions in western Canada. According to one missionary on the ground, the blankets "have been simply invaluable in covering the shivering and half-naked savages from the rigors of a northern winter ... and commending to otherwise unreceptive hearts the gospel which accompanies the gifts."[55]

Manitoba and the northwest were not foreign in a literal sense but, as Harvie had explained years earlier, missionary work in western Canada was also "work among the heathen." In "giving the red men of the prairie and forest the Gospel of our Lord Jesus Christ," she said, "we are presenting for their acceptance a richer heritage than their old hunting grounds which we now possess."[56] Harvie was hardly unique. Her assumptions – that what was theirs was now hers, that their gods were inferior to her God, and that residential schools were the answer to the "Indian question" – were the alibis of imperialism and of an "uncomprehending, unsympathetic, and insensitive" majority.[57]

Well before the professionalization of social work, the indefatigable Harvie established Toronto's Prison Gate Mission and Haven in 1878, serving as its president for seventeen years. Initially, the Haven was intended to meet the immediate material and spiritual needs of women who had been released from prison. But it quickly opened its doors to "every lost woman," from pregnant teenagers to prostitutes, making it one more response among many to Toronto's encounter with industrial capitalism. If the country's second-largest city was not to be forsaken, it would have to be saved, one fallen woman at a time. Stressing the transformative power of Jesus Christ, Haven administrators and volunteers talked in terms of good and evil, sin and redemption, confession and propitiation, and conversion and salvation.[58]

One volunteer was an "earnest, puritanical, and sanctimonious" nineteen-year-old University of Toronto undergraduate named Mackenzie King, who, in February 1894, resolved to save prostitutes from their "wicked life," a decision that brought him to the Haven, Lizzie Harvie, and Edna.[59] Nothing is known about Edna except that she was a prostitute living with another prostitute in a rented room on King Street when she first met this zealous university student who was determined to rescue her. According to King's version of events – which is the only version there is – he went to Edna's room, where they enjoyed "a long, earnest & extremely interesting talk." He pleaded with her "to give up the life" she was leading, which she was "perfectly willing to do" if only she could return to her old job as a nurse at an asylum. King, she believed, had been sent by God "in answer to her mother's prayers." Following this initial meeting, he "went to see Mrs. Harvie about Edna," who agreed to meet with her. That night King paid another visit to Edna. This time her roommate, Jennie, was there. "They had a grate fire burning, I sat opposite it. Edna sat beside me on the floor, Jennie to the right. We all cried. I spoke better tonight than ever before. Both girls feel very badly." The next afternoon Mackenzie King and Lizzie Harvie went to see Edna while Jennie was out and, together, persuaded her "to give up her bad life." That evening Edna was taken to the Haven, where "she broke down completely [and] asked for forgiveness" while King "rejoiced at bringing this tossed about little ship into a quiet harbour."[60]

V

As one brother carried the Gospel across Upper Canada, the other brother re-mained in North Dorchester, and it was there, in 1854, that James Creighton's wife, Mary, died one week after delivering her second baby. Without warning, James was left with two young daughters: Eliza, age three, and Mary Isabella, a newborn. Out of grief, necessity, and, no doubt, love, he turned to his wife's sister, Ann, and they were married a year and a half later. In England the law was clear: a man could not marry his deceased wife's sister, and any such mar-riage would be "null and void."[61] That law, however, didn't extend to British North America, and one was never passed in Upper Canada, a sparsely popu-lated colony where men outnumbered women. James and Ann Creighton – Donald Creighton's paternal grandparents – enjoyed a long, healthy, and fecund marriage. Their first child was born in 1856 and their fourteenth in 1886 when

Ann was forty-nine. Her granddaughter remembered her as a "wonderful character."[62] She must have been. She raised sixteen children.

Like the family, the farm also multiplied, becoming in Donald Creighton's words, "the main unit of economic activity and the principal agency of social security and welfare."[63] The census returns for 1861 and 1871, for example, indicate that James had become a prosperous, progressive farmer. By 1861 he had purchased another fifty acres. He now owned 150 acres, which, in the 1860s, was considered "a substantial farm."[64] Fifty acres were enumerated as under cultivation, twenty-four under pasture, and one under orchard. For whatever reason, Creighton didn't plant much wheat. His was a mixed farm with an almost equal acreage of peas (six acres), potatoes (five acres), and oats (five and a half acres). These three crops were useful in the household as well as on the market, where, at any given time, they earned a good price. They could also be fed to livestock, which were assuming more and more emphasis on the farm. In 1861 Creighton owned eleven steers or heifers under three years old, six milk cows, five horses, four pigs, and fifteen sheep.[65] Exercising caution and flexibility on a mixed farm with a nod to livestock, especially cattle, he was producing a surplus of beef and butter for market. According to the 1871 census, he owned 300 acres. In addition, he had purchased two "town or village lots." To the diversified agriculture of 1861, he had added barley (perhaps for Labatt in London) and corn (which, again, could be fed to humans and to livestock). Naturally, he continued to grow hay (thirty tons), but now for a much larger number of cattle and horses. In 1871 he owned eight horses, twenty-nine milk cows, and six other horned cattle, having "sold or killed" three others. His farm produced 1,200 pounds of butter, eight times what it had produced in 1851. And as a progressive farmer at that time would, he owned three ploughs or cultivators, one reaper, a horse rake, and a fanning mill. In addition to producing maple sugar (170 pounds) and apples (200 bushels), he was also using his wood lot: he produced 20,000 staves and 120 cords of firewood. Finally, his farm produced one hundred pounds of wool and forty-five yards of homemade cloth.[66]

In 1871, James Creighton was forty-nine years old and clearly successful, integrating all of the elements of his farm into a business. It was time to think about building a new house. At some point in the early 1870s, he and Ann built an eleven-room house with Middlesex cream bricks that had, as their name suggests, a distinctive cream colour. An 1889 county history boasted that this particular brick had attained some "celebrity" because of its unique whitish-yellowish colour.[67] James and Ann called their house Hillside, though, over time, it became better known as "the old Creighton home."[68]

Well suited to their needs and their personality, James and Ann Creighton built Hillside – a solid, unpretentious structure – in the early 1870s. Taken ca. 1905, this photograph shows Ann, seated at right, with some of her children and in-laws. The house was torn down in the 1990s. Too bad. Apparently it had a gorgeous staircase.

Hillside was set to the daily and seasonal rhythms of the farm and governed by the imperatives of religion, family, and education. Although James Creighton was a deeply religious man, he did not make a great show of it: "glibness," "posturing," and excessive "piety" were not his style. In simple and honest fashion, he "stuck by the little old church through thick and thin, worked for it, paid his money for its upkeep, and fairly well lived up to its principles and teachings in his own life." The Sabbath was a day to wear one's Sunday best, go to church, and, after the service, attend class meetings, where members would gather under the supervision of either a minister or a lay leader to grow in God's grace through testimony, discussion, and instruction. Sunday also meant a large family dinner, lively conversation, "gathering around the piano," and, for the children, invariably staying up past their bedtime. Playing the piano was one thing but playing cards was quite another. Cards were the devil's handiwork and thus not permitted in the Creighton household. James also emphasized the importance of education, or what he called getting "a good schooling." All of the Creighton kids attended the "old townline school" and, when it was time, attended high school in the city. Eventually, James rented a house on Hill Street in London, and "a second household was set up to which there was constant going and from which there was constant coming for years."[69]

No longer "tenants in time," James and Ann Creighton were now part of "an early, rural "middle class" in Ontario's heartland."[70] By the amount of land they owned, the house they built, the faith they adhered to, and the values of family, hard work, forbearance, and education they lived by, the Creightons had achieved a measure of opportunity, security, and respectability. The house was the "most visible" symbol of their "competency and social rank."[71] The piano was another. And the decision to establish a second household in the city in order to be closer to a high school reflected their ambitions for, and their expectations of, their children.

VI

"Closeness prevailed" between the two Creighton families.[72] Kennedy and Laura and their children often visited James and Ann and their children, and in the 1860s, until his early death in 1871, their eldest child, also named James, who was deaf and mute, lived at Hillside. When the two families got together, James and Kennedy retired to the porch, where they argued about politics and where, according to family history, they became "two brutes." Kennedy was a "capital L Liberal" and James a "capital C Conservative." For Kennedy, Sir John A. Macdonald could do no right; for James, he could do no wrong. At some point, compelled no doubt by the growing din, Laura would come out of the house and say, "Now, Kennedy." Although in the middle of "flipping John A. to the buff," he wisely complied with his wife's gentle reproach.[73]

This practice of making Hillside the centre for family gatherings continued into the next generation. Lizzie Harvie visited her uncle's farm as an adult and, in the summer months, her three children lived on it during their holidays. At a time when there was neither a religious nor a social stigma attached to such things, two sets of cousins fell in love and were married. John Kennedy Harvie, Lizzie's son, married Phoebe Creighton, his first cousin once removed. And Laura Creighton Harvie, Lizzie's daughter, caught the attention of William Black Creighton. "Each drew beads on the other" was how their daughter put it.[74]

Born in 1864, William Black Creighton was James and Ann's fifth child. His childhood was a happy, even idyllic one. It involved hard work, of course. All of the Creighton children were expected to contribute to the family economy. But it also involved the safe embrace of many brothers and sisters and an extended family of favourite uncles, loving aunts, teachers, ministers, eccentric hired hands, and a cast of characters in the community. And it involved exploring the countryside, finding the best swimming holes in the river that ran through the back of the farm, poking about old and abandoned houses, barns, and drive sheds, and, in the warm September sun, eating apple after apple in the orchard. The simple smell of an apple was enough to send William tumbling back through time to his childhood and adolescence and to the great crowded bins of apples stored in the cold cellar. It carried him back to "the Indians" who came to the farm "on several occasions" asking if they might have the "cool apples," those apples that had been exposed to the frost and, although "still clinging to the branches," had been "frozen quite solid."[75]

What Donald Creighton described as the "lush, green, unoccupied lands of southern Upper Canada" were never wholly unoccupied, and, by the last quarter of the nineteenth century, its original inhabitants had been reduced to foraging in the frozen orchards of its new owners. It was Locke's theory of property in practice.

Although attuned to the routine of farm life, William decided that it was not for him. He recalled how he would take books with him when he left in the morning to do his chores, and how, for example, he would read poetry when he should have been ploughing the back field. "Thinking back, certain fields on the old farm are associated even till this day with certain books."[76] At some point, Donald Creighton's father decided to pursue a college education.

As a Methodist, William attended Victoria College in Cobourg. Granted a royal charter in 1836 and given degree-granting powers by Upper Canada in 1841, Victoria College was part of the Methodist Church's attempt to reconcile revelation and experience with reason and knowledge through higher education. It was an attempt "to temper a religion that often exalted the emotional moment of conversion, and to link the vital, but at times transitory, Christian experience of the revival to the more enduring structure of sound learning and moral conduct."[77] In time, it added faculties of law, medicine, and theology. For its part, the Faculty of Theology was the institutionalization of changes taking place within Methodism itself. What had been a growing sense was now a firm conviction: ministers needed formal training in theology and church history if Methodism was going to remain relevant in the new, increasingly urban, and educated Canada.

William graduated in 1890 with a bachelor of arts and the determination to become a minister. Looking back, he described his four years at Victoria as the most "vital" of his life. The man who most influenced and inspired him was Samuel Nelles, the president and chancellor of Victoria. Nelles died unexpectedly in 1887, in William's second year, but he left an indelible impression. "I have never ceased to feel toward him as to one of the noblest and most human

souls that I have ever come into touch with."[78] As a teacher, Nelles "tried to in-
still in his students a vital piety and powerful moral sense." Although his sermons stressed the need for personal salvation, he reminded his many students
that salvation was not only the moment of conversion, the moment Jesus Christ
entered one's heart. Salvation was also a living thing. As disciples of Christ,
Christians had an obligation to lead a moral life free of sin and to live a charitable life in service of others. Heavenly grace and earthly justice were not the
same thing but they weren't separate either. Their union lay at the "core of the
Scriptures" and it was "the central theme of evangelical Christianity."[79]

Fifty years after the fact, William could still recall the sound of Nelles's
"strange, somewhat sepulchral voice." And he could still recall being moved by
one verse in particular that Nelles read in the college chapel:

> Now the long and toilsome duty
> Stone by stone to carve and bring;
> Afterward the perfect beauty
> Of the palace of the King.[80]

Was this, then, the moment that Creighton found his life's purpose? Growing
up, he would have known Jesus as an abstraction, as a name invoked, for example, in his bedtime prayers. And he would have known Jesus as the main
character in the story of God's only begotten son, his virgin birth, crucifixion,
resurrection, and ascension. But was this the moment when he knew, for the
first time, Jesus Christ as his personal saviour? Was this the moment that he
dedicated his life to serving God? The year he graduated, he was received on
probation by the London, Ontario, Conference of the Methodist Church. Four
years later, in 1894, he had completed his probationary duties and graduated
from Victoria with a second degree, a bachelor of divinity. He also carried away
the gold medal for highest standing in his class. After his ordination a few
months later, he received his first church in Tupperville, Ontario, a small village
near Chatham. It was time to think about marriage.

Initially, John Harvie – by this point an active congregant of Toronto's Knox
Presbyterian Church, a member of the benevolent St Andrew's Society, and
permanent secretary to the Upper Canada Bible Society – disapproved of his
daughter's choice: William Creighton was a Methodist. That William was also
his daughter's first cousin once removed apparently didn't matter.[81] Of course,
John's own wife had been a Methodist but she converted to Presbyterianism
and William was unlikely to convert. In time, however, John came around. By
all accounts, his future son-in-law really was a good and decent man whose
genuine faith in God was neither doctrinal nor sanctimonious. It was, a friend

William Black Creighton (1864–1946) graduated from Victoria College with a bachelor of arts (1890) and a bachelor of divinity (1894). After a brief and frustrating experience as a minister in rural Ontario, he was appointed assistant editor of the *Christian Guardian* in 1901 and elected editor in 1906, a position he would hold until 1937. As a teenager, Donald Creighton "began to appreciate the character and quality of the *Christian Guardian*" under his father's editorship. "What delighted me then, and what has never ceased to impress me since, were the range and catholicity of the paper's interests."

once said, both "simple and spacious."[82] William and Laura were married on 11 September 1895 at her parents' home on Bedford Road in Toronto.

They had been in Tupperville for about two years when they were moved to Guilds, an even smaller village. It was here that their first son was born in 1897, and, in honour of Laura's father, they named him John Harvie, or Jack. William, however, didn't particularly like the minister's life. Nor did Laura particularly like being a minister's wife. Their daughter, Isabel Wilson, remembered them talking about it in onerous terms, about how her father would come home from the district meeting and lay a handful of change – including pennies – on the mantel. It was a pittance, really, and it was all "that they had to live on." In those days, ministers were also paid in kind. But there was only so much head cheese that two people and an infant could eat. Under the cover of darkness – so that their neighbours couldn't see what they were doing – they would take "the whack of hog's head" and "literally bury it in the yard."[83] The community's gaze was an especially heavy burden for Laura. Since the congregation owned the house and its contents, "small groups of women could arrive to inspect it." The house, of course, was a pretence. The real purpose of their unannounced visits was Laura herself. She was the object of their gaze and she hated it. Unlike her mother, she had no instinct "for the taking on of a powerful management role in the life of the community," the sort of role that was expected of a minister's wife. As a result, she was left feeling anxious and inadequate. Years after the fact she could still recall – "with some emotion" – how, on putting a cake in the oven, she dropped "to her knees in prayer that it would not fall and bring disgrace when they entertained the choir that evening."[84]

Too academically inclined to be a minister in small-town Ontario, William needed to escape. As his daughter put it, he was "better with the pen" than he was with "the pulpit"; to have stayed would have led to "some tragic blowup."[85] Then fate intervened when William lost his voice in the fall of 1898. For one brief, terrifying moment, he suspected tuberculosis. Mercifully, it was only laryngitis.[86] But it was serious enough that it made preaching impossible. Seeking the restorative air of a more temperate climate, William went to the Okanagan Valley of British Columbia while Laura and Jack went to Hillside to live with his family.

Going to British Columbia, however, was not only related to his health. Through his father-in-law, who was active in the Upper Canada Bible Society, he became a colporteur, one of those dedicated servants – now mythologized in Bible societies around the world – who travelled enormous distances and endured endless privations to distribute the received word of God to remote locations. In just six months, William travelled 2,004 miles, paid 872 visits, sold 415 Bibles, gave away seven more, and met fifteen families who had been

Laura Harvie Creighton (1869–1946) was a quiet, thoughtful woman who introduced her children to the world of books. "I was born," Donald Creighton once said, "into a household in which books – history, biography, literature – were all about."

"destitute of scripture" altogether prior to his arrival.[87] Actually, the 1899 annual report of the Upper Canada Bible Society singled out the work being done in British Columbia. "The work of Colportage," it said, "has been extended during part of the year, most especially in British Columbia, where our Colporteurs have done excellent service along the new Railway lines, in mining districts, lumber camps, factories, canneries, Public Works, etc." But more than the miles travelled and the number of Bibles distributed, the colporteurs reported "many opportunities of personal conversation with infidels and others who were perfectly careless regarding their eternal interests."[88] William returned to Ontario six months later, in June 1899, still uncertain about his future. Preaching was always a possibility, but he didn't particularly like it and his voice was still weak. Indeed, "to the end of his days" he found it difficult to speak before a large congregation.[89] But colporteuring involved long absences from his family, meaning he would have to find a different way to serve.[90] Within a year – eleven months to be precise – that way presented itself when he left the pastorate for good and moved to Toronto to become the assistant editor of the *Christian Guardian*, the newspaper of the Methodist Church of Canada and the largest-circulation weekly in the country. Remarkably, he would remain at the *Guardian* – and after church union in 1925, the *New Outlook* – for the next thirty-six years. Although William described this course of events as the will of providence and although his obituary said that he had been "called," it was really the work of his mother-in-law, Lizzie Harvie.[91] She had learned of the initial open-ing and made things happen. William did the rest.

VII

Between 1832 – when John Creighton arrived in Upper Canada – and 1900 – when his grandson and great-granddaughter moved to Toronto – the Creighton family became Canadian. It was not a conscious decision. Nor was it the result of a single event. It just happened. Naturally, Ireland always resonated with John, Kennedy, and James. They had been born there. John would have liked his grandchildren and great-grandchildren to visit Northern Ireland and to see Tamlaght O'Crilly, the parish he had left so many years before.[92] For their parts, Kennedy could be reduced to tears when listening to old Irish songs like "Killarney," "The Wind that Shakes the Barley," and "An Irish Lullaby," while James played the flute and the fiddle and had a repertoire of "Irish songs and tunes and jigs" that seemed to be "without number." One of William's earliest – and clearest – memories saw him sitting on his father's knee out on the back stoop while he "hummed over those old Irish tunes," keeping time with his feet.[93] For the next generation, however, Ireland did not have the same reso-nance.[94] Indeed, for the Creightons that process began even earlier. John, Kennedy, and James all left the Presbyterian Church to join the Methodist Church. And when singing his favourite Irish songs, James liked to mix in a Methodist hymn. These "he could sing with considerable fervour."[95] As roots in the new country grew deeper, ties to the old country grew weaker. "The loyal-ties of the Old World were yielding to the vigorous interests of the New," Donald Creighton wrote, and "the immigrants of the past were becoming the British American citizens of the present."[96]

As Creighton intimated, being Canadian in the post-Confederation era meant being British.[97] When Sir John A. Macdonald famously said, "A British subject I was born, a British subject I will die," he was speaking as a Canadian nationalist, not as an obsequious colonial. Both as a British subject and as a Canadian, Macdonald understood that he was part of a larger British world premised on a shared set of assumptions, values, and institutions. Spanning the globe, and held together by an allegiance to the Crown, the British Empire was the greatest empire the world had ever known. As an inheritance, a sentiment, and an outlook, it offered tradition, power, and vision. And as an association of free states, it was a diplomatic, commercial, and military alliance that, for Canada, constituted an essential counterweight to the United States, ensuring Canada's independence and separateness in North America. Ultimately, the

Donald Creighton and his older brother, John (Jack) Creighton, 1902. "God, king, and country" was a living faith in the Creighton household. So too were the values of hard work, delayed gratification, and patient accumulation.

imperial connection shaped how English Canadians imagined themselves and their nation in North America and in the world.

Britishness was not something imposed from outside. It emerged from inside. Halifax, Fredericton, Kingston, Winnipeg, and Vancouver were British in composition and imperial in disposition. But, by all accounts, Toronto was the most imperial city in the country.[98] One prominent citizen described the Queen City as the empire's most loyal city.[99] Another described 24 May– "the birthday of our Gracious Queen" – as a great occasion in the city's calendar, featuring excursions, picnics, parades, and fireworks.[100] When Great Britain went to war in South Africa in 1899, Toronto responded in kind, its "valiant sons," the *Globe* reported, marching "forth to devote their strength, and if need be their lives, to the defence of the empire and the expansion of her power."[101]

William and Laura Creighton were living in Toronto – in a semi-detached house on Concord Avenue just south of Bloor Street – when their second son was born on Tuesday, 15 July 1902. They named him Donald Grant.

chapter two

Childhood and Adolescence

A rather quiet, thoughtful small boy – and yet, at times, full of exuberant fun and inventive mischief – he must have learnt to read early, for he quickly became passionately interested in books.

John A. Macdonald, vol. 1

"I was born," Donald Creighton once said, "into a household in which books – history, biography, literature – were all about."[1] After dinner, when his father retired to his book-lined study upstairs, his mother read aloud to him, his brother Jack, and his sister Isabel. Later, the pattern would change. Rather than reading to her children, Laura read with them. As Isabel recalled, she "began to bring us into her own world of books. She began to read *with* us. As soon as our homework was done, or said to be done, the session would begin."[2] The Creighton children never wanted for reading material. The *Christian Guardian* received dozens of books directly from publishers anxious to see them duly noted – and possibly even reviewed – in the pages of a Canadian newspaper. Creighton remembered how, "at certain seasons of the year, particularly in the early spring or in the last few weeks before Christmas, [my father] would bring home several large parcels of books." Tired after the long commute by streetcar from downtown Toronto to the city's west end, he would drop the parcels – all neatly wrapped in brown paper – in the front hall for his precocious son. "I was given the delightful privilege of opening them, and looking over, and sampling, the books inside. It was a very rare occasion, I seem to remember, when I did not discover at least two or three volumes that interested me."[3]

Dickens was an early and perennial favourite. While some writers are content, novel after novel, to "plow the same field," Charles Dickens set out to "map the world."[4] Ultimately, his great map of the world lay in his characters.

According to one count, he created 989 characters, both major and minor. A young Creighton explored Dickens's map of the world through Seth Pecksniff, Nell Trent, Ebenezer Scrooge, David Copperfield, Uriah Heep, Oliver Twist, Bill Sikes, and Miss Havisham, as well as M'Choakumchild, Pumblechook, Fagin, and Gaffer Hexam. Alfred Tennyson was another favourite: King Arthur and his sword Excalibur, Sir Galahad and his search for the Holy Grail, the Duke of Wellington and his service at the battle of Waterloo, and the tragic but noble charge of the Light Brigade captured the Victorian era's pieties of patriotism and duty, its certitudes of nation and empire, its promises of greatness and destiny, and its fondness for sentimentality and melancholy. In many ways, the age of Victoria was the age of Tennyson. When Prince Albert died, it was to Tennyson's poetry that Queen Victoria turned for consolation and comfort, keeping a copy of *In Memoriam* on her bedside table.

In time, Creighton committed to memory long passages from Dickens and Tennyson. He was especially fond of Dickens's opening sentences. "London. Michaelmas Term lately over, and the Lord Chancellor sitting in Lincoln's Inn Hall. Implacable November weather." Or, "Marley was dead, to begin with." And, of course, "It was the best of times, it was the worst of times, it was the age of wisdom, it was the age of foolishness, it was the epoch of belief, it was the epoch of incredulity, it was the season of Light, it was the season of Darkness, it was the spring of hope, it was the winter of despair." He also delighted in Dickens's character sketches, his uncanny ability to capture someone's inner being through their outer appearance. Uncle Pumblechook – that pompous, impudent, foolish figure in *Great Expectations* – was a "large hard-breathing middle-aged slow man, with a mouth like a fish, dull staring eyes, and sandy hair standing upright on his head, so that he looked as if he had just been all but choked." Tennyson's poetry was similarly wonderful.

> Bury the Great Duke
>   With an empire's lamentation,
> Let us bury the Great Duke
>   To the noise of the mourning of a mighty nation

Memorizing poetry was not something Creighton had to do. It was something he wanted to do.[5]

Laura Creighton turned to Charles Dickens and Alfred Tennyson because one was the world's greatest novelist and the other its greatest poet. As Northrop Frye observed, "There is no Canadian writer of whom we can say what we can say of the world's major writers, that their readers grow up inside their work without ever being aware of a circumference."[6] The novels of William Douw

Lighthall were strained and sententious, the poetry of Bliss Carman and Charles G.D. Roberts derivative and didactic. But if growing up inside the work of the world's major writers meant never being aware of a circumference, it meant being aware of a centre and knowing that it was someplace else. For Donald Creighton, it was Great Britain.

"Truth for any man," he said, quoting Oswald Spengler, "is the picture of the world which was born at his birth."[7]

II

On 15 July 1902 the Toronto *Globe* sold for two cents; a loaf of bread cost 10 cents; the Canadian Pacific Railway charged $59.25 for a return ticket to Vancouver; the war in South Africa had just ended; and a "confident consensus" governed the city, one marked by loyalty to Great Britain and the British Empire and by pride in Canada's past and a belief in its future.[8] Donald Creighton described Edwardian Toronto as a "cleanly, home-loving, self-centred, somewhat puritanical town, with a serious concern for education, and a growing interest in the arts." In other words, Toronto the Good was a boring place: prim, proper, and not a little strait-laced. And where Montreal was "imposing, complicated, and mysterious," Toronto was "solidly British."[9] According to the 1901 census its population was 208,040. One hundred and ninety thousand people, or nearly 92 per cent, described themselves as British to the enumerators that year.

In an editorial to mark Victoria Day in 1907, William Creighton celebrated the "imperial bond," reminding his readers that there was no contradiction between imperialism and Canadianism. "We are proud of our own land; we exalt in our own magnificent heritage, but we are also proud of the Empire to which we belong; and we honour and respect the grand old flag that floats everywhere the Empire's bounds extend."[10] King Edward VII's death a few years later, in May 1910, wasn't the death of a foreign sovereign. It was the death of his sovereign. Moved by the occasion's solemnity, he and Laura gathered Jack, Donald, and Isabel, and, as a family, they listened to the Ossington Avenue fire hall ring its bells.[11]

For his part, Wilfrid Laurier – the country's first French-Canadian prime minister – carefully balanced the imperialism of William Creighton and the nationalism of French Canada at the same time as he oversaw Canada's transformation. His national policy had been Sir John A. Macdonald's national policy: immigrants from across eastern Europe filled the prairies; the customs tariff both protected and encouraged industrial growth in central Canada; and not one but two new transcontinental railways were in the works. It was in this context, the context of Laurier's Canada, that Toronto emerged as a "nearly national" metropolis.[12] Although surpassed by Montreal and challenged by Vancouver and Winnipeg, Toronto's financial reach extended across the country, from the Atlantic to the Pacific, from northern mining operations to city utilities, from western farmlands to urban real estate.

Methodism too was transformed. Based on a new reading of the gospel that emphasized Christ's humanity and His service to humanity, the Methodist Church set out to build the kingdom of God on earth. It not only embraced but, to an extent, constituted the social gospel movement, the Christian reform movement of the late nineteenth and early twentieth centuries. Methodism's emphasis on the revival – on the very thing that had made it the largest Protestant denomination in Canada – gave way to an emphasis on social regeneration. "Methodism exists to make men holy," William Creighton wrote. But it is not enough to make men holy; society too must be made holy. The "problem of Methodism," therefore, is the problem of "society's regeneration."[13] The Methodist Church targeted the usual suspects in its effort to build His kingdom – alcoholism, poverty, and sexual deviance – but it also made children an important focus. "Take care of the children," advised one Methodist minister and Toronto child welfare advocate, "and the nation will take care of itself."[14] In effect, the Methodist Church had discovered children. And it saw them as little seeds that needed careful nurturing in order that they might grow into both successful adults and successful citizens.[15]

It wasn't just children from working-class families – children living, for example, in The Ward, the poorest district in Toronto – that became the object of the Church's attention. It was children from middle-class families as well. It was children like Jack, Donald, and Isabel Creighton. A 1905 article in the *Christian Guardian* commented – in earnest and concerned tones – on the decay of family discipline. It had become, the article claimed, a "thing of the past." Parents have become too busy, and, as a result, they "let their children grow up without that constant and loving oversight which is the very essence of true home life, and without which children cannot possibly be trained to habits of obedience, respect, and discipline." The stakes were high. The family, after all, "is the keystone of society, the keystone of the state. The result of laxity in the home is a shock to the whole future of the commonwealth."[16] The author's impression of family life was just that – impressionistic – but he intuited that the purpose of the family had changed over the course of the past thirty or forty years, that for urban middle-class families the purpose was the nurture of children, not economic production.[17]

William and Laura Creighton very much conformed to this ideal, which was, in fact, the ideal of the bourgeois family: he provided; she tended; and together they emphasized the values of discipline, hard work, personal responsibility, delayed gratification, patient accumulation, abstinence, and service. And together they placed their children's welfare – especially their education – above everything else.

III

In September 1906 the General Conference of the Methodist Church met in Montreal. Among the many items on its agenda was the election of a new editor of the *Christian Guardian*. When the previous editor resigned that winter because of ill health – an "affliction" according to one report – the paper became the full-time responsibility of William Creighton.[18] He had big shoes to fill and he filled them well. But this would not be an acclamation. Other men wanted the job, including a former editor. It took three ballots but, in the end, the General Conference elected Creighton as editor of its key publication. Donald was only four years old at the time but, some seventy years later, he could recall the "jubilation" and the "rejoicing" at 262 Concord Avenue when news of his father's election arrived.[19] For his part, William was naturally humbled by the awesome responsibility he had been handed. He thanked the Conference for its "trust and confidence" and asked its delegates for their help in making the paper "a great success."[20] His alma mater greeted his appointment with enthusiasm. The Conference had chosen wisely, the *Acta Victoriana* reported, because Creighton would bring his "philosophical insight," "literary grace," and "personal charm" to the task. "He is the type of man, of whom an Oxford lecturer recently said, that 'ought to have been an Oxford man.'"[21]

The General Conference could not have known that Creighton would remain as editor for the next thirty years, that he would see the paper, and in a sense the Methodist Church, through the First World War, the union of the Methodist, Presbyterian, and Congregational churches in the early 1920s, and the economic crisis of the early 1930s.

In the first paper that carried his name on the masthead, Creighton asked, "What kind of paper should this one aim to be?" In the long article that followed, he spelled out his vision. Echoing the reform movement's focus on the family and on children, he said that it should be a "family paper": "if it falls here, it must fall most signally."[22] Creighton especially wanted to make the *Guardian* more relevant to boys. To help them navigate what he called the "perplexities and fierce temptations" of adolescence, a place in the paper, he said, will be given over to their "encouragement," "instruction," and "inspiration."[23] His early decision to make the *Guardian* more relevant to teenage boys was part of

Methodism's attempt to confront what it called the "boy problem." Adolescence was an "emotional age." It was a "period of crisis." And too many boys, once they entered adolescence, left the church. If the boy isn't carefully guided, he "will drift away from Sunday school and church. He will become careless and indifferent, if not immoral."[24] Alcohol, cigarettes, pool halls, and penny theatres shouted their temptations, leading boys off the straight and narrow. Meanwhile, church leaders, clerical and lay alike, doubted "the ability of parents, whose own youth had been spent in rural or semi-rural environments, to fulfill their parental responsibilities."[25] If the Methodist Church was to remain a vital force in Canadian life, something had to be done. Special efforts had to be made to ensure that boys stayed in the church and that they were taught to lead a life of service.

"Are we teaching our boys," Creighton asked, "that they owe the world and their fellowmen a debt, great according to the measure of their ability and opportunity, and that service is the greatest and most honorable word in the whole calendar of human achievement, or are we allowing them to grow up with the idea that to get and to achieve is the be-all and end-all of living?"[26] His question implied its own answer. Ultimately, the source of the "boy problem" lay "in the home," Creighton said. "The father owes it to his boy to live a clean life in every sense." He should worry less about making money and more about getting "to know his boy." But suppose the father fails, what then? At this point, the church must be prepared to step in through special classes, clubs, and the Boy Scouts. Somebody, Creighton said, must "get a grip on Harry."[27]

William and Laura Creighton would get a grip on Harry and, for that matter, on Harriet too. It was, in part, for this reason that they left the city altogether in the summer months. The city, Creighton believed, failed children because it didn't provide enough opportunity for exercise. "Vice," after all, "is suppressed perspiration." To prevent vice, "let the boys and girls have plenty of vigorous exercise." Let them perspire and they will be "less apt to become law breakers" and more apt "to become good citizens."[28] Boys, especially, need the outdoors. As he explained on another occasion, the boy is "full of energy"; he is a "cyclone"; and the "titanic life forces at work in his small bundle of budding manhood" are really the voices "of the ancient Vikings unsilenced after fifteen centuries." He "must have room to grow. Somehow, somewhere, he must lose his surplus energy."[29] For Jack, Donald, and Isabel too, somewhere was Long Branch, a cottage community not far from Toronto.

In 1883 an entrepreneur named Thomas Wilkie "discovered" a wooded area on the lakeshore just west of the city. Here, he decided, was the ideal location for a summer resort. It was close enough to the city to be convenient but far enough away to be, in his words, "arcadian." He called it Long Branch. Premised on the principles of temperance and religious observance and surrounded by an iron fence – to prevent "incursions on the part of the rougher element" – the Long Branch Summer Resort featured a grand hotel with Japanese balconies and pagoda towers, generous cottages built in the Queen Anne revival style, a lovely beach, a boathouse, a picnic pavilion, and even a merry-go-round "on which the many children may ride in glorious rollicking delight." Tennis, lawn bowling, croquet, and archery were all made available to the discerning "pleasure seeker" who wanted "security against the thoughtless, the reckless, and, perhaps, the liquor-heated crowds."[30] Very quickly, Long Branch became a popular excursion destination for those seeking a reprieve from the unbearable heat of July and August. For the most part, people took day trips. It was, after all, only a forty-minute ferry ride from the foot of Yonge Street to the Long Branch pier. And it was an even quicker commute after the Toronto Railway Company built a radial line from Sunnyside to Long Branch in 1894. Because of its convenience and its moral foundation, Long Branch became an attractive spot to hold Sunday school picnics. A handful of people, though, would spend a night or two at the hotel, which boasted "all the latest improvements such as speaking tubes, electric bells, incandescent lights and a telephone connection direct to Toronto."[31] But for the very fortunate it was possible to spend the entire summer at their cottage. According to one advertisement, cottages would be sold on "strictly temperance principles" to people "who can be depended upon to maintain the [the Resort's] reputation." They were summer homes, really. Turrets, sun parlours, wrap-around verandas, and second-storey porches were common architectural features. Some even had names like Manitou and Idlewyld.

The Creightons were among the very fortunate. It is not clear how, exactly, they came to spend their summers at Long Branch. Presumably Laura's mother, Lizzie Harvie, made the arrangements. Although she did not own a cottage, she rented the same one each summer from 1906 or 1907 to 1912. Perhaps she knew Thomas Wilkie, who, like her, was active in Christian reform circles in Toronto. In any event, from mid-June to mid-September, the Creightons lived in a large cottage on Lake Ontario. William commuted back and forth to his office in the old Wesley Building on Richmond Street while Laura and the children spent long, wonderful summers on the lake. Donald Creighton's memories of Long Branch were many and vivid.

Although he rarely talked about his childhood – it was not something that interested him very much – when he did, Long Branch figured prominently. About two years before he died, he agreed to a lengthy interview with his son. On a reel-to-reel tape recorder, Philip Creighton gathered his father's childhood memories. Almost all centred on Long Branch. He remembered "the long sandy beach," of course. And the lake, too. Although it was "damned cold," he said. He and his brother and sister even named the landscape. There were groups, or clumps, of trees and these were named first clump, second clump, and third clump. At first clump, they liked to swim. At second clump, they liked to have a picnic lunch. And at third clump, they liked to wade deep into the lake. He remembered how "the literary ladies" would meet at the home of one Mrs Hills, a woman of "great authority" and "enormous bulk." Because his mother was the secretary of this little literary society, she read the minutes while he went off to busy himself. And he remembered how, in the middle of the summer, there would be a great carnival featuring races and contests of all shapes and sizes, including "the very dramatic 'walking the greasy pole' out in the middle of the lake." As a special treat, he was allowed to watch John Bunny movies in the grandstand. Preceding even Charlie Chaplin, Bunny was one of the first vaudeville actors to make the transition to film. "You went [into the grandstand] urged on by a man who called out, 'Hurry! Hurry! Hurry! The show is just commencing.'" One summer the *Turbinia* – the very first steam turbine ship ever built and, in its day, easily the fastest ship in the world – docked at Long Branch. It was a fantastic sight. "There it was long quarter! Lights gleaming! We were beside ourselves with the rapture of this."[32]

And then it ended. In 1912 Creighton spent his last summer at Long Branch. At the time, it had seemed "eternal." It was as if "the summer never ended, that it went on and on and on." Summers are like that in childhood. They never end. "Summers end when you get old," he said, making Long Branch something of a "lost paradise."[33] Of course, he wasn't talking about Long Branch. He was talking about his childhood and who he was as a child.

As a boy Donald Creighton had been the life of the party, full of exuberant fun and inventive mischief. "I was notorious for my high spirits," he said. On one occasion, in Toronto, he had been part of a church pageant. A number of the congregation children were. But he stole the show. "I went at it at a terrific dash and exaggerated every movement and, in effect, brought down the house." On another occasion, this one at Long Branch, he both wrote and performed in an end-of-the season musical. He danced, sang, and did a little comic routine. He was a hit. Indeed, his sister always described him as a happy, gregarious, outgoing boy who loved to carry on. But in that last summer at Long Branch, the summer he turned ten, he became violently ill. There was a huge bonfire one night, he said, "and I danced around the flames in my usual ecstatic way." But that night and and over the course of the next day, an infection developed in his neck. Soon great, open pustular lumps appeared. His mother took him into the city, where the doctors exposed him to massive X-ray radiation in an

Donald Creighton and his younger sister, Mary Isabel Creighton, at Long Branch, then a small summer community just west of Toronto on Lake Ontario, ca 1909. In those days, he said, summers "never ended"; summers end, he added, "when you get old."

effort to dry out what he described as "morbid," puss-filled lumps. It didn't work. Eventually, the lumps, whatever they were, had to be surgically removed. Then, in his convalescence, a prescription was incorrectly filled by the local chemist. "I was damn near poisoned," he said. In fact, he very nearly died.

The whole awful episode cost him a year at school. But more than this, it changed him fundamentally. He was never the same "gay guy" again, he said. Whereas before he had been the "extroverted member of the family," he was now "depressed."[34] According to Philip Creighton, it was at this point that his father's "view of the world darkens."[35] Donald Creighton's daughter, Cynthia Flood, agrees. Her father told stories about his childhood antics, she said, "to contrast his then sunniness with the gloom that descended" after the infection, the X-ray treatments, eventual surgery, and difficult convalescence.[36]

It is entirely possible that his illness and convalescence had nothing to do with the fundamental change that overtook him and, in the process, remade him. Perhaps it was the onset of puberty, the many physical changes of pubescence matched only by its enormous emotional changes that can alter a person's disposition and, in effect, remake that person. Perhaps, then, Creighton had confused his illness for something more profound and far-reaching.

At the very least, it can be said that his instinctive pessimism – his gloominess – came naturally to him. It came from his mother. His father was an eternal optimist who believed that the world, that God's creation, was "a decent, kind, and brotherly place."[37] In his words, "Unflinching, unconquerable, optimism is really the only truly Christian attitude."[38] Creighton's mother, however, harboured a more jaundiced view of the world. Where William always looked on the bright side, Laura always looked "on the dark side."[39]

Creighton used to say that people were born with different capacities for happiness. "Maybe," his daughter speculates, "that was how he explained to himself his own inability to be happy for very long."[40]

IV

Life went on, though. It didn't stop for Creighton's illness and it certainly didn't stop for his granite, intractable moods. In 1912 William and Laura Creighton bought a modest, undistinguished, but solid two-and-a-half-storey house on Hewitt Avenue, a quiet residential street in what was then a new development in the city's west end. There were schools in the area, of course. And High Park was a block or two away. But most importantly, Howard Park Methodist Church was just around the corner. In 1909 the Toronto Conference of the Methodist Church assigned Reverend Gilbert Agar to Howard Park. Initially, he led services in an old schoolhouse, but, in rapid succession, subscriptions were taken, a corner lot was purchased, the foundation excavated, and less than two years later, on Easter Sunday, 1911, Reverend Agar welcomed worshippers to the formal dedication of Howard Park Methodist Church.[41]

From the beginning, William and Laura Creighton were active congregants. He was an early member of Howard Park's Quarterly Board, which oversaw church governance, and led the Pulpit Committee, the committee responsible for guest pastors and visiting speakers. Meanwhile, Laura followed in her mother's footsteps by taking an interest in the Women's Missionary Society, serving variously as vice-president and president from 1913 to 1923. In 1917 she was made a life member in recognition of her service and devotion to mission work. Among other things, she read the scriptural lessons at monthly meetings; hosted social events at her home; arranged guest speakers, usually missionaries returning from the field; organized fundraising drives to support the long-term work of a missionary in Japan and the summer work of theological students at mission fields in western Canada; and led clothing drives for the Church's stations in the far north. In short, she encouraged the women of Howard Park to think, in her words, "more seriously of their sisters in heathen lands."[42]

In many ways, Howard Park was the church that Jack, Donald, and Isabel grew up in. Although Jack would have been too old, Donald and Isabel certainly attended Sunday school, "the garden in which God grows noble characters," according to one Methodist publication.[43] Howard Park's Sunday school organized an energetic program at the same time as it boasted a large membership. There were concerts, plays, games, crafts, lessons, activities, and outings. For example, in the summer of 1911 the Sunday school held its annual picnic in, of all places, Long Branch. And each Christmas, it ensured that every child received a small gift, usually a box of candy. In 1913 it reported an enrolment of 813 children with an average weekly attendance of 531; by 1914, 950 children were enrolled and 675 attended regularly.[44] William Creighton took Howard Park's Sunday school seriously and, for several years while his children were young, sat on its Board of Management. Part of the Sunday school's mission was to reach out to, and to connect with, "big boys." It's possible – indeed, likely – that Jack and later Donald were members of the Nikator Class, a special class designed to keep teenage boys interested in the church and to see them become "manly Christian characters." To quote its Howard Park leader, "these boys are now passing through the formative period of their careers, and if we can definitely hold them for the Church and Christian service during the next few years we will have them definitely tied up to active Christian service for their lives." With a room of their own, the boys had a place to gather in the evenings and on weekends that was not a street corner or a pool hall. Under "the immediate supervision of a loyal, earnest, and efficient Christian gentleman," they were warned about the temptations incarnate in alcohol and cigarettes.[45] Writing about Edwardian Toronto years later, Donald Creighton referred – derisively – to the "puritanical fanaticism" of the do-gooders and their various campaigns against alcohol and cigarettes.[46]

"God, king, and country" was not an empty phrase in Donald Creighton's childhood and adolescence. It was a living faith. And it was confirmed daily at home, at school, and at church by the example of his parents, by the lesson plans of his teachers, and by the prayers of his Sunday school leaders. It was also confirmed by his insatiable love of reading. Dickens, Tennyson, and the Bible may have been staples but so too were the many children's magazines published in Great Britain. According to Isabel Wilson, she and Donald devoured *Chums*, *Chatterbox*, and *Boy's Own Paper*. It was more like an "addiction," she said, especially to stories about English public schools. "For a time, we really inhabited a world of prefects and fagging, cricket matches and housemasters."[47]

Donald especially longed to attend an Eton, Harrow, Rugby, or Charterhouse, and, sadly, that longing never went away. Its focus changed and, for brief periods of time, was even satisfied, but it never went away because it never could go away. That is what it means to be colonized: one is led to believe that the action is someplace else.

When he and his friends learned that a neighbourhood boy was reading American comics, well, "we made his life miserable," he said.[48] And that, of course, was the point of British children's magazines: to fashion a shared membership in the imagined community that was the British world, to forge in children a stake in the imperial project, and, ultimately, to make them into loyal subjects. *Boy's Own Paper,* probably the most popular and successful children's magazine, carried endless stories of adventure featuring a cast of familiar characters, from explorers and soldiers to big game hunters and world travellers. Stemming from the white man's burden at the heart of late-Victorian and Edwardian imperialism, stories of British pluck in the face of adversity often turned on the racialized dichotomies of Self and Other, of Anglo Saxon superiority and African inferiority, of British fair play and Indian trickery, of British order and Chinese opium, of Christianity and heathenism. It wasn't just *Boy's Own Paper*. It was boy's literature in general that inspired dreams of adventure and legitimated deeds of empire in "a large and impressionable audience."[49]

For a year or two, though, Creighton's favourite children's monthly was *Little Folks*.[50] Although he "deplored" the title, he loved the magazine and its contents, each month waiting for its arrival with "great impatience" and, once he had it in his hot little hands, reading it "from cover to cover."[51] It contained the usual serial stories with predictable titles like "The Outlaws," "Pirates Three," "Castaways," "The Strange Doings of Benjie Brown," "A Nest of Malignants," and "Captain Dick Duck." The "Hobby Page" carried tips on how best to collect stamps; "Our Own Puzzle Page" presented word and number puzzles; and the "Post Office" printed letters from children in England, Scotland, and Wales and, for that matter, from children across the empire, from Australia, New Zealand, and Canada. Of course, that was the point, to bring Britannia's far-flung children together in one place. To quote the motto of *Little Folks*, "One Heart, Many Countries."

In 1913, *Little Folks* issued a special challenge to its readers, one that reflected the growing conservation movement in Great Britain and that movement's desire to extend its message of conservation and wildlife protection to children, when it invited them to create their own monthly nature journal: "The great point is that your journals should be the records of personal observation and that every page should be as beautifully neat as careful fingers can make it."[52] *Little Folks* didn't want accounts of "strange animals in far-off lands."[53] It wanted articles on the brown rabbit that lives in the field next door, on the birds that overwinter in the backyard, and on the multitude of insects that inhabit the vegetable garden. It wanted articles on the life cycle of trees, flowers, and plants of all varieties.

And so in the fall of 1913 and into the summer of 1914, Creighton designed, edited, and "published" what he called the "Canadian Nature Journal." He did most of the writing and provided all of the artwork. He wrote about squirrels, loons, and the autumn woods in High Park; he wrote a description of the chrysanthemum and a short reflection on frost; and because *Little Folks* had told its aspiring editors that it would be "capital fun" to have other people contribute to their journals,[54] he solicited stories from Isabel on the comings and goings of ants and the assigned tasks of the queen bee, the worker bee, and the drone. Listed on the masthead as a contributor, she also recounted watching two chickens engage in a tug of war over a worm. A regular feature in the "Canadian Nature Journal" was Creighton's Nature Notes, where he duly recorded the weather, the colour of the leaves, the names of butterflies, the items he had collected – "I picked up quite a curio today: two birch leaves had grown together"[55] – and the arrival of fall apples to the city. "5th Nov. [1913]: As I was going by the grocers I noticed the apples, boxes of apples stacked together, snows, russets, greenings, and spies and then I know there was a good apple harvest." Sounding a note of Canadian pride, he added, "In this north country the apples have a lovely taste and they are among the best in the world."[56] In one issue, Nature Notes included a list of the thirty-two different birds he had identified.

In the spring of 1914, Donald submitted the "Canadian Nature Journal" to *Little Folks.* Much to his surprise and delight, he won that month's competition. There, in the pages of *Little Folks,* was his name.

> Prize – Donald Creighton, aged 11, 32 Hewitt Avenue, Toronto, Ontario, for "The Canadian Nature Journal." A slender volume, but very well done. We were glad to see your nature notes.[57]

Looking back on the "Canadian Nature Journal," Isabel Wilson thought its significance lay in what it said about "the intensity of commitment" her brother "brought to everything he ever undertook."[58] Indeed, the three surviving issues reveal a neat, careful, and deliberate mind. And they reveal an abiding respect for the necessary detail – the different varieties of apples and the precise names of birds – and a fondness for the unnecessary, purely decorative detail. His cursive is clean and compact and the stories are carefully illustrated with elaborate lettering in the titles, little sketches in the margins, and bright watercolours.

That summer, Creighton and his family spent a few idyllic weeks tenting in Haliburton. Isabel Wilson remembered it as a "wonderful," "terrific" time.[59]

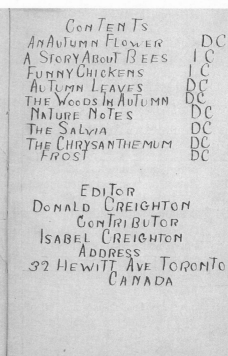

A young Donald Creighton loved British children's literature, especially a magazine called *Little Folks*. When it invited its many readers to create and submit their own nature journal, Creighton responded enthusiastically with stories about flowers, birds, and insects in "The Canadian Nature Journal."

Their days were spent swimming in Lake Kushog, exploring the woods, identifying birds, watching a local farmer plough his field, and walking into the nearby village of Ingoldsby to pick up supplies and to collect the mail. A little later in the summer, in late July and early August, the Creightons went to Lake Muskoka, where they stayed with Reverend Gilbert Agar, who, although no longer the minister at Howard Park Methodist Church, remained a close family friend. His boathouse had an upstairs with a bedroom or two and a small living area. Donald continued to keep nature notes for his journal. On 4 August 1914, for example, he recorded having seen "an immense bracket fungus about twenty inches long and twelve inches wide."[60]

A few hours earlier and several thousand miles away, Great Britain had issued a formal declaration of war against Germany. Europe had come undone. Sixty-four years later, Creighton could recall exactly where he was when he first heard the news. He was in Muskoka and Reverend Agar announced that the king had declared war against Germany, or as Agar pronounced it, against "the Keezer."[61]

V

Although Creighton did not serve in the war – he was only twelve when it started and sixteen when it ended – it became "a personal and family affair."[62] His father, as editor of the *Christian Guardian*, led a very public campaign in support of the war effort in general and of Robert Borden, Union Government, and conscription in particular; his brother served in the Canadian Expeditionary Force, was wounded at Passchendaele, and sent home; and he·worked as a farm labourer one summer. The war, in other words, was not an abstraction. It was real. And he followed events in Europe and at home with a keen and immediate interest. Half a century later he still wasn't sure what it all meant, "the macabre horror of Passchendaele," "the churned, oozing flats of the Ypres salient," and "the appalling mass slaughter" of the Western Front.[63] But the key to understanding the war lay, he suspected, in understanding its idealism. Not just Canada, he said, but the West in general "thought differently about the First World War than it had ever thought about any war in the past and will probably ever think about any war in the future. The idealism (misplaced, of course) of a whole generation of Westerners is what needs to be explained."[64]

He didn't say so, but Creighton was talking about his father. Canada's duty was clear, William Creighton believed: "We are British! And we will stand by the mother land in this greatest campaign of all time."[65] Like so many other Canadians, he thought that the war would be over in "a month or two,"[66] by Christmas at the latest. When it became obvious that the war would not be over quickly, that it would go on and on, he became convinced that it served a higher moral purpose. It was not simply a war *against* a ruthless enemy. It was a war *for* God. "Your country needs you," he said in June 1915. "That is the very same thing as saying your God needs you."[67] From this awful experience would emerge a new and better world. In February 1916, he described the war as a "blast from the very mouth of hell. It is licking up the best, the dearest, the noblest things in life and leaving behind it black ruin and unutterable misery." But might it not also "burn up something of the waste and rubbish and evil of our lives?"

The cruel and wicked class distinctions, the empty seeking after more pleasure, the indolent tolerance of drink and kindred evils – are there not many signs that in the fierce furnace of war these things are shriveling and passing away, and in their place are springing up an instinct for brotherhood and high and holy and self-sacrificing ideals and purposes of life? May we not make this great struggle a fire from God?[68]

His conviction was the conviction of the Methodist Church. In its transfigured form, the war was "a divine cause," "a crusade" even; it was "a clash between the eternal principles of good and evil"; ultimately, it was a holy war.[69] From the agony of the cross came salvation; from the agony of the front will come "the rule of God's laws."[70] And just as Christ could not have refused the cross, young men could not refuse the front. In effect, St Julien, Courcelette, Vimy Ridge, Hill 70, Passchendaele, and Amiens were so many Golgothas.

Jack Creighton was in Haliburton in August 1916 when his mother brought him the news: his regiment, the 48th Highlanders, had been called up for overseas service and he was to report immediately to Toronto. When he had enlisted that February, he was eighteen years old and a student at Victoria College. Because of his training in the militia – he had spent the previous summer at Camp Niagara in Niagara-on-the-Lake – and because of his education, he received a lieutenant's commission, the most dangerous rank of commissioned officers. It was the lieutenant who led platoons of fifty men "over the top." Within a few days of leaving Haliburton, Jack was in Halifax, where on 23 August he boarded the SS *Olympic*.

Once in France, the 48th Highlanders were "taken on strength" by the 15th Battalion.[71] All told, Jack Creighton was at the front for a little over twelve months, where he saw things that no man should have to see. In late 1916 and early 1917 the Canadian Corps prepared itself for a massive spring offensive, its objective a long, low ridge near Arras on the Western Front. General Julian Byng did not want Vimy Ridge to become another battle of attrition: infantry, artillery, and aircraft would be better coordinated; soldiers would be better trained; and officers would be better instructed. At one point, men rehearsed their steps on a mock battlefield. Jack was sent to the Army Corps School for one month, from late January to late February. As he told his sister, "I'm going on a course up near the sea coast, far, far away from the odd bullets and shell ... So tell mother that she needn't worry regarding her little boy for a few weeks at least."[72] In the end, he missed the attack against Vimy Ridge when he developed a severe case of paronychia, or a bacterial infection, in his toes. His case was so acute that he spent close to two months in two different hospitals before rejoining his unit in May. That summer the 15th Battalion made its way to the shattered town of Loos, where, on the night of 19 July, Jack led his men "up the line" to the immediate front. Out of nowhere, a German artillery shell exploded, sending pieces of shrapnel into his back and left shoulder. This time he spent just two weeks in the 18th Casualty Clearing Station before rejoining his unit for the attack against Hill 70, where the Canadian Corps was now led by a Canadian, Lieutenant General Arthur Currie.[73] Anxious to reduce the number of casualties, he too insisted on planning, training, and coordination: the attack would be carefully planned in advance; the soldiers would be thoroughly trained in their assigned roles; and infantry and artillery would be coordinated down to the second. It worked. But in the context of the First World War, to say "it worked" still meant 5,843 casualties in four days.

In July 1917, Donald Creighton turned fifteen and was both leaving behind "the awkward indecisions of adolescence" and coming into his own physically – soon he would be over six feet tall.[74] He was now capable of hard, physical work, and that summer his father had him clear brush in Muskoka. In the late nineteenth century, Muskoka underwent something of a transformation. Where it had been, in the words of one observer, a "frowning barrier of inhospitable rock,"[75] it was now a "rest cure in a canoe." Reimagined as a therapeutic tonic to the city, its rocks were "stupendous," its pine trees "health giving," and its water "soft for bathing."[76] Because of its proximity, it was dubbed an "instant north."[77] As early as 1902, the *Christian Guardian* carried an article on Muskoka, "The Lake-Land of Ontario," encouraging its readers to take every advantage of the clean air, warm water, and moderate temperatures that Muskoka offered to the weary city dweller in these "strenuous times." Here one could become something of an amateur ornithologist, entomologist, botanist, or geologist. To study nature is to study God, "the great architect of the natural world."[78]

For some time, William Creighton had wanted a cottage on Lake Muskoka. Long Branch was nice enough, but it was really a resort and was too close to the city. Besides, it was his mother-in-law who rented the cottage each summer. And so, in September 1916, he purchased an island on Lake Muskoka with James Endicott and T. Albert Moore, both prominent Methodist ministers. Endicott had been a missionary in China and was now head of foreign missions for the Methodist Church; Moore led the Department of Evangelism and Social Service. The war, meanwhile, was in its third year. According to family history, Creighton, Endicott, and Moore desperately wanted a break from the war's relentless presence in their lives and "so they said, 'let us go from this city and find a place of beauty and quiet, with clean water, beautiful trees and blue sky and white clouds.'"[79] The plan was to divide the property into thirds. Creighton's third was the middle third, sandwiched between the Moores at one end and the Endicotts at the other. In July and August of 1917, Donald Creighton and

Norman Endicott – James's youngest son – began clearing brush, cutting paths, and marking property lines. But William soon realized that not only was his third sandwiched, it was pressed. When he heard about a cottage for sale not far away, he had a look. Painted white and built on a small point, it didn't have electricity, running water, or road access. Without consulting Laura, he bought it on the spot. "It will be good for Jack," he thought.[80]

That fall, the Canadian Corps received its newest assignment: Passchendaele, a few acres of futility still linked with the wastefulness of the Western Front and, rightly or wrongly, with the vanity and incompetence of British military leadership. The Third Ypres campaign was supposed to be the long-awaited breakthrough when Allied forces would finally smash the German line, destroy Germany's submarine bases on the Belgian coast, and deliver a decisive blow. Instead, it turned into precisely what it was not supposed to be: another Somme, another slaughter. From the campaign's opening on 31 July to the capture of Passchendaele in early November, the Allies endured 310,000 casualties, or one soldier for every centimetre of ground gained. Although Field Marshal Sir Douglas Haig claimed victory, Britain's commander-in-chief on the Western Front failed to achieve his ultimate objectives. To Prime Minister David Lloyd George, he was the "planomaniac" who refused to let facts get in the way of plans. To subalterns, he was the Butcher. And although Lieutenant General Arthur Currie was reluctant to commit his soldiers to that sector's appalling conditions, he couldn't refuse Haig's demand, correctly predicting 16,000 Canadian casualties.

Jack Creighton would be one. The Canadian Corps had launched the first of its three "bite and hold" offensive actions on 26 October when the 15th Battalion arrived two days later. It was immediately broken up into work parties. For the next two weeks, the fighting was as awful as it was fierce. Companies were reduced to platoons and platoons to sections. On the first day alone, there were 3,400 casualties. At one point, No. 3 Company of the Princess Patricia Light Infantry lost so many men that, in the end, it was being commanded by a corporal. Because of the unusual amount of rain that October – and this after the wettest August in some thirty years – the battlefield was a massive sinkhole. Men were often swallowed by what the British war poet Siegfried Sassoon called "the bottomless mud." Horses that lost their footing on the duckboards disappeared. "The physical strain is almost beyond human endurance," one soldier wrote to his mother. "I am so weary and tired and homesick."[81] Four days later he was killed in action. Under near constant shelling, work parties laboured day and night trying to maintain supply lines. Exhaustion and frustration overwhelmed the men of the 15th. Some simply sat down and cried.

In early November, Jack's unit was reassigned from work detail to stretcher detail. On the morning of the sixth, stretcher parties "moved forward at 2 AM and followed the attack when it went over at dawn." According to the battalion's war diary, the "men worked hard all day, and by the night had cleared all the wounded from the field. The shelling was very heavy, and the men had the greatest difficulty in carrying through the muddy shell holes."[82] Normally, it took two men to carry a wounded soldier; at Passchendaele, it took four, six, and sometimes even eight men. The mud came up to their thighs and, at points, to their waists. One officer recalled how injured men would slide off the stretcher and have to be put back on again. A single trip could take a couple of hours, he said.[83] Three days later, Jack found himself in a captured German pillbox. The shelling had intensified that afternoon and seventeen men – fourteen soldiers and three officers – crowded into eight square metres of concrete in an attempt to "sit out the storm." The place reeked with "the stench of sweat" and was filled with a damp, heavy, acrid smoke from a portable coal heater. When a shell slammed into the doorway, the entrance collapsed and, in an instant, everything went black. A handful of men began the desperate scramble to dig themselves out. When light re-entered, they saw a heap of bodies beneath the rubble. Four men had been killed instantly. A piece of shrapnel had entered the skull of another man – he would die five days later – and the force of the explosion had thrown Jack against a wall.[84]

Casualty reports were slowly making their way to Canada. The morning list of 19 November contained Jack's name.[85] His mother also received a telegram, almost certainly by one of the many bicycle couriers who fanned out across the city each morning carrying their grim news. Two days later, William Creighton broke the news to his readers: "Lieut. John H. Creighton, wounded, son of the editor of this paper. No information is yet to hand save that conveyed by the words 'wounded in the head.'"[86] William, Laura, Donald, and Isabel were consumed. How serious were Jack's injuries? Would he even survive? Although shrapnel fragments were embedded in his scalp, his real injury was "a severe concussion" and he was evacuated to London's Prince of Wales Hospital. His war was over. While convalescing, he wrote to Isabel telling her that he was now able to sit up and that he should return to his old self soon enough, perhaps even as early as tomorrow. London, he added, was full of excitement. Church bells were ringing all over the place to celebrate Haig's victory at Cambrai. "A mighty silly idea to my mind. You'd really think we were winning the war, while as a matter of fact it's quite the reverse."[87] In December, a medical board noted that his physical injuries had healed nicely and that, after a period of insomnia, he was sleeping again. However, it also found him unfit for general service and recommended home service. "He is feeling pretty well now and *will be sure of himself* after a short period of home service."[88] Was being unsure of himself a euphemism for neurasthenia, or shell shock? Perhaps. After all, mental health issues in officers were taken far more seriously than in soldiers. In January 1918 Jack returned to Canada where, at 32 Hewitt Avenue, he received a hero's welcome. According to one story, he picked up the umbrella stand and danced about the front hall, shouting "You're still here! You dear old thing."[89]

In the summer of 1918, Donald Creighton was too young to serve overseas but he could still "do his bit." That spring the Canada Food Board and Ontario's wartime Organization of Resources Committee had announced its intention to place 15,000 boys on the province's many farms. The need for agricultural labour had been growing steadily and was now acute. Led by the YMCA's Taylor Statten, an organization called Soldiers of the Soil – or S.O.S. – recruited in schools and churches across the province.[90] As one advertisement put it, "Boys, this is your grand opportunity to do your bit. You're too young to serve in the trenches, but you can do something big – self-sacrificing – on the farm."[91] "Soldiers" had to be at least sixteen years old – although exceptions could be made for boys as young as thirteen or fourteen – and were expected to "serve" for at least three months. In his words, Creighton spent "an exhausting summer" on a farm east of Toronto.[92]

In the summer of 1918, it looked like the war would last another two years. Jack actually went back that fall, this time with the 2nd Tank Battalion. And then, just like that, it was over. "At last the long agony is ended," William Creighton told his readers. But it was obvious that the new world order that was supposed to have come out of this "long agony" would not materialize, that, in fact, the sun would not rise "upon a new day" and God would not "come into human history to achieve His great purposes and ideals."[93] Soon, he reached a painful conclusion: he had been wrong. War, he said, is "a hideous, utterly unchristian, unforgivable crime. And in so far as we did not feel quite that way about it just a few short years ago, some of us – many of us – are ready to acknowledge our fault in truest humility."[94] On another occasion, he said that he had been stupid to sing "Tipperary" in a crowded streetcar in August 1914.[95] Donald Creighton later described his father's sense of "betrayal" and "post-war disillusionment" as "extreme" as his wartime idealism.[96]

Donald Creighton was sixteen years old and in his junior year at Humberside Collegiate when the war ended. Because its most prominent architectural feature was an imposing tower and because it sat on a gentle rise, Humberside was known as "the castle on the hill."[97] But it was still Humberside and it was still in Toronto's west end. It was not Eton and it was not in England's Royal County of Berkshire. Humberside's motto is *felix qui potuit rerum cognoscere causas*, or happy is the person who has been able to learn the reasons of things. But

After being injured at Passchendaele, Jack Creighton (centre) returned to Canada in 1918 for home service. Donald Creighton recalled looking up to his brother as a kind of hero. "Sometime during the First World War, after he had returned wounded and was working as an instructor at Niagara-on-the-Lake, I went over on the steamboat from Toronto to see him. He made quite a fuss over me, introduced me to a number of officers … and treated me to ice cream and soft drinks."

Creighton knew that he would never learn the reasons of things in high school. High school was an obligation, a place to put in time. If he was going to find the answers to life's questions, he was going to have to look elsewhere.

He was going to have to look in those parcels of books – still neatly wrapped in brown paper – that his father left for him in the front hall, and he was going to have to look in the stacks of a university library.

chapter three

Vic

He had always been known as a bookworm; and now, when he was just
turning eighteen, he plunged into a wide variety of reading – novels, history
and biography, a sampling of the new books on economics and politics, and
quantities of poetry. He wrote some verses; he may have tried his hand at other
forms of literary composition.

John A. Macdonald, vol. 1

Armed with notions of imperial service, national destiny, and God's will, Victoria College marched to war. In all, some 642 students, alumni, and faculty served; 74 men never came home. For four years, the Union Jack flew at half mast. Afterwards, it was carefully preserved as a piece of Vic's material history. "This tattered piece of bunting registered [our] grief during the Great War," the president explained.[1] But young people breathed new life into Vic by attending classes, discussing ideas, joining clubs, running for student government, meeting for coffee, and flirting endlessly, although student conduct still came under the moral gaze of university authorities in the 1920s. Curfews were enforced, behaviour was policed, and transgressions were punished.[2] Donald Creighton remembered that in his day there were no student dances. There were, however, regular chapel services "where we sang robust Methodist hymns. And at least once a year a great campaign was launched on behalf of the Methodist missions in China."[3]

Creighton was eighteen years old when he entered Victoria College in 1920. Always something of a bookworm, he was now reading everything he could lay his hands on, from Thomas Hardy, Joseph Conrad, Ford Madox Ford, D.H. Lawrence, Ezra Pound, and T.S. Eliot to Honoré de Balzac, Marcel Proust, and Émile Zola. He admired Lytton Strachey's *Eminent Victorians*. He discovered

The Smart Set. And he emulated its most famous contributor, H.L. Mencken, the bad boy of Baltimore, whose contempt for mediocrity, admiration for great writing, and desire to aerate America's literary landscape confirmed his own interest in writing and its possibilities. Describing itself as "A Magazine of Cleverness," *The Smart Set* boldly declared that "one civilized reader is worth a thousand boneheads."[4] Creighton saw himself in much the same way, as a civilized reader surrounded by boneheads.

By now the dinner table at 32 Hewitt Avenue had become an arena for conversation and debate. The war, conscription, and prohibition; Borden, Laurier, and Mackenzie King; Dickens, Eliot, and H.L. Mencken: Creighton was being pushed to exercise his mind and extend its reaches. Looking back, Isabel Wilson recalled that sometimes "matters went too far," that her brother's "attacks" could be too "vigorous" and his "barrages" too "painful."[5]

Creighton's volatility was the volatility of adolescence, but it was amplified by his family dynamic. Jack was the handsome one; he was a soldier; he rowed on the Varsity crew; and he was his mother's favourite. Creighton once said that his mother "idolized" his brother "far more than she did Isabel and me ... I remember being a little envious of him."[6] For her part, Isabel was the baby, a girl in a family of boys, and the "apple of her father's eye."[7] This left Creighton stuck somewhere in the middle. To get attention, he would be the smartest. If that didn't work, he would be the loudest. And if that didn't work, he would be the angriest. Isabel Wilson always maintained that her parents had been too permissive with her brother, that they never set limits or established consequences, and that, as a result, he never learned to regulate his emotions or contain his anger.[8]

Perhaps, too, Creighton's short fuse and violent explosions lay in nineteenth-century Methodism, which was premised on the revival and what William Creighton once called the revival's good old-fashioned "explosive type of conversion."[9] The passionate intensity, the uninhibited outburst, the righteous declaration, the heated renunciation, and the lengthy harangue: all were features of early Methodism and all were features of Donald Creighton's personality.

II

Enrolled in the honour course in English and history, he did well, getting an A in English, a C in Latin, a B in French, a B in Italian, an a B in Greek. But he failed algebra and geometry, receiving an abysmal three on his term work and a fifteen on the final exam. Clearly, math wasn't one of his strengths: he had a number of failing grades in high school math as well.[10] In September 1921, he wrote the supplemental exams and, although he improved his grade to twenty-nine, he still failed. University regulations clearly stated that he couldn't enter second year until he passed this course, and so, in 1921–2, he registered for just two courses, algebra and geometry and physical training. Writing under the unfortunate pseudonym of Scarlet – the colour of shame – he wrote the final examination for algebra and geometry in the spring of 1922 and passed, though barely.[11]

In addition to taking a couple of courses that year, Creighton continued to write short stories and parts of novels, something that he had started doing in high school. "I always hoped and believed I would be a writer," he once said, and, like all writers, he was searching for his voice.[12] He copied Arthur Conan Doyle and P.G. Wodehouse. He even tried "to write a romantic poem, on the model of Scott's Lady of the Lake."[13] But he didn't look to Canadian writing for examples, finding it too provincial. In an essay published in *Acta Victoriana*, Vic's undergraduate literary journal, he used Canadian Book Week as an occasion to survey Canadian fiction. Depressed by what he found, he argued that, while there may be many Canadian authors, there is not an artist among them, making Canadian writing "didactic," "moralizing," "sentimental," "flat," "platitudinous," "insular," "conventional," and "patriotic." "Wholesome characters" do not "atone for bad characterization," he said. For example, Reverend Charles W. Gordon, who wrote under the pen name Ralph Connor, "could have been a very interesting preacher or a very interesting novelist, but in attempting to be both, he became uninterestingly neither." His sermons, Creighton said, are like stories and his stories are like sermons. Despite his "wearisome moralizing," Creighton concluded, Gordon deserves "the respect which is always due to the archaisms of the cloth."[14] In other words, the moderator of the Presbyterian Church, leading proponent of church union, best-selling author, and colleague of his father's, didn't deserve much respect at all.

Although not in fiction, Creighton was certainly finding his voice. It was opinionated, self-assured, even a little cocky; it delighted in wordplay; it took refuge in sarcasm and cleverness; and it was not his father's. To be sure, William Creighton held strong opinions but he never wielded them like a club, his voice calm, patient, and charitable. Where William Creighton was humble, Donald Creighton was imperious. And where his father looked for Christian virtues, Creighton found archaisms of the cloth. Indeed, the cloth itself – and the belief system it represented – became increasingly archaic to Creighton over the course of his undergraduate years.

In the meantime, he entered his second year in September 1922, his voice stronger and more distinctly his own. In a paper on *Gulliver's Travels*, for example, he applauded Jonathan Swift's condemnation of public moralizing and admired his "brutality."[15] And in a paper for E.J. Pratt, the Vic English professor and distinguished poet, Creighton considered the technical merits of Shakespeare's *Romeo and Juliet*. "It does not matter," he argued, "whether poetry succeeds by its rhythm or its ruggedness, its voluptuousness or its simplicity, so long as it does, indeed, give [the reader] that unmistakable emotional ecstasy." *Romeo and Juliet* succeeds brilliantly: its "romantic and vivid" poetry, he said, "clothes" the story. "The lovers are fired by neither a platonic, intellectual love, nor an equable, restrained affection, but by a fierce, startlingly sensuous passion that imperatively demands fervidness of diction." As well, there are no extraneous or minor characters who get in the way and the action unfolds quickly over the course of "two hot breathless weeks in mid-summer." Referring not to Shakespeare in particular but to playwrights in general, Creighton concluded that "the great playwright is not so much the dreamer, the man of moods and inspirations, as [he is] the coldly and scientifically impassioned worker that places one brick of plot upon its fellow."

> Under the careful hands of him whose mind is filled always with the splendid vision of its completion, the structure is built, brick by brick and stone by stone, as a great, polished whole up to the pinnacle of its climax.

Pratt awarded the paper an A+ for its "excellent" and "logical construction and phrasing."[16]

Creighton wanted to know how writing worked. To him, that was the more interesting question. Good writers, he seemed to be saying, were craftsmen, and good writing depended on the craftsman's ability to see and to seize "the splendid vision of completion." According to Philip Creighton, that was the essence of his father's genius, his ability to see "the big picture." "He saw the relationships. The connections. He saw the beginning, middle, and end. He had no reason to write an outline or a plan. He didn't need one. He saw it all in his mind."[17]

In addition to writing undergraduate papers, Creighton continued to write for *Acta*. In the fall of 1923 he reviewed *Newfoundland Verse*, Pratt's first collection of poetry. Pratt's Newfoundland was a hard land, but it wasn't T.S. Eliot's wasteland, and while life may not have been easy, it was noble. In this sense, Pratt avoided the themes of alienation and estrangement that animated modern poetry. Creighton admired Pratt's style, its "confidence of approach," and its "surety of touch"; he admired his refusal to engage in "that ponderous battle for "beautiful" diction that continues to characterize much of our Canadian poetry"; and he admired his "restrained and even calibre." Pratt, he said, is interested in "the thing" and not in "his emotional reaction to it." Still, there are weak poems, he added, some of which "leave me singularly unmoved." It took chutzpah for an undergraduate to critically assess his professor's poetry, but Creighton wasn't a typical undergraduate. "The pathetic panegyric to Carlo – 'the dog that saved the lives of more than ninety people in the wreck' – might have been conveniently omitted," he said, while "In Memoriam" "smacks a little too much of the sort of thing that might be read at the unveiling of a church monument." Creighton's reaction to "In Memoriam" – a conventional death-so-noble ode to the Great War and a statement of faith in a benevolent God – again pointed to his growing estrangement from that God and from the faith in which he was raised. Sensing, perhaps, that he had gone too far, Creighton quickly concluded that, when "set beside most of the insufferable stuff turned out mechanically by Canadian publishers," Pratt's poetry is pretty good. It is also "head and shoulders above vast tracts of the poetry of the great Republic to the South."[18]

Creighton wanted two sometimes opposing things: he wanted a national literature that would distinguish English Canada in North America and a great literature that aspired to art, not patriotism.

III

As Vic's senior English professor, Pelham Edgar was an important figure on campus. Tall, urbane, magisterial, and contemptuous of materialism and its flipside, philistinism, he devoted his life to fostering Canadian literature and Canadian literary criticism, to identifying and nurturing young talent, and to building the institutions necessary to support writers and writing. Through teaching, mentoring, and criticism, he influenced a generation of Canadian writers and scholars. E.J. Pratt, for example, had been an early protégé; the painfully shy and ultimately tragic Raymond Knister was a student in the 1920s; later, Earle Birney, Northrop Frye, Roy Daniells, Alfred Bailey, and Desmond Pacey all remembered him as an important person early in their careers.[19]

As a teacher, Edgar possessed the rare ability to see in students what they only sensed, and in Creighton, he saw an obvious critical talent to encourage: he loaned him copies of the latest periodicals from England; he invited him to give a lecture on modern American poetry to a meeting of the Canadian Authors' Association; and he arranged for him to teach a literature course at the Workers Educational Association. Not surprisingly, Creighton fondly remembered his old English professor, calling him one of Vic's "liberating spirits."[20]

In the essays he wrote for Edgar, a liberated Creighton pronounced and, like Émile Zola, accused. In a third-year essay, he condemned Canadian poetry to the dustbin of history or, failing that, to the living rooms of those "tea-party literary enthusiasts," the kind of women who used to gather at Long Branch to discuss bad poetry when he was a little boy. "What assaults, jars, and staggers the heroic reader, plodding through our verse, is its hopelessly derivative character, its absolute dependence, its colossal and dismal unoriginality." Canadian poetry, he said, "is mere imitation of Bliss Carman's imitation" of Percy Bysshe Shelley. Of course, its defenders will argue that Canada is a young country that has "not yet achieved its reverentially hoped-for national consciousness. But when, under God, that glorious day does dawn, then will the bards of this Dominion be aroused to unprecedented utterances." The problem, he said, is not the absence of national consciousness, but rather the absence of passion, or "that unashamed energy that must go to the creation of anything." Canadian "materialism and sour puritanism" sap that energy, and, as a result, Canada lacks great writers and great writing. It lacks a Sherwood Anderson and it lacks his novel *Winesburg, Ohio.*[21]

In a series of connected short stories, Anderson chronicled the frustrated and inarticulate lives of a handful of men and women in the fictional town of Winesburg, Ohio, their aspirations restrained by the limited horizons of small-town America and their desires repressed by an outdated Protestant morality.[22] As a criticism of American provincialism and materialism and as a call for personal and sexual freedom, *Winesburg, Ohio* spoke to Creighton. It articulated his own frustrations and longings and confirmed his convictions about Canadian provincialism and his suspicions of Methodist morality. "Sometimes when gloom descends upon me, I amuse myself by imagining the pained surprise, the Holy wrath, the righteous moral indignation that would arise in the breasts of all patriotic Canadians if their passionless existence were portrayed with one tithe the directness and simplicity of *Winesburg, Ohio.*"[23]

In another third-year paper for Professor Edgar, a presumptuous, even cocky, Creighton dismissed Jane Austen and Jane Austen scholars. Austen's characters are "types," he said, and she herself "never discerned anything but the painfully obvious; the subterranean pulses, the obscure and wonderful forces that exist beneath every period were totally beyond her." As for R.W. Chapman, who edited Austen's novels for a 1923 multi-volume series by Oxford University Press and who is now regarded as having revived Austen for a twentieth-century audience, well, he was no better. "The spectacle of a man apparently sane, healthy and not yet so old as to be unable to lift porridge to his mouth without spilling it – the spectacle, in short, of an ordinary male devoting some months of his doubtless not entirely useless life in annotating Jane Austen certainly offers mirth of a rare and precious variety." But what else should we expect? Creighton asked rhetorically. "As everybody knows, the history of English criticism is, in the main, a gloomy record of correct, "Christian" dictums and pompous, professional pronouncements."[24]

Creighton's contempt for "tea-party literary enthusiasts," for Jane Austen, and for "the old women, old-maidish men, and emasculated professors" who make up her audience, was a declaration of his independence and an admission of his youth.[25] Against those who were precious, effeminate, and Victorian, he would be honest, masculine, and modern. In his course for the Workers Educational Association, he included his favourite Thomas Hardy novels.[26] He liked Hardy's dark themes; he enjoyed his frank discussions of sex and of the hypocrisy of Victorian sexuality; and he connected with Hardy's characters as they struggle to lead their lives outside the conventions of marriage, religion, and class and who, ultimately, are punished for their transgressions. Young people always like Hardy because they "get" Tess Durbeyfield and Jude Fawley and because they like stories that end badly: happy endings are childish but unhappy endings are grown-up. Of course, liking stories that end badly is one of the privileges of being young and not being anywhere near dying.

In a fourth-year paper on American poetry, Creighton delighted in what Hardy had called the "ache of modernism" when he lauded the two ex-pats, Ezra Pound and T.S. Eliot. In Pound, he discovered a "botched civilization"; in Eliot, he negotiated a wasteland; in both, he revelled in an exciting mixture of scholarship, erudition, irony, and a complete lack of sentimentality. Eliot's pessimism, for example, was liberating and "philosophical," not resigned. It was "tortured and rebellious"; it was "wickedly deft and arrogant in its intellectualism." Creighton had hoped to quote from "The Waste Land," but he had misplaced his copy and, due to the "untiring vigilance" of Dr George H. Locke, chief librarian of the Toronto Public Library, the Reference Library's copy had been "prudently withdrawn." "Let us repair to our accustomed houses of worship," Creighton said in a riff on H.L. Mencken's well-known defence of Walt Whitman, "and there offer praises to God, who in his infinite wisdom and mercy, has created such Christian gentlemen to preserve our virtue."[27]

Thomas Hardy, Ezra Pound, and T.S. Eliot; sex outside of marriage, botched civilizations, and wastelands; a zealous librarian, Toronto's purity, and H.L. Mencken's refreshing sarcasm: like a sponge, Donald Creighton was absorbing everything in an attempt to navigate the world and to find his place in it. Literature, though, would not be his only compass.

IV

Headed by the anglophilic George Wrong, Toronto's Department of History was the largest in the country. It was also the best. Appointed in 1892, Wrong resolved to make Toronto Canada's answer to Oxford.[28] His faculty was, almost to a man, Oxford trained; the curriculum emphasized British and European history; instruction took place in small tutorial groups; star students were sent on to Oxford to finish their studies; and a lucky few were invited back to join the faculty. When a young Frank Underhill wrote to his former professor complaining about Oxford's remoteness from "real life" and its tendency to value "epigrammatic remarks" over the "truth," Wrong responded quickly: "I doubt whether the soul is after all much injured by the luxury of good pictures, carved furniture, comfortable easy chairs and beautiful rooms," he said. "Even Oxford luxury, if it does not lead to indolence and arrogance, may serve a useful educative purpose in leading to a desire for ease and beauty."[29]

By 1920 George Wrong had been joined by a number of junior members, by his son, Hume Wrong, and by George Smith and Bartlet Brebner. Educated at Toronto and polished at Oxford, these three men inspired a young Donald Creighton. They were, Creighton recalled, "sympathetic tutors and brilliant lecturers."[30] But perhaps more importantly, they were "young" and "enthusiastic" and "they managed to arouse an enormous interest in their students." In his third year, Creighton began, in his words, "to swing towards history."[31] Perhaps he could see himself in Smith, Brebner, and Wrong in a way that he couldn't see himself in Pelham Edgar, who was in his mid-fifties and suffering from rheumatism. Creighton remembered watching his English professor lumber into Vic's Annesley Hall and listening to him groan as he lowered his aching body onto a long leather couch at the front of the class.[32]

In his own words, Brebner taught "everything under the sun" as a junior in George Wrong's department.[33] But in the early 1920s, everything under the sun meant British and European history. The United States and Canada only existed as extensions of British history, while Latin America, Africa, and Asia were what early modern cartographers called "parts unknown." In a second-year paper for Brebner, Creighton compared Elizabethan and Early Stuart colonial policy: the Elizabethan era's preference for "reckless adventure and wild-cat, get-rich-quick scheming" was unfavourably compared to the Stuart era's policy of colonization and settlement. Still, Creighton argued, colonial Virginia survived despite James I, not because of him. Virginia "was a wonderful achievement," he said, "all the more wonderful in that the arrangements for the colony's government, in whose preparation James had lent a princely hand, showed such remarkable stupidity that it is a wonder the colony ever managed to exist for a day."[34]

Displaying his own preference for reckless opinion, impression, generalization, and wordplay, Creighton somehow managed to impress Brebner, who awarded the paper an A–. "You have a good touch and write interestingly," he commented. But, "We discussed the motives behind Stuart colonization" and these would have given "the part of your essay which deals with that considerable solid support."[35] Indeed, Creighton's paper didn't contain a single footnote.

In his third year, Creighton took Hume Wrong's popular course on the French Revolution. Everyone loved Wrong for his "vigorous style and acerbic wit." One student recalled that Wrong Jr attracted more students than Wrong Sr, while another described his lectures as "elegant performances."[36] It was in this course that Creighton fell in love with the French Revolution. Here was a subject that could hold his attention and fire his imagination. Complicated, dramatic, and endlessly busy with ins and outs and twists and turns, the French Revolution appealed to his instinct for big events, big ideas, and big men. It "thrilled me," he said, "to the marrow of my bones"; it was something "I never got over."[37]

For his term paper, Creighton selected the Estates General, Comte de Mirabeau, and the Declaration of the Rights of Man. "Was the Declaration of the Rights of Man wise and necessary?" he asked. No, he said, it wasn't. "The spectacle of a group of essentially ordinary men such as composed the States General, loftily proclaiming it as an incontestable truth [that all men are born with certain natural and inalienable rights], strikes one as not eminently wise but infinitely ridiculous." Mirabeau, he argued, was right to oppose the Declaration – "it was criminally asinine to fill the French peasant full of windy nonsense concerning his liberty without the salutary corrective of a generous list of duties and obligations." In short, Mirabeau was right to retain "a healthy suspicion of the mob."[38] Although he conceded that the paper was well written – "apart from an occasional too theatrical antithesis and forced emphasis" – Wrong wondered if Creighton had not been "too hard" on the Declaration of the Rights of Man. "Do you really disagree with its articles?" he asked. "Are not most of them now accepted as truisms? Don't you make a little too much of its errors, and lose sight of its real value as a charter in the history of liberty?"[39]

Creighton's assessment of the Declaration of the Rights of Man said more about him than it did about the French Revolution. Although attracted to modern writers and modern writing, he still respected the need for order amid the "ever-recurrent surges of the revolution."[40] Even as a young man exploring themes of freedom and alienation in literature, he rejected radical breaks with the past. Emphasizing continuity over rupture, he liked tradition, feared excess, admired moderation, distrusted theoretical approaches to politics, and acknowledged limits.[41]

In time, Creighton's conservatism – his respect for the wisdom of his ancestors – would define both him and his approach to the writing of Canadian history. But right now, he was a young man in his twenties and was having too much fun playing Vic's bad boy, the persona he adopted as editor of *Acta*.

V

Founded in 1878 when Vic was still in Cobourg, *Acta Victoriana* was a student-run literary journal. Today it claims the distinction of being the oldest such journal in the country and boasts an impressive list of contributors, including E.J. Pratt, Northrop Frye, Margaret Atwood, Dennis Lee, and Al Purdy. Donald Creighton had been a member of the editorial board when he was elected editor-in-chief in the spring of 1924, succeeding his old friend, Norman Endicott. Both were recognized as brilliant students, and, in 1924, Endicott received a Rhodes Scholarship to study at St John's College, Oxford. It was a path Creighton desperately wanted to follow.

In the meantime, he had big shoes to fill and, in October of that year, he established the tone that would mark his editorship. He confessed, in a laconic, stand-offish sort of way, that he didn't have "much of a policy" at all. However, he did have one "slight stipulation": "the editorial board," he wrote, "still preserves an unnatural prejudice against the stodgy and the profound." In other words, "if you compose a weighty article on the merits or otherwise of co-education, or indite an elaborate history of the Student Christian Movement, we do not actually bind ourselves to run it on the first page with suitable decorations."[42] And in an irreverent essay on the history of *Acta*, he reported that early editors had been expected to "sound the required note of high seriousness": there were plenty of articles on "the modern novel" that only went up to Sir Walter Scott; every December issue included an obligatory and earnest editorial on "the Christmas spirit"; and a lot of versification calling itself poetry had been published. At first, Vic's aspiring poets "had sought to justify the ways of God to man." Later, in "the first few years of the new dispensation," their poetry "assumed a faintly erotic character":

> Oh, she is the blessedest, dear little Methodist
> Ever knelt down to pray.

Eventually, it grew even naughtier and "more daring":

> Her little feet, that in and out
> Her comely gown play hide-and-seek.[43]

As Vic's H.L. Mencken, he made it up as he went along to make a larger point: there were no Ezra Pounds or T.S. Eliots out there, just a bunch of Babbitts pursuing middle-class mediocrity.

Douglas Duncan – a fourth-year student at Vic – sent a copy of *Acta* to Norman Endicott. "The tone of the first number was what one expected. And the November issue is to be more so." It will include, he said, "a vicious attack" against the Student Christian Movement, "which is about to have its campaign."[44] By today's standards, Creighton's November editorial was hardly vicious, but it was pointed. SCMers, he wrote, "are far too prone to imagine that their peculiar little hobby is of such vital importance that it should be adopted by everybody": "the mere fact" that a man attends "a college like Victoria does not necessarily mean that he is passionately convinced of the necessity of a student religious movement, or that he desires piously to attend their conferences, or that he will be infallibly eager to subscribe money for their projects among the heathen." SCMers, he said, would do well to remember "that the students of Victoria have not come here to support missionaries, but to get an education, and consequently that their money ought not to be confidently demanded, but modestly – very modestly! – solicited."[45]

At least one student was upset. Glenney Bannerman – a veteran and student-government-model-parliament-SCM type – complained that November's issue had been superficial and gratuitously critical. "Sir, I venture to assert that anyone reading the November number who was unfamiliar with true conditions at Victoria College would conclude that the students were bored with life, the religious motive was a matter of dollars and cents, and the student organizations empty and useless." Shocked and appalled, Bannerman added that "cleverness at the expense of good values is not justifiable."[46]

Indifferent, Creighton acknowledged the criticisms but refused to change course. Displaying his own knowledge of the Bible, in this case, the Book of Job, he imagined SCM discussions consisting of so many "driveling arguments about the respective merits of pearls or rubies." But "even in a Methodist college," Creighton argued, there is enough room both for the SCM and its efforts and for *Acta* and its efforts. Besides, the "devastating cleverness, which some seem to find in this paper, was never very obvious to me; I thought the stuff might be a little bit new, but that it was certainly very mild. Undoubtedly, there was a slight effort to avoid being ponderous and dull; but if one is 'smart' merely because one tries to avoid being dull, the editors will probably go on committing this unpardonable sin."[47]

Over fifty years later, Creighton recalled that his editorial on the Student Christian Movement's annual missionary drive had not been well received by the higher-ups and that he had been informed of their "displeasure."[48] No doubt the university authorities were displeased, but they neither silenced *Acta* nor sanctioned its editor. It was students being students, or, more to the point, it was Creighton being Creighton.

Among other things, he published a long book review by his brother Jack, an essay on the need for sororities by his sister Isabel, and an amusing defence of intellectual arrogance by one Megalopsychides.[49] He also published an essay on the cult of cleverness by Lester Pearson, at this point a lecturer in Toronto's Department of History and a residence don in Vic's Burwash Hall. Pearson scaled the heights of mock outrage to condemn the "spurious intellectualism" of cleverness and feigned disgust with "those tea-orgies where clever people smoke brown paper cigarettes out of twenty-inch holders; where sex and complexes hold the floor; where Aldous Huxley is "too divine"; where Sherwood Anderson is a far greater man than Hans [Christian Anderson]; and where jaded matrons, flaming flappers, and young university lecturers fall over each other in chasing culture." This cult of cleverness, he said ironically, "offends my sense of decency" in the same way that "dancing at a Victoria reception or drinking beer in Burwash Hall would do."[50] In a subsequent issue, Pearson published a response to his own article. This time he defended cleverness. Writing under a pseudonym, he stated that the real danger to Vic is not cleverness but crudeness, or "the Americanization of our college life," which is "turning our institution into a knowledge factory, a mill, and men go through the mill so that they may become more expert than their fellows in grubbing successfully in the gold pile."[51]

In the March 1925 issue, Creighton decided to have a little fun of his own. "We hear," he began, "that articles published in *Acta* this year tax the brains of some valued, not to say priceless, Burwash friends. The long words bother them." So as not to tax further Vic's beleaguered geniuses, he printed a "simple bed-time story" about Algernon, a dim-witted young man who attempted to hunt a bear with a popgun and who was, in the end, eaten. It was a play on the well-known children's poem, "Algy":

> Algy met a bear,
> The bear met Algy.
> The bear was bulgy,
> The bulge was Algy.

In the *Acta* version, Algy was a bit of a dandy who couldn't outrun the bear because his pants were too tight. "The moral of this little tale is: don't be too big for your breeches. Now scamper off to bed, children."[52]

Actually, Creighton had fun all year: he relished being the centre of attention. Like the bad boy of Baltimore, he intended to aerate Vic, and its many boneheads could like it or lump it. "From what I have heard," Norman Endicott wrote from Oxford, "if Donald had edited a hundred *Acta*s he would not have made the noise and reputation at Vic [that] he has." All told, he said, it was a "mighty achievement."[53] However, the next editor of *Acta* disagreed: Creighton had made too much noise. In his first editorial in October 1925, J.A. Irving announced that, on his watch, things would be different. *Acta* wouldn't be clever for the sake of being clever because cleverness is just disguised cynicism; nor would it aim to pick a fight for the sake of picking a fight because fights only alienate and ultimately bore everyone except "a small clique of intelligentsia." "*Acta* should represent Victoria, and not merely some section or sections," he said in a veiled reference to Creighton. It "should be the voice of the student body."[54]

Creighton's senior year also included the Hysterical Club, a spoof on the well-known, exclusive, and stodgy Historical Club. Founded by George Wrong in 1904, the Historical Club restricted its membership to twenty-five young men. Only the worthy were invited to join, and, every two weeks or so, they met in the home of a prominent Torontonian to debate the world. But the Hysterical Club had a very different mandate. Where the Historical Club was serious, the Hysterical Club was half-hearted; and where the former was uptight, the latter was up for anything. Surviving for only a year or two, the club didn't really have a membership at all. Rather, it was a handful of friends who met every now and then to discuss literature and to feel smarter than everyone else.

At one meeting of the Hysterical Club, Creighton read a paper on "The American Intellectual Contamination of Canada." Of course, he didn't mean H.L. Mencken or Sherwood Anderson. He meant American popular culture in the form of mass-circulation magazines like *Ladies Home Journal* and *Saturday Evening Post*. According to Douglas Duncan, it was a "great success."[55] At another meeting, he read Elmer Rice's 1923 expressionist play *The Adding Machine* after learning that the Players' Guild – University College's drama society – had refused to consider it because of its "starkness, blasphemy, and pitiful vulgarity."[56] The main character, Mr Zero, is a henpecked, emasculated office worker who, after twenty-five years of adding up receipts in the dingy office of a department store, is replaced by an adding machine. "The fact is," his boss explains, "that my efficiency experts have recommended" its installation. Feeling entirely justified, Mr Zero shoots his boss and, in due course, is executed for the crime of murder. But heaven turns out not to be the kingdom depicted by Jesus; instead, it is a variation of the hell that is earth. As one character says, "I might as well be alive."

Modern fiction's blasphemous and unsentimental look at the modern world repelled men like Lorne Pierce, a Methodist minister, the editor-in-chief of Ryerson Press, and a friend of William Creighton's. Writing in the *Christian Guardian*, he used the language of sin to describe modern fiction, warning readers that it contained no "philosophy of life," "soul-stirring beauty," or even an "atom of goodness." In fact, his advice was to read the dictionary instead.[57] But Donald Creighton didn't want to read the dictionary. He wanted insight into the human condition. He wanted J. Alfred Prufrock, Hugh Selwyn Mauberley, Jude Fawley, and Mr Zero. As a young man with all of the confusions, longings, and desires of a young man, he turned to Eliot, Pound, Hardy, and Rice for their validation, passion, and "restless nights in one-night cheap hotels."

VI

In his will, Cecil Rhodes mandated his trustees to create a scholarship that would allow students from the British Empire and the United States to study at Oxford, where they would receive "instruction in life and manners" and where the unity and wonder of the empire would be instilled "into their minds." Recipients, he added, "shall not be merely bookworms"; they shall also display the necessary "qualities of manhood," including "truth," "courage," "devotion to duty," and the "instinct to lead."[58] Overnight, the Rhodes Scholarship became a ticket to Oxford and a brilliant future in any number of fields.[59]

Creighton was certainly a strong applicant: he had excelled academically and had edited his college's literary journal. Indeed, the president of Victoria College, Reverend Richard P. Bowles, wrote him a generous letter of recommendation. Normally, university presidents don't know students, but Vic was a small place – there were only 522 students in 1924 – and Creighton wasn't a normal student. "We have not had in Victoria College for many years, if ever, a more brilliant student," President Bowles said. "In the estimation of all his teachers he holds a place of rare distinction. His gifts are not ordinary." These include a "wide reading of English literature" and an "ability to express himself in excellent style." "It is doubtful," he continued, "if we have ever had his superior among our students": "if he goes to Oxford, he will win distinction."[60]

The Ontario selection committee found itself "deadlocked" between two excellent young men: Donald Creighton on the one hand and Louis MacKay on the other.[61] A gifted student, a residence don, a lecturer in the Department of Classics, and an aspiring writer, MacKay cut an impressive figure, representing the best of Vic and the high ideals of the Rhodes Scholarship; in the end, the committee selected him. Losing the Rhodes proved a bitter pill for Creighton. Instinctively competitive, he could be petty and jealous. But he could be magnanimous as well, and in the January edition of *Acta* he congratulated MacKay, listing his many accomplishments and praising his "varied talents."[62]

Meanwhile, the Department of History in general and Hume Wrong in particular were determined to get Creighton to Oxford. Writing to A.D. Lindsay, master of Balliol College, Wrong inquired if a place might be found for a student who was applying for admission next fall: "His name is D.G. Creighton" and he is "abler than any other student I have had." "He has manners as well as brains"; he "would fit in well in college"; and "he would have a good chance for a first." That, by the way, "is also the opinion of my colleagues."[63] Wrong also wrote to Kenneth Bell, Balliol's tutor in modern history, asking him to "back" Creighton's application. Bell had taught at the University of Toronto from 1909 to 1911 and remained something of a conduit between the Department of History and Balliol College. In his letter to Bell, Wrong was more frank: Creighton "just missed getting the Rhodes by a hair (in my opinion they chose the worse of two very exceptional candidates)." Repeating what he had told Lindsay, and echoing the motto of Oxford's New College, that "Manners Makyth Man," Wrong described Creighton as "socially presentable with good manners and considerable wit."[64]

Wrong's letters must have worked because, in early February 1925, the master of Balliol College sent a short note to Creighton: "We have just had the pleasure of admitting you to the College and we are hoping to see you here next October. Term begins Oct. 8."[65] To Lindsay, it was a routine letter; to Creighton, it was the empire's acknowledgment of his genius.

Now that he had been admitted to Balliol, it was time to finalize the details of getting him there. With the Department of History's support and Vincent Massey's wealth, Creighton received the Edward Kylie Award in Modern History. Kylie had been George Wrong's favourite. A fine student with a keen mind, he went to Balliol College, where, in 1904, he obtained a rare first in modern history. That year, he also became Wrong's first appointment to the Department of History. When the First World War broke out, he enlisted in the 147th Infantry Battalion but never made it overseas: inoculated for typhoid in May 1916, he contracted the disease and died.[66] To honour his memory and what he stood for – idealism, imperial service, and loyalty – Vincent Massey and the Department of History created a fellowship in his name to take promising Toronto history students to Oxford.

With Oxford before him, Creighton put Vic behind him on a hot, humid, hazy day in early June. Officially, it was 94°; unofficially, it was over 100°; and the poor graduands baked in their heavy gowns.[67] Still, they dutifully applauded each other as they received their diplomas and as some among them received a prize, including Creighton, who carried away the prestigious Regents' Gold Medal in English and History. At an Annesley Hall reception that evening, a jealous-not-going-to-Oxford Douglas Duncan watched the self-assured-going-to-Oxford

"Mr. Creighton" hold court: "The spectacle of the aloof and presumably scornful Mr. Creighton, being assiduously gallant to divers ladies, in the broiling atmosphere of the refreshment room with little streams actually trickling down his face, was almost consoling," he told Norman Endicott. "Oh, won't you have a lovely time next fall welcoming, introducing, and generally doing the honours of Oxford to Mr. Creighton."[68]

That June, Creighton looked forward to a relaxing summer of reading, playing tennis, and spending time in Muskoka. His summer, though, was quickly overtaken by forces out of his control. In a few short "hot, breathless weeks," he fell in love.

VII

Luella Sanders Bruce decided at a young age that she would live her life on her terms and that, somehow, she would escape her stepmother.

Luella's father, James Walter Bruce, had been born in Scotland but emigrated as a child to Upper Canada, where his family settled in the Woodstock area and he was apprenticed to a blacksmith. At some point, he moved to Stouffville and met Sarah Luella Sanders. For James, it was a new beginning: his first two wives had died, the second in childbirth. For Sarah, it was a promising start: James was a kind man with a good trade. They were married in Stouffville's Methodist church on 6 February 1900, and nine months later, Sarah was pregnant. But the many joys of pregnancy and birth were overtaken by an irreparable loss: after delivering her baby on 25 August 1901, Sarah contracted puerperal fever, sometimes called childbed fever, and died two days later.[69] In the same red-brick Methodist church, mourners sang William Cowper's haunting "God Moves in Mysterious Ways," the entire congregation apparently in tears. Buried next to her sister in the Stouffville Cemetery, Sarah Luella Bruce left a grieving family and a husband unable to care for a newborn baby. But decisions had to be made: the baby would be cared for by her maternal grandparents while James moved to Winnipeg. Perhaps he would have better luck in the Gateway to the West, where the Laurentian Shield ends and the prairies begin.

By her own account, Luella's early childhood was a happy one. To John and Rachel Sanders, she was a daughter more than she was a granddaughter, and to William, Edward, and Blake Sanders, she was more of a sister than a niece. Not only was she named after her mother, she looked just like her. Among Luella's childhood memories were the wild buggy races with her uncles and her collection of forty dolls.

Donald Creighton graduated in 1925, winning the Regents' Gold Medal in English and History. "We have not had in Victoria College for many years, if ever, a more brilliant student," President Bowles said. "In the estimation of all his teachers he holds a place of rare distinction. His gifts are not ordinary."

Sarah Luella Sanders (1875–1901) died of puerperal fever two days after giving birth to a healthy baby girl, Luella Sanders Bruce. At her funeral a tearful congregation sang "God Moves in Mysterious Ways."

Luella Sanders Bruce with her father, James Walter Bruce (1860–1923), ca 1906. Luella was raised by her maternal grandparents after her mother died. Five years later her father remarried and collected his daughter. It was not a happy arrangement: a religious zealot, Luella's stepmother was determined to break her. "You do not know yet that you are wicked, and it is my business to teach you."

Five years later, James returned to Stouffville to marry Mary Ann Stouffer, a forty-one-year-old domestic servant and seamstress from a local German Mennonite family. With a house on Winnipeg's Beverley Street, a job as a blacksmith at a car works factory, and now a wife, James collected his daughter. To James, Mary Ann was a mother to his child. To Mary Ann, Luella was a burden. To Luella, it was all very confusing. "I was her job," she confided many years later. "And everybody said I was very spoiled ... My stepmother probably told my father I was difficult. I suppose I was."

Steeped in a harsh and unforgiving theology of fire and brimstone, and ill-equipped to raise a child, especially a wilful, precocious child, Mary Ann set out instead to break Luella. Among other things, she fed strychnine to the alley cats that Luella had befriended and then forced her to watch one die an agonizing death. In Mary Ann's mind, the dramatic contortions and grotesque convulsions associated with strychnine poisoning resembled the tortures of the damned that await sinners in Hell. On another occasion, she destroyed a small set of children's cutlery – presumably a gift from Luella's grandparents – because it was an unnecessary luxury item or, in her words, a "sinful waste." Poisoning the stray cats and burning a precious gift punctuated a longer and more insidious story of abuse: the female body is a site of shame and its normal desires are sinful, Mary Ann told her stepdaughter. "You do not know yet that you are wicked, and it is my business to teach you."

In 1915, James moved his family back to Stouffville, to a house on Main Street, just a few blocks down from Luella's grandparents. Now an adolescent, Luella was expected to finish school, get married, and start a family. But she had other plans. She wanted to become a teacher and, ultimately, go to university. When her parents said no, she ran away from home, at one point landing in Toronto, where she became part of its girl problem: working as discounted labour in a Toronto shirt factory, Luella represented a perceived threat to the city's moral order.[70] Who is minding the girls? asked reformer after reformer. It was a question Mackenzie King had asked when he "rescued" Edna, and it was a question he asked in 1918 when he connected "race degeneration" to the "new place of woman in Industry."[71] Finally, Luella's parents relented, and she attended the Toronto Normal School, where she received her "Certificate of Qualification as a Public School Teacher" in 1920.[72] When someone commented on the high calibre of the class of 1920, the principal of the Toronto Normal School responded, "Yes, but there is nobody like Miss Bruce." Her energy was as infectious as her enthusiasm was inspiring. For the next two years she taught in Siloam, a small village not far from Stouffville. Later, Luella would remember the experience of living on her own in a boarding house – despite the fact that it was freezing in the winter – as one of the most "valuable" in her life. She earned not only $800 in her first year and $1,000 in her second, she earned her independence.[73]

In the fall of 1922, Luella entered Victoria College as a first-year student in the Pass Course. Although the College nurse suspected that she had a "weak heart," Luella took the place by storm, quickly becoming something of a woman about campus. When she graduated four years later, she would be described as "permanently unsubduable."[74] In her first year, she sat on the organizing committee for the Joint Reception to the Freshman Class. In her final year, she served as vice-president of the Class of 2T6. In between, she represented Vic in the intercollegiate debating series (she once opposed the resolution that it would be better to be Agnes MacPhail than Mary Pickford) and, as a member of the Women's Undergraduate Association Executive, she organized a number of social events (including a massive Fancy Dress Skating Carnival featuring some 250 "gaily costumed" historical figures and fictional characters).[75] On a handful of occasions, she appeared in the Locals section of *Acta Victoriana*, which featured amusing accounts of campus comings and goings. "Luella Bruce," read one local, "complains that she doesn't know what is the matter with her eyes; they've hurt both times she has tried to study this year." A couple of months later an update was printed: "Luella Bruce wishes to request that no further inquiries be made as to the condition of her eyes. Ask her instead her opinion of leap year dances and the 'Vahsity stahff pahty.'"[76]

When Edward, Prince of Wales, visited Hart House, Luella joined what the *Globe* described as "a seething mass of undergraduates" on the front steps to catch a glimpse of England's next king and the "idol of the Empire." Edward's visit was partly informal (he played a game of squash) and partly formal (he enjoyed a "leisurely inspection of the building" and its newly completed memorial tower). He also paid his respects to the officers of Toc-H, a Christian service club that was founded by a British army chaplain in 1915 to meet the many needs of soldiers and that, after the war, spread across the empire. Luella was smitten. Handsome, athletic, and youthful, Edward represented the romance of the British Empire.[77] In her on-again, off-again diary, she recorded that she had fallen for him, "as they all do."[78]

Not surprisingly, Luella caught the attention of the boys. Vic's dean of women, Margaret Addison, took a natural interest in the appearance and behaviour of her girls, concerned about, among other things, "the boyish bob," "the pocket flask," and "the petting party."[79] While it is unlikely that Luella carried a pocket flask or participated in petting parties, she did wear her hair in a smart bob and briefly dated a young man named D.H. On one occasion, they took a "wonderful drive" out to the Scarborough Bluffs and, afterwards, they had tea by the fireplace in his room. It was "heavenly," she said. Everything was so "tremendously cozy." The next day he invited her to his fraternity dance. "Am learning a little about living – but there's an awful lot yet to learn."[80]

Of course, Luella's four years at university were not only about boys and Varsity staff parties. A determined student, she worked hard and got good grades. Vic was her ticket out. In a paper for Pelham Edgar on the supernatural in English poetry, she observed that "every man has his Secret Garden and the Spirit dwelling therein is a creature of weird fancies and wild thoughts." The garden represents, she said, "a poignant yearning for fulfillment," while the spirit possesses a "strange hunger" with "fierce cravings" and "far-off ineffable longings."[81] Although she was referring to John Keats and Samuel Taylor Coleridge, she was maybe referring to herself as well. To insulate herself from her stepmother's abuse, she started filling notebooks and scribblers with stories and poems when she was seven years old, once confessing that she had been "burdened since childhood with an obsessive urge to put words on paper."[82] Books also helped, especially *The Secret Garden*. Perhaps she saw something of herself in the story's main character, a lonely, difficult little girl who eventually finds happiness in a once beautiful garden that had been locked and allowed to become overgrown. Perhaps she gathered consolation from the book's themes of a fallen adult world, a garden's regeneration, and a happy, redemptive ending. Perhaps too the notebooks were her own secret garden, the one place where she could hide her "far-off ineffable longings."

Donald Creighton knew Luella in the way that everyone knew her. But they were in different years and travelled in different circles. Isabel Creighton, though, was in Luella's year and they became good friends. Shortly after her brother's graduation, Isabel invited Luella to 32 Hewitt Avenue for lunch. According to family history, it was Lizzie Harvie who played the role of matchmaker. "Don't you think Miss Bruce is nice?" she asked her grandson. Apparently he did because he invited her to Toronto's Centre Island, and, on the short ferry ride across the harbour, they fell in love. What followed was a *Romeo and Juliet*–like "fierce, startlingly sensuous passion": "It simply carried me off my feet," Donald confided to his best friend, Harold Wilson. "It was absolutely sudden and headlong." After three or four dates in Toronto, they spent ten days in Haliburton with the McMullens, Donald's cousins. "By the time the ten days were ended, we were both absolutely sure." Luella then had to leave for her job as a counsellor at a girls' summer camp, and for the next six, interminable weeks, they bided their time. After counting down the days until they could see each other again, they spent a week or so in Muskoka. Still, they hadn't been alone and so they escaped to Siloam, to what he described as "a little place out in the country." Almost certainly, Luella suggested it. Perhaps she wanted to return to the place where she first tasted her independence. Perhaps she knew someone there who

As a university student, Luella Bruce worked as a counsellor at a Canadian Girls in Training summer camp. Founded in 1915 by the YWCA and English Canada's Protestant churches, CGIT provided Christian education and leadership training to adolescent girls, making it part of Canada's discovery of adolescence in the early twentieth century.

wouldn't ask any questions about a young, unmarried couple sharing a room. Whatever the case, it was perfect and they became engaged on 22 August. All told, Donald and Luella were together for less than four weeks before he had to leave. "I am very glad that it happened so suddenly," he said. "I was just carried irresistibly along – I had no option in the matter."

Creighton was drawn to Luella's "intense, vividly-coloured personality." Swept overboard by her energy and her "inexhaustible store" of love, he also found himself attracted to her keen mind. Luella, he said, "is a brainy girl, and can give as good as she gets (and more) in conversation." She reads widely, but isn't a "literary lady." And "she isn't especially religious" either, "and hasn't the SCM fever." He acknowledged his earlier, more cynical pronouncements on love and the meaning of love, but he now found himself in love. In his words, he was "thrilled," he was "in the Seventh Heaven of delight," and was "happier" than he had ever been before. He now understood the "unmistakable emotional ecstasy" and the powerful intensity of *Romeo and Juliet*. Love wasn't an abstraction. It wasn't the stuff of an undergraduate essay. It was, he said, "like a recognition – as if you must have been two people who knew each other a long time ago."[83] It was like Romeo seeing Juliet on her balcony: "The brightness of her cheek would shame those stars / As daylight doth a lamp."

In the last weeks of August and over the course of September, Donald and Luella exchanged letters, uttered promises, and made plans: they would be married the following June, after Luella had graduated from Vic and Creighton had completed his first year at Oxford.

chapter four

Oxford and Paris

Macdonald carried away pleasant memories of Oxford in the June sunshine.

John A. Macdonald, vol. 1

Winters in Oxford are notoriously dismal. Thomas Hardy believed that all those cold, wet, rotten stones emitted "an extinct air."[1] But the summer sun seems to "fructify" Oxford's "golden stones" and the City of Dreaming Spires becomes a different place.[2] It was this Oxford that welcomed John A. Macdonald in 1865. In London for the final negotiations that would lead to Confederation, he received a pleasant bit of news: Oxford wished to grant him an honorary doctor of civil law at its June convocation. "This is the greatest honour they can confer," he told his sister. And so, on "a morning of cloudless skies and brilliant sun," Macdonald joined the other honorary degree recipients and the many graduands for a ceremony marked by solemn ritual and occasional cheers. Looking quite distinguished in his "gorgeous robes," Macdonald savoured the occasion.[3]

Located in the county of Oxfordshire, about eighty kilometres west of London, where the Cherwell joins the Thames, Oxford began as a convenient meeting place over 1,100 years ago. Slowly a town took shape. Curiously, though, its origins as a university city are opaque, the best estimate being sometime in the Middle Ages. Although teaching and learning had occurred at Oxford as early as the eleventh century, it was not until 1201 that the university was headed by a *magister scolarum Oxonie*, or, after 1214, a chancellor. In quick succession, a number of autonomous colleges were founded, notably University College in 1249 or perhaps more properly 1280, Balliol College in 1256 or 1269 or even 1284, and Merton College in 1264. Disagreement on how best to determine a founding date has led each college to claim bragging rights as Oxford's oldest. Of course, they were small affairs: Balliol had just sixteen students. In time, University College, Balliol, and Merton were joined by Exeter, Oriel, Queen's, and New College, and Oxford became Europe's leading university city, attracting the finest minds and most gifted students and surpassing Paris, Bologna, Coimbra, and Salamanca. From its accomplished alumni to its famous professors, and from its many authors to its equally many inventors, Oxford's distinctions are countless: it was an Oxford mathematician who invented ∞, the mathematical symbol for infinity. And it was in Oxford that John and Charles Wesley, both alumni of Christ Church College, founded Methodism in the mid-eighteenth century.[4]

Oxford's history and its reputation, its traditions and its ancient ways of doing things, its location and its status as the English-speaking world's greatest university, were not lost on Donald Creighton. He was where he wanted to be and where he thought he should be. He missed Luella desperately, though. "The truth is that we cannot stick two years apart: it would simply kill us."[5] They decided that, after their marriage, Luella would not return to Canada but would live in Paris and perhaps, at some point, teach English in Geneva while Donald returned to Oxford. Women were not welcome at Balliol. Holding the line on the woman question, it did not admit its first female student until 1979. Even the prim Eugene Forsey, then a Rhodes Scholar and later Canada's authority on all things constitutional, was surprised by Oxford's "medieval attitude about keeping men in monastic seclusion from the British female."[6] Perhaps, though, it was better that Luella lived in Paris: Donald needed to study. If he did well he might be invited back to the University of Toronto as a faculty member.

Although not in Oxford with her husband, Luella did not see Paris as some kind of consolation prize. After all, Paris in the 1920s really was what Ernest Hemingway said it was: a "moveable feast" where artists, writers, musicians, and ex-pats of all ages and hues gathered. It was, in short, where the action was. Luella fell in love with Paris. So too did Donald. And when they were older, they would speak about Paris in romantic and wistful terms. Before life's opportunities receded – before its injustices accumulated and its disappointments calcified – there was Paris.

II

Before "going up" to Oxford in October 1925, Creighton spent three or four days in London doing what tourists do. From his hotel on Bloomsbury Street, he explored the usual places – Mile End, Chelsea, Charing Cross, Putney, and the West End – and saw the usual things – Hampton Court, Big Ben, Trafalgar

Square, Westminster Abbey, St Paul's, and the National Gallery. "I'm just full of London," he told a friend, "and could very easily become a profound bore on the subject." In an effort to "avoid the obvious things," Creighton went for long, aimless walks. "I get the most joy out of merely wandering – especially at night." It was, he observed, a place of contrasts. "There's everything in this city, from luxury to disquieting poverty."[7] He had grown up with Charles Dickens and his descriptions of London's many waifs, beggars, orphans, and other assorted wretches, but nothing could have prepared him for the real thing or the fact that the centre of the British Empire was home to some of its poorest citizens.

From Paddington Station, Oxford was a short trip. The express train took only an hour and fifteen minutes, although the local train took twice that. If Creighton was anything like Charles Ritchie, another Canadian at Oxford in the 1920s, he was "shivering with excitement" at the prospect of seeing the famed city for the first time.[8] Alive with students and a sense of anticipation, Oxford in October is a magical place. "There are trunks everywhere, and shouts of recognition, and bespectacled freshman buying fountain pens. Porters' lodges are busy as railway stations." It is as if "the city is being recharged."[9]

From Oxford Station – where horse-drawn cabs still met the trains – Creighton made his way to Balliol College on Broad Street opposite the spot where the Oxford Martyrs – Hugh Latimer, Nicholas Ridley, and Thomas Cranmer – were burned at the stake in 1555 and 1556. Balliol's Gothic architecture, manicured quadrangles, and tidy footpaths radiated beauty, history, and academic excellence. Other colleges were known for other things, but Balliol was known for its high academic standards. At a 1908 dinner, British Prime Minister H.H. Asquith remarked that Balliol men were distinguished from their counterparts by a "tranquil consciousness of effortless superiority."[10] One did not have to look very hard to find evidence of that superiority: Balliol men occupied the highest seats of power in Great Britain and, for that matter, across the British Empire. Their influence, in other words, was as wide as it was deep. So too was their sense of obligation and mission. Some 900 Balliol men followed their ideals to the Western Front, where their mortality rate was 20 per cent, significantly higher than the national average of 12 per cent. Shortly after the war, a memorial tablet was mounted in the passageway leading to the chapel. On it Creighton could read the name of Captain Edward Kylie, Canadian Expeditionary Force.

Entering Balliol through the central gate tower on Broad Street, Creighton reported – like all undergraduates – to the porters' lodge. Someone there – presumably one of the scouts, or college servants, responsible for attending to the domestic needs of the undergraduates – would show him to his room. Originally, he had been assigned a room with Donald McDougall, another Toronto student. McDougall had enlisted in the CEF, served overseas, and, in the language of his service records, been "struck in the face by bits of shell casing" at Courcelette on the morning of 15 September 1916: his blue eyes were "destroyed" and he became one of Canada's 24,000 casualties at the Battle of the Somme.[11] Although completely blind, he entered university and, in 1925, received a special Rhodes Scholarship. Because McDougall required readers to study, Creighton didn't think that he could share a room with him. "It would be practically impossible for both of us to use the room for studying purposes at the same time."[12] Balliol's tutor of admissions duly reassigned Creighton to a single room.

Undergraduate living quarters at Balliol were small, quaint, and antiquated. There was a bed, of course. And a writing desk. But each room contained a chesterfield, a couple of armchairs, and a sitting table. Gas lights flickered and hissed while a reluctant coal-burning fireplace kept the room in perpetual coldness. Eugene Forsey recalled never having been so cold in his life as he was at Oxford.[13] And although at different colleges, Norman Endicott likened his bedroom to an "iceberg,"[14] while Gordon Robertson described the heating in his room as "positively medieval."[15] Balliol's plumbing was similarly medieval. The rooms themselves had none, forcing students to cut 200 metres across the quad day and night to the lavatories in "The Perriam," a building named after Lady Elizabeth Perriam, one of the college's benefactors. Meanwhile, taking a shower meant putting on a robe and slippers and queuing up behind other shivering undergraduates. After leaving Oxford, Raymond Massey – Vincent Massey's younger brother – amassed a collection of chamber pots as so many reminders of Balliol.[16]

Creighton next reported to his tutors in the Honour School of Modern History. The study of history at Oxford was divided into modern and ancient. Modern history attracted the most students, convinced, perhaps, by its claim "to provide the best humane education of all the schools, by its broad and continuous survey of life and thought and action." Teaching, meanwhile, was based on the tutorial, "the keystone of the Oxford educational arch": undergraduates met with their tutor once a week for about an hour to discuss the material at hand; an essay would be assigned and, the following week, read aloud. In the process, "some of the older man's wisdom and experience" was supposed "to alight like a mantle on his pupil."[17] Stephen Leacock famously likened the tutorial meeting to a smoking session. "I gather that what an Oxford tutor does is to get a little group of students together and smoke at them. Men who have been systematically smoked at for four years turn into ripe scholars." Why, a "well-smoked man" can both speak and write with unusual "grace."[18]

Creighton's principal tutor was Kenneth Bell, who had been one of George Wrong's early appointments to the University of Toronto as part of his project to transform Toronto's Department of History into Canada's answer to Oxford. "If young men could be imbued with the ideology of Oxford," Wrong always said, "they would just naturally think imperially and would prevent Canada from becoming a second U.S.A."[19] Although he returned to Oxford in 1911, Bell continued to keep in regular touch with his Toronto colleagues and, later, his Canadian students.

As a man, he was a bluff, pipe-smoking, larger-than-life sort of figure who had served in the Royal Field Artillery, won distinction, and returned to Balliol a war hero. With tremendous reserves of energy, an "irrepressible enthusiasm,"[20] a bibulous bent, and a penchant for swearing "like a Billingsgate fish porter," Bell initiated his students into the other side of university life: drinking. "Gentlemen," he opined, "you have come to this ancient university to study a very large number of different subjects. It is our duty to see that you get the best opportunities for studying [them]. But there is one which you will have in common, and that is what we propose to teach you in this college. And that is to take your drink like gentlemen." It was a lesson learned by the great British writer and Balliol alumnus Graham Greene, who added, "I've never known a man I've admired more."[21] Raymond Massey remembered his former tutor as "a remarkable human being, kindly, witty, humorous, and understanding."[22] Eugene Forsey described Bell as a "hearty" who had a sign on his front door that read "Balliol men enter." Bell meant it, but the abstemious Forsey never took up the invitation: by his own admission, he "felt at a loss" with the hearties. [23]

As a tutor, Bell conformed to the larger Oxford ethos which stressed the "liberal or humanistic purposes of higher education." Conceived out of an idealized past, history was taught "as a text which demonstrated the origins and evolution of private and public obligations," instilling in students a sense of "nation, duty, character, and confidence."[24] Change was acknowledged but continuity was emphasized. Technical training was eschewed in favour of broad learning. Students were not expected to master a particular methodology; rather, they were expected to appreciate the past for its association with the national character and its ability to impart confident idealism. Meanwhile, it was not the special responsibility of an Oxford tutor to publish academic articles and scholarly monographs.[25] Their job was to introduce young men to what Bell once called the "pageant" of history.[26] In this sense, Oxford was outside of the professionalization imperative that was transforming the practice of history in Germany, the United States, and, for that matter, even Canada.

At Oxford, young men were not trained in history. They were steeped in it. It wasn't extinct air that emanated from Oxford's stone walls – it was history.

III

Working at a feverish pace, Creighton did well. In a letter to his father he proudly announced that he had received "a very good report" from one of his tutors, C.G. Stone. Some students found Stone "disconcerting" because of his "speech impediment, deafness and idiosyncratic mannerisms."[27] But Creighton liked him and was pretty chuffed when Stone told him that his work had been "admirable" and that he had "no criticisms to offer." "Not so dusty, eh?" Creighton told his father.[28] Privately, Stone reported that his young Canadian student "has been doing v. good essays," though he "struggles agst. his natural respect for authorities." Another tutor, F.F. Urquhart, reported that Creighton was doing "excellent" work, that it was easily "1st class."[29]

But if Creighton was committing to memory the names, dates, events, and facts of British and European history, he was also deepening his interest in how history was written. As a student, first at Toronto and now at Oxford, Creighton developed a lifelong appreciation for narrative history and for the great narrative historians, Edward Gibbon and Thomas Macaulay.[30] He admired historical writing that organized itself "in a chronologically sequential order," that arranged "the content into a single coherent story," that was "descriptive rather than analytical," that aspired to "stylistic elegance" and was "directed by some pregnant principle."[31] For Gibbon, that principle was the decline and fall of the Roman Empire; for Macaulay it was the rise and expansion of constitutional liberty. For both, history was not only a rational encounter with the past; it was also an imaginative reconstruction of that past, and, together, they confirmed Creighton's suspicion that history was, in fact, a branch of literature.

It took Gibbon twenty-four years, from original inspiration in 1764 to final publication in 1788, to complete his six-volume *History of the Decline and Fall of the Roman Empire*. Taking what he called "the greatest, perhaps, and most awful scene in the history of mankind," he made 1,300 years of history readable.[32] With a craftsman's design, he selected, arranged, and narrated his material. He didn't break the decline and fall of the Roman Empire into a series of discrete topics, themes, and causes. Rather, he juggled all three simultaneously and braided them into "a single coherent story." After all, the past unfolds simultaneously and chronologically, not topically, thematically, or monocausally.

Although he didn't think that Macaulay could be "ranked in the same class" as Gibbon, Creighton similarly admired the nineteenth-century historian as a writer.[33] According to Macaulay, too many historians "miserably neglect," in his words, "the art of narration, the art of interesting the affectations and presenting pictures to the imagination." Historians, however, "may produce these effects without violating truth" because history can be both an art and a science, appealing to both the heart and the mind. The distinctions were false ones. "The perfect historian is he in whose work the character and spirit of an age is exhibited in miniature." But historians must be prepared to reclaim those tricks – for example, the judicious placement of details to convey a mood or to establish a setting – "which have been usurped by fiction."[34] Practising what he preached, Macaulay wrote a five-volume *History of England* using the techniques of the novelist, including suspense, climax, and resolution. He changed the pace of his writing to reflect the story that he was telling and employed carefully contrived opening sentences to draw readers in and point them forward.[35] "The whole *History* is a long, superbly sustained piece of narrative," Creighton once said. "Begin at almost any page and you become absorbed: you want to go on reading."[36]

The same things that attracted Creighton to Gibbon and Macaulay attracted him to the great French novelists, especially Émile Zola. At Toronto and now at Oxford, he read Zola's novels, wanting to understand how they worked. Zola wrote nearly forty books, but his greatest accomplishment was *Les Rougon-Macquart,* a twenty-novel cycle that follows the lives of an extended family across five generations and against the backdrop of the Second Empire and the enormous disruptions and dislocations associated with France's industrialization. It was a self-consciously ambitious project. "These are troubled times," Zola wrote. "It is the trouble of our times I portray." Over the course, the Rougon-Macquart family is overwhelmed by forces it can barely discern let alone control. They become, Zola said, "unhinged."[37] Each novel is self-contained but also part of a sweeping narrative arc. How did Zola do it? That question animated Creighton as a young man and continued to animate him throughout his adult life. How did Zola contain the uncontainable? How did he reconcile the goal of unity, order, and coherence with the goal of portraying "the whole of reality"?[38] Although Creighton never attempted to answer this question, he confided that "Zola is certainly a very inspiring example to me."[39]

As craftsmen, Gibbon, Macaulay, and Zola struggled to achieve the elusive balance of form and content. It did not come effortlessly. It was the result of careful planning, deliberate execution, and a lot of hard work.

IV

Oxford was not only about tutorials, essays, and being smoked at; it was also about exploring different horizons, meeting new people, and seeing something of England and the Continent. Normally unathletic, Creighton took up field hockey ("You'd laugh if you saw the funny little stick," he told his father)[40]; he enjoyed going for long walks in Christ Church Meadow, a bucolic green space bounded by the Thames, the Cherwell, and Christ Church itself; and he liked to poke about Oxford's many bookstores, including Blackwell's, a favourite undergraduate haunt. Initially, Creighton found the English "all right." "At times, however – particularly when I am at tea somewhere – I do wish I had a bomb to explode and wake them all up. They're nice, but very satisfied."[41] Within a few weeks, however, he had made a number of friends, including Kenneth Matthews, the son of an Anglican vicar from Newport, a small town on the Isle of Wight.

At the end of Michaelmas term in December 1925, Creighton and Matthews took part of their six-week vacation together in the tiny village of Bicknoller in Somerset in southwest England. They stayed in an old farmhouse – which Creighton described as "a delicious old place, thatched, of course, like all of the cottages around here, and terribly ancient." There they ate "the most abundant and substantial meals," enjoyed "a constant supply of thick Somerset cream," and made their way through a pile of books. In the afternoon, they took long walks through the rolling Quantock Hills, where Samuel Taylor Coleridge had ushered in the Romantic movement in British literature, a movement that emphasized the eternal beauty of nature and its power to console the human spirit. As he often was when he encountered something beautiful, Creighton found himself moved, in this instance, by the landscape. It was, he said, "more beautiful" than any countryside he had ever seen. It was somehow "wilder" and "more romantic." "I am," he added, "absolutely happy."[42]

It was in the Quantocks that Creighton wrote a long letter to his friend Harold Wilson. Exposing himself, he confessed that he had fallen in love and that he and Luella Bruce planned to get married. "I wanted to tell you that last day when we had lunch together but, somehow or other, the time didn't seem propitious and I missed my last chance." Sharing the details of he and Luella falling in love, including their daring escape to Siloam, Creighton wrote that he hasn't "felt a moment's doubt": "I know that my life may be rather stormy or unsuccessful or humdrum, but I'm sure it will be happy."[43]

After two weeks in Somerset, Creighton went to London for a few days. Like a sponge, he absorbed everything. He went to the theatre a couple of times, once to see a production of Anton Chekhov's *Three Sisters,* a play about the dissolution of one family and, ultimately, of an entire social order. Affected by its themes of loneliness, alienation, and nostalgia, Creighton described it as "a simply colossal drama."[44]

From London, he went to Paris, the City of Light, where he found a cheap room at the Hôtel Jeanne d'Arc, a little place on the Left Bank not far from the Seine and Île Saint-Louis. As he had done in London, he now did in Paris: he walked and walked and walked. He looked in the shop windows, admired the architecture, and visited the great monuments. His hotel was two minutes from the Place des Vosges, the oldest planned square in Paris, and five minutes from the Place de la Bastille, where, in some ways, the French Revolution began. He took in low culture by attending a cabaret at the Moulin Rouge and experienced high culture by attending what he described as a "spiritual concert" at the Église de la Sorbonne.[45] He also met up with Douglas Duncan, who had moved to Paris to study the craft of bookbinding and who had turned his Montparnasse studio apartment into a meeting place for travellers from any and all parts.[46] Creighton and Duncan weren't particularly close at Vic. It was Duncan who found consolation in watching a not-at-his-best Creighton hold court before a number of women at their graduation. Still, they at least knew each other and, in such a large city, that was enough. According to Duncan, Creighton "seemed delighted" with his hotel and anxious to take in Paris. Creighton suggested that they go to the opera on New Year's Eve, to see a production of *Faust* at the Opéra de Paris. But the tickets were too expensive and they went to the Opéra-Comique instead, where, sitting in the cheap seats, they saw *Carmen* for seven francs.[47] Creighton had already been to a production of Mozart's *Marriage of Figaro*, a comic story about love, and to a production of Wagner's *Tristan und Isolde*, a passionate story about forbidden and ultimately tragic love.

Creighton's interest in opera began at Vic and was now being indulged in Paris. Over time, it would become an obsession. He would know the works of Verdi, Puccini, and Strauss backwards and forwards; he would visit the great opera houses of Europe; he would assemble an impressive collection of different recordings; and he would melt when a performance reached its emotional climax. But it was Richard Wagner who seized his imagination. As an undergraduate, he admired Wagner's "colossal" "outbursts of ego"; later, a journalist would describe him as a "Wagner freak."[48] Because Wagner's music provided an expanded emotional range and a different emotional outlet, Creighton let its intoxicating genius wash over him and allowed himself to be picked up, swept away, and transported to another world and into another dimension.

Macaulay, Zola, and Wagner were from different times and from different places but they had one thing in common: they were artists who pushed the limits of their form and, in the process, reinvented it.

V

Calling themselves the Hotbed of Virtues and Vices, Creighton and a group of friends formed a club over the course of Hilary term and into Trinity term. It was part of Oxford's undergraduate culture to form clubs of all shapes and sizes and for all manner of purposes, the clubs coming and going with the students themselves.[49] The most renowned was the Hypocrites, whose most famous member was Evelyn Waugh. Meetings of the Hypocrites Club were alcohol-soaked affairs often ending in homosexual encounters. "A sort of mist of homo-sexuality does hang over Oxford like the mist of the Thames Valley," Charles Ritchie wrote in his diary.[50] Meetings of the Hotbed, though, were very different. Its members were neither the bluff "Hearties" who drank too much beer and got into fights with the Other nor the feminine "Aesthetes" who drank too much champagne and got into bed with each other.[51] Rather, its members discussed books, ideas, politics, and history. The Hotbed was also a social club, an excuse to get together for an elaborate dinner at the Candied Friend, a restaurant on Cornmarket Street, not far from Balliol. Giving each other names after the Seven Deadly Sins, one member was Superbia, or Pride, and another was Invidia, or Envy. But Creighton was Ira, or Anger.[52] His anger, his inability to contain his outbursts or to manage his feelings, followed him to Oxford. Like his parents, his peers didn't attempt to rein him in and, like his parents, they indulged it. Calling him Ira only legitimated his anger by making it seem, well, funny.

Hilary term also found Creighton trying to arrange the details of his wedding. Because Luella was still in Toronto finishing her final term at Vic, the task fell to him. Neither one wanted a large affair. Naturally, Laura Creighton wanted to at-tend her son's wedding. But he delicately discouraged the idea in a letter to his father. He conceded that she would be a great help, especially to Luella. However, it would be a costly trip and the money that would be spent on her passage and her accommodation in London could be better spent in other ways. (Creighton worried desperately about money while at Oxford. His scholarship barely cov-ered his battels – the bill he received from Balliol at the end of each term for tu-ition, living expenses, and miscellaneous items – and he was always asking his parents for a little more here and there.) Besides, he and Luella wanted to get married by themselves, in their own way and on their own terms.

Although they didn't want a large wedding, the idea of getting married in a registry office didn't appeal to them either. Creighton's estrangement from the faith of his parents – which first emerged at Vic – was a process, not an event. Later he would tell people that he never liked the Methodists, that they were a "bunch of tub thumpers," and that he got out "as soon as possible."[53] That wasn't true, though. Yes, the tree was coming down, but its roots ran deep, meaning it didn't seem right not to get married in a Methodist church, and so Creighton asked his father to call in a favour or two.[54]

Meanwhile, Luella got a pleasant surprise that winter when she received a small legacy from her father's estate. James Bruce had died a few years earlier, in November 1923, and now, in January 1926, his only daughter finally obtained a modest inheritance. It wasn't much but it meant that she could afford to live in Paris. All she had to do was hand in a few more essays and write her final exams. When that day finally came, when the last essay had been submitted and the final exam written, she was free. She had done it. Despite the many obstacles in her way, she had done what she set out to do: get a university education and close the door on Stouffville. Printed on the program of her graduation dinner party was a quotation: "We wonder if the world is very cold; we will soon know." Beneath it Luella wrote, not defiantly, but matter of factly, "I personally, myself, for instance, register no fear."[55]

A few months later she was in Liverpool, England, where she was met by Donald. He had been "very restless and naturally a bit excited"[56] before leaving Oxford, but now, as they made their way to London, everything was falling into place: on 23 June 1926, they were married at Wesley's Chapel. Through his many connections, William Creighton had arranged it. Built in 1778 and located on City Road, it was John Wesley's place of worship. If not the birthplace of Methodism, it was an important site in the history of Methodism and the Methodist movement. The service was deliberately simple: Donald didn't have a best man; Luella didn't have a maid of honour; and their witnesses were the minister's sister and his son. In effect, it was just Donald and Luella. To save money, Luella refused to carry a bouquet. Instead, she picked a small handful of mock orange blossoms from a bush in the chapel's garden. In her various gardens over the course of her long life Luella always planted a mock orange bush, the scent of its summer blossoms carrying her back to London, England, her wedding day, and her youth.

Young and in love, Donald and Luella had the summer to themselves. Immediately after the wedding service, they went to Bicknoller, the village in Somerset where Donald had spent part of his Christmas vacation. Waiting for him was an amusing telegram from his friends in the Hotbed of Virtues and Vices. "This is too bad," they told him. Later, though, they would give him "a magnificent cigarette box." "It is oak," he said, "with the Balliol crest carved on the top, and inside a little copper plate with my name, and the names of all the club members, and the date of our marriage."[57] From their rented cottage with its thatched roof and courtyard garden, Donald and Luella explored the surrounding countryside famous for its romantic associations. They took long walks through the Quantock Hills to the neighbouring villages of Stogumber, Wilton,

Luella Bruce graduated from Victoria College in 1926. Printed on the program of her graduation dinner party was a quotation: "We wonder if the world is very cold; we will soon know." Beneath it Luella wrote, "I personally, myself, for instance, register no fear."

and Crowcombe, where they visited a church built in the fourteenth century. "Somerset was simply beautiful," Donald later reported.[58] They also befriended a small black kitten that they named Humphrey Bigot. Luella was always befriending cats, protecting them, if only for a period of time, in a way that she had been unable to protect those alley cats from her stepmother's strychnine.

After Somerset, they went to London for a couple of days and then to Paris, where they visited the Louvre, Notre Dame Cathedral, and the Samaritaine, one of the enormous department stores that inspired Zola's novel *The Ladies' Paradise.* In the eleventh book in the Rougon-Macquart cycle, Zola set his characters against the much larger canvas of consumer culture and opulent palaces of consumption. "Don't you see," Creighton once enthused, "Zola's characters are multitudinous, and always move against a background, either the inception of the great department stores, or the changes in peasant life due to industrial development, or the growing self-consciousness of the working-classes or the political, social, and military collapse of an era."[59]

From Paris, they went to Saint Malo, a city famous for its "narrow, twisting streets," its "substantial merchant houses," and its "walls and great defensive towers."[60] It was from Saint Malo that Jacques Cartier left for the new world to become the first European to map the shores of the St Lawrence River. But Donald and Luella found the famous port city too touristy. Cutting their stay short, they went to Paimpol, a small fishing village farther down the coast, where, for the next seven weeks, they rented half of a house from an elderly woman, a Madame Blake. Situated on a hill, their rooms overlooked the town. They christened one room the Seaward Room because it looked out on to the turquoise waters of the Brittany coast.

Luella chose Paimpol. At Vic she had read Pierre Loti's novel *An Iceland Fisherman,* a story about the Britanny fishermen who leave Paimpol each February for the cod grounds off Iceland and who return – or don't return – in September. It is a sad, haunting, romantic story of one fisherman in particular, Yann, and the woman he must leave behind, Gaud. They are young lovers, passionate and hopeful, but also doomed. Pulled by the sea, Yann leaves with the other men but never returns, becoming, instead, one more drowned fisherman in a village full of drowned fishermen. As a story about nature's indifference and as a story about love, separation, and death, it spoke to Luella. Perhaps she identified with Gaud, who was raised by her grandmother after her mother had died. Perhaps the novel reminded her of her own mother, whose death from an indifferent infection had robbed a child of a mother's love and forged an unbridgeable expanse. Luella made a point of visiting Pierre Loti's house.

For the next several weeks, Donald and Luella explored Brittany, its churches, its castles, and its ruins; they fell for a kitten named Lulu and her mother,

Donald and Luella spent their wedding night in Bicknoller, a small village in Somerset. "This is the cottage, with roses at the door, where they went immediately after they were married" Luella wrote.

In Somerset, England, on their honeymoon, Donald and Luella befriended a black kitten that they named Humphrey Bigot.

Mademoiselle Minette; and they spent long, lazy afternoons reading. Afterwards, Luella assembled a detailed photo album and scrapbook. It chronicled their peregrinations and their adventures from the exciting to the mundane, from watching a beautiful religious procession to buying milk, potatoes, and choux pastry. She called it "La Lune de Miel 1926." Beneath a picture of Donald – smoking a cigarette and surrounded by a great stack of books – she wrote "The Great Man at Work."[61]

In exploring Somerset, London, Paris, and Paimpol, Donald and Luella were really exploring each other. Their summer romance the year before had been fast and intense, or "swift and absolutely sure" in Luella's words. But, except for those few days in Siloam, it had unfolded under the gaze of his family. Now, they were free to do what they wanted when they wanted to do it. "Marriage," Luella explained, "has been a revelation of abundant living. And the wonder grows instead of diminishing."[62]

VI

After "a perfect summer," Luella went to Paris. Oxford was alright, she explained. Indeed, she "loved the old place." However, she didn't "care to be a woman undergrad there." Oxford was a male sphere and she knew it. Except for a "few stunning Scandinavian blondes," the only women in Oxford were "undergraduettes and whores," Charles Ritchie explained. And the "undergraduettes are hardly regarded as girls": they bicycle to lectures "with unpowdered noses" and wear "hideous regulation Tudor-style black velvet caps." No one, he remarked with an adolescent's double entendre, had ever "penetrated" one of the women's colleges.[63] Luella would have been a fish out of water in Oxford. But in Paris she was in her element.

Renting a tiny apartment on the Left Bank's Avenue Denfert-Rochereau, an "exuberant" Luella reported that she was "happier than she ever thought a girl could be." Actually, her apartment was two furnished rooms in the larger apartment of an old woman, a Madame Paparin, but it was a stone's throw from the Montparnasse Cemetery, a short walk to the Luxembourg Gardens, and a million miles from Stouffville. Although she took a course or two at the Sorbonne, she majored in Paris itself, where, she said, "everything is spinning." She mastered the complicated system of buses and trams, and learned French. Her only complaint was having nothing to wear: her clothes, she explained, "come back from the laundry so beautifully done – all tucks and pleats and things – that I simply haven't the heart to wear them."[64]

Although Donald and Luella faced another separation, it was not like the year before. "Our summer has simply made everything right," Creighton told his mother. "The old tension has absolutely gone." They could see each other more often – already they were planning their Christmas vacation – and they could get a letter to each other in one day. "Isn't that marvellous," he said. More assured and more relaxed, he found that he was able to work "about twice as well." He was managing to keep three subjects going and, somehow, he wrote "several mammoth essays" in just a few short weeks. "Life is strenuous – but I am having a very good time." All told, marriage agreed with him. It is, he pronounced, "a most excellent institution."[65] But his tutor, B.H. Sumner, found him "in bad form" and a bit "testy" because his wife was in Paris.[66] He probably was. Some fifty years later, Creighton could still picture his visits to Paris, the anticipation of getting there, the delight in holding Luella again, and falling to the floor in front of the fireplace.[67]

Creighton's goal was an ambitious one: get a First at Oxford and secure an academic appointment at Toronto.[68] In March, he wrote a letter to George Smith, who had succeeded, on a temporary basis, George Wrong as the head of Toronto's Department of History, explaining that he was tucked away in Saujon, a "tiny little village" in the south of France, where for the next five weeks he planned to undertake a "strenuous review." Schools – Oxford's word for final examinations – "seem rather frighteningly near." He also let it slip that nothing had come from his "various feelers" to American universities and that he still hadn't lined up anything for the fall, although "Kenneth Bell – who has been most awfully good in the matter – still has hopes." In fact, Bell quite liked Creighton; his work, he said, isn't "getting stale" and he himself is "full of things."[69] In any event, Creighton finally came to the real point of the letter. He could not be crass and come right out and ask about an appointment at Toronto, but he could drop the hint. He had heard, he said, that Hume Wrong had arranged a leave of absence to serve as the first secretary to the new Canadian legation in Washington. "The work should be interesting," Creighton added.[70]

Meanwhile, Kenneth Bell was busy writing letters on Creighton's behalf, including to his former student Frank Underhill, who at this point was at the University of Saskatchewan. Underhill was interested: "With regard to your man Creighton, you might send some particulars, although I am not sure there will be any vacancy here." Perhaps, though, there might be one down the road in English and imperial history. Still, Underhill remained unhopeful: Creighton's Oxford pedigree would be a strike against him. "Our president, as he grows older, becomes more desirous of tranquility, and Oxford men in the universities of this continent seldom make the atmosphere more tranquil."[71] Bell responded right away: "My man Creighton," he said, "is a thorough Canadian rubberneck though he has been at Oxford for a year and a half."[72] By rubberneck, he meant tourist or sightseer. Although a pejorative, Bell didn't mean it that way: Creighton hadn't become so Oxonofied that he couldn't fit in at Saskatchewan.

Actually, Bell's various letters didn't matter because Creighton's hint to Smith worked: a few weeks later he was offered a one-year appointment as a lecturer in Toronto's Department of History. Curiously enough, Creighton hadn't been Smith's first choice. In a lengthy letter to Robert Falconer, president of the University of Toronto, Smith had detailed his staffing needs for the coming year – Creighton's name was one of six names on a list of possible candidates for a junior position – and, in a follow-up letter, he explained his desire for someone "not from Toronto who has had post-graduate training in the United States."[73] He didn't say so but certainly implied that Toronto's tradition of hiring its own was not healthy, that, perhaps, new blood was needed. In the end, neither of the young men Smith had wanted – both of whom were at Cornell University – were available and Creighton got the nod. He was still in Saujon when he received Smith's telegram.

Everything was coming together. As Smith reported to the president, "Creighton wires from France that he will accept your offer of a junior lectureship. I made it perfectly clear in my wire and in a subsequent letter that the appointment was for one year only."[74] His salary would be $1,800. About a month later, Underhill accepted a position at Toronto with a salary $4,500. He was older and more experienced but the seeds of jealousy and resentment were sown at the beginning.

VII

In Evelyn Waugh's *Brideshead Revisited*, Charles Ryder receives a bit of advice from his cousin Jasper before going up to Oxford. "You're reading History? A perfectly respectable school. The very worst is English Literature and the next worst is Modern Greats. You want either a first or a fourth. There is no value in anything between. Time spent on a good second is time thrown away."[75] For his part, Creighton was determined to get a First and not "a good second."

In a long letter to her mother-in-law, whom she called Mother, Luella reported that "Don is working at a terrific rate. I don't know how he keeps it up – and there are still two and a half months till the ghastly strain is over. I shall certainly be glad when it is done." Among other topics, he was studying France's foreign policy under the July Monarchy and, as Luella put it, a handful of "obscure occurrences in Spain and Portugal some one hundred years ago." Then, in jest, she joked about her own ignorance of such things and the problems it might pose to a faculty wife. "What if G.M. Smith should find out that I don't know what happened the morning of June 12, 1831, in Rustchuk, Wallachia? Life would be scarcely worth living after that."[76]

Laura Creighton responded quickly, describing Luella as a "perfect bride" for helping Donald prepare for his exams (she made study notes, for example) and for attending to quotidian matters (it fell to her to get the day's milk and bread). "I do not think any girl could have done any more, or indeed half as much, for her husband as you have been doing since you arrived at Saujon." Laura too worried about the pace Donald had set and the toll it was taking. "Like you, I wish the awful strain of it all was over and, at times, I fear that Don will overtax himself and go to pieces before the whole thing ever comes off." But she took comfort in the thought that Donald was like her, and like the rest of the family for that matter: "we can usually do better at a critical time than any other."[77]

The five weeks in Saujon disappeared, according to Luella, "at a most prodigious rate," and before they knew it she and Donald were preparing to move. Leaving, though, meant abandoning a new friend, "namely a gaunt and mangy hound answering to the name of Margarine." Donald and Luella had more or less adopted the stray dog after it snuck into their kitchen one afternoon and consumed "almost a pound" of margarine. Hence its name. Luella couldn't resist his "sweetly sympathetic face" peering in the kitchen window after the crime had been committed, and, for the next few weeks, Margarine was made an honorary – and useful – member of their family: he "acts as our living garbage can and consumes every remnant of all known comestibles."[78]

They both returned to Paris for a few days, where Luella found a one-room apartment with a tiny kitchenette on rue du Cardinal Lemoine – the same Left

Bank street that Ernest Hemingway had lived on a few years earlier. Her previous landlady had been a bit difficult and the apartment itself lacked real privacy. But she adored her new place, and, although the building itself dated to the seventeenth century, the apartments were brand new. Hers overlooked a little courtyard garden which, at the end of April, was "full of lilacs." She was, she said, "happy as a King." "Really, you've no idea how marvellously independent I feel with this little place to live in as I please."

From Paris, Creighton went back to Oxford for the start of Trinity term, his final term at Balliol. Schools were just a few weeks away. Lester Pearson had sat the exams a few years before and hated every minute of it. "You write them one after another, morning and afternoon, day after day, until the frightful ordeal, physical as well as mental, ends."[79] Lasting as long as six days, Schools were a "bruising" rite of passage.[80] Although Creighton had prepared tirelessly, he didn't get a First. He got a Second. No doubt, it was a disappointment. In some ways, though, it didn't really matter. He had secured an appointment at his alma mater and had learned a lot about British and European history and about the writing of history. Perhaps he consoled himself with the knowledge that very few Canadians received a First. Pearson got a Second. So too did Vincent Massey and Arnold Heeney, future clerk of the Privy Council. The brilliant polymath F.R. Scott actually received a Third. Pearson, Massey, Heeney, and Scott were all exceedingly bright men but the Oxford system may have worked against them: they did well on the written examinations but fared less well on the oral examination because they lacked the fluency and the dexterity, the smoothness and the ease, of their British counterparts, and it was the Viva that usually tipped the scales for or against a First.[81]

It is difficult to say what, exactly, Oxford meant to Creighton. On the one hand, he didn't adopt a fake accent in an effort to out-English the English, which is to say he didn't overcompensate for his colonial background by pretending to be someone he wasn't. Nor did he feel inferior or defensive because Canada wasn't England, Toronto wasn't Oxford, and Vic wasn't Balliol. But, on the other hand, he wanted to fit in by wearing the right clothes. Jasper's academic advice to Ryder was followed closely by sartorial advice: "Dress as you do in a country house. Never wear a tweed coat and flannel trousers – always a suit."[82] It was in this context that Creighton not so subtly asked his mother for more money: "If you could send a little extra," he wrote, "I might be able to get a new suit – Ahem!"[83] (When he was at Oxford, Frank Underhill felt the same pressure "to upgrade his wardrobe in keeping with the upper-class English students.")[84]

But more fundamental than Oxford's pressure to wear a nice suit was Oxford's influence on Creighton's nationalism, his Canadianness, and his Britishness.

In fact, Oxford shaped an entire generation of Anglo-Canadian elites whose experience was a double one: Oxford's snobbery and brutal class system strengthened their Canadian nationalism and their hope in Canada's future, but Oxford's reputation as the English-speaking world's greatest university and its mystique – or what Vincent Massey and Lester Pearson called its "spell" and Bart Brebner called its "imprint"[85] – reinforced their Britishness and their appreciation for Britain's place in the world. Their identities were characterized by hybridity and doubleness. Canadianness and Britishness combined to form a Canadian British identity that was no less Canadian for being British. In short, "Oxford repelled but also attracted, strengthening colonial nationalism while reinforcing Britishness."[86]

In this sense, Creighton's experience resembled Eugene Forsey's. Forsey had gone to Oxford in 1926 and was a year behind Creighton. Although he and Creighton knew each other, they didn't know each other well. Actually, Forsey wasn't all that taken with Creighton when they first met, telling his mother that three Canadian students had come around to introduce themselves. He quite liked the first two but "I wasn't so keen about another Toronto man named Creighton."[87] Forty years later, in the 1960s and 1970s, they became confidants in the fight against Quebec nationalism, Forsey describing him as "one of my closest and most revered friends." That fight was in part related to their defence of Canada's imperial connection. And that connection, which was fashioned in their childhood, was confirmed and strengthened at Oxford. In Forsey's words, Oxford "reinforced my pride in England, 'her glory and her message' (to use Churchill's words), in which I had been brought up. It made me understand more fully just what that glory and that message were." Quoting Tennyson, he said that it gave him "a stronger determination that Canada also should be a 'land where, girt with friends or foes, a man may speak the thing he will.'"[88] In other words, Forsey was both Canadian and British. So too was Creighton. For them, Canadianness and Britishness were not mutually exclusive identities.

All told, Creighton loved Oxford. It had cast its spell on him, just as it had cast its spell on Vincent Massey, Frank Underhill, and Lester Pearson before him and on Eugene Forsey and Charles Ritchie after him. Its beauty and its architecture – "ever crumbling but ever renewed" – were "imprinted" on him.[89] "I'd like to put myself on record here (if I haven't done it sufficiently before) that coming to Balliol is the second best thing I've ever done in my life," he told his mother. (The best thing he had ever done was, obviously, marrying Luella.) "If I had to borrow two thousand dollars, I shouldn't have regretted it – the whole experience is marvellous. And I am really getting to know a thing or two."[90] He was happy at Oxford. There was no trace of the underlying bitterness that marked – and marred – so many of his later interactions with family members, friends, and colleagues.

And although he didn't get a First, he could now, like Sir John A. Macdonald, "regard Oxford as his alma mater; and the memories that he carried away from it … were very pleasant ones."[91] That July, Donald and Luella returned to Toronto.

VIII

Donald Creighton was just twenty-five years old when he was assigned Room 22 in Baldwin House, Toronto's Department of History. Not far away was Frank Underhill in Room 19. Although in the Department of Political Economy, Harold Innis also had an office in Baldwin House, a small room really, crammed with books, maps, and research notes on the history of the fur trade. Just a few years before, Creighton had been an undergraduate in the same building. Now he was on the other side of the lectern as a lecturer in modern British and European history. In those days, Canadian history was taught as part of the history of the United States in the first year and not again until the fourth year. Initially, at least, Creighton didn't care. His interest was in French history, in particular the French Revolution, which had been his "special subject" at Oxford. France mattered in the same way that Canada didn't matter, and the Revolution mattered in the same way that the Rebellions of 1837 didn't matter. Because his appointment at Toronto was temporary, Creighton decided to pursue a doctorate. Although uncommon – there was only one PhD in the department in the 1920s – it was increasingly seen as a necessary degree for an academic appointment, especially in the United States. And so he set his sights on the Sorbonne: if he enrolled in a doctoral program, the Doctorat de l'Université, he and Luella could get back to Paris.

After the final grades had been submitted, Donald and Luella returned to Paris. It was the summer of 1928 and Paris was still spinning. It was still the Paris of Ernest Hemingway, Gertrude Stein, F. Scott Fitzgerald, Man Ray, and Josephine Baker, of James Joyce, Ezra Pound, and Ford Madox Ford, and of the Canadians Morley Callaghan and John Glassco, and of Dada and surrealism. Callaghan likened the city to a "giant crystal" that was always refracting light in different ways and showing people new ways of looking at things.[92] Donald and Luella went to the Café Dôme and the Café de la Rotonde, the epicentres of cultural life in Montparnasse. They ate borscht at La Vieille Russie, drank Dubonnet at the Lutèce, and went to the Théatre du Grand Guignol, a theatre famous for its production of horror shows and for its special effects, including eye-gouging, throat-slashing, and blood-soaked climaxes. They took a boat trip down the Seine and saw the largest advertisement in the world, the Eiffel Tower lit up with over 250,000 light bulbs spelling Citroën, the French car maker.[93]

Creighton began his doctoral studies at the Sorbonne with Albert Mathiez, the great historian of the French Revolution. A large man with broad shoulders, a fraying, untidy moustache, and a distinctive pair of tinted and very-much-out-of-fashion pince-nez eyeglasses, Mathiez was a leading, if notoriously difficult, short-tempered, and opinionated figure in French academic circles.[94] But behind an enigmatic and gruff exterior lay a brilliant, original, and controversial man who attracted students from far and wide who regarded him with a mixture of fear, trembling, and awe.[95] Another Canadian student, W.K. Lamb, took a course with Mathiez which he found, curiously enough, a bit boring, but he conceded that the great man "was a master of his subject."[96] As a committed socialist – and, for a brief period of time in the early 1920s, a member of France's Communist Party – Mathiez revitalized the life and career of Robespierre, that equally brilliant, original, and controversial member of the Committee of Public Safety who attempted to defend the Revolution through the Terror. His three-volume history of the Revolution presented a materialist interpretation and, to this day, occupies an important place in French historiography: following Marx, he argued that the Revolution was, in fact, a bourgeois revolution.

In a paper written for one of his Balliol tutors, Creighton had considered what he called "recent tendencies" in French historical writing with a particular focus on the scholarship of François-Alphonse Aulard, Jean Jaurès, and Albert Mathiez. While he found something to admire in all three, it was Mathiez and his approach to the writing of history that captivated him. Where Toronto – and Balliol too – had stressed constitutional and political history as a series of events unfolding according to their own logic, independent of their economic and structural contexts, Mathiez attempted "to see political events within their structural context."[97] In addition, Creighton admired his "exactitude," "insight," "savage logic," and "bitter intensity."[98] But if Creighton found in Mathiez and his approach to the writing of history a "breath of fresh air,"[99] he could not bring himself to admire his conclusions. For Mathiez, the Terror was necessary and justifiable; for Creighton, it was excessive and unrestrained. Bloodletting begat bloodletting, meaning, he said, it was "an impossible vehicle for a socialist revolution." He also believed that Mathiez had been too quick to dismiss the Girondins – the Revolution's moderates who vainly sought to establish the rule of law – as "the last stubborn and belated defenders of the old bourgeois liberalism."[100]

Creighton's proposed dissertation was a study of the economic policies of Jean-Marie Roland, minister of the interior in the Girondin government and an opponent of the Revolution's eventual excesses. It was a topic "dictated" to him by Mathiez, who had just published *La vie chère et le mouvement social sous la Terreur*, an important book on the economic and social conditions of Paris during the Terror.[101] Roland's wife, Madame Roland, was every bit her husband's intellectual equal, turning their Paris salon into a meeting place for many of the Revolution's leading figures. When they found themselves condemned as enemies of the Revolution, he escaped from Paris but she did not. Arrested, convicted, and sentenced to death, she was eventually guillotined in the Place de la Révolution. Upon receiving the news of his wife's death, Roland committed suicide and the Terror claimed another victim.

While Creighton spent long hours at the Bibliothèque Nationale, Luella continued her love affair with Paris. She met with her French tutor, read "piles of books" on art history, collected reproductions, and visited the Louvre as often as she could.[102] At one point, she even mused about writing a book herself. Madame Roland was a fascinating, even romantic, figure who defied the conventions of her time and place to live a meaningful life even if it cost her her life. Luella's book would be a companion volume to Donald's, a sort of his and hers book set.

That summer, Donald and Luella met up with a number of their Toronto friends, including Douglas Duncan, Louis MacKay, Harold Innis, and Harcourt Brown, a Toronto alumnus and aspiring academic. One evening, after Donald had gone to bed exhausted after another long day at the library, Luella went to Harcourt's apartment. Dressed "in an old blue middy" with her "stockings rolled" down, Luella made "herself comfortable on the bed." For the next couple of hours, she and Harcourt discussed the meaning of marriage and how "the conduct" of a woman or a man "could be misconstrued."[103] According to the mores of small-town Ontario, Luella's actions were unbecoming: the church ladies would surely frown upon a married woman visiting a married man late at night. But Luella wasn't in small-town Ontario. She was in Paris. And because she had stopped going to church, she didn't care what the church ladies thought. She was modern. And her marriage was going to be different. It was going to be based on mutual trust and personal freedom, not on old-fashioned ideas of male authority and female submission. Of course, there were limits: unlike that group of Montreal moderns – for example, the painter John Lyman and his wife, Corrine, or the journalist John Bird and his wife, Florence – neither she nor Donald were prepared to swim in the nude with their friends just to prove that their marriage was not their parents' marriage.[104]

Focused, driven, and granite-like, Creighton worked steadily. Harcourt Brown reported that he has his "points" and that he "is as much of a radical as anybody," but "he seems curiously matter of fact about his work." Brown was right: Creighton was not a poser and had no interest in being a perpetual graduate student. While Morley Callaghan boxed Ernest Hemingway and while John Glassco performed live sex shows for men behind peepholes, Creighton

went to the library.[105] "He is at present," Brown said, "plowing through procla-
mations and pamphlets."[106] At times the heat could be insufferable – Creighton
liked to recount how a man armed with a deodorant spray gun would walk
through the reading room of the Bibliothèque Nationale freshening its fetid air
– but he persevered. Although he found his subject "prosaic" and suspected
that Mathiez was "an out and out communist," he was determined to finish
what he started.[107]

Then he and Luella had run out of money. Despite their cheap digs – they
paid 500 francs a week for their tiny west bank apartment – and despite their
frugal efforts – they ate meals of bread, cheese, and fruit in their room – they
returned home, empty-handed and in steerage. Fortunately, Luella had stashed
$85 in a Yonge Street bank for precisely this contingency: she knew that they
would be returning home broke and that they would need a little money to see
them through to September when Donald resumed teaching.

Donald and Luella always referred to their summer in Paris as "that summer." Fifty years later, he remembered "the blissful weather" and how the sun
"just poured down without interruption."[108] What he was really remembering,
of course, was his youth, now long gone. In any event, Creighton's failure to
complete his thesis confirmed his suspicion that, in the absence of granting
agencies and research funding, he would have to give up French history. But if
he couldn't write French history, he could write Canadian history as if it were
French history; he could write Canadian history as if it were large, multilayered,
and important. In short, he could write it as if it mattered.

SUMMER

We are only beginning to realize the central position of the Canadian Shield.
Harold Innis, *The Fur Trade in Canada*

chapter five

Historian

The craft had its traditions, its conventions, its techniques, its stock of forms and variations – all of which were historical products. It found its raw material in the problems of a particular landscape and a particular people. It was the task of a politician to work within the tradition, and to respect the limitations and exploit the possibilities of the medium. He might remain a competent craftsman; he might become a great, creative artist.

John A. Macdonald, vol. 1

Donald Creighton was just twenty-six years old in September 1928, and restless with the desire to write a book. It had been his dream for years, since he had been a high school student at Humberside Collegiate. He still had vague ideas about doing a PhD as well. Perhaps, he thought, he could kill two birds with one stone. And so he began to cast about for a subject, one that was closer to home but big enough to satisfy what he called his instinct for the "grandiose."[1] He would soon find it in the empire of the St Lawrence, and, in the process, history would become his art. At Toronto, Oxford, and the Sorbonne, he had come to appreciate history as a craft. And, like all crafts, it had its "traditions," "conventions," and "techniques." It also had its limitations, including aridness, recitation, and tedium. But history could be more than the sum of its limitations and greater than "its stock of forms and variations." As a branch of literature, it could not only instruct readers, it could touch their emotions as well. In other words, the historian might be content to "remain a competent craftsman" or "he might become a great, creative artist."

Then Luella discovered that she was pregnant, meaning the PhD and the book would have to wait. Right now, it was a matter of getting through the academic year before the baby arrived. Over the fall and winter terms, Luella grew bigger and bigger, or more "portly" according to her mother-in-law.[2] Finally, on a Saturday morning in mid-May she was admitted to the East General Hospital, where that evening she delivered by Caesarian section a 9 lb. 10 oz. baby boy. Luella was naturally exhausted and ecstatic. It used to be said that a woman who had a C-section could not feel the same love for her child as a woman who had experienced what Marie Stopes called "the full torture of childbirth." What nonsense, Luella thought. Stopes, she said, didn't know what she was talking about. Her baby was hers. She adored his little features, his distinctive cry, and his patch of light-brown hair.[3] At first, she and Donald named him Somerset, perhaps after Somerset, England, where they had spent their wedding night, or perhaps after Somerset Maugham, the English writer.

Luella's recovery was proceeding apace – she was now sitting up and eating liver and onions – when she became violently and inexplicably ill. Her fever spiked to 105° and she couldn't nurse the baby. For a few frantic days, no one knew what, exactly, was happening. Like her own mother, Luella had delivered a perfectly healthy baby and now, like her mother, she had become desperately sick. A "terribly anxious" and "much worked up" Donald could only watch.[4] The doctors speculated that it was a infection in her breasts, an extreme case of mastitis, perhaps. Then, slowly, the fever began to abate and Luella recovered her strength. But it meant an extra week in the hospital. Finally, she was sent home, and, a few days later, a name was settled on: Philip William Bruce Creighton, or Philip W.B. Creighton in honour of Donald's father and in memory of Luella's father. William Creighton seemed, Luella said, "highly gratified at the appearance and demeanour of the new scion of his noble race."[5] But Philip would not be baptized. The church of Donald's and Luella's youth had become, at last, irrelevant. Just three years earlier, they couldn't imagine not getting married in a Methodist church; now they couldn't imagine baptizing their son.

Adjusting to life with a baby wasn't easy. In late June, it was decided that Philip was not gaining enough weight and that he had to be supplemented with a bottle. Luella was, understandably, "discouraged over her failure as a dairy."[6] And, of course, there were countless sleepless nights. In the spring of 1930, when Philip was just ten months old, Donald and Luella reached their breaking point. They "have finally come to the conclusion that there is no God, no Santa Claus, and almost nothing of value in life." They are, Donald's sister Isabel reported, "simply shrouded in gloom." Philip is "rather active and that seems to be the primary cause of trouble." Luella, in particular, found herself at the end of her rope. Exhausted and perhaps feeling the effects of post-partum depression, she felt "disgusted" with herself and with her "inability to manage the house and infant with some degree of efficiency." Isabel diagnosed it as an "aggravated case of slump" and, in part, blamed her brother who, she felt, was "too doting" and too "uncritical."[7]

The sphere of necessity – of shopping, cooking, ironing, folding, tidying, sweeping, scrubbing, cleaning, washing up, and looking after the baby – was Luella's, not Donald's, and she found it overwhelming. To ease her relentless domestic assignment, they hired a maid to come every afternoon and supper hour and for a couple of hours on the weekend. "I have ceased to do any housework to speak of," Luella announced. Fifty-odd years later, she would tell her granddaughter – with a mixture of pride and defiance – that she had never in her life used a vacuum cleaner.[8]

Meanwhile, Creighton's position at the university was year to year, and, although the threat to publish or perish hadn't been made, the Department of History expected its members to be researchers as well as teachers. He had already lost one summer. He couldn't afford to lose another.

II

In June of 1930, Donald Creighton made his first of what would be many trips to the Public Archives in Ottawa. His colleague, W.P.M. Kennedy, had suggested a study of Lord Dalhousie, who had been governor-in-chief of British North America in the 1820s and whose papers had been recently acquired by the Archives. Perhaps they contained a PhD – and a short book – on the constitutional development of Canada. Neither sophisticated nor particularly interesting, English-Canadian historical writing was what it was: traditional, political, constitutional, at times sentimental, and too focused on the story of self-government, its development over time, and its ultimate achievement. Arthur Lower once described it as "state-the-terms-of-the-Quebec-Act" history. If it wasn't dry-as-dust constitutional history, it was after-dinner expressions of loyalty to Great Britain, heroic accounts of great men, and patriotic renderings of the Plains of Abraham and General Wolfe or of Queenston Heights and General Brock.[9]

Still, there were hopeful signs of history's professionalization and maturation. The *Canadian Historical Review* had been launched in 1920, the Canadian Historical Association was created two years later, graduate programs were invigorated, and the boundaries between professional and amateur historians were drawn and policed. In 1922 A.L. Burt began making the long trip from Edmonton to Ottawa each summer, from the University of Alberta to the Public Archives of Canada. At first, he was alone. Later, he would be joined by colleagues from across the country. "Certainly all the professional historians in

Canada," he said in 1926, "are turning their eyes on the Archives during the summer and a revolution is bound to come as the result." Indeed, the Archives had become "a sort of clearing house of research," "mutual criticism," and "suggestion." He likened the excitement and the sense of possibility to a "renaissance": Bill Mackintosh had started his lifelong interest in Canadian economic history; Bart Brebner was getting set to publish an important book on colonial Nova Scotia; Harold Innis had completed the research for his magnum opus on the history of the fur trade; Frank Underhill had begun to ask important questions about Canadian liberalism and the reform tradition; and Burt was methodically making his way through eighteenth-century Quebec.[10]

At first, Creighton found himself out of sorts. "After Paris, I hated the runty little town," he recalled.[11] It didn't help that Ottawa was "as hot as hell," or that staring him in the face were mountains of impossible-to-read petitions, dispatches, letters, and reports. "There seems to be about 1,500 tomes that I must read before I shall ever be able to write a word. And the handwriting of these terrible politicians, who are supposed to have made Canadian history, doesn't give one a good temper." He was also lonely. And so he pleaded with his best friend, Harold Wilson, to make a quick trip to Ottawa some weekend because he couldn't, he said, "stand drinking alone."[12]

On more than one occasion he was on the verge of packing it in. "It was the most awful summer I ever spent in my life."[13] Then something caught his eye. Later, it would fire his imagination. When petitioning Lord Dalhousie, the Montreal merchants were not talking about constitutional development and self-government. They were talking about tariffs, taxation, trade, navigation, and transportation. They were talking about a commercial empire based on the St Lawrence River and the Great Lakes, the only waterway to connect the centre of British North America to Great Britain and, in turn, Great Britain to the centre of its greatest prize – the northern half of North America. "Suddenly I realized I had an enormous and wonderful subject. I saw it extended back in time to the start of the French regime and forward into the future." His epiphany came while he was taking the train out of Ottawa, out of the old Union Station and along the Rideau Canal. "'West, west,' I thought to the rhythm of the wheels. 'We're going west.' And I saw it all in a flash. It was a moment of pure rapture."[14]

Actually, the genesis of Creighton's one great thesis – what Bill Morton would call the Laurentian thesis in 1946 – was more prosaic than it was epiphanic, the creative process being less about eureka moments than it is about long hours of work punctuated by moments of frustration, disappointment, and immobility. Moreover, economic history, the importance of geography, and even the meaning of rivers were all very much "in the air" in the late 1920s and early 1930s.[15]

Harold Innis had published *The Fur Trade in Canada* in 1930, which contained, Creighton said, "a whole new interpretation of Canadian history."[16] The key to Canada's past, Innis argued, lay in its economic history, specifically in the history of its staple commodities, first fish, then fur, and later timber, wheat, and minerals. Explicit in *The Fur Trade* was geography. The networks of rivers, lakes, and drainage basins made an east-west economy possible by connecting the interior of the continent to the metropolitan centres of Europe and, especially, Great Britain. "The northern half of North America remained British because of the importance of fur as a staple product," Innis concluded.[17] Sprawling, ambitious, suggestive, and working by induction from the specific to the general, *The Fur Trade in Canada* inspired an entire generation. The problem of Canada became the problem of staples.[18] "Few scholars wrote about Canada without wondering what Innis would think of their work," Bart Brebner said. "I know that I never did."[19]

Neither did Creighton. Writing in the pages of the *New Outlook* – which, amazingly, his father still edited – he described *The Fur Trade* as the first scholarly study of "the first great staple." The whole thing was "immensely important," he said, but it was the conclusion that animated the twenty-eight-year-old, green-as-grass historian. A notoriously clumsy, even ham-fisted, writer, Innis achieved a rare moment of clarity and simplicity: "The present Dominion emerged not in spite of geography but because of it." It was as close as Innis ever came to poetry. Creighton described it as "a remarkable piece of synthesis."[20]

It was not just Innis who shaped Creighton's early thinking. The Scottish geographer Marion Newbigin had published *Canada: The Great River, The Lands, and The Men* in 1927. "How is it that Canada today is an entity distinct from the United States?" she asked. Because "the French had established themselves on the St. Lawrence." The river had opened the interior of the continent and made its riches accessible. Without it and the mobility it made possible, New France would have been an impossibility. In a suggestive comment, she observed that Canada's western expansion "could only take place with safety into an area whose products would find a natural outlet by the St. Lawrence." She seemed, Brebner later said, to be "glimpsing" the Laurentian thesis: fur, timber, wheat, and minerals all found their natural outlet by the St Lawrence. Creighton acknowledged Newbigin's book at the time and – just a few months before he died – he told a researcher curious about its impact on his thinking that, while he had read it, it confirmed more than it shaped his thinking. "The basic idea," he said, "had already been laid down."[21]

What Creighton called "the basic idea" also appeared in George Brown's University of Chicago doctoral dissertation. As only the second PhD to be appointed in Toronto's Department of History, Brown had examined attempts by the British, the Canadians, and the Americans to capture the natural advantages of that "great highway between the interior of North America and the Atlantic Ocean."[22] Creighton was surely aware of Brown's thesis and would have had easy access to it. At the very least, he had read Brown's article in the *Canadian Historical Review* which gave "a leading part" to the St Lawrence River in "the drama" of early Canadian history and which used the phrase "commercial empire."[23] No doubt the two men also exchanged ideas at Baldwin House when Freya Hahn, the departmental secretary, served afternoon tea in the staff room, a shallow, oblong-shaped room that faced west on to St George Street. Perhaps, over a cup of tea and a biscuit or two, Creighton and Brown discussed the St Lawrence River, the fur trade, commercial empires, and colonial politics. Perhaps too they were joined by Harold Innis, before the Department of Political Economy moved in 1933.

In early 1934, Creighton reviewed *Toronto during the French Regime*, which argued that Toronto, as the terminus of an important river and portage route connecting the lower lakes to the upper lakes, was part of the much larger commercial and military struggle for the northern half of North America. Creighton's review was largely sympathetic and, for the most part, simply described the book's contents. But it contained his first use of the phrase that he would later make famous: Toronto, he wrote, was an important point in a "commercial empire" based on the fur trade. Together the St Lawrence River, the Great Lakes, the Humber River, and the Toronto portage provided a vast and interconnected "transportation system which made this western empire possible."[24]

No scholar lives and works in isolation. Books, ideas, methods, sources, and conversations on Canadian history, the St Lawrence River, the merchant class, and a great western commercial empire percolated and then coalesced. Over lunch at the Public Archives, during tea in Baldwin House, through a chance encounter on campus, and in two early articles and a couple of book reviews, Creighton shared his insights, tested his ideas, and refined his arguments.[25] Fuelled by the sensation that he was breaking new ground in the writing of Canadian history, that Canada was not the story of responsible government, that it was, instead, the story of the Montreal merchants and their successive efforts to build a commercial empire, he clocked long hours at the Archives, the library, and the office. Over time, he amassed and then arranged by subject and by date hundreds of pages of research notes, each one emanating a steady, focused, and deliberate sense of purpose.[26]

As he gathered and arranged his research notes, Creighton did not have, in his words, "the remotest idea of where and how [my book] might be published." In those days, the market for Canadian history seemed "permanently depressed," and, in the absence of financial assistance, few publishers were interested in academic monographs with small print runs.[27] Then fortune smiled.

James Shotwell was an ex-pat living in New York City, where he taught medieval history at Columbia University and served as the director of the Division of Economics and History at the Carnegie Endowment for International Peace. As a Canadian living in the United States and as a committed liberal internationalist, he looked on anxiously as Ottawa and then Washington erected a high tariff wall along the 49th parallel in response to the depression. Determined to do something, Shotwell envisioned a multi-volume research project on Canadian-American relations, past and present. "The time has come," he said in April 1932, "for a very important shaping up of Canadian-American questions."[28] In fact, he wanted the series to demonstrate to the world the example and the genius of the Canadian-American border.

Shotwell next turned to Innis, English Canada's leading social scientist and the person who would oversee the Canadian half of the series formally known as The Relations between Canada and the United States. Before committing himself, Innis spelled out the conditions of his participation. Research, he believed, could not be bought and sold.[29] If scholars surrendered their independence for a research grant and the promise of publication then they surrendered everything. Innis also told Shotwell that it didn't make sense to study Canadian-American relations when basic studies in the history of the Canadian economy had yet to be done. The two economies are distinct, he insisted, and the Canadian economy must be studied in and of itself before there can be comparative studies or studies in relations. "I have argued that at considerable length elsewhere ... that the boundary line is not accidental and that the economic background is fundamentally different in the two countries."[30] What were needed, Innis believed, were specialized monographs on fish, timber, minerals, and pulp and paper.[31] And so Shotwell's series on Canadian-American relations became in part Innis's series on Canadian staples.

Innis also insisted on Creighton's participation. No longer a junior lecturer, Creighton had been made an assistant professor in 1932; he had an active research agenda; and he had published a handful of articles and book reviews. As Innis told Shotwell, Creighton is "alive" and does "excellent work."[32]

Shotwell wasn't so sure. What did Creighton's proposed study on the "Commercial and Financial Organization before the Concentration of Capital Stage" have to do with Canadian-American relations? And so he sought the advice of his colleague in Columbia's Department of History, Bart Brebner. Also an ex-pat, Brebner knew the Canadian scene well. He admired Innis and had taught a young Donald Creighton when he had been a Toronto lecturer in the early 1920s. But he was inclined to agree with Shotwell: Creighton should be dropped because his work fell outside the parameters of a series that purported to be on Canadian-American relations.[33]

But Innis was adamant, and, as he so often did, he got his way when Shotwell sent a formal invitation to Creighton in April 1934.[34] Naturally, Creighton was thrilled. He now knew where and how his book would be published – by Ryerson Press with Carnegie money. In addition, he would receive a $500 honorarium. To an assistant professor earning just a couple of thousand dollars a year, $500 was, in his words, "extremely generous." And echoing Innis, he added that his work would be his own and that he would not bend it to fit Shotwell's agenda: it will be, he said, "an independent piece of research."[35] With a $200 advance from the Carnegie Endowment, Creighton went to Ottawa in June 1934 for his "final summer's work" at the Archives.[36]

III

Donald's priority was his career. It was Luella's priority too. And so she made it possible for him to spend long days at the office and to be away for weeks at a time in June and July. But they both knew that her intelligence and energy needed an outlet and that, as much as she loved and wanted children, she needed to live a creative life.

Luella's decision to write stemmed, naturally enough, from her interest in literature. But it also stemmed from a need to keep Stouffville and her painful childhood and adolescence at bay. In an unpublished novel – which was, really, a veiled autobiography – an older woman gives Harriet, the novel's heroine and a struggling writer, some strong advice based on her own experience. Unable to support her husband, look after her children, and pursue her promising art career, she did what was expected of her: she stopped painting, she met the needs of others, and she ceased to exist. "It is the tragedy of my life that I did not insist on going on with it," she says of her painting. "But there were reasons, of course. Children to be got into this world, to be fed, loved, and to absorb time and energy. And a husband must be supported, encouraged too. They do not realize what it means to be a woman, to have something of her own. Don't let your work go," she implores Harriet. "It is a justification of one's existence, really. Nothing takes its place."[37]

It was the same advice that Virginia Woolf had delivered to the London branch of the National Society for Women's Service in 1931: if they are going to lead creative, artistic, and full lives – if, in short, they are going to exist – women must kill the Angel in the House, that inner voice instructing them in the "difficult art of family life," in the ways and means of self-denial and self-negation.

"Killing the Angel in the House," she said, is "part of the occupation of a woman writer." Luella, like Harriet, needed to kill the Angel in her house; she needed "to turn upon her and catch her by the throat."[38] By hiring a maid and by refusing to vacuum, Luella did precisely that.

Initially, Luella wrote children's stories for the Boys and Girls Page of the *New Outlook*. The first series featured Gutrik, a 600-year-old gargoyle at Paris's Notre Dame Cathedral. From his panoramic perch, he teaches children about Paris and its many sites and sounds, its boulevards and parks, its squares and fountains, and even its Bird Market where people gathered once a week to buy and sell animals, flowers, and, of course, birds. In one story a little boy and his mother select "a warm and friendly kitten," just the kind of kitten "who might sleep in a hump on your bed." Another series featured Blue Rabbit, a stuffed rabbit belonging to a little boy. Blue Rabbit and a small cast of other stuffed animals teach him about the meaning of friendship; they help him overcome his fear of going to the hospital; and they offer him advice on how to plan his first sleepover. A third series centred on a little boy named Peter and his kitten named Spuddie.[39]

Luella also wrote short stories, and, in these, her themes were darker. In "Miss Kidd" the main character is a proper church-going schoolteacher who marries a man she knows to be rough around the edges but whom she hopes to reform and to refine. When things don't go according to plan, she finds herself trapped in a loveless marriage to a man who drinks, swears, and forces sex on her. "Miss Kidd was ill with fear and shame. But it is the duty of a good wife to submit to her husband. He fell asleep in his dirty blue shirt, without even taking his socks off." Only when they are both killed in a car accident is she released; when the bodies were found, it was said that "Miss Kidd looked serene and happy."[40]

Luella next published "The Cornfield." Told from the perspective of a ten-year-old girl, it deals with a challenging subject: a girl's dim and inarticulate awareness of her sexuality. The story opens with Virginia's arrival at the Mennonite farm of her step-aunt, a zealot who uses religion as a weapon. When, for example, Virginia puts flowers into her hair, she is told by her scripture-quoting step-aunt that it is "vain and wrong." According to Paul's first epistle to Timothy, women should "adorn themselves in modest apparel, with shamefacedness and sobriety; not with braided hair, or gold, or pearls, or costly array" (1 Timothy 2:9). Virginia is at once confused and defiant. "Something within [her] told her that what the woman said was false." Later, Virginia feels her first romantic interest in a fourteen-year old boy. While playing hide-and-seek in the cornfield with a group of children, they find themselves alone. Although perfectly innocent, there is a connection, and, as they walk in silence through the field, she can see "his rough, light hair near the tassels of the corn." Coming out of the field, they are confronted by her step-aunt. Instantly enraged, she slaps Virginia "sharply on the cheek," screaming that she "ought to be ashamed" for walking with a boy. Then she pulls at Virginia's dress in such a way that allows her to peer down into it "with her hateful eyes," the girl's prepubescent chest eliciting demeaning laughter. Stamping her foot "furiously," Virginia screams, "Don't you dare touch me." For once silent, the step-aunt cannot respond. During all of this, Virginia's uncle does nothing. A pathetic figure, he remains passive and unresponsive. But Virginia doesn't hate him. Rather, she feels sorry for him.[41]

Published in the *Canadian Forum* in 1937, it won a $50 prize for the best story published that year, the judges acknowledging the difficult subject matter and the challenge of depicting "the subtleties of a child's inner life."[42] What Morley Callaghan, Earle Birney, and Bertram Brooker couldn't know is that Luella's story drew on her own inner life. The step-aunt was her stepmother; the uncle was her father; the sexual humiliation was her humiliation; and Virginia's refusal to be defeated by her step-aunt's religious tyranny was her refusal.

IV

Donald and Luella were building a rich and full life in Toronto. They had each other; they had Philip; they had their work; and they had a lovely circle of family and friends. They spent a lot of time with Donald's parents, who were doting grandparents, with Isabel who became a devoted aunt, and with Jack and his wife, Sally Murphy.

After the war, Jack completed his undergraduate degree and, in a way, went into the family business when he got a job with Oxford University Press in its education division. On a business trip to Vancouver in early 1927, he reconnected with Sally Murphy, an old flame from Toronto. As the daughter of Denis Murphy, the first native-born British Columbian to be appointed to the BC Supreme Court and long-time member of the University of British Columbia Board of Governors, Sally had been told from the day she could walk that the world of higher education was also a woman's world.[43] After completing her undergraduate degree at UBC in 1923, she did graduate work in English at the University of Toronto, where she and Jack first met. In Luella's words, they used to "trot around" together. When they saw each other again in Vancouver, they fell in love and were married almost immediately in the Murphy home on Vancouver's Davie Street. Jack barely had time to send a quick telegram to his parents: "Marrying Sally March 17. Both arrive in Toronto March 28."[44] Although a Catholic, and thus a source of some initial consternation, Sally was welcomed into the fold. Indeed, Luella went out of her way to compliment her mother-in-law for being so accepting.[45]

In some ways, the Creighton boys married similar women. Like Luella, Sally was smart, assertive, interested in books, and had boundless reserves of energy. She was the sort of person who could raise six children and run a hospital at the same time.[46] And like Luella, she started to write, publishing in the late 1920s and early 1930s several essays and book reviews in the *New Outlook*, including a celebration of the female novelist from Jane Austen and George Eliot to Virginia Woolf and Edith Wharton.[47] In 1930, Jack and Sally had a son. After his great-grandfather and his grandfather, he was named Denis and became a much-loved addition to the family. Isabel delighted in watching her nephew enter childhood and found herself quite amazed at his "volubility": "He pursues me with a series of questions which are sometimes staggeringly keen."[48]

The family cottage on Lake Muskoka took on a new importance in the late 1920s and early 1930s. William – now the family patriarch – built a croquet lawn which provided no end of fun, and Laura – now the family matriarch – looked forward to gathering her children and her grandchildren under one roof at least once a summer. In the dogs days of August, when Donald got back from Ottawa, that tiny piece of the Laurentian Shield became a place for the growing Creighton family to read a ton of books, discuss writing, solve the problems of the world, swim, take long naps, and play rummy after the dishes were done and the children put to bed.

Family dynamics, though, could be tense and unpleasant. Donald and Sally especially did not get along. Luella by experience, and Jack and Isabel by instinct, knew how to manage his personality but Sally didn't and, almost certainly, refused to learn. Strong-willed and not likely to back down, Sally found him impossible; difficult and self-centred, Donald found her insufferable. He simply couldn't see her "better moments," Isabel said at the time. It cut both ways: she couldn't see his better moments either. Years later, Denis remembered how, whenever Donald's name came up in conversation, his mother would bristle.[49]

After his family, the most important people in Donald and Luella's life were Harold and Mary Innis. With a shared interest in art, books, and writing, Luella and Mary formed a deep friendship that included the Women's Art Club, Greta Garbo movies at Loew's, ginger ale at the Honey Dew, Christmas shopping at Eaton's, and long, aimless drives in the country.[50] The Innises often entertained the Creightons at their North Toronto home on Chudleigh Ave. After dinner, Donald and Mary would retire to the living room to listen to classical music, especially the operas of Wagner, while Harold, who was tone deaf, and Luella stayed in the dining room talking about any manner of things. The Innis children adored Luella. She had so much energy and seemed so full of life. "Hello, boys and girls," Luella shouted when entering the Innis house. And she meant

William and Laura Creighton in Muskoka, ca 1930s. At least once a year, usually in August, Laura liked to gather her children and grandchildren at the family cottage on Lake Muskoka, one of the countless lakes dotting the Laurentian Shield, and situated close enough to Toronto to make it a therapeutic tonic, or an "instant north."

it. She genuinely liked children and was interested in their comings and goings, their new toys, and their hidden treasures. And while she sat at the kitchen table having a cup of tea with Mary, she let the Innis girls braid her hair.[51] The Creighton-Innis friendship continued into the summer months when Donald, Luella, and Philip went to Lake Muskoka and Harold, Mary, and their brood rented a cottage on Lake Joseph.

The constant flow of family and friends to and from the cottage may have been great fun but it was an obvious distraction too. Much as Creighton wanted to be in Muskoka, he desperately needed to work. And so, in 1933, Luella had a small writing hut built close to the lake's granite shoreline. Although rustic, it was functional. A long, narrow table, a chair, a couple of shelves, and a window that looked west across the lake were pretty much the sum of it. Carefully arranging his notes and a handful of books, Creighton took out his fountain pen. He never learned to use a typewriter because, he said, he needed to feel the words on the page: "When, in the course of a September day in 1759 ..."

Built just a few metres from the shoreline, Donald Creighton's writing hut on Lake Muskoka allowed him to escape the comings and goings at the cottage and gave him the peace and quiet he needed to write.

V

Four years and 850 manuscript pages later, he had completed his first book. Once he found his pace, Creighton wrote quickly and deliberately. He was just thirty-five years old but already he had the unusual and enviable capacity to see an entire book, from beginning to end, in his mind's eye. There were no false starts, dead ends, or aborted efforts, and there were no lengthy rewrites. Working from an inner sense of design and proportion, he knew exactly what he wanted to say and where he wanted to say it.

When he read a portion of the manuscript in the spring of 1937, James Shotwell found himself "stirred." Describing it as "high literature," he compared its author to Francis Parkman, the great nineteenth-century American historian. He had a couple of quibbles – for example, he thought that Creighton might have included more biographical information on certain figures in Canadian history who were not as well known to American readers – but he had no substantial criticisms.[52]

Shotwell's enthusiasm was important, but what Creighton really wanted was Innis's approval. Although he and Innis were intellectual equals, Creighton looked up to Innis as a kind of mentor and wanted to be like him. He wanted to lead a life of research and scholarship. He wanted to lead a life of the mind. But Creighton also wanted to be a writer and worried that Innis wouldn't like or even approve of his attempt to produce a work of art. It was one of Creighton's firmest convictions that history should be accessible and that it should be written for a general audience. History's professionalization brought benefits but it also carried costs, including its privatization, or its tendency to become a private conversation between experts.[53] The editor of the *American Historical Review* complained that historians had become too obsessed with facts and had lost an interest in form, while the editor of the *Canadian Historical Review* could not cite a single PhD thesis that even approximated a "great book."[54] Resisting history's privatization, Creighton had set out to write a great book, not a monograph and certainly not a PhD thesis.

Meanwhile, an avuncular Bart Brebner told him not to worry about what Innis thought. "He has such an appetite for his 'political arithmetic' that he can't bring himself to care much about how he presents his sums. He can see what is wrong just as clearly as any of his critics, but with the best will in the world on his part there is no inner urge to artistry."[55] Of course, Brebner was right because Innis didn't care how he presented his research findings. But Innis admired Creighton's manuscript and cracked the whip at Ryerson Press to ensure its quick publication.[56]

Published in December 1937, *The Commercial Empire of the St. Lawrence* was, by any definition, a great book.[57] In the morality tale of Canada's steady march to self-government, the Montreal merchants were the bad guys, the Chateau clique, that small group of men who had the ear of the imperial authorities, who distrusted the motivations and policies of Lower Canada's elected House of Assembly, and who effectively retarded responsible government. According to Creighton, however, it was the merchant class and not the Assembly – now firmly in the hands of the Parti canadien and, after 1826, the Parti des patriotes – that understood the logic of Canadian history. From this vantage point, Creighton went back in time to document the successive attempts by the merchants to build a commercial empire through the fur trade and later through the trade in timber and wheat between 1760 and 1849, from the advent of British sovereignty over the northern half of North America to the advent of free trade and the appeal to union with the United States, from the imperial connection to the triumph of continentalism, from vast possibility to ultimate failure, from beginning to end.

Divided into three parts, *The Commercial Empire of the St. Lawrence* reads quickly. Creighton likened it to "a drama with lofty ambitions" that unfolded in clearly defined "stages."[58] The opening act finds British merchants entering the empire's newest colony and being "drawn northwards by the promises of the river." Despite their initial success, they encounter defeat in the form of a new international boundary. Negotiated after the American Revolution, it divides British North America and the United States and cuts the merchants off from the fur trade's great hinterland south of Lake Erie between the Ohio and Mississippi rivers. "Devoid of geographical and historical meaning," the new boundary "cut through the commercial empire of the St. Lawrence." In the second act, the merchants regroup to capture the fur trade in the northwest. But again, they are met with inevitable defeat: by 1821, the fur trade was directed through Hudson Bay by the Hudson's Bay Company and not through Montreal by the North West Company. "Montreal, the incredible little city which had won half a continent, was now – what it had always seemed – a small provincial town." The third and final act sees a new generation of merchants seeking their own empire through the new staples trade in timber and wheat. But their ambitions end in a spectacular collapse when they prove unable to rival American trade through the Erie Canal, or what Lord Durham had called New York's "own St. Lawrence,"[59] and when Great Britain, for its own reasons, abandons imperial preferences and mercantilism for free trade. Recoiling from an "unnatural mother country," the merchants concede final defeat: "the commercial empire of the St. Lawrence was bankrupt" and the dream of a territorial empire was exhausted.[60] Out of anger, confusion, and desperation, they pin their hopes on a continental over an imperial trading system and embrace annexation to the United States.[61]

Central though the merchants were to Creighton's historical calculus, they are curiously absent in the book itself. They appear, of course – the McGills, the McTavishs, the Richardsons, and the Merritts – but they appear as names. They don't come alive because Creighton neither animated them nor provided their back stories. Indeed, he didn't show any interest in them as individuals. As a result, they remain "like-minded to the point of being interchangeable."[62] They are the heroes of the story, but they are treated as a collective hero and not as individual heroes. Creighton's decision not to animate the merchants was a calculated one. After all, he wanted to highlight the deeper logic of Canadian history: the movement westward via the St Lawrence River and the Great Lakes.

Jacques Cartier, the first European to explore the St Lawrence River Valley, called it the River of Canada and, believing that it was "the largest river … ever to be seen," he followed it westward. So did Creighton. He saw Cartier's "great

River of Canada"[63] as a force in history and transformed it into a sentient being with a will and personality of its own. With "acquisitive fingers," the St Lawrence "groped into the territory of the plains"; "it entrenched upon the dominion of the Mississippi"; "it grasped the Shield"; it "reached southward into the valley of the Hudson"; and finally, it "rolled massively" past Quebec City and into the Atlantic. "Youthful, willful, turbulent," the river "shouted its uniqueness to adventurers." It "invited," "promised," "commanded," and "inspired." It even "consoled." "The dream of the commercial empire of the St. Lawrence runs like an obsession through the whole of Canadian history," Creighton wrote. "The river was not only a great actuality: it was the central truth of a religion."[64]

There were other truths, though. One was the imperial connection; another was the inescapable presence of the United States. In a 1932 essay – which was really a version of his Hysterical Club paper on Canada's intellectual contamination – Creighton considered contemporary Canada as a colony of both Great Britain and of the United States. Although critical of Great Britain – he had been, he later said, influenced by all the talk of isolationism in the early 1930s – he understood that the far greater threat to Canada came from south of the border and not from across the pond. "American movies dominate Canada, if anything, even more completely than they do the United States," he wrote. "And every month American magazines are dumped in hundreds of thousands across the border"; "every winter the barons of Canadian industry trek to California and Florida; and every summer visiting Americans deposit hundreds of millions at Canadian hotels, service stations, liquor stores and hot dog stands." The only thing worse than American tourists stuffing their faces with hot dogs were the countless "Rotarians, Shriners, Kiwanisans, Oddfellows, Laundrymen, and Morticians [who] cross the border joyfully for the back-slapping orgies and carnivals of service." Creighton was still playing the bad boy and Canadians were still a bunch of Babbitts who "believe the Royal York Hotel is superior to the Cathedral at Rouen for the sufficient reason that it is higher"; who think that "bathtubs, tiles, electric gadgets, and radios are the most sacred features of interior decoration"; and who eat "baked beans, pancakes, milk-shakes, and ice-cream" in "tiled and infinitely tedious restaurants."[65]

Creighton's insistence on the importance of Great Britain and his emerging anxiety about "Americanism" in Canada – which was not at all atypical for his time and place – were projected onto the past and found expression in his first book.[66] Over and over again, he emphasized the St Lawrence River and Great Lakes as an imperial trade route and stated that, without Great Britain, Canada lay exposed and vulnerable to truculent, aggressive, and predatory American trading practices. Today's movies, magazines, and hot-dog-eating tourists were yesterday's Erie Canal: both carried American goods, ideas, and ways of doing things into the Great Lakes, the symbolic heart of the empire of the St Lawrence.

If the "central problem of Canadian history [was] the problem of building a continental dominion on the basis of the St. Lawrence and the Laurentian Shield," the solution, Creighton believed, was the imperial connection. It alone was capable of offsetting the continental challenge. Running throughout *The Commercial Empire of the St. Lawrence* is a constant tension – imperialism versus continentalism, Great Britain versus the United States, the St Lawrence versus the Hudson. That tension is only resolved when Great Britain repeals the Corn Laws and Navigation Laws in 1849 and the merchants, bewildered and desperate, turn to union with the United States. Canada, Creighton wrote, "was virtually meaningless apart from the imperial connection."[67]

Many years after the fact, Creighton said that he had been attracted to the St Lawrence River because it possessed "a kind of romantic dream" of nation.[68] Summoning the ancient metaphor of rivers as "the arterial bloodstream of a people," he saw Canada in the same way that Herodotus saw Egypt, as "a gift of the river."[69] And drawing on the national "fluvial myths" of the Rhine, the Danube, the Vltava, the Seine, the Thames, and closer to home, of the Hudson, the Ohio, and the Mississippi, he imagined the St Lawrence as the one great stream "on which you could found an enormous territorial empire, either commercial or political."[70] In this sense, the merchants were the first Canadians. Although the merchants who initially set up shop in Montreal came with the "single, simple objective of making money," they soon became "the only Canadians in the modern sense of the term; they alone thought in terms of a distinct and continental northern state."[71]

Yet they were destined to fail. British North America had to lose and the United States had to win. Failure was built into the landscape itself. "Two worlds lay over against each other in North America and their conflict was not only probable but certain," he wrote.

Between those who possessed and those who were denied the single great entrance to the continent, the hostility of war could subside only into the competition of peace. With the whole pressure of its material and spiritual being, each society was impelled to maintain its separateness and to achieve its dominion. They contradicted each other, they crowded each other; and the wars and raids of the seventeenth and eighteenth centuries are but outward manifestations of a great, essential, and slowly maturing conflict ... Here were two geographic provinces occupied by culturally distinct peoples; here were two economies controlled by antagonistic national states. Of their essence, the St. Lawrence and the seaboard denied each other. Riverways against seaways, rock against farmland, trading posts against ports and towns and cities, habitants against farmers, and fur traders against frontiersman – they combined, geography and humanity, in one prime contradiction.[72]

"That's pure Spengler," Creighton admitted.[73] All the actualities of the past – people, events, victories, and defeats – are, Oswald Spengler believed, "secondary" to, or "derivative" of, the deeper logic of a particular historical grouping.[74] In this case, that historical grouping was embodied in what Creighton called a "prime contradiction": the commercial and political empire of the St Lawrence versus the commercial and political empire of the eastern seaboard, or British North America versus the United States.

For all of its strengths and possibilities, the river harboured weaknesses and limitations. As a single waterway, it stretched 3,800 kilometres into the centre of the continent, but its "continuity was broken at Niagara [and] it stumbled and faltered at the Cascades, the Cedars, and Lachine" while the upper lakes were indefensible and the lower lakes were easily accessible by competitors. As a whole, the St Lawrence River and the Great Lakes had no definite boundary and no bold frontier, only a "smudged faint tracery" that bled into upstate New York, the Ohio Valley, and the Laurentian Shield. In short, the river had a "root defect" and a "fundamental weakness" making defeat geographical and unavoidable. "The St. Lawrence was a stream which dashed itself against the rocks and broke the hopes of its supporters; and all the long struggle, which had begun when the first ships of the French sailed up the River of Canada, had served, in the end, to establish a tradition of defeat." That "tradition of defeat" achieved its violent climax in the stunning events of 25 April 1849, when a passionate mob, not knowing what to do or where to turn, burned the Montreal parliament buildings to the ground. "The accumulated sense of failure was so oppressive that it drove men to repudiate their unavailing loyalties and to destroy the cherished system which had failed them. The fire which broke out on that April evening in 1849 was symbolic of the blind urge towards disavowal and destruction; and the hopes of successive generations of Canadians, consumed in a last blaze of anger, were reflected in the red sky over Montreal."[75] Nothing lasts forever; civilizations rise and fall; the commercial empire of the St Lawrence once extended across the continent and now it was gone. "Spengler was very much in vogue" in the 1930s, Creighton later said.[76]

The final sentences also owed a debt to Richard Wagner and his four-opera Ring Cycle. For that matter, the entire book owed a creative debt to Wagner. In the same way that the Ring opens with the Rhine River, *The Commercial Empire of the St. Lawrence* opens with "the one great river which led from the eastern shore into the heart of the continent." And in the same way that the Ring ends with the final destruction of the world, *The Commercial Empire of the St. Lawrence* ends with the "disavowal and destruction" of an empire which, for generations, had been the one great hope of Canadians. In the Ring, the prophesied war of the gods brings the world to a burning end when Brünnhilde orders the building of a funeral pyre on the banks of the Rhine. Riding her horse into the fire, she fuels an inferno; flames shoot up, engulfing the earth and filling the sky. As Valhalla burns in the distance, the horizon glows bright red. But in the world's destruction lay its redemption as the Rhine flows majestically on. In *The Commercial Empire of the St. Lawrence,* the burning parliament buildings "were reflected in the red sky over Montreal" while the St Lawrence flows to its appointed destination. Inspired by Wagner, Creighton understood that everything contained its own opposite: day/night; light/darkness; good/evil; love/hate; birth/death; beginning/ending.

Creighton could have easily extended the story past 1849 because, obviously, the political crisis in Lower Canada was overcome, the United States did not annex the Canadas, the imperial connection was not severed, and British North America survived to become Canada. In an otherwise glowing review, Arthur Lower said as much: the book is "brilliant," he said, but 1849 was not an end point. The "draw of the St. Lawrence was still felt," he wrote. "For canal and bateau were substituted the Grand Trunk and the C.P.R."[77] Creighton obviously knew this. But like all great artists, he also knew where he wanted to stop. If not pinpointed, 1849 was at least prophesied by the limitations and defects of the St Lawrence River and Great Lakes basin. To have extended the story – even in an epilogue – would have destroyed the book's unity and violated its design. And it would have erased the aura of immediacy he was striving for. The desire that drove Creighton to write history was the desire to feel the reality of the past, to follow its paths, to participate in its events, to sense its actualities, to feel the warmth of its summers and the cold of its winters, to hear its shouts and cheers, to visualize its forms and gestures, and to reconstruct its passage through time. He wanted, he said, "to write history for its own sake, not from the backward glance of the present, but as if what I was describing had happened the day before yesterday."[78]

Creighton knew what he was doing when he emplotted *The Commercial Empire of the St. Lawrence* as a tragedy. History was an aesthetic practice, he maintained, not a scientific one; it was an imaginative reconstruction, not a falsifiable experiment; it was narrated by the historian, not found in the archives; and, finally, the form was the content. Constituting a deliberate choice on the part of historians, a book's "mode of emplotment" reflects not only their apprehension of the past but their view of the world and their place in it. Moreover, the plot structure of tragedy demands that, after the fall, the hero not only recognize the limits of human action but also accept "the conditions under which [humans] labor in the world." These conditions are "inalterable and eternal," setting "the limits on what may be aspired to and what may be legitimately aimed at in the quest for security and sanity in the world."[79]

In its quest for security and sanity, the merchant class recognized and accepted the limits of the river as the basis for a commercial empire. But the river was indifferent. When the parliament buildings are set on fire and the city erupts in clamour and confusion, there was "the darkness and movement of the St. Lawrence." Later, when the merchants circulate the annexation manifesto, again there was the river "which cared not whether it was valued or neglected" and "which would outlast all the ships that sailed upon it and survive all the schemes which it could possibly inspire."[80]

VI

Hit by the originality and forcefulness of its argument and moved by the quality of its prose, readers found themselves gripped from beginning to end. Although he wished that Creighton "had dipped his pen less frequently in purple ink," Herbert Heaton from the University of Minnesota described *The Commercial Empire of the St. Lawrence* as "a brilliant piece of analysis, synthesis, and interpretation." Charles Stacey considered it "a most important contribution to the literature of Canadian history and the most distinguished volume so far published in the great survey of Canadian-American relations." Daniel Harvey exclaimed that it was "a brilliant book." And Yale's Gilbert Tucker called it "an extremely good book and a really important contribution to the understanding of Canadian history."[81]

Privately, one friend told Creighton that he had read his book with "great profit"; another thought that it was the best book in Canadian history published in the last twenty years; and yet another placed *The Commercial Empire of the St. Lawrence* on his bookshelf next to *The Fur Trade in Canada* "as one of the most significant contributions to Canadian history." A.L. Burt, who had watched the renaissance in Canadian historical writing unfold at the Public Archives, called it "a grand piece of work."[82] Frank Underhill considered it "the best book ever written" in Canadian history and described its author as the "white hope" of Canadian historical writing.[83]

Amid the chorus of praise, however, there were discordant notes. Although he genuinely liked the book, Stacey noted that "the reader is sometimes allowed to lose sight of the opposing interests," including the interests of French Canadians, because the author had told the story so consistently from the perspective of the merchants. Gilbert Tucker was more pointed: "The [British] decision to respect the cherished institutions of the French Canadians is run through the mill of adverse criticism and comes out ground exceedingly small." "Surely," he added, "the decision has a smack of generosity and tolerance about it which merits a kind word."[84]

Unwittingly, Stacey and Tucker had struck at Creighton's Achilles' heel: his inability to understand French Canada on its terms. His unbreakable, granite conviction that the empire of the St Lawrence was the essence of Canadian history, that it ran backward and forward in time "like an obsession through the whole of Canadian history," meant that everything else was inessential, or epiphenomenal, including the Conquest. Whereas Lionel Groulx, the great French-Canadian historian, interpreted the Conquest as Quebec's "supreme catastrophe," Creighton argued that it "could not change Canada." If anything, "it strengthened the dominant impulse of Canadian life" by tying Montreal and its vast hinterlands to a far stronger and far richer metropole. Injecting "fresh enthusiasm, new strength, and different leadership," into Canada, the Conquest was serendipitous, not catastrophic; it was an opportunity to be taken, not a defeat to be nursed. "It was certain that the British Canadians would fight to realize the commercial empire of the St. Lawrence," he wrote; "but it was equally certain that they would be forced to fight in company with the Canadians of French descent."[85]

However, French Canadians didn't share that same dream of commercial empire. On the one hand, Creighton sympathized with their plight: "They were opposed in principle to rapid and intensive exploitation, to a greedy dissipation of lands and resources, which, in their opinion, ought to be conserved as the rightful inheritance of unborn generations of French Canadians. They wished to save their patrimony for the society of the future; and they soon came to realize that the laws and customs of their forefathers were the best protection against the domination of an acquisitive, speculative, and alien race." On the other hand, he buried that sympathy beneath an insensitive and parsimonious depiction of French Canada and French Canadians. Creighton shared more than narrative skill with Francis Parkman. He also shared Parkman's dark suspicions about French-Canadian "absolutism" and the character of the "French Celt." Eighteenth-century French Canada, according to Creighton, was a feudal society and "not yet an osseous growth in the living tissue of a young, new, vital social body." But its "charm" soon wore thin when its quaintness became backwardness and its backwardness retarded the Laurentian ambitions of the merchant class. In this context, in what Creighton saw as a backward-looking society sharing the same geopolitical space as a forward-looking society, he turned to a series of stereotypes to describe French Canadians. In exactly the same way that Lord Durham had described French Canadians as "sullen," "in-ert," "hostile," and "unprogressive," Creighton described them as "simple, doc-ile, and politically unambitious"; "aloof, dogged, and apprehensive"; "sullen, suspicious, and unresponsive"; "simple, untutored, and biddable"; "obstructive, unprogressive, and anti-commercial"; and, by turns, "inert," "hostile," "distrust-ful," and "apathetic."[86]

Creighton didn't ignore French Canada, but he didn't attempt to understand it either. Indeed, his unwillingness to consider French Canada on its own terms had appeared in his very first academic article published some six years earlier. The political struggle between the elected assembly and the imperial authorities for financial control in Lower Canada, Creighton argued, was really a struggle between the Frenchness of the French Canadians and the Britishness of the British. French Canadians were "a pastoral people dominated by professional groups"; the British were a commercial people motivated by "the urge for pros-perity"; and conflict was inevitable. "A peasant and professional community, unambitious, parsimonious, and unmoved by the lush economic possibilities of a new land, was confronted by a governing class whose deepest instincts were towards improvement, expansion, and prosperity."[87]

Creighton's refusal to look at French Canada as anything other than the Other to English Canada points to a central irony in the Laurentian thesis: "The centre of the commercial empire of the St. Lawrence, its very lynchpin, lay in Quebec, in French-speaking Canada."[88] There is yet another irony. Because French Canada never got misty-eyed over Great Britain and because it insisted on its political autonomy, its historians largely ignored the Laurentian thesis because it emphasized the imperial connection and political centralization.[89] In the 1930s, Creighton could conveniently ignore all of this. He wouldn't be able to in the 1960s and the 1970s.

VII

Holes in the Laurentian thesis were apparent from the beginning. In an impor-tant – and now classic – 1946 essay, Bill Morton wondered aloud about what he called its "implications" for the teaching and writing of Canadian history. As a western Canadian, Morton knew what it was like to grow up in a colony of central Canada. And as a historian, he knew that the Laurentian thesis couldn't explain western Canada. It was a form of intellectual imperialism that, like all imperialisms, was indifferent to local identities and local knowledges. "Teaching inspired by the historical experience of metropolitan Canada cannot but de-ceive, and deceive cruelly, children of the outlying sections." Against this backdrop, he famously said, "the West must first work out its own historical experience." It must "free itself and find itself."[90]

And although the St Lawrence River and the Great Lakes are acknowledged as an important transportation route, historians didn't believe then and don't believe now that the merchant class ever possessed a national vision or aspired to anything other than making money.[91] Arthur Lower not only questioned Creighton's decision to end his book with the destruction of the parliament buildings, he questioned his insistence that the merchants were in fact nationalists: their patriotism, he said, was really self-interest and their loyalty was "geared to their pocket books." What else could have been expected from men accustomed to judging right from wrong "by the columns of a ledger"? Another and more recent author put it more bluntly: the merchants were members of "a parasitical class" who followed the British army "into the defeated colony to feed off the spoils"; and according to Bill Eccles, Creighton's sleight of hand stemmed from a methodology that began "with an answer, not a question." Gerry Tulchinsky neither called the merchants parasites nor accused Creighton of a sleight of hand, but he did argue that Montreal's "river barons" thought in terms of their bottom line, not in terms of an "incipient Canadian nationalism." To them the river was "merely a convenient transportation system" and not "the fact of all facts in the northern half of the continent" and certainly not "the central truth of a religion." The invigorating nationalism of *The Commercial Empire of the St. Lawrence* was, Michael Bliss said, a "romantic fantasy."[92]

But that nationalism, or romantic fantasy, was very much part of English-Canadian historical writing. Despite history's professionalization, historians continued to labour under two masters: the past and the present. As a massive and unforgiving land mass covering half a continent, as a colony first of France and then of Great Britain, as a nation with two distinct nationalisms, one French Canadian, the other English Canadian, and as a country sitting next to the United States, Canada was a question. The writing of Canadian history, therefore, was characterized not simply by the effort to explain the past, but by the imperative to transform the present from a question into an answer, to narrate a reason for being, a purpose, and sometimes even a mission.

Aristotle defined history as "what was" and poetry as "what ought to be." But Creighton never accepted what he saw as a false distinction. History was both, because the unfolding of events – or what was – took place within larger moral imperatives – or what ought to be. Canada, Creighton believed, ought to be connected to Great Britain; it ought to be separate from the United States; it ought to resist continentalism. *The Commercial Empire of The St. Lawrence,* therefore, should be read as both history and poetry. As history, it is the story of Canada's origins. As poetry, it is the expression of its purpose.

Like all poetry, *The Commercial Empire of the St. Lawrence* can be reread and new meanings divined: in its pages is an implicit environmentalism. Creighton was not a proto-environmentalist and, despite his moving evocations of the St Lawrence River and the Laurentian Shield, and despite his abiding love for Muskoka, he was always more at home in the built environment than he was in the natural environment. But his first book carries a powerful environmental message: listen to the river, learn its limits, and live within them. The historian who sets out to write the twentieth-century history of the St Lawrence River and the Great Lakes will be unable to use tragedy as a mode of emplotment because tragedy, by definition, demands the recognition of limits. It demands that the hero recognize and live within the laws that govern the natural world or suffer a severe reversal of fortune. But to a century that refused to set "limits on what may be aspired to" – to a century that simply re-routed a river if it had the temerity to flow the wrong way – that recognition didn't occur and tragedy as a mode of emplotment will be impossible.[93]

Not only did the twentieth century fail to recognize limits, it denied the existence of limits. And in the process, human beings contravened every law of nature, including the supreme proscription: do not soil your own nest. Unchecked wills and voracious appetites have resulted in the near death of the St Lawrence River and the Great Lakes. Persistent toxic chemicals, undrinkable water, condemned beaches, deformed birds, cancerous fish, invasive species, falling water levels, disappearing waterfowl habitats, and deoxygenation are today's St Lawrence River and Great Lakes. Jacques Cartier described the great vessels of dried eels the Iroquois prepared in the short summer months to eat during the long winter months. But in the past half-century, the eel population in the St Lawrence River and Great Lakes has declined by something like 90 per cent. According to one expert, "The eels are sending us a message."[94]

chapter six

Professor

*Macdonald became a typical, overworked professional man, away to the office
by nine o'clock in the morning and absent until six at night.*

John A. Macdonald, vol. 1

A few weeks before the publication of *The Commercial Empire of the St. Lawrence*,
Donald Creighton received a telephone call from the director of research for the
Royal Commission on Dominion-Provincial Relations inviting him to write a
background paper on the origins of Confederation. Although Alex Skelton's invitation meant a departure from Creighton's immediate interest in the Montreal
merchants, it represented an extension of his larger interest in nineteenth-
century economic and political history. And although it would mean repeated
absences in Ottawa and long hours at the office, Creighton was used to hard
work. Just thirty-five years old, he still had the energy of a young man, his unlined face, tall, lanky frame, and boyish enthusiasm giving him a certain youthful appearance. All told, it was too good an opportunity to miss and so, in late
November 1937, Creighton agreed to participate in what is still considered to be
one of the most important royal commissions in Canadian history.

For years after the fact, the entire Creighton family referred to 1937 as their
annus mirabilis. To be closer to Donald, Luella, and Philip, William and Laura
sold 32 Hewitt Avenue and moved into an apartment on Delisle Avenue in the
Yonge and St Clair area. After a year in Vermont where he taught at Bennington
College, Jack accepted a position in the Department of English at the University
of British Columbia. For their part, Isabel and Harold Wilson were finally married in May after an on-again-off-again five-year engagement. And, of course,
Donald published his first book.

Although Luella was enjoying success as a writer – her short story "The Cornfield" had won the *Canadian Forum* Fiction Prize – she also found herself at something of a crossroads in the late 1930s. She desperately wanted more children but, for whatever reason, wasn't able to conceive. Unable to bring herself to admire a new baby and to pretend that nothing was wrong, she would deliberately cross the street to avoid a mother pushing a baby carriage. And each month she lamented the onset of her period – or, as she called it, "the curse."[1] With Philip in school and no baby in tow, Luella needed to find an outlet for her prodigious energy. At some point in the mid-1930s, she began selling real estate when she and a partner opened a small office above the old public library on St Clair Avenue, just east of Yonge Street. Her interest in real estate stemmed from her interest in houses, in their architecture, floor plans, curtains, and wallpaper. One of her favourite books was *The Personality of a House*, Emily Post's sprawling 500-page manual on turning a house into a home; she once gave a talk in Stouffville entitled "Housing and Interior Decorating." Two decades later, she could drive around the neighbourhoods where she used to work as a realtor, point to a particular house, describe its layout, and tell elaborate stories about the people who bought it.[2]

Although Creighton didn't like his wife working outside the home, he didn't give it much thought either. He had been too busy with his book and now he was too busy navigating Confederation, which, to him, was still "a new and unfamiliar building."[3]

II

The Depression forced Ottawa's politicians and policymakers to rethink both federalism and the federation. R.B. Bennett had proposed a New Deal in 1935 that included, among other things, unemployment insurance, a revised old-age pension, and a minimum wage. In effect, it proposed an expanded regulatory role for the federal government in the new and growing arena of social welfare. To some, it was about time. To others, it was a blatant power grab by the federal government and an unconstitutional intrusion into provincial spheres of jurisdiction. As predicted, Bennett's New Deal ended up before the Judicial Committee of the Privy Council, where the majority of it was declared ultra vires.

The ball was now in Mackenzie King's court. Returned to power in 1935, he had adopted a wait-and-see attitude while the Supreme Court and later the JCPC deliberated. But he also recognized that, having "outgrown" the clothes it had been given in 1867, Canada "needed a new suit," and so he appointed the

Royal Commission on Dominion-Provincial Relations, or the Rowell-Sirois Commission after its two chairs, Newton Rowell and his successor, Joseph Sirois. Charged with re-examining "the economic and financial basis of Confederation and the distribution of legislative powers," the commission undertook an ambitious research program.[4] Led by its brilliant if also mercurial director of research, the commission held hearings in every provincial capital, received 427 briefs, and generated 10,702 pages of testimony. Taking advantage of Ottawa's recent discovery of the unused research and policymaking capacity of Canadian academics, Skelton also commissioned twenty-eight specialized studies on a range of topics including the economic history of the Maritimes, the demographics of the prairie provinces, the difficulties of divided jurisdictions, and the origins of Confederation.[5]

With a leave of absence from the university, Donald Creighton spent the month of January at the Public Archives. Working quickly and efficiently to meet Skelton's spring deadline, he returned to Toronto, where he wrote the first draft. Although it didn't meet the literary standards of *The Commercial Empire of the St. Lawrence*, it was, in fact, an epilogue to his first book. Railways, he said, had been built "in accordance with that continental strategy which had been for generations the distinguishing feature of the commercialism of the St. Lawrence." But they placed an unsustainable financial burden on British North America. Meanwhile, British North America confronted an "ominous" United States – "a vast and encroaching organization, politically truculent [and] economically aggressive" – at precisely the moment Great Britain was looking to offload its North American obligations and responsibilities.[6]

Against this backdrop, British North America turned to federal union as a solution to its many problems. It alone would realize the ancient and elusive objective housed in the St Lawrence River and Great Lakes basin: a national, transcontinental economy. "The Fathers of Confederation," he wrote, "believed that they were creating a structure which would be stronger financially, commercially, and politically – a structure which would command the confidence of investors, as well as the interest of merchants and the respect of statesmen." They also believed that the federal structure they were building must have a clear division of powers and "that all matters of a general or national importance should be entrusted to the general legislature, and that all matters of merely local significance should be confided to the local legislatures." Although John A. Macdonald would have preferred a legislative union, he understood that politics was the art of the possible and that a single government for all of British North America simply wasn't possible. Still, Macdonald sought a strong, even paramount federal government: "We have strengthened the General Government," he declared in 1865. "We have given the General Legislature all the great subjects of legislation." Or, in Creighton's words, "The surrender of legislative union was to be repaid by the abandonment of extreme sectional pretensions."[7]

Creighton's views on Confederation coincided with the emerging academic consensus in English Canada. The Fathers of Confederation, according to this consensus, knew precisely what they were doing when they devised the British North America Act, when, for example, they divided legislative powers between the federal and provincial governments in sections 91 and 92: they intended to create a strong central government and subordinate provincial governments.[8] Creighton's views also confirmed the assumptions of Alex Skelton. "Resolutely centralist in his views of Dominion-provincial relations," Skelton envisioned an activist federal government that was constitutionally capable of playing a leading role in building the social welfare state.[9]

If Creighton's report confirmed Skelton's assumptions, it contradicted the assumptions of the provinces which harboured a competing conception of Confederation. According to the provincial governments, the provinces were coordinate with, not subordinate to, the federal government, and, further, each level of government was sovereign in its respective spheres of jurisdiction.

New Brunswick in particular objected to Creighton's interpretation of Confederation.[10] Just a few years earlier, in 1935 and again in 1936, it had been the only province to oppose a plan to patriate the Constitution with an amending formula. A.P. Patterson – New Brunswick's point man on federal-provincial relations – refused to back down: Mackenzie King's proposed amending formula, he believed, favoured Ontario and Quebec. Patterson didn't think that New Brunswick should be asked "to sign a blank cheque."[11] The prime minister was not amused. Patterson, he said, is a "very narrow minded man."[12] Although a political neophyte, Patterson wasn't stupid. His doctrine of provincial rights stemmed from his larger frustration with national policies that consistently worked against the interests of the three Maritime provinces: "Confederation has been for the Maritimes," he said, "one of the worst commercial disasters ever experienced by an Anglo-Saxon country."[13] One particularly galling policy was the federal government's wartime decision to merge the Intercolonial Railway with the newly created Canadian National Railway and to undo the system of preferential freight rates. The Intercolonial had been Canada's promise to the Maritimes in the 1860s, and its dismantling not only disrupted the region's economy, it also left many rallying behind the cause of Maritime Rights.[14]

It was against this backdrop that W.P. Jones, New Brunswick's legal counsel, prepared the province's May 1938 submission to the Rowell-Sirois Commission. Jones's affable-small-town-lawyer disposition belied his tough, legal, and historical mind. Calling for increased cooperation between the two levels of government, he also made it clear that New Brunswick would not tolerate "any encroachment by the Dominion on provincial rights." In a lengthy discussion he articulated a New Brunswick variant of the compact thesis which held that the provinces entered into a treaty, or compact, in 1867, that they did not surrender their autonomy, and that they were not, after 1867, the mere custodians of local matters. And yet, "the Dominion has persistently ignored the rights of the Maritime provinces." For example, the failure to develop the port of Saint John had weakened New Brunswick. Had Saint John been developed as had been promised, Jones argued, "it would have given rise to the development of all kinds of industries in the province. There would have been a market for our farm products close at hand. Manufacturers would have been encouraged. Our population would probably have reached more than a million souls."[15]

Six months later, Jones prepared a supplementary submission to the Royal Commission in which he reiterated New Brunswick's belief that Confederation had been a compact. In fact, New Brunswick saw itself as the defender of Confederation and the federal government as its "destroyer."[16] It was the federal government – through its national policies and its instinct for centralization – that represented the greatest threat to Canada. In addition, it had failed to live up to the promise of 1867. Specifically, it had failed to honour Resolution 66 of the London Resolutions, which obligated the federal government to make "the improvements required for the development of the trade of the great west with the seaboard."[17] New Brunswick had been misled in 1867 and it now wanted financial compensation.

At the same time, Jones prepared a confidential submission: Donald Creighton was wrong. The professor had written his paper, Jones said, from a "local standpoint and with a disregard for the fundamental principles upon which Confederation was founded." He erroneously assumed that the purpose of Confederation had been to create a strong central government and subordinate provincial governments. Nothing, Jones argued, could be further from the truth. In his initial submission, Jones had referred to the provinces as "sovereign nations," a fact confirmed by the Judicial Committee of the Privy Council. In a series of decisions made in the first thirty years of Confederation, it had clipped the wings of the federal government, restored provincial autonomy, and effectively contradicted Creighton's interpretation: "With respect, we submit that it would have been expected that a commentator of the standing of Professor Creighton should have indicated the contrary views of the Judicial Committee and which must govern us in our construction of the compact entered into at the time of Confederation." As well, Jones pointed out, Creighton had not addressed the matter of Resolution 66, which constituted the crux of New Brunswick's demand for compensation.[18]

Skelton almost certainly slipped Creighton a copy of Jones's confidential sub-mission, but, for obvious reasons, this couldn't be acknowledged in the pub-lished version of *British North America at Confederation*.[19] However, the meaning of Resolution 66 had to be addressed in light of New Brunswick's ini-tial submission. According to Creighton, the "improvements required for the development of the trade of the great west with the seaboard" referred not to the development of Saint John as a winter port. Rather, it "was held at the time to imply the improvement of the Canadian canals."[20] Similarly, the term sea-board included Montreal and Quebec, not simply Saint John and Halifax, meaning Ottawa was not in material breach of the Confederation agreement.

But what about New Brunswick's defence of provincial rights? After all, one did not have to subscribe to the compact thesis to believe in provincial rights and provincial autonomy. As a French Canadian sensitive to provincial auton-omy, Joseph Sirois insisted – "very keenly," in fact – that the final version of *British North America at Confederation* at least acknowledge the existence of competing interpretations of Confederation in general and the division of pow-ers in particular. Creighton gladly obliged.[21] He knew that history can never be conclusive and that there are always going to be different versions of the same event – "There is no final historical court of appeal," he said, "whose decisions are absolute and binding" – and he was extremely grateful that the commission didn't seek to transform itself into such a court, telling Sirois that the conditions for research had been "ideal."[22]

In its final report, the commission accepted neither the compact thesis of Confederation nor New Brunswick's claim for compensation.[23] Indeed, the fi-nal report, especially Book I, bore Creighton's influence: the Fathers of Confed-eration intended to create a strong central government.[24] But, at the same time, its Creightonian overtones were necessarily muted. With a Quebec chairman, the commission had to concede the existence of competing interpretations of Confederation, or, put another way, it "had to hedge on matters of historical interpretation."[25] It also had to hedge on its specific recommendations, and, to this end, it struck a balance between what it called "reasonable national unity" and "legitimate provincial autonomy."[26]

Moreover, it wasn't just Joseph Sirois who insisted that the final report must acknowledge and defend provincial autonomy. J.W. Dafoe did as well, and, in many ways, he was the commission's most important member. The long-time editor of the *Winnipeg Free Press* described Creighton's paper as "admirable," but felt that it needed "a little wider scope."[27] Dafoe didn't subscribe to the compact thesis, nor did he think much of what he called New Brunswick's "harangue," but he developed, over the course of his experience with the com-mission, "an ingenious and innovative argument": there were actually two

Confederations.[28] The first Confederation occurred in 1867; the second Confederation occurred over a longer period of time, from 1870 to 1905, and included the creation of Manitoba, Saskatchewan, and Alberta. Furthermore, this Confederation had to be studied on its own terms. In his focus on the first Confederation, Creighton had ignored the second Confederation. If Dafoe commended Creighton's "additional researches," he didn't alter his conviction that "the treatment of the western provinces" cannot be fit "into the original Confederation scheme."[29]

If *British North America at Confederation* confirmed Creighton's growing stature, it also revealed his advancing rigidity. New Brunswick's W.P. Jones, Quebec's Joseph Sirois, and Manitoba's J.W. Dafoe, in their own ways and for their own reasons, pointed to gaps, weaknesses, and problems of emphasis in Creighton's history: either he refused to see or he couldn't see beyond his own centralist bias. From Creighton's point of view, though, he saw the big picture, and with a granite determination he stared them down. "The Dominion was to become a great corporation," he wrote, "upon which would be piled all the burdens, past and future, of defence, development and consolidation in British North America."[30] The Canadian purpose was to realize the Canadian nation from sea to sea, and it was only small-town lawyers from Woodstock, New Brunswick, law professors from Quebec City, and journalists from Winnipeg who, out of provincial pettiness, French-Canadian nationalism, and regional loyalty, refused the Laurentian dream.

III

At some point in 1938, Luella stopped selling real estate after a minor dispute with her business partner. Besides, Donald never really supported her work as a realtor – it was a little crass, perhaps – and so, out of boredom and necessity, Luella began a diary. From the outside looking in, she had a happy marriage, a healthy son, and a host of friends. But something wasn't right. Keeping a diary – something she hadn't done since college – might help.

Luella began with a description of her cat Toby, "his lovely pale gray and black paws" and his "green intelligent eyes." A few weeks later, though, he was hit by a car and a devastated Luella cried uncontrollably. Reacting angrily to her mother-in-law's lack of sympathy, she wrote "Damn her!" Luella's grief surprised even her. Obviously, Toby's death had triggered something – the memory, perhaps, of her stepmother feeding strychnine to the alley cats. Resolving "never to become so attached again," Luella concluded that "you are only safe when you don't love anything."[31]

Donald told her that she needed to start writing short stories again. Maybe he was right, she decided. And so, on 1 January 1939, she made an impossibly ambitious New Year's resolution to write one short story every month for the next twelve months. Later, Luella toyed with the idea of writing a novel as well. At first, she simply called it "The Mennonite," and, because she intended to set it in nineteenth-century Upper Canada, she spent long afternoons reading general histories. On a couple of occasions she did archival research, taking notes on Mennonite settlement patterns and religious practices. From some unidentified source she copied the following injunction: "Abstain from flagrant sins, ungodly conversations, extravagance in habits or living, excesses, fleshly and worldly lusts, and the use of liquor and tobacco."[32] Luella had been running away from Stouffville for nearly two decades, but, now that she was more settled, Stouffville was catching up to her. If "The Cornfield" had been one attempt to make sense of her childhood, "The Mennonite" would be another.

By the summer Luella was thoroughly discouraged: she had made no progress on either the short stories or the novel. "Feel very low," she wrote. Perhaps, she said, her New Year's resolution had been made too "rashly."[33]

Meanwhile, events in Europe only increased her uncertainty and hesitation. "The newspapers scream that we are on the brink of war," she wrote in April: Mussolini had invaded Albania; Hitler threatened Poland; and Chamberlain finally drew a line in the sand.[34] The last war – the one that was to have ended all wars – was a part of Toronto's landscape, the memorials, cenotaphs, Remembrance Day services, and wounded veterans all serving as constant reminders of the city's very real connection to Great Britain.

To confirm and strengthen that connection, King George VI and Queen Elizabeth visited Toronto in May 1939 as part of their nineteen-day royal tour of Canada and the United States, the first visit to North America by a reigning monarch. The city welcomed the royal couple with open arms. "From rooftops, windows, trees, and grandstands, from every little crevice or corner which afforded a spot to which any one could cling, the men, women, and children of Toronto watched as the King and Queen passed," the *Globe and Mail* reported.[35] Donald, Luella, and Philip dutifully joined the large crowds to watch the royals arrive by train; later, they waited for hours at the corner of St Clair and Avenue Road. "I got a very good view," Luella wrote. "The Queen looking very lovely indeed, in an upturned hat and filmy outfit of soft light blue. George looked very alert and pleasant and the two of them simply slew the entire population."[36]

That, of course, was the point of the tour: to slay Canadians and, in the process, to shore up support for the coming war against Germany. Although he was a young man, there was never any suggestion that Creighton would serve. The Canadian Army did not have any use for a thirty-seven-year-old with bad eyesight, he once said.[37] But this was an after-the-fact justification: the truth was he didn't want to enlist. His reluctance to serve, he would later tell a junior colleague, stemmed from "the inexplicable mental transformation of a cherished family friend by his experiences during the First World War."[38] In a small country like Canada, every family knew someone – a father, a son, a favourite uncle, a next-door neighbour – who was never the same again. Perhaps he was referring to Harold Innis, who, just a few years earlier, had collapsed with "nervous exhaustion."[39] Or perhaps he was referring to his own brother. Although Jack had got on with his life after the war, he was not unaffected by Passchendaele. Watching young men go off to war in the same way that he had gone off to war some twenty-five years earlier led to recurring nightmares; it was "simply too much" for him.[40]

Creighton didn't seek war work as an expert or as a planner in Ottawa either, a decision influenced by his friendship with Harold Innis. Innis had served with the Canadian Expeditionary Force and was nearly killed at Vimy Ridge when a piece of shell casing smashed into his right leg just above the knee. Like so many other men who had witnessed the horrors of the Western Front, Innis often fell into sinking depressions. And he would spend the rest of his life hating war and everything about it, its violence and brutality, its wastefulness and futility. With Europe rushing to a second war in his lifetime, "the memory of the blood and mud and hunger and danger came back in a violent gush of feeling." His lonely quest to protect the university from the demands of war now became his personal obsession: with every ounce of his being, he believed that the tradition of free intellectual inquiry was essential to the survival of Western civilization and that it must not be allowed to atrophy. He therefore urged his colleagues to resist the temptation to go to Ottawa as a planner – a breed of human being that he held in contempt – at the same time as he told them to get on with their research.[41]

It was in this context – in the summer of 1939 – that Innis wrote to Henry Allen Moe, director of the John Simon Guggenheim Memorial Foundation: Donald Creighton, he said, is an ideal candidate for a fellowship. Because Innis's recommendations carried such weight with the great American philanthropic foundations, with the Carnegies, the Rockefellers, and the Guggenheims, Moe promptly contacted Creighton, inviting him to submit an application.[42]

Although something of a long shot – he had published only one book and had just been made an associate professor a few weeks earlier – Creighton prepared his application and solicited letters of recommendation from Chester Martin, head of the Toronto History Department, James Shotwell at the Carnegie Endowment for International Peace, Robert MacKay at Dalhousie University, and John Dafoe. The letters were effusive. The avuncular elder statesman

Chester Martin described his junior colleague as a "very attractive chap" and as "one of the most promising young scholars in Canada," who is at once "modest" and "ambitious." James Shotwell called him "just about the most promising" young historian in North America and described his book as "one of the most thrilling performances in recent years in the field of history. Anyone who can read the opening section without the thrill of emotional uplift might just as well stop reading history altogether." Why, Robert MacKay declared, *The Commercial Empire of the St. Lawrence* marks not only "a contribution to Canadian scholarship, but to Canadian literature as well."[43]

In his statement of research, Creighton explained his intention to carry forward into the present the themes that he had developed in his first book. He wanted, he said, "to analyze the interplay of forces in the development of Canadian nationality," forces that were centred in the St Lawrence River Valley and Great Lakes basin. "The St. Lawrence remained the symbol of the chief economic forces which were making for the unification and expansion of Canada. The river had once been the centre of an international trading system reaching far into the American west; it now became the chief support of the national, British-North American economy which was planned by the Fathers of Confederation." In addition, he intended to study those "cultural and political characteristics" which contributed to the making of modern Canada. Ultimately, his proposed book would be "an interpretative account of modern Canadian history."

By any definition, it was an ambitious research project, yet it suited his instincts as a historian for large, complicated, and dramatic history, for the multiplicity of forces and factors meeting and colliding on a towering stage, in this case, "the effort to build a nation in the northern half of the North American continent." When asked by the Guggenheim Foundation to discuss his "ultimate purpose as a scholar," he talked about his desire to write history that both analysed "the interplay of forces" and attained "some of the characteristics of literature."[44]

IV

Even as talk of war filled lecture halls, corridors, stairwells, and offices, life at the University of Toronto carried on. There were changes, of course. Some events were scaled back while others were cancelled altogether. And the Canadian Officers Training Corps and the Red Cross had a visible – and audible – presence as men and women in uniform marched, drilled, and performed any number of training exercises on the fields behind University College. But unlike in the First World War when they were pressured to enlist, students were now told to finish their studies.

In September 1939 Creighton began his thirteenth year of teaching. His initial efforts in 1927 had been awkward and difficult. In time, though, he grew more self-assured, becoming more comfortable with the material and with himself. Wearing a dark suit and an academic gown, Creighton believed that lectures were an important occasion in the life of the university. (The sartorial decline of the professoriate beginning in the 1960s appalled him: "No member of the Department," he opined, "should ever be seen in anything less than a suit and tie.")[45] Lectures themselves, meanwhile, were to be carefully crafted. They were not to be written in haste the night before and were certainly not to be extemporized. He once advised a graduate student to write out his lectures in long hand as opposed to point form.[46] This would allow him to develop a rhythm and a tempo appropriate to his teaching style and to craft a beginning, middle, and end appropriate to the material. Lectures were not opportunities to communicate information, they were performances and the performance was as important as the content.

Curiously, Creighton didn't teach Canadian history in the 1930s. Despite his growing reputation in the field, Canadian history was taught by Frank Underhill and Chester Martin. Instead, he taught survey courses in both early modern and modern British and European history. A young Northrop Frye was only "tepidly interested" in Creighton's course on Tudor England because it was taught in an "orthodox" and "linear" fashion.[47] But in his upper-level course on European history, Creighton came into his own.

In 1939 Maurice Careless was in his senior year when he enrolled in History 4b: Europe since 1789. He remembered Creighton as an "imposing" figure. But he also remembered him as a wonderful teacher. Behind the gruff exterior lay a "lively and approachable" man who was "eager to talk and ready to listen." Years later, Careless could still summon Creighton's "insight and enthusiasm" and could still picture how "his eyes would light up and his laugh roll out." Inside the classroom Creighton could be a "dramatic performer." From beginning to end, his lectures "seized" us, Careless said. They were, in a word, "gripping" precisely because they were "tightly-organized literary products." "But one never felt that he was merely reading. The lectures shone with vivid descriptions, deft, sardonic turns of phrase, the power of rising climax – until he reached the incisive end and swept out the door in a swirl of black gown." One of Creighton's favourite tricks saw him bring students to the edge of their seats and then leave them hanging: what happened after Charlotte Corday plunged the kitchen knife into Jean-Paul Marat's chest while he sat in his bathtub? Because he took lectures seriously, he expected students to do so as well. Students who arrived late were greeted with an "awesome" frown while students who disrupted him were publicly reprimanded.[48] "Put that away!" he shouted at one poor kid who had the temerity to read a newspaper during class.[49]

In late 1939, Creighton published an essay in a festschrift for George Wrong, the dean of Canadian history. "Conservatism and National Unity" was both a summation of *The Commercial Empire of the St. Lawrence* and *British North America at Confederation* and a projection of his future books. It was all here: the St Lawrence River, Confederation, John A. Macdonald, federalism, a strong central government, Great Britain, and a menacing United States. Describing the thirty years between the repeal of the Corn Laws in 1846 and the inauguration of the National Policy of tariff protection in 1879 as a "critical transitional period," he posed his own version of the Canadian question: "Where was the best substitute for the political and economic connection with Great Britain to be found? Was it to be found in the union of the provinces among themselves, or in the closer association of each of them with the United States? Could the loyalties of nationalism and the techniques of industrialism be used to unite the provinces, or were they to remain separate and tributary to the triumphant success of these forces in the United States?"[50]

Of course, Creighton was writing about 1939 as much as he was writing about 1879: Great Britain was not the world power that it had been and the United States was set to become the world's leading power. That is why King George VI and Queen Elizabeth included the United States in their royal tour. There was a state dinner at the White House and a garden party at the British embassy followed the next day by a visit to the World's Fair in New York City and a tour of Columbia University. But it was the hot dog picnic with President Roosevelt at his estate in Hyde Park that captured the nation's imagination. To be seen eating a hot dog was a brilliant exercise in public relations: the royals weren't so royal that they couldn't enjoy a good old-fashioned picnic complete with paper plates and paper napkins. Great Britain not only needed to shore up Canada's support in the coming war against Germany, it needed "to chip away at American isolationism."[51]

On 25 December 1939 King George VI delivered his Christmas message to the empire. Acknowledging "the dark times ahead of us" and citing the necessity of "sacrifice," he summoned "the spirit of the Empire," that "great family of nations."

V

In an otherwise dark world, the new year brought good news to Donald and Luella. First, Luella learned that she was pregnant. When she had been unable to conceive, she made an appointment with Marion Hilliard, an old friend from Vic who had gone to medical school and was now an obstetrician at Women's College Hospital and whose areas of specialization included helping women overcome sterility. Then, a few months later, Donald learned that he had been awarded a Guggenheim Fellowship for the 1940–1 academic year. "This is the best news I have heard for a long, long time!" his brother Jack shouted. "I read your letter to Sally over morning coffee and we positively cheered when we reached the dramatic climax. The Guggenheim fellowships are something – kudos, my boy, kudos."[52]

As part of his fellowship, he intended to tour a handful of Maritime universities before going to Virginia, where he would be based for six months and where his family would eventually join him. That September, Donald left a very pregnant Luella in Toronto when he began his lengthy trip to New Brunswick and Nova Scotia. Thirteen days later, Luella delivered a baby girl at Women's College Hospital: Laura Mary Cynthia, or Cynthia. Donald's mother was obviously pleased to have her name passed on. "Cynthia," Laura reported, "is growing in stature and in favour with God and man." She has "dark eyes," "dark hair," and a "sunny disposition"; "she really cries quite infrequently." Luella, meanwhile, is "a marvel of health and efficiency." In other words, she told her son, "do not worry about [your] family."[53]

Although a devoted husband, Creighton took more than he gave. Indeed, he was largely oblivious to what he once called the "ordinary duties of parenthood."[54] He was not the kind of father who invented elaborate games, who got down on the floor, who wrestled, or who built tree forts. And because he "found children a bit bothersome,"[55] the imperatives of apple juice and breakfast cereal, of crayons and crafts, belonged to Luella. True, he read the novels of Charles Dickens to Philip, the very novels that he had devoured as a boy. And when Cynthia was a little girl, he invented a wonderful series of stories about Mr Jumpy and the four Jumpy children, Angela, Pamela, Richard, and Eric. Mr Jumpy could jump as high as a house, but his jumps were spontaneous, creating all sorts of social mishaps and embarrassments. Another set of stories centred on Oswald Leftover, whose mother packed him a lunch of leftovers as he raced out the door on little-boy adventures involving caves, castles, dragons, and giants. But, in the main, Philip and Cynthia were their "mother's problem."[56] By Creighton's own admission, children were "mysterious things."[57] He might have added that he didn't have much interest in solving or even appreciating their many mysteries.

From the small town of Fairfax, Virginia, Creighton commuted into Washington, DC, where he spent long days in the main reading room of the Library of Congress looking for what he called "a suitably big subject to peg his research on." He had told the Guggenheim Foundation that he intended to study the development of Canadian nationality since 1850. But how? It was such a massive topic and he couldn't find an organizing subject. He had thought about the Canadian Pacific Railway but decided in the end that it wasn't "comprehensive enough."[58]

Like everyone else, he read the newspapers and listened to the radio for news coming out of London: the phoney war had ended and the real war was advancing into eastern and southern Europe and into North Africa. He also watched American politics unfold. It was like watching, he said, "a remarkable exhibition in the workings of democracy – all under the klieg lights."[59] When Joseph Kennedy, the American ambassador to Great Britain, resigned in early December because of the controversial remarks he made about Britain's future, Creighton cheered: Britain needed support and encouragement in its hour of need, not defeatism.[60]

And through letters with his colleagues, Creighton followed events in Canada. The Royal Commission on Dominion-Provincial Relations had issued its report in May 1940, but it never stood a chance: Ontario, Alberta, and British Columbia objected to the report's centralist bias and pretty much told Ottawa to take a hike. Still, a federal-provincial conference was held in January 1941 to discuss the report but it was, in the words of one observer, "the god damnedest exhibition and circus you can imagine."[61] Writing to Creighton, a Toronto colleague informed him that the report, "if not actually dead, is pretty comatose at the moment"; meanwhile, one of his Ottawa contacts told him that the only thing to come out of the federal-provincial conference was "a lot of back biting."[62] Creighton could follow the ups and downs of the Royal Commission on Dominion-Provincial Relations with a bemused detachment: he had written a decent research report which enhanced his reputation as a talented young historian, and in the process he had learned a lot about the origins and purposes of Confederation. In this sense, what the belligerent and bullish premier of Ontario said about the report didn't really matter.

More troubling, however, were the attacks that both Mitch Hepburn and the University of Toronto unleashed against Frank Underhill.[63]

VI

Underhill's anti-capitalism and anti-imperialism hardly endeared him to Canon Henry J. Cody, the Anglican clergyman and president of the university. In fact, just prior to Cody's appointment in 1931, Underhill correctly predicted that the people associated with the *Canadian Forum* – a small, progressive periodical – "will have to watch [their] step."[64] On at least four separate occasions he was hauled in to the president's office to explain himself. But with the spectre of war hovering over Ontario politics, he suddenly became an easy target for politicians, including the premier, who was on the brink of coming mentally undone. On 13 April 1939, members of the Ontario legislature out-bellowed each other in their condemnation of Underhill's four-year-old assertion that "the poppies blooming in Flanders Fields have no further interest for us" and that another war in Europe would be another "meaningless slaughter."[65] Although he had served with the British army, fought at Passchendaele, been wounded at the Second Battle of the Somme, and returned to active duty for the final Allied offensive, Underhill was now being accused of treason. A "disappointed" Hepburn told the legislature that the university ought to discipline Underhill for "the crime he has committed. It smacks of rank sedition." Another MPP called him a "rat" "trying to scuttle our ship of state."[66]

That night, Donald and Luella got together with Harold and Mary Innis where the discussion centred on Hepburn's bellicose demands for Underhill's "scalp."[67] Creighton had not taken much interest in politics, left or otherwise, in the 1930s – he neither contributed to the *Forum* nor participated in the League for Social Reconstruction (he attended a meeting or two in 1931 but quickly decided that it wasn't for him). Instead, he had followed the lead of Innis, who insisted on research as the professor's first and only obligation. However, he took seriously the principle of free speech. Eight years earlier, he had been one of sixty-eight Toronto professors to sign a letter to the editor objecting to the Toronto Police Commission's anti-communist campaign. For Creighton, at least, it was not about the Communist Party of Canada; it was about free speech which, "for generations," has been considered "the proudest heritage of the British peoples."[68] That heritage was again threatened, this time by the furious denunciations of Underhill from the self-appointed defenders of the realm at Queen's Park. Creighton and Innis feared that the threats emanating from the Ontario legislature represented "the thin edge of fascism."[69]

Despite Cody's angry accusations that his remarks were costing the university untold sums of money, Underhill escaped dismissal in 1939. But less than a year and a half later, he found himself fighting to save his career. At the August 1940 meeting of the Canadian Institute of Economics and Politics, held every year on the shores of Lake Couchiching, Underhill observed that Canada would have to alter its defence policies and seek a closer relationship with the United States: "We can no longer put all our eggs in the British basket." In many ways, he was simply stating the obvious: France had fallen to Germany in June, the Battle of Britain had begun in July, and an early invasion of Great Britain appeared imminent. But his remarks were distorted in the press – he never suggested that Canada should abandon Great Britain – and his head was placed on the proverbial chopping block. A furious President Cody didn't care what he had or hadn't said. He was nothing but a "trouble maker" and that, Cody told him, was his "real crime."[70] In a venal effort to find some dirt on Underhill, he even demanded to see his "personal page" – the list of books that a faculty member had borrowed from the library – but was refused by the university's head librarian.[71] The former prime minister, Arthur Meighen, believed that Underhill should be interned for the duration of the war, while the attorney general of Ontario ordered the police to investigate him for possible prosecution under Defence of Canada regulations. By this point, an unstable, paranoid Mitch Hepburn now saw sympathizers, collaborators, and fifth columnists everywhere he looked. A few weeks earlier "the cocksure, temperamental politician with a puffy, petulant face" had told journalists that there were hundreds of thousands of Nazis in the United States waiting for orders from Germany to invade Ontario.[72]

All Creighton could do was watch. He was about to leave for New Brunswick and Nova Scotia when the scandal broke. "Don't let it get you down," he advised an obviously upset Underhill. At first, everyone assumed that it would blow over. A few days later, though, Creighton arrived in Fredericton, where he was told by Larry MacKenzie, the president of the University of New Brunswick and former Toronto law professor, that Underhill was actually in a lot of trouble; in Saint John, Creighton anxiously read the *Telegraph-Journal* and learned that, for the time being at least, the Board of Governors had decided not to take action; and in Wolfville he wrote a long and sympathetic letter to his colleague: "The whole thing looks like an even more senseless and vindictive piece of witch-hunting than the 1939 episode."[73]

Underhill's September reprieve ended in December, when the Board of Governors voted to dismiss him; at the same time, it sought and received provincial support. Although now in Virginia and thus far removed from Toronto, Creighton was livid: "Your dismissal will be a black reflection upon the state of Canadian universities in general and, indeed, upon the whole intellectual life of the country."[74] In an effort to be useful, he met with an official at the Washington office of the American Association of University Professors. The AAUP was, Creighton reported, honestly "interested and surprised at conditions as they exist in our great Dominion."[75]

When he was asked to resign in early January, Underhill refused. When they realized the fight they would face from the faculty and the political price the university would pay for firing a professor who was also a veteran of the First World War, President Cody and the Board of Governors backed down. "Can the university make a contribution to this war," Innis asked, "by dismissing a veteran of the last?"[76]

The extent of Mitch Hepburn's personal involvement remains an open question, but it is unlikely that his minister of education would have supported the Board's December decision to dismiss Underhill without the premier's consent. Certainly Underhill always thought that the premier and his "gunmen" on the Board of Governors were out to get him. He had once – privately, of course – called Hepburn a dictator and looked forward to the day when someone published stories about his "adventures with wine and women."[77]

Ironically, it was Hepburn who intervened at the last minute to stop Underhill's dismissal after experiencing a sudden change of heart: in a rare lucid moment, it dawned on the normally vindictive premier of Ontario that firing a professor for making pro-American comments might injure Canadian-American relations. As Creighton later noted, the man Underhill "regarded as the instigator of the plot against him became instead the agent of his deliverance."[78] In other words, if the principle of academic freedom had been preserved, it had been preserved only at the expense of another important principle: university autonomy.[79] Thanking Creighton for his support, a shaken Underhill felt safe for the time being but also asked his young colleague to let him know of any openings in the United States.[80]

A few months later, in mid-April, Creighton returned home. He was sorry to leave Virginia, where the "cherry trees, magnolias, and quite a few flowers" were already blooming, but he had to get back to Toronto.[81] Arriving a few weeks ahead of Luella and the children, he attended to university matters, caught up on departmental gossip, and rented a house on Glenrose Avenue, just a short streetcar ride away from his parents. Shortly after collecting Luella and the children at Toronto's Union Station, he boarded a train for Vancouver. His Guggenheim Fellowship also included visits to university campuses in western Canada. It was his first trip across northern Ontario and the prairie provinces, which, in his mind, represented the western reaches of the empire of the St Lawrence. Once in Vancouver he was able to spend a couple of days with his brother and his family before returning to Toronto in early June. A few weeks later, he was gone again, this time to the Public Archives in Ottawa.

Creighton could look back on the past twelve months with a sense of accomplishment. He had travelled the length of the country, made a number of new contacts at both eastern and western Canadian universities, played a minor role in the Underhill affair, and accumulated a healthy stack of research notes at the Library of Congress and the Public Archives. But he hadn't written a single word.

chapter seven

Mid-Career

His powers had matured and he had grown increasingly expert in their use.

John A. Macdonald, vol. 1

In the fall of 1941, Donald Creighton returned to the university. At thirty-nine, he was no longer a junior member of the department, but he wasn't a senior member either. He was, however, the most promising. *The Commercial Empire of the St. Lawrence*, the Royal Commission on Dominion-Provincial Relations, and the Guggenheim Fellowship were tremendous accomplishments. In a sympathetic review of *British North America at Confederation*, Bart Brebner announced that his former student "has given us every reason to expect another fine book." Privately, Brebner told him what Frank Underhill had told him, that he was "the white hope" of Canadian historical writing and that he would be the one to rescue it from the smothering grip of traditional constitutional history.[1]

Although it was a hierarchical place with an established pecking order, the Department of History continued its tradition of meeting for afternoon tea, still dutifully prepared by Miss Hahn. Naturally, everyone talked about the war. Japan had joined the Axis the year before; Germany had invaded Russia in June; and slowly but surely, the United States was being drawn in. For its part, Canada had rushed to the defence of Great Britain in 1939 and, through a series of complicated arrangements, had committed vital industrial and financial support to a weakened mother country. Now, two years into the war, it was sending troops to defend the British Empire in Hong Kong. At the same time, Canada deepened its military and economic relationships with the United States. The Ogdensburg Agreement created the Canada–United States Permanent Joint Board on Defence while the Hyde Park Declaration linked the two countries through the production of war-related materials. If the defence of North

As a writer, Donald Creighton's "powers had matured and he had grown increasingly expert in their use." His former professor, Bart Brebner, called him the "white hope" of Canadian historical writing, telling him that he would rescue it from traditional constitutional history.

America demanded cooperation, it also demanded coordination and even a measure of integration.

Creighton tried to discern the implications of the endless string of announcements coming out of London, Washington, and Ottawa. Maybe Frank Underhill had been right after all. In his address to the Couchiching conference the year before, he said that Canada had two loyalties, an old one to Great Britain and a new one to North America. He also said – and this is what very nearly got him fired – that "the relative importance of Britain is going to sink no matter what happens."[2] But if Underhill was right, if Britain did sink, what would it mean for Canada? Canada's "membership in the British Commonwealth of Nations" and its "location on the North American continent" were not complementary, Creighton believed, but antithetical. And since the first was historical and the second geographic, would geography defeat history in the context of a world war?[3]

Creighton instinctively turned to the past for an answer when a publisher's representative from Boston paid a courtesy call to his office in early October. In the course of their conversation, he not-so-innocently asked if Houghton Mifflin had ever considered publishing a general history of Canada. Two weeks later he received an encouraging letter from an editor asking him to keep Houghton Mifflin in mind as his manuscript neared completion.[4] An "astonished" Creighton had found the solution to his problem: instead of a sequel to *The Commercial Empire of the St. Lawrence*, he could write a survey of Canadian history using the Laurentian thesis as a narrative thread to connect early Canada to modern Canada.[5] In other words, Canada itself was the "suitably big subject" he had been looking for all along.

At first, he didn't even know where to begin. He could, he explained, begin at the beginning, which in those days meant European exploration and discovery, or he could begin at the Conquest and the origins of British North America. If his book was going to be a college text it would have to be the former, he said, but if it was going to be a trade book, it could be the latter. His publisher, however, believed that a college text and a trade book were not mutually exclusive and that such a book could expect to "enjoy a substantial sale."[6]

Over the Christmas holidays, Creighton wrote the first chapter from discovery and exploration to tenuous beginnings and eventual settlement. Although he was less comfortable with New France than British North America, the writing went surprisingly well. His powers as a writer "had matured." Indeed, he confidently predicted that he could finish the manuscript in eighteen months, perhaps even less. His editor, meanwhile, was thrilled, describing the opening chapter as "excellent," "well written," and "very convincing." In the end it took nineteen months, but in July 1943 Creighton mailed the entire manuscript to Boston. "It has breadth, excellent proportion, and a complete grasp of the subject," his editor enthused. Its style is "uniformly grand" and "sometimes really eloquent."[7]

Although he had a manuscript, Creighton didn't have a title. Initially he suggested *A History of Canada*, which had the advantage of being "simple and straightforward" but the disadvantage of being "flat and uninteresting." His editor agreed. The book needed something more "provocative." Going back to the drawing board, Creighton returned with two possibilities: *Dominion from Sea to Sea* and *Dominion of the North*, a phrase that he had used in *The Commercial Empire of the St. Lawrence*. It had been Leonard Tilley – the teetotaller from New Brunswick – who had proposed Dominion of Canada as an alternative to Kingdom of Canada at the London Conference in 1866 when British officials worried that Kingdom might antagonize the American republic. Tilley had received his inspiration from Psalm 72 and its promise of "dominion from sea to sea." The British did not object because the word dominion had been used to describe any territory belonging to the British Empire since the seventeenth century. Following the Canadian example, other self-governing colonies, including New Zealand and Australia, adopted the title Dominion, leading Eugene Forsey to describe it as "the only distinctive word we have contributed to political terminology."[8] On balance Creighton preferred his first suggestion to his second, but he also confessed that he didn't like either one very much. He did know one thing, though: he didn't want a title with democracy or civilization in it because they look "cheap." His editor responded immediately: he loved *Dominion of the North: A History of Canada*, adding that it was "just about perfect."[9] Capturing the book's recurring themes, "dominion" linked Canada to Great Britain and the British world while "north" situated Canada on the northern half of North America, separate from the United States.[10]

II

Shortly after Creighton sent his manuscript to the publisher, he learned that the house he was renting at 161 Glenrose Avenue had been sold out from under him. Finding a new house in wartime Toronto – where a general housing shortage had driven up prices – wouldn't be easy, meaning he would need all the money he could lay his hands on. Believing that he didn't have a choice, he called in the loan that he had made to his sister a couple of years earlier.

When Isabel married Harold Wilson in 1937 she lost her position as a reference librarian at the Toronto Public Library because of its marriage bar. Everyone, including Isabel, assumed that her husband would support her. But nothing ever seemed to work out for Harold. Despite his many gifts and obvious intelligence, he couldn't hold a job. When a career in sales didn't pan out, he went to law school and, with a partner, opened a firm. He never really liked being a lawyer, though, and his practice floundered. Next, he tried his hand at publishing when he and his father-in-law, William Creighton, started their own magazine of ideas, *The New Canadian*. Letterhead was ordered and plans were made, but not a single issue was ever printed. Without two nickels to rub together, Isabel and Harold moved in with Donald, Luella, and Philip. It was a disaster. The house was small; the added burden of cooking and cleaning fell to Luella; and Harold disappeared for extended periods of time only to return drunk, wreaking of alcohol and cigarettes. Isabel was beside herself. If she had denied it before, she couldn't now: her husband was an alcoholic and a depressive. Acting quickly, she convinced Harold to see a psychiatrist, borrowed money from Donald, and found an apartment.

Harold's mental and physical health only worsened. In early 1941, Laura Creighton remarked that she "got a shock" when she saw her son-in-law. Harold, she told Donald, "has lost a good deal of weight and looks pale," adding that "one cannot help feeling sorry for him."[11] Two years later Isabel made the enormously difficult decision to leave her husband when she accepted a position at the University of Saskatchewan library. In a lengthy exchange of letters, Harold told her that he loved her and that he wanted to work things out; Isabel assured him that she had not left him "in any spiritual sense" but she needed time and distance to reassess their "situation"; and they both talked about maybe moving to western Canada and starting a family.

Isabel was crushed when she received Donald's letter demanding $500, confessing that it was "sharp" and it "hurt." He knew very well that her marriage had broken down and that she didn't have that kind of money. Harold proposed making a series of small payments. But Isabel refused and so, against her salary, she borrowed the entire amount from the University of Saskatchewan. Donald and Luella would have their money. She couldn't endure another minute of his judgment or of her off-handed comments about not having enough money to buy a new dress.

"You know Donald as well as I do," she told Harold. "You know the moral indignation and complete outrage such an incident would produce in him. That God should allow people to deal with him in this manner isn't to be borne. He doesn't see the fact that this housing situation is just one aspect, an unpleasant but very minor one, of a war which, in the main, doesn't affect him at all. He has never suffered a great deal and certainly never in silence."[12] Isabel knew her brother well, his sense of entitlement, and, in this case, his notion that he was somehow immune to the realities of wartime Canada.

All told, it wasn't one of his finer moments. Although he later apologized, the damage had been done. For a moment they had reverted to their roles at 32 Hewitt Avenue where he demanded and she deferred. This time, Isabel's decision to pay him back wasn't out of deference. It was out of defiance – he wouldn't have that power over her anymore, and, for that matter, neither would his wife.

With the money from Isabel and with money that he borrowed against a life insurance policy, Donald and Luella bought their first house on Walmer Road for $5,800. He grumbled about the price, of course, but she insisted.[13] A stunning, three-storey semi-detached house built in the Richardson Romanesque style, it had arched window and door frames, a distinctive stone belt course, and a second-storey tower. Inside it had gracious living and dining rooms perfect for entertaining. But more importantly, it had what Luella desperately needed: a room of her own, a place to read and write and think.

If Luella needed her own room, she also needed her own bed. Indeed, she and Donald never shared a bed again, and sex, when it happened, was at her invitation. She loved Donald with every ounce of her being, but her stepmother's abuse had filled her with persistent and contradictory ideas about the body, desire, and women's proper roles, making "physical closeness hard for her."[14] Luella's decision must have been difficult for Donald – he was, after all, so passionate about so many things, about art, literature, music, and opera – but he adored Luella and never sought the comfort of another woman. He used to say, in a resigned sort of way, that in love there is one who kisses and one who offers the cheek. It was his way of saying that, although he kissed and Luella offered the cheek, he would wait until Luella kissed him.[15]

After Cynthia was born, Luella had stopped writing, but her idea for a novel about Ontario Mennonites continued to percolate. Cynthia was now four years old and would be starting school in a year or two, making it possible to resume the book that she had started in the spring of 1939. That her career was always second to her husband's didn't bother her. It was what it was. Philip, Cynthia, and the house were her responsibilities. Writing was something that she did when the kids were at school or after they had gone to bed. Cynthia remembers that her mother's door was always open and her father's always closed. "We would no more have knocked on that door than we would have thrown ourselves in front of a tractor!" For his part, Philip remembers watching his mother set up a clothesline in her bedroom and pinning manuscript pages to it. Because she could only write in bits and pieces here and there, hanging her manuscript gave her a better view of the whole.[16] "There was considerable pinning, unpinning, and re-pinning before she was satisfied."[17]

Set in the fictional village of Kinsail, Ontario – which was really Stouffville, she later admitted – Luella's first novel centres on Tillie Shantz, a young

Mennonite woman who decides to follow her own path even if it means leaving both her family and her faith. Engaged to one man, she loves another man. Tillie's romantic awakening, however, is part of her larger awakening to a world of books, music, and knowledge, to a world not governed by biblical injunctions and religious repression. At one point, she acquires a library card. It is a symbolic ticket out, and by now there is no turning back: she ends her engagement and marries the man she loves. When her husband takes her to Toronto in his new car – one of the very first cars in Kinsail and an obvious symbol of modernity – they visit the university, stay in a hotel, and go dancing. From their hotel room they can see the lake and the lights of the ferry taking people to and from Centre Island, a reference, perhaps, to the ferry Luella and Donald took to Centre Island on their first date. Eventually the novel ends with an emotional reconciliation between Tillie and her father, Levi Shantz. When he learns that Tillie has lost her baby, he goes to her while her mother, to whom she was never close, refuses, insisting instead that Tillie is dead to her. Holding her as if she were still "his little girl," Levi tells his daughter that God has not, in fact, punished her.[18]

Tillie's need to escape the limited horizons of her family and her determination to live her life on her terms were Luella's. Certainly, Jack Creighton read it this way, telling Luella that Tillie reminded him of her.[19] Perhaps, too, Levi was the father Luella never had. Although set in his Mennonite ways, he was also capable of forgiveness and stood up to his wife in a way that Luella's father never stood up to his wife. Luella needed Tillie to have at least one person in her life who loved her unconditionally. It was too painful otherwise, and, as a writer, she couldn't go there. She once told Philip that although she was sure there were Mennonites like Levi Shantz, she had never met one.[20]

It took six or seven years and it marked one more attempt to understand, if not resolve, her childhood, but *High Bright Buggy Wheels* was published by McClelland and Stewart in 1951.[21]

III

The day after Donald and Luella Creighton bought 92 Walmer Road, *Dominion of the North* was published. Creighton's second book displayed his ability both to make connections across time and space and to sustain multiple narrative threads over several hundred pages. Because the past didn't unfold in political, economic, and cultural units, history shouldn't be written as a series of so many units. The past, he told his editor at Houghton Mifflin, possessed "a basic unity," and to break it into topics "is both historically and artistically bad."[22] Later, he would describe history written in the topical form as "a confession of weakness" on the part of the historian.[23]

Dominion of the North begins with the Norsemen "who first discovered the giant stepping stones which link northern Europe with northern North America." Creighton's decision to lead with Leif Ericsson and early Viking exploration was a curious one. Every nation requires a beginning, but this presented a problem for Europe's offspring, for the world's so-called "white settler" nations: their origins lay in the recent past. By locating Canada's origins in the Norse expeditions of the ninth and tenth centuries, Creighton both deepened Europe's claim to North America and lengthened Canada's history. It also reinforced Canada as a northern nation by attaching it to the history of "those dynamic Scandinavian peoples" who had been "driven outward from their homeland by repeated explosive bursts of energy."[24]

Of course, Creighton could have accomplished the related goals of deepening and lengthening Canadian history by opening his book with Canada's Aboriginal peoples, with, for example, the early migrations across the Bering Strait. In 1932, Diamond Jenness had published *The Indians of Canada*, a pioneering work of anthropology and history which argued that Aboriginal peoples first crossed the Bering Strait some 15,000 to 20,000 years ago and, over enormous stretches of time, migrated across North and South America.[25]

But Creighton was blind to Aboriginal history. In *The Commercial Empire of the St. Lawrence*, Aboriginal people are occasional actors but they never assume a leading role, playing instead the romantic and unproblematic supporting role of the Disappearing Indian, a people outside the march of history and doomed to disappear beneath the steady advance of civilization. "White settlement had conquered the empire of the St. Lawrence," he wrote, "and the Indians had been driven before it, driven irresistibly through defeat and shame towards their final degradation – towards the reserve, the shapeless alien clothes, the crafts debased and meaningless in a new age, and the dull, uncomprehending, haunted search for something which had irrevocably vanished." Insisting that land must be "cleared and sowed and tidied," the doctrine of improvement could not accommodate the aspirations of Aboriginal people.[26]

In *Dominion of the North*, Aboriginal people make cameo appearances and perform occasional if brief solos before leaving the stage altogether after 1885. They are partners in the fur trade, enemies of New France, and allies of the British; they are "childish," "unspoiled," "primitive," "stoic," "alien," "strange," "wild," "hostile," "savage," "devious," "secretive," "envious," "barbarous," "dissolute," "promiscuous," and "gluttonous"; they wander, they dance, and they torture.[27] Once their threat or their usefulness disappears, Aboriginal people disappear, or "inevitably dwindle away."[28] But "inevitability" is an assertion, not an explanation; it is teleological, not historical; and it exculpates both the author and the reader: because it happened, it therefore had to happen and no one has to take responsibility for what happened or even attempt to explain it.

The final suppression of Aboriginal peoples occurred after the Northwest Rebellion. Led by a "megalomaniac" named Louis Riel, the rebellion was quickly defeated but not before "the Indians, under Big Bear and Poundmaker, [had] terrorized the valley of the North Saskatchewan." The rebellion's defeat confirmed that the "old order was gone forever" and that "the Indians would have to learn to live on their reservations." In a narrow, technical sense, Creighton was right: the old order was gone forever and Aboriginal peoples would have to make the difficult and protracted transition to reserves. But he didn't extend an ounce of sympathy. Although he acknowledged that Ottawa had not been generous and that the Plains Indians were left in a state of "suspicious bewilderment," Creighton depicted the North West Mounted Police as men of "honour and fair dealing," Louis Riel as a madman, and Big Bear and Poundmaker as terrorists.[29] Like his grandmother who, in 1894, had visited the Presbyterian missions in the northwest, he was the product of a particular time and place, of an "uncomprehending, unsympathetic, and insensitive" majority.[30]

The erasure of Aboriginal people in *Dominion of the North* was part of the larger erasure of Aboriginal people in English-Canadian historical writing and, for that matter, in the historical writing of British settler societies, making it a twentieth-century example of nineteenth-century settler historiography.[31] When one Australian scholar referred to the absence of Aboriginal people in his country's historical writing as the Great Australian Silence, he could have expanded his address to include the Great Canadian Silence.[32]

Still, there were important exceptions in Canadian scholarship which Creighton simply ignored. Harold Innis assigned "a significant and prolonged"[33] role to Aboriginal people before concluding that scholars "have not realized that the Indian and his culture were fundamental to the growth of Canadian institutions."[34] Because the more important knowledge and technology transfer was Aboriginal to European, not European to Aboriginal, Diamond Jenness maintained that the early explorers and settlers were initially dependent on Aboriginal peoples. In the long run, though, contact was a "wreck," exploration "an invasion," and settlement "an occupation."[35] And New Brunswick's Alfred Bailey broke new ground in his 1937 book, *The Conflict of European and Eastern Algonkian Cultures, 1504–1700*. Where Creighton plotted the discovery, exploration, and settlement of what is today eastern Canada, Bailey decentred Cartier, Champlain, Intendant Talon, and Bishop Laval, focusing instead on the Mi'kmaq, the Maliseet, and the Montagnais. His themes were conflict, decline, and disintegration, and his topics included the devastating impact of foreign pathogens, the tragic introduction of alcohol, and changing conceptions of property and ownership in Aboriginal society.[36] In Creighton's historical arithmetic, however, it was the Aboriginal people who debased the French. The coureurs de bois, he said, learned new and unfortunate "modes of behaviour, traits of character, [and] attitudes to life. "Uneasily and with an exciting sense of degradation, they took part in the gluttonous feasts, the drunken orgies, the sexual promiscuity of the tribes. They acquired something of the Indian's stoical fatalism, his superstition, his secrecy and savagery in battle." New France itself, he concluded, was a place of "violent contrasts" where French finery met North American barbarism, where "exquisite *toilettes* and civilized license confronted the plumed scalplocks, the greasy buffalo robes, and the barbarous codes of the Indians."[37]

Despite its contradictions, however, Creighton's New France had discovered the fundamental purpose of Canadian history: the creation of a vast commercial and territorial empire stretching the length of the continent.

> Cartier climbed the hill high back of Hochelaga, which he named Mont Royal, and surveyed the landscape for more than thirty leagues around. He could see the St. Lawrence, "grand, large, et spacieux" – the waterway to the rich Laurentian Lowlands, to the Great Lakes, to the heart of the entire continent – flowing from the remote horizon of the south-west, flowing in white violence through the rapids at Lachine and onwards towards the ocean.

One of history's great prizes – maybe even its greatest – the continent was there to be claimed by successive generations of French explorers, traders, administrators, and settlers and its key lay in the St Lawrence River Valley. "From the first," Creighton declared, "the French seem to have understood the meaning of the region they had occupied." "Conscious of the river and of the enormous continent into which it led," Intendant Talon, for example, submitted "to that instinct for grandeur, that vertigo of ambition, that was part of the enchantment of the St. Lawrence."[38]

Impervious in the same way that granite is impervious, Creighton refused to engage French Canada, relying instead on the same simple stereotypes that he had employed in *The Commercial Empire of the St. Lawrence*. An "apathetic conservatism" and a "stubborn adherence" retarded nineteenth-century French Canada, he argued. The place lacked "enterprise and initiative"; it "defended" the old regime; and it "refused to vote money" for canals and other "public improvements." Afraid of the future, it clung to the past. Meanwhile, the Acadians were a "simple minded" people and – at least "in the subject of political theory" – "particularly dense."[39]

But it was Creighton's depiction of the Catholic Church that infuriated one reviewer. According to Reverend John O'Reilly, the source of Creighton's indifference and, at times, hostility to French Canada and French Canadians was simple anti-Catholicism. Emphasizing "racial hatred" and "clerical domination," Creighton was a "pamphleteer" and his book a "tract for our times."[40] To make his case, Reverend O'Reilly compared Creighton's parsimonious depiction of Bishop Laval in *Dominion of the North* to A.L. Burt's generous depiction in *A Short History of Canada for Americans*. Burt had presented the first bishop of New France as a man of "great natural ability" who used his "powerful influence with the government" to pull the fledgling colony back from the brink, who "vehemently denounced" the liquor trade with Aboriginal people, and who, in his final years, "lived the life of a saint."[41] Creighton's Bishop Laval, however, was "a man of burning religious zeal" and "almost superhuman austerity" who freely chose to sleep "between thin blankets well filled with fleas" while "the frigid atmosphere of his unheated church in the early winter morning [inspired] him to interminable supplications." Imitating Charles Dickens, Creighton deliberately exaggerated Laval's countenance. His nose was "big," his lips were "firm" and "pursed," and his eyes "cold" and "protruding." Revealing an "assertive ecclesiastic determined to preserve and increase the authority of the church," his face was an index to his entire career and a reminder of the power and place of the Catholic Church in New France.[42] Creighton's fondness for insulting historical figures to make a point first appeared in *The Commercial Empire of the St. Lawrence*, where Robert Gourlay, the agrarian radical who championed land reform in Upper Canada, possessed an "abnormal psychology," and where Robert Baldwin, the nineteenth-century politician and champion of responsible government, was a "barnacle."[43]

Although Creighton didn't use footnotes, his reference to Laval's austerities and self-mortifications almost certainly came from Francis Parkman, the great nineteenth-century American historian.[44] In Parkman's New France, Laval "represented clerical absolutism incarnate, the worst of all the enemies of Progress." Not surprisingly, Parkman was often accused of anti-Catholicism. When Laval University announced its intention to grant him an honorary degree in 1878, it ignited a storm of controversy and was forced to rescind its offer. But Parkman's anti-Catholicism was really anti-clericalism. Although he distrusted the participation of priests in politics because he saw them as the "enemies of liberty, of conscience, [and] of Progress," he actually harboured an admiration for the ancient church and its many good works.[45]

In this sense, Creighton followed Parkman, or, as Hilda Neatby put it, he dealt "unhappily" with the Church in New France.[46] As a result, there was always a "but" in his assessment. He acknowledged the importance of the Catholic

Church to "the defence of French civilization in America," *but* he condemned "the frown of clerical control." He noted Laval's opposition to the brandy trade, *but* he argued that the fur trade and western expansion constituted the very purpose of the empire of the St Lawrence. He conceded that Quebec's "distinctive faith" was essential to its survival after 1759, *but* he criticized the Church's systematic attack against the Enlightenment, "that spirit of philosophic doubt, of urbane skepticism, [and] of cultivated worldliness." At one point he mocked the Church for its role in the Guibord affair. Joseph Guibord had been a liberal and a member of the Institut Canadien – a literary and scientific society – and, because his conduct had been "tainted with the vicious principles of reason and tolerance," the Church denied him a Catholic burial. The matter ended up before the courts, and, in due course, the Judicial Committee of the Privy Council ordered that Guibord be given a Catholic burial. However, Bishop Bourget deconsecrated the burial plot immediately after the service. The concrete and scrap metal that had been poured over Guibord's coffin to protect it from vandalism was, Creighton said, "no defence against the ghostly powers of the priests."[47]

In a letter to A.L. Burt, Reverend O'Reilly thanked him for his fair-minded treatment of Catholics and Catholicism. *Dominion of the North* was surely written "in a rage," he said, and, as a result, it has undone the important work of Abbé Maheux, the French-Canadian historian who promoted mutual understanding between the two solitudes. Abbé Maheux's intellectual opposite, Abbé Groulx, would never have written "such an invidious blast as Creighton's," not even in "his wildest moments."[48]

Conflating anti-clericalism and anti-Catholicism and equating anti-Catholicism to anti–French Canadianism, Reverend O'Reilly failed to read *Dominion of the North* as a sustained essay in the importance of an English-French entente to the successful defence of Canada. In *The Commercial Empire of the St. Lawrence*, Creighton had identified "the central problem of Canadian history" as "the problem of building a continental dominion on the basis of the St. Lawrence"[49] on a continent dominated by the United States. Building that dominion of the north required cooperation between English and French Canadians at the same time as it required a permanent connection to Great Britain. The Quebec Act of 1774 represented a frank acknowledgment of Quebec's "curious individuality" and constituted an important "first victory over continentalism." Quebec had forced Great Britain to acknowledge that its northern colony was not one of its Thirteen Colonies and, in the process, had ensured that Great Britain would have a presence in North America after the American Revolution. But the Quebec Act represented only a first victory over continentalism, not a final victory. There could be no final victory, Creighton believed. The United States was a living, breathing, menacing, imperial power "against which" British North America and Canada "were to struggle from that time forward."[50]

That struggle, for example, animated British North American politics in the 1860s. According to Creighton, Confederation constituted the fulfilment of Jacques Cartier's Laurentian epiphany on the top of Mont Royal: the northwest belonged to the empire of the St Lawrence. When delegates gathered in Quebec in October 1864 to plan a general federation of British North America, they met in the Canadian legislature overlooking the river:

> Through the tall windows of the second-storey room in which the delegates sat, they could see the St. Lawrence – the River of Canada – moving slowly through its broadening estuary towards the sea. The rain drummed persistently on the windows; but nothing could destroy the overpowering effect of that panorama. The rock was the beginning and end of everything in Canada – the first outpost of expansion, the last citadel of defence. Quebec had been the origin of the empire of the St. Lawrence; it was to be genesis of the Dominion of Canada.[51]

But Confederation was also driven by the American Civil War. British North Americans largely sympathized with the Confederacy not because they liked slavery but because they feared that a Yankee victory "would unleash American expansionism once again."[52] Creighton likewise sympathized with the South because it represented a conservative bulwark to the North. Inspired by the Progressive historians – especially Vernon Parrington in the stirring conclusion to volume two of his three-volume masterpiece *Main Currents in American Thought* – Creighton admired the agrarian democracy of Thomas Jefferson over the industrial capitalism of Alexander Hamilton. The Jeffersonian ideal represented a check on the Hamiltonian pursuit of national consolidation and expansion. When living in Virginia, Creighton took his son Philip to Monticello, Jefferson's magnificent estate located just outside of Charlottesville. The mansion, the gardens, and the 5,000 acres of rolling hills, green forests, and rich farmland of Monticello invoke the lost world of the Old South. That South, Creighton wrote, "had managed to keep a precarious balance of economic and political power within the United States and hence upon the North American continent as a whole"; it "had taught the continent its ideas of equalitarian democracy"; and it "had stood for the interests of agriculture, commerce, and international trade." Its defeat, therefore, would mean a victory for the North's coercive policy of "vigorous national expansion"[53] and "territorial aggrandizement."[54] British North America, therefore, had no choice but to federate in order to defend both itself and its "enormous inheritance" in the northwest.[55]

Like the War of 1812 before it and the defence of Great Britain in South Africa and in the trenches of western Europe after it, Confederation was a chapter in the larger story of the Dominion's desire to remain separate in North America and connected to Great Britain.

In the same way that some readers questioned Creighton's depiction of French Canada and the Catholic Church, other readers questioned his depiction of the United States. Still something of a mentor to him, Bart Brebner noted that in overemphasizing the threat of continentalism, Creighton had underemphasized "the North Americanism of Canada" and the "beneficent aspects" of the Canadian-American relationship.[56] As an expat at Columbia University, Brebner didn't fear continentalism. To him, it was a useful category of analysis. Where he saw similarities between Canada and the United States, Creighton saw differences, and where he encouraged a comparative approach, Creighton drew a line in the sand. Clearly, the view from New York's Upper West Side was different than the view from Toronto's St George Street.[57]

The view from Madison, Wisconsin, was different as well. In the early 1940s, Gordon Skilling was a junior professor in Wisconsin's Department of Political Science, where he taught a class in Canadian politics. Although he thought that *Dominion of the North* was a "brilliant historical summary," his students had a different reaction. "Why is Creighton so anti-American?" they asked. Skilling was genuinely puzzled and chalked it up to "the fact that American students are not accustomed to looking at their own history through the eyes of foreigners and consider critical statements of their past to be anti-American." In one instance, though, Skilling was inclined to agree with his students. In his discussion of the 1911 election on reciprocity, Creighton had rebuked "a number of irrepressible American congressmen" for "intoning the discordant strains of Manifest Destiny." Their comments, he said, "aroused that unsleeping hatred of North American continentalism which is one of the strongest elements in Canadian nationality."[58] Surely, Skilling said, it is "an exaggeration to say that most Canadians harbour an 'unsleeping hatred of North American continentalism."[59] He was right, of course. As he often did, Creighton had exaggerated for effect and, in the process, drawn raised eyebrows in his readers.

But Creighton didn't care if he annoyed a handful of American students at some Midwestern university. By his own admission, he had written *Dominion of the North* in order "to show why Canada is and will desire to remain a separate North American nation."[60] After the United States entered the war in December 1941, it was clear that Underhill had been right: because of its enormous power and wealth the United States had effectively replaced Great Britain at the head of the Western world.[61] The implications of a weak Great Britain and a hegemonic United States terrified Creighton. After all, Canada was an autonomous country in the British Commonwealth but it was a junior player in North America. Still, *Dominion of the North* did not end with Canada's imminent defeat in the way that *The Commercial Empire of the St. Lawrence* had ended with an enraged mob setting fire to the parliament buildings. Instead, it ended on a note of imperial and national unity when Canada declared war against Germany. The country remained true to "the British Empire and the values for which it stood," at the same time as the French-Canadian minister of justice, Ernest Lapointe, stood beside the English-Canadian prime minister, Mackenzie King. "Once again, the two races, whose association had given Canada its distinctive character and history, were jointly committed to an enormous and dangerous task. They were well aware that latent differences of opinion lurked between them. The whole course of the War of 1914–18 had taught them the gravity of the difficulties and possible disagreements which lay ahead. But they went forward together to meet them."[62]

Saturday Night described *Dominion of the North* as "well-built and admirable in style"; the *Montreal Gazette* praised its "brilliantly worked pages"; the *New York Times* admired the high quality of its prose; and the *United Church Observer*, the newspaper that his father had edited for so many years, called it a "lofty, light, airy fabric of graceful, balanced proportions." In addition to the public recognition, Creighton received numerous letters from his friends and colleagues. A.L. Burt called it "a capital piece of work" while Irene Spry considered it "magnificent." A.G.B. Claxton – the prominent Montreal lawyer and father of Brooke Claxton, a Liberal cabinet minister – wrote an enthusiastic letter to say there wasn't a "dull paragraph" in it, an assessment also shared by his son, who felt that it was "easily the best" history of Canada available right now. Jack Creighton proudly reported seeing it displayed in the window of a downtown Vancouver bookstore. "You are really building up a first-class reputation as a Canadian historian and a good many people consider *Dominion of the North*, by long odds, the best history of Canada." Although Creighton complained that Houghton Mifflin might have done more to promote it in the United States, *Dominion of the North* sold 9,081 copies in its first five years. And negotiations with an Argentinean publisher for a Spanish translation to be called *El Dominio del Norte* were completed in early 1946 when the Canadian Information Service agreed to purchase the first 750 copies for distribution throughout Latin America.[63]

IV

As a narrative of discovery, exploration, consolidation, settlement, and nationhood, and as a narrative written in the omniscient, third-person Voice of God,

Dominion of the North conformed to a well-established tradition of historical writing dating back to the Middle Ages and the early modern period. Chroniclers and historians had used history to narrate the nation into existence, to invent a temporal and spatial entity, and to imbue it with both an essence and a purpose. After 1750 writing the nation became the dominant historiographical tradition when the nation itself triumphed over competing religious, feudal, and dynastic allegiances. In turn, the disciplinization and professionalization of history in the nineteenth and twentieth centuries gave history – and historians – even greater authority in the ongoing process of national invention. History became "a kind of mirror in which the nation could see itself," and historians "were the ones holding up the mirror."[64] That mirror, however, never provided an accurate or complete reflection, and, as a result, national histories, despite their certainties and self-assurances, were always full of stretches, exaggerations, compressions, and omissions.

Because of its threat to "harmonizing tales of the nation," one obvious omission was class.[65] Although no one seriously suspected Creighton of being a crypto-Marxist, some readers had detected a distinct leftward lean to his early scholarship. Herbert Heaton, for example, thought he saw "shades of Marx" in *The Commercial Empire of the St. Lawrence* because of its emphasis on economic history, teasing that he intended to recommend it to the Left Book Club. Privately, Bart Brebner described *The Commercial Empire of the St. Lawrence* as a Marxian analysis of Canadian history. Publicly, he compared its author to Charles Beard, the great American historian who had provided a brilliant reinterpretation of American history. The Constitution, Beard had argued, was the calcification of elite economic self-interest, not a statement of abstract political principles. Canada's political history, Creighton seemed to be implying, was a function of its economic history. When F.R. Scott – a law professor at McGill University and one of the early founders of the Co-operative Commonwealth Federation – read *British North America at Confederation* he quipped that its author had adopted a "dangerous approach to Marxism!" because he had argued that "it was only natural" for a society to be affected by its economic activities.[66]

But Heaton, Brebner, and Scott were relying on a pretty thin definition of Marxism – one that ignored the complexity of historical materialism and equated it instead with the simplicity of economic determinism – when they caught a whiff of Marxism emanating from between the lines of *The Commercial Empire of the St. Lawrence* and *British North America at Confederation*.

For his part, Creighton didn't think that Marx – whom he once dismissed as a "German Jew" – had much to offer the writing of Canadian history, an opinion he made clear in his review of Stanley Ryerson's first book, *1837: The Birth of Canadian Democracy*. A member of the Central Committee of the Communist Party of Canada, Ryerson wanted to recover the revolutionary spirit of 1837 for the class struggle in 1937, or as he put it, the struggle against "the entrenched powers of organized greed." Creighton, however, panned Ryerson's effort, dismissing it as "a kind of garbled translation in the Canadian vernacular of what Marx thought about the class struggle in Europe."[67]

In Creighton's estimation, the Rebellions of 1837 were not indigenous at all. They were foreign, which is to say they were American. Ideologically, they were a mixed bag of republican creed, revolutionary cant, and Lockean rhetoric about natural rights; practically, they were misguided, misdirected, "almost accidental" affairs lacking purpose and direction. The Lower-Canadian patriotes wore "their homespun garments, leather mittens, and long toques" while they "strolled aimlessly up and down St. Eustache, carrying their rusty, broken-down muskets and smoking stumpy black pipes." The Upper-Canadian rebels were equally comical, and their "pikes, pitchforks, and cudgels" were no match for the "formidable" Lieutenant Governor Sir Francis Bond Head or his "loyal" militia of "merchants, mechanics, and labourers." When their abortive rebellions were defeated both Louis-Joseph Papineau and William Lyon Mackenzie hightailed it to the United States, where Mackenzie at least tried to incite American support for "the cause of Canadian freedom." It backfired, Creighton asserted, because it linked both rebellions "with the foreigner and with a kind of disreputable violence."[68]

It was a neat narrative trick: the American threat is invoked, Stanley Ryerson's revolutionary moment is suppressed, and the fiction of national unity is magically preserved. Put another way, because he couldn't ignore the Rebellions of 1837, Creighton made fun of them.

All told, Creighton mentioned labour just twice, once when he discussed the Toronto printers' strike of 1872 and once when he referenced the Winnipeg General Strike of 1919. In neither instance did he study labour in and of itself. The printers' strike presented the politically astute Sir John A. Macdonald with an opportunity to pass the progressive Trades Union Act. In one deft parliamentary move, be could buy labour's electoral support and stick it to his Liberal and anti-labour nemesis, George Brown.[69] Meanwhile, the Winnipeg General Strike was simply part of a larger pattern of postwar unrest that needed to be contained and ultimately absorbed into a new national interest via one of the two main political parties. In both 1872 and 1919 nation trumped class and History trumped histories: "Despite the class conflicts and ethnic divisions of the new Dominion," Creighton argued, there was "a transcendent sense of nationhood which seemed, in some degree at least, to reconcile and integrate the whole."[70]

But Creighton's "transcendent sense of nationhood" is the lie, or at least the illusion, at the heart of all national narratives. Because "that deep, horizontal comradeship" necessary to all nations doesn't exist, it has to be imagined, while conflict, dissent, and even rebellions have to be mocked, minimized, or ignored. Indeed, that is the point of a national narrative – to resolve internal contradictions, to extinguish objections, to make molehills out of mountains, to project a coherent picture, to naturalize territorial expansion and dispossession, to proclaim the integrity and inviolability of national boundaries, to wed state, people, and territory, and, ultimately, to "ensnare ordinary people in a giant web of nationhood pretending to a common interest." Creighton was not a propagandist, but his narrative had what all national narratives have: "seductive power."[71] Its beauty, its confidence, and its movement across the page seduced readers into believing that there really was such a thing called Canada, that there really was a community of people with a shared history and a common purpose, and that there really was a "we" and an "us."

In this sense, Donald Creighton's *Dominion of the North* wasn't any different than Arthur Lower's *Colony to Nation*. Both narrated in the same problematic ways a "transcendent sense of nationhood." Lower's nation, though, was very different. Where Creighton emphasized the imperial connection, Arthur Lower emphasized North America, and where Creighton's stressed Canada's historical efforts to achieve autonomy in the British Empire, Lower stressed Canada's historical efforts to end its colonial status. After all, Lower had served in the First World War and had done his postgraduate work at Harvard, meaning he neither sentimentalized Great Britain nor feared the United States. Although he admired Britain for its liberalism, for "its democratic tradition, its strong sense of individualism, and its parliamentary form of government," his imagined Canada wasn't British – it was Canadian.[72] Gustave Lanctôt, the French-Canadian historian and Dominion archivist, wrote a nice letter to Lower saying how pleased he was to learn that he was writing a history of Canada. It will no doubt be "un véritable Histoire du Canada," which, he added, is even more necessary "après la version tory de notre ami Creighton dans *Dominion of the North*."[73] By tory, he meant colonial. But Lanctôt was wrong. Creighton wasn't a colonial; he was a nationalist, and his imagined nation was no less Canadian for being British. The tension between Creighton's British nationalism in *Dominion of the North* and Lower's Canadian nationalism in *Colony to Nation* could be contained in the 1940s and 1950s, but not in the 1960s.

V

A few weeks after the publication of *Dominion of the North*, Creighton received a telegram from New York City: the Executive Committee of the Rockefeller Foundation had just approved a $6,500 research grant. Although "very happy to get the good news," he wasn't surprised.[74] The Rockefeller Foundation had been looking for a way to support him and his research for the better part of two years.

In November 1942, John Marshall spent three days at the University of Toronto. It was not uncommon for a program officer from the Rockefeller Foundation to visit Canada as part of the foundation's mandate to support research in medicine, the sciences, the social sciences, and the humanities in the United States and around the world. In Toronto, Marshall met the usual suspects – President Cody, Principal Wallace, and, of course, Harold Innis, who served as something of a broker between American philanthropic foundations and English-Canadian social scientists and humanists. It was through Innis that Marshall met Creighton. The two men had a long conversation about Toronto, the war, research, and writing. Afterwards, Marshall reported that Creighton was "vigorous and articulate" and almost certainly "the ablest historian" in Canada. Innis later confirmed his impression. Creighton, he said, carried a heavy teaching and administrative load and if anybody should be released it should be him, both for his benefit and "the benefit of scholarship." Because Marshall already intended to provide teaching release and research support to a handful of promising American historians, men who were in mid-career and who had made significant contributions to their field, it would be easy enough to expand the program to include Canadian historians. And so he invited Creighton to be part of a new Rockefeller Foundation initiative in the study of values in history.[75]

Creighton was obviously delighted. For the past two or three years, the Canadian historical profession had been talking about values, Western civilization, and the role of the historian.[76] After all, for the second time in a century that had not yet reached its halfway mark, Western civilization had imploded and the world was at war. There is, he told Marshall, "a good deal of interest in the problem of those fundamental values or objectives in the history of our country which historians should strive to make its citizens realize." The historian, in other words, is not only a teacher, he is a public moralist, especially in wartime when the "permanent values of a society" are either "distorted" or "overlooked." It is the historian's duty "to remind his fellow citizens of the values for which his nation has consistently stood."[77]

In another century, Creighton would have become a minister. Instead, he was born in the twentieth century and he became a historian. His colleague in the Department of Political Economy, Del Clark, looked to "the strength of Canada's evangelical religious tradition" to explain the inclination of historians to proselytize, adding that "it is perhaps not insignificant" that Creighton was the son of a Methodist minister.[78]

But if William Creighton could write a homily for the *Christian Guardian*, what kind of book could his son write? The study of values in history was awfully vague. Initially, Creighton toyed with the idea of writing a book on Canadian foreign policy or a book on the history of Canadian education. He also thought about writing a history of the Anglo-French rivalry in the new world or a biography of Sir John A. Macdonald. It was Innis who discouraged a book on New France, suspecting, perhaps, that his friend's "treatment would resemble Parkman's."[79] A biography of Macdonald, however, would be a logical sequel to *The Commercial Empire of the St. Lawrence*. Besides, Macdonald appealed to Creighton's instincts as a historian and as a writer: he was a large, powerful figure whose career spanned several decades and whose vision animated an entire generation. Canada's first prime minister embodied the "permanent tendencies" in Canadian history, Creighton believed, and his biography would stand as a kind of national monument. Later, he admitted to being a "little dazzled" by the prospect that was before him.[80]

Good historians have good instincts but great historians have great instincts and Creighton was a great historian. He wasn't interested in minor figures and didn't want to write a book that no one would read. He wanted to write a book that mattered. Macdonald, he confessed, was "a big subject"; he came with "a large cast" of supporting characters; and he acted on a "wide stage."[81] In *The Commercial Empire of the St. Lawrence*, he had written the myth. It was time to give that myth a hero.

But the excitement of a new research project was dampened by the reality of aging parents in the late summer and early fall of 1944. In the early stages of age-related dementia, almost certainly Alzheimer's disease, Laura Creighton had become confused and disoriented, at times quick-tempered and acidulous. Her increasing demands placed an overwhelming weight on William, whose own health declined when he began to experience occasional dizziness and moments of confusion. That summer he had at least two falls and made a couple of inexplicable financial decisions that, while not ruinous, cost him a lot of money. Frustrated with his father, Donald also tried to be useful. A few years earlier he had made a point of always shovelling his parents' driveway and had taken over the maintenance of the family cottage. But he couldn't possibly put his life on hold to care for his parents. And no one expected him to. His career, his work, and his writing were too important. Jack, meanwhile, lived on the other side of the continent and everyone understood that his job, his family, and his life were in Vancouver. Besides, they were sons and sons didn't do that kind of thing. Daughters did, and so the burden fell to Isabel.

In the fall of 1944, she left the University of Saskatchewan, returned to Toronto, took a job at the Canadian Association for Adult Education for $150 a month, repaired her marriage, moved into her parents' home, and assumed responsibility for them and for her husband. Although Harold had worked as a night watchman at Inglis for a year or so, he was now unemployed. Caught in the horrible spiral of depression and alcohol, he was always on the verge of a nervous breakdown and was never able to work again. To her credit, Isabel didn't complain, and, if she felt sorry for herself, she didn't say so. It may not have been how she had imagined her life but she accepted it with equanimity.[82]

Freed again from the sphere of necessity, in this case the necessity of caring for his elderly parents, and freed from the obligations of teaching, Creighton threw himself into his work with, in his words, "fanatical conviction." For the better part of a year, he ploughed his way through Macdonald's correspondence. The Public Archives even provided him with an office.

Although careful not to put the cart before the horse, Creighton also began to think about the many challenges of writing a biography. When the University of New Brunswick invited him to deliver the 1945 Founders' Day Address, he spoke about the need to write history that was both scholarly and accessible. "The real historian," he told his Fredericton audience, "will aim to know his period as well – or almost as well – as if he had lived in it himself." Of course, he will spend long hours in the archives but he will also immerse himself in his particular period, in its art forms, its fashion, its architecture, even its domestic furniture and kitchen utensils. At the same time, he must strive to "meet the requirements of literature." He must always remember that history "is not made by inanimate forces and human automatons; it is made by living men and women, impelled by an endless variety of ideas and emotions, which can best be understood by that insight into character, the imaginative understanding of people, which is one of the great attributes of literary art."[83]

It was one of his deepest convictions that history was no less a science for being artistic and no less an art for being scientific. And because he understood that "all great works of literature either dissolve a genre or invent one," he set an ambitious goal: to marry the research of history to the insight of fiction through the genre of biography.[84] It devoured the next eleven years of his life, but Creighton would reinvent Canadian biography and *Macdonald* would become a great work of literature.

chapter eight

Macdonald

Once again, as had happened with such tragic frequency in the past, the Anglo-Canadian resistance to the United States had been weakened, at the crucial moment, by the distracting events in Europe. And once again Macdonald feared, and with reason, that the United States would attempt to exploit the British desire for appeasement by extracting ruinous concessions at Canada's expense.

John A. Macdonald, vol. 2

After an "extremely successful" research leave, Donald Creighton resumed his many responsibilities at the university in September 1945. That summer he had been appointed to the rank of full professor – but only after McGill had offered him a full professorship with a higher salary, a reduced teaching load, and the promise of more time to write. Although he felt that his promotion was long overdue and that some of his colleagues weren't worth the offices they occupied, he still loved Toronto. He first came to the university in 1920 as an undergraduate and now, twenty-five years later, he was a full professor earning $4,900. Knowing, perhaps, how much things like salary, rank, and status mattered to him, the head of the department informed him that while he wouldn't be its highest-paid member, he would be one of its highest paid.[1]

The campus was a busy place that fall, and from his office window Creighton could hear students walking up and down St George Street. New government programs encouraging service men and women to attend university dramatically increased enrolments. Lecture halls and classrooms were so crowded that even students who arrived on time had to stand at the back or sit on the floor.[2] It was a minor inconvenience, though, because Europe had been liberated, Japan had been defeated, and Canada had avoided a national unity crisis. But Canada's celebrations were punctuated by apprehension: the British Empire was in tatters.[3] Even as King George VI delivered his Victory in Europe speech a sense of unease haunted the corridors of power in London and Ottawa. The empire's "will power and vitality" were not, in fact, "inexhaustible."[4] John Maynard Keynes would declare that Great Britain had reached its "financial Dunkirk" in August, and, two years later, the world's greatest empire would ration potatoes. The United States now led the Western world and was embarking on a dangerous standoff with a Soviet Union that was determined to expand its spheres of influence in eastern and central Europe and in the Middle East. The postwar world was not only different from the pre-war world, it was also more dangerous. The United States had proven its willingness to use nuclear weapons, and in 1949 the Soviet Union would demonstrate its own nuclear might. Geography, self-interest, and the logic of Cold War politics meant that Canada would align itself with the United States. It couldn't be a British nation in North America; it would have to be a North American nation that was only nominally British. As one senior military official reported in August 1945, Canada could neither defend every outpost of the British Empire nor "preserve the Indian Ocean as a British lake."[5]

The Laurentian thesis would be tested in the new world order. Would Canada's "primitive desire for separateness" in North America survive a sustained test of its strength? Could the Anglo-Canadian alliance mount a successful resistance to American demands and pressures? Or would the United States exploit British weakness to exact ruinous concessions from Canada? According to a young George Grant, Canada's very survival depended on its membership in the British Commonwealth of nations: without it, "no power on earth can keep us from being absorbed by the United States."[6]

Creighton's growing conviction that Canada risked being absorbed by the United States was confirmed and strengthened by his friendship with Harold Innis. In the 1940s, Innis began what would be the final leg of his long intellectual journey when he turned to the study of communications, monopolies of knowledge, limitations, biases, time, and the rise and fall of civilizations. His emerging critique of modernity became in part a critique of the United States after 1945. Rejecting Cold War orthodoxies and brooding over Canada's fate, he identified the United States "as the chief threat to peace."[7] What he said in private in 1946 and 1947, he would say in public in early 1948: American foreign policy is "disgraceful," "irresponsible," and "promises little for the future stability of the western world"; Canada has succumbed to "American domination"; Canadian opinion "has become very largely a reflection of American opinion"; and no one questions "the implications of joint defence schemes with the United States." In short, Canada has gone "from colony to nation to colony."[8] It is, he said, little more than a "stool pigeon" to the United States.[9] In a later essay, he grew even more pessimistic. "We are indeed fighting for our lives. The pernicious influence of American advertising reflected especially in the periodical press and the powerful persistent impact of commercialism have been evident in all the ramifications of Canadian life," he warned. "The jackals of communication systems are constantly on the alert to destroy every vestige of sentiment to Great Britain holding it of no advantage if it threatens the omnipotence of American commercialism. This is to strike at the heart of cultural life in Canada."[10] Continentalism, he argued, was a greater threat to Canada than imperialism ever was.

Creighton didn't understand Innis's larger intellectual project – very few people did – but he certainly understood his references to pernicious influences, stool pigeons, and jackals. It was in this context – the context of Britain's decline, America's rise, the Cold War, and Canada's shifting allegiance – that the biography of John A. Macdonald began to take shape.

As early as the fall of 1947 Creighton indicated what direction his biography would take and what his Macdonald would look like when he spoke to a meeting of the Graduate History Club at the University of Toronto. Although he hadn't done any writing yet, he had been thinking about Canada's first prime minister for nearly three and a half years and had formed a basic thesis not just about Macdonald but about Canadian historical writing as well. Despite the rich collection of Macdonald papers at the Public Archives and despite the renaissance in Canadian historical writing, Creighton explained, historians have been content to rely on the popular image of "an easy-going, pleasure-loving, and none too scrupulous opportunist, who survived a half-century of political conflict by means of a dubious series of compromises, appeasements, and reconciliations."

Unimaginative and lifeless, Canadian historical writing didn't aspire to anything other than being factual. Echoing Lytton Strachey's preface to *The Eminent Victorians,* Creighton described Canadian biographies as "solemn works of commemoration, usually in two fat funereal volumes," written by "historical undertakers." Historians showed no interest in their subjects as living, breathing, complicated human beings. And they showed no interest in the genre of biography and its close relationship to the novel. Instead, they dutifully fit their subject into the simple story of Canada's constitutional history. "Are there really biographies of Baldwin, Hincks, and Laurier, or are these merely lives of Robert Responsible-Government, and Francis Responsible-Government, and Wilfrid Responsible-Government?"[11] But Bloomsbury writers had transformed biography – once "noble, upright, chaste, and severe," in the words of Virginia Woolf – into life-writing and, in the process, freed it from its Victorian death grip. Where the old biography draped velvet robes "decorously over the recumbent figures of the dead," the new biography "promised to tell the truth about the dead," "a task that called for gifts analogous to the poet's or the novelist's."[12]

Historians hadn't ignored Macdonald only because they were lousy writers, Creighton added, they had ignored him because he was a Conservative and they were Liberals. At one point, he snidely referred to the author of Wilfrid Laurier's biography as the "eminent scholar Dr. Oscar Douglas Skelton, Ph.D." (In response, Skelton's not-at-all amused widow called Creighton a "shallow, pompous, imperialist.") The Liberal Interpretation, or the Grit Interpretation, of Canadian history stressed Canada's struggle to unshackle its colonial chains, to emancipate itself from Britain, achieve national independence, and bury imperialism once and for all. Content to ignore or dismiss other imperialisms, meaning American imperialism, Grit historians wanted to rid Canada of its British past and "rehabilitate it as a decent American community." But they forgot one thing, Creighton said. "Canadian nationality depends as much upon the separateness of Canada in North America as upon its autonomy within the British Empire."[13]

Creighton's Macdonald never forgot Canada's separateness in North America; he always appreciated the imperial connection; and, to the very end of his days, his favourite holiday destination was London, "the capital of the Empire."[14]

II

A biography of Canada's first prime minister naturally attracted interest from publishers. First Longmans and then Oxford University Press expressed polite interest: if authors need publishers then publishers need authors and good publishers are always looking for good authors. For his part, John Gray was a good publisher. In 1946 he returned from active service in the Second World War and resumed his career at Macmillan of Canada, where, that June, he was promoted to general manager. It was a powerful position that gave him considerable – if not absolute – freedom to nurture Canadian writers, including Hugh MacLennan, W.O. Mitchell, and Robertson Davies. At a cocktail party that fall, he spied Donald Creighton and Frank Underhill, and the conversation soon turned to writing and publishing. Creighton told him that he was working on a biography of John A. Macdonald, and a few days later Gray invited him to lunch. Twenty-four years after the fact, he could still recall "the shared excitement of that first long talk" in the Oak Room at the King Edward Hotel, where, for several hours, they talked about the world of authors, publishers, books, history, biography, and fiction. Gray left the table "coveting the privilege" of being Creighton's publisher, but Macmillan had recently signed a contract with another writer for a biography of Macdonald.[15] When that manuscript finally arrived in 1948, Gray cancelled the author's contract – the thing was unsalvageable – and he promptly informed Macmillan's London office that he intended to sign a contract with Creighton. Daniel Macmillan advised caution. There were already a number of biographies of Macdonald and he doubted very much if there was room for another one. Gray agreed to wait and see, but, he added, "it would be a great pity if we lost this book."[16]

In the end, of course, Macmillan didn't lose the book and Creighton and Gray became close friends. Their personal friendship, though, would be strained by their professional relationship. Indeed, Gray likened their publisher-author relationship to that of "a fairly experienced scuba diver and a basking shark": the diver wants to get close but not too close. Creighton was more than an author. He was an artist, and, like all artists, he thought always in terms of the whole. Parts, even small parts like the balance of a sentence, the choice of words, grammar, and even punctuation, couldn't be altered without altering the whole. But Gray was an experienced and brilliant publisher: he knew when to advance and when to retreat; he appreciated the difference between a suggestion and an instruction; he quickly learned to navigate the shoals of Creighton's "wrath"; and, most importantly, he respected the decision of English Canada's leading historian to write a biography as if he were writing a novel.[17]

In his Founders' Day Address and in his talk to the Graduate History Club, Creighton claimed for the biographer the novelist's right to imagine. Why, he asked, shouldn't the biographer be allowed to imagine? History, after all, is not the past. It is an account of the past. It is, R.G. Collingwood said in 1946, "a picture of the past" and "it is the artist and not nature that is responsible for what goes into the picture." History, like the novel, is an "imaginative reconstruction" and the historian, again like the novelist, constructs "a picture" of events, situations, motives, and characters.[18] *The Idea of History* confirmed Creighton's instincts, and by his own admission he took his stand beside its Oxford author: from a vast and imperfect archival record, the historian selects what goes into history, not the past.[19]

III

The beginning of any book is a threshold – on one side is the real world of the reader; on the other side is the imagined world of the author. To cross that threshold, to willingly suspend disbelief, the reader must trust the author. But how does an author establish that trust and, in the process, draw the reader into the story? Creighton wrestled with that question in each of his books. In

Macdonald, he used the image of immigrants travelling westward by the river, brilliantly inviting the reader to enter what is still considered to be one of the best books ever written in Canada: "In those days they came usually by boat. A few immigrants may have made the long journey by land, taking several weeks and stopping at a score of friendly farm-houses as they pushed their way through the green forest. But most people travelled westward by the river." Evoking the St Lawrence River and the Laurentian Shield – "a huge knotted fist" thrusting itself "southward across the river" from its "rocky highland" – he linked *Macdonald* to *The Commercial Empire of the St. Lawrence* and Macdonald to the Laurentian thesis: every myth requires a hero and every hero requires a myth.[20] The St Lawrence River had made New France and British North America possible. It had "shouted its uniqueness," "invited journeyings," "promised immense expanses," and opened the continent to adventurers, explorers, traders, and now immigrants, including a young boy from Scotland who, like Moses, would one day deliver his people.[21]

When the reader first meets him, Macdonald is not yet six years old. He is "tall for his age, slight yet sturdy, with an increasingly lanky and almost angular frame." Even then, his otherwise smooth face carried "rugged lines," although his character "was still a new, unknown land." It would be revealed in time, though, during adolescence, "that primitive period of upheaval and subsidence" when "a few solid, rocky contours" emerged. Macdonald's "lanky almost angular frame," the "rugged lines" on his face, and the "solid, rocky contours" of his character evoked the Laurentian Shield, that "huge triangle of rocky upland" featuring "great, crude, sweeping lines and immense and clumsy masses." In other words, he was marked by destiny, something Creighton showed by pairing stories about the future prime minister with descriptions of the landscape. One Christmas, a young Macdonald brings home a group of friends and, in his convivial way, welcomes everyone into the fold. "It was the last Christmas but one that they were to spend at the Stone Mills. The fires burned brightly; and outside the dark trees rose behind them, tier on tier, to the crest of the mountain, and in front the waters of Adolphus Reach lay spread out still and white with ice."[22] Of course, Creighton had no evidence indicating that the fires were bright, that the trees were dark, or that the river was frozen. But he didn't care because he wanted to communicate a different truth about Macdonald: his destiny was waiting for him in the vast boreal forest, the endless waterways, and the relentless granite reaches of the Laurentian Shield.

"I cannot help feeling that novelists have taught me more than historians have about the craft of narrative," or storytelling, Creighton admitted.[23] Although it has some of the features of historical writing – a preface, a table of contents, footnotes, a list of sources, and an index – *The Young Politician* lacks a thesis statement and a sustained argument, and the text is neither burdened by historiographical posing nor cluttered with references to secondary sources. History, Creighton famously said, "is the record of an encounter between character and circumstance," and that record is "essentially a story."[24] Analysis and exposition get in the way of narrative and storytelling. At best, they slow readers down. At worst, they turn them away. Besides, history is not a problem to be solved. It is, Creighton repeated over and over again, a story to be told. Stories require characters; characters require circumstances; circumstances require description; and description requires details. The darkness of the trees, the lines on someone's face, the curls in someone else's hair, the wallpaper in a particular room, and the sound of rain against a window denote physical exteriors but they also connote emotional interiors. The great nineteenth-century writers made details an essential feature of the modern novel. Honoré de Balzac brilliantly captured the mood of a Parisian boarding house through its stale air and dingy furniture. Jane Austen's "cold, stormy rain" mirrored Emma's inner turmoil. And Charles Dickens's "implacable November weather" said what needed to be said in just three words.[25]

Envious of novelists for their godlike ability to create new worlds, to give life to characters, and to explore their moods and motivations through any number of techniques, from backstories to interior monologues, Creighton confessed that sometimes the historian has to invent in order to tell the truth. The inventions were not falsehoods. They were embroidery. "You have to write biography and history as though it were fiction, as though it were a novel, because that is the only way the human mind can deal with it. You have to backtrack and embroider along the sides and the embroidery isn't necessarily a lie, but the embroidery isn't drawn from the moment."[26]

IV

In 1951 Creighton received a generous research fellowship from Britain's Nuffield Foundation which allowed him to spend the 1951–2 academic year in Oxford. Although he hadn't been back to Oxford since 1927, he still earned an important psychic income from its colleges and libraries, its narrow and confusing streets, its surrounding countryside, and its rivalry with Cambridge. The timing couldn't have been better. He had already written six chapters; Luella had just published *High Bright Buggy Wheels*; Philip had finished his studies at Toronto's Trinity College and been accepted at Balliol; and Cynthia was nearly eleven years old and about to enter middle school. Donald and Luella acted quickly: in just a few short weeks, they sold their house, put their belongings in storage, booked their transatlantic passage, enrolled Cynthia at a girls' boarding school in Bournemouth, and found a room to rent at the Derbyshire, an Oxford guest house that provided long-term accommodations, cleaning and laundry service, and even meals. They had considered renting a flat but – as Creighton later admitted – the day-to-day routine of shopping, cooking, and washing up would have fallen to Luella.[27]

For Luella, Oxford was like a dream. With no meals to prepare and no washing up to do, she could explore the city, drive to neighbouring villages, and, in the evenings, go to the theatre or enjoy a long walk with Donald. She could also start her next novel. The reviews of her first novel had been mediocre at best. Des Pacey wrote that if *High Bright Buggy Wheels* wasn't a great novel, it was nonetheless a good novel. And Northrop Frye tried to be encouraging but bluntly reported that its "dialogue runs to clichés," its "analysis doesn't go very deep," and "the characters are drawn with a hand that still needs a lot of practice in drawing characters."[28] Discouraged, perhaps even a little bruised, Luella had to keep writing. Although still very much in its infancy, *Turn East, Turn West* would take her back to the fictional town of Kinsail in turn-of-the-century Ontario and the themes of family, religion, sexuality, repression, and hypocrisy.

Meanwhile, Creighton picked up where he had left off in June. Sometimes he went to the Bodleian Library and sometimes he worked in the small office that Balliol College had made available to him, but for the most part he stayed in his room. On a good day, he could write nine, ten, or even eleven pages. Recording in his diary how many pages he had written was his way of both pacing himself and pushing himself. Like a long-distance runner, he maintained a consistent pace by keeping his eyes focused not on the immediate but on the distant horizon. Curiously, he never reflected on what he had written, perhaps because he didn't have to. He now had an absolute command of the material and knew exactly what he wanted to say and where he wanted to say it.

That fall and early winter, he made a couple of short research trips to the Royal Archives at Windsor Castle and to a number of English country estates that still had family papers containing original material on Confederation. On one occasion he and the butler lugged several tin boxes from Highclere Castle's attic to its "magnificent library," where he spent the afternoon reading the personal papers of the fourth Earl of Carnarvon; on another occasion he visited Hughenden Manor, the beautifully restored estate of Benjamin Disraeli, where the Victorian era seemed to emanate from the library's flock wallpaper, settees, embroidered chairs and footstools, and its view out across the terrace to the garden beyond. He and Luella also received an invitation to dine with Lord Beaverbrook – one of the wealthiest and most powerful men in England – at Cherkley Court, his country home in Surrey. Beaverbrook had first noticed

Jack McClelland – that master of promotion – hired an actor and actress to give away copies of *High Bright Buggy Wheels* while driving a horse and buggy down Toronto's Yonge Street. Although in Oxford at the time, Luella could not have been more delighted and often told the story with a mixture of pride and pleasure.

Creighton in 1948 when he read his essay on the treatment Macdonald had received at the hands of Canadian historians and he now wanted to meet him.[29]

To accelerate the publishing process, Creighton had delivered the first six chapters to John Gray before leaving Canada, and Gray, in turn, sent them to a number of readers. For the most part, the assessments were positive, at times effusive: Creighton had succeeded in telling a compelling story and in making John A. Macdonald come alive. But the readers were not uncritical. One didn't like the excessive use of adjectives. It gives the manuscript, she said, "a verbose and even amateurish suggestion." Another felt that he was reading a Conservative biography, not the biography of a Conservative. "It is slanted history," he said. And yet another hated the opening sentence. "'In those days they came usually by boat.' In what days? Who came by boat?" he asked.[30] Knowing how thin-skinned his author was, Gray didn't send him the individual reports. Instead, he and his editors assembled a seven-page document entitled "Editorial Notes" containing only the most salient suggestions for revision.

Creighton exploded, threatening to kill Gray or, at the very least, "wring his neck." He was, Luella reported, "smoulderingly angry."[31] "It sometimes seems to me," Creighton fumed, "that about half the population of Toronto has read my manuscript – each person feeling perfectly qualified to send in his two cents worth of criticism." Of course it was slanted history, he intimated. But that was the point: to rescue Canadian history from the Grit Interpretation. "I gather that the real trouble with my biography is that it doesn't correspond to what [the reader] remembers of his public school history. I am prepared to admit this, but it doesn't interest me greatly. However, to pacify the gentleman and his kind, I have stuck in the pontifical commonplaces which I suppose he likes."[32] But the revisions were minor and, in a couple of places, represented improvements. Creighton loved how an adjective could enlarge or restrict a noun and, in the process, cast it in a different light, but his fondness for adjectives also led to what one review of *The Commercial Empire of the St. Lawrence* had called purple writing. In the end, Creighton agreed to make some changes, but he refused to make other changes, especially to the opening paragraph, which Macmillan editors had described as "over elaborate," suggesting that it should be stripped "of all meaningless and vague trimmings."[33] Meaningless and vague! The entire biography, including its ending, grew out of the opening description of the St Lawrence River and Laurentian Shield. In his mind, it wasn't over-elaborate. It was perfect.

As a friend, Gray told him not to "shoot the referee"; but as a publisher, he wisely dropped the question of the opening paragraph and the book's larger interpretive slant. After all, Creighton had completed the first volume in record time and it was now on its way to publication sometime in the fall. If he privately quibbled about a particular word or phrase, Gray also conceded that the manuscript "reads exceedingly well."[34]

The Young Politician presents two Macdonalds – the public figure and the private man. After his apprenticeship and eventual admission to the bar, Macdonald became one the brightest, most capable lawyers in Kingston, where he won public recognition by taking difficult, unpopular cases which nonetheless required legal counsel, including the defence of a man accused of raping a child. At twenty-nine years of age, he entered politics and was elected Member of Parliament for Kingston. Clever, outgoing, and gregarious, he quickly established himself as someone to watch when he became a minister of the Crown at thirty-two. Politics suited him and he suited politics. It was a game with established rules and he played it well. A natural tactician, he deliberately cultivated relationships with French-Canadian members because he understood that the road to power led through French Canada. He also understood that the Conservative Party would have to moderate its conservatism along more progressive lines if it was going to match the growing appeal of the Reform Party. And finally, he understood "the problem of survival against the imperialist designs of the United States" and the related "problem of British North American defence." Although a late convert to the idea of a wider union between the Canadas and the lower provinces, he successfully steered the Confederation movement and, in 1867, became Canada's first prime minister.[35]

Macdonald's public success was offset by private tragedy. As a child he witnessed the murder of his older brother when the two were left in the care of a family acquaintance – the old man, it turned out, was a violent, angry drunk who, in a fit of rage, struck and killed James when he refused a drink of gin. His father believed that he "was made for success," but he was, in fact, "invariably susceptible to failure" and the family seemed to be just one step ahead of creditors and always on the brink of financial ruin. As the only son, Macdonald discovered that the reality of supporting his family would fall on his young shoulders. "I had no boyhood," he once remarked, confirming Charles Dickens's dictum that "the poor have no childhood."[36] When Macdonald married and started his own family, he reasonably expected to live happily ever after. But his wife Isabella developed a mysterious, chronic illness. In constant pain, often bedridden, and dangerously reliant on opium, she could never fulfil her domestic assignments as a wife and mother. Then their infant son – and his namesake – died suddenly. They had another son, but her poor health precluded anything like a normal family life. Finally, after twelve years of illness, convalescence, doctors, and prescriptions, she died. By this point, Macdonald had turned to alcohol. "He had become a family man whose home was a hotel or a lodging-house; a bachelor husband who had to go for companionship to bars and lounges and smoking-rooms; a frustrated host who drank too much on occasion, partly because it was an easy way to forget."[37]

Creighton worried about the references to Macdonald's drinking. Was it even appropriate, especially when he lacked direct evidence and had to infer?[38] In the end, he decided that it couldn't be avoided. After all, Macdonald's earlier biographers had alluded to it, and, as a biographer, Creighton wanted to walk in Macdonald's shoes. He wanted to see what he saw, to hear what he heard, to feel what he felt, and to imbibe what he imbibed. In his words, he "poured" himself into his subject.[39] Arnold Bennett – one of the twentieth century's most brilliant novelists – once said that the "essential characteristic of the really great novelist" is "a Christ-like, all embracing compassion."[40] Creighton's compassion for Macdonald was Christ-like precisely because it was forgiving. In looking past Macdonald's minor sins, petty corruptions, and little transgressions, he effectively forgave them; in sympathizing with his over-consumption, he humanized it. Creighton's forgiveness, however, stopped at Macdonald's political rivals, and, as a result, Macdonald's hates became his own. Robert Baldwin carried himself with a "solemn, slightly Pecksniffian air of conscious rectitude"; Oliver Mowat, that "plump, bespectacled, rather self-important little man," was still the "fat boy" with whom Macdonald had gone to school; Joseph Howe's "big face with its rather coarse features" had become "dull and heavy" with "fatigue"; and George Brown, editor of the *Globe,* leader of the Reform Party, and Macdonald's antithesis and nemesis, "was an awkward, red-haired, extremely tall, extremely serious young Scotsman"; he was "a difficult colleague" who was by turns "reserved, sensitive, moody, and impulsive"; why, when the "terrible," "humourless" thing rose to speak in the House, his "stiff arm jerked monotonously up and down like a dull saw on an obstinate log of hardwood."[41]

Creighton's treatment of Confederation was similarly problematic: Macdonald's role is emphasized; his point of view is privileged; and opposition is either ignored altogether or marginalized. In the final climactic chapters, when the United Province of Canada descended into an acrimonious political stalemate and when a "general fog of uncertainty" obscured everyone else's vision, Macdonald "clearly" saw the future: the formation of a coalition government with the purpose of negotiating a wider federal union. In Creighton's estimation, Canada's destiny depended on one man. Only John A. Macdonald understood the logic of the St Lawrence River and only he could fulfil the promise of the Laurentian thesis. When delegates from across British North America gathered in Charlottetown in 1864 to discuss a wider federal union, they were bathed in the warm assurance of September's sun. But when they gathered in Quebec City five weeks later to negotiate a federal union, they were accosted by October's rain. Through the tall, arched windows of what had been designed as a post office but now served as their meeting room, the Fathers of Confederation could only dimly make out the river below and the horizon beyond. Drumming relentlessly against the large windows, the rain "drowned the curves of the river and the long line of the Laurentians in pale washes of indigo." But Macdonald "seemed to have a truly architectonic view of the entire structure." His whole career "had been an unconscious preparation" for this moment. There was no turning back now. Like some Biblical prophet, he would deliver in law what he could see through the rain and mist: a great, transcontinental, British nation. His life's purpose was the preservation of British North America against the United States, and Confederation represented the partial fulfilment of that purpose. In Charlottetown, Quebec, and London; in the colonial buildings of British North America, the meeting rooms of a London hotel, and the drawing rooms of Highclere Castle – an estate he once described as "one of the swellest places in England" and where much of Canada's Constitution was actually drafted – Macdonald stayed the course. And when it was clear that the British North America Bill would become the British North America Act, he received a private audience with Queen Victoria. "We have desired in this measure," he said, "to declare in the most solemn and emphatic manner our resolve to be under the Sovereignty of Your Majesty and your family forever."[42]

In the same way that Creighton crafted a particular opening, he crafted a particular ending. On the first of July 1867, the weather cooperated and the hot summer sun shone brightly on the new Dominion. For a brief moment, it even seemed to stop its movement across the sky, he said. There was a swearing-in ceremony and a reading of the proclamation in Ottawa; there were military parades in Toronto, Montreal, Quebec, and Halifax; there were cricket matches in Trois-Rivières and Kingston; there was a sailing race in Barrie and a harness race in Dunnville; and there were picnics and games in every village and every hamlet, where, "for an hour or two the small boys who were later to drive the Canadian Pacific Railway across their country and who were to found the first homesteads in the remote prairies, jumped across bars and ran races." As darkness fell, people reassembled for fireworks, roman candles, rockets, and bonfires.

> Parliament Hill was crowded once again with people who had come to watch the last spectacle of the day. The Parliament Buildings were illuminated. They stood out boldly against the sky; and far beyond them, hidden in darkness, were the ridges of the Laurentians, stretching away, mile after mile, towards the northwest.[43]

In the final sentence, Creighton took his readers back to the very first page and pointed ahead to the second volume; he reminded them of the book's main theme and prepared the ground for what was to come; he directed them to the origins of Canada in the St Lawrence River and Laurentian Shield and invited them to its appointed destiny in the northwest. His description of 1 July 1867 wasn't indulgent. In weaving together 481 pages and some 190,000 words, it served a vital integrative function and was essential to the narrative's larger meaning.

V

With the first volume in the Macmillan pipeline, Donald and Luella went to London for a much-needed holiday in early February. He worked on and off at the British Museum and the Public Records Office, but, for the most part, they simply enjoyed the city. They visited the Victoria and Albert Museum and the British Museum of Natural History; they took in the theatre and the opera; and they made a point of going to Charles Dickens's house because Creighton wanted to see where his boyhood hero had written *Oliver Twist* and *Nicholas Nickleby*. And more by instinct than by choice, they participated in the events marking the sudden death of King George VI. He was their king, whose example during the war had inspired millions of men and women across the empire. Thirteen years earlier Donald and Luella had been among the scores of thousands to welcome him to Toronto; now they listened to Winston Churchill address the nation, went to Charing Cross to hear the accession proclamation of Queen Elizabeth II, and braved the massive crowd to watch his last journey to London in a coffin made by his carpenters at Sandringham, the Norfolk estate where the royal family liked to spend Christmas and where he had died. It was, of course, public theatre, a carefully scripted display of a dead king and a living crown, of a deceased sovereign and his grieving subjects, of Britain and its empire. It was, Donald confessed, "superbly done."[44]

A few weeks later, they returned to Oxford, where, on a cold afternoon, he tuned into the BBC for "The Boat Race," the annual rowing race between the Oxford and Cambridge eights held on the last Saturday in March on the River Thames. The weather was awful. One commentator described the conditions as a "blinding blizzard." Cambridge had been favoured going into the race, but Oxford somehow managed to keep abreast its ancient rival and, led by Chris Davidge, one of Britain's all-time great rowers, pulled ahead in the final stretch to win by a length. It was all very exciting, Creighton reported. "Oxford's dramatic victory" was "perhaps the most thrilling finish in the entire history of the race." It was like a dream: being in England, living in Oxford, visiting country estates, dining with Lord Beaverbrook, enjoying London, delivering guest lectures at London, Oxford, Bristol, and the London School of Economics, reconnecting with old friends, meeting new colleagues, and celebrating his alma mater's "magnificent" victory on the Thames.[45] Creighton even talked about moving to England, about leaving Canada and the University of Toronto. If he could secure an appointment at an English university, he would leave Toronto in a heartbeat. The petty rivalries were taking their toll. Yes, he loved the place. But he was also colonized. He believed that British history mattered in a way that Canadian history didn't matter because it stretched back in time to the Saxons, Romans, Normans, and Celts; he believed that the British literary tradition was the world's greatest literary tradition and that, unlike Canadian writers, British writers were held in a hushed and reverential embrace by a grateful nation; and he believed that British universities were better than Canadian universities because they were older.

Then a devastating letter from Mary Innis interrupted his dream and brought him crashing back to reality: Harold was dying. His sore back, fatigue, and weight loss were not the usual complaints of middle age and overwork. They were the symptoms of metastasized prostate cancer. To Creighton, Innis had been a mentor, a role model, and a friend. The thought that he might never see him again was "dreadful"[46] and it forced him to revisit their twenty-five-year friendship, which had grown into a friendship between their two families. It had been Innis who arranged for him to deliver his very first paper on the commercial class in Canadian politics. And when everyone else was chasing rabbits through the *Canadian Forum* and the Canadian Institute of International Affairs, it had been Innis who taught him to put scholarship first. That night Creighton made the decision to dedicate *John A. Macdonald: The Young Politician* to his friend. "I think that it is the best thing that I have done – at any rate, I don't think I can do any better – and for that very reason I should like it to be inscribed to you."[47] Because he didn't want something saccharine, the dedication simply read "To Harold Adams Innis." From his hospital bed, Innis told him that his gesture meant a lot to him "in the siege of this time." Indeed, he regarded it as "the highest honour, academic or otherwise," that he had ever received. Creighton may have been his protégé in the early 1930s, but that was a long time ago. Now, he shaped Innis's thinking, especially on the subject of Canada, Britain, and the United States. Innis was especially pleased to learn that Creighton had declined to participate in a volume of essays on Canada's British inheritance and its creeping Americanization. The Macdonald biography would be the best contribution he could make to the ongoing debate about Canada, its history, and its future, and he must not allow himself to be sidetracked by small writing projects.[48] Innis's hopes were confirmed when Creighton arranged for a galley proof to be sent to him. In a brief reprieve that summer, he managed to read it and found himself absorbed by both its style and content. Writing to John Gray, he said that it will "compel a re-writing" of Canadian history "which has been slanted toward the liberal view."[49]

Creighton left England in late August and arrived in Toronto on the morning of 3 September 1952. That afternoon, he visited Innis at his North Toronto home. Somehow a terribly frail Innis found the strength to stand up and greet his old friend. They enjoyed a long talk about university politics and about the comings and goings of their families. It had been decided that Luella and Cynthia would stay in England while Philip finished his studies at Balliol, that Donald would rent a room at Hart House, and that he would return to Oxford in the spring.[50]

When *The Young Politician* was finally published in early October, Creighton delivered a copy to Innis. But what little strength Innis had in early September was now gone. Too weak to hold the volume, which to him felt like a piece of granite, Innis directed him to lay it on his chest and, thanking his friend, he ran his hands over the yellow dust jacket. They talked for a minute or two but Innis quickly tired and Creighton was overcome. Returning to Flavelle House, he bumped into one of his graduate students and, needing someone to talk to, invited him for a walk. It was a lovely fall afternoon. The maple leaves had turned their distinctive red, orange, and yellow hues and were now gathering in great piles against fences and along walls. Walking through Queen's Park, Creighton unburdened himself. No one, he said, fighting back the tears, could replace Innis.[51] Not even the death of his parents a few years before had affected him so deeply. Parents live into old age and their adult children bury them. That is the order of things. Innis wasn't supposed to die.

But there was a book to promote, and, a few weeks later, he took the train to Ottawa, where his hotel room happened to overlook the Rideau Canal, a key link in the commercial empire of the St Lawrence. The last time he had been in the Château Laurier it was to meet Innis. In December 1950 the two men found themselves in the nation's capital – Innis was a member of the Royal Commission on Transportation and Creighton was deep into the Macdonald papers at the Public Archives. At the end of their respective work days, they liked to meet for dinner at the Château. The Korean War had started that June, and, by the fall, Canada had committed ground troops. Both Innis and Creighton viewed the war as an American war, not as a United Nations war, and were deeply troubled by Canada's willingness to participate in what they interpreted as "an obvious adventure of American military imperialism."[52] Following the United States into war constituted an "unprecedented step"[53] in Canadian foreign policy and proved – in their minds at least – that Innis had been right all along: Canada had gone from colony to nation to colony, or from empire to empire. That day's *Globe and Mail* carried a sombre front-page story: Canadian forces had engaged in a fierce fire fight and suffered some of its heaviest casualties to date.[54]

In the morning, Creighton visited a Sparks Street bookstore for a meet-and-greet and book signing but the main event took place that evening when he presented a leather-bound copy of *John A. Macdonald: The Young Politician* to Prime Minister Louis St Laurent. The idea had been John Gray's. Initially, he had requested just a few minutes of the prime minister's time. Perhaps, he suggested, the prime minister could receive the book in his office or, failing that, on the steps of the East Block. But someone in the Prime Minister's Office had a sense of occasion. John A. Macdonald wasn't any prime minister, he was the first prime minister, and Donald Creighton wasn't any historian, "he was one of Canada's eminent historians." In other words, there would be a formal ceremony followed by a short reception at the prime minister's new residence, 24 Sussex Drive.[55]

Nine days later Harold Innis died, and the next seventy-two hours were a blur: Creighton went instantly to see Mary; he met with senior university administrators; he spoke to the undertaker; he helped Mary select a burial plot; and he served as an honorary pall-bearer. "Brief, dignified, and moving," the funeral service at Convocation Hall was "remarkably good," he said. Afterwards, he drove with the Innis family to the burial itself, where, with a small handful of mourners, he huddled around the edge of the grave as a "bitter" November wind blew and the casket was slowly lowered into the ground.[56]

Creighton was completely "worn out," physically and emotionally. And yet he still confronted an "endless succession of duties": lectures, seminars, thesis chapters, and committee meetings pressed in on him and, on top of everything else, he had agreed to write Innis's obituary for CBC Radio. It was too much, but what choice did he have? Exhausted, lonely, and "depressed," he wrote two long letters to Luella from his small room in Hart House. He had been reading, "of all things," he said, the time plays of the British playwright, J.B. Priestley, a series of four plays that explore the meaning of time through flashbacks, flash forwards, stoppages, reversals, and recurrences. In one play, the undertaker keeps looking at his watch – an obvious reference to the pitiless march of time – while the main character, although dead, plays the lead role in the re-enactment of his life. Priestley believed that time was not only linear, it was also circular and simultaneous. If Priestley was right, if the past recurs in the future and the future unfolds in the present, then maybe Innis wasn't really dead. But of course Innis was dead. Macdonald was dead too. That was the point: everyone dies. Time can't be stopped any more than the dead can come back to life.

Donald missed Luella desperately and he wanted the release of making love when, for a brief moment, time stands still.

> My sweet, sweet darling, I want you so badly that I can hardly bear it. I wish that you were in my arms, and that your body was naked and that my face was pressed against your full white breasts. It is a lovely body, so smooth and womanly, and I wish I could kiss all its adorable hills and curves and hollows. And I am so damned hungry for the delight of making love to you that I don't seem to be able to think of anything else.

A few days later, he reported that the weather had turned, that the temperature was dropping and Toronto was being pelted with a heavy rain.

> I wish we were together tonight, and that you would let me come into your bed, and that you would slip your nightdress down from your bosom, and press my face against your full smooth breasts and tender nipples. I feel so damned lonely.[57]

He used the language of the Canadian landscape – of hills and curves and hollows – because he knew it so well. And he acknowledged that *she* must let him into *her* bed because he knew the rules.

VI

The Young Politician received glowing reviews in newspapers and magazines across Canada, the United States, and Great Britain. The *Kingston Whig-Standard* called it "careful and perceptive"; the *Winnipeg Free Press* described it as "indispensable"; and the *Saskatoon Star-Phoenix* predicted that "it will occupy a unique place in Canadian letters for a long time to come." "Definitive," said the *New York Times*; "dramatic," said the *Nation*; and, at long last, a Canadian biography that is not "stiff, tedious, and cold," said the *Times Literary Supplement*. The *Manchester Guardian* happily announced that Canadian history was not dull after all. *Canadian Business* reported that *The Young Politician* had all of "the excitement of a who-dun-it," while *Saturday Night* called its author a "literary artist."

Only the *Globe and Mail* carried a critical review. William Arthur Deacon may have harboured odd Theosophical notions about the dawning of a New Age and the promise of universal brotherhood, but he functioned as a gatekeeper in the world of Canadian writing because, as the *Globe*'s literary editor, he determined what got reviewed and who got to review it. Through Ryerson Press, he had known W.B. Creighton; years before, he had given Jack Creighton the opportunity to write book reviews in *Saturday Night*; but now he proceeded to trash *The Young Politician*. It was neither "brilliant" nor "imaginative"; it wasn't even a "narrative." Instead, it was a "sober, scholarly, plainly written record of the facts." It was, he gratuitously added, the sort of "solid statement we should expect from a professor of history at the University of Toronto and even more from the author of *Dominion of the North* and *The Economic* [sic] *Empire of the St. Lawrence.*" Deacon's assessment was supercilious and catty; in Creighton's words, it was "stupid" and "semi-literate," but it still sent him into a "very real depression."[58]

But he was quickly cheered by the numerous congratulatory letters he received from Canadians across the country, including Maude Grant, George Grant's mother, Bruce Hutchison, Arthur Meighen, John Diefenbaker, Davie Fulton, and Lester Pearson, his former colleague in Toronto's Department of History. An avuncular, almost paternal, Lorne Pierce – who had been a friend of his father's – said that he was proud of him. During a House of Commons debate on a memorial to Robert Borden, a CCF Member of Parliament invoked *The Young*

Politician as, in its own way, a memorial to another great prime minister. In a later debate on Canadian broadcasting, the leader of the CCF, M.J. Coldwell, reminded his honourable friends in the Progressive Conservative Party that Sir John A. Macdonald had defended Canada through thick and through thin and that they could do worse than read Professor Creighton's new book.[59]

Bill Deacon's "stupid" and "semi-literate" review notwithstanding, Creighton was delighted by his book's reception. He had done something that no other Canadian historian had done: he had transformed the genre of biography; he had written a book that people actually read; he had been cited in the House of Commons; he had met with the current prime minister; he had received a kind note from a former prime minister; and he had been described as "one of the half-dozen best historians now writing anywhere in the English-speaking world" in *The Spectator*, a British journal of ideas and culture. "Elated" by Max Beloff's "beautiful review," he pasted a copy into his diary.

Not surprisingly, *The Young Politician* did exceptionally well: it sold 11,387 copies; it earned $7,197.28 in royalties; and it received the 1953 Governor General's Award for Academic Non-Fiction. Although anyone else would have been pleased by the award, Creighton found the whole thing "annoying." The category "academic non-fiction" as distinct from "creative non-fiction" was, he said, "offensive," "stupid," and "invidious" because it implied that academic writing couldn't be creative and that creative writing couldn't be academic. Had he not demonstrated that academic writing could aspire to more than the sum of its footnotes and the length of its bibliography? It's a good thing, he added, that he had been unable to attend the banquet dinner because he might have flung the "damned medal back in their faces!"[60]

If *The Young Politician* struck a resonant chord with readers, it struck a different chord with historians. Some loved it and some hated it, but no one was indifferent to it. Arthur Lower admired his colleague's accomplishment but also described it as over-written: "The adjective kills the noun. The adverb mutilates the verb." Taking her cure from Matthew 19:23, Hilda Neatby conceded that it is "easier for a camel to go through the eye of a needle than for a biographer not to be partisan" but Creighton's treatment of George Brown surely compromised "the principles of scholarship." George Stanley really liked the book but he too questioned Creighton's depiction of Brown, admittedly a bigoted and unsympathetic character, he said. In their respective reviews, C.P. Stacey and Albert Corey observed that Creighton never really attempted to understand Canadian-American relations, while a Barnard College professor detected a "censorious" attitude to the United States. Stating that he was going to be "very severe" in his criticisms, the University of Montreal historian Michel Brunet attacked Creighton's Achilles' heel. As he had in his previous books,

Creighton depicted French Canadians as "sullen" and "reluctant." One French-Canadian politician was simply "incompetent" while two others were "undistinguished mediocrities." Surely, Brunet asked, there were lightweights and nobodies from English Canada? Brunet admitted that his English-Canadian counterpart had consulted a tremendous range of sources but had ignored other sources, especially French-language sources. As a result, his treatment of Confederation was one-sided because it failed to include French-Canadian opposition to Confederation.[61]

In a thoughtful review, W.L. Morton grasped *The Young Politician*'s larger purpose: to articulate and defend Canada's separateness in North America. Creighton's Macdonald knew that there were only two defences against nineteenth-century American "insolence" and "aggression." One was the British connection. The other was British North American union. "To desire to be Canadian by preserving the British tie and British values was not to be anti-American, and Macdonald was not anti-American. But he was British and by remaining British became Canadian." Against the backdrop of the Cold War, the Korean War, and continental defence initiatives – against the backdrop of what Morton called an "aroused and swollen American power" – *The Young Politician* was a "timely reminder" of Canada's primitive instincts and its vital connection to Great Britain.[62]

VII

Donald's two pleading letters to Luella led to a change of plans: she would return to Canada in February, and together they would return to Oxford in May. He needed her; by his own admission, he didn't like being a widower. When they finally met at Montreal's Windsor Hotel, they couldn't stop talking. She told him about Philip and Cynthia and about the progress of her novel. He told her about receiving a $2,000 grant from the Rockefeller Foundation and about his plans for the second volume. And of course, they talked about Harold Innis. In fact, they were going to rent a room from Mary Innis for the next three months. Returning to Toronto by train, Donald and Luella unpacked their suitcases at 92 Dunvegan and fell into their routines. She worked on her novel; he resumed chapter one of volume two; and in the evenings they read to each other.[63] She wanted to get the dialogue right and he wanted to hear the words on the page. As writers, they understood that the sequence of words, their arrangement and their rhythm, prepares the reader for certain further sequences. The sound of a word doesn't matter in analytic prose. But it matters in narrative prose. The right word propels readers forward; the wrong word stops them in their tracks.

That spring they returned to Oxford. They still talked about moving to England and about maybe buying a house. Creighton even made discreet inquiries at Oxford, Cambridge, London, and Bristol. All told, it was a marvellous couple of months: he got caught up in the excitement of Eights Week, the annual rowing regatta between Oxford's many colleges; he dined with the master of Balliol College; attended several functions at Rhodes House; toured the private gardens of Christ Church Cathedral; went to Stratford to see *Richard III* and *King Lear*; and attended a meeting of the Commonwealth University Congress at St John's College and King's College in Cambridge, England's other ancient university city. Meanwhile, his work took him to London and the Institute of Historical Research, where he met Lewis Namier, one of the great British historians; it took him to Kimberley House in Wymondham, where, in a room with windows that stretched from the floor to the ceiling, he read the 1st Earl of Kimberley's diary; and it took him to Bowood House in Wiltshire to consult the papers of the 5th Marquess of Lansdowne, Governor General of Canada in the 1880s. The estate caretaker led him to the current Lord Lansdowne's study, which looked towards the lake, past terraces, neatly trimmed hedges, and a perfectly manicured lawn. At one point, he was even served a meal of grouse that had been shipped from Scotland.[64]

It was both a constant delight and a massive lie. The England of Oxford and Cambridge and eighteenth-century country estates wasn't England. It was a dream-like version of England made possible by a rigid class system and a hereditary peerage. The realities of rationing, austerity, working-class resistance, rural poverty, and industrial pollution neither obstructed Creighton's view from Lord Lansdowne's personal study nor interrupted his meal of Scottish grouse. Ultimately, his romanticized and idealized England would clash with the realities of a post-1945 England unable to maintain its imperial power. But that lay in the future. Right now, he had to get back to Toronto, and, in mid-September, he, Luella, and Cynthia boarded the *Empress of France*. Six days later, they entered the Gulf of St Lawrence and, from the forward deck, watched as the "high hills of the Laurentians began to gradually appear" on the horizon.[65]

It had been decided that Luella and Cynthia would rent an apartment and that Donald would take a room at Hart House. He needed time to finish the book that had consumed him and, at times, overwhelmed him. If he had been writing the biography of a Liberal prime minister, it would have been different, he explained. He would have had the munificent services of Grit Historical Enterprises. Like Richard Dawson writing the biography of "Billy King," he

Donald, Luella, and Cynthia on the *Empress of France* returning to Canada in 1953. From the forward deck, they watched as the "high hills of the Laurentians began to gradually appear" on the horizon.

would have had "stenographers, typists, and filing clerks" at his beck and call; he would have had "really able historians" preparing "indexes, calendars and digests of the documents"; and he would have had "people to get material" for him and "other people to verify" everything he had written. But no, he was writing the biography of a Conservative prime minister, meaning he had to do his own research, his own note taking, and his own fact checking. "*I have done every damned bit of this work myself,*" he thundered.[66]

For the next two years he worked around the clock. In addition to teaching a full course load, supervising a handful of graduate students, and chairing a Graduate School committee, he was writing nearly a chapter a month. It was a cruel pace sustainable only at the expense of his physical and emotional health. At one point, his face and chest erupted in a painful rash. At another point, he collapsed. Describing it as "a crisis of depression and nerves," he felt "dreadful." He was "sick of everything," he said, and "wept" frequently and inconsolably. Two days later, he went to Muskoka, where, on a warm spring afternoon, he sat on the veranda reading Charles Dickens. He hadn't read *A Tale of Two Cities* since his mother had read it to him as a small boy.[67] He loved the cottage for its many associations and memories: his mother and father, his brother and sister, and now Luella, Philip, and Cynthia. It was his own little piece of the Laurentian Shield where he could enjoy lazy afternoons on the lake and long evenings in front of the fire, where, in short, he could recharge his batteries.

But the relentless pressure of high expectations never went away. He wasn't just writing a biography of John A. Macdonald. He was writing his country's reason for being.

VIII

Published in 1955, *The Old Chieftain* opens in Ottawa, where politics confronts geography and where the Laurentian thesis would or would not be realized. It was a "raw, overgrown, lumber town" consisting of "rows of ugly mid-Victorian terraces and semi-detached villas and a fringe of untidy lumber-yards." The Parliament Buildings were cold, the heating system was hopelessly inadequate, and it was already feeling cramped. As for Confederation, it too was a "new and unfamiliar building." "One was always blundering into new passages, bumping up against unexpected walls, discovering unfinished rooms; and periodically the uneasy suspicion returned that not enough provision had been made for this or that need, or that something had been completely forgotten." As its architect and "chief author" it fell to Macdonald to transform Confederation from a legal document into a great nation.[68]

Donald Creighton's Muskoka cottage was his own tiny piece of the Laurentian Shield and one of his favourite places on earth, both for its natural beauty and its many memories of his childhood and adolescence. In this undated picture, he is sitting on the veranda looking south across the lake at the opposite shoreline of pine, fir, and spruce trees.

The Old Chieftain follows both the public and private Macdonald through the vicissitudes of politics and the disappointments of life; it employs the same neat tricks and literary devices; and it has the same prejudices and weaknesses. Because heroes demand villains, Creighton dutifully provided his hero with a host of irritants, opponents, and enemies. To realize his Laurentian vision of a transcontinental British nation linked by the longest railway in the world, Macdonald must overcome that small-minded collection "of beards, whiskers, moustaches, bald heads, oiled locks, and tall tile hats" sitting on the Liberal side of the House; he must outsmart their leader, the "thick-set," "fat-faced," "near-sighted" Edward Blake; he must out-manoeuvre the "pestilent" Joseph Howe and his band of anti-Confederates from Nova Scotia; and he must somehow extricate himself from that pit of his own digging, the Pacific Scandal and the graft of railway politics.

The railway became Macdonald's obsession. It would extend the St Lawrence River and Great Lakes to the Pacific Ocean; it would carry settler after settler to the west; and it would fulfil the Laurentian thesis. From it everything stemmed and to it everything was owed. Indeed, the Canadian Pacific Railway wasn't a railway at all. It was "the track of destiny." When Louis Riel resisted Macdonald's vision a second time, he was met with a swift and violent response. "Deep in the final privacy of his being, [Macdonald] refused to believe that a single half-breed megalomaniac could destroy the west as a homeland for British Americans."

Meanwhile, there were other challenges and other villains. Oliver Mowat – the "fat boy" with whom Macdonald had gone to school – was now the premier of Ontario and his ongoing defence of provincial rights threatened Macdonald's federal design of a strong Ottawa and a string of subordinate provincial capitals. Following his victory over Ottawa in a protracted legal dispute over Ontario's northern boundary, Mowat "returned to Toronto in triumph, like some fabulous eastern war-lord, laden with booty and rich in territorial conquests."

And so it went: Macdonald vs Blake, Howe, Riel, and Mowat among others. In the election of 1891 – in what turned out to be his last election – Macdonald asked Canadians to reject the Liberal promise of reciprocity with the United States. Reciprocity, he believed, was another word for annexation. Indeed, Creighton added, that was "the fundamental purpose of the United States": "to starve Canada into annexation." Meanwhile, Macdonald's private life was a source of heavy emotional burdens and crushing financial obligations. It was, in short, a life marked by "failure after failure."[69] His second marriage to Agnes Bernard in 1867 and the birth of their daughter in 1869 were supposed to have marked a new beginning, but their baby was horribly ill and would never lead anything like a normal life; alcohol and debt exacted a heavy price; and poor health haunted him.

Fifteen days before he died, Macdonald made what turned out to be his final appearance in the House of Commons. On his way home that evening, he stopped to chat with Mackenzie Bowell, his minister of customs. "It was like a summer night. The laden lilac bushes rimmed the crest of Parliament Hill, and beyond that the land fell steeply away to the river below and rose on the other side to the low dark hills of the Precambrian Shield," Creighton wrote. "And somewhere out there, hidden in the rock and forest, bright under the moonlight, was the railway, his railway, the track of Canada, the track of destiny, thrusting its way forward, mile after mile, towards the north-west."[70] As the last sentence of the last chapter in volume two, it connected to the last sentence of volume one, where the still "unconquered"[71] Shield stretched "mile after mile, towards the north-west."[72] Now, twenty-four years later, it had been "mastered," he said, by the railway.[73]

Atoning, perhaps, for his earlier review, Bill Deacon told his many readers that *The Old Chieftain* was "twice as good" as *The Young Politician*. Meanwhile, the *Victoria Daily Times* pronounced it "a Canadian masterpiece"; the *Ottawa Journal* compared its writing to that of Ernest Hemingway; the *Manchester Guardian* described it as "a valuable contribution to history and literature"; the *New York Times* said that it was "thrilling"; the *Economist* called it "absorbing"; the *Times Literary Supplement* reported that it carried not a hint "of archival dust"; and, writing in the *Spectator*, Max Beloff likened it to a novel.[74] In addition to the generous reviews, Creighton received equally generous letters from, among others, Vincent Massey, Arthur Meighen, and Isabella Gainsford, Macdonald's granddaughter. Hugh MacLennan told him that his book could hold its own when measured against world standards, while Mary Innis admitted that it brought her to tears. Harold, she added, "would have been very proud of you."[75]

In its first four years, *The Old Chieftain* sold 10,371 copies and Creighton pocketed $7,433.11 in royalties.[76] He also earned his second Governor General's Award, albeit for academic non-fiction. It had taken eleven years, two volumes, and 450,000 words, but he had become his country's greatest historian. However, beneath the praise, the hefty sales figures, and the Governor General's Award lay a number of problems.

IX

Creighton's depiction of Louis Riel and the Métis was not simply problematic, it was grotesque. Not less than eleven reviewers – including George Stanley, C.P. Stacey, and the broadcaster Gordon Sinclair – felt that he had been unfair to the leader of the Red River and Northwest Rebellions.[77] In Creighton's estimation, Riel was an "evil genius," "a self-interested American adventurer," "an arrogant dictator," and a "half-breed megalomaniac" leading a "sullen," "impressionable," "unpredictable," "restless," and "improvident" Métis people. He acknowledged that the Métis saw themselves as a nation and admitted that the transition to farming constituted a "revolutionary change." But Riel and his followers could not be allowed to refute the Laurentian thesis: the "empty prairies" belonged to the empire of the St Lawrence, not to the descendants of French traders and their Aboriginal wives.[78] On two separate occasions, John Gray had urged Creighton to reconsider his treatment of Riel and the Métis. What comes through, he told him, "is your own complete lack of sympathy" when surely "you have more sympathy for their confusion in a world they couldn't understand."[79]

Macdonald certainly did. "All these poor people know," the prime minister wrote in 1869, "is that Canada has bought the Hudson's Bay Company, and that they are to be handed over like a flock of sheep to us … and they are told that they may lose their lands and everything they value. *Under these circumstances it is not to be wondered at that they should be dissatisfied, and show their discontent.*"[80] Macdonald didn't sanction rebellion but he did, at least, extend a bit of sympathy. Creighton had read this letter and even quoted the first part. But he omitted the second – and more significant – part, which invites the reader to see events through Métis eyes. Was it an act of suppression? Probably not. After all, Creighton acknowledged that "discontent was almost inevitable" in the transfer of Rupert's Land from the Hudson's Bay Company to the Dominion of Canada.[81] Still, it was an obvious omission.

In a second letter – written, he joked, "after much prayer and fasting" – Gray invited his author to revisit his discussion of Riel's execution. It is too "violent" and too "studied," or contrived, he said.[82] But Creighton refused. He had staked his entire career on the Laurentian thesis and, like Macdonald, he wasn't going to let the Métis leader escape the noose: "The sprung trap gave and Riel dropped to his extinction."[83]

Riel may have dropped to his death but he didn't drop to his extinction. His life and the meaning of his life have continued to fascinate historians, writers, and artists for over a century, and, by the 1950s, he was well on his way to martyrdom.[84] When a Winnipeg high school teacher objected to what he called Creighton's "cavalier treatment of our own folk-hero" – the "Canadian stage," he said, is surely big enough for both Riel and Macdonald – Creighton responded that the people of Winnipeg in 1885 would be "astonished" to learn that the man behind two rebellions had become a hero.[85] Indeed, Creighton never understood the reinvention of the Métis leader and, eight years later, declined to review George Stanley's biography of Riel. He had, he explained, attempted to set the record straight in *The Old Chieftain* but had only received "a lot of abuse from journalist reviewers." Even his friend C.P. Stacey accused him, he said, of being the hanging judge. (Actually, Stacey had called him the prosecuting attorney but it was very much like Creighton to file every slight.) That a man tormented by religious visions, hallucinations, and prophecies had become one of the "sacred myths" of Canadian history seemed to him "the stupidest nonsense": "The best that can be said for Riel – a strange recommendation for a hero – is that he ought to have been in the loony-bin!"[86]

Creighton's depiction of Riel as, in part, "a self-interested American adventurer" points to another problem: his depiction of the United States. Indeed, Canada's southern neighbour haunts volume two in the same way that it haunts volume one; its manifest destiny is a continuous threat lurking between the lines and along the margins, stalking the realization of Canada's own manifest destiny – that is, its Laurentian destiny. Every so often Uncle Sam rears its ugly self, making Macdonald's task – which was and always had been "the task of building a separate and distinctive nation on the northern half of the North American continent" – that much more difficult. Against this backdrop, Creighton deliberately transformed Macdonald's National Policy – which was only a tariff policy to protect Canadian industry – into an integrated national policy of high tariffs, a transcontinental railway, western settlement, and the building of "a separate and distinctive nation" in North America. His Macdonald never underestimated the American threat and never forgot Great Britain and all it had done for British North America. He never forgot "Brock leading the volunteers up the heights at Queenston, Mackenzie toiling north towards the mouth of his great river, Colonel By driving the canal through the forest towards the Ottawa River, and Carnarvon rising in his place in the House of Lords to move the first reading of the British North America Bill." In a brilliant review of *The Old Chieftain,* Guy Frégault cut to the chase: the author's anti-Americanism and his imperialism were as obvious as they were polemical and said more about him than Macdonald.[87] As part of his own ongoing defence of the nation, Creighton had fashioned a Macdonald and a National Policy for the 1950s.

Creighton's faith in the Laurentian thesis and his Christ-like compassion for his hero excluded Macdonald as *homo politicus* and, as a result, in a biography about a prime minister, politics are oddly absent. Because everything his Macdonald did was directed at a higher purpose, Creighton missed the grubbiness of politics – party machines, vulgar Senate appointments, kickbacks, toll-gating, conflicts of interest, slush funds, vote buying, greased palms, gerrymandering, patrons, clients, brokers, troughs, pork, and the spoils of office. Of course, Creighton couldn't ignore the Pacific Scandal – a sordid affair even by nineteenth-century standards – but he blamed the opposition Liberals and a dubious businessman with connections to American railway interests. Dirty pool in the form of a break-and-enter followed by calumny and blackmail led to Macdonald's resignation in 1874, he argued. Yes, Macdonald's hands were dirty, but so what? Everyone's hands were dirty. "Everybody knew that elections were fought with money."[88] The subtext was clear: building the railway and fulfilling Canada's Laurentian destiny outweighed a lousy few thousand dollars, making *Macdonald* exculpation by biography.

Returned to power in 1878, Canada's first prime minister was not so much reformed as he was better at not getting caught because, "under the microscope, Macdonald's handiwork sometimes crawled with maggots."[89] Indeed, it may have been a breaking scandal – one that involved an inflated government contract with a fictional businessman to build a dry dock in Kingston with the real Connolly brothers, who, in turn, had kicked back contributions to the Conservative war chest – that led to Macdonald's death.[90] It wasn't like Creighton didn't have access to the grubbier underside of Macdonald's career. It was in his correspondence and it was discussed in the House of Commons. At one point, Creighton cited the nefarious connection between the Department of Public Works and the corrupt Connolly brothers but quickly moved on because it didn't conform to his romantic view of history as the story of sweeping forces, tides of change, mighty events, great men, and destinies fulfilled, which is to say that it didn't conform to his idealized vision of Macdonald as the incarnation of the Laurentian thesis.[91] But making Macdonald stand in for the Laurentian thesis came at a price because, over the course of 1,089 pages, his Macdonald becomes unbelievable. He may have been a great man, but he was not a Great Man because there are no Great Men. As a biographer, Creighton demanded too much from his subject: no one, not even Sir John A., not even Old Tomorrow, can bear the burden of the meaning of Canada.

Finally, Creighton did in volume two what he had done in volume one: he invented conversations, reactions, and private moments. He fabricated dialogue between the prime minister and a man outside his bedroom window; he put thoughts into Macdonald's head when he suspected that something was wrong with his daughter; he conjured a scene of violent pain, of a man "twisting" and "writhing" before finally "dropping into a dark void of agony" at an attack of gallstones; he imagined a shocked prime minister "shaking his head in bewilderment" while reading allegations against him in the *Globe;* and he pictured a defeated man staring in disbelief at a letter from the governor general intimating that he had lost confidence in his first minister. In one very powerful scene towards the end of the book, Agnes hands her husband a small toy that had belonged to his first son. Creighton seizes this moment as an opportunity to transport an old man back in time:

And suddenly thirty years had rushed away, and he was back in the "Italian villa" Bellevue, and the soft summer breeze from Lake Ontario was blowing in from the open window, and his first-born was playing boisterously on the bed by Isabella's side … He did not notice Agnes's departure. The room was empty. And he was staring at the floor.[92]

Like Arnold Bennett in *The Old Wives' Tale*, Creighton wanted to foreground time and its relentless passage. That he had no evidence indicating that thirty years had rushed away didn't matter. The image of an open window, a soft summer breeze, and a child playing with his toys connected by an ellipsis to the image of an empty room and an old man staring at the floor told a higher truth than historical truth: Macdonald was once a young man and had now become an old man.

Passages like this led Arthur Lower to roll his eyes. Writing in the pages of the *United Church Observer*, he asked for less Lytton Strachey and more "cold-blooded examination" of the facts.[93] In a sense, Lower was right – Creighton's many inventions, embroideries, and fabrications violated the rules of evidence, or what Hilda Neatby called "the principles of scholarship." In a 1971 lecture, Creighton acknowledged his critics.

I have been reproached on occasion for putting particular thoughts, aims, and plans in the heads of my historical characters at particular moments. How do I know, is the decisive question, that these specific ideas were passing through their minds at this exact point of time? The answer is, of course, that I don't know.[94]

He might have added, too, that he didn't care because fictional truth, he believed, could be greater than historical truth. If literature is "a process of producing grand, beautiful, well-ordered lies that tell more truth than any assemblage of facts," then lying is the "best way of telling the truth."[95] To communicate the truth as he understood it, Creighton had to do more than assemble facts. He had to lie. He had to push the limits of the form and, in the process, invent a new form. As a writer, he knew that his two selves, his artist self and his historian self, often collided. Driven by an inner urge to create *and* to understand, he never attempted to reconcile the one with the other because he also knew that his best writing came out of those very collisions. And if his imagination occasionally overwhelmed his evidence, it didn't matter because his genius was Thomas Carlyle's genius – it was the rare ability "to bring dead things and dead people back to life; to make the past once more the present, and to show us men and women playing their parts on the mortal stage as real flesh-and-blood human creatures."[96]

Despite its faults, or perhaps because of its faults, Creighton's two-volume biography of Canada's first prime minister remains a remarkable accomplishment. It is still in print and still casts a shadow over Macdonald scholars. In the same way that Virginia Woolf predicted that "Lytton Strachey's Queen Victoria will be Queen Victoria," Donald Creighton's John A. Macdonald became John A. Macdonald, and the problem of all Macdonald biographers is the problem of Donald Creighton.[97]

When Macdonald became ill, Agnes summoned the doctors. But her husband's condition was more serious than a cold, and, when he suffered a series of strokes, there was nothing they could do. He had lost his mobility and his speech. Then, as the sun sank beneath "the long blue line of the Laurentians," his breathing grew slow and shallow, his burdens lifted, and he was carried "past care and planning, past England and Canada, past life and into death." Macdonald was buried in the family plot in Kingston, which stood, Creighton observed in volume one, "at the head of the St. Lawrence" and "at the foot of the vast, interconnecting system of the Great Lakes."

> It was nearly seventy-one years since Hugh and Helen Macdonald and their small family of children had first set foot on the dock at Kingston. Beyond the dock lay the harbour and the islands which marked the end of the lowest of the Great Lakes; and beyond the islands the St Lawrence River began its long journey to the sea.[98]

In the final two sentences of volume two, Creighton brought the reader back to the opening sentence of volume one, invoking the Laurentian thesis for a final time.

Although he acknowledged its beauty, John Gray also felt that it was too "studied" and wondered if readers would make the connection between the river and Macdonald. Perhaps, he suggested, another sentence or two could be added. But Creighton refused to spell it out: as an artist, he knew that art is never made clearer by the insertion of an explanation and that, in this case, an explanatory sentence would violate the effect he wanted. He had deliberately conceived the final paragraph, he said, as a diminuendo – a musical term for a sudden decrease in volume – in order to give the reader an opportunity for quiet reflection and contemplation of the biography's ultimate purpose. "The St. Lawrence is a symbol of Canadian unity – a symbol of an east-west transcontinental system, a symbol of our relationship with Great Britain and separation from the United States."[99]

When that symbol could no longer contain Canada's many faultlines, it collapsed. So too would its author: the burden of being Donald Creighton was not an easy one, especially since he had agreed to take on a major administrative responsibility.

FALL

"My God," he said once, his voice suddenly breaking with emotion. "What a country we could have been. What a country we were one time."

Wayne Johnston, *Baltimore's Mansion*

chapter nine

Chairman

The Reform leader was a difficult colleague: reserved, sensitive, moody, and impulsive; touchy about everything that concerned superiority and precedence, and already quite obviously jealous of Galt.

John A. Macdonald, vol. 1

In June 1954 the president of the University of Toronto invited Donald Creighton to the York Club. Over gin and tonics on the veranda, Sidney Smith informed him that, effective January 1st, he would be the next chairman of the history department with a salary of $9,000. Describing it as "a very important day" in his life, Creighton had achieved one of his greatest ambitions. A few years earlier he had been bitterly disappointed when he didn't get the nod, when it went instead on an interim basis to Ralph Flenley, a much older and more senior member of the department. But as the department's most accomplished scholar, Creighton believed that he had a stronger "claim," that he was Chester Martin's heir apparent, not Flenley and certainly not that Brit, Bertie Wilkinson, or that writer of textbooks, George Brown. By turns "annoyed" and "depressed," he remarked that "age seems to be all you need to get you places these days."[1] However, Creighton wanted the job for the wrong reasons because what he really wanted was the recognition it implied. His desperate need to be recognized meant that he could never be happy or, at least, that he could never be happy for very long. In this instance, it also meant that he couldn't see his own inability to manage men and his emotional unfitness to negotiate conflict.

Even as he and Luella celebrated his appointment they talked about its "implications."[2] Administering a large department, in a complex arts faculty, in an expanding university, would mean less time for writing, the very thing he enjoyed most in life. Of course, Creighton was no stranger to hard work. In a few weeks he would be fifty two. If no longer a young man, he wasn't an old man either and he still had – or, more to the point, he believed that he still had – the reserves needed to carry out his many university assignments and maintain an active program of research and writing. But his emotional collapse that spring should have been a sign. Had he been able to look into a crystal ball, he never would have accepted Sidney Smith's offer.

And had Luella been able to look into the same crystal ball and seen its catalogue of disasters, she would have put her foot down. But she wanted the position for the same wrong reasons that he wanted it. In a way, it was more important to her because it increased the distance between her life in Toronto and her childhood in Stouffville. And yet, her writing kept taking her back.

II

In February, Luella had published her second novel. Like *High Bright Buggy Wheels, Turn East, Turn West* is set in the fictional town of Kinsail and follows the story of Laura Paparin, a high-spirited, red-haired young woman who has returned from Red Wing, Manitoba, also a fictional town, just outside of Winnipeg. Laura's mother, Emma Paparin, is a cold, emotionally distant woman who openly resents both her husband and her daughter, blaming them for her own unhappiness. Although Laura's father, Johnny Paparin, is a kind man, he has been broken by his wife and by his own drinking. Later he will effectively abandon Laura when he dies in a bizarre, alcohol-soaked riding accident that was almost certainly a suicide. Meanwhile, Laura's mother has a stroke and loses her mobility and her speech. Literally and figuratively silenced, she can no longer stop her daughter from living her life on her terms. At one point, Laura announces that she won't clean the same house day after day for the rest of her life, declaring that she will not "be a sacrifice to chairs and tables and floors and ceilings." But the town gossips: Laura Paparin is a fallen woman. Determined to save her, the Methodist minister invites her to a private meeting where, in a moment of anger and lust, he throws himself at her. He "crossed the small space between them, put out his hand to steady her, and caught the swell of breast that moved the circling lace. Horror mounting in his eyes, he clasped her roughly to him, kissing her again and again on the mouth, and the slender throat, on the little triangle of white flesh beneath her ear, and in the hollow of her lace-bound bosom." The town continues to gossip when the minister is reassigned to a new church and Laura falls further into confusion and isolation. Meanwhile, the boy Laura loves doesn't care about the gossip because he only wants what he assumes she had given the minister, telling her that he too wouldn't mind a little "fun." At that moment, the "memory of the minister's hot hands pressing through the lace on her back, his broken tortured face, and his mouth on her breast," compels Laura to throw herself into a fast-moving river. But something tells her to fight the current, and, in the end, she marries the young man who had always loved her from a distance and they move to Red Wing.[3]

Like all of Luella's writing, *Turn East, Turn West* mined the themes of her childhood and adolescence: a cruel mother, an ineffectual father, a hypocritical church, and a determined young woman. In an address to the Empire Club of Canada that April, Luella admitted that her writing grew out of her necessity to tell a story and that it drew on her own experiences and on her own memories, memories, she said, that she didn't even know she had until something triggered them.[4] It was as close as she ever came to acknowledging that her heroines – Virginia, Tillie, and Laura – represented some aspect of herself.

By this point, she had resolved that her next book would be very different. She was tired, she said, of girls. And she was tired of Kinsail. It was time to examine the interior life of a middle-aged woman.[5]

III

In December 1954, Moffat Woodside met with the Department of History in his capacity as dean of arts to announce that Donald Creighton would be the next chairman. According to one member, the news hit the place "like a thunderbolt." A "visibly shaken" Wilkinson was furious that his younger colleague had been appointed ahead of him. And a "much upset" George Brown called an emergency, invitation-only, early-morning meeting at his home to discuss what, if anything, might be done. Of course, nothing could be done. The senior administration had made its decision, and, as "bewildering" as it was, its decision was final. "Top brass will be top brass," said a resigned Donald McDougall. In a sense, his colleagues knew Creighton better than he knew himself: "reserved, sensitive, moody, and impulsive," he was completely ill-equipped to lead a department marked by strong personalities, ancient animosities, ambitious juniors, and brewing resentments.[6]

For his part, Frank Underhill resigned on short notice when he was appointed curator of Laurier House in Ottawa. "I haven't looked forward with great joy to continuing in the present department with Don Creighton as head," he confessed.[7] And who could blame him? Creighton and Underhill had never been close, but there had been an initial and mutual respect: when Underhill was threatened with dismissal, Creighton rallied to his defence. But in the late 1940s and early 1950s, that respect evaporated, leaving behind a residual tension punctuated by occasional outbursts, intemperate remarks, and, on Creighton's part, name calling. If everyone respected Creighton, they adored Underhill. One member of the department even told him that, had there been an election, he would have been the department's next chairman.[8] He was approachable, irreverent, and a wonderful lecturer with a somewhat "salty style" and dry sense of humour.[9] Because the students looked up to him with an awe bordering on hero worship, an "obviously jealous" Creighton brooded, never seeing in Underhill what other people saw.[10] In his eyes, he was at best a journalist and at worst a phoney: why, "the pot-bellied little bastard" still hadn't completed his biography of Edward Blake, the nineteenth-century Liberal leader. In fact, he would never complete a major work of scholarship. Years later, Creighton asked one colleague what, exactly, had made Underhill so popular with students? It was a "poignant" moment, Ken McNaught recalled. "I had no better answer than the man who was asked if he had stopped beating his wife."[11]

The Creighton-Underhill feud was personal – they simply didn't like each other – but it was also intellectual: the editor of the *Canadian Forum*, the founder of the League for Social Reconstruction, and the author of the Regina Manifesto had become a Mackenzie King Liberal. In a way, Underhill's intellectual transformation from interwar socialist to postwar liberal was not a transformation at all: his liberalism had always come before his socialism, and he now defended Mackenzie King and endorsed American leadership in the Cold War. According to Underhill, King had been right to put Canada's eggs in a North American basket. Canada was a North American nation and its "fundamental interests" were "identical with American interests." Fears of the American bogeyman and of the American empire, he argued, were red herrings pursued by a collection of lonely communists, a diehard rump of English-Canadian Tory nationalists, and a handful of professors "who are still thinking up nasty wisecracks about American imperialism regardless of the fact that most of their own pet research projects are apt to be financed by money from Rockefeller or Carnegie or Guggenheim" or, in Creighton's case, all three.[12] Underhill didn't have to refer to his colleague by name because everyone knew whom he was talking about.

Although he has been dismissed as a "venomous" anti-American whose anti-Americanism "was arguably the fiercest of any in the last half of the twentieth century," Creighton was much more thoughtful.[13] Refusing the brutal and simplistic Us versus Them logic of the Cold War, he took his intellectual cue from Herbert Butterfield's 1953 Beckly Social Service Lecture, *Christianity, Diplomacy, and War*. The Cold War, Butterfield said, was a "war for righteousness," "for the vindication of morality," and "for the destruction of the wicked." Like all wars for righteousness and great holy crusades against moral evils, it was also an "unlimited" war marked by "hatred," "viciousness," and "the refusal to compromise." The greatest threat to "our civilization" wasn't communism; it was "the conflict between giant organized systems of self-righteousness – each system only too delighted to find that the other is wicked – each only too glad that the sins give it the pretext for still deeper hatred and animosity." The real test of moral courage, he said, was not the demonization of the Other; it was "the exposure and the condemnation of our own sins as a nation and an empire."[14]

To expose and condemn American sins of nation and empire, Creighton delivered a public lecture at a conference organized by Westinghouse Canada in November 1953. Entitled "Canada's Tomorrow" and held at Quebec City's Château Frontenac, the conference brought together a handful of public intellectuals to consider Canada's possible futures. Although he hadn't finished the Macdonald biography, Creighton agreed to participate not least because it carried a $1,000 honorarium, or about an eighth of his 1952–3 salary. Starting from the premise that Canadian foreign policy had two historical objectives – to achieve autonomy in the British Empire and to remain separate in North America – he argued that the "squat," "solid," and "unremarkable" Mackenzie King had committed the country to the first objective at the expense of the second in the interwar years. Following his lead was a "new generation of politicians, publicists, journalists, and professors," men like Oscar Skelton, John W. Dafoe, and, of course, Frank Underhill. As "professional Canadian nationalists," they extolled "the sufficiency and normality of our North Americanism."

> It was pointed out on numerous occasions and with the greatest possible complacency that the Canadian now played baseball, ate dry cereals, chewed gum, smoked blended cigarettes, drank rye whiskey and lager beer; and it was intimated hopefully that if he only persevered in these respectable American activities for a sufficiently long time, he would eventually realize his true personality in the image of his great neighbour, the United States.

From the vantage point of North American conformity – of baseball, blended cigarettes, and lager beer – "Great Britain was an alien and sinister world, crowded with a deplorable collection of snobs, imperialists, and trouble-makers generally, with whom, obviously, we should have as little as possible to do." But the American mission to save the world from communism was neither wholly benevolent nor purely altruistic. It stemmed from its own economic and military interests, especially in Asia. As an imperial power, the United States "put itself and kept itself in that most odious of all political roles, the role of the wealthy foreigner who supports the hated counter-revolution. The prolonged American intervention in the politics of the Far East enabled the Communists to enlist the potent force of Asian nationalism on their side and to hold up the United States as the last and worst of the foreign imperialist oppressors." America's – and Canada's – subsequent refusal to recognize China, he said, was like refusing to admit that Everest was a high mountain or that yesterday was a rainy day. Because the United Nations risked becoming an anti-communist alliance for the pursuit of American foreign policy objectives, Creighton placed his faith in the British Commonwealth, "a truly cosmopolitan organization" that "unites contrasted cultures" and "bridges rival continents."[15]

Buoyed, perhaps, by the success of his Quebec City address – Lester Pearson had read it and he too seemed "baffled" and "alarmed" by the direction and tone of American foreign policy[16] – Creighton delivered a follow-up performance at the annual meeting of the Canadian Institute of Economics and Politics, better known as the Couchiching Conference. Sounding a familiar note, he criticized the United States for its aggressive actions in Korea, its recent incursion in Guatemala, and its refusal to recognize China. He also described the Chinese nationalist regime in Taiwan as a "discredited satellite" and reproved both the United Sates and Canada for the "self-righteous fiction that the Chinese are diplomatic untouchables." Likening the word of Washington to the word of God, he said that it had the force of "divine revelation" when it was really just a great "sales campaign to sell the Cold War, in an exclusive American package, to the rest of the world."[17]

Creighton got as good as he gave. As chair, John Diefenbaker "took the occasion to announce publicly that he completely dissociated himself from" the professor's "strange opinions."[18] But it fell to Marcus Long, a Toronto philosophy professor, to deliver the formal response. He was "astonished," he said, by the anti-American and un-Canadian tone and content of the paper, calling it "a sustained and bitter attack on the United States." Condemning its extreme language – Creighton had depicted the United States as a "diplomatic gangster" patrolling the world with "sawed-off shotguns"[19] – Long towed the official line. The United States does not patrol the world, he said, it defends the "right of nations to determine their own form of government based on the consent of the governed."[20] In a way, both Diefenbaker and Long confirmed Creighton's point that public criticism of the United States was outside the perimeter of permissible discourse.

When the *Globe and Mail* reported Creighton's speech on the front page, it received at least one furious letter to the editor demanding his immediate resignation from the University of Toronto. As a "professor of lying propaganda," he should not be allowed to teach history to "the youth of this country."[21] In an editorial entitled "Professors get out of focus, too," the *Vancouver Province* accused Creighton of distorting American foreign policy and of towing a Red line.[22] An anonymous letter writer told him to pack up and go live in Russia, while someone else sent him a deranged three-page rant. Calling Creighton "a miserable and vile mouthpiece and dupe blowing the communist's red bugle," he pictured him "in the first row with those who gladly will kiss dirty boots and lick, with a watering mouth, the backsides of the red invaders." But all the boot-kissing and ass-licking in the world won't save you, he said, when Canada is overrun by those "savage hordes of reds": "At this moment, you will receive a final reward – a shot in your half-rotten brains from a small calibre gun from a professor of history of the Bolshevik party."[23]

On the whole, though, Creighton received a favourable response. The *Globe and Mail* explicitly defended Creighton's academic freedom and printed four letters in response to J.F. Boland's initial letter. "Since when, outside of Communist Russia, Fascist Italy, Nazi Germany and lesser vicious political entities, has state control of universities meant that professors must conform with the state or party line in their opinions?" one person asked. And because it had broadcast his address on national radio, the CBC received seventy-one letters, seventy favourable, one unfavourable.[24] Meanwhile, the historian George Stanley congratulated him. "When you were speaking my enthusiasm rose," he said. "And when Diefenbaker made his little comment and Long his little sneers I choked with rage. All of which simply says that I was glad to hear somebody speak out as you did and say things that needed to be said."[25] Although Creighton was generally "gratified by the support" he received, he also learned that public "dissent from the orthodox Canadian belief in the disinterested wisdom of the American leadership of 'the free world' was highly unwelcome" in official circles, making it on balance a "disturbing experience."[26]

In a way, it was his own fault. Ad hominem attacks against Mackenzie King and comparisons of American diplomats to Chicago gangsters with mono-syllabic vocabularies overwhelmed his larger ethical argument: the Cold War was a war for righteousness that demanded blind allegiance to a dangerous and Manichaean world view of Good versus Evil. Like Herbert Butterfield, Creighton saw through the fanatical hypocrisy of a war "for the extermination of all those heretics who refuse to accept our principles and share our way of life." And like Harold Innis, he worried about the blind faith in technology as the solution to every problem. Our "reliance on the machine," he said, conditions us to accept "instant retaliation by the terrible devices of push-button warfare" and to accept force as both a means and an end. "The most complimentary adjective which an American newspaper correspondent can apply to the foreign policy of his country is 'tough.'"[27] But Creighton lacked Butterfield's calm moral vision and never fully grasped Innis's dark but equally moral vision. As a result, where Butterfield was measured, Creighton was excessive, and where Innis was thoughtful, he was shrill.

By his own admission, Innis's death in November 1952 represented "a tremendous loss." It not only robbed him of "the support that can come only from a long friendship," it left him feeling "very much alone" at precisely the moment he assumed the chairmanship of English Canada's largest and most important department of history.[28]

IV

Creighton had been chairman for less than ten months in the fall of 1955 when he began to wonder what he had gotten himself into. Frank Underhill's sudden resignation that September meant that he had to scramble to fill a hole, and Maurice Careless's leave of absence meant that he couldn't accept an invitation from the government of West Germany to visit a number of German universities that November and December. As well, the department found itself bogged down in a curriculum fight that divided members by rank and by field. Although sympathetic to the junior members who wanted to broaden the curriculum and reduce its emphasis on North America, Great Britain, and western Europe, Creighton was bound by a committee of senior members that didn't see what the fuss was all about. Of course, the fight was not about adding Asian history to the curriculum. Nor was it about where and when to divide the British history survey. It was about power, the future of the department, and Creighton's own inability to mediate a happy solution. "My chairmanship so far seems to have been nothing but a record of misfortunes," he told Dean Woodside.[29]

What he really wanted was time to write. The publication of *The Old Chieftain* in September had lifted a tremendous weight off his shoulders, but even before its completion, he had agreed to write a short single-volume history of Canada for the British publisher Faber and Faber, in part because he didn't want Arthur Lower or Edgar McInnis or anyone else to have the opportunity. In his mind, he was the only historian worthy of the assignment. But what about his next big book? Sidney Smith wanted him to write the biography of Robert Borden, putting tremendous pressure on him to commit himself. And for years, Lord Beaverbrook had been after him to write the biography of another Conservative prime minister, Richard Bennett. In November 1954, he informed Creighton that he would be in Toronto and that he would like to meet with him. Creighton was duly received in Beaverbrook's suite at the King Edward Hotel. Although a powerful man who was used to getting his way, Beaverbrook was disappointed by Creighton's answer. A few weeks earlier, English Canada's leading historian had met another wealthy person at the King Eddie, Mrs James A. Richardson, wife of the late James Richardson. Actually, this was their second meeting.

Brokered by a young Jack McClelland, Creighton had gone to Winnipeg in early October to meet the Richardson family and to hear their proposal for a company history of James Richardson & Sons Ltd., a venerable Canadian company based in Winnipeg with roots in Kingston. Because of its connection to the commercial empire of the St Lawrence – it was the first company to ship western Canadian grain overseas by the Great Lakes – Creighton instinctively gathered the possibilities of a subject that would allow him to carry the Laurentian thesis into the first half of the twentieth century. To cement the deal, the Richardson family agreed to pay him $30,000 plus a $5,000 bonus, or in today's dollars, $301,000. Not even Lord Beaverbrook could match that.

In addition to the single volume history of Canada and now the Richardson history, Creighton had agreed to write a short memoir of Harold Innis as well. Within days of Innis's death, several of his friends and colleagues pressed Creighton to put Macdonald aside to take up the biography of English Canada's most important thinker. But Creighton rightly refused. Still, he agreed to advise Mary Innis on the organization of her husband's papers and indicated that, once the Innis papers were catalogued, he could maybe envision writing what he called a short "interpretive biography."[30] He also agreed to sit on a committee that administered a five-year $215,000 grant from the Rockefeller Foundation to honour Innis's research on Canadian problems. Finally, the University of Toronto established its own Harold Innis Memorial Fund to make possible the republication of Innis's key books and the production of a memorial volume that would include a short account of his life by Creighton, essays on his contribution to the study of economics and politics by Del Clark and Alexander Brady, and a selection of his letters.

Although he confronted the problem of time, he continued to take on commitments one after the other. It was as if he wanted to be the next Harold Innis. In 1955 he became chairman of the Humanities Research Council just as the Rockefeller Foundation announced that it would not renew its grant. Canadian scholarship, it intimated, should be a Canadian problem. Creighton conceded that the picture of Canadian academics going cap in hand to American foundations was "an embarrassing one," but, like Winston Churchill and the British Empire, he didn't intend "to preside over the dissolution of the Humanities Research Council." Rolling up his sleeves, he wrote a series of letters to the foundation on behalf of Canadian scholarship; he solicited the support of Lester Pearson, who knew Dean Rusk, the president of the Rockefeller Foundation; and, at the eleventh hour, he negotiated a new three-year grant in an urgent long-distance telephone call from Muskoka to New York City.[31] A few months later, he agreed to act as the Canadian editor of the *Encyclopedia Americana,* an assignment that required a tremendous volume of correspondence with its

American publisher and its many Canadian authors (but which paid a $1,000 annual honorarium). When the Canadian Historical Association selected him as its vice-president in 1955 and as its president in 1956, he gratefully accepted. And although his instincts told him to run in the opposite direction, he couldn't say no when Bill Morton asked him to serve as the advisory editor to the multi-volume Centenary Series to be published by McClelland and Stewart.

Everyone wanted a piece of Creighton. At its January 1956 annual meeting, the Progressive Conservative Party passed a unanimous resolution praising *Macdonald* as an "outstanding contribution" to Canadian political history and as "a true appreciation of the history of the Conservative Party, its origin, guiding principles, and contribution to the building of Canada." A few weeks later, the prominent Tory MP and leadership aspirant Davie Fulton introduced Creighton to party faithful at an Ottawa luncheon. In his remarks, Creighton reminded his audience that they were heirs to the vision of John A. Macdonald. Apparently Ellen Fairclough – MP for Hamilton West – "broke down and wept" when he "connected the spirit of Sir John" to the party of today. According to Nova Scotia's George Nowlan, Creighton was "tall, thin, bald, homely" and looked like "a typical college prof" but he was "a damn good writer" and a "damn good Tory."[32]

Creighton's young colleague, Jack Saywell, looked on with bemused interest. The Conservatives, he said, "have boosted Creighton as the historian-prophet, as the man who might lead the party intellectually back to the promised land." He also sensed something of his chairman's conceit. "Little snippets of information suggest that he is not unwilling to play the part."[33]

The Faber and Faber volume, the Richardson book, the Innis biography, the Humanities Research Council, the Canadian Historical Association, the *Encyclopedia Americana,* the Centenary Series, the speaking engagements, and, of course, the Department of History piled one on top of the other. By the fall of 1956, Creighton found himself overwhelmed by the combined weight of his many responsibilities. As early as that summer, he began to experience the first awful symptoms of a chronic intestinal complaint, or in his word, "disturbance." First diagnosed as an ulcer and later as a gastrointestinal infection, it defied treatment. The bloating, discomfort, pain, and bouts of diarrhea would have to be managed. His graduate students watched him take great swigs of some horrid-looking green medicine while his colleagues experienced his short fuse getting even shorter. If something set him off – an unpleasant meeting with the dean, a chance encounter on campus, a casual reference to Underhill, a routine administrative task, or even a friendly inquiry about his own work – he would storm up the stairs of Flavelle House and slam his office door behind him. Like a petulant child, he wanted attention. But he was also self-aware enough to know that he was in over his head. "For my own piece of mind, I must try to end this feeling of pressure and obligation," he told one friend.[34]

But how? His administrative responsibilities were relentless and thankless. Budget estimates, hiring decisions, salary negotiations, office assignments, library acquisitions, leaves of absence, grant applications, reference letters, committee work, curriculum debates, and student requests plagued him day and night. He once wasted an entire afternoon in the attic of Flavelle House looking for office space. Eventually, he settled on the department's tiny map room. But it didn't matter how many meetings he attended or how long he rummaged through the attic because no one was happy. The senior members of the department never accepted his appointment as chairman, and through the Senior Committee – an archaic but powerful committee with real decision-making powers – they made both short-term and long-term planning difficult. One person likened it to the Politburo and another to the House of Lords because its members were appointed according to age and rank and because it constituted an anti-democratic institution at the centre of departmental governance. Had Creighton been willing to stoop to conquer or had he possessed the necessary guile, he could have managed the Senior Committee or run end-runs around it. Instead, he nursed the memory of its support for either Frank Underhill, Bertie Wilkinson, or George Brown. Meanwhile, the junior members were frustrated by their precarious employment, low pay, and small offices. Looking back, Willard Piepenburg recalled the emotional and financial frustrations of being hired and rehired on a series of nine-month contracts. Going to the Honey Dew for a 50-cent meal was, he said, a real treat.[35] At the time, he compared the intricate and "idiotic" ins and outs of Flavelle House politics to the War of the Roses. The place, he wrote, "is a seething nest of discontent." John Cairns talked about the "dreary pessimism" hanging over every interaction, every conversation, and every gathering. And, calling himself Mercury, the much-respected and much-liked Maurice Careless played a game of shuttle diplomacy, running messages back and forth between the juniors, the seniors, and the chair.[36] Even Luella got drawn into departmental politics when she cornered John Cairns, imploring him to look at things from Donald's perspective.[37] But there was only so much that she could do because, ultimately, the problem was not the Senior Committee, or the curriculum, or the lack of office space, or the low salaries: it was her husband.

Led by his vanity, he found himself trapped in the petty but vicious game of university and departmental politics, a game for which he had no instincts and from which he couldn't seem to extricate himself. Where John A. Macdonald enjoyed "an easy, generous tolerance for men and the infinite variety of their views and ways," Creighton suffered from an obvious impatience for most people. But he and his hero shared one unfortunate trait: both liked to personify their problems. For Macdonald, it was George Brown and later Oliver Mowat.[38] For Creighton, it was Frank Underhill and, ironically enough, Jack Saywell.

Initially, Creighton had taken Underhill's successor under his wing, working closely with him as he edited his first book in the summer of 1956. Although it was incredibly hot and his house didn't have air conditioning, he invited Saywell to his home on Parkwood Avenue almost every afternoon, and together they went through his manuscript line by line. Saywell appreciated the interest in his work, especially since he knew that Creighton was writing a biography of Harold Innis. But throughout the fall and into the winter he noticed that the man who had been a mentor to him began to pull back. At times, Creighton was merely indifferent; at other times, he was cold; and at yet other times, he was openly hostile. Saywell was young, brilliant, bibulous, and, because he wasn't "above challenging" the chairman on matters concerning seniority and precedence, something of an unofficial leader among the Young Turks.[39] He was also a wonderful lecturer whose courses attracted a lot of students, and this, as much as anything else, provoked Creighton's jealousy. When Saywell was offered a position in the United States that fall, Creighton didn't encourage him to stay, a fact not lost on Robert Spencer, who reported that the chairman didn't care one way or the other if the department lost one of its brightest lights. It was different for the others – for Spencer, Cairns, and Piepenburg – because they weren't Canadianists and Creighton didn't perceive them as threats. But Saywell was a gifted scholar, a fantastic teacher, and a natural leader. One colleague described him as "the most promising historian" in the country while another colleague referred to him as "a man to be reckoned with." In the end, he declined the University of Washington's offer because he wanted to stay in Canada, but part of him regretted that decision because Creighton continued to "ride" him.[40]

V

Miss Hahn's afternoon tea – a tradition that survived the department's move from Baldwin House to Flavelle House – became brittle affairs that fall, marked by shouting matches, finger pointing, and angry accusations: everyone had an opinion on the disaster unfolding in the Middle East. The Suez Crisis – or the Tripartite Aggression as it is called in the Arab world – constituted a colossal and immoral blunder and represented the worst instincts of a fading empire desperate to reassert its hegemony in a region that it still viewed as its backyard. When the Egyptian leader, Colonel Nasser, had nationalized the Suez Canal Company a few months earlier, the British prime minister, Anthony Eden, read it as an act of aggression and resolved to respond in kind. A joint military response was cobbled together, and on 29 October Israel attacked first, followed by France and Great Britain three days later. The Commonwealth was hopelessly divided – Australia and New Zealand supported Great Britain but India refused to back such an obvious imperial fantasy – and the world confronted the terrifying prospect of a war between the United States and the Soviet Union. Desperate to avoid being drawn into that nightmare scenario, a furious President Eisenhower apparently asked Prime Minister Eden if he was out of his mind. The United States – although well versed in gunboat diplomacy – wanted a diplomatic solution and soon found one in Lester Pearson's proposal to send UN peacekeepers into the canal zone.

Now remembered as a golden moment in Canadian diplomacy, at the time many Canadians rejected Pearson's statecraft, believing that Canada, like Australia and New Zealand, had a duty to support Great Britain in its hour of need. Arthur Lower chalked it up to an "unregenerate," "choleric," and, frankly, racist imperialism: "Canada at Britain's side ... show these niggers ... etc. The *Globe and Mail* is full of it."[41] According to one poll, 43 per cent of Canadians supported the Anglo-French invasion while 40 per cent opposed it. Speaking for perhaps the majority of Canadians, Conservative MP Howard Green accused the government of turning its back on Great Britain to curry favour with the United States. Canada, he declared, had become a "chore boy" to Uncle Sam. Pearson responded that he was neither a chore boy to the United States nor "a colonial chore boy running around shouting 'Ready, aye, ready.'"[42] Although stating an obvious truth, Louis St Laurent didn't help his government's cause when he referred to Britain and France as "the supermen of Europe," telling the House of Commons that their day was over.

For Donald Creighton, the Suez Crisis confirmed his worst fears – Canada had become a colony of the United States – and, needing a target, he found it in Jack Saywell. In Creighton's mind, he personified the bloody Liberals. He personified Louis St Laurent and Lester Pearson because, like them, he was willing to sell Britain out to do America's bidding. But Saywell rightly understood that Britain had "destroyed" the Commonwealth and alienated the United States. British imperialism "has not changed," he said, and Canada and the United States were correct to seek a diplomatic solution. Because Saywell wasn't afraid to state his opinions, he became, in his words, Creighton's "whipping boy." Creighton, he said, remains "extremely difficult" and "still harps on Korea, how we were 'sucked in' by the Americans, and how we dare to criticize the British when we accept American actions."[43] Working "himself into a frenzy of hate over American policy," Creighton turned to Saywell, shouting that "it would take a train full of insecticide to make an American fit to enter a dog kennel."[44]

The American bitch, in other words, was covered with her own fleas, including the escalation of the Korean War and a host of ham-fisted imperial misadventures in Central and South America, a region that it freely called its backyard.

A few days later, the discussion of a recent anti-war demonstration in London's Trafalgar Square ignited yet another round of "fireworks" at afternoon tea. Creighton launched into his usual tirade, and, "as he raved on," it became clear: "the American villain" was to blame for the mess Britain now found itself in. Three years earlier, Creighton had argued that the United States shouldn't interfere in Guatemala but he now implied that it should either support British interference in Egypt or mind its own business.[45] Either way, he made no sense. Sometimes, he reiterated the logic of the editorial writers at the *Globe and Mail* who argued that President Nasser had been the aggressor, not Prime Minister Eden, and that Britain had gone to Egypt "not to make war, but to make peace";[46] at other times, he admitted that Eden had made a costly mistake. Creighton's numerous, contradictory, and bilious explosions were toxic. Some people simply stopped going to afternoon tea while others found excuses not to go into the department at all. John Cairns "pulled down the shades" and kept his "mouth shut." And Willard Piepenburg kept a low profile, hoping not to get sucked in by "the currents of hatred and passion that swirl about indeterminately in the background of everything."[47]

Had Innis been alive, he might have moderated Creighton's anger. But Creighton had no close friends in the department and, without an ally or two, he found himself isolated. His mood darkened and his health worsened – in addition to his persistent and unpleasant intestinal problems, he required medicated creams and prescription shampoos for psoriasis, and, because of shooting pain in his lower back, he had to wear a bulky, tight-fitting corset. Although largely of his own making, the swirling currents of hatred and passion threatened to pull him under. "If DGC is not careful this job will kill him," Saywell remarked.[48]

Creighton's contempt for the United States reached a new low a few months later when the Canadian ambassador to Egypt and one of the key players in negotiating a diplomatic settlement to the Suez Crisis, climbed to the top of a downtown Cairo building and jumped seven storeys to his death. Desperately overworked, Herbert Norman was also dogged by American accusations of communism and espionage. Although he had been cleared in the past, the same accusations resurfaced in the United States Senate; rather than face another witch hunt, he killed himself on the morning of 4 April 1957. Canadians were rightly outraged. Lester Pearson, who had been a close personal friend of Norman's, condemned the United States in diplomatic but certain terms. This time the *Globe and Mail* got it right when it expressed its "disgust" and described the much-vaunted Canadian-American friendship as a "long series of insults and injuries." Norman's death and the circumstances leading up to it were tragic reminders that the Cold War was in part what Creighton said it was: a war for righteousness fought by zealots in which suspected heretics could be burned at the stake, or compelled to jump from a Cairo rooftop. His death was also a poignant reminder of Creighton's own childhood and adolescence. Norman had been a son of the manse and, although he had grown up in Japan where his father was a missionary with the Methodist Church, he attended Victoria College, where he won distinction and was awarded the Kylie Scholarship to pursue graduate work in England.

A few months after the fact, Creighton received a lovely letter from Howard Norman, Herbert Norman's older brother, whom he had known briefly at Vic. Having just finished reading *John A. Macdonald: The Old Chieftain*, Norman wrote that it had "fired" his anti-Americanism. "My brother's death is only the last event in a long history of injustice, bullying and insult. Right now I feel that I never want to set foot in the States again." Creighton knew exactly what he meant, telling him that his letter had "touched a very responsive chord." "It has always seemed to me that this fine man and distinguished public servant was quite literally hounded to death by malignant and bullying meddlers in Washington." That Herbert Norman had convinced President Nasser to accept Canadian peacekeepers and, in that sense, was complicit with St Laurent and Pearson in the betrayal of Great Britain did not matter. What mattered was the death of a good and decent man. "His tragedy is not the only calamity which has fallen upon us from that particular quarter but it is one of the saddest."[49]

VI

The nation's capital was in a state of silent disbelief in early June 1957 when the Canadian Historical Association met at the University of Ottawa. Not even the prime minister was granting interviews. When Louis St Laurent dropped the writ in late April, he and everyone around him assumed that he would coast to another easy mandate before handing the reins to Lester Pearson. There hadn't been a Conservative prime minister in over twenty years, and no one seriously believed that the newly minted leader of the Progressive Conservatives could pull it off. But the maverick prairie lawyer ran a brilliant campaign, condemning Liberal arrogance, attacking its foreign policy, and defending the British connection at every turn. Denouncing the suspicion and innuendo of Washington's inquisition, he even claimed to be fighting for the soul of Herbert Norman. On election night, Donald Creighton watched the returns with C.P.

Stacey. As more and more Liberals were defeated, he grew more and more excited, "repeatedly bouncing out of his chair with hoots of unholy joy." According to Stacey, it was more fun watching Creighton watch the returns than it was watching the returns.[50] When the results were finally confirmed, the unthinkable had happened: the Liberals had been defeated and the governor general was poised to invite John Diefenbaker to form a government. Although it would be a minority government, it would be a Tory government.

For the next few days, Creighton simply "crowed": the tide of history had turned, deliverance was at hand, and the long nightmare of Liberal rule was over.[51] The Suez Crisis and the perceived poor handling of the Herbert Norman tragedy were the most recent Liberal sins in a long line of Liberal sins that included the wartime agreements with the United States, the parliamentary shenanigans during the infamous pipeline debate when the government invoked closure to force a vote on its controversial legislation, and the decision to quietly drop "Dominion" from official nomenclature and to rebrand the Royal Mail as Canada Post on delivery trucks and mail boxes. Although historic words, the Liberals saw them as undignified reminders of Canada's colonial past. To Creighton, "Dominion" and "Royal" were national symbols that reinforced his identity as a Canadian. Sharing Eugene Forsey's view that the assault on "Dominion" was an indignity "characterized by bad law, bad history, and bad logic,"[52] he deliberately wrote the prefaces to both *The Young Politician* and *The Old Chieftain* on Dominion Day. After all, English Canada's protracted identity debate in the post-1945 period was never a debate between nationalists and imperialists, between those who were independent thinking and those who were colonial minded: it was a debate between two competing nationalisms.

The sight of so many Liberals losing their seats – including C.D. Howe, the American-born cabinet minister and architect of the government's parliamentary strategy to force a vote in the pipeline debate – emboldened Creighton's delivery of his presidential address. It was as if he were back at Vic delivering a paper on Canada's intellectual contamination to the Hysterical Club. Wearing a tuxedo, despite the oppressive summer heat, and "leering" like some cock of the walk, his voice "nasty and biting," he revisited one of his favourite themes: the Liberal Interpretation or the Authorized Version of Canadian history.[53]

Just a few months earlier Creighton had delivered a similar talk at Carleton University. Worried that his anti-Americanism was "a portent of things to come," the United States Embassy in Ottawa actually reported his remarks to Washington. "Purportedly historical," Creighton's lecture was "obviously political," an embassy official wrote. And while his assertion that American bases in Canada were a "primitive form of military imperialism" was standard fare from "the Communists," it was surprising from "a man of unquestioned intelligence who is held in the highest regard in Canadian academic circles."[54]

In both lectures, Creighton excoriated Liberal politicians, Liberal journalists, and Liberal historians for rewriting Canadian history in their own self-image. The story of Canadian history, according to the Authorized Version, was the story of Canada's emancipation from Great Britain and discovery of North America. It didn't matter that this collection of self-appointed Liberal oracles had gone after the wrong imperialism and ignored American imperialism because Canadians were now told that they had been part of one big, happy North American family all along. The whole thing, he said, smacked of a "gigantic international Elks convention where all the delegates went around hand-shaking and back-slapping and exuding cordiality from every pore." It was in the context of Canada's discovery of North America that Canadians were recently informed by a government member – "speaking *ex cathedra*," of course – that "Dominion" was a foreign word and that the Fathers of Confederation hadn't intended to call Canada the Dominion of Canada or to refer to the federal government as the Dominion government. What tripe, to borrow Eugene Forsey's favourite word. Creighton reminded his audience that the Fathers of Confederation had intended to call Canada the Dominion of Canada, but in the brave new world of Canadian history, words now meant whatever the Authorized Version said they meant. To keep the Authorized Version alive and well, to enlarge and perfect its Sacred Texts, a national headquarters was needed. What better place than Laurier House in Ottawa, Creighton asked? And who better to carry "the Word" into the indefinite future than "those scholars who had dedicated themselves to the lives of the blessed Liberal saints and martyrs of the past?"[55]

In case anybody missed it, Creighton leaned his tall frame over the lectern in the University of Ottawa's Salle Academique to point a long, granite index finger straight at Frank Underhill, the recently appointed curator of Laurier House.[56] Leaving the lecture hall, Underhill turned to one of his former graduate students asking, "What makes a man do that?" Margaret Prang didn't have an answer and instead muttered something about what a shame it had been.[57] That evening, Underhill organized a small reception at his Ottawa home. Everyone talked about Creighton's presidential address and its digital gesture and, like their host, wondered what would make a man publicly insult a former colleague.[58] Perhaps they identified his pettiness, his insecurity, his need to be the smartest person in the room, his reluctance to forgive and forget, or his tendency to nurse old wounds and to pick at old grievances. Or perhaps they said it was simply Donald Creighton being Donald Creighton. Underhill said that if he had that much venom, he would at least try to do a better job of containing it. John Cairns described his chairman's performance as "a cheap, low-comedy, vulgar attack on everything and everyone, a music-hall routine that had a sweltering audience rolling in the aisles with its venom and buffoonery."[59] But Jack Saywell reported that people weren't laughing with Creighton, they were laughing at him, making what should have been an important occasion in his professional life – the delivery of his presidential address to a gathering of his peers – an unpleasant and uncomfortable affair. Allowing his pettiness to triumph over his better instincts, he had ruined everything. "I'll always see that tuxedoed figure leaning forward in that tropical hall firing off one rotten egg after another," Cairns said.[60]

A few weeks later, Hilda Neatby apologized to her former professor for the fact that the Canadian Historical Association had become so "intemperate." Creighton's real problem, she told Underhill, was his need to approach Macdonald as a "faithful clansman" who "must have his knife into every enemy of the clan."[61] But Creighton's capacity for venom was matched by an equal capacity for love, and in the summer of 1957 he put the finishing touches on the short biography of Harold Innis he had started the previous spring.

VII

Before putting pen to paper, Creighton first needed to see Innis's childhood home, and so, on an overcast, wet day in April 1956, Mary Innis and her youngest daughter, Anne, rented a car and took Donald and Luella to Norwich Township and the old Innis farm in the village of Otterville. Despite the grey cold, they explored the farm's outbuildings, pastures, and woodlot. As Creighton walked ahead across an open field, Mary pulled Anne aside, instructing her to watch closely. This is what great historians do, she explained. They collect details, take mental pictures, measure distances, visualize sightlines, and, ultimately, imagine what it was like. That afternoon, they had tea with Harold's sister, Hughena, and coffee with his brother, Samuel. Creighton collected their childhood memories; he gathered stories about their older brother and about their parents, Mary Adams and William Innis; and he examined old family photographs, taking notes on the shape of someone's face and the colour of someone else's hair. Afterwards, they drove to the neighbouring village of Hawtrey, where Harold had worked in his uncle's general store. Next, they drove to Woodstock, some twenty miles from Otterville, where Harold had completed his secondary education at the Collegiate Institute. Creighton wanted to get a sense of the distance a young Innis had to travel each day and to see the red-brick, two-storey building on Riddell Street that, in its modest way, set Innis on his life's path. All told, it was a "very good day," Mary wrote in her diary.[62]

Creighton opened his biography of Harold Innis in the same way that he had opened his biography of John A. Macdonald, with the Canadian landscape, in this case the rolling tableland of southwestern Ontario: "The house stood a little below the crest of a long ridge. Ages before, the glacier had paused in its sluggish career southward; and the detritus of its moraine had solidified in the long low elevation which became known as Oak Ridge." By pairing a house and a glacier, Creighton paired human time and geological time – time that the Scottish geologist James Hutton described in 1785 as having "no vestige of a beginning and no prospect of an end" – and he symbolically linked the Innis family farm to Canada's Precambrian beginnings. Through the careful use of the word "career," he also implied that, like the Laurentide Ice Sheet, the influences of his friend's career would continue indefinitely. Meanwhile, the house itself was small and, practically speaking, too far from the concession road, a fact not lost on William Innis, who had to make the difficult ascent in good weather and bad. But his wife had insisted that it be built near the crest of the ridge because she loved the view, which, in Creighton's imagination, stretched beyond southwestern Ontario to include the distant reaches of northern Canada. "One could see the whole landscape spread out in a simple, satisfying pattern of roads and fields, houses and barns, orchards and woodlots; and away to the north the blue border of the horizon was sombre with remoteness." In other words, Harold Innis was marked in the same way that Macdonald had been marked: the little boy who absorbed the "enormous landscape" outside the windows of a small farmhouse in Otterville, Ontario, would one day unlock its secrets.[63]

Recognizing her son's unusual gifts, Mary Adams Innis ensured that he continued his studies beyond Norwich's one-room schoolhouse and Otterville's insufficient high school. Despite the cost, Harold would go to the Collegiate Institute in Woodstock and, from there, to McMaster University in Toronto because his mother was determined that he would be a Baptist minister, not a farmer. But he had other plans; with much of Europe sinking in the mud of France and Belgium, he enlisted. The "tall slight young man" with a "thin mobile face" and a "sensitive humorous mouth" would never be the same person again.[64] The First World War was like a gigantic magnet and the men who passed through it had their lives bent and redirected. Injured at Vimy Ridge and invalided back to Canada, Innis decided that he would not go into the ministry. Instead, he would spend the rest of his life inside the university in a desperate quest to understand the world through political economy, history, and, eventually, communications theory.

Although his quest took different forms, it was singular in its obsession, a fact not lost on his biographer. Creighton clearly envied Innis's endurance and his capacity to travel the lengths of Canada's great rivers; he admired his ability to see patterns in the masses of evidence he collected; he revered "the last great chapter" of *The Fur Trade in Canada* and its promise that the country emerged because of its geography, not despite it; he applauded his academic principles and his vigorous defence of them; he praised his monastic devotion to the cause of scholarship and to the integrity of the university; he enjoyed his company and his delight in delicious academic gossip; and he grieved his final diagnosis and untimely death.[65] To capture his friend, he used simple, unadorned, accessible prose. He didn't clutter the text with references to secondary sources; he didn't even use footnotes because he wanted readers to connect with the book's subject and not be distracted by the conventions of scholarly writing. In effect, he told a story with a compelling narrative arc: the little boy who studied the landscape of southwestern Ontario and pondered its northern horizons became the rare genius who proposed an overarching theory of Canada and who, as death closed in on him, was approaching a theory of everything.

When Del Clark and Alexander Brady read Creighton's manuscript, they quickly shelved the original plan to publish a memorial volume of three essays and a collection of Innis's letters. Looking past the mountain of essays, articles, books, manuscripts, university reports, research notes, government documents, newspaper clippings, and correspondence in the Innis archive, Creighton had written an extended love letter to a remarkable human being.

Published in the fall of 1957, *Portrait of a Scholar* was read with the same warmth and affection as it was written. The Innis children were, in their own ways, incredibly grateful to receive it. In a sense, it was Creighton's gift to them for the years of friendship between two families, for the many Sunday dinners in Toronto and "the long summer evenings" in Muskoka.[66] Some fifty-odd years later, Mary Rutledge and Anne Innis Daag still talk about the book's simple and graceful depiction of their father.

Creighton's ability to bring the dead back to life through the arrangement of words on a page prompted a long letter from Gerald Graham, an old friend now teaching at King's College, London. Finding himself "strangely moved and disturbed," he told Creighton that he had read it in one sitting, that he had been transported back in time, and that, when he woke up the next morning, he was "haunted" by the sudden realization that Innis was still dead.[67] Not surprisingly, the reviewers also had kind words. George Grant described it as "a portrait of Canada's greatest academic written by our finest historian"; John Kenneth Galbraith admired its "literary skill"; the great Australian historian Keith Hancock praised its "fine craftsmanship" and "deeply moving" prose; and both the *Times Literary Supplement* and *The Economist* carried glowing assessments.[68] Even today, Creighton's slim volume is considered "the best overall work" and "the best summary biography" by the author of *Marginal Man: The Dark Vision of Harold Innis*.[69]

Because Creighton wrote, in his words, "under a fresh, deep sense of personal bereavement and loss,"[70] he was able to give his book an emotional undertow that drew the reader into the story. Had he waited, he said, he would not have been able to recover those feelings. But mixed with his bereavement was his anger, and, unfortunately, he allowed it to creep though in a handful of places.

In the 1930s, Innis had conducted a perfectly civil academic exchange with Frank Underhill: where Innis believed that the proper place for the scholar was in the university, Underhill believed that it was out there, in the trenches of social activism and party politics, in the League for Social Reconstruction and the Co-operative Commonwealth Federation. Creighton had sided with Innis in the 1930s and again in the 1950s, this time by reducing the thoughtfulness of Underhill's position to a caricature and by dismissing him as one more hot gospeller who preached the received truth and the promise of salvation to all true believers. He also revisited the historiographical debate between those historians who saw Canada as a North American nation and those who saw it as a British nation. Although he didn't employ his stock phrases – for example, Liberal Historical Inc. or the Authorized Version – he dismissed the story of Canada's ascension from "dependent" colonialism to "serene" autonomy as a "beautiful fable" told by nationalist historians untroubled by mere facts.[71] Unable to let it drop, he committed the sin of ventriloquism. Through a dead Innis, he voiced his personal and intellectual war of words with a still very much alive Underhill.[72]

More problematic, however, was Creighton's depiction of the later Innis, the Innis of communications theory, monopolies of knowledge, and the rise and fall empires. Although he caught occasional glimpses, he still didn't appreciate what had driven his friend back to the ancient civilizations of Mesopotamia, Greece, and Egypt. Instead, he cherry-picked his criticisms of the United States, rehashed his opposition to the Korean War, took potshots at Lester Pearson, and largely ignored everything else. This had the unfortunate effect of misrepresenting Innis's massive scholarly output in the last ten years of his life and the even more unfortunate effect of transforming him into a knee-jerk anti-American. Like God, Creighton had made Innis in his own image. But Innis wasn't anti-American. He was anti-war. And his criticisms of the United States were always directed at higher targets, including the concentration of power in a centralized state and the easy application of military solutions to international problems. Ultimately, his difficult journey "into the most distant countries of the mind" was an attempt to save Western civilization from itself, from its relentless commercialism, its fixation on technology, its present-mindedness, and its numerous and dangerous nationalisms.[73]

Boris Swerling, an economist at Stanford University, had been Innis's student in the late 1930s and early 1940s and had remained, in his words, "devoted" to him ever since. For this reason, he simply couldn't reconcile Innis the anti-American with Innis the author of *The Cod Fisheries,* a book that took a dim view of nationalism. Tom Easterbrook, Innis's junior colleague in the Department of Political Economy, had a similar reaction: Innis the anti-American wasn't the Innis he had looked up to. But both men admitted that *Portrait of a Scholar* was a beautiful book. It "moved me deeply," Swerling acknowledged, "more than once to the point of tears."[74]

Indeed, no one could have been left unmoved by Creighton's affecting description of Innis's battle against an unstoppable cancer, of his operation and convalescence, of his brief reprieve and awful descent into the black days of dementia and powerful sedatives, or of his final release: "The lad who had set out on the train to Woodstock that golden September morning long ago had at last finished his journey."[75]

VIII

In January 1958, Creighton's chairmanship had entered its fourth year when Graham Spry invited him to sit on the executive of a reincarnated Canadian Radio League to be called the Canadian Broadcasting League. For strategic purposes, Spry wanted the author of *The Young Politician* and *The Old Chieftain* on the league's letterhead because both Creighton and Creighton's Macdonald stood for nation building, and that, he reasoned, was in short supply. Despite the strains of administration, the weight of unfinished manuscripts, and the unhealthy stress of overwork, Creighton couldn't resist the persuasive Spry. "Count me in," he said.[76] The new League, Spry explained, would have a similar mandate to the old League – to promote a publicly owned Canadian broadcasting system with sufficient resources to offset imported American programming. Because the government was considering a new Broadcasting Act, the league would have to act quickly.

By this point, Creighton's many obligations had spilled into his family life. Luella once confessed that her husband's physical and emotional needs left her with little time for anything else. It wasn't really true because she was deep into her third novel, but, because his "disturbances" never fully went away, she had to prepare special meals. To avoid obvious triggers, dinners were plain, not rich or heavy, and never fried. Cynthia remembers eating steamed fish and boiled potatoes every night for what seemed like an eternity. She also remembers her father's galoshes. "Coming home from school and entering the house, I looked for his galoshes. If they were there I had to prepare myself, brace myself, for whatever might be waiting for me. He could be in one of his sour, difficult moods. But if the galoshes weren't there, well, I could relax and go upstairs to see my mother." It was like living in a minefield where even the smallest misstep could set off an explosion: "It was unhealthy for him, but it was unhealthy for all of us."[77]

Creighton had settled into a permanent state of overwork that winter when he exploded in anger at Alfred Knopf, one of the most distinguished publishers in the English-speaking world. Knopf had wanted a history of Canada on his list for a number of years and, in 1952, had written to C.D. Howe – of all people – asking for his confidential opinion of Creighton. Had the powerful cabinet minister known what Creighton thought of the bloody Liberals, he wouldn't have told Knopf that *Dominion of the North* was easily the best book of its kind or that its author was a gifted writer.[78] Initially, Creighton declined Knopf's invitation because he needed to finish *Macdonald*, but Knopf persisted and, in late 1956, signed him to a contract; now, in early 1958, he had the manuscript in hand and a tentative plan to publish it in early 1959 with Faber and Faber in Great Britain and Macmillan in Canada. Describing it as a "brilliant essay," Knopf was genuinely pleased, although, he added, American readers may not like its "anti-United States attitude." But then Knopf invited Creighton to consider a number of stylistic changes. "It would read much better for the general reader for whom it is addressed if there were not so many sentences and clauses beginning with "it"; if many passive verbs were made active and if you would avoid again and again describing a situation of crisis by a paragraph beginning, "It seemed that ..." and balancing it immediately afterwards with a paragraph beginning "But under the surface ..." or some equivalent of this."[79]

Passive verbs? Sentences beginning with "it"? Creighton fired off an ill-tempered letter. His book wasn't anti-American, he said, unless anything but "the grossest flattery" is anti-American. And "if you wanted a historian of Canada who didn't begin sentences with 'it' and who always used active rather than passive verbs, then why did you waste my time by making an agreement with me?" Unable to restrain himself, Creighton let Knopf know what he thought of his "suggestions for smartening up my history for a popular American audience": "They resemble the kind of advice which might be handed out in a freshman course in short-story writing at a middle-western American university." Because he didn't have "the slightest intention" of making any revisions, he demanded his manuscript's return. Knopf sat on Creighton's letter for two weeks in the hopes that its volatile author would come to his senses and recant. But when it became clear that Creighton wouldn't undo his decision, Knopf returned the manuscript and cancelled the contract. "I have been in the publishing business now for nearly forty-six years, and I have never had from any writer as rude, nay as boorish, a communication as yours." Creighton, though, had the last word. "You spoke your mind plainly. I did likewise." In other words, what is your problem? But he didn't have the last laugh because he had lost the prestige of the Knopf imprint and now had to find another American publisher.[80]

Exhausted and oversensitive, Creighton had bitten the hand that fed him and, in the process, created more work for himself at the very moment the Canadian Broadcasting League called him to Ottawa. When Spry secured a meeting with the prime minister and his minister of national revenue, George Nowlan, he asked Creighton to chair the delegation. As Macdonald's biographer, he would "serve as a link" between the past and the present, between Canada's first prime minster and its current prime minister. He also asked him to lead with a five-minute presentation on the "Macdonald east-west axis theme in contemporary terms."[81] What had seemed like a good idea in early January had become a lot of work in early July. But Creighton was convinced that Canada was, in Harold Innis's words, "fighting" for its life against American "jackals."

In his presentation on 18 July 1958, Creighton appealed to the prime minister's ego by reminding him that some eight million Canadians had watched him win a massive parliamentary majority just a few months earlier; he appealed to his sense of history by sketching a Laurentian picture of Canada based on the St Lawrence River and Great Lakes; and he appealed to his sense of destiny by telling him that he had an opportunity to do "in the realm of the mind and the spirit" what Sir John A. Macdonald had done in the realm of the economy. Taking his final inspiration from Psalm 72, and sounding not unlike an Old Testament prophet, he told the prime minister that the "steady flow of live programmes along the east-west life line will express Canadian ideas and ideals, employ Canadian talent, and help unite our people from sea to sea and from the river unto the ends of the earth."[82]

In a House of Commons debate on broadcasting a few weeks later, Minister Nowlan summoned the Laurentian thesis when he invoked Canada's "separateness in North America," its "unity from ocean to ocean," and Sir John A. Macdonald's commitment to nation building. This time, Macdonald's biographer wasn't a tall, thin, bald, and homely college professor. He was a "distinguished Canadian scholar" whose views "represent the views of this government with respect to the functions, maintenance, and strengthening of the Canadian Broadcasting Corporation."[83] When the government passed the 1958

Broadcasting Act, which, among other things, set Canadian-content rules, the league was largely happy and even took credit for a couple of late amendments to strengthen the independence of the CBC president and vice-president.

For Creighton, it was an important intervention because it presented an opportunity to play the part of a national sage who kept the country's story, shared its secrets, and revealed its destinies.

IX

In the fall of 1958, the Department of History settled into the predictable routine of lectures, seminars, and meetings. There were no explosions, but no one was particularly happy either. And there was at least one new person who was trying to find his way. A few months earlier the department had to make a last-minute hiring decision and – like all hiring decisions – it opened up fault lines. Originally, Creighton had hoped to appoint either Margaret Prang or Alan Wilson, both of whom had been his PhD students. No one objected because Toronto had a lengthy – and probably unwise – tradition of hiring its own. But neither Prang nor Wilson was available and so the department decided to interview a newly minted PhD from the University of Illinois. After meeting him at Hart House, Creighton announced that he now knew why the young man was still on the job market: he was one of "God's chosen people."[84]

Creighton's anti-Semitism was the anti-Semitism of Wasp Toronto, meaning it was habitual, reflexive, and contradictory more than it was straightforward and vicious. It was the anti-Semitism of Frank Underhill, who once wanted to hire someone because, although a Jew, he was at least a Jew that everyone knew. It was the anti-Semitism of Harold Innis, who didn't want to hire Jews because it would only encourage more Jews to pursue academic careers. And finally, it was the anti-Semitism of Luella, who took Cynthia to Toronto's University College, pointed to the Jewish students in the cafeteria, and asked if this was really where she wanted to study but who, in the end, relented when Cynthia said yes.[85] In short, Creighton's anti-Semitism was complicated. He had wanted the department to hire David Spring in 1952 and was desperately disappointed when Spring's contract negotiations with the university fell apart; later, he supported Chester Martin's decision to hire Morris Zaslow because he was quite fond of him. Zaslow had been one of his students in the late 1940s, and, according to Zaslow, they "got along very well." "I had heard that he was anti-Semitic, but I never saw that side of him. He didn't like stupid people, that's true. But he liked me."[86] On one occasion, Creighton "went to the wall" in an effort to secure a raise for Zaslow and was "livid" when the president refused his request.[87]

Meanwhile, the department was favourably impressed by the quiet, thoughtful Ed Beame, and it was agreed that he should be hired. Creighton didn't object, but he reiterated his concern that the department was missing a golden opportunity: Prang and Wilson may not have been available, but Tom Symons was. Smart, cultured, and ambitious, Symons had been one of Creighton's favourites. Like Creighton, he had done his BA at Toronto and had studied at Oxford. Being Toronto-bred and Oxford-polished meant that he was, in Creighton's mind, "civilized" in a way that the Brooklyn-born, Illinois-manufactured Beame wasn't.[88] But Symons didn't have a PhD, and this, more than anything else, played against him: he was a well-rounded generalist at a time when the profession demanded research specialists. The department's reluctance to hire Symons became an open source of friction.[89] Creighton didn't throw a fit but declared that "in putting so much stress on specialization," the department was "embarking on a dangerous course." That Beame was an American Jew influenced Creighton's lack of enthusiasm, but he genuinely believed that the tradition of humane scholarship was a better model than hyper-specialization. A few months later, he would echo Harold Innis in a public address to welcome Toronto's new president; defending an idealized university tradition, he urged his audience to be wary of "a modern world which presses clamorously in upon us with its insistent needs and demands."[90] After the hiring meeting, one colleague said that he wouldn't put it past Creighton ensuring that Beame "flopped" so that he could say, I told you so.[91]

Because he had been appointed the Harold Adams Innis Visiting Professor for the 1958–9 academic year, Creighton didn't have any teaching obligations that fall but he still had a long list of administrative obligations. Over the Christmas holidays and into the new year, he considered his future. By his own estimation, he was devoting three-quarters of his time to university matters and, as a result, wasn't getting ahead with his research and writing. In a perfect world, he told the president in a letter marked "Private and Confidential," he would be made a Research Professor "with no administrative duties and a reduced teaching load." At the very least, "I feel I should resign the chairmanship." It had been what he wanted in 1954, he said, but he now realized that he had been wrong, that his strengths lay elsewhere, and that, for his mental and physical health, he needed to unburden himself.[92]

Although Claude Bissell was new to the president's office, he wasn't new to Toronto. Indeed, he had known Creighton for years and had experienced first-hand how prickly and petty his colleague could be. Some fourteen months earlier, the two men had crossed swords over a volume of essays that Bissell had edited. *Our Living Tradition* contained both Creighton's Carleton University address on John A. Macdonald – the one that had led the American embassy to report his anti-Americanism to Washington – and Frank Underhill's address on Edward Blake. When he received his copy, Creighton was miffed to see that Underhill's essay was nearly twice as long as his. Yes, Underhill's essay was longer, Bissell responded. But so what? It is, he said, "neither here nor there."[93] Now, as president of the University of Toronto, he accepted Creighton's resignation effective 1 July 1959.

In one of his final acts as chairman, and after much back and forth with the administration, Creighton secured the appointment of Ken McNaught. Although McNaught was a socialist and a close friend of Underhill's, he and Creighton shared an abiding mistrust of the American empire. Creighton also admired McNaught's principled decision to resign from Winnipeg's United College when it dismissed Harry Crowe in one of Canada's most famous battles over the precise meaning of academic freedom. In a December letter to the *Globe and Mail* signed by all twenty-two members of the Department of History – including the recently arrived Ed Beame – Creighton protested "the deplorable situation at United College" and called upon its Board of Regents to extend an olive branch of conciliation.[94] Now, he had the chance to hire McNaught and he grabbed it.

Meanwhile, Dean Woodside had the chance to repair the department and, in March, invited Maurice Careless to be the next chairman. He was "the best port in the storm" and, at thirty-nine years old, signalled a generational shift.[95] The announcement of Creighton's resignation was as big a shock as the announcement of his appointment five years earlier. This time, however, the decision was greeted with a collective sigh of relief. "It will be a much happier department for the change," Jim Conacher told Ken McNaught, "and you come at a good time."[96]

Conacher was right but, in Creighton's defence, he had inherited an impossible department in 1955. Saddled with a petrified Senior Committee that never accepted his leadership and surrounded by a collection of precariously employed juniors, Creighton had no place to turn and lacked the people skills needed to create those places. George Brown always maintained that he should have been appointed chairman ahead of Creighton and, when Careless was appointed, wished him well but muttered something to the effect that it should have been him.[97] For his part, Jack Saywell may have felt unappreciated by Creighton, but he didn't appreciate Creighton either. When he received the offer from the University of Washington, Creighton didn't get down on his hands and knees and beg him to stay but he did pressure the administration to make a counteroffer.[98] Two years later, Saywell returned the favour by *not* informing his chairman that he had an offer from the University of California at Berkeley, leaving it instead to the academic gossip mill to break the news. Creighton was stunned. He acknowledged that Saywell wasn't "bound" to tell him anything,

Donald Creighton and Claude Bissell, president of the University of Toronto, had been colleagues for many years and were on friendly terms. Although he admired Creighton's many gifts, Bissell did not hesitate when he accepted his resignation as chairman of the Department of History.

but it would have been nice. Besides, he would like to have had the chance to make an "alternative proposal on Toronto's part."[99] In other words, if Donald Creighton was difficult, then the George Browns and Jack Saywells weren't easy either.

In the spring and summer of 1959, Creighton spent a lot of time at the cottage. He resigned as chairman of the Canadian Broadcasting League; he wrote a chapter or two of the Richardson book; and he corrected the proofs to *The Story of Canada,* but otherwise he didn't exert himself. He desperately needed the rest and, as he told one friend, he was "already feeling a good deal better."[100] His tenure as chairman – which he later described as "a storm of weeping" – was finally over.[101]

That July Creighton also celebrated his fifty-seventh birthday. Time was creeping up on him. It seemed like only yesterday that Philip was a young man about town; now, he too was a husband and a father. Cynthia had just finished her sophomore year at Toronto's University College and was coming into her own as a young woman. Maybe, Creighton thought, he should take early retirement and dedicate himself full-time to writing. The Richardson book was still unfinished and he had recently signed a contract with Macmillan to write two books, one to mark the one hundredth anniversary of the Charlottetown and Quebec conferences and the other to celebrate Canada's centennial. But academic pensions were small in those days, and so he returned to the department in September. However, he returned a happier man. Jim Conacher reported on the "disappearance of the tensions that have plagued us since 1955." Creighton has rejoined the fold, he said, and, though his "views and personality have not changed," he is "glad to be rid of it all and is the better for it."[102]

That fall, *The Story of Canada* was published in Canada and Great Britain.[103] Despite its occasional bursts of brilliant colour, Creighton's seventh book was the work of a tired scholar who hadn't been able to keep up with the historiography or get to the archives. As a result, it clung to old themes, sounded familiar notes, reused certain phrases, repeated the same prejudices, and followed a standard narrative route: Canada's origins lay in Europe; a "youthful" St Lawrence River made westward expansion possible; "primitive" Aboriginal peoples were doomed to disappear beneath the Laurentian tide; the United States represented "encroachment" and "aggression"; John A. Macdonald understood the "enormous continental task" ahead of him; the "empty" northwest was opened to settlement; Canadians answered the call of empire in the Great War; Mackenzie King was a "short" and "bulky" man who, over the course of a lengthy career, ignored the Commonwealth of British Nations for the Trojan Horse of North America; Louis St Laurent emitted an "indiscreet" and "angry" ejaculation when he announced the end of Europe's supermen; and the Liberal Party never appreciated the threat of "American continentalism."[104] However, Creighton concluded his story of Canada with a hopeful ode to a young Queen Elizabeth and to the newly elected John Diefenbaker. All was not yet lost.

The reviews were mixed. Bill Morton admired its verve but the journalist Walter O'Hearn described it as "the work of a scholar who tries to survey" all of Canada from the University of Toronto campus. Downtown Toronto, he said, is "singularly flat" and has a "short horizon," meaning Creighton could see neither Quebec nor western Canada. As a result, French Canadians disappear after 1759 and the North West Rebellion is a problem to be solved in the construction of the Canadian Pacific Railway.[105]

But one review in particular stuck in Creighton's craw. Although the *Globe and Mail's* review was unsigned, he suspected its author was Arthur Lower. He and Lower were never confidants, but they had been collegial and even helpful to each other in the 1930s and 1940s. As late as 1954, Creighton wrote a very positive letter to the Rockefeller Foundation supporting Lower's proposed book in the new field of Canadian social history. But then something happened. Or

When his chairmanship, or what he called that "storm of weeping," ended, Donald Creighton returned to full-time teaching in the fall of 1959 and was happier for it. He could be a mesmerizing teacher. One of his doctoral students compared him to "a sorcerer around a campfire telling the story of a great adventure."

nothing happened. Either way, Creighton stopped speaking to him in 1955 and their relationship was, in Lower's word, "terminated." Even Lower, who had the hide of an elephant, was surprised by Creighton's "impossible" behaviour.[106] In any event, the offending review described *The Story of Canada* as "a simplified history of Canada" that "any bright teenager could understand" and it "regretted" the fact that Professor Lower's many books were not included in the list for further reading.[107] As he so often did when he received a negative review, Creighton fell into a funk and let everyone know exactly what he thought of the "pestiferous" professor from Queen's University.[108] Jim Conacher was right: his views and personality hadn't changed. In Creighton's mind, Arthur Lower and Frank Underhill were the enemies of Canada and he was its defender against the Liberal establishment and its court historians.

But his defence of Canada was the defence of a disappearing definition of Canada, something Lower had always hoped for and Underhill clearly saw. In the late 1930s, Lower wished that just one man of "public prominence" had the "guts" to say that "the British connection" was too "damn dangerous" and that the country could no longer "afford" it. In the autumn 1959 issue of *Queen's*

Quarterly, Underhill identified the "illusion" at the heart of Canada's self-understanding. Canada is not British, he argued; it is "inescapably" North American. "Do historians in Toronto never go to the movies or look at television or read our trade statistics," he asked with specific reference to his former colleague. The commercial empire of the St Lawrence has "disintegrated," while Canada's economic, political, and military links to London have been severed. No longer part of the sterling area, Canada "is now part of the dollar area," and its trade "is mostly with the United States." As for the Commonwealth, it has become a Pavlovian term in English Canada. Its mere mention sets mouths panting and tails wagging. Yet it embodies a host of contradictions: the majority of its population live under republican governments; South Africa and, if it is admitted to the Commonwealth, the Central African Federation of Rhodesia and Nyasaland, deny the principles of freedom and equality; and most members seek their own special relationship with the United States. "All roads in the Commonwealth now lead to Washington, for the simple reason that we all depend on American power for our security."[109]

At least one important Liberal appreciated Underhill's critical response to the Laurentian dream of nation and its "neurotic" anti-Americanism.[110] Mike Pearson congratulated him "for reducing some of Donald Creighton's views to historical perspective and accuracy," adding that, in future speaking engagements, he intended "to borrow from it shamelessly."[111] Had Creighton seen Pearson's letter, it would have confirmed his worst suspicions: Grit Historical Inc. was alive and well and bent on destroying Canada by wrecking whatever connections it had to Great Britain and the Commonwealth.

chapter ten

Decolonization

As for myself, my course is clear. A British subject I was born, a British subject
I will die.

John A. Macdonald, vol. 2

When John A. Macdonald made his famous profession of faith in 1891, Great Britain spanned the globe. The sun never set on the empire and no one could imagine ever letting it set, at least not without a fight. A few years earlier, a small contingent of Canadian boatmen had participated in the ill-fated rescue of General Charles Gordon at Khartoum. A few years later, a much larger contingent of Canadian soldiers would defend imperial interests in South Africa's Transvaal. But in the two decades after the Second World War, the British Empire met its Waterloo when decolonization, independence, and the end of empire repainted the world's map, making it suddenly a lot less red. Frank Underhill joked that the British flag should have been made of wool so that it could shrink with the British Empire. That kind of humour annoyed Donald Creighton, getting as it did under his skin: he had been born a British subject and, like Macdonald, intended to die a British subject because the alternative was to die an American subject, if not de jure then at least de facto. But what did it mean to be British at the end of empire? There was never a single answer, but in the late 1950s and early 1960s, Creighton looked to a revitalized Commonwealth and that Commonwealth unexpectedly looked to him.

Shortly after becoming prime minister of Great Britain in 1957, Harold Macmillan described nationalism "as a tidal wave surging from Asia across the ocean to the shores of Africa," and although he understood that it couldn't be "driven back," he believed that it could be "led."[1] Despite its retreat from Asia, its Suez misadventure, and its grant of independence to the West African colony of

Ghana, an attenuated and chastened Great Britain still clung to late-Victorian notions of its place in world history and world politics. Indeed, "the dream of a British world-system, updated and modernised, haunted Harold Macmillan."[2] In 1959, he momentarily pinned that dream on the Central African Federation of Rhodesia and Nyasaland: after all, Southern Central Africa was always more important to British economic and strategic interests than West Africa.[3]

Pieced together by imperial fiat out of Southern Rhodesia, Northern Rhodesia, and Nyasaland in 1953, the Central African Federation constituted an attempt to halt Afrikaner nationalism at the Limpopo River by creating a British buffer state between South Africa and its northern neighbours.[4] Ideally, the federation would be a Central African Australia, New Zealand, or Canada, meaning it would be "dynamic, stable, and 100% British."[5] In reality, though, the federation was "a bizarre construct of imperial grand strategy" and the seeds of its breakup were sown at the beginning: Southern Rhodesia had been self-governing since 1923 while Northern Rhodesia and Nyasaland were still protectorates under British direct rule; African opposition to federation in the two northern territories was simply ignored; both Rhodesias had sizeable European minorities but Nyasaland was overwhelmingly African; and, finally, the federation's constitution required a full review in not less than seven years and not more than nine years.[6] The British admitted that the federation was a "hybrid," its critics called it a "bastard," and by 1959 everyone conceded that the thing was coming undone.[7] African nationalism in Nyasaland and Northern Rhodesia and settler nationalism in Southern Rhodesia were miles apart. Meanwhile, the prime minister of the Central African Federation, Sir Roy Welensky, desperately wanted to preserve the federation. Although he was from Southern Rhodesia, his political base was in Northern Rhodesia, and he refused to abandon its European minority to African majority rule. Besides, Northern Rhodesia sat on top of one of the world's greatest deposits of copper and Nyasaland had vast reserves of cheap labour. But Hastings Banda had other ideas. As the leader of Nyasaland African Congress, he feared the apartheid leanings of Southern Rhodesia and demanded nothing less than the dissolution of the federation and independence for his country. When a state of emergency was declared in all three territories in early 1959 and Banda was imprisoned on bogus charges of plotting the murder of government officials, both the Central African Federation and Whitehall went into crisis mode.

Donald Creighton was at his cottage in July 1959 when Harold Macmillan announced his intention to create an advisory commission on the constitutional future of Rhodesia and Nyasaland and indicated that it would have Commonwealth representation, ideally from a multi-racial federation like Canada. As the Commonwealth's senior member, and as a country with an

NIGERIA

AFRIQUE EQUATORIALE FRANCAISE

SUDAN

ETHIOPIA

SOMALIA

UGANDA

KENYA

• Nairobi

CONGO BELGE

TANGANYIKA

• Mombasa

Brazzaville•

• Leopoldville

• Dar-es-Salaam

ATLANTIC OCEAN

• Luanda

Elisabethville•

RHODESIA

NYASALAND

ANGOLA

NORTHERN

MOÇAMBIQUE

SOUTHERN RHODESIA

• Beira

Tananarive •

MALGACHE REP.

SOUTH-WEST

BECHUANA LAND

Walvis Bay•

• Windhoek

AFRICA

Pretoria•

• Johannesburg

• Lourenco Marques

INDIAN OCEAN

UNION OF SOUTH AFRICA

• Durban

Cape Town•

• East London

• Port Elizabeth

SOUTHERN AFRICA
SHOWING
THE RELATIVE POSITION
OF
THE FEDERATION
SCALE 1:32,000,000

This 1960 map shows Northern Rhodesia, Southern Rhodesia, and Nyasaland. The British described the Central African Federation as a "hybrid"; its critics called it a "bastard"; but everyone agreed that it was coming undone.

English-speaking majority and French-speaking minority, it had made a virtue out of federalism. Macmillan also intimated that he wanted the Central African Federation to survive. Regardless of what one now thinks of the scramble for Africa, he told Parliament, the fact remains that European – and especially British – imperialism has improved Africa. Why, in Rhodesia, there had been "no schools, no roads, and no hospitals"; its resources had not been developed; and its agriculture had been "primitive." The choice was clear, he said: Great Britain could continue its "fruitful partnership" with Rhodesia and Nyasaland or it could let the federation descend into chaos. Privately, his Commonwealth secretary had told Welensky that the appointment of a commission "with no axe to grind" and "hearing evidence in public from all and sundry" would show "the world that there are two communities in Central Africa," one white and the other black, "and that Africa for the Africans is the very negation of partnership."[8] Although Welensky doubted the wisdom of a commission – it would accelerate the already "excessively fast pace" of African advancement and it would harden "opinion in the Federation against" interference from Great Britain – he had to play ball with Macmillan.[9]

Initially, Britain wanted to appoint Douglas Abbott, a Supreme Court judge and a former cabinet minister in the governments of Mackenzie King and Louis St Laurent. Actually, it had been Roy Welensky who first suggested Abbott after one of his colleagues had spoken highly of him. To appease the federation's prime minister, Britain agreed, but, as the Colonial Office pointed out, Abbott had been a minister "in a Canadian government whose general attitude on 'colonialism' in the United Nations was not always as helpful as we might have wished."[10] Put another way, he had been a member of a government that didn't say "ready, aye ready" in 1956. As a diplomatic courtesy, the British high commissioner informed John Diefenbaker that his government wished to appoint Justice Abbott, but the thin-skinned Chief clearly remembered Abbott sitting on the opposite side of the House. The high commissioner invited other suggestions, but Diefenbaker said that he would have to consult his colleagues. Much to the high commissioner's frustration, he took his time. Events were unfolding quickly in Rhodesia and Nyasaland – indeed, the political landscape was becoming more volatile by the day – and the British government was anxious to finalize the commission's membership. Diefenbaker had either forgiven or forgotten the "strange opinions" in Donald Creighton's 1954 address to the Couchiching Conference because, ten days later, he recommended him to the British high commissioner.

In turn, Whitehall floated Creighton's name to Welensky. As long as he was a he and he came from Canada, the former Rhodesian heavyweight boxing champion didn't care. Throughout the process, he had asked Whitehall to limit the number of women and to rule out Commonwealth representation – meaning "coloured" representation – from Malaya, India, or the West Indies.

When the British high commissioner met Creighton in Toronto in early November, he received a polite but incredulous response. Neither a student of African politics nor an expert in constitutional law, Creighton could not understand why Great Britain wanted to appoint him to its advisory commission. The high commissioner told him that he would bring an informed impartiality to the table. He also explained that the commission would be addressing some of "the most important problems affecting the Commonwealth in the next decade" – the problems of African nationalism, settler nationalism, multi-racial democracy, independence, and the preservation of British influence in a strategic corner of the world that linked the North Sea nation to the Indian and Southern Pacific Oceans, or what used to be called the Southern British World. Overwhelmed by the invitation and the issues it raised, Creighton agreed to sleep on it.[11]

Privately, the high commissioner reported his impressions of Canada's leading historian. Creighton is not "a dynamic personality nor will his name carry great weight in the Commission," he said, but "he is an excellent chap," at once "serious-minded and painstaking." Moreover, the high commissioner added, he is "sympathetically disposed to the Commonwealth connection."[12]

Despite his reservations, Creighton let his name stand on 11 November, or Armistice Day, and, two weeks later, Harold Macmillan stood up in the House of Commons to announce his appointment. Calling him a "distinguished citizen," the British prime minister thanked him in advance for his service to "this arduous but vital task."[13] Although Creighton would not be hauling a boat up the Nile to Khartoum or manning an outpost in the Transvaal, he would be defending British interests in an economically important and politically sensitive part of the empire.

And then he got, in the words of one British official, "cold feet."[14] From the moment Harold Macmillan announced his intentions, the Advisory Commission had become a lightning rod both in Great Britain and the Central African Federation, and now the Labour Party openly questioned its membership and its terms of reference. Labour had a point: only five of twenty-six commission members were African, and according to its terms of reference the commission could not consider the federation's dissolution. Ultimately, Labour decided to boycott the commission altogether. Meanwhile, Africans across the federation announced their own boycott. The commission's mandate was too narrow, its African members were "stupid dogs," and Hastings Banda was still in jail.[15] From their perspective, the federation had been a shotgun marriage and they wanted a divorce. Although some British newspapers supported the government's intention to press on, others questioned the wisdom of a commission that, before it even convened, had divided British and African opinion. The *Manchester Guardian* argued that the commission required a broader mandate and called its membership "respectable but not inspiring." The *London Observer* went further, describing the two Commonwealth members as "unexciting federal experts from Canada and Australia."[16]

Alarmed by the "violence" of the opposition both in Great Britain and Central Africa, Creighton asked the British high commissioner to be "relieved" of his appointment. It was now the high commissioner's turn to be incredulous. Creighton may be a "man of scruples," he informed the Colonial Office, but he is quite "unversed in political matters." Not having the stomach for politics, he now finds himself "in a somewhat emotional state."[17] The Colonial Office instructed the high commissioner to do whatever he had to do to prevent Creighton's resignation: tell him that it will embarrass Harold Macmillan; tell him that the creation of "a politically stable multi-racial society" in Central Africa "will have repercussions in the Union of South Africa and indeed throughout the continent"; tell him that, when it is prepared, this report will do for Africa what the Durham Report did for British North America; and, finally, tell him that it "will make history."[18] It was a clever strategy: in appealing to Lord Durham's famous Report on the Affairs of British North America, Whitehall was appealing to Creighton's sense of purpose and destiny. In a subsequent telephone conversation, the high commissioner "pulled out all the stops" and, in the end, convinced him not to resign. The last thing he wanted to do, Creighton told the high commissioner, was to create "difficulties" for the government of Great Britain.[19]

His appointment to the Advisory Commission was, he told John Diefenbaker, "a great honour" and confirmed his authority as a public intellectual. According to the *Globe and Mail*, it also confirmed Canada's transformation from a colony into the Commonwealth's "senior Dominion."[20] Apparently no one had told the *Globe* that "dominion" was four-letter word in certain political circles after previous Liberal governments decided that it connoted Canada's colonial status. But the Liberals were in the wilderness of opposition and Creighton now had the opportunity to carry the benefit of Canada's experience as a British dominion to Central Africa.

II

Over the Christmas holidays and into the New Year, Donald and Luella talked a lot about his coming trip. All told, he would be out of the country for the better part of seven months. Because he needed her company and her attention, Donald wanted Luella to come with him. He could make a cup of tea for

Appearing in *Punch*, a British magazine of humour and satire, this political cartoon problematically draws on the stereotype of Africa as the dark continent. But it also pokes fun at the hubris of empire, the idea that a British commission could solve the "problem" of African nationalism. Sitting in the tree are Labour leader Hugh Gaitskell (left) and deputy leader Nye Bevan (right). The Labour Party boycotted the Monckton Commission and is here presented as a lurking political threat.

himself, but that was pretty much the extent of his domestic skills. Both he and Luella worried about his stomach. How would it adapt to a new diet? Could it tolerate African dishes? And who would look after him if he had a "disturbance"? When he finally learned that, while she was welcome to meet him in London, she could not go to the Central African Federation, he "found it rather hard to take."[21]

Right now there were a million things to do: he had to finalize the details of his leave of absence, finish chapter five of the Richardson book, and get a series of inoculations against typhus, typhoid, and yellow fever. He also had to pack. Among the different clothing items the Colonial Office recommended were a dinner jacket and cummerbund.[22] Buried in the request to bring evening attire were assumptions about British supremacy. After all, imperialism was always more than a set of political, economic, and military forces. It was also cultural, and it was reproduced in art, literature, architecture, and even clothes. To project British power, commissioners were expected to dress the part of gentlemen at sundowners and formal events.

On 31 January Luella hosted a family farewell dinner for Donald. Cynthia was there, of course. Philip, his wife Phyllis, and their two little girls came. And so did Harold and Isabel. Donald's departure was a source of both excitement and apprehension. Like David Livingstone – the nineteenth-century explorer who, in Creighton's words, "plunged into the depths of central Africa" and, in the process, came to occupy an iconic place in the British world's imagination – he would be a long way from home. What if he became lost like Livingstone? Who would rescue him? And what would his rescuer say? "Dr. Creighton, I presume?"[23] It was like something out of *Boy's Own Paper* and *Little Folks*, only it wasn't. The imperial project was never innocent, and as it neared its end, the stakes were huge: unscrambling Africa would not be easy, violence was imminent, and security was on everyone's mind. The Mau Mau revolt in Kenya – with its atrocities against both Europeans and Africans and its brutal mass suppression by the British – had unnerved everyone. Politicians passed emergency legislation; armed patrols readied themselves for the coming race war; and anxious children listened to their parents whisper about Europeans who had been murdered in those countries to the north that had "fallen."[24]

Five days later, Creighton arrived in London, "delighted," he said, "to be back again." He had first been to the city in 1925 and now, thirty-five years later, he was there as a guest of Her Majesty's Government. In addition to seeing old friends, taking long walks, and going to the opera, he met some of the other commissioners, including the chairman, Viscount Monckton of Brenchley. An alumnus of Balliol, a veteran of the First World War, a close friend to King Edward VIII, and a seasoned politician, Walter Monckton was a go-to person in moments of panic because of his ability to mediate competing opinions. Indeed, he had been the king's confidant and legal adviser during the abdication crisis. Vincent Massey had known Monckton at Balliol and remembered him as a "brilliant" and "versatile" man who also happened to be "a first-class cricketer."[25] In a private – and sobering – letter to Monckton, Harold Macmillan outlined the enormity of the problem: "If we fail in Central Africa to devise something like a workable multi-racial state, then Kenya will go too and Africa may become no longer a source of pride and profit for the Europeans who have developed it but a maelstrom of trouble into which all of us will be sucked." The Africans, he acknowledged, cannot be "dominated permanently," but the Europeans cannot be "abandoned." With classic British understatement, Monckton told a group of journalists that he had been handed "a pretty hard assignment."[26]

After a nearly twenty-four-hour flight that stopped in Tripoli, Khartoum, and Nairobi, the commission and its support staff finally arrived in Livingstone, Northern Rhodesia, only to be greeted by a violent thunderstorm. Named after the famed explorer, Livingstone sits on the Zambezi River just ten kilometres from Victoria Falls, the highest waterfall in the world. To cultivate moderate African opinion, or what one Cabinet briefing note called "sensible" African opinion,[27] Whitehall decided not to begin in Salisbury, the largest city in Southern Rhodesia and the federation's capital; it also ensured that the Victoria Falls Hotel would be desegregated and declared multi-racial for the duration of the commission's stay. According to the logic of imperialism, colonial opinion was either sensible – meaning it conformed to imperial expectations – or it was insensible – meaning it didn't – and Whitehall retained the prerogative to make the distinction.

From its base at the "palatial" Victoria Falls Hotel – where King George VI and his family had stayed in 1947, where mist from the falls can be seen rising hundreds of metres into the sky above the rainforest, and where, at night, when everything is quiet, their faint roar can be heard above the crickets – the commission began its work.[28] After a few introductory remarks and other pleasantries, it ran into a point of order that threatened to derail everything when the commissioners representing the federation demanded that evidence on secession be made inadmissible. Elspeth Huxley – the only woman on the commission – suspected that Roy Welensky had put them up to it: from the beginning, the pugnacious prime minister had been frustrated by his British counterpart's unwillingness to explicitly exclude evidence on secession in the commission's terms of reference.[29] Harold Macmillan had told the House of Commons that the commission was "free, in practice, to hear all points of view from whatever quarter and on whatever subject," and he had told Welensky that "no one, in practice, can prevent that."[30] Diplomatic cables were exchanged between Livingstone and London seeking clarification while Monckton used his skills of persuasion and conciliation to keep the discussion moving forward and to prevent the resignation of any commissioners. But even he was concerned that the commission might "disintegrate" before it began. According to one diplomatic cable, the dispute "threatened to wreck the whole exercise at the start."[31]

It was at "this critical moment" that Creighton intervened, lending "powerful support" to Monckton and "to the idea of making evidence on the question of secession admissible."[32] He didn't know very much but he knew that to exclude it was to exclude African majority opinion. As an early and measured intervention, it signalled his intention to be a full member of the commission and may have averted a disaster.

In order to cover more ground, the commission broke into three groups, and for the next twelve weeks it criss-crossed the federation. Travelling by Land Rovers and Beaver bush planes – made by de Havilland Canada – the twenty-six commissioners logged 27,000 kilometres, heard from approximately 750 groups and individuals, and gathered two and half tons of material. They met witnesses in hotels, offices, grass huts, open fields, and, at least once, beneath the shade of a single tree. It was exhausting work, physically and emotionally, especially since it was obvious from the outset that African nationalism and settler nationalism were two very different languages. Despite six or seven decades of British settlement, Southern Rhodesia was still a place where a white child could grow up without ever fully understanding that eight million Africans "really existed."[33]

When they didn't boycott the commission, most African witnesses in Northern Rhodesia and Nyasaland reiterated their opposition to the federation. Demanding its immediate dissolution, the Choma Tonga Native Authority in Northern Rhodesia pointed a collective finger at Roy Welensky, "his short-sighted European Cabinet," and its "discriminatory and vexatious laws." It also bitterly resented the federal government's use of the label "extremist" to describe anyone who challenged the federation. But in its brief, Welensky's United Federal Party (UFP) reiterated its defence of the federation and its belief that "African opposition is based on narrow African nationalism." Relying on the doctrine of improvement, the UFP argued that "the energy, initiative, skill, and capital of the Europeans" had transformed the two Rhodesias and Nyasaland "from a wilderness into a modern state."[34]

One man implicitly critiqued that doctrine when he feared that the arrival of European farmers to Nyasaland would mean large estates for them and poverty for everyone else, adding that he simply wanted to be left alone to raise his children and cultivate his gardens. But to a white farmer in Southern Rhodesia,

Appointed by the British prime minister in 1959, the Advisory Commission on the Review of the Constitution of the Federation of Rhodesia and Nyasaland had an impossible assignment – to reconcile African nationalism and settler nationalism in the Central African Federation. Convening in Livingstone in February 1960, the commission posed for a group photograph on the back lawn of the Victoria Falls Hotel. The mist from the falls can be seen on the left rising above the rainforest canopy. Seated in the centre and wearing glasses, Lord Monckton kept the commission moving forward. Seated second from the left, Donald Creighton took his responsibilities seriously.

estate farming was the definition of progress, an idea, he explained, that is beyond the "psychology" of the average African, who is "impulsive," "superstitious," "inadequate," "disappointing," and, after the age of twelve or thirteen, absorbed "in matters of sex."[35] A Northern Rhodesian witness went further, warning that Mau Mau's "reign of terror" in Kenya – its rapes and its murders – could happen in the federation at any moment. The African, G.L. Lipschild explained, has a "nerve-wracking habit of walking up on you, whether barefooted or shoe-shod, in absolute silence, just slinking about and appearing suddenly seemingly out of nowhere." Once the "fateful drum" is played indicating a general and bloody uprising, will "women and children" be safe? he asked the commissioners. The fear of the black rapist was never far from the surface.[36]

As a member of the Monckton Commission, Donald Creighton travelled across the Central African Federation, sometimes by Land Rover, often by airplane. "We then said good-bye to the D.C. [district commissioner] and took off from the bumpy stubble field," he wrote after one flight. "More enormous herds of antelope on the way back. In addition, the pilot took us over the Victoria Falls, and the aerial view is the only complete one. We were back in time for dinner."

Hoping to find the elusive middle between settler nationalism and African nationalism, Donald Creighton read the briefing documents and background papers contained in what one commissioner called the "appalling flood of memoranda";[37] he listened to witness after witness, asked thoughtful questions, and took detailed notes.[38] In the words of a Commonwealth Relations Office document, he wanted to identify those "Europeans and Africans of common sense and goodwill."[39] He therefore dismissed the North-Eastern Rhodesia Agricultural Association as "utterly unyielding and intractable" because of its claim that Africans were not "civilized" and therefore not fit to govern.[40] And after listening to the Settlers and Residents Association of Nyasaland assert that "the average African has absolutely no conception" of the meaning of the phrase "political freedom," Creighton called them "reactionaries, pure and simple."[41] But he didn't have much time for T.D.T. Banda either, the leader of Nyasaland's Congress Liberation Party and one of the few Nyasa nationalists to appear before the commission, despite being called a "stooge" by opponents of the "Mockery Commission." Accompanied by a dozen "lieutenants" who clapped and shouted during his presentation, Banda condemned the federation, the colour bar in Southern Rhodesia, the use of his country as "a reservoir of cheap of labour," and the imposition of emergency rule. He also demanded the right of secession and the grant of independence. Describing Banda's four-and-a-half-hour presentation as one "long harangue,"[42] Creighton was "disgusted" by some of its wild assertions about the federation, the division of powers, and Nyasaland's economic viability.[43]

But even Creighton had to admit that Banda's responses to specific questions were "more sensible," making it impossible to isolate extreme from moderate opinion or to locate the elusive middle. Whitehall's battle to cultivate sensible African opinion was lost before it began. Listening to the Anglican bishop of Nyasaland defend the federation in principle but pronounce it dead in practice was, Creighton said, "very gloomy and depressing."[44]

The commissioners also toured hospitals, schools, farms, and factories, although security was tight and they were guarded "like the crown jewels."[45] At one point, Creighton explored a "pre-historic" cave with 2,000-year-old wall paintings of animals; a week later, he entered a very different kind of cavern when he descended 200 metres into the earth to see the massive Kariba dam, then the largest dam in the world; he was shown the stone palace of the ancient kingdom of Zimbabwe; and he spent Easter at a game reserve where he saw "zebras, giraffes, wildebeest, antelope, buffalo, [and] ostriches." The elephants, though, were the most impressive, his driver taking him "quite close" to one large herd of fifteen or twenty.[46]

The African people, however, were largely Other to him. At the Nairobi airport he recorded his "first sight of Africans in numbers walking about." And although he interviewed hundreds of African witnesses, he never actually had a conversation with anyone. Instead, they were the objects of his gaze. After visiting a small peasant farm, he noted that it didn't have a bathroom – always a signifier of "civilization" – but the farmer had three wives and a "marvellous" leopard-skin coat.[47] When he watched members of the Chewa tribe dance, Creighton couldn't take his eyes off one man wearing a long red mask and a short grass skirt with dried gourds tied to his ankles: "His shoulders remained absolutely still but his hips wiggled in a most amazing fashion." And at a garden party, he was surprised to see a woman "unconcernedly give her baby the breast."[48] Creighton was out of his element; he was, Elspeth Huxley said, "a fish out of water." Because she had grown up in Kenya's White Highlands, leopard-skin coats, grass skirts, wiggling hips, and bare breasts were not strange to her in the way they were to Creighton.[49]

But what most affected Creighton was the landscape. It was so unlike the landscape of central Canada, the Laurentian Shield, and the boreal forest. Flying at low altitudes and driving for long stretches, he found himself moved by the rocky uplands, the long, green river valleys of the Zambezi, and the immense reaches of open grassland that seemed to go on forever. It is an "almost empty country," he commented after his first plane trip.[50] And after a 600-kilometre journey by Land Rover, he observed the vastness of the landscape and the lack of any settlements. It is, he wrote, a "seemingly unoccupied and desolate country" where everything "conspires to strengthen the general impression of empty immensity."[51]

The language of emptiness – like the legal fiction of *terra nullius* and the doctrine of improvement – was not a neutral language describing an objective reality. Rather, it was an essential part of the larger language of imperialism, colonialism, and the great land rush,[52] a point made over and over again by witnesses to the commission. A "special example of African suffering," I. Kandanda told the commission, is the fact that Africans "have been driven from a great deal of their land" in Southern Rhodesia and he didn't want to be driven from his land in Northern Rhodesia. The Chewa Lundazi Native Authority reported that Southern Rhodesia had been taken by conquest, and "our fear is that eventually the Northern Territories [will] be dominated and over-swamped": "We do not trust these settlers in sheep's clothes." Damon Mtonga didn't trust the settlers either. They think that Northern Rhodesia is "empty," he said, and he didn't want to be "cheated" of his land. When the commission asked G.S.J. Ngoma why he opposed federation, he responded that federation meant that "the land can be taken." He also said that had David Livingstone done in the last century what Roy Welensky is doing in this century, he would have been killed.[53]

The commission not only listened, it was being listened to: technically a liaison officer assigned by the federation to assist the commission, A.D. (Taffy) Evans doubled as Welensky's man on the ground tasked with befriending the commissioners. In regular communiqués sent directly to the prime minister, Evans divulged what individual commissioners were thinking. "I like the Canadian," he said in an early communiqué. "I think he is sound; he has not as yet expressed any views to me but I like his openness and his willingness to be persuaded of what he sees and hears."[54] By "sound," Evans meant that Creighton was not disposed to prejudge the federation as a colossal mistake. Evans's initial assessment was shrewd: although he found him "shy" and felt that he sometimes lived in "the clouds of constitutional academics," he nonetheless

At one of the many receptions held for the commissioners, Donald Creighton chatted with fellow commissioner, the writer Elspeth Huxley. In a letter to her husband, she described Creighton as a "fish out of water," implying that he was out of his element in Africa. In 1963 she published *The Merry Hippo*, a satirical murder mystery. Set in the fictional African country of Hapana on the eve of independence, it follows the ups and downs of the Connor Commission, the Royal Commission on Constitutional Changes in the Protectorate of Hapana.

appreciated Creighton's instinctive defence of the federal government over the territorial governments.[55] "He is a firm believer" in federalism, "and I think it would very much go against his wish to see any dismemberment of any federal system."[56] Although Evans hadn't read the biography of Sir John A. Macdonald, he had pegged its author: in both *The Young Politician* and *The Old Chieftain,* Creighton defended the idea of a strong federal government, at one point referring to provinces as "foreign bodies" and to premiers as "insolent provincialists."[57]

III

When the commission reconvened in London in late May it somehow had to reconcile the racist fantasies of a G.L. Lipschild to the legitimate worries of a Damon Mtonga, and the reactionary opposition of the Settlers and Residents Association of Nyasaland to the insistent demands of the Congress Liberation Party. It would be more than "a pretty hard assignment" – it would be an impossible assignment.

For the next three and half months, the commission worked at a feverish pace. Creighton was tired and didn't feel well much of the time. On two separate occasions, he had been ill – or "indisposed" in the words of one diplomatic cable – in the Central African Federation and had to miss a number of hearings and social events, including the final sundowner in Salisbury. Now, in London, the familiar "disturbances" were back. Some days he felt fine but other days he was confined to his room on a restricted diet of weak tea and dry biscuits. The stress was overwhelming. Like the Fathers of Confederation in London in 1866, the commissioners were trying to build a durable federation, and each day they had to tackle something else: the division of powers, the right of secession, the location of the capital, the franchise, and even the name of the future country. At times, Creighton found it "depressing" because the discussion kept going in circles: everyone had an opinion on everything and no one seemed to know the difference between "responsive" and "responsible" government.[58] But he also knew that the commission was not just laying the groundwork for a durable federation, it was laying the groundwork for a multi-racial state. In this sense, it saw a very different future from the one Lord Durham envisioned in 1839 when he recommended French Canada's assimilation.

Despite the heavy workload, London had many wonderful distractions, including Luella. She had met him in Italy for a ten-day vacation in mid-May, and now they had their evenings and weekends together. Despite his many commitments and his periods of ill-health, they had a wonderful summer.

They did the usual things – going to the theatre, the opera, and the Tate, and reading the Sunday papers in Hyde Park – but they were also given tickets to the women's semi-final at Wimbledon. They sat in the Royal Box at the Earls Court Military Tournament, and, from a private stand at Ascot, they watched the King George VI and Queen Elizabeth Stakes. At Fishmongers Hall, they met the Queen Mother; at 10 Downing St., they chatted with the prime minister; at Buckingham Palace, they were presented to Queen Elizabeth and Prince Philip; and on a perfect weekend in July, they were the guests of fellow commissioner Lord Crathorne at Crathorne Hall in North Yorkshire. After touring the massive estate, including an aviary for hatching and releasing game birds, Donald and Luella enjoyed a dinner of roast mutton, lovely wine, and a "perfectly marvellous" 1912 vintage port.[59]

On 2 September, the commission held its final meeting. A few days earlier, Creighton had been asked by the commission's vice-chairman to move a vote of thanks to Lord Monckton. The task was a small one, but it carried the symbolic recognition of his hard work and his many contributions, including his initial intervention in Livingstone on the question of hearing evidence on secession. Creighton duly thanked the Viscount of Brenchley for his patience, his help, and his encouragement, adding that he had wanted to say that, as a chairman, he had been "inspiring, but I thought that some of my British colleagues might regard that as an example of North American over-emphasis."[60]

One commissioner believed that Monckton's patient leadership could "calm an angry buffalo,"[61] but it couldn't calm "the winds of change" blowing across Africa. In a letter to Prime Minister Macmillan, Monckton conceded that Britain's most controversial large-scale exercise in state building was all but dead and that the chances of "reviving" it were "thin."[62] Curiously enough, the commission maintained that the federation's only hope lay in the right of secession. In recommending the right of secession, the commission was not recommending dissolution. That would have been a clear violation of its terms of reference. In fact, the commission bent over backwards to defend the federation, hoping instead that the right of secession would never be used and that it would function as a sort of constitutional "safety valve" obviating the resort to violence: "A right to secede would, far from weakening a federation, enable it to survive."[63] The commission knew that secession was an explosive subject, but it also knew that "the dislike of federation among Africans in the two Northern Territories is widespread, sincere, and of long standing. It is almost pathological."[64] Because it implied that African opposition to white rule from southern Rhodesia was somehow diseased, the word pathological was an unfortunate if honest attempt to describe what the commission heard. Despite their "great disappointment and anger," even the European Rhodesian commissioners signed the final report.[65]

Although he considered himself a "federalist" rather than a "territorialist," Creighton fully supported a constitutional right of secession, a division of powers that favoured the territorial governments over the federal government, and the inclusion of a Canadian-style bill of rights to protect basic human rights and freedoms.[66] He also wanted to ensure – and the final report recommended as much – that the federal government retained the taxation room necessary to nation building. At one point in the London deliberations, he had arranged for an expert from the Canadian High Commission to explain Canada's tax-rental system to the commission, a system which gave the federal government the fiscal capacity it needed to finance the Second World War and Canada's postwar development.

Actually, Creighton was happy with the final report. If its recommendations tilted towards the territories, that was the price of keeping the federation together. The alternative to federation was not just its break-up, it was the "admission that there is no hope of survival for any multi-racial society on the African continent and that differences of colour and race are irreconcilable." It was the admission that South Africa was right. And it was the admission that British imperialism had not been beneficial to Africa. Southern Rhodesia, the report asserted, "has been ruled with efficiency and energy by its white community of settlers and their descendants, who are justly proud of their achievements in turning wilderness into fertile farms, in founding industries and cities, and in promoting African welfare and education."[67]

Clearly, the commission could not break the settler contract, the original – and racial – contract of occupation and settlement that "gave" this corner of Africa to British settlers in the late nineteenth century. Similarly, the commission could not think outside the logic of improvement as a universal model of economic development. In this sense, it echoed Lord Durham, whose own report was animated by the desire to "lay the foundations of order, tranquillity, and improvement."[68]

Lord Monckton delivered the final report to Prime Minister Macmillan in early September, but Taffy Evans – Roy Welensky's personal conduit to the commission – had gleaned that its recommendations were controversial, warning his boss that he would be "infuriated" when he received a copy. Actually, Welensky didn't have to wait for his copy because, a few days later, Whitehall leaked some of its contents. Welensky was indeed furious: to appease African nationalism, Her Majesty's Government had abandoned Her Majesty's Central African subjects.[69] Despite Whitehall's desire "to keep the temperature of public discussion as low as possible," Welensky publicly denounced the commission for going beyond its terms of reference and betraying "the tenets of British justice."[70] Privately, he said that the federation had been "stabbed right in the back," adding that, from now on, it was going to be up to "us" – meaning European

Rhodesians – to shape our destiny: "I am not relying on any comfort or help from the United Kingdom."[71]

From Canada, Donald Creighton watched events unfold in the Central African Federation: if the Monckton Commission couldn't rewrite the settler contract, Africans could, and that is precisely what happened over the next three or four years. But if his sympathies lay with the federation, Creighton didn't sympathize with white minority rule. The South African solution was not a solution at all, and, in February 1961, he communicated this to the prime minister. When he met John Diefenbaker in Ottawa, he assumed their conversation would be about the Central African Federation, but the Chief quickly turned to the question of South Africa's membership in the Commonwealth. Confessing that he hadn't given the matter much thought, Creighton agreed to write a position paper. In a brief six-page document, Creighton argued that although other Commonwealth countries – including Canada – "have sinned" against the principles of multi-racial democracy, apartheid is "unique" and Sharpeville indicates the depths of South Africa's willingness "to enforce" a policy that has "all the authority of a religious dogma." Because it has shown itself indifferent to the weight of world opinion, South Africa should be excluded from the Commonwealth, he concluded, otherwise the Commonwealth as a multi-racial association of independent states is meaningless.[72] In its analysis, however, the Department of External Affairs had urged a more cautious approach. Indeed, this was the position of Diefenbaker's own external affairs minister, who argued against South Africa's exclusion.

Going into the Commonwealth Prime Ministers' Conference in London that March, Diefenbaker still hadn't made up his mind, but, in the end, he stood beside the prime ministers of India, Malaya, Ghana, and Nigeria when the prime ministers of Great Britain, Australia, and New Zealand didn't, and South Africa was effectively excluded from the Commonwealth. For Harold Macmillan, who "had nourished high hopes of being able to steer the Conference into accepting the request of the S.A. gov't that S.A. should remain in the Commonwealth," it was "a most exhausting and most painful affair."[73] For John Diefenbaker, it "marked a high point of his prime ministership."[74]

Creighton did not tip the prime minister's hand – his voice was one among many pressing Diefenbaker to reject South Africa's application for readmission – but he was on the right side of history when the Department of External Affairs advised caution. "I am pretty certain," he told Eugene Forsey, "that the Dept. of External Affairs was opposed to the policy [Diefenbaker] pursued at the Conference. I think this fits in clearly with the Department's policy, consistently pursued since the days of [Oscar] Skelton, to prevent or avoid anything which will give the Commonwealth meaning or significance." Forsey agreed that the prime minister's "stand on South Africa was excellent": "no doubt you had a good deal to do with that."[75]

With South Africa out of the Commonwealth and the Central African Federation heading towards dissolution, "the long British moment in South-Central Africa ended."[76] It was about to end in Canada as well.

IV

Donald Creighton was fifty-eight years old in April 1961 when he and Luella decided to look for a new house. The timing made sense: they had been renting the same upstairs apartment at 11 Parkwood Avenue since 1954; Cynthia had been awarded a Woodrow Wilson Fellowship to pursue graduate work at Berkeley in the fall; and, although he had no definite plans, Donald was inching closer to retirement. Actually, it was Luella who pushed the issue. She desperately wanted a big house in a small village, a place to write, to entertain, and to plant a rose garden. She wanted, she said, to live in a place where she could borrow a cup of sugar from her neighbour.[77]

But mostly Luella wanted to get Donald out of the city. His stomach seemed to be in a perpetual state of contorted misery and his familiar rash had come back. Unable to diagnose a physical cause, one doctor suggested that he was "obsessive-compulsive" and prescribed tranquillizers, but their side effects included fatigue and depression so he stopped taking them. He wasn't obsessive-compulsive but he was overworked. The Richardson book was still not done, and the family had intimated that it was unhappy with the draft chapters. The book on Confederation that he had agreed to write in 1958 had not been started yet. And, of course, he carried a heavy teaching and administrative load, at one point confessing that university teaching had become "a drag" on his "health and spirits."[78] When he repeated his wish to be made a research professor, an "unsympathetic" Vincent Bladen all but laughed: "Everybody would like to be a research professor, he said, and he himself would like to be a 'research president.'"[79] If the university wouldn't relieve her husband's burden, Luella would. Living outside the city, she reasoned, would mean less time at the department; less time at the department would mean less time debating the undergraduate curriculum; and less time debating the undergraduate curriculum would mean more time to enjoy life.

For the next ten or eleven months, Donald and Luella looked at houses in Palgrave, Georgetown, Maple, and King. They even looked at a house in Siloam, that tiny dot on the map they had escaped to as young lovers in the summer of 1925. When an offer on a house in Uxbridge fell through, they decided on a whim to look at a house in Brooklin, a small village east of Toronto near Whitby. It was perfect. Located on a quiet, tree-lined residential street, the red-brick, two-storey Victorian farmhouse backed on to Lynde Creek. Donald described it as an "Old Ontario house." Outside, it featured white brick lintels, decorative barge-boarding, and wooden shutters. Inside, it had generous rooms downstairs and a couple of bedrooms upstairs, meaning they could each have a room of their own. Luella especially liked the pine floors. "There is a quality of timelessness about them," she wrote. "They suggest security and are undemanding."[80] Two days later, Donald and Luella offered $18,500, and in May 1962 they moved in.

Built in 1877, 15 Princess Street represented a symbolic link to a very different Canada and to a very different world. In those days, John A. Macdonald led the Conservative Party; Benjamin Disraeli played the Great Game; and Queen Victoria presided over a confident empire. Now, eighty-five years later, John Diefenbaker led a divided Tory caucus; Harold Macmillan conceded Britain's inability to play any game; and Queen Elizabeth stood at the head of a confused Commonwealth. Within a few years, Elspeth Huxley would describe the Commonwealth as "the remnants of a tattered dream of imperial glory," and Great Britain, she argued, would be wise to "bow out" of an organization that had become, at best, a "platitudinous after-dinner speech" and, at worst, "a shouting match."[81] No one knew what the thing stood for after Great Britain, when faced with the choice of Europe or the Commonwealth, chose Europe in 1961. With his dream of a British world system floundering in the wake of the Monckton Commission and the imminent collapse of the Central African Federation, Macmillan stunned his Commonwealth trading partners when he announced his government's intention to join the European Economic Community. Loyalty, it seemed, was a one-way street.[82]

Decolonization was not only a political and economic process, it was also a psychological process that asked difficult questions about national identity. Creighton once described it as "vast and painful." And if it reshaped post-colonial Asia and Africa, it also reshaped Australia, New Zealand, English Canada, and French Canada.[83] The Quiet Revolution may have had its own logic but that logic drew on international examples and comparisons. As Canada's largest province transformed itself into a modern, secular, and nationalist jurisdiction anxious to flex its economic and constitutional strength in a redefined federation, many French-speaking Quebeckers wanted more. Inspired by anti-colonial movements around the world, they demanded not constitutional reform but Quebec's liberation. In October 1960, the Rassemblement pour l'Indépendance Nationale, or RIN, issued its manifesto calling for "the total independence of Quebec": just as Asian and African nations are "throwing off the colonial yoke," French Canada must also free itself from "foreign" control.[84]

Although it would be another six years before Pierre Vallières published *White Niggers of America*, nationalist intellectuals were already describing French-speaking Quebeckers as the "nègres blancs" of Canada.

Meanwhile, the Other Quiet Revolution witnessed the disappearance of English Canada as an ethnically British nation and its eventual replacement by a civic definition of nation premised on equality, bilingualism, and multiculturalism.[85] It was in this context that John A. Macdonald's old war cry – "A British subject I was born, a British subject I will die" – lost its ability to rally English Canadians. Of course, it never had the ability to rally French Canadians, and in 1962 Pierre Trudeau urged his counterparts on the other side of the national divide to change or face the consequences. "English Canadians, with their own nationalism, will have to retire gracefully to their proper place, consenting to modify their own precious image of what Canada ought to be."[86]

But the view from 15 Princess Street was different than the view from downtown Montreal. From their study windows, Donald and Luella saw the old Canada. By this point, Luella's writing had undergone a major shift. In 1956, she completed her third novel. Despite an earlier promise, "Music in the Park" took her back to Kinsail, although this time the story focused on a young man's difficult but ultimately successful adjustment to village life after being wounded in the Second World War. Later she would describe Kinsail as "something of a literary concept," as "an image small enough to be carried in [her] heart," and as a little treasure that could be taken out, examined, and put back again.[87] But when "Music in the Park" wasn't published, Luella put it in a drawer and turned instead to writing history for a juvenile audience. Perhaps it was a way of avoiding the hard work of writing fiction. By her own – and sad – admission, she regretted not having "really worked" at her writing.[88]

When it was presented to her, Luella jumped at the invitation to write a textbook for children in grades seven and eight – frankly, it was easier than trying to revise her novel. Published in the early 1960s, *The Struggle for Empire* and *Trial and Triumph* followed a predictable narrative of discovery, exploration, settlement, and nationhood. "The French Canadian," she wrote, "was likely to be a short man, strong and lively, obstinate and gay, a singer, a dancer, [and] a lover of horses." Fortunately, the Conquest brought the British – a more dynamic, less folkloric people – to the northern half of the continent, and in very little time French Canadians "learned to respect and trust their new government." In fact, "they and their new masters became friends." The Loyalists, however, were the real Canadians. Their opposition to the United States and their loyalty to Great Britain anticipated modern Canada. In her words, "the Dominion of Canada was born in the minds and hearts of her people many years before Confederation."[89]

Luella Creighton's depiction of French Canada as static, conservative, and Catholic, as a province somehow frozen in time, and her view of English Canada as essentially British, as a nation loyal to the empire, meant that her textbook was out of date the moment it was printed. Of course, she didn't see it that way but she was content to "retire gracefully to her proper place" in a way that her husband was not. Instead of accepting change as normal and inevitable, he drew an unforgiving line in the sand: the old Canada was his Canada and he would defend it tooth and nail against the bloody Liberals and their French-Canadian allies.

His malignant need to focus his anger on a single individual soon found a new target in that "giggling bow-tied bastard," Lester Pearson.[90]

V

In the 1963 election, Lester Pearson's Liberal Party defeated John Diefenbaker's Progressive Conservative Party: the Tory interregnum was over and Liberal rule had been re-established. Except on one or two occasions, Diefenbaker had been a "tragic disappointment," Creighton maintained, primarily because he had failed to revive the old Empire-Commonwealth connection. "I am not even sure that poor old Alexander Mackenzie," the man who kept the seat warm for Sir John A. Macdonald, "failed more dismally at the job."[91] But Creighton never suggested what Diefenbaker might have done to resuscitate what was pretty much dead and what Great Britain had no interest in. In any event, if Diefenbaker had been a disappointment, Pearson was worse. Despite the prime minister's service in the Great War, his Balliol pedigree, and his distinguished career as a diplomat, Creighton hinted that the "bastard" was really an American and that his Oxford degree hid his real preference for cowboy movies and baseball games. Moreover, the decision to appoint a royal commission to investigate the country's "fundamental bicultural character" was as a monstrous act of appeasement; the promise of a new flag was sop to Quebec; and both enervated the country in its struggle against the rising tide of continentalism. In a way, Creighton took it personally, as if the prime minister were doing it to him. "I feel positive hatred towards that man."[92]

As part of Pearson's response to the national unity crisis, which was itself a response to the far larger process of decolonization, the Royal Commission on Bilingualism and Biculturalism was asked to recommend "what steps should be taken to develop the Canadian Confederation on the basis of an equal partnership between the two founding races."[93] Because everyone, it seemed, even people who ought to know better, had an opinion on two nations, associate states, a bi-national Senate, and other such "nonsense," Creighton feared that the commission would either wittingly or unwittingly premise its recommendations on a misunderstanding of what actually happened in 1867. If it "asserts, or implies," he told Eugene Forsey, "that the generation that made Confederation – and its members lasted to the 1890s – ever intended, or even thought, of making a 'bicultural state,' they will be imposing upon the Canadian people the most monstrous example of the Hitlerian 'big lie' in our entire history." And that individual commissioners had been appointed on the basis of their ability to speak and write in both English and French, well, that was about the most "incredibly asinine" thing he had ever heard because it excluded a huge segment of English-Canadian public opinion from its membership. Forsey shared some of Creighton's misgivings – he was especially worried about those "well-meaning idiots" who knew nothing about the Constitution saying God knows what to the commission – but he still hoped that French-language rights could be expanded in a united Canada.[94]

One person who should have known better, Creighton said, was Ramsay Cook. Cook had been his PhD student in the 1950s, and over the years their supervisor-student relationship had grown into a friendship that included Sunday brunches in Brooklin and weekends in Muskoka. Creighton never expected idolatry from his graduate students, but he did expect common sense. And that, he believed, was lacking in Cook's July 1963 essay in the *Canadian Forum,* a left-liberal-Underhillish journal that he loathed. Actually, Cook showed a far deeper understanding of Quebec history – and Canadian history – than his former supervisor when he encouraged English Canadians to respond creatively to the "changed circumstances of the 1960s." To do nothing, to remain silent, to pretend that French-Canadian nationalism doesn't exist, is to deny that Canada is "a country which belongs to French and English Canadians."[95]

"I cannot help but feel you are wrong – terribly wrong," Creighton told his junior colleague. "It seems to me that these fanatical French-Canadian 'nationalists' will never be satisfied except by concessions which only the provinces can give and which no province will give, or can give, without plunging [the country] into a violent controversy the likes of which – thank God! – we have not had for half a century." Creighton concluded his mini-diatribe with an open-ended – but eerily prescient – question. "Do you really think that it is possible to turn back the clock in the western provinces, or even Ontario?" In Creighton's opinion, the plea for French-language rights outside of Quebec and the "radical modification" of Canadian federalism were non-starters. "I cannot help but feel that this is folly – and dangerous folly at that."[96]

Holding his ground, Cook admitted that the Royal Commission's English-Canadian membership was largely "a disgrace," that it was top-heavy with

Liberal hacks. But he wasn't prepared to sit down and idly watch his country go down the drain. To him, it wasn't a question of turning back the clock, but rather of finding a practical solution to a real problem. "The trouble is that I don't see anyone on the scene who can take the situation and use it creatively."[97]

A couple of years later, Pierre Trudeau would emerge as that person, and both Ramsay Cook and Eugene Forsey embraced his vision of one nation, two languages, and many cultures. By that point, though, Creighton's line in the sand had become too wide and too deep for him to cross. He never "got" Trudeau. Convinced that he was right and everyone else was wrong, Creighton's position calcified to the point where it could reach blind rage and he could become English Canada's answer to the white Rhodesian who dug in his heels, shouting "Never, Never, Never."

As a member of the Monckton Commission, Creighton had been prepared to respond creatively to the challenges of decolonization, African nationalism, and the end of empire in Central Africa. Recognizing that the federation had to accommodate the legitimate aspirations of Africans, he had urged Southern Rhodesia to moderate its racist laws and had supported the right of secession. When Northern Rhodesia became Zambia and Nyasaland became Malawi in 1964, and when Southern Rhodesia, now just Rhodesia, issued a Unilateral Declaration of Independence in 1965, Creighton was disappointed, but he wasn't angry.[98] Ultimately, Central Africa was an abstraction. But Canada was real. It was his country, God damn it. And arguments about French-language rights in Ontario, Quebec's secession, and national symbols weren't theoretical, they were visceral. "Everything that hurts the things I love I react against violently – violently!"[99]

VI

In a May 1964 address to the Canadian Legion in Espanola, a small town in his northern Ontario riding of Algoma, Lester Pearson indicated his intention to fulfil his promise of a new Canadian flag when he "talked about the need to introduce symbols of national unity."[100] Creighton wasn't surprised by the prime minister's remarks – after all, Pearson had been talking about a new flag since at least 1960 and in the weeks leading up to his address, he had revealed his preferred design. Dubbed the Pearson pennant, it featured three red maple leafs in the centre and two blue bars, one on either side, symbolizing the Atlantic and Pacific oceans. But in Creighton's opinion, there was nothing wrong with the Red Ensign. It wasn't a foreign flag and, all things considered, had served Canada well. In one letter, Creighton described the idea of a new flag as "deplorable stupidity"; in another letter, he said that the Pearson pennant resembled the label of a beer bottle.[101] The whole thing "disgusted" him.[102] Canada had been a "wretched birthplace" and he now wished that "that he had lived anywhere else."[103] What kind of country deliberately rejects its history?

When Denis Smith, then a professor of political science at Trent University, invited him to sign an open letter to the prime minister, Creighton couldn't say no. Neither could Bill Morton, Eugene Forsey, Tom Symons, or his brother, the writer Scott Symons. The proposed design, they said, is "innocuous," "insipid," "tepid," and "mild." It inspires "indifference" and negates the sum of Canadian history, which, they believed, emphasized order, restraint, and tradition over progress, freedom, and experiment. "We are not in the position of a country with a revolutionary tradition, creating itself anew; we exist because we have inherited the past without revolutionary upheaval." We are conservative, not liberal; we are British, not American; we are Canadian, and the maple leaf will "undermine" our "will to survive."[104] Printed in newspapers across French and English Canada, including on the front page of the *Globe and Mail*, their letter reached the floor of the House of Commons. When asked by a Tory MP for his opinion, the prime minister simply shrugged it off, saying that he knew something about "the weakness of professors of history when they start mingling with contemporary events."[105] Creighton and company, in other words, didn't know what they were talking about.

Wrapping himself in the Red Ensign, John Diefenbaker led the fight against what he called Pearson's disregard for "Canada's heritage," what Creighton called his "plot," and what one scholar has called his "coup."[106] But if Diefenbaker was fighting a rear-guard action, he wasn't an anachronism. Nor was he alone. Polls indicated that the majority of English Canadians supported the Red Ensign.

The flag debate was really a debate about the meaning of Canada, and it overshadowed the Queen's royal visit to mark the centenary of the Charlottetown and Quebec conferences. Five years earlier Queen Elizabeth had been greeted by large and enthusiastic crowds, but her "last great royal tour" hadn't been seamless. One CBC journalist had pointed unwittingly to the Other Quiet Revolution and the emerging division on the place and purpose of the monarchy in English Canada when she told an American television audience that the royal tour left her "indifferent."[107] But if the controversy over Joyce Davidson's remarks was limited to the opinion pages of English-Canadian newspapers, the controversy generated by the Queen's 1964 visit spilled into the streets of Quebec City. In the context of the Quiet Revolution and the growing separatist movement, her visit was seen by many French-speaking Quebeckers as an insult to their national aspirations. Even before the royal yacht entered the St Lawrence River and docked at Wolfe's Cove below the Plains of Abraham where over two hundred years earlier the British had defeated the French, the Queen's visit aroused an angry response. When death threats were made, talk of another Dallas hit the newspapers. Some people wanted to cancel her visit altogether. But Pearson persisted. The cancellation of a royal visit that had been in the works since 1961 would mark a victory for the separatists, he said. It would be, the *Globe and Mail* argued, an admission that "a tiny bunch of French-speaking terrorists" controlled Quebec.[108] And so the visit went ahead as planned, though under tightened security. But when protesters – many of them RIN members – carrying signs that read "Elizabeth Chez Vous!" or "Elizabeth Go Home!" were attacked by the police, they became martyrs, and the sight of uniformed agents of the state beating young men and women entered Quebec mythology as "Samedi de la matraque," or "Truncheon Saturday."[109]

Creighton did not see it that way, of course. It was the Queen who had been "humiliated." And it confirmed his suspicion that Canada was suffering from what he had described in 1961 as "a spiritual and moral depression."[110] In *The Story of Canada* he had placed his hope in a new "Elizabethan Era." But that was then and this was now. "I have gone through another bout of acute depression over the state of our unhappy country," he told Bill Morton, "with black moods equally compounded with anger and sorrow."[111]

A few weeks later, the flag debate finally ended. Through clever tricks and the use of closure, the Liberals out-manoeuvred the Tories and Canada got a new flag. Diefenbaker dismissed it as a flag that Peruvians might salute, while Scott Symons felt like his country had been stolen. He had been "annulled," he said, reduced, even, to "a belated second-class American burdened by a specific Canadian nostalgia that is irrelevant." Quick, decisive, and irreversible, it was "like losing one's virginity." Forty years later, Symons's wound still hadn't healed: "When I first saw that piece of shit maple leaf, I wanted to kill that fucking bastard Pearson!"[112]

To Creighton, it was another humiliation. He thought the single maple leaf looked like someone had squashed a tomato on a handkerchief and that it "bore a disturbingly close resemblance to the flag of a new 'instant' African nation, a nation without a past and with a highly uncertain future."[113] It was a stupid remark that undermined both his work on the Monckton Commission and his opposition to apartheid. But it contained an accidental insight: signifying "the last gasp of Empire" in English Canada,[114] the flag debate represented a key moment in Canada's decolonization in the same way that Zambia's new flag represented a key moment in its decolonization.

Arthur Lower welcomed the new flag as the "crowning step" in Canada's independence from Great Britain and its march from colony to nation.[115] But he assumed that the flag debate had pitted nationalists against colonialists when it had set nationalists against nationalists. The debate was not about a Canadian flag over a British flag. It was about two Canadian flags.[116] Ultimately, it was a variation on an old theme: Lester Pearson versus John Diefenbaker; Oscar Skelton versus Stephen Leacock; Wilfrid Laurier versus Robert Borden; and Goldwin Smith versus George Monro Grant.

On 15 February 1965, the new flag was raised for the first time on Parliament Hill. At home in Brooklin nursing an awful cold, Creighton was too ill to comment. But he never forgave Pearson and, for years after the fact, found it hard to attend funeral services for men who had served in the military because the Red Ensign and sometimes the Union Jack would be draped over the casket. Not even Pearson could take that away from them. On one occasion he was so overcome with depression that Luella took him for a long drive through the back roads north of Brooklin, through the Lynde Creek watershed. Formed some 10,000 years ago when the Laurentide Ice Sheet began its slow retreat – when deglaciation left behind masses of scarred granite, drumlins, kettles, lakes, and waterways – Lynde Creek snakes its way to Lake Ontario from its headwaters on the Oak Ridges Moraine. It was January and there was snow on the ground. The little farms dotting the landscape were quiet and, for a few minutes, Creighton could forget about the end of empire.

chapter eleven

Confederation

*Treat them as a nation and they will act as a free people generally do –
generously. Call them a faction and they become factious.*

Sir John A. Macdonald, vol. 1

If Confederation marked the beginning of modern Canada, the Quiet Revolution marked its moment of truth. How the country responded to Quebec's urgent demands would determine its fate, a fact not lost on the Royal Commission on Bilingualism and Biculturalism when it took the unusual step of issuing a preliminary report. Canada, it said, "is passing through the greatest crisis in its history."[1] Both as leader of the opposition and as prime minister, Lester Pearson instinctively understood the need to accommodate Quebec. He also understood that the "real separatists" were not the young men and women who told the Queen to go home. The real separatists were those English Canadians who told Quebec to go home, who denied that French-speaking people constituted "a nation," and who insisted "on talking about our country, race, and nation as one and indivisible." Pearson even summoned the political wisdom of Sir John A. Macdonald: "Treat them as a nation and they will act as a free people generally do – generously. Call them a faction and they become factious."[2]

Ironically, Macdonald's biographer never fully grasped the first rule of Canadian politics. Instead, Donald Creighton called French Canadians a faction and couldn't understand why they became factious. Departmental meetings, Hart House lunches, and family dinners often ended with raised voices and unpleasant exchanges when the conversation turned to Quebec and Creighton became, in the words of one friend, "so amazingly unreasonable."[3] Like a massive granite wall, he couldn't be moved: the answer to the Quebec question would not be found in the 1960s by an "asinine" royal commission; it would be found in the 1860s, in the three or four years immediately preceding Confederation, when the French language received its final accommodation in Section 133 of the British North America Act permitting the use of French in Parliament and in federal courts.

And so on a clear, cool day in August 1961, Creighton sat down at his writing table. Although narrow and even a little wobbly, the long brown table was certainly adequate. He hated clutter and the table's length allowed him to arrange his research notes, a number of books, and a few sheets of unlined writing paper. Besides, it overlooked one of his favourite places on earth. Lake Muskoka had been a part of his life since childhood. Its hard granite shoreline and its low line of distant pine trees inspired some of his best writing in the same way that Algonquin Park's Canoe Lake inspired some of Tom Thomson's best paintings. At first, the writing went slowly. In fact, he only wrote a page and a half. Two days later, he decided that the opening was all wrong, that the story didn't begin quickly enough and that the reader wasn't drawn into a compelling narrative. And so he started over again, this time, he said, "along better lines."[4] For the next three years, Creighton worked incessantly. Luella, of course, worried about his health. But she also knew that she couldn't stop his obsessive need. He needed to set the record straight; he needed to tell Canadians what the Fathers of Confederation had "actually said and done in those crucial years."[5] His new book, he told Eugene Forsey, "will be called *The Road to Confederation*, and – though this definition may sound a little pompous – it is my contribution to the centenary of Confederation and to the current debate over Canadian federalism."[6]

Published in October 1964 to coincide with the centenary of the Quebec Conference and the Queen's royal visit, Creighton's book was an outstanding – if also flawed – contribution to Canadian historical writing. He told one colleague that he had enjoyed writing it more than *Macdonald*, that the material had completely absorbed him, and that he liked it better than anything else he had done.[7] When John Gray sent him the very first copy, Creighton admired the binding, the jacket, and the pictures. For a few minutes he was a little boy again opening the packages of books that his father had left for him in the front hall of 32 Hewitt Avenue. That afternoon he arranged all of his books on the dining-room table, from *The Commercial Empire of the St. Lawrence* to *The Road to Confederation*. It formed an impressive sight and represented a lifetime of thinking about Canada and about the writing of history.

Brilliant, engaging, and wonderfully written, *The Road to Confederation* struck a resonant chord with readers. One Toronto colleague told him that he formed part of historiography's Holy Trinity: "Thucydides the Father, Creighton the Son, and Gibbon the Holy Ghost." Another compared his description of

Charlottetown's red-coloured cliffs, generous streets, and impressive government buildings to Thomas Babington Macaulay's Trial of Hastings. Writing
from Vancouver, his brother told him that it was "the best thing" he had done;
for that matter, "it's the best thing anybody has done on the curious complexity
that is Canada's essential nature."[8] Of course, Creighton welcomed the praise.
More than that, he needed it. Writing was, for him, an act of creation, of par-
thenogenesis even. His books weren't external to him, they were extensions of
him. They were his flesh and blood. Writing meant exposing himself. It meant
making himself vulnerable. And in the context of the Quiet Revolution and
the struggle to redefine the meaning of Confederation, it meant making himself a target.

II

The Road to Confederation mined familiar themes – Maritime Union, political
logjam in the Province of Canada,[9] railway debt and the threat of insolvency,
western expansion, the desire of Great Britain to unload its North American
obligations, and the military threat of the United States; it introduced a familiar cast of characters – John A. Macdonald, George-Étienne Cartier, George
Brown, Alexander Galt, Leonard Tilley, and Charles Tupper; it followed a familiar timeline – the Charlottetown Conference begat the Quebec Conference, the Quebec Conference begat the London Conference, and the London
Conference begat the Dominion of Canada; and it sounded familiar notes – the
enduring wisdom of Confederation's proponents, the parochialism of its ossi-
fied opponents, the need for a paramount central government, and the necessity of maintaining the imperial connection. In this sense, it was not, strictly
speaking, an original book. Stan Mealing may have been blunt, but he wasn't
wrong when he said that it contained "no new information of consequence
and no new ideas at all." Nor was Albert Tucker when he observed that, for all
its beauty, *The Road to Confederation* failed to turn our understanding of
Confederation in a "new direction."[10]

And yet it constituted an important book. It represented years of research
and writing by English Canada's leading historian; it carried the imprint of his
authority; it brought together in one place all of the specialized research – including his own – on the 1860s; and it defended the Laurentian thesis.[11]

Creighton believed that Confederation and its concomitant, a "great transcontinental northern nation," lay, like a sleeping giant, in the land itself, in the
St Lawrence River Valley and Great Lakes basin, in the rocks and lakes and
trees of the Laurentian Shield.[12] At key moments in the story, he conjured the

St Lawrence River and the heavy blue sweep of the Laurentian mountains, giving them a quiet, continuous presence. When, for example, Macdonald, Cartier, Brown, and Galt left Quebec City bound for Charlottetown in August 1864, they travelled by government steamer. "That evening, as the sun went down behind them, the Canadians sat out on the deck and watched the gradually receding shores, with the steepled churches and whitewashed cottages of the little struggling French-Canadian villages, and, beyond and above them, growing bolder and more precipitous, the massive and sombre ranges of the Laurentian Highlands. This was the St. Lawrence, the River of Canada, as Jacques Cartier had called it; and for generations and centuries ships sailing up and down the river had founded Canada, peopled it, [and] nourished it."[13]

The reference to steepled churches and whitewashed cottages reveals one of the most distinctive features of Creighton's writing: the self-conscious use of the unnecessary detail. It was George Orwell who identified "the unnecessary detail" as the "unmistakable mark" of a Charles Dickens novel. How, Orwell asked, does a particular detail, often buried in a long sentence, advance the story? "The answer is that it doesn't. It is something totally unnecessary, a florid little squiggle on the edge of the page." But "it is by just these squiggles that the special Dickens atmosphere is created," making, therefore, the unnecessary detail necessary.[14] Thomas Babington Macaulay employed the same trick. "Precision in dates, the day or hour in which a man was born or died, becomes absolutely necessary," Macaulay argued. "A slight fact, a sentence, a word, are of importance in my romance."[15] In the same way, even the slightest fact and the smallest detail mattered to Creighton. What did Macdonald, Cartier, Brown, and Galt see when they made their way from the Charlottetown harbour to the Colonial Building? What did the women wear to the many social functions at Quebec? And what was the weather like on 1 July 1867? The "low, red-coloured cliffs" of the harbour, the "fashionable coiffures and the coquettishly elaborate gowns" of the women, and the "brilliant" sunshine of July 1st were neither accidental nor incidental.[16] They were the deliberate squiggles on the edge of the page that allowed readers to imagine that what they were reading happened the day before yesterday.

Of course, some "squiggles" jar our contemporary sensibilities. At one point, Creighton reported that an Island delegate to the Quebec Conference had been disappointed by French women, finding them "remarkably plain," "usually quite short," and "almost invariably much too stout." But Edward Whelan, Creighton said, was something of a "Tupman-like" character, a reference to Tracy Tupman, the corpulent bachelor in Dickens's *Pickwick Papers* whose fondness for the fair sex leads to various mishaps. Maybe, Creighton wrote, French women weren't that "stout and hearty" after all. Maybe their billowing crinoline dresses only exaggerated "their stout figures." Maybe, just maybe, these "short, dimpled, vivacious creatures" possessed "as much of that precious mid-Victorian quality of femininity as the less robust and more languid beauties of Halifax and Saint John."[17]

Writing history as if it happened the day before yesterday also allowed Creighton to build suspense into the story of Confederation. Although the ending was obvious – Confederation happened – it wasn't obvious to that small group of colonial politicians from the Canadas and the lower provinces. Doubt, therefore, haunts *The Road to Confederation* in the same way that it haunted the road to Confederation itself. Creighton highlighted setbacks, disappointments, and obstructions; he used chapter titles like "Uncertain Reception," "Imminence of Failure," and "Summer of Frustration"; and he routinely reported that the future looked "confused" and "contradictory," that it was "depressingly uncertain" and "as dark" as it ever had been.[18]

But the doubt animating *The Road to Confederation* was more than a narrative device. It mirrored Creighton's own doubt. The Quiet Revolution, the Other Quiet Revolution, the end of empire, continentalism, and the impossible-to-square circle of national purpose, provincial autonomy, and federalism all contributed to his "vague sense of impending failure."[19] By late 1962 Creighton had come to the conclusion that his Canada was nearing its end. "It seems silly," he told Eugene Forsey, "to be writing a book about Confederation when doubts are freely expressed that the nation will ever reach its centenary."[20]

As a result, the language question, provincial autonomy, and a bruised United States make repeated and ominous appearances in *The Road to Confederation,* making it as much about the 1960s as the 1860s. The language question, Creighton argued, had been settled in the 1860s when the Fathers of Confederation decided that the French language could be used in the federal parliament and in federal courts. But this decision was not a declaration that Canada should be "a bilingual, or a bicultural, country." "Nobody suggested that the legal status of the French language in the national parliament should be extended to the legislatures and courts of any or all of the other provinces – provinces either already existing or yet to be created – of what, it was intended, was to be a truly transcontinental British American federation."[21] The provinces, meanwhile, were to be clearly subordinate to the central government. The creation of a centralized federation, Creighton maintained over and over again, had been the intention of the Fathers of Confederation from the beginning. To the general legislature they assigned "the great national tasks of the future"; to the provincial legislatures, those "simple, inexpensive, and unostentatious little affairs," they assigned local matters.[22] Finally, the United States and its threat to Canada's survival played a recurring and exaggerated role. Like some horrible ghoul lurking in the darkness, the great republic stalked the road to Confederation. Projecting his fear of the United States onto the Fathers of Confederation, Creighton covered the Civil War, reporting on troop movements, battles, victories, and defeats. As it had in *Dominion of the North*, his sympathy lay clearly with the South. A Confederate victory would have created a healthy balance of power on the continent, but General Robert E. Lee's surrender in 1865 meant that Canada "would have to stand for all time in the deep, permanent shadow of the colossus to the south."[23]

That permanent shadow now obscured Creighton's vision of both the past and the present. "I increasingly regret the fact," he told Eugene Forsey, "that I have given my time to the interpretation of Canadian history. Continentalism, 'the wave of the future,' may become so strong that Canadian history will appear simply as a trivial and obstructive side-issue, something like the resistance of the Southern Confederacy, but without its romantic appeal."[24] To lament the Confederacy, to see both it and Canada as two of history's lost causes, reflected his anti-Americanism and his indifference to race; to regret his decision to write Canadian history reflected his unfortunate capacity for self-pity. Yet, he didn't conclude his story on an unhopeful note. The American shadow was momentarily lifted on the morning of 1 July 1867 when the day broke, revealing the promise of "the pale blue sky of morning."[25]

Roger Graham described *The Road to Confederation* as a "beautifully written book"; Bill Morton called it an "immense piece of scholarship"; and Ramsay Cook proclaimed it the "crowning achievement" of a long and distinguished career. Creighton was naturally delighted. Morton's review, he said, was "wonderful," while Cook's was "simply splendid."[26] Fifty years after its publication, Christopher Moore still considers it "the most readable account of the Confederation process," while Peter Russell describes it as "a great piece of history."[27] But Creighton's eighth book attracted strong criticisms. Arthur Lower wished that Creighton had paid more attention to French Canada, to what he called "the other side." Margaret Ormsby declared that "only an English-speaking Canadian" could have written this book. In an editorial in *Le Devoir,* Claude Ryan accused Creighton of minimizing the importance of autonomy to Lower Canada in the 1860s. Michel Brunet conceded that the Fathers of Confederation had intended to create a centralized federation, but their intentions, he argued, shouldn't dictate constitutional reform in the 1960s. And in a perceptive review, Paul L'Allier took up the metaphor of a road. Every road, he said, has two sides and history depends on what side of the road the historian stands. For his part, Creighton – "un ontarien avec assurance" – stood on the Ontario side, an assessment Lionel Groulx would have shared.[28] In a 1965 photograph Quebec's national historian posed with a copy of *The Road to*

Confederation as a reminder, perhaps, that there was more than one interpretation of 1867.

Unlike Arthur Lower, who insisted on reading French-language monographs, journals, and newspapers and who corresponded with French-Canadian historians, Creighton relied on a series of stereotypes – rural, Catholic, quaint, and inert – to understand French Canada. But when those stereotypes lost what little explanatory power they had, he found himself confused and disoriented. Instead of seeking to understand Quebec's growing opposition to the idea of Canada in the 1960s by studying Lower Canada's opposition to the idea of Confederation in the 1860s, Creighton ignored it. He made a handful of passing references to Antoine-Aimé Dorion – Lower Canada's leading opponent of Confederation – but he doggedly refused to take Dorion's objections seriously because they violated the logic of the Laurentian thesis.[29] Instead, George-Étienne Cartier – Lower Canada's leading proponent of Confederation – functioned as a representative figure. But, as Lower asked, "How typical was he?"

In addition, Creighton ignored Maritime opposition. Prince Edward Island initially refused union. Nova Scotia was bitterly divided. And New Brunswick voters actually rejected Confederation in 1865. Yet Creighton dismissed opposition in the lower provinces as "parochial," "suspicious," "jealous," "mutinous," and "fanatical."[30] His treatment of Albert J. Smith, for example, the leading anti-Confederate in New Brunswick and, from 1865 to 1866, the premier of the province, reflected his assumption that what was good for Upper Canada was good for New Brunswick. A successful lawyer and politician, Smith wasn't a crusty reactionary and his opposition wasn't unfounded. Confederation, he said, was a solution to the problems of Upper and Lower Canada, and the proposed scheme – cooked up by the "oily brains of Canadian politicians" – would make New Brunswick "a mere municipality."[31] But according to Creighton, Smith embodied "the dead, unyielding weight of provincial loyalty, provincial distrust, and provincial inertia." Throughout New Brunswick – "a dreary, unenterprising, poverty-stricken place" – "there were copious deposits of a peculiarly hard and resistant parochialism." Not only were Smith's politics objectionable, he was objectionable, his "wide, plump, jowly" face "aflame with righteous indignation."[32]

Smith may have been on the wrong side of the Laurentian thesis, but he wasn't necessarily wrong.[33] A version of Old Ontario's sense of mission, the belief that British North America was a political and economic unity, and that Confederation existed for the fulfilment of both its and Ontario's appointed national destiny, the Laurentian thesis was always more teleological than it was logical.[34] Moreover, the opponents of Confederation were not "stupid"; in fact, they were capable of "disconcerting brilliance."[35] Smith's commitment to

Taken in November 1965 on the occasion of a lecture marking the fiftieth anniversary of his appointment to the University of Montreal, Lionel Groulx posed with a copy of *The Road to Confederation*. Where Creighton viewed Confederation as the logical outcome of the commercial empire of the St Lawrence, Groulx viewed it as a failure, emphasizing instead Quebec's autonomy. Still, Groulx appreciated that in historical writing there is never a final word. "I am a French-Canadian Catholic, indeed a priest," Groulx told his audience, "but I do not know that this has affected my impartiality any more than another historian who would happen to be an Anglo-Protestant Canadian. Both, I hope, would be above pettiness."

provincial rights and, once the die was cast in favour of Confederation, his wish to see established some kind of court to settle federal-provincial disputes, have proven more far-sighted than near-sighted. Similarly, it was Lower Canada's Louis Auguste Olivier, a minor figure on the road to Confederation, who got it right when he predicted that the general government, "with its power of purse," will "stretch its prerogatives" and "trench upon the domain of the local governments." And it was John A. Macdonald who got it wrong when he pronounced that, by the proposed division of powers between the general and local legislatures, "we have avoided all conflict of jurisdiction and authority."[36] If the story of Canadian federalism has been anything, it has been the story of the federal government's spending power and the conflict over jurisdiction and authority.

Confederation represented a key moment in the Laurentian dream of nation when the political consolidation of British North America opened the west to settlement, or when "the great scheme of territorial expansion and material advancement" came into view.[37] In *The Commercial Empire of the St. Lawrence*, Creighton had promised that "the whole west, with all its riches," would be "the dominion of the river."[38] In 1867, however, it was still a "howling wilderness." It had yet to be tamed and opened to "commercial exploitation": "The great wheat-lands of the North West, which only the stars looked down on, had never been touched by the plough." To the Plains Cree, of course, the northwest didn't belong to the river. It wasn't even the northwest. It was the Centre and it belonged to them. Blind, as always, Creighton referred to Aboriginal people only once when, on a rainy Wednesday, the wives and daughters of the delegates to the Quebec Conference made "a dismally damp expedition" to the Huron village at Lorette (now Wendake). Aboriginal people, in other words, were a tourist attraction just off Confederation Road.[39]

III

A few weeks after the publication of *The Road to Confederation*, Donald and Luella received a telephone call from Cynthia: she had fallen madly in love and was engaged to be married. At first, they didn't know what to make of her sudden and, to them, inexplicable announcement. For that matter, they didn't know what to make of her. As the daughter of Professor and Mrs Donald Creighton, she was supposed to marry a nice young man – a doctor, perhaps, or a lawyer – live in North Toronto and have babies. Instead, she did an MA at Berkeley, worked in San Francisco for a couple of years, and then moved to New York City. Inspired by the civil rights movement and the nascent anti-war movement, her view of the world had started to change and her politics had started to radicalize.[40] She wasn't who her parents wanted her to be and now she intended to marry a man she had just met in the cafe at the Museum of Modern Art.

Although Luella had never seen her daughter so happy, her class bias was immediate and obvious. Maurice Flood was a poor Irish Roman Catholic from the Bronx who had not gone to university and who worked as a security guard at the MoMA. What could he possibly "offer" Cynthia, she wondered. Meanwhile, Donald didn't record his reaction. As a father, he couldn't bring himself to go there, and as a writer, he couldn't bring himself to put it into words. Maybe if he didn't write it down, it would go away. So, shortly before going to bed, he recorded the events of that day in his diary, including a dinner with Ramsay Cook and Craig Brown, but he didn't mention Cynthia's telephone call. According to Luella, though, he was "absolutely crushed." He couldn't "believe that *his* daughter means to marry a poor American Roman Catholic." It was as if someone had taken a giant knife and "struck" him in the heart.[41]

Donald and Luella had forgotten their own "hot, breathless" affair in the summer of 1925.[42] They had forgotten what it was like to be young, in love, and determined to live one's life on one's own terms. Luella had forgotten how much she had admired Laura Creighton's equanimity when Jack announced his sudden decision to marry a Roman Catholic. And Donald had forgotten that he had rebuked Sir John A. Macdonald for his less than magnanimous reaction to his son's engagement to a Roman Catholic.[43]

Over Christmas and into the new year, plans were made for a spring wedding. Because Maurice was, as Luella put it, "an R.C.," Cynthia agreed to get married in a Catholic church. Of course, she didn't care one way or the other. She didn't care, she said, if she was married by "a justice of the peace, a rabbi, or a milkman."[44] Trying to see things from Cynthia's perspective, Luella admitted that her daughter was "easily bored by the conventional," that she was really an academic – perhaps "too much" so – and that Maurice was anything but conventional. For Cynthia to have married a dentist and lived in North Toronto would have meant a slow death by suffocation. At least initially, Luella made an effort to accept Maurice. Even if "he is an oddball," he is "a GOOD young man," she wrote in an effort to convince herself. However, Luella also knew that Donald would never accept Cynthia's decision to marry an American Roman Catholic.[45] To protect himself emotionally, he had built a wall between himself and Maurice. But that wall would keep Cynthia out as well.

The wedding took place in Whitby's St John the Evangelist on Saturday, 22 May 1965. Everyone was there. Philip's daughters were bridesmaids. Isabel and Harold sat close to the front. Luella looked smashing in her red dress and "gorgeous" red hat. And Donald wore a morning coat and tails. Cynthia, he said, looked "lovely" in her white gown. But he never once mentioned Maurice. He simply couldn't. Even if the wedding itself "had been a tremendous success" – even if everyone had behaved themselves and no one had talked about Quebec – it had been "an exhausting and at times painful experience": "It is especially difficult for a father to part with his only daughter," he told Bill Morton, "and I felt a harder pang than I had expected when the final moment came in church."[46]

Two days later, the *Globe and Mail* printed a picture of Cynthia and Maurice signing the registry with the headline, "Professor's Daughter Marries." To see it, Creighton had to thumb through several pages. Perhaps he noticed the brief report of Daniel Johnson's speech to a group of university students in Quebec. As leader of the opposition, he upped the ante when he criticized Premier Lesage's approach to federal-provincial negotiations. "Why does he not demand for the state of Quebec," he asked, "the true status of a national state?"[47]

IV

Jean Lesage may not have demanded Quebec's status as a national state, but he was no pushover. At the 1964 federal-provincial conference in Quebec City, he surrounded himself with a team of advisers who knew everything there was to know about shared-cost programs, taxation agreements, and amending formulas. The premier of Ontario looked across the table at his Quebec counterpart and realized that he had no one. Later, John Robarts would say that he felt "naked."[48] To defend Ontario's interests, he needed his own brains trust and so, with Ian Macdonald, chief economist for the province, he assembled a committee of experts. Although its formal mandate was to advise the government on "matters in relation to and arising out of the position of Ontario in Confederation," the real purpose of the Ontario Advisory Committee on Confederation was to answer the Ontario question – what does Canada's most populous province want? Its membership included, among others, the Toronto professor Paul Fox, the political scientist John Meisel, the legal scholar Ted McWhinney, the university president Tom Symons, the Franco-Ontarian lawyer Roger Séguin, the Jesuit priest and educator Lucien Matté, the historian John Conway, the walking encyclopedia of constitutional history Eugene Forsey, and Donald Creighton.[49]

At first, he didn't want to accept Robarts's invitation. Forsey notwithstanding, the committee's membership was, in his opinion, uninspiring. John Conway, for example, gave him the pip when, at a preliminary meeting, he proposed that Canada become a republic.[50] He "appears to feel that God has called him north to carry out the political and moral transformation of the Canadian people. I

Seated second from the right, Donald Creighton served on the Ontario Advisory Committee on Confederation from 1965 to 1970. Although he admired Eugene Forsey, seated fourth from the right, he felt that the other members were a bunch of "second- and third-raters" who practised the politics of "appeasement" and who suppressed competing opinions with "loud cries of righteous indignation."

find these people and their pretensions both boring and annoying; and I refuse to waste my time discussing the basic institutions of my country with a recent immigrant from the United States." Actually, Conway was a Canadian citizen and a decorated war hero, but he had come to York University via Harvard and that, apparently, made him a recent immigrant. In the end, though, Creighton accepted the invitation. It confirmed his role as a public intellectual and it would give him access to Ontario's decision makers at a critical moment in both the province's and the country's history. "The only government that can speak with any force for the old conception of Canada is the government of Ontario, and personally I feel that I am bound to do anything I can to help it."[51]

By "the old conception of Canada," Creighton meant the conception that he had outlined in *Macdonald* and *The Road to Confederation*: British, anti-American, Ontario-driven, and Laurentian. Old Ontario's sense of national destiny, its sense of itself as the dominant centre of British North America and, after 1867, the Dominion of Canada, animated Creighton's work.[52] At one point in *The Old Chieftain,* he painted a powerful – and revealing – picture of an election rally in Uxbridge. People had come from all over, from Toronto, Greenbank, Blackwater, and Port Perry, to catch a glimpse of the great man. Macdonald was at his best, working the crowds, shaking hands, kissing babies, exchanging pleasantries, and swapping stories. These were his people. "He knew the

Canadians better than anybody had ever known them before – and better than anybody would ever know them again." Of course, the assembled crowd was not, in Creighton's words, "a cross-section of the nation"; it wasn't even a cross-section of Ontario.[53] But in Creighton's mind, Canada was Ontario writ large and Canadians were English-speaking Ontarians.

However, the days of Old Ontario and the old conception of Canada were over, making Creighton's five-year membership on the advisory committee an exercise in frustration. Unwilling to consider the extension of French-language rights beyond Section 133 of the British North America Act, he found himself backed into an uncomfortable and unhappy corner. The committee's younger members – Tom Symons, Paul Fox, Ted McWhinney, and John Meisel – lacked Creighton's seniority, but their openness to French Canada in general and to French Ontario in particular gave their views greater credibility.[54] Looking back, Tom Symons concedes that Premier Robarts had been right to appoint Creighton – he was the country's leading historian, he had just published the book on Confederation, and even if the days of Old Ontario were over there were still a lot of Old Ontarians around, meaning his views were not unrepresentative – but he also admits that Creighton wasn't an easy person to work with. When, for example, Symons recommended that Ontario and Quebec develop a language-exchange program for young people, Creighton stopped speaking to him for a couple of months. It was "provincial aggrandizement," he said. It was "province building."[55] Ultimately, it was an admission that there was a problem.

From the beginning, the committee confronted the question of French-language rights in Ontario, including French-language education rights at the secondary level. Roger Séguin – an Ottawa lawyer and president of l'Association canadienne-française d'éducation d'Ontario – insisted that French-language secondary schools were essential if Franco-Ontarians were to be more than "labourers," "elevator operators," and "char workers."[56] Most committee members agreed. It was both the right thing to do, they said, and it would send a positive message to Quebec. But Creighton didn't buy it. He argued that primary schools were one thing, but secondary schools were quite another because of their proximity to the labour market. "Bilingualism," by which he meant French, "is not an asset in Ontario." And "if it is carried so far that it impairs a citizen's power of speaking fluent and idiomatic English, bilingualism becomes a positive liability. Such people are handicapped in all the main activities of Ontario. They compete for jobs at a decided disadvantage. They become second-class citizens." The very people that French-language education rights were supposed to benefit would become its ironic victims, he said. Besides, Quebec doesn't care about French Ontario. It doesn't even care about Canada. "For the past five years, English Canada has been treated to a sequence of truculent demands, assertions, threats, and blackmail. Institutions and their symbols, beloved by many English Canadians, have been openly derided as in the mass discourtesy shown to the Queen." Quebec, he said, has a "limited and strictly pecuniary attitude to Confederation," treating the federal government "as a machine for collecting and handing out money" and leading the provinces "up the garden path to frustration and humiliation."[57]

At an April 1966 committee meeting, Creighton reiterated his argument – French-language secondary schools will "handicap" Franco-Ontarians in an English-speaking labour market and prevent them from achieving their full human potential. Drawing on census data, he pointed out that some 200,000 Franco-Ontarians had adopted English as their mother tongue because it was to their advantage to do so. In other words, it was precisely because they didn't want to be "elevator operators" and "char workers" that they stopped speaking French. It was the same argument that Lord Durham used in 1839. "The language, the laws, [and] the character of the North American Continent are English," he wrote, and French Canadians will remain in a suspended state of "inferiority" and "dependence" unless they learn English. "It is to elevate them from that inferiority that I desire to give to the Canadians our English character." And it was the same argument that George W. Ross – Ontario's minister of education in the 1880s and 1890s – used when he urged a policy of voluntary assimilation. Taking steps to increase instruction in English in Ontario's schools, he believed that French-speaking parents wanted their children to learn English.[58]

Creighton's remarks led to an angry exchange. Paul Fox accepted his census figures but said that it was a matter of assimilation, not voluntary assimilation. John Meisel "deplored" the "ethnic disappearance" of French-speaking Ontario. And Roger Séguin bluntly declared that Franco-Ontarians had no intention of going anywhere.[59]

To hell with it, thought Creighton. He would resign from the committee. He had better things to do, he said, than waste his time with a bunch of "second- and third-raters" who practise the politics of "appeasement" and who suppress competing opinions with "loud cries of righteous indignation." In a long letter to Eugene Forsey, who had been unable to attend the meeting, he reported that Fox and Meisel had made "a few sorrowful remarks" but Séguin had what could only be described as "an emotional outburst": "I could not help but feel that [he] had shown a definite personal hostility to me."[60] What did Creighton expect from a French-speaking Ontarian when he accepted with, in his words, "no feelings at all," the disappearance of French-speaking Ontario?[61]

Forsey urged him not to resign – his opinion was an important one, he said, and they carried more weight together than they did alone. But he also restated his support for French-language secondary schools. In an earlier letter, he had told Creighton that Franco-Ontarians "have a right to insist that their children get an adequate French education," and, "if we refuse, they'll become fanatical and bitter," or, in a word, factious.⁶²

Although tempted, Creighton didn't resign from the committee and, in time, he became a valuable member. According to Ted McWhinney, he encouraged a dialectical approach to problem solving. Yes, he could be "insufferable," and he didn't know how "to retreat gracefully," but by taking the positions he did, and by sticking to his anti-bilingualism guns, he forced other members to clarify and defend their own positions. In other words, he was "important" to the committee's success because of his hard line, not despite it.⁶³

But speaking out against bilingualism and what he saw as English Canada's "will to disintegration and extinction" carried a personal and professional cost.⁶⁴

V

On 15 July 1966, Donald Creighton turned sixty-four years old. He had the usual aches and pains of a man that age, but, for the time being, his health was pretty good and his capacity to spend long hours at his desk was undiminished. He didn't intend to retire just yet and he certainly didn't intend to stop writing. In the fall he had been named the Sir John A. Macdonald Professor of History – but only after Tom Symons had tried to lure him to Trent University with the Vanier Professorship of Canadian History and the promise of an apartment at Champlain College. From Creighton's perspective, the Macdonald Professorship was long overdue, but he welcomed the gesture, especially since he knew that he would have been a fish out of water on the banks of the Otonabee River. Symons's early commitment to bilingualism at Champlain College and in the *Journal of Canadian Studies* was, he said, "bogus." He wouldn't feel "comfortable" at Trent and, as attractive as the idea of being a "historian in residence" was, he didn't want to be an "embarrassment."⁶⁵

Bilingualism, biculturalism, two nations, associate states, and special status may have been well intentioned, Creighton thought, but they were also misguided, if not fat headed. The time had come to speak out. In late June and into early July, Creighton wrote a deliberately provocative essay for *Saturday Night* entitled "The Myth of Biculturalism or The Great French-Canadian Sales Campaign." Calling it a "bombshell," Kildare Dobbs – *Saturday Night*'s managing editor – suggested that a reply be solicited, perhaps from René Lévesque, then a popular figure in nationalist circles for, among other things, his decision as a minister of the Crown in the cabinet of Jean Lesage to boycott the Queen's

1964 royal visit. Creighton didn't think much of Dobbs's suggestion because it implied that "there was only one orthodox belief and heresies had to be corrected every time anybody dared to utter one." Besides, Quebec nationalists have been "offered all the platforms and forums they deserve in English Canada. They don't pay the slightest attention to us. Why should we show them such submissive deference?" But, he added, if a response is necessary then the best bets are Claude Ryan, the editor of *Le Devoir*, or Ramsay Cook, who, incidentally, "dissents strongly from my views."[66] In the end, Dobbs didn't seek a response, although he held on to Creighton's essay until September when people returned from their summer holidays.

Starting from the premise that English-Canadians had been sold a bill of goods, Creighton accused French-Canadian nationalists and their English-Canadian fellow travellers of being so many snake-oil vendors: the Confederation agreement was not an agreement between two nations; the French-language received a fair and equitable settlement in Section 133; associate-statehood or special status for Quebec is tantamount to "virtual independence"; bilingualism at its "fullest" will mean the provision of French-language education "from the nursery school to the graduate school"; French-language education rights for Franco-Ontarians will handicap them in the long run; and, finally, the French language has survived only because Canada has survived. "The Fathers of Confederation reached a settlement which gave the French language the best chance it will ever have on this continent."[67]

At long last, Creighton had become George Brown – Macdonald's political and intellectual opposite – and Brown's furious rants against French domination had become his own. In fact, he now believed that Brown had been crucial to the Confederation agreement and that had language rights been extended beyond Section 133, he would have withdrawn his support and, in the process, scuppered Confederation for another generation, or "perhaps for all time." A few years earlier, Creighton had appealed to Ramsay Cook not to give up on him as "as an unreconstructed Brownite."[68]

Originally, he had written a much stronger final paragraph when he invented what he called "a hypothetical good-bye to French Canada": "You say that you are a distinct people and a separate nation. You have insisted on this through a long campaign of demands, threats, abuse, blackmail, and terrorism. Very well then, you are a distinct people! Henceforth you will be foreigners to us! Break up Confederation, form a separate nation, and in God's name leave us in peace!" Dobbs, however, thought that it was too much and Creighton agreed that, yes, it probably was too "brutal," although, he noted for the record, it's the way "a good many people, including a lot of Westerners, really feel."[69]

In the end, the decision not to commission a response didn't matter because *Saturday Night* received several letters to the editor denouncing what some clever headline writer called "The Myth of Creightonism." Solange Chaput-Rolland – a well-known Quebec journalist – criticized the "anger," "arrogance," and "ignorance" of English Canada's leading historian and even intimated that he was, well, a white Rhodesian. According to John Trent – a political scientist at Queen's University – Creighton's selection and interpretation of historical facts were so "narrow and biased" that the only myth he managed to debunk was the myth "of himself as a truly Canadian historian."[70] A letter writer from Saskatoon described "The Myth of Biculturalism" as an example of "English separatist polemics," while a letter writer from Ottawa said that it contained "enough ammunition" to keep "French-Canadian nationalists going for another generation at least."[71]

But, curiously enough, it was Claude Ryan and, by association, Ramsay Cook, who offered a rebuttal after all. Instead of relying on the work of Henri Bourassa, Thomas Chapais, or, closer to the present, André Laurendeau, to refute Creighton's interpretation of Confederation, Ryan turned to Cook, who had just published *Canada and the French Canadian Question*. According to Cook, the meaning of Confederation lay in its acknowledgment of Canada's linguistic and cultural duality and its respect for minority rights; its genius lay in federalism and a constitutional division of powers; and its hope lay in the willingness to cooperate across the national divide to ensure both English and French Canada's survival. Where Cook's approach was fresh, Creighton's was "dry," and where Cook's interpretation was imaginative, Creighton's was "literal." And, Ryan added, perhaps rubbing salt in the wound, where Cook was a young man, Creighton was an old man, a prisoner of a no-longer-viable status quo.[72] He didn't say it because he didn't have to, but the apprentice had overtaken the master.

Although Creighton received several letters of support from Canadians who appreciated his willingness to speak out – including a request from the grand secretary of the Orange Lodge of British America to reprint "The Myth of Biculturalism" in pamphlet form – he was, in the eyes of his friends and colleagues, a bad Canadian. Good Canadians supported bilingualism. Bad Canadians didn't. That had been the thrust of John Trent's "abusive" letter to the editor. And it was the thrust of John Gray's remarks when, over lunch at the Royal York Hotel, he questioned his friend's "patriotism."[73]

But it was Bill Morton who dealt the "wounding blow."[74] He and Creighton had been friends for years, sharing similar views on Mackenzie King, the British connection, and the United States. Morton once said that Canada was "so irradiated by the American presence that it sickens and threatens to dissolve in cancerous slime."[75] But where Creighton said no to bilingualism and minority-language education rights, Morton said yes. In a 1964 address to students in Quebec City, Morton confessed that the flag debate had shaken his assumptions about the meaning of Canada, that his world, "the English-Canadian world," had collapsed, and that he had become "a man without a world." "I have become aware over the past few months that a prestige I once unconsciously possessed, I have now consciously not got. I have become a Canadian like any other, a member of an ethnic minority, and am obliged to make such way in the world as my personal merit permits."[76] Although it would not be easy, Morton recognized that English Canadians had to give up their sense of entitlement and privilege – or what he called their "prestige" – if Canada was to survive. By retiring gracefully to his "proper place" and modifying his image of what the country "ought to be," he was, in effect, following Pierre Trudeau's advice. But Creighton couldn't, and Morton knew it. Shortly after reading "The Myth of Biculturalism," he charged his old friend with denying French Canada "a full and free role within Canada" in a preface to Solange Chaput-Rolland's book *My Country, Canada or Quebec*.[77]

A few weeks later, Creighton happened to be Christmas shopping when he picked up a copy of Chaput-Rolland's account of her travels across the country. It was as if someone had punched him in the stomach. Not only did Morton accuse him of denying French Canada, he accused him of distorting his own career in the process. John Gray, moreover, had been complicit because Macmillan had published *My Country, Canada or Quebec*. Calling his preface a "gratuitous and uncalled for" attack, he told Morton to stuff a sock in it. "You write as if you alone were doing God's good work for this country and that your mission entitled you to pronounce moral judgements on people like me who have relapsed from their former virtue." And he told John Gray that he shouldn't have published it, that what he had done was very "serious." An unrepentant Morton responded that he had not made his comments lightly, that he knew they might jeopardize their friendship, but he refused to accept Creighton's charge of delivering a "low blow." His comments were based on what he called "considered opinion."[78]

Creighton may have been wrong about bilingualism, but he wasn't wrong about his reputation: he had become the reactionary tory to the enlightened liberal, the bigoted Other to the virtuous Self, the fallen one to the chosen few, the bad Canadian to the good Canadian. The abuse bothered him, but it also emboldened him. He was right, God damn it. He didn't make this stuff up. It was history and he was still the country's leading historian at the very moment Canada was getting ready to celebrate its centenary.

VI

Despite the freezing temperatures, several thousand people gathered on New Year's Eve to watch the prime minister light the Centennial Flame and officially launch Canada's one hundredth birthday party. In cities and towns across the country Canadians listened to speeches, lit bonfires, rang bells, honked horns, and watched fireworks. In Fredericton, people huddled on the steps of the just-constructed Centennial Building to witness the premier light the province's own centennial flame. In Victoria, residents sang "O Canada." But the towns-folk of Bowsman, Manitoba, stole the show when they set fire to their out-houses in a double celebration of the town's new sewage treatment plant and Canada's birthday. For its part, the Quebec government had decided in advance that there would be no New Year's Eve festivities marking Canada's centennial, although some municipalities went ahead anyway. In Montreal, however, the new year was barely an hour old when a bomb shattered a mailbox in the financial district, a violent reminder that not everyone welcomed Canada's one hundredth birthday.

If 1967 was marked by celebrations, it was also marked by an ongoing debate over the meaning of Confederation and, for the matter, of Canada itself. The history wars had several fronts, took different forms, and drew politicians, journalists, and historians into the fight, including Donald Creighton. On 11 january 1967, he flew to Winnipeg, where that evening he delivered an address to the Manitoba Historical Society marking the 152nd anniversary of Sir John A. Macdonald's birth and the one hundredth anniversary of Confederation.

After exploring a number of possibilities for his talk, Creighton eventually settled on Manitoba's entry into Confederation and the limits of biculturalism and bilingualism. According to his interpretation, Sections 22 and 23 of the 1870 Manitoba Act guaranteeing denominational schools and the use of the French language in provincial institutions had been hastily conceived and unfortunately imposed by those "fanatical emissaries from Red River" and their "ruthless dictator," Louis Riel, whose name Creighton deliberately mispronounced as "Lewis" Riel. Sections 22 and 23 were historical accidents, he argued, not the solemn fulfilment of a promise made by the Fathers of Confederation. "There was nothing in the Quebec Resolutions or the British North America Act which remotely approached a general declaration of principle that Canada was to be a bilingual or bicultural nation."[79]

Although Creighton felt that his "speech seemed to go over fairly well," not everyone agreed. Maurice Arpin, a prominent Franco-Manitoban lawyer and self-described amateur historian, could hardly believe his ears. Listening to an Ontario professor dismiss the Manitoba Act's guarantee of French-language rights made his blood boil. Russell Doern, a history teacher turned MLA, condemned Creighton's treatment of Louis Riel – "the father and founder of Manitoba" – as "derogatory" and as "the exact opposite" of what is now taught in high schools. Moreover, Creighton's "slam" against French-language education rights led Doern to publicly support a proposal "for the use of French in elementary schools now before the legislature." In fact, Creighton's speech made him "more receptive to the ideas of French Canadians generally," Doern said. A few days later, the *Winnipeg Free Press* carried a long article by Cornelius Jaenen of the Department of History at United College. Young and brash, Jaenen argued that the decisions of the 1860s should not limit the options of the 1960s. Had he stopped there, Creighton wouldn't have cared. It was nothing that Eugene Forsey, Bill Morton, and Ramsay Cook hadn't told him. But Jaenen described him as an "imperialist-nationalist Tory interpreter" from Ontario and accused him of self-delusion, "political pontification," and the wilful selection of "facts to buttress a preconceived thesis." "One suspects that Professor Creighton's views have not ranged much beyond a concept of a commercial empire of the St. Lawrence centred on Toronto with occasional glimpses of the borderlands awaiting exploitation." Then the *Ottawa Citizen* entered the fray with an editorial entitled "Come Off It, Professor" and an op-ed piece by the journalist Tim Creery describing Creighton's Winnipeg address as an extended plea for Quebec's secession and as a betrayal of Sir John A. Macdonald's legacy.[80]

Creighton was furious. Who did Jaenen think he was? And what did Creery know anyway? In an angry letter to the editor of the *Winnipeg Free Press*, he denounced Jaenen's deliberate misrepresentation of his views on French Canada.[81] In an earlier interview, Creighton had said that he didn't care one way or the other if French Canadians celebrated John A. Macdonald's birthday were it made a national holiday but that is not what Jaenen reported. Using Toronto as a pejorative, he implied that the Toronto historian did not see French Canadians as participants in the past and didn't care if French Canadians participated in the present. It was certainly a cheap shot. But was it also defamatory? Creighton called Bora Laskin, whom he knew from the Ontario Advisory Committee on Confederation; Laskin sent him to Horace Krever, a Toronto law professor; and Krever told him that a lawsuit would be pointless. In the end, Creighton neither sent the letter to the *Winnipeg Free Press* nor sued Jaenen for defamation for the same reason that he didn't complain to the *Ottawa Citizen* about its "vulgar and vicious journalism": he didn't want to prolong the controversy.[82]

Following the controversy from a distance, Michel Brunet wrote a short note to Jaenen. As a professor of history in Montreal and as the author of the decapitation thesis – the idea that the Conquest had been a tragedy because it resulted in the replacement of a French-speaking elite by an English-speaking elite

– Brunet obviously disagreed with Creighton's interpretation of Canadian history.[83] Now he wondered if he had not lost his mind. "Souffre-t-il de sénélité?" he asked Jaenen. "Je pense plutôt que sa réaction est celle d'une nationaliste raciste anglo-saxon." A few months later he wrote to Creighton. He conceded that he was right – the British North America Act did not create a bilingual or bicultural Canada – and he conceded that French Canadians outside of Quebec, existing in a suspended state of vegetative survival, or "survivance végétative," were destined to assimilate. But the Canada of 1967 was not the Canada of 1867, meaning that today's language rights should not be yesterday's language rights. "Un historien doit savoir que la constitution et les institutions politiques d'un pays se modifient constamment."[84]

Of course, Brunet was right: a historian should know that constitutions and institutions change over time. But that didn't make Creighton a racist. It made him a particular kind of English-Canadian nationalist: British, tory, wary of change for the sake of change, and, by 1967, unbending, pessimistic, and, at times, shrill. In Winnipeg, it made him one more Ontarian in a long line of Ontarians who brought their cultural baggage to what was then the northwest, unpacked their assumptions about the place of the French language and the Catholic faith, and repeated them in newspapers, assembly debates, and legal measures limiting the use of French and the continuation of denominational schools.[85] For example, Bill Morton always pointed the finger at Ontario's D'Alton McCarthy and Manitoba's "British-Ontario majority" for the bitter school question of the 1890s.[86] But where McCarthy found a receptive audience in 1889, Creighton found a hostile one in 1967.

Once he had decided not to pursue legal action against Jaenen, Creighton felt a great sense of relief. Every time he spoke he stirred up "a hornet's nest of vilification and abuse" and, frankly, he had had "enough."[87] He had better things to do with his time, including figuring out how to spend a small fortune.

In early February, Creighton received a letter from James Richardson, chairman of James Richardson & Sons, containing a much larger cheque than he had anticipated. Holding up his end of the bargain, Creighton had completed the Richardson manuscript in 1966 – twelve years after he had first agreed to write it – but the family decided not to publish it. Although no reason was ever given, he wasn't surprised. For years the family had indicated its unhappiness with draft chapters. As early as 1960, they told him that he hadn't succeeded in telling the story and that "the characters did not come to life"; now, six years later, they told him that it wasn't really what they wanted after all.[88]

The manuscript may not have marked an original contribution to Canadian historical writing, but it did recount the rise of a successful family business from its humble beginnings in Kingston – "a main station on the long lake and river transport system" – to national dominance in Winnipeg. And because the Richardsons understood that the problem of Canadian history was the problem of transportation and the movement of men, capital, goods, and information across enormous distances, it linked their story to the Laurentian thesis. Of course, Creighton assumed that western Canada was a colony of eastern Canada, that it was the river's dominion, and, by portraying the Richardsons as nationalist entrepreneurs in "the exploitation of Canadian resources," he emphasized the building of an east-west economy.[89] Still, he told a compelling story about, among other things, the creation of Western Canadian Airways and the introduction of airmail, the west being just as entitled to fast mail service as the east. Perhaps the family objected to a handful of private revelations inserted here and there, but they were minor details that could have been negotiated. In any event, a deal was a deal. In addition to the $5,000 bonus – which Creighton refused but which Richardson sent anyway – he received a cheque for $35,747.24.[90]

Because it was 1967, everyone, or so it seemed, was undertaking a personal centennial project. Some men grew centennial beards; others re-enacted the Battle of the Thames; and one proud Canadian celebrated the nation's birthday by "throwing a hammer through the window of the U.S. Consulate in Toronto."[91] As much as he might have liked to make a similar statement, Creighton took a more cautious route when he and Luella put an addition on to their house. With the Richardson money, they hired the heritage architect Napier Simpson, who respected the architectural and historical integrity of 15 Princess Street when he designed Creighton's new study, a large room with built-in bookshelves, a fireplace, lots of windows, and French doors that opened into Luella's rose garden. And because it had been fifty years since his father bought the Muskoka cottage, they undertook a couple of centennial projects there as well, including much-needed repairs to the writing hut and the completion of a log cabin that had been started in the late 1940s.

VII

To mark July 1st, Donald Creighton went to the south lawn of Queen's Park where – amid the statues of Queen Victoria and George Brown and the war memorials to the North West Rebellion and the 48th Highlanders – he listened to a one-hundred-gun salute and watched the daytime fireworks. A few years earlier, he had participated in a wreath-laying ceremony at the statue of Sir John A. Macdonald with the prime minister, John Diefenbaker, and the premier, Leslie Frost. He even had been cajoled into giving an impromptu speech.

Now he was just one more person in a large crowd of people when he bumped into a former student. But Michael Bliss precipitated a "bitter monologue" when he asked if Ottawa had any plans to recognize either *Macdonald* or *The Road to Confederation*. Creighton angrily explained that he expected nothing from Pearson in the same way that he got nothing from Diefenbaker. Why Diefenbaker, he said, had only "pretended to be a Sir John A. buff." He had been perfectly prepared to "exploit my books" for his own purposes but he had never used "my talents": "you might have expected that a senior conservative intellectual would have been made a senator."[92] It was a childish, self-indulgent response to a polite question. It was his way of getting attention. It was 32 Hewitt Avenue all over again, his bottomless need for attention. What more did he want? The CBC had paid him $1,000 for the right to use *The Road to Confederation* in a series of centennial broadcasts, while Diefenbaker had appointed him to the Historic Sites and Monuments Board, had offered him an appointment to the Board of Broadcast Governors, and had recommended him to the Monckton Commission. Ultimately, Creighton's response was that of an old man feeling sorry for himself. Despite receiving two honorary degrees that spring – one from St Francis Xavier University and the other from the University of Victoria – and despite being named a Companion of the Order of Canada just nine days earlier, he still felt that his country had ignored him, that it had never appreciated his unique genius or duly lauded and magnified him.

And then, just like that, his mood lifted. The morose rendition of his neglect had been for Bliss's benefit because, that afternoon, he returned to Brooklin, where, with family and friends, he celebrated Canada's birthday with a bottle of champagne. By his own account, he had a nice time drinking to Canada and talking about his recent trip to the Yukon with the Historic Sites and Monuments Board and about Cynthia's recent trip to Expo with Maurice.

Of course, the whole country was talking about Expo 67. According to one count, there were 2,860 federally funded centennial projects to mark what Pierre Berton famously called Canada's "last good year," but nothing matched the audacity and ambition of Expo. Attracting over 50 million visitors, it brought the world to Canada and Canada to the world. Sixty different countries displayed their history, geography, art, and scientific accomplishments in ninety pavilions. Although a celebration of "Man and His World," Expo was not without controversy. When the French president cried "Vive le Québec libre" to a cheering crowd, Creighton – like every other English Canadian – was disgusted, but he was equally disgusted by the Quebec premier's fawning "performance": having to watch Daniel Johnson welcome a foreign head of state was simply "incredible."[93] That was Ottawa's prerogative, not Quebec City's. But to Solange Chaput-Rolland, the problem wasn't de Gaulle; it was English Canada's

Despite Donald Creighton's assertion that John Diefenbaker only "pretended to be a Sir John A. buff," the prime minister admired *Macdonald*, even presenting a special boxed set to his British counterpart, Harold Macmillan, on the occasion of their first meeting in 1957. The following year he embarked on a six-week, fourteen-country world tour bearing gifts of maple syrup, Aboriginal handicrafts, and leather-bound copies of *Macdonald*. In 1961 he attended the opening of the E.J. Pratt Library at Victoria College, Creighton's alma mater, with E.J. Pratt, Creighton's undergraduate English professor, and Margaret Ray, librarian.

"visceral," hate-filled, francophobic response to de Gaulle, an indication of just how much distance separated French and English Canada.[94] Still, Donald and Luella wanted to experience Expo even if it meant crossing the national divide and going to Montreal.

As the host country, Canada had one of the largest pavilions. An inverted pyramid, it included displays, panels, films, music, and the People Tree, an exhibit of ordinary Canadians at work and play. But it also included a separate – and contentious – pavilion. In the shape of a massive tepee, the Indians of Canada Pavilion was yet another chapter in the global story of decolonization. Staging a very different "Indian-ness" and telling a very different story than the one most Canadians were used to, it was also another front in the history wars. Instead of the benevolent white father in the form of brave explorers, kind missionaries, and Indian agents, there were realistic depictions of dispossession, forced religion, broken treaties, and poverty. The gaze had been reversed, forcing viewers to see themselves in a new and uncomfortable light. The root of the "Indian problem" wasn't the Indian, it was the non-Indian.[95] According to one newspaper account, "photographs of tattered, unhappy-looking Indian children placed beside pictures of white Canadian children playing in the comfort of suburbia" were supposed "to provoke questions." After previewing the exhibit, a furious minister of Indian affairs threatened to shut the thing down. According to a DIA official, he "just about shit."[96] But one Haida organizer didn't care. "If it is making people angry," he said, "then the message is coming through."[97] During her thirteen-minute tour, an obviously well-briefed Queen Elizabeth "carefully ignored" that message by looking in the opposite direction at key moments, although she did admire the handiwork on display, remarking that "Indians are so adept with their hands."[98] Creighton, however, got the message, calling it "nothing but propaganda for the Indians."[99]

Creighton's reaction to the Indian Pavilion was part of his larger reaction to the 1960s. Canada no longer made any sense to him. It didn't conform to his understanding of it. Native people weren't supposed to challenge the settler narrative of discovery and ultimate nationhood. They were supposed to disappear, or in his words, "dwindle away."[100]

Canada didn't conform to Luella's understanding of it either, but instead of getting angry, she retreated into an idealized past when she completed her own centennial project, a social history of 1867. Blending real and invented people with actual diary entries and made-up letters, *The Elegant Canadians* used history, fiction, and epistolary fiction to decentre John A. Macdonald, George Cartier, and constitution making. In her words, she wanted to identify "the cadence of the times" through fashion, travel, food, and leisure. Everything was so much simpler back then. "Public order, social discipline, and private restraint" were society's hallmarks. Men and women were governed by "a definite code of conduct," and, unlike the noisy, ill-mannered, and inelegant Canadians of the 1960s, they were gracious, well dressed, and endowed with impeccable manners. They were, in a word, elegant, keeping neat diaries, writing interesting letters, hosting beautiful dinner parties, and attending balls where the gentlemen all bowed and the ladies all curtsied. The French were "gay"; the Indians were "romantic"; and the one African Canadian was "devoted" to the family he worked for (although the Americans were still ostentatious).[101] Dressing modestly and deferring to their social betters, people knew their place. They didn't blow up mail boxes or take to the streets.

One journalist described Luella's seventh book as a look "at a vanished Canada."[102] Donald Creighton might have added that his Canada had vanished, too, a fact that was confirmed a few weeks later when he attended a joint session of the Canadian Historical Association and the American Historical Association in late December.

Because the AHA was holding its 1967 annual meeting in Toronto, he felt obligated to make an appearance. Afterwards, he wished he hadn't. His former student, Margaret Prang, "took a side swipe" at him when she referred to his "accurate" but "irrelevant" analysis of the "language issue" and the intentions of the Fathers of Confederation.[103] To protect himself, he dismissed her paper as "silly and sentimental."[104] However, Maurice Careless's paper was harder to dismiss. In an early version of his seminal article on limited identities and the writing of Canadian history, he argued that Canadian historians have been "too hung up on the plot of nation building."[105] Not only is the story line teleological, its main characters are either good guys or bad guys, either forward-thinking nation builders or backward-looking colonials. The dream of nation, he said, has been the dream of historians, not the Canadian people, whose primary identities have been the limited identities of region, class, and ethnicity. Historians, therefore, should abandon the fruitless search for a single national identity in favour of Canada's limited identities.

Creighton had devoted his entire career to the articulation and defence of what he had called, in *Dominion of the North*, Canada's "transcendent sense of nationhood." Now he was being told by his colleague that his past efforts had been misguided and that his current effort – a single-volume history of Canada since 1867 – would be out of date the second it hit the shelves. He felt, he said, "very depressed": "I am a very old fashioned nationalist who is completely out of tune with the present."[106]

Not surprisingly, he didn't feel like celebrating New Year's Eve. Instead, he wrote a lecture and went to bed. It hadn't been Canada's last good year at all. Indeed, he couldn't remember Canada's last good year. Maybe Luella was right. Maybe it had been 1867. Or maybe it was 1883. The CPR was nearing completion, Macdonald was at the top of his game, and both the French and the Métis were quiet.[107]

WINTER

Historians have a peculiar duty towards losers, not out of mere perversity, but because much is to be learned from them.

S.F. Wise, "Upper Canada and the Conservative Tradition"

chapter twelve

Despair

Deep within him there lay the inarticulate assumption that the history of Canada during its most important half century was a plot which he, as its chief author, must hasten to complete. He had always known what he wanted to do. The design had been there from the beginning. All he needed now was a few years in which to finish it.

Sir John A. Macdonald, vol. 2

When he was invited to deliver a keynote address to the 1969 annual meeting of the Canadian Historical Association, Donald Creighton jumped at the chance to survey his career and the writing of Canadian history. But as the date approached, he grew increasingly uneasy. He had trouble sleeping, and at one point a heavy depression settled over him.[1] He couldn't back out now, though. What he had to say was too important. As he entered the York University lecture theatre, his mood lifted. The place was packed. Someone told him that there were 700 people in the audience. Latecomers had to sit on the stairs, lean against the walls, or stand at the back. To some, it represented an opportunity to hear – perhaps for the last time – English Canada's greatest historian.[2] To others, it had the look and feel of a "happening."[3]

Opening with a brief description of his initial interest in French history and his switch to Canadian history, he now said that the history of his own country had been a "bad second or third choice."[4] Of course, that hadn't been true at all. In the late 1920s, he had been young, ambitious, and hungry to write a big book that contributed to Canada's self-understanding. Revelling in the thrill of discovery, he had enjoyed writing *The Commercial Empire of the St. Lawrence*. Any sense of disappointment he felt at having to abandon French history had been fleeting. But in the late 1960s, he rewrote his own life story. In this version, he had been the victim of unfair circumstances – had he been a young historian today he would have had scholarships and travel grants and he could have written the history of a country that mattered. Canada hadn't been worthy of his genius and he had wasted his time writing the history of an ungrateful colony. It was a familiar lament. "Great authors," he always said, are "born in great countries" where publishers compete for manuscripts and people actually read books.[5] Britain lauds its great writers, magnifying them with honorary degrees from Oxford and Cambridge and burying them in Westminster Abbey. But Canada couldn't recognize greatness to save its life. "I suppose there is hardly a Canadian author who hasn't, at one time or another, bemoaned the fact that he had the misfortune to be born in this country."[6] It was as if he needed a past injustice – some great betrayal – at the beginning of his career to explain his unhappiness at the end of his career.

Calling his address "The Decline and Fall of the Empire of the St. Lawrence," Creighton now seemed to be saying that Canada had been too much to hope for. After all, the Laurentian thesis had been both a story of Canada's origins and a prophecy of its defeat. Great Britain had been too weak, the United States too strong, successive Liberal prime ministers too indifferent, and John Diefenbaker too ineffectual. This was what had been keeping him up at night. This was what had led to his sinking depression. And this was why he hadn't been looking forward to his address: the Laurentian prophecy had been fulfilled and Canada had entered "the final struggle of its existence."[7] The Montreal merchants had been right all along – the country couldn't escape its destiny.

The audience didn't know how to respond. What had looked like a "happening" turned instead into a wake. Only one person was inspired to ask a question, and even then it was an unrelated comment about hiring practices at Canadian universities. Someone else booed. Others snickered. And although most people clapped politely, it was clear that they saw the author of the Laurentian thesis as "a relic from the past."[8] Uninterested in history as a vehicle of national consciousness or in narratives of national declension,[9] the profession wanted to hear what Irving Abella – then a newly minted Toronto PhD – had to say about the Committee for Industrial Organization, the Communist Party, and the Canadian Congress of Labour.[10]

Creighton, however, never cared about the minutiae of social history, and a few days later he returned to the book that he had been writing for the past three years, a single-volume history of Canada since 1867. The going was tough. At one point, he told Luella that he felt as if he were trying to write in Latin, that even simple composition had become difficult and progress agonizingly slow. Although he was sixty-seven years old and no longer had the powers of concentration or the stamina that he had just four or five years earlier, that wasn't the real problem. The real problem was the terrible conclusion staring him in the face: the final defeat of Canada. He had always known it was there. It had been there from the beginning. All he needed now was a few months in which to complete the story.

Finally, the damn thing was done. Although he knew that Macmillan would publish it, he also knew that John Gray wouldn't like its treatment of French Canada or its bleak conclusion. The original vision had been a celebration of the country's first one hundred years by its leading historian. The end result was something else. Brooding and pessimistic, *Canada's First Century* was probably mistitled, Creighton explained, because it "implies" that there will be a second century, a "more than slightly doubtful" assumption.[11] When Gray urged him to soften his tone here and alter his perspective there, he exploded. Soon the two men were having a screaming match that ended only when Creighton stormed out of Gray's office, shouting "I bid you good day." A month or two later, he became violently ill and had to be hospitalized. As his fever spiked and he slipped in and out of consciousness, he began to hallucinate: John Gray was in his hospital room telling him that, while he intended to publish *Canada's First Century*, he also intended to include two essays by French-Canadian historians refuting his arguments. Trying to stop him, a terrified Creighton found himself immobilized, unable to get out of bed.[12] For years afterwards, he dined out on this story, proving that, when he wanted to, he was capable of laughing at himself.

II

Luella had her own worries. That August, she turned sixty-eight years old, and, although never obsessed by her appearance, she became anxious about her weight. A few months later she ate too many Christmas treats, berating herself for being "terribly fat" and pressuring herself to "take off many pounds." By May she had lost fourteen pounds and, despite her resolution to "hold the line," started to gain them back again.[13] Soon her dress size was 18. "It's my big rib-cage," she said. "I could have been an opera singer, if I had had a nice voice and a sense of music."[14]

Of course, Creighton didn't care if her dress size was 8 or 18. He loved her with all of his heart. A wonderful cook and generous hostess, she transformed every one of their apartments and houses into homes, hosting luncheons, dinners, and parties for his colleagues and his students. He genuinely appreciated her many efforts, commenting endlessly on what a wonderful meal she had prepared, or what a lovely party she had organized, or how beautiful she looked in this or that dress. He could be difficult but never unappreciative, because he also knew that her strength and endurance grounded his moodiness and intractability. To show his appreciation, he bought her gifts, usually jewellery or clothes, sometimes books or prints, and once a portable transistor radio. He always remembered their anniversary and never forgot her birthday. For Valentine's Day, he sent flowers. But one year, he bought her a black nightdress. That morning she slipped into it, modelling it for him. He thought she was beautiful and she seemed "pleased."[15] She was sixty-one years old and he still found her sexually attractive, if not as sexually available as he might have liked. But he had accepted long ago her need to have a room – and a bed – of her own. After twenty-odd years, that wasn't going to change. Besides, it didn't matter, because they were happy. Sometimes, after dinner, they drew the curtains, lit a few candles, and danced to the CBC Orchestra.

If fulfilled in her marriage, Luella was alone in her writing. Her textbooks hadn't been very successful, and her social history of 1867 – while technically interesting – hadn't been a commercial success either. "Writers are fools," she said.[16] Meanwhile, finding the conviction needed to write serious, adult fiction was still a burden. To put off again the responsibility of another novel, she turned to juvenile fiction and, in late 1969, published what would be her last book. A poignant novella about love and magic, *The Hitching Post* tells the story of a little girl looking for a mother she barely knew. "Cecilia could not really remember how she looked, or the sound of her voice, or how her hand felt when she was holding it. Cecilia thought of her often, with a terrible longing, almost like a pain."[17]

It was Luella's own terrible longing. A year or so earlier, on a hot, breezy July afternoon, she had collapsed in the Stouffville Cemetery, "shattered," she said, "by the sight" of her mother's grave.

Sarah Luella Sanders
wife of J.W. Bruce
born July 8, 1875
died August 27, 1901
in her 27th year

Unable to move, she stood there "crying" and "wishing hard on the stone as if communication could somehow be possible after nearly sixty-seven years."[18] If Luella couldn't be reunited with her mother, her character could be, and in the book's final pages Cecilia's mother returns, holds her closely, and makes her understand that she will never leave again.[19]

Luella Creighton holding a tabby kitten: in her life and in her early children's fiction, she was always protecting cats. McClelland and Stewart used this picture on the dust jacket of *The Hitching Post*.

In a 1968 or 1969 talk – to the Heliconian Club, perhaps, or a Women's Institute – Luella referred to Virginia Woolf's diaries and their "almost painful loneliness." The true writer, meaning the writer of fiction, not the writer of textbooks, "writes to satisfy oneself" and one's overwhelming need to tell a story. To not tell that story is to "betray" a trust; it is to "sin."[20] And so, with Donald's encouragement and her own inner determination, Luella found the courage to begin a new novel that took her back for a final time to Kinsail and the hole at the centre of her emotional existence.

Written in the first person, "Prelude" is about many things – love, grief, marriage, family, and the writer's life – but it is really about one woman's need for her mother. In a heartbreaking scene Harriet Chisolm – or Hallie – attempts to find her mother's grave, "wishing and wishing that I could see her there below, with her shawl of bright brown hair about her shoulders." Unable to find it, she becomes inconsolable: "A woman thirty-nine years old, not given to tears, I was crying because I could not find the gravestone of a mother I had never known." Unlike in *The Hitching Post*, there can be no tender reunion across the years, and eventually Hallie resolves never to write again. "The muscles of my mind have petrified, I think, and I shall force my heart to turn to stone also. Certainly I shall never write another book. To write there must be a fermentation, a boiling up which must be released. I am dried out and shrunken within. But I am free, too, free from the terrible crushing burden of response."[21] Hallie's resolve was Luella's resolve: she never published her final novel because she had freed herself from the need to. She had atoned her earlier betrayals and sins; she had eased her "painful loneliness"; and she had accepted that her mother's death was what it was, and that all the wishing and all the writing in the world couldn't undo it. But it was a pyrrhic victory because, in freeing herself "from the terrible crushing burden of response," she had turned her heart to stone.

Luella's grief was complicated by her crumbling relationship with Cynthia. In the last four or five years, Cynthia and Maurice had lived in New York, Toronto, and Montreal. At one point, they talked about moving to Nova Scotia and becoming writers; at another point, they talked about returning to Toronto and opening a bookstore; and now, in 1969, they had moved to Vancouver where Cynthia, a feminist, joined the Vancouver Women's Caucus and Maurice, an open bisexual, entered the gay liberation movement. It was too much for Luella. Needing someone to blame, she blamed Maurice. But it wasn't Maurice's fault. It was no one's "fault." Cynthia was simply leading her life on her terms. She didn't want a comfortable middle-class existence in North Toronto; she wanted to change the world.

Because she never had a mother's unconditional love, Luella didn't know how to love Cynthia in that way. Instead, she withdrew emotionally.[22] Maybe it is possible to read her last two books differently. Maybe the physical closeness in *The Hitching Post* is what Luella wanted with Cynthia; maybe that explains why she dedicated it to her; maybe it was her way of saying what the heart of stone in "Prelude" prevented her from saying, that she loved her.

III

When *Canada's First Century* was published in March 1970, Donald Creighton had been at war, for the better part of a decade, with a country that he simultaneously loved, and it was from this coincidence of opposites that came the brilliant sweep of his ninth book.

> The great pine forests which had first brought the timber merchants up the river sixty years before still loomed over the settlement that had been built to exploit them. To the north, across the deep valley of the Ottawa, and beyond the low-lying meadows on the other side, the Laurentian hills rose slowly, deliberately, in ridge after darkening ridge of pine trees.

In effect, his last great book began where *The Road to Confederation* had ended, with the promise of the Laurentian thesis steadily revealing itself. Also emerging in the opening pages were the same four themes that he had developed over the course of his long career: the need for a strong central government to oversee the building of a great transcontinental nation; the limited but sufficient language guarantees of Section 133 of the British North America Act; the importance of Great Britain to Canada's survival; and the relentless "pressure of a resentful and predatory United States." Of course, they weren't really themes at all. They were leitmotifs in the Wagnerian sense. At times quiet and unobtrusive, at other times urgent and demanding, they appear and reappear over 350-odd pages, always moving deliberately to their final, deafening crescendo: the triumph of continentalism and the defeat of Canada. The provinces prevail over the federal government; French-Canadian nationalists demand official bilingualism; the imperial connection is severed; and the United States dominates all aspects of Canadian life.[23]

In *The Commercial Empire of the St. Lawrence*, Creighton had taken his inspiration from Richard Wagner's four-opera masterpiece *Der Ring des Nibelungen*, but it had come in broad strokes. In *Canada's First Century*, he again turned to Wagner, but this time his inspiration came in the form of individual characters. Cast as Wotan, the supreme god and creator, John A. Macdonald was a giant among men, a visionary leader "of exceptional gifts." When most of Macdonald's

Although Donald Creighton and John Gray were good friends, their relationship was strained by Creighton's hard line on Quebec. Prior to its publication, Gray had urged Creighton to soften his position in *Canada's First Century*; soon the two men were having a shouting match. Taken at a happier moment, this photograph shows a pleased publisher and a content author. *Canada's First Century* would be Creighton's last great book.

contemporaries "followed the mid-Victorian fashion of beards, whiskers, and moustaches, he was invariably clean-shaven." It was yet another example of Creighton's deft use of the unnecessary detail, the squiggle on the edge of the page: Macdonald wasn't a garden-variety, dime-a-dozen, run-of-the-mill politician. He stood out, and, more importantly, he stood above. Alone among his peers, he perceived the new Dominion's "enormous territorial inheritance" and grasped the potentialities of the St Lawrence River and its iron extension, the Canadian Pacific Railway.[24]

Because everything contains its own opposite in Wagner's universe, every hero demands its own anti-hero, a role Creighton reserved for Mackenzie King and his successors, Louis St Laurent and Lester Pearson, all Liberal prime ministers and all blind to Macdonald's Laurentian vision. They were the ones who unfastened the country from Great Britain, tied it to the United States, and appeased Quebec's professional blackmailers.

Casting King in the role of Alberich, the ugly, wretched dwarf who renounces love for power, Creighton described Canada's longest-serving prime minister as a "short, stoutish man, with a torso like a barrel" and an "audible wheeze" for a voice. As a young man, King had talked in terms "of serving suffering human-ity" but quickly outgrew his "humanitarian and reformist youth" to become a vicious practitioner "of the mean devices" of realpolitik.[25] (Parenthetically, Creighton never knew that his grandmother, Lizzie Harvie, and his nemesis, Mackenzie King, had "rescued" a young woman named Edna, a prostitute liv-ing on King Street, in 1894. Later, though, he delighted in the public specula-tion that the man who saw himself as chosen by "divine providence" to save his country from itself wasn't just rescuing prostitutes.)[26] King, or at least Creighton's King, would do anything to stay in power, and the series of wartime agreements he negotiated with the United States "effectively shackled" Canada to its southern neighbour. He was, Creighton concluded, "one of the shrewdest, hardest, and most ruthless political operators in the entire history of the British Commonwealth."[27] Where Macdonald was prime ministerial, creative, and he-roic, King was calculating, destructive, and small.

But it fell to St Laurent and Pearson to finish the job. Together, they are Hagen, Alberich's son, who plunges the spear into Siegfried's back, killing the youthful grandson of Wotan or, to extend the character assignments, killing Macdonald's Dominion of the North. Following his political father's lead, St Laurent quietly removed the word Dominion from official nomenclature at the same time as he oversaw "the close integration of Canada into a North American economy dominated by the United States." Pearson was no better and probably worse: "His slight lisp, his pleasant, slightly deprecating manner, and the mild idiosyncrasy of his bow tie" obscured an ugly truth. Canada's fourteenth prime minister was really an American philistine whose "favourite indoor relaxation was watching western dramas and football and hockey games on television." As "products of the American sports and entertainment industry," they revealed both "his bland acceptance" of North American life and his refusal to "indulge in pretentious notions about Canadian sovereignty or nostalgic longings for the old Britannic connection." Like King and St Laurent before him, he accepted as "natural and beneficial" the "invasion of American capital and the authority of American leadership in international affairs."[28]

Although Creighton acknowledged Britain's weakness in world affairs, its growing indifference to the Commonwealth, and its decision to seek member-ship in the European Economic Community, he tenaciously blamed the bloody Liberals. In fact, the closer he got to the present, the more biting he became, his judgments fast and furious, his insults cheap and gratuitous, and his conclu-sions severe and unfair. He hated Pearson and it showed. As a historian, he was always more comfortable in the nineteenth century than he was in the twenti-eth century. His loud, powerful voice worked best at a distance. The twentieth century didn't belong to Canada, as Wilfrid Laurier had predicted; it belonged to the Liberal Party and it had ruined everything by selling the country's birth-right, appeasing Quebec nationalism, and failing to defend the Constitution. In a veiled reference to himself, he noted that anyone who attempted to expose the myths and distortions uttered by men and women who ought to know bet-ter "were promptly rebuked as narrow-minded bigots or denounced as dis-loyal Canadians."[29]

In the final pages, the original promise of the Laurentian thesis – "the enor-mous expanse of rock and water, forest and plain, which made up the half-continent that the Dominion of Canada had inherited and hoped to occupy as its own" – is forsaken. Canada had always been an impossibility. It had always been a pipe dream. The "tradition of defeat" had overwhelmed the promise of immense expanses, and now, at last, continentalism, that rough beast, was slouching "towards its final triumph."[30]

An instinctive fear of continentalism – that "American urge towards conti-nental empire" in the form of "armed invasion, commercial competition, politi-cal pressure, financial takeover, cultural influence" – informed all of Creighton's books and, at times, approached simple anti-Americanism.[31] This was espe-cially true for *Canada's First Century*. His treatment of the Kennedy administra-tion, for example, was brutal and unforgiving. In fact, he never liked the Kennedy family. He never forgave the father's unhelpful remarks about Great Britain in 1940 and didn't lose any sleep over the son's assassination in 1963. "All the world mourns," Luella recorded in her diary, "but Red China and Donald Creighton." According to his historical arithmetic, the Kennedy ad-ministration equalled the Berlin crisis (which "risked the extinction of the hu-man race") plus the Cuban Missile Crisis (which saw the president of the United States speak as "the voice of God, revealing God's perfect truth") plus the "sav-age" intervention by State Department officials in Canada's 1963 election (which facilitated Lester Pearson's ascent to 24 Sussex Drive). "That's the kind of thing I think of when I think of New Frontiers," Creighton told a national television audience.[32]

Despite his deserved reputation as a blind critic of the United States, Creighton was capable of critical insight. He belonged to an impressive group of intellectuals that included Harold Innis, Hilda Neatby, W.L. Morton, and George Grant. As tories, they distrusted modernity and its commitment to secularism, its faith in technology, its mass culture, its consumer culture, and its promise of self-fulfilment. And as tory nationalists, they distrusted the United States. In their view, it represented the epicentre of modernity.[33] From this van-tage point, Creighton's concern about Canadian reliance on American technol-ogy was also a critique of technology; his reference to the "anarchy and license" of the United States was also a plea for "public order and private restraint"; his commentary on the penetrative power of American mass media was also a commentary on the philistinism of mass culture; and his criticism of "sophisticated city dwellers" and their "continentalist interest and values" was rooted in conservative conceptions of community and traditional values.[34] Unfortunately, he never pushed his analysis, relying instead on one-liners and cheap shots at the Kennedys.

Canada's First Century received a handful of thoughtful reviews that sought to place it within the larger contours of Creighton's career and within the larger contexts of English-Canadian thought,[35] but it received more than one negative review: it lacked "objectivity" and its author was "didactic and overly assertive"; it was "depressingly consistent with conventional neurotic nationalism"; and it displayed a "hypnotic preoccupation" with our neighbour to the south. The *Financial Post* declared that it was "more dirge than history," while the *Ottawa Citizen* described its author as "a cranky propagandist, as ready as any Soviet encyclopedist to rewrite, distort, select, or ignore the facts in order to serve a theory." Not to be outdone, the *Winnipeg Free Press* called Creighton "an ill-informed loon" who was "as out-of-date with information as the housewife on a phone-in radio show." And the *Edmonton Journal* noted that in Alberta "we can see more readily the benefits of Imperial Oil than we can of Ottawa."[36]

And yet *Canada's First Century* sold exceptionally well. In July it earned a spot on the best-seller's list ahead of David Reuben's *Everything You Always Wanted to Know about Sex*, Masters and Johnson's *Human Sexual Inadequacy*, and J's *The Sensuous Woman*. For a few heady weeks it even outsold the Bible. By August over 5,400 copies had been sold and the Book of the Month Club announced that it would be placing an order for 2,500 copies. Within a year nearly 13,000 copies would be sold and Creighton would receive a cheque for $15,622.21, his biggest royalty cheque ever.

Clearly, *Canada's First Century* struck a resonant chord with English Canadians. While his draw-a-line-in-the-sand position on Quebec nationalism drew fire from many corners, even George Woodcock had to concede that Creighton showed real courage. At least he has "the honesty to speak what many believe but have not the courage to say at a time when criticism of Quebec has come to be regarded as sheer bigotry."[37] But it was Creighton's loud denunciations of American foreign policy and American ownership of the Canadian economy that made his book so popular and him something of a hero. In the context of the brutal and bloody war against Vietnam, young Canadians in particular saw the United States in the new and terrifying light of what Creighton rightly called the "tragedy" and the "carnage" of "American military imperialism."[38] In fact, Creighton's tory nationalism and the New Left nationalism of the late 1960s and early 1970s shared common nationalist ground: both distrusted the

American empire and American ownership of the Canadian economy.[39] Creighton even said that he would have voted for the NDP had it supported Mel Watkins's Manifesto for an Independent Socialist Canada, better known as the Waffle Manifesto.[40] Apparently, Watkins was "overjoyed" by the endorsement. And one NDP MLA in Manitoba cited Creighton's economic nationalism to defend his government's modest scheme for public automobile insurance. All we are proposing, he said, is a Crown corporation for auto insurance. "We're pikers compared to Creighton!"[41]

Canada's First Century remains a great book because of its intimacy and its honesty and because it emanates Creighton's passionate and distinctive voice. In many ways, it is his most autobiographical book precisely because it documents the disappearance of his picture of the world: the picture of God, King, and Country; of his parents taking him to the Ossington Avenue fire hall to mark the death of King Edward VII; of his mother reading to him from the novels of Dickens and the poetry of Tennyson; and of a little boy devouring *Chums*, *Chatterbox*, and *Little Folks* for their stories about cricket matches and prefects. Perhaps this explains why both his brother Jack and his sister Isabel considered it his best book. Perhaps they not only heard their brother in its pages, perhaps they saw him as well.[42] Ultimately, it implies a picture of what Canada might have been had the bloody Liberals not sold it, had the Quebec nationalists not weakened it, and had that "bastard" Lester Pearson never been born.[43]

In the final analysis, *Canada's First Century* is Donald Creighton's lament for a nation.[44] And if it lacks the philosophical insight of George Grant's more famous lament, it has all of its tragic beauty. History may have been Creighton's profession, but it was also a cross he was unable to refuse. When the burden became too great, he indulged his anger or drowned in self-pity, diminishing himself either way. But as a constant reminder of the land – of the St Lawrence River, the Great Lakes, and the Laurentian Shield – it gave him the courage to stand up and be counted as the Last English Canadian.[45]

IV

After the publication of *Canada's First Century*, Donald and Luella took a much-needed vacation to England and France. Actually, Great Britain and Europe had become an annual thing. Although their 1960 trip to Cambridge had been a disaster – Luella broke her leg when the impossibly massive oak door at the Ely Cathedral closed on it and Donald landed in the hospital with an irregular heartbeat, which, in the end, turned out to be nothing – they enjoyed exploring new cities, visiting old haunts, and spending long, lazy afternoons in

DONALD CREIGHTON - THE OLD CHIEFTAIN

Donald Creighton's defence of Canada wasn't lost on the artist Isaac Bickerstaff, who depicted him as Sir John A. Macdonald, as a modern day chieftain ready to lead his clan into battle.

the Victoria and Albert, the Jeu de Paume, or the Uffizi Gallery. In many ways, this vacation would be more of the same. But they also intended to visit Brittany and the little village of Paimpol where they had spent part of their honeymoon in 1926. And they would be travelling with Robert Finch, a French professor at University College and one of Creighton's dearest friends. They had been close forever. In the early 1950s, they used to meet for what they called "Lodge Night" in Finch's room at Wycliffe College, often after a gowned high table dinner in hall. Creighton would write *Macdonald* and Finch would write poetry. It was their way of pushing each other and fighting back against the isolation of the writer's vocation. Afterwards, they would go to the Honey Dew for a cup of coffee or the Park Plaza for a drink. When Cynthia was confirmed in the Anglican Church – a decision she came to on her own but which her parents supported – Finch was asked to be a godparent.

Almost immediately, Finch began to wonder what he had gotten himself into. For years after the fact, he referred to that trip to France as "That Trip."[46] Thunder Cloud – his secret nickname for Creighton – was impossible: he didn't feel well; he fretted about money; he disliked the hotel; he hated the food; he complained about the service; and he threw a fit when he lost his room key (which turned out to be in his pocket the whole time). Paimpol, meanwhile, was a dirty, one-horse town with too much traffic, Creighton now said. And the house he and Luella had rented in 1926 had been allowed to fall into miserable disrepair. It was "dingy" and "run-down," he said.[47] Still, Luella wanted to knock on the door. But Donald wouldn't allow it. Clearly, something was bothering him. It wasn't the traffic or the service or even his stomach. It was time and its relentless passage. It was his mortality. Forty-four years earlier he had been a young man with his whole life ahead of him and now he was an old man. Instead of seeing Paimpol as it had been, he saw it as it had "disintegrated"; instead of delighting in a flood of memories, he became "morose and silent." And then he became "angry, almost livid." When Finch asked him why he and Luella had chosen this particular Brittany village so many years ago, he thrust "himself forward in his chair," shouting something about being "poor" and having "nothing."[48] And there it was: that toxic bile and familiar bitterness he carried inside him. He and Luella may have been poor but they were young, happy, and in love. But his accumulated resentments and calcified disappointments wouldn't let him see any of that.

Something else was bothering him as well. It was Cynthia. Before going to Paimpol, Donald, Luella, and Robert took a day trip to Chartres, a city not far from Paris famous for its magnificent cathedral. As he wandered through its cavernous interior, he remembered the last time he had been there. It was Easter 1952, and he and Luella had taken Cynthia to Paris and, from there, to Chartres. At one point, he saw an eleven-year-old Cynthia sitting by herself at precisely the moment a beam of sunlight fell from the South Rose Window, bathing her in a golden blue light. The image of his angelic little girl had stayed with him all those years. Now, she was a thirty-year-old woman, a feminist, and a member of the Trotskyist League for Socialist Action. At the very moment he was in Chartres, she and Maurice were driving back to Vancouver after attending the Toronto convention of the Canadian section of the Fourth International.

Thinking about Cynthia as a child was like reading the casualty lists in old newspapers, he told Finch, adding that it made him "inexpressibly sad."[49] In a way, Cynthia was dead to him. Having idealized his daughter, he couldn't reconcile the angel he had invented with the woman she had become.

Returning to Canada and a mountain of mail, he opened a letter from, curiously enough, Cynthia that set him off. A few months earlier, he had raised with Philip the possibility of selling the Muskoka properties, and Philip, in turn, had told Cynthia, who wrote that she was "extremely surprised" and "very upset." Of course, Creighton objected to the tone of her letter. He also reminded her that they were his properties and that inflation had reduced the value of his pension. Unlike Philip, who could slide out of confrontations with his father, Cynthia couldn't, and she let him have it: "You and mother are among the financially privileged, and that is why I find this sort of monetary crepe-hanging so extraordinary."[50] It was a silly miscommunication: Creighton had raised the matter of selling the cottages as a possibility; Cynthia had interpreted it as a likelihood. Her feelings were hurt because she felt that she hadn't been consulted; and his feelings were hurt because he felt that he had been reduced to "a member of the bloated capitalist class": "I am offensive to her both as a socialist and a feminist."[51]

In the end, the cottages weren't sold but it was a revealing moment: driven to despair by his own feelings, he couldn't communicate with his own daughter. Luella once said that Donald was "too strong" for Cynthia, that his temperament and large personality didn't leave her the emotional and intellectual space she needed. "I don't think she can settle where he is a factor." "Both are too sensitive to each other."[52]

V

On 30 June 1971, Creighton formally retired from the University of Toronto after forty-four years of teaching. He wasn't disappointed. In fact, he had wanted out for years. After the department moved to Sidney Smith Hall in 1961, he resolved to "avoid the place." The old department may have had its frustrations, but at least it was a department: everyone knew each other, and, God bless Miss Hahn, there was afternoon tea. But Sid Smith was all concrete and glass.

Describing it as "a terrible disappointment" and "extremely depressing," he dubbed it the "Cell Block."[53] Almost immediately, the department undertook what turned into a multi-stage curriculum review. This time, Creighton found himself defending the old curriculum against a proposal that introduced more choice to accommodate the research and teaching interests of a large professoriate and to broaden it beyond Western Europe, Great Britain, the United States, and Canada. The whole damn exercise was, by turns, "depressing" and "boring," he said. Before the final vote was taken in May 1966, he had insomnia and indigestion, tossing and turning all night. He had prepared a historical explanation and defence of the old curriculum, but when the moment came he couldn't be bothered. Instead, he spoke "briefly and forcefully" against the proposed changes and bowed out.[54] It wasn't his department anymore; it belonged to a new generation. Freya Hahn had retired; the tradition of afternoon tea went with her; and the place was now "completely dominated" by "American imports," including a "cocksure" specialist on the Reformation.[55] He felt, he said, "very alienated."[56] After his appointment as a University Professor in 1968 – an honour held by only a handful of scholars, including Northrop Frye – and his appointment as a Fellow of Massey College a year later – also an honour that gave him a new office and a small bedroom – Creighton left the department altogether. When he learned that he no longer had the highest salary, that Maurice Careless, his former student, made more than he did, his decision to get out was confirmed (although Careless's salary stuck in his craw).

As chairman, Archie Thornton posed a "delicate" question to his colleagues: how should the department mark the retirement of its two most senior members, Donald Creighton and Dick Saunders? Bill Eccles – a brilliant scholar of New France – responded immediately: for Dick, "a crystal decanter and a case of malt whiskey to go with it"; for Donald, "a set of sterling silver buggering irons."[57] Creighton, he always said, was a "francophobe."[58] In the end, Thornton chose neither buggering irons nor a decanter, inviting instead department members to make a cash contribution towards a new stereo for Creighton and a new camera for Saunders. Most people contributed equally to each gift, but several members contributed more to Saunders's gift. Eccles, for example, gave $5 towards Creighton's stereo, but $10 towards Saunders's camera. As a result, Thornton collected just over $300 for Creighton and nearly $450 for Saunders. Had Creighton known any of this, he would have been crushed. *Et vos, collegae? And you, colleagues?*

A few months later, Thornton hosted a dinner for Donald and Luella at his home. Luella described it as a "marvellous party" – although she got mad at herself for eating too much, insisting that she put on three pounds. When presented with his gift – that also included a cheque for $45 to buy some new records – Creighton "made a graceful acceptance speech." It was, he said, a "very lovely" event, and he thoroughly enjoyed himself.[59] Later, he bought a new recording of Wagner's Ring Cycle.

Creighton's only connection to the university now were his graduate students. In fact, he had been saying this for years. Viv Nelles, Richard Clippingdale, Paul Rutherford, Donald Page, Angus Gilbert, Jim Miller, and Ken McLaughlin formed his final batch of students, and he had wanted to see them through the program. In the case of Gilbert, Miller, and McLaughlin, he agreed to supervise their work after his retirement. Forty-odd years later, his students fondly remember his encouragement, his letters of recommendation, his attention to detail, and his little kindnesses. It was a side of him that the Bill Eccleses of the department didn't see, or, if they did, didn't appreciate. After encouraging a precocious Nelles to give graduate school a shot, Creighton worried about the effect that reading so much microfilm might have on the poor boy's eyes, and as Clippingdale was preparing to write his thesis, he welcomed him to Brooklin on a Sunday afternoon to discuss possibilities and directions. When McLaughlin announced the arrival of his first child, Creighton urged him to forget the thesis and to enjoy his daughter in a long, emotional letter about Cynthia as a baby, about seeing her for the first time on the platform of the Washington train station, and about not being as present as maybe he should have been.

It was always understood that his students were writing their thesis, not his. They weren't expected to ride his hobby horse or copy his style. Rather, they were expected to undertake an exhaustive program of research and develop an original argument. When Clippingdale wrote a biography of J.S. Willison – a leading journalist in late Victorian-Edwardian English Canada and one of the early authors of the Liberal Interpretation of Canadian history – Creighton admired his independent intelligence and fine writing.[60] When McLaughlin used the University of Waterloo's computer lab and an early program called Statistical Package for the Social Sciences to correlate religion and voter behaviour at the level of individual polls, Creighton was thrilled. Although a narrative historian, not a quantitative historian, he appreciated that his student was breaking new ground, and he found himself "much impressed by the novelty" of McLaughlin's research "and the cumulative effect of his evidence."[61] And when Jim Miller was still a fourth-year student, Creighton saw something in him – a spark, a fine mind, a seriousness of purpose – and encouraged him to apply to the PhD program. He would be his last student. "I liked the old guy," Miller now says. "He was good to me."[62]

Always prepared to go to bat for them, the old guy was good to his graduate students. He was furious, for example, when Robert Bothwell read the penultimate draft of Angus Gilbert's thesis and refused to let it go to a defence. That "bearded barbarian" with his "minor" and "absurd" criticisms, Creighton said with Dickensian flair, had drawn "a knife" on both him and his student. It's not clear what happened next: according to Bothwell, Creighton went "ballistic"; according to Creighton, he "managed, with difficulty, to keep [his] temper."[63] Whatever the case, he rolled up his sleeves, and he and Gilbert prepared the thesis for a successful defence.

Except for Margaret Prang, all of Creighton's doctoral students were men. "Unfailingly polite," he never flirted or otherwise carried on with his female students as some of his colleagues did.[64] But he didn't tap them on the shoulder either in the way he had tapped Viv Nelles or Jim Miller. An undergraduate in the 1960s, Bernadine Dodge recalls that "if his classrooms were not hostile to women, they were certainly chilly."[65] He once said that women didn't make very good teachers because their voices couldn't reach the back of large lecture halls. He was wrong, of course, but in a profession that deliberately excluded women, he was hardly unique.[66]

Creighton's graduate students looked up to him and wanted to achieve his high expectations and his equally high standards. Nelles, for example, told him that *The Commercial Empire of the St. Lawrence* had confirmed his interest in the relationship between economics and politics and that it "served as a constant guide, example, and companion."[67] And if his students worshipped him, it was because they owed him a portion of their daily bread. Remembering, perhaps, his own search for an academic position in the 1920s, he wrote countless letters on their behalf. He once apologized to Eugene Forsey for failing to answer his letter. In addition to a million other things, he said, "I have written to practically every head of a History Department in Canada on behalf of my four doctoral students who were seeking jobs for this autumn. The market is suddenly very restricted, but thank God! my students were all placed."[68] It wasn't only about ego gratification, or empire building, or, even worse, silly ideas about achieving professional immortality through his students, although all of this may have played a part. He genuinely liked his students; he took an interest in their families; and he wanted to see them succeed in their chosen careers. They were his friends.

This explains, in part, why he got so upset after an article appeared in the September 1971 issue of the *Canadian Historical Review*: not one of his students defended him. After reading *Canada's First Century* – especially its unforgiving assessment of bilingualism and biculturalism – Ralph Heintzman wrote a paper making the historical case for precisely that, bilingualism and biculturalism. As co-editor of the *CHR*, Craig Brown encouraged the York University doctoral candidate to submit it for publication, although he also advised him to send a copy to Creighton first. To his credit, Creighton advised his former student to accept Brown's invitation. Of course, he didn't agree with Heintzman's argument – in his opinion, Confederation did not constitute a bicultural compact – but, he said, "I don't think I used my seminars to teach historical dogmas. And I was always pleased when a student applied a new approach or suggested a fresh interpretation or gave other evidence that he had a mind of his own."[69]

Describing his paper as "eminently just and wholly generous," Bill Morton likewise encouraged Heintzman to accept Brown's invitation, although he warned him that it will be "used by critics of Creighton in ways you would not approve." Still, Heintzman equivocated. He didn't want to come across as "an ambitious little beast," but he didn't want to remain silent either. "At such a critical moment in our national life, can Professor Creighton be allowed to speak out, repeatedly and vigorously as he has done, without a word of criticism from his own profession?" he asked. "Would silence represent yet another chapter in the *trahison des clercs?*"[70]

After the publication of "The Spirit of Confederation: Professor Creighton, Biculturalism, and the Use of History," Creighton had hoped that one of his colleagues or one of his students would write a response.[71] Eugene Forsey intimated that he would dearly love to take a "whack" at "Master Heintzman," but he never found the time, something he later regretted: "I am afraid that you and I, more and more, find ourselves 'among new men, strange faces, other minds.'"[72] Meanwhile, when no response appeared, Creighton felt betrayed, eventually convincing himself that the *CHR* had suppressed a response. It was an example of distorted, almost paranoid, thinking. Although he had told Heintzman that his paper "was an interesting and well-written piece of work," he now called it "a disingenuous piece of special pleading." Worse, the profession seemed to accept that no response was possible and that Heinztman's article was the "true bill." The profession had turned its collective back on a relic from the past. "This thought was hard to bear."[73] At the University of Saskatchewan to give a series of public lectures in February 1973, he gently rebuked Jim Miller. Deliberately slowing his delivery for effect, he said, "And not one of my students [long comma] Jim Miller [long comma] came to my defence."[74] Craig Brown assured him that the *CHR* hadn't suppressed anything because it hadn't received anything to suppress. What it had received, he said, was not acceptable for publication in its current form.[75]

Brown was referring to a paper by his doctoral student David Hall. Reading Heintzman's article, Hall noticed several factual errors and was surprised by the *CHR*'s willingness to publish such a "sloppy" piece of work.[76] When one of his senior colleagues at the University of Alberta took perverse pleasure in seeing Creighton reduced to size in the pages of the country's most important journal of history – as Morton had predicted would happen – he decided to write a response.[77] But when it was sent back with a number of suggestions for revision, Hall put it aside in order to finish his thesis. It wasn't until September 1973, some eighteen months later, that he was able to resubmit it. For its part, the *CHR* duly sent the revised version to an external reader. Maurice Careless largely agreed with its argument, "no doubt because my view of Confederation has always been that it was an 'act' by and for the majority limited by a necessary 'pact' with the minority to enable it to maintain its own defences." Designed to overcome a political crisis and confined to specific language guarantees and a division of powers in Sections 91 and 92, that pact – such as it was – did not form the basis of Confederation. "In this sense, much Fr. Can. contention about a compact, pact, or whatever, is wishful thinking, as is Heintzman's 'spirit.'" But surely Creighton's hard line had invited Heintzman's response, he added. "My real quarrel with DGC – the start of this debate – is that he tries to bind the future by his analysis of what 1867 was all about. Has anyone noticed that this Red Tory oracle of both the Wafflers and the Diefendoofers is really a Whig historian? Who else so sees the past as leading to his present – even if it is a tale of disaster, not freedom, slowly broadening down." It was a perceptive comment: Creighton's dark reading of Canadian history was an inversion of Whig history, and his winner-take-all approach to the Quebec question was a variation on original intent – a literal, parsimonious, approach to American law and politics designed to limit progressive public policy by appeals to the intention of the founding fathers. Still, Careless hadn't answered the question: should the paper be published? "I don't basically quarrel with this author's views – only with the fact that he thinks it necessary to prove the obvious at such length – and to go in for overkill." But, on balance, yes, "publish and be damned!"[78]

Despite Careless's final recommendation, the *CHR*'s co-editors – Michael Cross and Robert Bothwell – rejected Hall's paper on the grounds that "it used an atom bomb on a gnat."[79] Perhaps it did. But maybe Creighton's thinking wasn't that distorted after all.

Eventually, "The Spirit of Confederation: Ralph Heintzman, Professor Creighton, and the Bicultural Compact Theory" appeared in the *Journal of Canadian Studies*, the same journal that Creighton had called "bogus" in 1966 because of its early commitment to bilingualism.[80] Incredibly, its associate editor was a magnanimous Ralph Heintzman. Although Hall refuted Heintzman's history, he too made the case for greater generosity in the present, something Creighton could neither summon nor stomach. As the Last English Canadian, he intended to hold the line.

VI

In February 1973, Donald and Luella received a "wonderful" piece of news from Vancouver: Cynthia was pregnant.[81] Although naturally excited, they weren't the kind of grandparents who cultivated special relationships with their grandchildren or even spent much time with them. Reserved and cool, they were the opposite of "warm" and "cuddly."[82] When Philip's four children were still young, Donald and Luella moved to Brooklin in part because distance was easier for them. Family get-togethers tended to be formal and obligatory: Christmas, Easter, and the occasional Sunday dinner. At Muskoka, Donald and Luella used one cottage while Philip and his family used the other cottage. If Donald was swimming, Philip and his children avoided the lake because interactions could turn into altercations at the drop of a hat. On one occasion, Donald became "enraged" with Angus for doing what teenage boys do: yelling, shouting, carrying on, and otherwise having fun. Even Donald conceded that it was an "unpleasant scene."[83] Looking back, Philip acknowledges that his father was a "difficult" man and that, by necessity, he tried to limit the number of days that he overlapped with him at Muskoka.[84]

Isabel Mary Flood was born on 27 September 1973. Isabel Wilson was, of course, "touched" to have a great niece named after her.[85] Luella was always a bit jealous of Cynthia's relationship with Isabel, of her admiration and genuine affection for her aunt. "Cynthia loves me," she once told Isabel, "but she admires you." And it "hurt" when her daughter told her that she didn't want her in Vancouver for the birth.[86] As a vulnerable new mother, Cynthia knew enough to know that she couldn't handle her mother's unforgiving judgment. Had Luella been a different person, had her love been unconditional, had she not rationed it, Cynthia would have welcomed her. But she was never going to be that person. Exactly one year earlier, Luella had gone to Vancouver, and although the visit passed without incident Cynthia felt her disapproval. It was obvious to everyone that Luella's "feelings" for her daughter had "settled into a hardened gloom."[87]

Despite his own disapproval and his barely concealed contempt for his son-in-law, Creighton quickly booked an airline ticket. That he didn't have business in Vancouver or a lecture to deliver at UBC didn't matter. He needed to see his daughter. Actually, his visit went well: he was instantly smitten with little Isabel, her "dark blue eyes" capturing his heart. Later, he would tell Luella that she was the "most beautiful baby" he had ever seen, rivalled only by Cynthia as a baby.[88] To be useful, he bought a couple of things for their Nicola Street apartment, including a rather expensive carpet. But there was one uncomfortable moment. As he was leaving, he quietly asked Cynthia how she was feeling "down there," an awkward reference to vaginal tearing. "Because I didn't know and, after Philip was born, I hurt your mother." It was an incredible confession: he had been carrying that regret for forty-four years, and now finally he had an opportunity to unburden himself. Unable to pursue that kind of intimacy with her father, Cynthia deflected the question. "My defences were just too high. I couldn't go there. Not with him. Not after everything. The fights. The arguments. The anger."[89]

Creighton's question may have been misdirected, but it was an honest attempt to protect his daughter, not the radical feminist, but the little girl at Chartres.

VII

Creighton's retirement from the university didn't mean his retirement from writing, and in November 1974 he published his eleventh book, *Canada: The Heroic Beginnings*.[90] Although a handsome coffee table book, Creighton could hardly bear to look at the thing. From the outset, it had been a test of his patience, and he had never been very patient. Three years earlier, he had received an invitation from George Robertson, a producer at CBC Television, to narrate a feature-length documentary on what he called Canada's "heroic beginnings." Modelled on the BBC series *Civilisation*, Creighton would act as a tour guide to a handful of representative historical sites and monuments across the country. His journey across time and space would be the viewer's journey. Precise locations had yet to be determined, Robertson explained, "but the aim of the program is, of course, the same: a look at some of Canada's heroic beginnings through the eyes of one of its most distinguished historians." Creighton had never been particularly comfortable on camera, but he had rather enjoyed the experience of being in Ramsay Cook's film on the writing of Canadian history. Besides, Robertson's invitation carried a $5,700 honorarium and represented a chance to travel across the country, from L'Anse aux Meadows to Dawson City. Moreover, he liked being cast as the national historian lecturing to a national audience. It appealed to his sense of who he was and what his role was: a prophet who carried a people's past and who saw its future. In the film's opening sentences, he reminded his audience that Canada's beginnings didn't come easily, that they often involved "difficulty or danger." In the film's final sentences, he repeated his warnings about the dangers of continentalism and the rapid depletion of "our" natural resources, particularly energy resources. "We have a last chance to safeguard our future," he counselled. "We can survive only by a new departure which must be as resolute as any of the heroic beginnings in our past."[91]

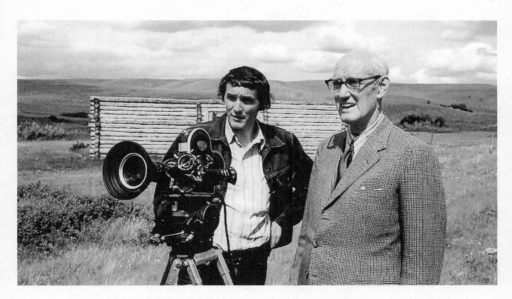

In 1972 Donald Creighton travelled the length and breadth of the country with the film-maker George Robertson. He had a lot of fun that summer, not least because he liked being cast as the national historian telling the nation's story. Broadcast in February 1973, *Canada's Heroic Beginnings* received very favourable ratings.

A few months later, he was "exhilarated" to learn that between one and a half and two million Canadians watched the February 1973 broadcast of *Heroic Beginnings* and that it received a much higher "appreciation rating" than had been anticipated. His need for attention and ego gratification was endless. But now came the hard part: converting the script into a book-length manuscript. Although he had research assistance from Parks Canada, he was left largely to his own devices. By the end, he was glad to be done with it. But when he received the proofs, he couldn't believe what had happened: someone at Macmillan, a junior copy editor, had "monkeyed" with his text. He was by turns annoyed, furious, and depressed. Because of "Macmillan's bungling," he had to read the proofs word by word against his original typescript. Returning the proofs to Macmillan – with strict instructions not to touch a single word – he was handed a final insult: a "perfectly dreadful," "commonplace," and "badly written" preface from the minister of Indian and northern affairs which he wanted "killed."[92] Of course, that wasn't possible: Parks Canada had co-sponsored the book and the minister expected visibility.

In at least one way *Heroic Beginnings* is an interesting book: it starts from the premise that Canadian history is multiple, not singular, that there is no "single beginning" but a "number" of beginnings. There are Aboriginal and European beginnings; military, economic, and political beginnings; and Atlantic, Pacific, and Arctic beginnings. But Creighton quickly abandoned the book's premise and, for that matter, its promise, when he framed Canada's multiplicity in the tired, and frankly uninteresting, frame of heroism, that spirit of "initiative, perseverance, endurance, and courage." As a result, the book is a pedestrian account of exploration, possession, settlement, and development by courageous, forward-thinking men like Jacques Cartier, James Cook, David Thompson, Sir George Simpson, and Sir Isaac Brock, whose "fighting spirit" and "rapid decisive action" won "the campaign of 1812 and saved Upper Canada." Aboriginal people in the form of Big Bear, Poundmaker, and even Louis Riel are presented in a sympathetic light but they are also cast as "restless," "resentful," and "sullen."[93]

Heroic Beginnings received largely generous reviews: the *Winnipeg Free Press* expressed its gratitude to Creighton for reminding readers that Canada does indeed have heroes; the *Saskatoon Star-Phoenix* welcomed its "unique" approach to the breadth of Canadian history; the *BC Library Quarterly* recommended it to anyone who intends to visit "Acadia, Queenston Heights, or Head Smashed In Buffalo Jump"; and the *Canadian Geographical Journal* celebrated its "shining prose." But writing in the *Ottawa Journal,* Dillon O'Leary expressed both his surprise and his regret that Canada's leading historian had been reduced to writing a guidebook for tourists. Lacking its author's distinctive and at times "truculent" voice, it doesn't belong, he said, in the same league as the "epic" *Commercial Empire of the St. Lawrence*, the "monumental" *Macdonald*, or the "polemical" *Canada's First Century*. It also exposes his "unfamiliarity" with the Cree and the Métis. So put "this book aside," O'Leary advised, "and take up the tomes of the Creighton" we once knew, "the crusty doyen of our historians": at least he was "interesting."[94]

Heroic Beginnings is problematic for another reason: only one woman is mentioned, "a pretty and vivacious" mother whose ambition was directed at her son, Mackenzie King, who she believed was "destined by providence to restore her family's name."[95] The daggers were drawn and the subtext was clear: Canada's longest-serving prime minister was a mama's boy.

That Creighton's heroic beginnings were masculine wouldn't have surprised Barbara Roberts, a young historian trained in the field of women's history who charged the "crusty doyen" of Canadian history with projecting his own gendered assumptions about women's roles onto John A. Macdonald's two wives, Isabella Clark and Agnes Bernard. Although some of her criticisms fell wide of their mark, Roberts's basic point was fair: uncritically accepting the male public sphere and the female private sphere, Creighton didn't see the past through the eyes of either Clark or Bernard.[96] But Roberts's essay is more interesting for what it says about Canadian historical writing in the 1970s than for what it says about Creighton's biography of Macdonald. After just five or six years, Maurice Careless's brilliant essay, "Limited Identities in Canada," needed to be updated: Canadian history was not only the history of region, class, and ethnicity; it was also the history of gender.

Creighton's decision to participate in the making and the writing of *Heroic Beginnings* reflected his sense of himself as the author and the keeper of Canada's national story. But Roberts's essay was one more indication that he wasn't. No one was. And no one is. National histories are never singular, always plural, and constantly being rewritten because changing who tells the story changes the story, a truth Creighton never grasped. His assumption that Canada was a plot and that he was its chief author was like a piece of granite: hard and unbending.

But even granite breaks.

VIII

In January 1976 Creighton delivered the Dunning Trust Lecture at Queen's University. He was "very pleased" to have been invited because it confirmed one more time his stature as an important public intellectual, especially since past lecturers included Herbert Butterfield, John Kenneth Galbraith, and Northrop Frye. In keeping with the lecture's theme of freedom and responsibility, Creighton delivered a wide-ranging talk on the individual and the welfare state.

Two things characterized the post-1945 period, he said: steady economic growth and the equally steady expansion of the welfare state. But at what cost? he asked. Largely freed from material concerns and now dependent on any number of social welfare programs, the suddenly untethered individual was free to indulge his or her passions, including sexual passions. "The varieties of human indulgence and human depravity," he said, "grow without ceasing." Although he didn't quote George Grant, he effectively echoed his dark assessment of "our absolute freedom": "Nobody minds very much if we prefer women or dogs or boys, as long as we cause no public inconvenience," Grant wrote in *Lament for a Nation*.[97] Adhering to the moral standards of his Methodist childhood, Creighton believed that Canada's "old-fashioned pre-war morality" – that is, individual responsibility, perseverance, religious observance, hard work, delayed gratification, and personal restraint – had been replaced by young couples living freely together, high divorce rates, drug and alcohol abuse, juvenile delinquency, and violent crime. No one needs to work. No one needs to save. The state will take care of us. As an example of an over-generous welfare initiative, he cited the Trudeau government's controversial decision to extend unemployment insurance benefits to seasonal workers and to ask everyone else to pay for it. Against this backdrop, he reminded his audience that economic growth and its concomitant, a welfare state, were dependent on a material base, on natural resources, especially energy resources. But Canada's resources were finite, not infinite, and the country must learn the discipline of conservation if it is going to survive.[98]

Creighton was pleased with his performance. The evening, he said, seemed "to go very well." He was playing the part not only of the public intellectual, but also of the public moralist, something he had been doing for the past six or seven years, really since his 1969 address to the Canadian Historical Association. In a series of convocation addresses at different universities across the country and in a handful of articles published in *Maclean's* magazine, he told Canadians to repent now before it is too late.

"Every generation is the mental prisoner of the age in which it lives," he said, quoting Oswald Spengler, and this generation is the mental prisoner of the logic of economic growth predicated on consumption.[99] Painting "a very grim future," he castigated Canadians for filling their houses and garages "with assorted unused junk, which they had never needed, or had discarded and forgotten, or which was now useless because its manufacturer, despite his lifetime guarantee, had thoughtfully ensured its rapid obsolescence." If a purchase remained unconsumed or neglected, it was of no consequence; it had been bought, and that fulfilled the one real purpose of its creation. Meanwhile, "credit cards, charge accounts, bank loans, and instalment purchases all helped Canadians to keep on buying more than they could afford." The citizen, he said, has been remade into a consumer. It didn't matter if that citizen had "religious beliefs, or political convictions, or intellectual interests, or artistic talents" as long as he continued to consume.[100] Again, he sounded like George Grant, who argued that when "the purpose of life is consumption," "most human beings" will be "defined in terms of their capacity to consume."[101] Overconsumption was not only personal, it was national, Creighton said, pointing a finger at the country for its complacent willingness to "squander" its natural resources "for a quick buck" and its proposed development of the Athabasca tar sands.[102] Indeed, he worried about the looming environmental catastrophe across impossibly large swathes of Canada's north. Imploring Canadians "to alter the tenor of their ways," he applauded those men and women who had "entered the ranks of the conservationists and environmentalists," who had "joined the fight against the contamination of air and water," and who had protested "against the continual American takeover" of Canada's energy resources. What is needed, he said, is "a new conception of the purpose of life," one that accepts limits to growth and consumption.[103] But first, Canadians need to escape the clutches of the American empire and its insane, religious "belief that progress is the only good in life and that progress means the liberation of man through the progressive conquest of nature." He wasn't hopeful: "The American Empire is taking over the birthright of Canadians; and its imperial religion has taken over their minds."[104]

That he had claimed a prophetic voice was not lost on his contemporaries. Gerald Graham noted his "righteous indignation" and "evangelical fervour"; John K. Elliott likened him to Jonah, the Hebrew prophet called by God to preach to the ancient city of Nineveh; Phillip Buckner compared him to Cassandra; Viv Nelles called him the "voice of doom"; and Ramsay Cook rejected his self-inflicted "need to be so despairing" so much of the time. "There is much sadness," he said, "in the sight of a great historian" having fallen "into such depths of despair."[105]

But historians often become prophets, especially historians who have achieved a profile outside the academy and who have become associated with the national story. Frederick Jackson Turner and Charles Beard were, in their own ways, Jeremiahs profoundly depressed by the course of American history; Manning Clark wrote Australia's future as much as he did its past; Pierre Nora's work on sites of memory mourns a lost France; and predicting a future dominated by environmental and economic crises, Eric Hobsbawm darkly warned that "time is not on our side."[106]

Yet Creighton's dire warnings and dark predictions failed to resonate. Phillip Buckner astutely observed that, as a writer, Creighton's genius was always narrative history, that he was ill-suited to the confined space of the essay where "his interpretations" were "too sweeping" and his "judgements on men and events too one-sided."[107] If his anger and, frankly, his meanness, undid his larger arguments, if they turned readers off, so too did his anti-Americanism. Ramsay Cook rightly argued that he oversimplified "the issue of technology and the religion of progress," attributing it wrongly to the United States. "Surely the idea of progress and the conception of technological mastery came to Canada not on the wings of the United States Air Force or even with the multinational corporation. They came to Canada, and the United States, from Europe where they were born";[108] they came with the Montreal merchants who envisioned, and for many years realized, the commercial empire of the St Lawrence; they came with Lord Durham, whose Report was an extended plea for improvement; and they came with his great-grandfather, John Creighton, who, in Durham's words, turned the forest from a "state of waste" into a productive farm linked to a market economy.[109] Although Creighton admired both *Lament for a Nation* and *Technology and Empire,* his anti-Americanism unfortunately blinded him to George Grant's basic point: "North Americans have no history before the age of progress."[110]

Creighton's prophetic voice came naturally to him from his father, William Black Creighton.[111] But where his father saw a brighter future, he saw a darker future. Perhaps, then, it is not a surprise that beginning in the late 1960s and through the 1970s, his interest in Richard Wagner became an obsession. He loved to sit on the chesterfield, fill the living room with Wagner's music, and for the remainder of the afternoon allow himself to be transported to another dimension where the great forces of the universe are at war one with the other. He once described listening to the Met's *Götterdämmerung* – the Ring's final opera – as a "nearly prostrating experience."[112] In a way that no other artist could, Wagner allowed him to escape – intellectually, emotionally, and, to an extent, physically – from the petty debates and picayune concerns of the present. In the Ring, Canada didn't matter.

Perhaps, too, it is not a surprise that he rediscovered his Christian faith. Although Luella never returned to church – her fanatical stepmother forever alienated her from organized religion – Creighton joined St Thomas' Anglican Church in Brooklin. No doubt he was attracted to the perceived status of the Anglican Church – until 1955, the Church of England in the Dominion of Canada – but it was more fundamental than that. The beauty of the Anglican liturgy and of the Anglican vestments satisfied his need for ceremony and ritual while the promise of the Anglican litany – especially the words, "as it was in the beginning, is now and ever shall be, world without end" – eased his terrible conviction that Canada had ceased to be anything other than a name on a map. When time is everlasting, when it is understood in terms of eternity, the here and now are pinpricks on a vast and unknowable continuum.

As Creighton's faith matured and deepened, he asked to be confirmed as an adult. A few years earlier he had been denied communion by a visiting minister to St Thomas' because he hadn't been confirmed. The incident bothered him, and for several months he stopped going to church. But in 1974 he reached a new point in his relationship with God, and so, on a grey November day, he went to the Synod Office Chapel on Adelaide Street in Toronto, where Bishop Garnsworthy – "a tall, handsome man" with "a pleasant, warm manner" and "a good voice" – conducted the Service of Confirmation. Today, the Anglican Church of Canada would never turn someone away from the Lord's table, but it did then and Creighton decided that the Sacrament mattered more than whatever reservations he had about adult confirmation. Afterwards, Bishop

Garnsworthy told him that it had been his "personal pleasure" to conduct the service, adding that it is "a very meaningful moment" in one's faith, especially "when one has made his own decision" and not had that decision made for him.[113]

Yet Creighton was rarely at peace with either himself or his country. And, as its chief author, he still needed to write its history.

IX

In February 1976, a few weeks after the Dunning Trust Lecture, Donald and Luella were at home when the phone rang: Cynthia was pregnant again and due in October. It was all very "dramatic," Donald said. Luella, however, "announced that she is certainly going to Vancouver for this birth."[114]

But that winter Creighton's stomach had begun to bother him. After a merciful reprieve of several years, the familiar symptoms returned: bloating, cramping, sharp intestinal pain, and diarrhea. Then, his skin broke out in an ugly rash around his waist, chest, and upper back. Describing the pain as "intolerable," he took pills, used ointments, and sought ultraviolet radiation. In March he began to experience, for the first time, dizziness when he stood up. On Good Friday, he went to church. The service, he said, was very "simple," and the minister retold the story of Christ's crucifixion "very effectively."[115] Afterwards, Creighton spoke to him about a burial plot in the Anglican cemetery. Did he sense that something was wrong with him? His blood work and physical examinations had been normal. Still, his doctor ordered more tests. Luella thought that he was working too hard, that the stress of trying to finish his volume for the Centenary Series was the cause of his many complaints.

Despite his poor health, Creighton desperately wanted to finish what he called his "unending labour."[116] As far as he was concerned, the series had been one damn thing after another, and now he was under pressure to finish his own manuscript. When it was first conceived in 1955 and formally announced two years later, the multi-volume history of Canada was one of Jack McClelland's many publishing projects commemorating Canada's centennial. But as an academic project involving several authors, it took much longer. "I cannot forget the fact that the series got under way exactly twenty years ago," Creighton remarked. "There have been repeated changes of authorship. There have been delays, procrastinations, evasions, and downright lies. Authors have broken their word and violated their contracts." Why, two French-Canadian authors "have signed contracts with French-Canadian publishers after signing our contract": "To my mind," he said, the story of the series "is a very sorry story indeed." When, for example, Marcel Trudel announced that he needed two volumes on New France to 1663, Creighton rolled his eyes. Not only would it upset the series' delicate balance, it would be "a laborious record of the particular and inconsequential, with lots of room for dubious guesswork and inferences and appalling amounts of genealogy." Trudel's announcement, he said, was "an awful example of French-Canadian local piety gone mad!"[117] In the end, Morton held Trudel to one volume, but the three-way exchange between Trudel, Morton, and Creighton highlighted the profession's competing conceptions of national history, Creighton's ignorance of French-Canadian historiography, and the reason why John Herd Thompson once joked that the Centenary Series risked becoming the Bicentenary Series.[118]

Initially, Creighton was supposed to conclude the series with a general history of Canada between 1939 and 1967. But he quickly realized that the twenty-eight-year stretch between the start of the Second World War and Canada's centennial celebrations was "too crowded" and that he would need a second volume, an irony he never appreciated: two volumes on contemporary Canada was acceptable, but two volumes on early New France would upset the series' balance. Jack McClelland was only too happy to accommodate the country's leading historian, and when he received the final manuscript in mid-July he was thrilled. Throughout the process, he played the same role John Gray had played, stroking the ego and feeding the vanity of a vulnerable artist. After reading the first two chapters some fifteen months earlier, he described their felicitous prose as "vintage Creighton." As more chapters came in, he grew more enthusiastic. The writing "absorbed" him from beginning to end, especially the sections on Mackenzie King, that "cunning political strategist" described by Creighton as a leader prone to "verbal flatulence": it "is really great stuff," McClelland said, adding that he could "see no problems of libel."[119] Of course, he was reading the manuscript as a publisher with an eye to sales, at one point instructing his staff to generate advance "controversy."[120]

As late as April 1976, Creighton still hadn't settled on a title. Possibilities included "Decline of the Commonwealth," "Sell Out," or "The Forked Road to the Future." Each title captured an aspect of the book: the Liberal Party's indifference to the imperial connection; its willingness to sell Canada out; and its decision to take that fork in the road leading to a country that, to Creighton, was unrecognizable.

The Forked Road: Canada, 1939–1957 was an awful book and, not coincidentally, Creighton's only major book that didn't draw on the Laurentian thesis. Instead, it drew on a reservoir of anger and disappointment, making it little more than a barely researched series of bitter laments for a nation that might have been and easy shots at the "unidentified," "nondescript" and "almost anonymous" nation that was. Unable to see beyond his own prejudices, Creighton lashed out at the bloody Libs, the damn Yanks, the feckless Brits, new immigrants, pushy women, young people, cigarettes, alcohol, marijuana, and the substitution of an old-fashioned work ethic for a newfangled "pleasure principle." His wrath and his range of disapproval were breathtaking. Everything was a target: the Commonwealth was in "dissolution"; the Liberals were "rampant"; and planners by the thousands had gone to Ottawa to transform the federal government into "a kind twentieth-century benevolent despot." He even managed to indulge his disappointment at not being able to write French history when he wrote that in the interwar years there were no granting agencies and that "Canadian scholars were quite literally on their own financially." Meanwhile, American bases in Newfoundland "were sovereign political enclaves, very much like the duodecimo principalities of the Holy Roman Empire"; US Secretary of State Dean Acheson "had a hawk-like nose, beetling eyebrows, an aggressive chin, and a small, close-clipped moustache"; and General MacArthur was "a preposterous mixture of Genghis Khan and Louis XIV." Mackenzie King's principal secretary, Jack Pickersgill, had been a "fairly slim" United College lecturer when he went to Ottawa, but "a long succession of good dinners at public expense had notably increased his girth"; Brooke Claxton, a powerful Liberal cabinet minister, was "a tall, shambling, rather maladroit Montrealer"; and Louis St Laurent's "strained, chalk-white countenance" and his "harsh, nasal accent" gave him all the charm of a "company chairman." Worse, he and Maurice Duplessis – the "short, spare" premier of Quebec who had gained and kept power through "blatant electoral fraud" – only dimly understood the complexities of fiscal federalism, acting more like a couple of "old clowns chasing each other around a circus ring" than statesmen negotiating a tax-rental agreement.[121]

What Frank Underhill once said about *Macdonald* could have been said about *The Forked Road:* "as a work of history," it would have been "more impressive" had its author not cast his enemies as "deficient," "delinquent," and "physically repulsive." But even if Creighton had restrained his Dickensian impulses, it wouldn't have mattered because *The Forked Road* was what Marg Conrad said it was – "a bigoted and often unreliable account of Canada's recent history" that ignored region, labour, the Japanese internment, and Aboriginal people among other things. Michael Cross described it as a good example of the Wasp school of history, meaning it was "flawed in almost every conceivable way"; writing in the *Canadian Historical Review*, Reg Whitaker called it a "major disappointment"; Jack Granatstein dismissed it as a "depressing" collection of "memories, reflections, and might have beens"; and Fred Soward was frankly stunned by its "disturbing" lack of research, privately telling one colleague that it was littered with "misjudgements" and "dubious interpretations." Even Denis Smith, who was sympathetic to Creighton's larger interpretation of Canadian history, acknowledged the book's "unsatisfactory" and "inadequate" research. A handful of newspapers reviewed it favourably, but most were just as critical. "When McClelland and Stewart hired their flunky to write the dust jacket," wrote one reviewer, "they must have blackmailed the poor fellow" because nothing else could have led him "to spout such drivel." A work of "discerning insight"? A work of "major historical significance"? Writing in the *Globe and Mail,* Paul Fox accused Creighton of being "out of joint with the times" and of longing for "an age that is past." Several people noted that the book's metaphor didn't work, that Creighton never demonstrated that there was ever a fork in the road. And if there was a fork in the road, Davidson Dunton said, most Canadians preferred the maple leaf to the Red Ensign. Besides, and as Creighton himself conceded, Winston Churchill never appreciated the Commonwealth, leading Michael Cross to quip that only English-Canadian tories were able to divine its "mystical" purpose.[122]

"Badly disappointed" by his book's reception, Creighton hit back. The reviewers were "incompetent," he said. Paul Fox, in particular, had a mind "made up of alternating slabs of concrete and cast iron."[123] That wasn't true, of course. Fox was a brilliant scholar and an energetic administrator. But Creighton needed to shoot the messenger because he couldn't bring himself to read the message. Ramsay Cook was right: "the sight of a great historian" mired in "the depths of despair" wasn't pretty.

X

After sending the final manuscript to McClelland and Stewart in July, Creighton took a well-deserved break. He had pushed himself too hard, and in August he and Luella made plans to go to Stratford. He had always liked the Stratford Festival because it could hold its own against "international standards" and because it showed that Canadians weren't only a bunch of Babbitts.[124] Leaving Brooklin on the morning of 24 August, they stopped for a little picnic in Acton, a small town in Halton founded by two itinerant Methodist ministers and their families in the 1820s. Suddenly, Creighton started to feel unwell. Something was dreadfully wrong. His underwear filled with blood. He and Luella returned home as quickly as possible and, four days later, he was admitted to Toronto's Wellesley Hospital on the corner of Wellesley and Sherbourne for another battery of tests.

While in the hospital, he read, of all things, *The Mediterranean* by Fernand Braudel, a book that casts Europe's Mediterranean basin as a protagonist in a narrative combining geological and human time. Wars, politics, and national boundaries are, Braudel famously insisted, "surface disturbances," mere "crests of foam" on "the tides of history."[125] Maybe it comforted Creighton to know that, like the mountains, plateaus, plains, and peninsulas of the Mediterranean, the St Lawrence River and Great Lakes basin would always be there. At the bottom of Sherbourne Street was the Toronto harbour and, beyond it, Lake Ontario. It takes about two hundred years for a drop of water to travel from Lake Superior to the Atlantic Ocean. When the water that was now flowing past Toronto to its appointed destination in the Gulf of the St Lawrence first began its journey, the Montreal merchants were just beginning to gather the "shining" if "ever-receding possibilities" before them: they were the new northerners and the empire of the St Lawrence was theirs. But their dream of a vast commercial empire was eventually lost, and, as far as Creighton was concerned, the dream of a separate Canadian nation built on that same river had been lost as well. Since the publication of his first book in 1937, he had been its chief author and now both he and it were nearing their inevitable conclusions. His test results could be good or they could be bad. Either way, that "one great river" – "which would outlast all the ships that sailed upon it" – still "rolled massively" into the sea, "as it was in the beginning, is now and ever shall be, world without end."[126]

On the evening of 30 August, Creighton received the grim diagnosis: a malignant tumour had been discovered in his colon. That September, he was admitted to the Oshawa General Hospital, where he underwent two operations. A day or so after his second operation, a horrified Luella confessed that she had never seen a human being "look so wretched": wires and tubes ran in and out of his emaciated and parched body.[127] Heavily sedated, he didn't know where he was and, at one point, started to hallucinate: this time it wasn't his publisher orchestrating an elaborate conspiracy against him, it was his doctor. Fearing that he had been kidnapped and taken to Montreal, Creighton didn't know where to turn. All told, he was in the hospital for five weeks. His convalescence was slow and fitful, and early in the new year he had to be readmitted for yet another procedure, this one to remove his prostate. When, he wondered, would this ordeal ever end?

The only good news that fall and early winter was the announcement that Cynthia's baby had arrived safe and sound on 12 October. Obviously, neither he nor Luella could go to Vancouver. But he liked looking at pictures of Margaret Theresa. Cynthia, he said, "looks very young and happy" while Margaret appears "majestic," with adorable "bulging cheeks" and "a most complacent, self-satisfied expression."[128] Luella wanted to have the picture framed, but neither one of them could bear to part with it.

Finally, in late January, he felt well enough to start writing. In addition to a couple of short articles for the *Globe and Mail*, he began a novel. He also began to follow Canadian politics again. A lot had happened, including the election of René Lévesque in November. For the first time, Canada confronted the real possibility of Quebec's independence. Good riddance, Creighton thought, as he readied himself to speak out. This time he wouldn't pull his punches.

chapter thirteen

Endings

Then, when once more the sun had gone down behind the long blue line of the Laurentians, the last change came. Up to then his breathing had been shallow and rapid. Now it grew slower, slower still, and, as the watchers clustered around him, died away in the last, faint, lingering prolongations. He was going now. He was borne on and outward, past care and planning, past England and Canada, past life and into death.

John A. Macdonald, vol. 2

Donald Creighton was good copy. Journalists could count on him to say something contentious; editors knew that he would never miss a deadline; and readers found themselves either nodding in agreement, shaking their head in disbelief, or pounding their fists on the kitchen table. So when the editor of *Maclean's* magazine commissioned an article from him in March 1977 on what René Lévesque's victory portended, he knew what to expect. Peter Newman had always admired Creighton's "Captain Ahab intensity" because, "unlike most of his milquetoast colleagues," Canada's "best historian" actually had an opinion and knew how to express it.[1]

But Canada's best historian was still very weak. Even simple things – like doctors' appointments, errands, and church – required considerable effort. Luella, though, was fully in charge. She managed his health and kept the house up and running. Creighton talked on and off about writing a general history of Canada from 1957 to 1967 to conclude the Centenary Series, but he also knew that it would never happen and that he had written his last history book. Time was not on his side. If he was going to meet Newman's deadline, he would need to conserve his energy and focus his convictions. Yet what could he say that he hadn't already said?

Three or four days later, Creighton received a frantic telephone call from an "almost beside himself" Hugh MacLennan: the Parti Québécois had just released its controversial white paper on the French language. Invoking the Conquest, Lord Durham's dream of assimilation, and the ghost of Louis Riel, it declared that French will be Quebec's official language and that there "will no longer be any question of a bilingual Quebec."[2] The writer who had hoped that Canada's two solitudes would "protect, and touch, and greet each other," and who had admired the Quiet Revolution, now saw the thin edge of "fascism" in Quebec City.[3] That night Creighton went to bed early. He was, he said, "very tired" and "deeply depressed." "The sun had gone down behind the long blue line of the Laurentians" and he was a man without a country. He woke up the next morning, though, feeling curiously refreshed and with a renewed determination to write the article with what he called a "new emphasis." Lévesque's November victory had been bad enough, but his proposed language bill was "a provocation" that needed a clear "reply."[4] Creighton called it a "manifesto of independence"; the *Globe and Mail* described it as a "monstrous gamble"; and Eugene Forsey was "appalled," adding that English-speaking Quebeckers "face a pretty dim prospect."[5] After sending the final version to *Maclean's*, Creighton confessed that he didn't "repent a single word of it" and rather hoped that it would cause "something of a furore."[6] A thrilled Peter Newman featured a granite-looking Donald Creighton on the front cover with the headline, "Canada's Pre-Eminent Historian Speaks Out: NO MORE DEALS FOR QUEBEC."

Since the end of the Second World War, Creighton began, Quebec has practised "the politics of blackmail" and English Canada has responded with "the politics of appeasement." The new flag was one example; the failure to patriate the Constitution with an amending formula was another. But that twin-headed monstrosity, bilingualism and biculturalism, was "the ultimate turn of the screw"; and its offspring, the Official Languages Act, has wasted "vast amounts of money," "aroused" the "angry resentment" of English-speaking civil servants, created a new bureaucracy staffed by "a robust army of dedicated snoopers" bent on finding infractions, and led its commissioner to "think that his most important public duty lay in abusing and hectoring English Canadians for their neglect of a language only an infinitesimal minority would ever have occasion to use." There is no point, Creighton argued, in waiting for the results of Lévesque's promised referendum. If its proposed language charter – the one that led Hugh MacLennan to despair – becomes law, "Quebec will legally, as well as morally, have declared its independence." In this event, English Canadians who wish "to survive as a distinct people" should replace the policies of "appeasement" with "the policies of self-defence and self-preservation" and they, not "the separatists," should set the terms of Quebec's separation. What he

When Alain Masson was sent by *Maclean's* to photograph Donald Creighton at his home in Brooklin, Ontario, he was warned that Canada's "pre-eminent historian" didn't particularly like French people. However, Creighton could not have been more charming and the photo shoot went off without a hitch.

had said in private – that the time had come "to boot them out, on our terms, not theirs" – he now said in public.[7]

According to Creighton's terms, Quebec will leave Confederation "with exactly the same boundaries" that it had when it entered Confederation, meaning its "vast northern territory" will remain a part of Canada; the St Lawrence Seaway will require something like a Panama Canal "protective zone" extending one mile on either side since it is both a "vital" artery and a Canadian "obligation"; bilingualism at both the federal and provincial level will be terminated since it never had any purpose other than a "political" one; and, finally, Quebec can forget about an economic association with the rest of Canada. That kind of logic, the idea that Quebec could enjoy both "the political liberties of independence" and "the economic advantages of union," is "peculiarly offensive."

Eleven years earlier, he had agreed to cut the final sentence to his defiant article in *Saturday Night*. But not this time. Once a tariff barrier is erected along the new border, he said, and capital continues its relentless flight, "René Lévesque, his associates, and his deluded followers will be left to themselves in the stagnant economic backwater of independence."[8]

Creighton certainly got what he wanted because his article did raise a furore: Newman called it a "storm" and *Maclean's* was flooded with letters.[9] According to its count, 66 per cent of the letters agreed that "it was time to draw the line." Support was highest in western Canada and, "not surprisingly," lowest in Quebec. To his fans, Creighton was a tough, no-nonsense, straight shooter. One person intimated that he was our Churchill; "Hurray for Donald Creighton!" someone else shouted. "I wonder if he has ever considered running for Joe Clark's job." But to his detractors, he was a crank. He "spews and sputters the philosophy that built and then brought down the Empire: imperial self-righteousness"; his article was "a disgusting example of the harnessing of history to the cause of self-justification"; and, if he is our pre-eminent historian, "then Canadian historians must be a pretty wretched group."[10]

As well, Creighton received a handful of supportive letters from people who had tracked down his address. One woman remarked that it was a "disgrace" to see a "French-Canadian draft dodger tearing our country apart." Trudeau, she said, "is Canada's answer to Benedict Arnold." He should be "stuffed" and fed to "the seals," said a Newfoundlander. Your article was "magnificent," wrote a man from St Catharines, Ontario. "I have almost decided that I would like to see Quebec secede"; as it is, there are too many French labels on "packaged and bottled goods."[11] And an outfit calling itself the Preparatory Committee for an Eleventh Province whose aim was to create a new English-speaking province with its centre in Montreal also appealed to him.[12] Indeed, Creighton's public profile made him an unfortunate ally of the francophobic right. The author of

Bilingual Today, French Tomorrow: Trudeau's Master Plan and How it Can Be Stopped wanted him to sign an open letter calling for Joe Clark's resignation; a retired captain in the Canadian Air Force "pestered" him "with absurd solutions" to the Quebec question; and the Alliance for the Preservation of English in Canada invited him to address its Halifax convention. Even worse, he lent respectability to every anti-French nutjob with a pen and an axe to grind. The disgraced ex-mayor of Moncton – whose opposition to bilingualism led university students to deliver a severed pig's head to his front door – addressed a 1978 APEC meeting in Toronto. Proudly calling himself a "bigot," Leonard Jones proceeded to quote "the well-known Canadian historian, Donald Creighton," on the Official Languages Act.[13]

Creighton's article met with an equally mixed response from English-Canadian journalists, politicians, and intellectuals: calling for "reason, not rage," the *Globe and Mail* compared him to Lionel Groulx, the French-Canadian historian whose dream of nation made him the spiritual father of modern Quebec; the *Winnipeg Free Press* condemned him as a "negative historian of despair" for, ironically, betraying Sir John A. Macdonald's vision; the *Regina Leader-Post* lamented his "waspish style" and "prejudiced outpourings"; but the *Hamilton Spectator* congratulated him for calling René Lévesque's "bluff." Meanwhile, the federal cabinet minister John Roberts said that he was "ashamed" of Creighton's latest contribution to the national debate, and Senator Maurice Lamontagne added that its various prescriptions would "very likely lead to civil war." Publicly, George Grant accused Creighton of declaring war "in the wildest, craziest way"; privately, he regretted his remarks but still felt that the article had been "unwise." In *Lament for a Nation*, Grant had described the French fact as the "keystone of a Canadian nation," adding that English Canada's survival was tied to French Canada's survival. However, one of the country's best legal scholars and a member of the Royal Commission on Bilingualism and Biculturalism maintained that Creighton's article had been "important." F.R. Scott also found it particularly rich that while the PQ freely talks about breaking up Canada, it greets any suggestion of breaking up Quebec with righteous indignation. Bill Morton "rejoiced" when he read Creighton's "splendid effort" and, in a long letter to the editor, protested the *Free Press*'s "hysterical" editorial. Finally, Eugene Forsey raised a handful of objections but, on balance, maintained that his old friend had stated "some hard truths that needed to be stated."[14]

Creighton reacted as he had always reacted, with a mixture of hurt and defiance: he didn't like the *Globe*'s "abuse" and found George Grant's "denunciation rather hard to bear," but he was cheered by the many letters of support he had received, especially from Frank Scott, whom he counted as one of the Liberal Party's court intellectuals. He was so cheered, in fact, that he pitched a "very short book" on the subject of Canada and Quebec to Jack McClelland, who wisely passed after one of his editors intimated that it would be "blasted as the wrong book for the times and probably even laughed at as the dying tirade of a tired old man."[15]

Ramsay Cook said pretty much the same thing. "Donald's article was simply pathetic," he told Eugene Forsey. It was so bad, he didn't know where to begin. For example, he said, the St Lawrence Seaway is also an American seaway, meaning the United States will protect its interests in an independent Quebec. "I just love the idea of Donald on the bridge welcoming American marines, his long time friends, as they arrive to share supervision of the canal." Surely, he wrote, the article was intended as "a bad joke." "Donald reminds me of the Montreal Tories between 1837 and 1849" because, like them, he jealously refuses to accommodate French Canada and its aspirations. In the same way that the Montreal Tories wanted to join the United States, threatening that "Lower Canada must be English, at the expense, if necessary, of not being British," Donald Creighton wanted to boot Quebec out, in effect saying that Canada must be British, at the expense, if necessary, of not being Canada. But where Lord Durham sympathized with the Tories' intention to "protect themselves" against "French dominion," Cook dismissed Creighton's intention to protect himself against bilingualism: "to him, all French Canadians look the same," he said.[16]

A few months later, Creighton gave an address to the Arts and Letters Club in Toronto. In recent years, the club had become an important part of his weekly routine. Almost every Tuesday, he met a handful of friends – including John Gray, Lovat Dickson, and Barker Fairley – for a long lunch of literary gossip and martinis. Now, though, he was terribly frail. Weakened by a lack of balance, he struggled to climb the small set of stairs. But for the better part of an hour, he delivered a history of Canadian federalism from the Royal Commission on Dominion-Provincial Relations to the constitutional challenge represented by Quebec's language law, Bill 101; he itemized Liberal sins; he enumerated national humiliations; and he repeated his terms of separation. Finally, even he had had enough. There is only "one thing" left to do, he said, and that is to "obliterate the fanatic Trudeau and his Montreal gang under such an avalanche of rocks that even their ghosts will cease to haunt us."[17]

On that note, his audience gave him a standing ovation, oblivious to the sadness of it all. Creighton wasn't only a man without a country, he was a historian without a thesis, or, at least, a thesis capable of explaining contemporary Canada. In *The Commercial Empire of the St. Lawrence*, the Montreal merchants understood the logic of Canadian history. Now, Canada's capitalist class thought in continental terms, and a very different group of Montreal citizens intended to remake Canada along bilingual lines. Backed into a corner, Creighton lashed out. Cook was right. It was pathetic. But it was also pathetic in the older and original sense of the word, in the sense that the dying tirades of old men arouse compassion and sympathy.

II

In late September 1977, *Saturday Night* published a feature article on "the man who invented Canada" by the journalist Heather Robertson. Of course, Robertson acknowledged Creighton's controversial essay in *Maclean's* and his "reputation as a cantankerous old curmudgeon," but she rather liked him as a person, finding him "fragile" and "shy," almost "diffident" and "boyish." Covering familiar ground – from his many books to his thirteen honorary degrees and back-to-back Governor General's Awards – she depicted "Canada's greatest historian" as a modern day biblical prophet warning his people about the coming day of judgment when all nations shall be gathered before the Son of Man "and he shall separate them one from another, as a shepherd divideth his sheep from the goats" (Matthew 25:32). The apple, Robertson implied, hadn't fallen very far from the family apple tree: his great-grandfather, Kennedy Creighton, had been an itinerant Methodist minister; his grandmother, Lizzie Harvie, had been a tireless servant, scouring "the streets of Toronto for fallen women"; and his father, William Black Creighton, had edited the *Christian Guardian.* "Honest, moral, and fearless," Donald Creighton, she said, was "a soldier of the Lord." The "rolling thunder" of his prose, "his brimstone vocabulary," and his "compulsive need to preach the truth" can be traced back to "his rigorous biblical education" and, before that, to "the hellfire preachers of the Ontario bush."[18]

Creighton appreciated the article, describing it as "sympathetic" and "fair." He was especially "pleased" by the picture of him standing in his study, in front of the fireplace and a Claude Monet print of Argenteuil, a small village not far from Paris on the Seine River.[19] But the article also saddened him because, two days before its publication, he received an unbearable telephone call from Vancouver: Jack had died. His brother would have liked the article and, as he had done on so many occasions in the past, would have written a generous letter commending him. Although he had been ill for several months, his death was still a shock and, for a few moments, Creighton was "overcome with regret and despair," wondering "what remaining purpose" he had in life. For the rest of the day, he didn't do much of anything. As a teenager and as a young man, he had looked up to his big brother as "a kind of hero." Jack told him what books to read and how far to swim to improve his endurance; he once advised him to have fun and to keep his "pecker up"; and he took an early and honest interest in his writing, even showing one of his very first articles on Canada and the Canadian identity to, curiously enough, the editor of *Saturday Night*.[20]

Creighton's generation was disappearing. Six years earlier, Harold Wilson – who had been his best friend at Vic and his brother-in-law for over thirty years – had died. Afterwards, he and his sister Isabel spent a long afternoon reading old family letters and looking at photographs of their grandparents and parents, of 32 Hewitt Avenue and Lake Muskoka, of Jack as a lieutenant in the 48th Highlanders, and of Philip and Cynthia as babies, the past moving under their fingertips. Frank Underhill died in 1971 and Lester Pearson died in 1972. God knew, Creighton had no love for either one of them, but their deaths were reminders of his own mortality. Mary Innis's death in 1972 tore him apart, sending him back to the lost thirties and forties when the Creighton and Innis families spent so much time together, when Harold was still alive and, together, they were rewriting Canadian history. Norman Endicott's sudden death in 1976 was another painful reminder of time disappearing. As teenagers, they had cleared brush in Muskoka; as young men, they had excelled at Vic and later Oxford; and as professors, they had built their careers at Toronto. After the memorial service, he reported that only one other person from the old department was there. Everyone else was either dead or didn't care.

Unable to attend his brother's funeral, Creighton did the only thing he could do. He resumed the book that he had started a few months earlier, a mystery set in Toronto. For the past eight or nine months, he had been writing a novel as a way of keeping busy during his prolonged convalescence. As a high school and university student, he had written narrative poems and started two novels; and, years later, in the early 1940s, he wrote parts of a gothic novel set in Edwardian Toronto. Philip Creighton still remembers the main character, Libby Rivington, standing at a window doing absolutely nothing. "The whole thing was just awful." Frustrated and overwhelmed by other commitments, Creighton threw the manuscript in the garbage and, several years later, "handed the torch" to a young Cynthia, telling her that "she must write the novels" and stories that he had failed to write. Still, the desire to write a novel never went away. And in late 1977 he finally realized a lifelong dream when he sent the manuscript – minus the last chapter – to McClelland and Stewart, confessing that he didn't know what to make of something that was so unlike anything he had ever written. One editor hated it. "This is BAD," Anna Porter said. But Ellen Seligman liked it. "It's an old fashioned story"; there is "no sex, no violence, and no bad language." And where Porter found herself bored, Seligman found herself hooked: "Will you ask Dr. Creighton how the story ends?"[21]

Lacking the stentorian anger that had marred parts of *Canada's First Century* and later ruined *The Forked Road* and "No More Concessions," *Takeover* centres

Donald Creighton in his study in Brooklin. Designed by the heritage architect Napier Simpson, it featured built-in bookshelves, a fireplace, and windows that looked onto Luella's rose garden.

His brother's death in 1977 left Donald Creighton wondering "what remaining purpose he had in life." In an emotional letter to his sister-in-law, Sally Creighton, he referred to his brother as one of his early heroes. "Hero worship is a part of youth, and doesn't long outlast it; but for a good many years, as college student, soldier, oarsman, and young man about town in Toronto, Jack was a very romantic figure in my eyes."

on Hugh Stuart and the proposed sale of Stuart & Kilgour, a venerable Canadian distillery. Located on Toronto's King Street, Hugh's office is the symbolic centre of a "commercial empire" founded by his great-grandfather after the final defeat of the Tories in 1849 when an enraged mob torched the Montreal parliament buildings.[22] In effect, his great-grandfather was assembling a new empire of the St Lawrence out of the ashes of "disavowal and destruction."[23] On the walls of Hugh's office are an impressive collection of paintings by the Group of Seven and their contemporaries, "the intense green" of Emily Carr's British Columbia complementing "the romantic blues and greys" of Fred Varley's northern Ontario. From his office windows, Hugh can see the railway tracks below Front Street, a reminder of Sir John A. Macdonald's Laurentian vision. But he is "bored to tears" and desperately longs to "escape" the daily routine of running a large company. What he wants, more than anything else, is his freedom. Then, out of nowhere, James Pettigrew, the owner of an American distillery anxious to expand his company and to improve his line, offers to buy Stuart & Kilgour for a staggering sum of money. Although an American, Pettigrew is a southern gentleman whose family fought for the Confederacy at Gettysburg, which makes him at least palatable to Hugh. To sell or not to sell? From beginning to end, Hugh is haunted by the past in the form of family portraits, particularly the "magnificent" portrait of his great-great grandfather by George Romney, the fashionable eighteenth-century British artist. The founding patriarch had been a United Empire Loyalist from Massachusetts and a staff member to John Graves Simcoe, the first lieutenant governor of Upper Canada. One hundred and seventy-five years later, he casts a heavy shadow of obligation.[24]

Determined to escape that obligation, Hugh soon wins his family's consent, even from his son, an NDP supporter and an economic nationalist. His spinster aunt Cecilia, however, quickly recants. Her "two recognized and loved countries were Canada and Britain"; she didn't like Americans, especially those "uncouth and illiterate boors" in the midwest; and she took an instant dislike to one of Pettigrew's business associates, Dimitrios Papadopoulos, a "stout," "overdressed," "vulgar," "suave," and "common type of Levantine" who wore "too much jewelry." As the family archivist and historian, Aunt Cecilia presides over an important collection of personal and business papers as a sort of modern-day Vestal Virgin. In fact, she is negotiating their transfer to the Public Archives in Ottawa, not, she says, to the provincial archives. The Stuarts aren't a "provincial family"; they belong to "the Canadian nation." And so too does Stuart & Kilgour. After denying her consent, Cecilia is murdered by Hugh's "stormy," "calculating," and self-absorbed daughter, who pushes her down a flight of stairs in a desperate attempt to secure her inheritance. As she falls to her death, the past both repeats and exerts itself: over a century before, another Stuart woman had killed her much older husband for his money. Discovering the awful truth, Hugh decides that he can't possibly sell Stuart & Kilgour: despite his best efforts to escape, "the past had reached out and clutched him, and held him fast."[25]

Drawing on familiar themes, especially the many dangers of continentalism and the psychic importance of Great Britain, the novel refers to the takeover of a Canadian business by an American business and, ultimately, to the take-over of Canada by the United States. Because Montreal had forsaken its history and geography and was unable to defend his conception of Canada, Creighton looked to Victorian and Edwardian Toronto. Although the novel is set in 1966, Hugh Stuart belongs to a different time and place and still thinks of Canada as a British country rooted in a yet older tradition of loyalism. It isn't an ac-cident that he never changed the names of Stuart & Kilgour's two most popu-lar brands, Stuart Regal and Loyalist Rye, or that he preferred to lunch at the old-money Brock Club over the nouveau-riche City Club. After all, he was a "Toronto merchant."

Although it contains a couple of neat tricks, especially the use of portraits to set a scene, convey a mood, or summon a parallel between the past and present, *Takeover* met a swift and unkind reception. The *Globe and Mail* panned it; *Quill & Quire* trashed it; and *Maclean's* called it a bad cross between a tract for the times and an Agatha Christie novel. But it fell to *Saturday Night* to deliver the fatal blow. Ramsay Cook now wishes that he had never agreed to review it.[26] But he did, calling it "unconvincing," "unsatisfactory," and "unfinished," and de-scribing it as a statement of Wasp nationalism. In this sense, he said, it resem-bles Lionel Groulx's 1922 novel, *L'appel de la race*, itself a statement of defensive French-Canadian Catholic nationalism. Both novels examine national sur-vival in the context of a single family; both evoke "the past as the teacher of the present and the determinant of the future"; both draw on a narrow, racialized national identity; and, finally, both end badly. In *L'appel de la race*, the hero embraces his French-Canadian identity but loses his marriage and two of his children; in *Takeover*, Hugh yields to the weight of history, but his aunt is dead, his daughter is a murderer, and he is chained to the family firm.[27] According to Cook, Canada's two national historians were the flip sides of the same ideologi-cal coin: for every Groulx, a Creighton; for every Creighton, a Groulx.[28]

Reading his former student's review wasn't easy, and in a letter Creighton expressed his "deep hurt."[29] By this point, their friendship had been strained by mutual disappointment. Creighton's outbursts had disappointed Cook, and Cook's Liberal leanings had disappointed Creighton. In fact, he had lost the battle for Cook's intellectual soul to Grit Historical Enterprises years before. When, for example, he learned that Cook – who "had already provided ample proof of his devotion to the good old cause" – spoke at an event to mark Frank

Underhill's eightieth birthday party, he took it personally. His selection as the third speaker after Lester Pearson and Frank Scott was, he said, "the symbolic equivalent of his appointment as the historian who would carry forward the Liberal torch – *vitai lampada* – of continental unity into the beckoning future."[30] Although he admired Cook's many intellectual gifts, and although he was terribly fond of both him and his family, it was as if Underhill's birthday party were somehow about him.

Anyway, Creighton didn't understand Cook's reaction to his novel. He had had a lot of fun writing what he called his "little yarn" and, in his opinion, it neither invited nor deserved a comparison to *L'appel de la race*.[31] But to Cook, it wasn't an innocent little yarn at all: it was the expression of a particular brand of English-Canadian nationalism that had run its course. Through his scholarship and teaching, Cook wanted to explain French Canada to English Canada with an eye to building an open, bilingual, multicultural, and, above all, decent Canada. He had the future on his side, and the future is always a more powerful ally than the past when that past has calcified into ancestor worship, or resentment, or both. The past that had "reached out and clutched" Hugh Stuart was the same past that held Donald Creighton. Leading nowhere, it prevented him from imagining different futures, exploring new identities, and, well, from saying yes.[32]

III

In January 1979, Donald began to feel unwell. First, he blamed his novel's "very disappointing" sales; then he blamed the "bitterly cold" weather; next, he instructed his lawyer to ensure that his personal and family letters were destroyed after his death to keep PhD students "from rooting around" his private exchanges and intimate confessions; finally, he made an appointment to see his family doctor. Not liking what he saw, his doctor ordered more tests. In the meantime, Donald and Luella did what needed to be done. She went upstairs to get a box of old letters while he lit a fire and opened a bottle of champagne. For a few hours, they were young lovers again. He was in Oxford; she was in Toronto; and together they were making plans for their wedding. Half a century later, the letters seemed "terribly obvious and adolescent": "The fact is," he said, "we were two different people then." Maybe. But everyone is different in their twenties. In his case, he was in love, he was at the best university in the world, and he was happy; she too was in love and preparing to take on the world. What happened next isn't clear. Did they burn them one at a time or all at once? "God help us," Luella wrote afterwards.[33]

"Protesting every step of the way," Donald was admitted to the Oshawa General Hospital on 4 February. In fact, he was given the same room he had been given three years earlier. Although familiar, room 6108 meant tests, examinations, consultations, and, almost certainly, surgery. The cancer had returned, his lower descending colon would have to be removed, and he would need to be fitted with a colostomy bag. Had it been up to him, he would have said no, there is "a time to be born, and a time to die." But after nearly fifty-three years of marriage, Luella couldn't imagine him gone. The next five weeks were a suspended state of misery, convalescence, boredom, and hospital food, which he "loathed."[34] After he was discharged, he was told that the cancer had metastasized and that he would need chemotherapy. Christ. What was the point? He could barely walk; he couldn't control his bladder; and the stupid colostomy bag leaked. But Luella insisted. He fought back though, believing that it should be pronounced "kemmo-therapy," as in chemistry. It was his way of showing that he was still smarter than everyone else.[35]

In early May, Cynthia visited her parents. "She looks wonderful!" Luella said. And for the next few days they simply enjoyed each other's company. At one point, Cynthia saw her father sitting on the stairs and thought to herself, that's not my dad. "He was always so powerful. But that person on the stairs was an old man, exhausted and defeated by cancer, too weak even to stand up." Sitting down beside him, she put her arm around his shoulder and, for a few minutes, they just sat there. "Don't ever let them do this to you," he told Cynthia, still trying to protect his daughter.[36]

May and June were cruel. Instead of getting stronger, he was getting weaker. His rector from St Thomas's paid a pastoral visit and, following the Book of Common Prayer, he read Psalm 23, which had always been Creighton's favourite, its words "dissolving" him:

> Yea, though I walk through the valley of the shadow of death,
> I will fear no evil: For thou art with me;
> Thy rod and thy staff they comfort me.

A few weeks later, Creighton "begged" his doctor for something – a pill, an injection, anything – to "end it all."[37]

His many friends sent letters and cards, including Ramsay Cook, who was in Connecticut as a visiting professor at Yale University. "I have been a little reluctant to write, since I know that I have infuriated more often than I have pleased you in recent years," he said. "Still, I hope you realize that my fondness for you has not changed, nor have I forgotten all of the things that you have done for me over the many years."[38] Donald appreciated the gesture. In mid-June, Ramsay, now back in Toronto, and his wife Eleanor visited Donald and Luella in Brooklin, where they enjoyed a lovely Sunday afternoon. Like they had done on so many occasions in the past, they fell into a familiar conversation about literature, history, music, and people, carefully avoiding certain subjects and known landmines, and never once mentioning Ramsay's offending review.[39] Afterwards, Ramsay thanked Donald and Luella, telling them that their friendship meant a lot to him.

That is why it bothered him to know that Charles Taylor and Scott Symons had visited Brooklin a few weeks earlier. Taylor was writing a book on the conservative tradition in Canada and Symons was along for the ride. Cook feared – rightly, it turns out – that they were preying on the loneliness and vanities of a vulnerable man, that Symons in particular was winding Creighton up, pressing his buttons, and getting him going. Afterwards, Symons acknowledged that their "mission" had been "precise": "under guise of paying a social visit," or "a social picnic," to the Creightons, "we were really trying to know more about Donald (and hear more from him) for the sake of Taylor's Tory book." To get the copy they wanted, they went as "spies," a role Symons "loved." In other words, it was a set-up. Knowing that their prey was "explosive," Taylor and Symons lit the fuse, sat back, and watched the fireworks as Creighton made a series of truly awful remarks that surpassed anything he had said in the past.[40] Taylor admitted that Creighton's anti-Liberal, anti-American, anti-French, and anti-everything explosions were surely "the rantings of a dying old man" that "could be excused" but "never be reported."[41] Yet, incredibly, he reported them anyway, in part reducing the man who had written *The Commercial Empire of the St. Lawrence*, *Macdonald*, and *The Road to Confederation* to a handful of racist eruptions. Shakespeare's Marc Antony called that sort of thing the "unkindest cut of all."

And so it went, Creighton's long, painful slide. In mid-July, he wished that he could go to sleep and not wake up. In late August, he "broke down," overcome, he said, by "the weight of the past." But in September and October, he rallied, resuming his correspondence, receiving visitors, and listening to Wagner. He also talked about writing a memoir of his mother, who had introduced him to the written word through Dickens, Tennyson, and the Bible; he promised Peter Newman an article on television and changing speech patterns in English Canada; he resumed his second novel, another mystery set in Toronto; and he and Luella even managed a four-day trip to Vancouver to see Cynthia and her family. Luella, though, was physically and emotionally exhausted. Sleeping on the chesterfield and eating poorly, she was also drinking too much, on one occasion becoming "very drunk."[42] On most nights, she was up once or twice to change Donald's bedding or just to hold his hand. On a bad night, she could be up three or four times.

In early November, Creighton fell down, hitting his head. The next day, he fell twice. The day after that, he was taken to the hospital by ambulance. He hated the hospital and wanted to go home, unable to understand why he was there. He complained that the doctors didn't know his name, and if they did, they called him Mr Creighton. "We're supposed to call them Dr. Smith or Dr. Jones," he said, not bitterly, but almost sardonically. "They should have to address me as Professor Creighton."[43] Six days later he was sent home, again by ambulance, in a "total rage" that he had been admitted in the first place. In mid-November, a male nurse was hired to sit with him at night. "I am so tired I would have accepted a gorilla to do bedside nursing," Luella said. But the attendant didn't know what he was doing and Luella found herself alone at the very moment Donald's condition deteriorated "beyond measure": five days later he told Luella that he was ready.[44]

Still, he agreed to see Robert Finch, whom he had known forever, and John Cairns, a former colleague from the Department of History. Somewhere he found the strength to shave himself and to put on a suit and tie, and together they enjoyed a pleasant visit. At first, he began a familiar lament about Canada never recognizing him. However, Luella gently reproached him, reminding him that he had had his share, and the conversation moved on.[45] His need for recognition was instinctive, close to the surface, and layered with a romanticized picture of England, where he would have been Sir Donald Creighton. In Canada, he was just one more professor from a provincial university. After lunch, he announced his need to lie down, and Robert and John, one on either arm, helped him to the bed that had been put in his study. He loved that room, its built-in bookshelves, its fireplace, its Monet print, and its photograph of his father carefully placed on the mantle. But he especially loved its many windows looking out onto the backyard and Luella's rose garden, now covered in snow. John wanted to remove Donald's jacket, but he was already lying down, wrapped in a wool blanket, trying desperately to stay warm. That night and into the next day, he entered the final stage, his shallow breaths punctuated by violent gasps, his emaciated body fighting to stay alive. And then, just like that, he grew oddly peaceful, his breathing rapid but calm: he was going now, past words and books, past England and Canada, past life and into death.

Not knowing what to do, Luella opened her diary to 19 December and began to write. "Donald is dead. In the early hours of Wednesday morning at about 3 o'clock he was breathing quietly – at about 5:30 – just now – I went in and he is cold."[46] Officially, the northern hemisphere was still two days away from the winter solstice. But in the St Lawrence River Valley and the Great Lakes basin winter had already arrived.

IV

Designed by Frederick William Cumberland – whose St George Street home became Baldwin House – the Chapel of St James-the-Less on Toronto's Parliament Street was built in the Gothic Revival tradition, an architectural movement premised on a return to the churches and cathedrals of medieval Britain. When construction on it began in 1857, Confederation was still ten years away and John A. Macdonald had yet to be converted to the idea of a wider union of British North America. The funeral service was deliberately simple. Luella felt that it had been "superb," finding enormous comfort in the "glorious words" of John, Peter, Paul, and, of course, Psalm 23.[47] Afterwards, Philip Creighton hosted a reception at his North Toronto home, where people remembered a man who had dared to imagine that he could turn history into literature, who had written two or three of the best non-fiction books ever published in Canada, who had been called one of the half-dozen best historians in the English-speaking world, and who had been appointed by the British prime minister to repair the Central African Federation but who was himself undone by Canada's own decolonization. Perhaps, too, people talked about the stunning events in national politics: Lévesque had promised a spring referendum, the Clark government had fallen, an election had been called, and Trudeau had taken back his resignation. "No one cares what happens to Canada anymore," said Donald Creighton a day or two before he died.[48] As the reception ended, his former students and colleagues expressed their final condolences to Luella, Philip, and Cynthia, and to his sister, Isabel, before walking into the gathering darkness. On the December solstice, Toronto gets less than nine hours of daylight.

Not wanting to be alone, Luella spent Christmas with Philip's family. The tree was lovely and there were a lot of gifts, but she was cold, she said, and on Boxing Day she felt "an urgent need" to go home: what if Donald comes back and the house is empty and dinner isn't ready? "I still don't believe he is dead." Friends told her not to make any major decisions for at least a year and not allow herself "to be pressured into selling the house." Right now, though, she had other things to worry about, like writing thank-you notes, cleaning out Donald's safety deposit box, straightening up his desk, and, as he had instructed, burning a batch of letters that he had written to her in the 1940s.[49]

A few weeks later, the University of Toronto held a memorial service for one of its intellectual giants in Convocation Hall, a building influenced by the

Sorbonne grand theatre in Paris and the Sheldonian Theatre in Oxford. But the interior plan of Convocation Hall is very Canadian, the seating arrangement taking its inspiration from nature north of the 49th parallel, from, in fact, the snowflake.[50] The last time Luella had been in Con Hall was in 1974 when Donald received an honorary doctorate and he regaled the audience with a self-deprecating confession of his secret and unfulfilled desire to have been elected chancellor. Maurice Careless, Ramsay Cook, and Robert Finch were invited to speak at the memorial service, each man casting Donald Creighton in a different light, revealing a teacher, colleague, writer, and, above all, a friend.[51] Quoting from "Little Gidding," T.S. Eliot's brilliant meditation on the meaning of time, Cook pointed to Creighton's unshakeable belief in the importance of history and memory.

> A people without history,
> Is not redeemed from time, for history is a pattern
> Of timeless moments.

But Eliot also implies that history has a darker self, that, yes, it "may be freedom" but it "may be servitude" as well. For Creighton, history began as freedom in *The Commercial Empire of the St. Lawrence*, found its fullest expression in *The Young Politician* and *The Old Chieftain*, and ended as servitude in *The Forked Road* and *Takeover*. Trapped in a thesis that no longer led anywhere, and not knowing where to turn, he sank into despair.

When the president of the university invited the audience to stand for the singing of the national anthem, Luella lost her composure. She had "stood up pretty well," she said, "but O Canada brought me to my knees." Later, she doubted that she would ever be able to sing the national anthem again because it reminded her of Donald's overwhelming sadness: *his* home and native land was gone. "He grieved so for Canada," she wrote afterwards.[52]

In the months and years after her husband's death, Luella rebuilt her life. Although she sometimes wondered why she bothered to live at all, she enjoyed the company of her many friends and of Philip and his family, busied herself with community projects in Brooklin, and delighted in her garden and its many different varieties of roses. Cynthia, however, had a different experience. With two young children, a collapsing marriage, and a million political commitments, she didn't have time to properly grieve her father's death. Instead, she packaged it up and put it away. Eight or nine years later, though, she listened to a recording of an interview Donald had done with the CBC a year or so before he died. Hearing his distinctive voice sent her into an emotional tailspin; by her own admission, she cried for the better part of a week.

Sent by *Saturday Night* to photograph Donald Creighton at his home in Brooklin, Ontario, in 1977, the photographer Arnaud Maggs took a series of artistically and symbolically brilliant photographs of him standing at the end of a hallway. Through the artist's use of perspective, the great man is reduced in size at the same time as he is backed into a physical corner which was also a symbolic corner, the Laurentian thesis leading nowhere. He died a little over two years later.

To make sense of her father and her complicated relationship to him, she did what writers do: she wrote a short story. Later someone asked her how long it took to write it, and she responded, "About forty years." Moving backward and forward in time, from Toronto to Oxford to Paris to Brooklin, "My Father Took a Cake to France" depicts an old man – haunted by lost causes, convictions of failure, and imminent death – looking back on his younger self in Oxford, en route to Paris, with a cake for the woman he loved. When Cynthia won the 1990 Journey Prize for the best short story published by an emerging writer, Luella proudly watched her daughter step onto the stage at the Harbourfront Centre in Toronto to accept the award and a cheque for $10,000. Earlier, she had told Cynthia how much she liked the story for its depiction of Donald, telling her, while fighting back the tears, "you got him."[53] Perhaps, too, Luella admired Cynthia's courage as a writer, for her willingness to go places that she wasn't able to. In her short stories and novels, Luella had always pulled back from her mother's death and its emotional scar. The one time she did go there, she resolved never to write again.

After Donald died, Luella continued to keep a daily diary out of habit and necessity. She also wrote a short poem, a sort of last will and testament:

> Leave me my roses when I am dead
> When I am lying on the south side of the hill
> Roses blanketed above me white and yellow and red
> Speak to the women who would take them away
> To furnish some hot sick chamber
> Better for the living than the dead
> They say. It is not so.
> I shall need my roses when I am dead
> Their sweetness trickling down will comfort me.[54]

Luella Sanders Bruce Creighton died in 1996 and was buried next to her husband in Brooklin's Anglican cemetery, about thirty kilometres as the crow flies from the Stouffville Cemetery, where her mother was buried ninety-five years earlier.

St. Paul's Anglican Cemetery, Brooklin, Ontario. "Yea, though I walk through the valley of the shadow of death, I will fear no evil: for though art with me; thy rod and thy staff they comfort me." Psalm 23:4.

appendix one

Donald Creighton, Selected Bibliography

"The Struggle for Financial Control in Lower Canada, 1818–1831." *Canadian Historical Review* 12, no. 2 (June 1931).

"The Commercial Class in Canadian Politics, 1792–1840." *Papers and Proceedings of the Canadian Political Science Association* 5 (1933).

"A Study of History." *Canadian Journal of Economics and Political Science* 2, no. 2 (May 1936).

"The Crisis of 1837." *Canadian Banker*, April 1937.

"The Economic Background of the Rebellions of 1837." *Canadian Journal of Political Science* 3, no. 3 (August 1937).

The Commercial Empire of the St. Lawrence: A Study in Commerce and Politics. New Haven: Yale University Press, 1937; reprinted with a new introduction by Christopher Moore, University of Toronto Press, 2002.

"The Victorians and the Empire." *Canadian Historical Review* 19, no. 2 (June 1938).

British North America at Confederation: A Study Prepared for the Royal Commission on Dominion-Provincial Relations. Ottawa: King's Printer, 1939.

"Conservatism and National Unity." In Ralph Flenley, ed., *Essays in Canadian History.* Toronto: Macmillan, 1939.

"Federal Relations in Canada since 1914." In Chester Martin, ed., *Canada in Peace and War.* Oxford: Oxford University Press, 1941.

"The Course of Canadian Democracy." *University of Toronto Quarterly* 11, no. 3 (April 1942).

"Economic Nationalism and Confederation." *Annual Report*, Canadian Historical Association, 1942.

"George Brown, Sir John A. Macdonald, and the Workingman." *Canadian Historical Review* 24, no. 4 (December 1943).

Dominion of the North: A History of Canada. Boston: Houghton Mifflin, 1944.

"Ontario" (with Helen Marsh). *Canadian Affairs*, September 1944.

"Canadian History in Retrospect and Prospect" (with G.W. Brown). *Canadian Historical Review* 25, no. 4 (December 1944).

"The Writing of History in Canada." Founders' Day Address, University of New Brunswick, 1945.

"Canada in the English-speaking World." *Canadian Historical Review* 26, no. 2 (June 1945).

"Sir John Macdonald and Canadian Historians." *Canadian Historical Review* 29, no. 1 (March 1948).

"An Episode in the History of the University of Toronto." *University of Toronto Quarterly* 17, no. 3 (April 1948).

"Sir John A. Macdonald and Kingston." *Annual Report*, Canadian Historical Association, 1950.

"The Dominion: Genesis and Integration." In G.W. Brown, ed., *Canada*. Toronto: University of Toronto Press, 1950.

John A. Macdonald: The Young Politician. Toronto: Macmillan, 1952; reprinted with a new introduction by P.B. Waite, University of Toronto Press, 1998.

"Canada in the World." In G.P. Gilmour, ed., *Canada's Tomorrow*. Toronto: Macmillan, 1954.

John A. Macdonald: The Old Chieftain. Toronto: Macmillan, 1955; reprinted with a new introduction by P.B. Waite, University of Toronto Press, 1998.

"Education for Government." *Queen's Quarterly* 62 (Winter 1955).

"Old Tomorrow." *The Beaver* (Winter 1956).

"Towards the Discovery of Canada." *University of Toronto Quarterly* 25, no. 3 (April 1956).

"Macdonald and Manitoba." *The Beaver* (Spring 1957).

"Sir John A. Macdonald." In Claude Bissell, ed., *Our Living Tradition*. Toronto: University of Toronto Press, 1957.

"Presidential Address." *Annual Report*, Canadian Historical Association, 1957.

Harold Adams Innis: Portrait of a Scholar. Toronto: University of Toronto Press, 1957.

Dominion of the North: A History of Canada. Revised and enlarged. Boston: Houghton Mifflin, 1958.

"The United States and Canadian Confederation." *Canadian Historical Review* 39, no. 3 (September 1958).

The Story of Canada. Toronto: Macmillan, 1959.

The Road to Confederation: The Emergence of Canada, 1863–1867. Toronto: Macmillan, 1964; reprinted with a new introduction by Donald Wright, Oxford University Press, 2012.

"John Alexander Macdonald: The Father of His Country." *Historic Kingston* 14 (1965).

"Confederation: The Use and Abuse of History." *Journal of Canadian Studies* 1 (May 1966).

"The Myth of Biculturalism or The Great French-Canadian Sales Campaign." *Saturday Night*, September 1966.

"Introduction." In J.B. Brebner, *North Atlantic Triangle*. Toronto: McClelland and Stewart, 1966.

"John A. Macdonald, Confederation and the Canadian West." *Historical and Scientific Society of Manitoba Transactions*, series III, 23 (1966–7).

"The Decline and Fall of the Empire of the St. Lawrence." *Historical Papers* 4 (1969).

Canada's First Century. Toronto: Macmillan, 1970; reprinted with a new introduction by Donald Wright, Oxford University Press, 2012.

"Reflections on the Americanization of Canada." *Laurentian University Review* 3 (February 1971).

"Watching the Sun Quietly Set on Canada." *Maclean's*, November 1971.

Towards the Discovery of Canada: Selected Essays. Toronto: Macmillan, 1972.

"Is Canada More Than We Can Hope For?" *Maclean's*, September 1973.

Canada: The Heroic Beginnings. Toronto: Macmillan, 1974.

"We've Been Fat for Too Long and Now It's Too Late." *Maclean's*, April 1975.

"Prostitutes Left Out in Account of Mackenzie King's Career." *Globe and Mail*, 28 February 1976.

"The Ogdensburg Agreement and Frank Underhill." In Carl Berger and Ramsay Cook, eds. *The West and the Nation: Essays in Honour of W.L. Morton.* Toronto: McClelland and Stewart, 1976.

The Forked Road: Canada, 1939–1957. Toronto: McClelland and Stewart, 1976.

"No More Concessions." *Maclean's*, June 1977.

Takeover. Toronto: McClelland and Stewart, 1978.

The Passionate Observer: Selected Writings. Toronto: McClelland and Stewart, 1980.

Donald Creighton's Doctoral Students

Peter Waite. "Ideas and Politics in British North America, 1864–1866: A Study of Opinion on the Subject of Federal Government" (1953).

John Moir. "The Relations of Church and State in Canada West, 1840–1867" (1954).

Goldwin French. "Wesleyan Methodism in Upper Canada and the Maritime Provinces: The Heroic Age, 1780–1855" (1958).

Margaret Prang. "The Political Career of N.W. Rowell" (1959).

Alan Wilson. "The Political and Administrative History of the Upper Canada Clergy Reserves, 1790–1855" (1959).

Ramsay Cook. "The Political Ideas of John W. Dafoe, 1866–1944" (1960).

Alan MacIntosh. "The Career of Sir Charles Tupper in Canada, 1864–1900" (1960).

Robert Craig Brown. "Canadian-American Relations in the Latter Part of the Nineteenth Century" (1962).

Francis Bolger. "Prince Edward Island and Confederation, 1863–1873" (1964).

R.A. (Ray) MacLean. "Joseph Howe and British-American Union" (1966).

Lovell Clark. "A History of the Conservative Administrations, 1891 to 1896" (1968).

H.V. (Viv) Nelles. "The Politics of Development: Forests, Mines and Hydro-Electric Power in Ontario, 1890–1939" (1969).

Donald Page. "Canadians and the League of Nations before the Manchurian Crisis" (1972).

J.R. Miller. "The Impact of the Jesuits' Estates Act on Canadian Politics, 1888–1891" (1972).

John Eagle. "Sir Robert Borden and the Railway Problem in Canadian Politics, 1911–1920" (1972).

Paul Rutherford. "The New Nationality, 1864–1897: A Study of the National Aims and Ideas of English Canada in the Late Nineteenth Century" (1973).

Angus Gilbert. "The Political Influence of Imperialist Thought in Canada, 1899–1923" (1974).

Appendix 2

Richard Clippingdale. "J.S. Willison, Political Journalist: From Liberalism to
    Independence, 1881–1905" (1974).
Ken McLaughlin. "Race, Religion and Politics: The Election of 1896 in Canada" (1974).

appendix three

Luella Creighton, Selected Bibliography

· "The Observations of Gutrik the Gargoyle: The Bird Market." *New Outlook,*
27 November 1929.

"The Observations of Gutrik the Gargoyle: The Luxembourg Gardens." *New Outlook,*
29 January 1930.

"The Seller of Magic Seeds." *New Outlook*, 16 April 1930.

"The Observations of Gutrik the Gargoyle: The First of May on Mouffetard Street."
New Outlook, 30 April 1930.

"Once in a Magic Moon." *New Outlook*, 28 January 1931.

"Once in a Magic Moon: Part II." *New Outlook*, 4 February 1931.

"The Tale of Mrs. Brown Ruffle Duck." *New Outlook*, 16 September 1931.

"Two Christmas Stories: The Gingham Pig and The Tiny Bear." *New Outlook*,
16 December 1931.

"Christmas Eve in No-Name Town." *New Outlook*, 23 December 1931.

"The Blue Rabbit." *New Outlook*, 23 March 1932.

"The Bear Who Went to the Hospital." *New Outlook*,18 May 1932.

"Susie." *New Outlook*, 6 July 1932.

"The Blue Top." *New Outlook*, 9 November 1932.

"Nicholas Spends the Night." *New Outlook*, 15 March 1933.

"Nicholas Visits the Dinosaur." *New Outlook*, 10 July 1933.

"Black Magic." *New Outlook*, 30 May 1934.

"The Coming of Spuddie." *New Outlook*, 13 June 1934.

"McCork and Mrs. McCork." *New Outlook*, 8 August 1934.

"Miss Kidd." In Bertram Brooker, ed., *Yearbook of the Arts in Canada*. Toronto:
Macmillan, 1936.

"The Cornfield." *Canadian Forum*, June 1937.

High Bright Buggy Wheels. Toronto: McClelland and Stewart, 1951; reprinted with a
new introduction by Cynthia Flood, Oxford University Press, 2013.

Turn East, Turn West. Toronto: McClelland and Stewart, 1954.

Canada: The Struggle for Empire. Toronto: Dent, 1960.

Canada: Trial and Triumph. Toronto: Dent, 1963.

Tecumseh: The Story of the Shawnee Chief. Toronto: Macmillan, 1965.

Miss Multipenny and Miss Crumb. London: Peal Press, 1966.

The Elegant Canadians. Toronto: McClelland and Stewart, 1967; reprinted with a new
   introduction by Donald Wright, Oxford University Press, 2013.

The Hitching Post. Toronto: McClelland and Stewart, 1969.

Notes

Introduction

1 Donald Creighton to Eugene Forsey, 12 November 1972, Library and Archives Canada (LAC), Donald Creighton fonds, MG 31 D 77, vol. 26, file Correspondence with Eugene Forsey, 1965–1975; *Globe and Mail,* 13 December 1963; Creighton to Forsey, 12 November 1972. On biographies of historians, see Doug Munro, "Biographies of Historians – or, The Cliographer's Craft," *Australian Historical Studies* 43, no. 1 (2012): 11–27.

2 Donald Creighton, Diary entry for 29 March 1977, LAC, Donald Creighton fonds, MG 31 D 77, vol. 66, file 4. See also Donald Creighton to Ramsay Derry, 26 April 1977. Original in possession of Ramsay Derry. The Public Archives of Canada is now Library and Archives Canada.

3 For example, see Robert Bothwell, *Laying the Foundation: A Century of History at University of Toronto* (Toronto: University of Toronto Department of History, 1991); Paul Romney, *Getting It Wrong: How Canadians Forgot Their Past and Imperiled Confederation* (Toronto: University of Toronto Press, 1999); Philip Massolin, *Canadian Intellectuals, The Tory Tradition, and The Challenge of Modernity, 1939–1970* (Toronto: University of Toronto Press, 2001); Donald Wright, *The Professionalization of History in English Canada* (Toronto: University of Toronto Press, 2005); and Jon Suffrin, "The Canadian Apocalypse: Nationalists and The End of Canada, 1963–1983" (PhD thesis, York University, 2009); Cara Spittal, "The Diefenbaker Moment" (PhD thesis, University of Toronto, 2011). See also Kenneth Dewar, "Where to Begin and How: Narrative Openings in Donald Creighton's Historiography," *Canadian Historical Review* 72, no. 3 (1991): 348–69; and Donald Wright, "Donald Creighton and the French Fact, 1920s to 1970s," *Journal of the Canadian Historical Association* 6 (1995): 243–72.

4 Barker Fairley, "Donald Creighton," in Gary Michael Dault, ed., *Barker Fairley Portraits* (Toronto: Methuen, 1981), 2.

5 Peter Waite, "Introduction" in Donald Creighton, *John A. Macdonald: The Young Politician* and *John A. Macdonald: The Old Chieftain* (Toronto: University of Toronto Press, 1998), viii; Ramsay Cook, "Donald Grant Creighton: Tribute to a Scholar," University of Toronto *Bulletin* (25 February 1980): 4; Michael Bliss, "Privatizing the Mind: The Sundering of Canadian History, the Sundering of Canada," *Journal of Canadian Studies* 26, no. 4 (Winter 1991–2): 5.

6 "An Interview with Donald Creighton," in Eleanor Cook and Ramsay Cook, eds, *The Craft of History* (Toronto: Canadian Broadcasting Corporation, 1973), 145.

7 William Creighton, "On Reading Books," *Christian Guardian*, 24 November 1909.

8 Charles Taylor, *Radical Tories: The Conservative Tradition in Canada* (Toronto: Anansi, 1982), 24.

9 Luella Creighton, "Prelude," unpublished manuscript, ca 1968–70, University of Waterloo, Doris Lewis Rare Book Room, Luella Creighton fonds, GA 99, series 5, box 9, file 86.

10 Personal communication from Lynda Franklin, 8 February 2005; author's interview with Margaret Prang, 18 January 2005.

11 Isabel Creighton to Harold Wilson, n.d., ca March 1930. Original in possession of Philip Creighton.

12 Taylor, *Radical Tories*, 28.

13 François-Xavier Garneau, *History of Canada*, 3 vols, trans. Andrew Bell (Montreal, 1860), 1:xxii.

14 Donald Creighton, *The Empire of the St. Lawrence* (Toronto: University of Toronto Press, 2002), 6. When it was republished by Macmillan in 1956, Creighton shortened the title to *The Empire of the St. Lawrence*.

15 Donald Creighton, "The Colony of Great Britain and the United States," LAC, MG 31 D 77, Donald Creighton fonds, vol. 14, file The Colony of Great Britain and the United States 1932. Creighton, *The Empire of the St. Lawrence*, 6; Ralph Heintzman, "Political Space and Economic Space: Quebec and the Empire of the St. Lawrence," *Journal of Canadian Studies* 29, no. 2 (1994): 19. Updating Heintzman's observation, the Laurentian thesis and the liberal order framework are the only two genuinely arresting paradigms ever to emerge from Canadian historical scholarship.

16 J.L. Manore, "Rivers as Text: From Pre-Modern to Post-Modern Understandings of Development, Technology and the Environment in Canada and Abroad," in T. Tvedt and T. Oestigarrd, eds, *A History of Water*, vol. 3: *The World of Water* (London: I.B. Tauris, 2006), 229.

17 Donald Creighton, "Macdonald and the Anglo-Canadian Alliance," in Donald Creighton, *Towards the Discovery of Canada* (Toronto: Macmillan, 1972), 212; Max Beloff, *The Spectator*, 6 March 1953; Frank Underhill, "The Revival of Conservatism

in North America," *Transactions of the Royal Society of Canada* 52, series III (June 1958): 17.

18 The full inscription reads "Presented / To the Library of / Her Majesty The Queen at Windsor / this biography of / the first Prime Minister of Canada / With the homage and loyal good wishes / of the author / Donald Creighton / Toronto, Canada, June 23, 1959." I would like to thank the Royal Library for providing the inscription and allowing me to quote from it.

19 Author's interview with Diane Mew, 21 October 2004.

20 Donald Creighton to Eugene Forsey, 9 May 1971, LAC, MG 31 D 77, Donald Creighton fonds, vol. 26, file Correspondence with Eugene Forsey 1965–75.

21 Donald Creighton to Eugene Forsey, 2 May 1970, ibid.

22 Séraphin Marion, *Péchés d'omission d'un historien canadien* (Ottawa, 1966); Arthur Lower to Séraphin Marion, 13 August 1966, Queen's University Archives, Arthur Lower fonds, Collection 5072, box 5, file A67; Hugh Keenleyside, *Memoirs of Hugh L. Keenleyside* (Toronto: McClelland and Stewart, 1981), 1:197; C.P. Stacey, *A Date with History* (Ottawa: Deneau, 1983), 228; Stephen Clarkson and Christina McCall, *Trudeau and Our Times: The Magnificent Obsession* (Toronto: McClelland and Stewart, 1990), 71; Desmond Morton quoted in Michael Valpy, "Is the National Dream Over?" *Globe and Mail,* 11 March 2006; George Fetherling, "Remembering Charles Taylor, A Red Tory," *New Brunswick Reader,* 16 September 2006; Veronica Strong-Boag, "Contested Space: The Politics of Canadian Memory," *Journal of the Canadian Historical Association* 5 (1994): 7–8; Ray Conlogue, *Impossible Nation: The Longing for Homeland in Canada and Quebec* (Stratford: Mercury Press, 1996), 39; Ray Conlogue, "A Dialogue of the Deaf between the Conqueror and the Conquered," *Globe and Mail,* 21 January 1995; and Claude Charron, *La partition du Québec: de Lord Durham à Stéphane Dion* (Montreal: VLB, 1996), 72. So obsessed is Charron with Creighton that his book might have been called *La partition du Québec: de Lord Durham à Stéphane Dion via Donald Creighton.*

23 Gerald Graham to Bartlet Brebner, 12 May 1952, Columbia University Rare Book and Manuscript Library, J. Bartlet Brebner fonds, box 5, file H.A. Innis: cuttings (obituaries, etc.) and correspondence about him.

24 Author's interview with Jim Miller, 26 March 2004.

25 Author's interview with Ramsay Cook, 3 December 2004; Ramsay Cook, Review of *Towards the Discovery of Canada, Globe and Mail,* 13 May 1972.

26 Sam Solecki, "Homage to the Runner," CBC Radio, *Stereo Morning,* 6 January 1981.

27 Carl Berger, *The Writing of Canadian History: Aspects of English-Canadian Historical Writing since 1900* (Toronto: University of Toronto Press, 1976), 237; Donald Creighton to John Gray, 30 January 1977, LAC, John Gray fonds, MG 30 D 266, vol. 2, file Correspondence 1977.

28 William Faulkner, "The Art of Fiction XII," *Paris Review* 12 (Spring 1956): 28–52.

29 Brian Nelson, "Zola and the Nineteenth Century," in Brian Nelson, ed., *The Cambridge Companion to Zola* (Cambridge: Cambridge University Press, 2007), 4.

30 Northrop Frye, *The Anatomy of Criticism* (Princeton, NJ: Princeton University Press, 1957), 36.

31 Northrop Frye, "The Decline of the West," *Daedalus* 103, no. 1 (1974): 6. It was as an undergraduate in the early 1930s that Frye first discovered Spengler. He was supposed to be in Creighton's class on Tudor England but, in fact, spent his time in the library of Hart House reading *The Decline of the West*. See John Ayre, *Northrop Frye: A Biography* (Toronto: Random House, 1989), 65. George Woodcock, "The Servants of Clio: Notes on Creighton and Groulx," *Canadian Literature* 83 (1979): 131; Donald Creighton, "A Study of History," *Canadian Journal of Economics and Political Science* 3, no. 2 (May 1936): 220.

32 Oswald Spengler, *The Decline of the West* (New York: Knopf, 1926), 117.

33 Ibid., 118.

34 Donald Creighton, "Somerset Maugham and His World," in Donald Creighton, *The Passionate Observer* (Toronto: McClelland and Stewart, 1980), 89.

35 See G.M. Trevelyan, *Clio, A Muse and Other Essays* (New York: Books for Libraries Press, 1968), 148. "Clio, a Muse" was first published in 1914. Donald Creighton, "History and Literature," in Donald Creighton, *Towards the Discovery of Canada* (Toronto: Macmillan, 1972), 23, 21.

1 Family Tree

1 Between 1825, the year reliable statistics become available, and 1845, the year immediately preceding the Great Famine, nearly 475,000 men and women left Ireland for Britain's North American colonies. Donald Akenson, *The Irish in Ontario: A Study in Rural History* (Montreal and Kingston: McGill-Queen's University Press, 1984), 23.

2 Donald Creighton, *The Empire of the St. Lawrence* (Toronto: University of Toronto Press, 2002), 259; Donald Creighton, *The Story of Canada* (Toronto: Macmillan, 1959), 117.

3 Francis Evans, *The Emigrant's Directory and Guide to Obtain Lands and Effect a Settlement in the Canadas* (Dublin: William Curry, 1833), 30.

4 William Black Creighton, John Creighton's grandson, described Tamlaght O'Crilly as perhaps the most beautiful place on earth. "As we drove along from Ballymena to Portglenone and afterward to the little village of Tamlaght O'Crilly and gazed upon those green Antrim hills shining in the sunlight with the noble Bann river flowing through the midst of them we felt that we had never seen anything so utterly beautiful … The glens of Antrim – who has a pen to describe them!" William Creighton, "Through Ireland by Motor Bus," *New Outlook*, 22 July 1931.

5 In technical terms, Tamlaght O'Crilly Parish had a high population density per unit of cultivated land, making improvements to agricultural practice difficult.

6 There were famines in 1816, 1821, and 1831.

7 See James H. Johnson, "Population Movements in County Derry during a Pre-Famine Year," *Proceedings of the Royal Irish Academy* 60, no. 3 (1959): 141–62.

8 "Extract from old book of Kennedy Creighton and written in his own writing," n.d. Original in possession of Philip Creighton.

9 Northrop Frye, "Conclusion to a *Literary History of Canada*," in Northrop Frye, *The Bush Garden: Essays on the Canadian Imagination* (Toronto: Anansi, 1971), 217.

10 Akenson, *The Irish in Ontario*, 14.

11 Creighton, *The Empire of the St. Lawrence*, 259, 260.

12 Cecil Houston and William Smyth, *Irish Emigration and Canadian Settlement: Patterns, Links, and Letters* (Toronto: University of Toronto Press, 1990), 112.

13 Donald Akenson, *An Irish History of Civilization*, 2 vols (Montreal and Kingston: McGill-Queen's University Press, 2005), 1, 617.

14 Creighton, *The Empire of the St. Lawrence*, 261.

15 Gerald Craig, ed., *Lord Durham's Report* (Montreal and Kingston: McGill-Queen's University Press, 2007), 112.

16 Evans, *Emigrant's Directory*, 30. Italics in original.

17 *History of the County of Middlesex, Canada* (Toronto and London: W.A. and C.L. Goodspeed, 1889; reprinted 1972), 799.

18 See Wilbert Harold Dalgliesh, "The Economic History of the County of Middlesex, Canada, Prior to the Building of Railways" (MA thesis, University of Western Ontario, 1923).

19 Houston and Smyth, *Irish Emigration*, 127.

20 1842 Census and Assessment of Canada West, London District, Township of Dorchester, 3. Although the census listing is for John Claton, I believe that this is incorrect and that it is, in fact, John Creighton. Two lines down in the census is William English. Although the lot numbers are not included in the census, I know that English purchased the north half of lot four, concession two, in 1835 from the Canada Company. Given that James Creighton purchased the south half of the same lot in 1848, and given the close relationship between the two families (Nancy married Thomas English and James married Mary English and, after her death, Ann English), it is likely that the two families were living one near the other and thus listed in the census one near the other.

21 Catharine Anne Wilson, *Tenants in Time: Family Strategies, Land, and Liberalism in Upper Canada, 1799–1871* (Montreal and Kingston: McGill-Queen's University Press, 2009), 56.

22 This figure – 24.5 acres under cultivation – suggests that the Creightons had been on this farm for some time, perhaps even as early as 1834 or 1835. On average, a farmer could clear one and a half acres of crop land per year.

23 1851/2 Census of Canada West: Middlesex County, North Dorchester Township, Part 3, 113–14; Agricultural Schedule, 121–2.

24 See Karl Polanyi, *The Great Transformation* (New York: Rinehart, 1944); and John Weaver, *The Great Land Rush and the Making of the Modern World, 1650–1900* (Montreal and Kingston: McGill-Queen's University Press, 2003). See also the chapter on Upper Canada in Cole Harris, *The Reluctant Land: Society, Space, and Environment in Canada before Confederation* (Vancouver: UBC Press, 2008).

25 Akenson, *The Irish in Ontario*, 335.

26 Creighton, *Story of Canada*, 143. In point of fact, the Great Western Railway – which was completed in the early 1850s and connected Hamilton to Windsor – ran through the Creighton farm.

27 Polanyi, *Great Transformation*, 41. See also Weaver, *Great Land Rush*, 356.

28 J. David Wood, *Making Ontario: Agricultural Colonization and Landscape Re-recreation before the Railway* (Montreal and Kingston: McGill-Queen's University Press, 2000), xx.

29 See William Westfall, *Two Worlds: The Protestant Culture of Nineteenth-Century Ontario* (Montreal and Kingston: McGill-Queen's University Press, 1989).

30 Michael Gauvreau, *The Evangelical Century: College and Creed in English Canada from the Great Revival to the Great Depression* (Montreal and Kingston: McGill-Queen's, 1991), 45.

31 Donald Creighton, *Dominion of the North* (Boston: Houghton Mifflin, 1944), 219.

32 Ibid.

33 Neil Semple, *The Lord's Dominion: The History of Canadian Methodism* (Montreal and Kingston: McGill-Queen's University Press, 1996), 443.

34 The Reformed Presbyterian Church came out of seventeenth-century Scotland and the many and often violent struggles both to resist state interference and to preserve spiritual independence. Covenanters ultimately rejected the Revolution Settlement of 1691 because of the role it assigned to government within the Church of Scotland. To them it was a surrender of the very spiritual independence they had fought for and so they made a covenant to resist the Crown. See Adam Loughridge, *The Covenanters in Ireland: A History of the Reformed Presbyterian Church of Ireland* (Belfast: Cameron Press, 1984), and Eldon Hay, *The Covenanters in Canada: Reformed Presbyterianism from 1820–2012* (Montreal and Kingston: McGill-Queen's University Press, 2012).

35 "Extract from Old Book of Kennedy Creighton and Written in His Own Writing," n.d. Original in possession of Philip Creighton.

36 See "A Pioneer Gone Home," *Christian Guardian* (17 February 1892): 104.

37 Kennedy Creighton, *Annual Report, Indian Missions, Methodist Church of Canada, 1885–6*. I want to thank Donald Smith, who sent me copies of his own research notes.

38 See Donald Smith, *Sacred Feathers: The Reverend Peter Jones (Kahkewaquonaby) and the Mississauga Indians* (Toronto: University of Toronto Press, 1987), and Donald Smith, *Mississauga Portraits: Ojibwe Voices from Nineteenth-Century Canada* (Toronto: University of Toronto Press, 2013).

39 In 1882 Kennedy was sixty-eight years old and "a respected preacher known for his moderate views" when he led a revived but again unsuccessful effort to see an itinerant's term extended to five years, an effort no doubt stemming from his own experience. Semple, *The Lord's Dominion*, 235.

40 Quotation in Marilyn Färdig Whitely, *Canadian Methodist Women, 1766–1925: Marys, Marthas, Mothers in Israel* (Waterloo, ON: Wilfrid Laurier University Press, 2005), 51.

41 Kennedy and Laura had three boys and two girls. Their second daughter, Mary Isobelle, drowned in 1865. She was seventeen.

42 Johanna Selles, *Methodists and Women's Education in Ontario, 1836–1925* (Montreal and Kingston: McGill-Queen's University Press, 1996), 223.

43 Philip Creighton's interview with Isabel Wilson, 12 February 1978. Copy in author's possession.

44 Quotation in Philip Creighton, "John Harvie," *York Pioneer* 81 (Summer 1986): 1. Many decades later his abstemious son-in-law, William Creighton, visited Campbeltown. It was 1931 and the distilleries had largely disappeared. "The dying down of this industry is, of course, bitterly complained against here and there but it was rather easy for us to see the bright side to all that." William Black Creighton, "Land of Cold Winds and Warm Hearts," *New Outlook*, 15 July 1931.

45 G. Mercer Adam, *Toronto: Old and New* (Toronto: Mail Printing Company, 1891), 173.

46 See Philip Creighton, "Harvie (Harvey), John," *Dictionary of Canadian Biography*, available online at www.biographi.ca.

47 See Westfall, *Two Worlds*. See also Denis McKim, "Boundless Dominion: Politics, Providence, and the Early Canadian Worldview, 1815–1875" (unpublished dissertation, University of Toronto, 2011).

48 Author's interview with Philip Creighton, 30 September 2004.

49 Lizzie Harvie to John Harvie, 22 November 1880. Original in possession of Philip Creighton.

50 See Judith Young, "A Divine Mission: Elizabeth McMaster and the Hospital for Sick Children, Toronto, 1875–92," *Canadian Bulletin of Medical History* 11 (1994): 71–90; Philip Creighton, "Creighton, Eliza Jane (Harvie)," *Dictionary of Canadian Biography*, available online at www.biographi.ca; and "Harvie, Mrs. Elizabeth J." in H.J. Morgan, *The Canadian Men and Women of the Time* (Toronto: William Briggs, 1912).

51 Ruth Compton Brouwer, *New Women for God: Canadian Presbyterian Women and India Missions, 1876–1914* (Toronto: University of Toronto Press, 1990), 13.

52 *First Annual Report of the Women's Foreign Missionary Society of the Presbyterian Church of Canada* (Toronto: n.p., 1877), 26.

53 Andrew Baird, *The Indians of Western Canada* (Toronto: n.p., 1895), 28.

54 *Nineteenth Annual Report of the Women's Foreign Missionary Society of the Presbyterian Church of Canada* (Toronto: n.p., 1895), 22.

55 Baird, *Indians of Western Canada*, 28.
56 *Eighth Annual Report of the Women's Foreign Missionary Society of the Presbyterian Church of Canada* (Toronto: n.p., 1884), 3–4.
57 J.R. Miller, *Shingwauk's Vision: A History of Native Residential Schools* (Toronto: University of Toronto Press, 1996), 87–8.
58 The phrase "every lost woman" is quoted in Creighton, "Creighton, Eliza Jane (Harvie)," *Dictionary of Canadian Biography*. See John R. Graham, "The Haven, 1878–1930: A Toronto Charity's Transition from a Religious to a Professional Ethos," *Histoire sociale/Social History* 25, no. 50 (November 1992): 283–306.
59 Donald Creighton, *Canada's First Century* (Toronto: Oxford University Press, 2012), 162; Mackenzie King, Mackenzie King's Diaries, 8 February 1894. For two very different interpretations of King's early association with prostitutes see C.P. Stacey, *A Very Double Life: The Private World of Mackenzie King* (Toronto: Macmillan, 1976), and Michael Bliss, *Right Honourable Men: The Descent of Canadian Politics from Macdonald to Mulroney* (Toronto: HarperCollins, 1994).
60 Mackenzie King's Diaries, 11 October 1894; 19 October 1894; 20 October 1894. See also John Graham, "William Lyon Mackenzie King, Elizabeth Harvie, and Edna: A Prostitute Rescuing Initiative in Late Victorian Toronto," *Canadian Journal of Human Sexuality* 81, no. 1 (Spring 1999): 47–60.
61 See Margaret Banks, "Marriage with a Deceased Wife's Sister – Law and Practice in Upper Canada," *Western Ontario Historical Notes* 25, no. 2 (Spring 1970): 1–6. Passed in England in 1835, Lord Lyndhurst's Act banned marriages within prohibited degrees of consanguinity and affinity, including marriage between a man and his deceased wife's sister.
62 Philip Creighton's interview with Isabel Wilson, 12 February 1978. Copy in author's possession.
63 Creighton, *Canada's First Century*, 6.
64 Gordon Darroch, "Scanty Fortunes and Rural Middle-Class Formation in Nineteenth-Century Central Ontario," *Canadian Historical Review* 79, no. 4 (December 1998): 629.
65 1861 Agricultural Census of Canada West: Middlesex County, North Dorchester Township, 55.
66 1871 Census of Ontario, Canada, Schedule 3, 17.
67 *History of Middlesex County*, 15.
68 Louise Gillies to Donald Creighton, 27 October 1952, LAC, MG 31 D 77, vol. 6, file Correspondence John A. Macdonald: The Young Politician.
69 W.B. Creighton, *Round 'bout Sun-Up: Some Memories That Live* (Toronto: Ryerson Press, 1946), 6, 9, 8, 25, 7.
70 See Wilson, *Tenants in Time*; Darroch, "Scanty Fortunes," 623.
71 Darroch, "Scanty Fortunes," 641. In one respect, however, the Creightons did not fit the pattern of middle-class formation in central Ontario. Although fertility rates declined rapidly beginning around 1840, they had sixteen children.

72 Philip Creighton's interview with Isabel Wilson, 12 February 1978. Copy in author's possession.

73 Philip Creighton's interview with Isabel Wilson, 12 February 1978. Copy in author's possession.

74 Ibid.

75 W.B. Creighton, *Round 'bout Sun-Up*, 48.

76 Ibid., 53. On the occasion of his retirement in 1936 a number of tributes were published in *The New Outlook*, the newspaper of the United Church of Canada. James Endicott referred to his old friend as a "veritable bookworm. He loves books. He loves to look at them and to handle them." James Endicott, "William Black Creighton: The Man," *New Outlook*, 6 January 1937, 7.

77 Gauvreau, *Evangelical Century*, 49–50.

78 William Creighton, "Memories of Half a Century," *United Church Record*, February 1937, 6.

79 Neil Semple, *Faithful Intellect: Samuel S. Nelles and Victoria University* (Montreal and Kingston: McGill-Queen's University Press, 2005), xiv, 121.

80 Creighton, "Memories of Half a Century," 6.

81 Philip Creighton's interview with Isabel Wilson, 12 February 1978. Copy in author's possession.

82 Endicott, "William Black Creighton: The Man," 7.

83 Philip Creighton's interview with Isabel Wilson, 12 February 1978. Copy in author's possession.

84 Isabel Wilson, untitled six-page memoir of her childhood. Original in Ramsay Derry's possession.

85 Philip Creighton's interview with Isabel Wilson, 12 February 1978. Copy in author's possession.

86 Ibid.

87 The figures are taken from *The Fifty-Ninth Report of the Upper Canada Bible Society* (Toronto: n.p., 1899), 6, and *The Sixtieth Report of the Upper Canada Bible Society* (Toronto: n.p., 1900), 6.

88 *The Fifty-Ninth Report of the Upper Canada Bible Society*, 4.

89 Donald Creighton, "My Father and the United Church," in Donald Creighton, *The Passionate Observer: Selected Writings* (Toronto: McClelland and Stewart, 1980), 94.

90 See William Black Creighton, Diary of Trip to Revelstoke, British Columbia, 1899. Original in possession of Philip Creighton.

91 William Creighton, "Thirty Years as an Editor," n.d. Original in possession of Cynthia Flood. "Rev. William Black Creighton," *United Church Observer*, n.d. Copy in United Church Archives, Vertical File Collection, W.B. Creighton.

92 See Lizzie Harvie to John Harvie, 22 November 1880. Original in possession of Philip Creighton.

93 W.B. Creighton, *Round 'bout Sun-Up*, 4, 6.

94 In his classic study of the Irish in Ontario, Donald Akenson observed "a sharp decline in ethnic affinities among the first generation born in Canada." Akenson, *The Irish in Ontario*, 339.
95 W.B. Creighton, *Round 'bout Sun-Up*, 6.
96 Creighton, *Canada's First Century*, 7.
97 See Carl Berger, *The Sense of Power: Studies in the Ideas of Canadian Imperialism, 1867–1914* (Toronto: University of Toronto Press, 1970).
98 Ibid., 5.
99 George Taylor Denison. See George P. de T. Glazebrook, *The Story of Toronto* (Toronto: University of Toronto Press, 1971), 183.
100 C.S. Clark, *Of Toronto the Good: A Social Study* (Montreal: Toronto Publishing Co., 1898), 76.
101 Quotation in Glazebrook, *Story of Toronto*, 185.

2 Childhood and Adolescence

1 "Out of the turmoil comes a new awareness of ourselves: Donald Creighton Interviewed by Allan Anderson," *University of Toronto Graduate* (June 1968): 43.
2 Isabel Wilson, untitled six-page memoir of her childhood. Original in Ramsay Derry's possession.
3 Donald Creighton, "My Father and the United Church," in Donald Creighton, *The Passionate Observer: Selected Writings* (Toronto: McClelland and Stewart, 1980), 96.
4 Jane Smiley, *Charles Dickens* (New York: Penguin, 2002), 209.
5 Cynthia Flood, "It was her fingers gave the pickles their peculiar green," unpublished manuscript, 1997. Original in possession of Cynthia Flood. Sixty-odd years later, the journalist Heather Robertson was impressed by Creighton's ability to quote long passages from Dickens, Tennyson, Shakespeare, and T.S. Eliot. See Heather Robertson, "The Man Who Invented Canada," *Saturday Night*, October 1977, 20.
6 Northrop Frye, "Conclusion to a *Literary History of Canada*," in Northrop Frye, *The Bush Garden: Essays on the Canadian Imagination* (Toronto: Anansi, 1971), 214.
7 Donald Creighton, "The Future in Canada," in Creighton, *The Passionate Observer*, 23.
8 J.M.S. Careless, *Toronto to 1918* (Toronto: James Lorimer, 1984), 122.
9 Donald Creighton, *Dominion of the North* (Boston: Houghton Mifflin, 1944), 419–20.
10 William Creighton, "Empire and Victoria Day," *Christian Guardian*, 29 May 1907.
11 Philip Creighton's interview with Isabel Wilson, 21 January 1978. Copy in author's possession.

12 Careless, *Toronto to 1918*, 149.
13 William Creighton, "The Problem of Methodism," *Christian Guardian*, 22 May 1907. See Phyllis Airhart, *Serving the Present Age: Revivalism, Progressivism, and the Methodist Tradition in Canada* (Montreal and Kingston: McGill-Queen's University Press, 1992), and Ramsay Cook, *The Regenerators: Social Criticism in Late Victorian English Canada* (Toronto: University of Toronto Press, 1985).
14 Quotation in Neil Sutherland, *Children in English-Canadian Society: Framing the Twentieth-Century Consensus* (Toronto: University of Toronto Press, 1976), 17.
15 See Neil Semple, "'The Nurture and Admonition of the Lord': Nineteenth-Century Canadian Methodism's Response to 'Childhood,'" *Histoire sociale / Social History* 14, no. 27 (1981).
16 "The Decay of Family Discipline," *Christian Guardian*, 13 September 1905.
17 Sutherland, *Children in English-Canadian Society*, 27. See also Cynthia Comacchio, *The Infinite Bonds of Family: Domesticity in Canada, 1850–1940* (Toronto: University of Toronto Press, 1999).
18 "Price of Guardian Increased," *Christian Guardian*, 3 October 1906.
19 Creighton, "My Father and the United Church," 94.
20 "Assist Guardian Editor," *Christian Guardian*, 3 October 1906.
21 "The General Conference – A Sketch," *Acta Victoriana* 30, no. 1 (October 1906): 18.
22 William Creighton, "A Personal Word," *Christian Guardian*, 17 October 1906.
23 Ibid.
24 G.W. Kerby, "The Boy Problem," *Christian Guardian*, 29 April 1903.
25 Patricia Dirks, "'Getting a Grip on Harry': Canada's Methodists Respond to the 'Big Boy' Problem, 1900–1925," *Canadian Methodist Historical Society Papers* 7 (1990): 69–70. See also Patricia Dirks, "Reinventing Christian Masculinity and Fatherhood: The Canadian Protestant Experience, 1900–1920," in Nancy Christie, ed., *Households of Faith: Family, Gender, and Community in Canada, 1760–1969* (Montreal and Kingston: McGill-Queen's University Press, 2002); and Nancy Christie, "Young Men and the Creation of Civic Christianity in Urban Methodist Churches, 1880–1914," *Journal of the Canadian Historical Association* 17, no. 1 (2006): 79–106.
26 William Creighton, "Citizenship and Service," *Christian Guardian*, 24 October 1906.
27 William Creighton, "Tobacco, Pool-Rooms, Profanity, and Boys," *Christian Guardian*, 8 May 1912.
28 William Creighton, "The City and the Children," *Christian Guardian*, 1 January 1907.
29 William Creighton, "The Inside of a Boy," *Christian Guardian*, 27 February 1907.
30 "A Souvenir of Long Branch Summer Resort" (1889): 5, 17, 1, 9. Copy in Toronto Public Library, Long Branch, Local History Collection. The carousel, "with its strange and handsomely caparisoned figures of birds and animals," eventually found a new home in Port Dalhousie, Ontario. To this day, a ride only costs five

cents. My daughters took many rides on that carousel, the very carousel that Donald Creighton surely rode as a child.

31 "Summer Resort," n.d., ca 1886. Copy in Long Branch Public Library, Local History Collection.

32 Philip Creighton's interview with Donald Creighton, 22 January 1978. Copy in author's possession.

33 Ibid.

34 Ibid.

35 Author's interview with Philip Creighton, 30 September 2004.

36 Personal communication with Cynthia Flood, 7 September 2008.

37 G.S. French, "Creighton, William Black," in Nolan B. Harmon, ed., *Encyclopedia of World Methodism* (Nashville: United Methodist Publishing House, 1974), 604.

38 William Creighton, "Can We Be Optimistic?" *Christian Guardian*, 28 June 1911.

39 Isabel Wilson, untitled six-page memoir of her childhood. Original in Ramsay Derry's possession.

40 Personal communication with Cynthia Flood, 19 January 2006.

41 See "Dedicates Building without a Mortgage," Toronto *Globe*, 17 April 1911. William Creighton was a subscription captain, that is, someone responsible for raising money through subscriptions. He raised $5,710. Of the five captains, he raised the most. Today, Howard Park is the Abbey, a twenty-four-unit loft-style condominium where units list for a million dollars.

42 United Church Archives, Accession no. 1977-074L, Howard Park United Church fonds, box 2, file 2, Minutes of the Women's Missionary Society, 21 September 1916.

43 *Happy Days*, 29 December 1906.

44 United Church Archives, Accession no. 1977-074L, Howard Park United Church fonds, box 2, file 4, Minute Book Howard Park Sunday School, 1908–1916. In 1924 Howard Park had the largest Sunday school in Canada: 10,335 Sunday schools were surveyed; Howard Park claimed an enrolment of 1,621 children. See Hugh D. McKellar, *Our Cloud of Witnesses: The Centennial History of Emmanuel-Howard Park United Church* (Toronto: n.p., 1990), 4.

45 United Church Archives, Accession no. 1977-074L, Howard Park United Church fonds, box 1, file 3, Leonard Ball, Superintendent, Secondary Division, Howard Park Sunday School, to Board of Trustees, Howard Park Methodist Church, 11 March 1914.

46 Creighton, *Dominion of the North*, 421.

47 Isabel Wilson, untitled six-page memoir of her childhood. Original in Ramsay Derry's possession.

48 Charles Taylor, *Radical Tories: The Conservative Tradition in Canada* (Toronto: Anansi, 1982), 34.

49 Martin Green, *Dreams of Adventure, Deeds of Empire* (New York: Basic Books, 1979); Patrick Dunae, "Boys' Literature and the Idea of Empire," *Victorian Studies*

(Autumn 1980): 121. See also Kathryn Castle, *Britannia's Children: Reading Colonialism through Children's Books and Magazines* (Manchester and New York: University of Manchester Press, 1996); and Robert H. MacDonald, "Reproducing the Middle-Class Boy: From Purity to Patriotism in the Boy's Magazines, 1892–1914," *Journal of Contemporary History* 24, no. 3 (1989): 519–39.

50 For a history of *Little Folks* see Gretchen R. Galbraith, *Reading Lives: Reconstructing Childhood, Books, and Schools in Britain, 1870–1920* (New York: St Martin's Press, 1997), esp. chapter 4, "Creating a Magazine World."

51 Isabel Wilson, untitled six-page memoir of her childhood. Original in Ramsay Derry's possession.

52 *Little Folks* 80 (1914): 313.

53 *Little Folks* 79 (1914): 79.

54 Ibid., 153.

55 Donald Creighton, "Canadian Nature Journal," August 1914. Original in possession of Philip Creighton.

56 Donald Creighton, "Canadian Nature Journal," n.d, ca fall 1913. Original in possession of Philip Creighton.

57 *Little Folks* 79 (1914): 316.

58 Isabel Wilson, untitled six-page memoir of her childhood. Original in Ramsay Derry's possession.

59 Philip Creighton's interview with Isabel Wilson, 21 January 1978. Copy in author's possession.

60 Donald Creighton, "Canadian Nature Journal," August 1914. Original in possession of Philip Creighton.

61 Philip Creighton's interview with Donald Creighton, 22 January 1978. Copy in author's possession.

62 Creighton, "My Father and the United Church," 97.

63 Creighton, *Dominion of the North*, 443, 444; Donald Creighton, *Harold Adams Innis: Portrait of a Scholar* (Toronto: University of Toronto Press, 1957), 29.

64 Donald Creighton made these comments on a graduate paper written by Michael Bliss. University of Toronto Archives, J. Michael Bliss fonds, B2006-0015, box 19, "Their Ploughshares into Swords: The Methodist Church in World War I," February 1965.

65 William Creighton, *Christian Guardian*, 26 August 1914.

66 William Creighton, "Memories of Half a Century," *United Church Record*, February 1937, 6.

67 William Creighton, *Christian Guardian*, 30 June 1915.

68 William Creighton, *Christian Guardian*, 9 February 1916.

69 Michael Bliss, "The Methodist Church and World War I," *Canadian Historical Review* 49, no. 3 (September 1968): 216–17.

70 Neil Semple, *The Lord's Dominion: The History of Canadian Methodism* (Montreal and Kingston: McGill-Queen's University Press, 1996), 396.

71 For details of Jack Creighton's service, see LAC, RG 150, Accession no. 199293/166, box 2133, file Creighton, John Harvie.
72 Jack Creighton to Isabel Creighton, 14 January 1917. Original in possession of Denis Creighton.
73 LAC, RG 150, Accession no. 199293/166, box 2133, file Creighton, John Harvie.
74 Donald Creighton, *Sir John A. Macdonald: The Young Politician* (Toronto: Macmillan, 1952), 36.
75 Quotation in Roy I. Wolfe, "The Summer Resorts of Ontario in the Nineteenth Century," *Ontario Historical Society* 54, no. 3 (September 1962): 153.
76 E. Herbert Adams, *Toronto and Adjacent Summer Resorts* (Toronto: Frederick Smily, 1894), 8.
77 See Patricia Jasen, *Wild Things: Nature, Culture, and Tourism in Ontario, 1790–1914* (Toronto: University of Toronto Press, 1995).
78 See "Muskoka: The Lake-Land of Ontario" and "God in Nature," *Christian Guardian*, 16 July 1902.
79 Luella Creighton, one-page typed manuscript on the Creightons in Muskoka. Original in possession of Denis Creighton.
80 Ibid.
81 "In the Casualty List," *Christian Guardian*, 21 November 1917.
82 LAC, RG 9, series III, D-3, volume 4924, file 391, part 2, 1917/01/01–1917/12/31, 15th Canadian Infantry Battalion, War Diary, 6 November 1917.
83 Kim Beattie, *48th Highlanders of Canada: 1891–1928* (Toronto: Southam Press, 1932), 278.
84 Ibid., 279–80. See also LAC, RG 9, series III, D-3, volume 4924, file 391, part 2, 1917/01/01–1917/12/31, 15th Canadian Infantry Battalion, War Diary, 9 November 1917.
85 "Toronto Casualties, Morning List," *Toronto Daily Star*, 19 November 1917.
86 "In The Casualty List," *Christian Guardian*, 21 November 1917.
87 Jack Creighton to Isabel Creighton, 24 November 1917. Original in possession of Denis Creighton.
88 LAC, RG 150, Accession no. 1992–93/166, box 2133, file Creighton, John Harvie. Italics mine.
89 Personal communication with Cynthia Flood, 7 September 2008.
90 See C.A.M. Edwards, *Taylor Statten: A Biography* (Toronto: Ryerson Press, 1960).
91 "Can't You Hear Them Calling – Boys?" *Toronto Daily Star*, 15 March 1918.
92 Creighton, "My Father and the United Church," 97. Donald Creighton did not specify when, exactly, he worked as an agricultural labourer. However, I assume it was 1918. In 1917 he was in Muskoka for much of the summer. Nor did he specify if he was, in fact, one of Taylor Statten's Soldiers of the Soil. But given Statten's Methodist background and the support of the Methodist Church for the S.O.S. initiative, it's a reasonable assumption.

93 William Creighton, *Christian Guardian*, 13 November 1918.
94 William Creighton, *Christian Guardian*, 20 February 1924.
95 Creighton, "Memories of Half a Century."
96 Creighton, "My Father and the United Church," 97.
97 Mel Grief, "More Than Just a Building," in Kristina Hidas, ed., *Humberside: The First Century, 1892–1992* (Toronto: n.p., 1992), 3.

3 Vic

1 Quotation in C. Vincent Massey, "Victoria College and the War," in Nathanael Burwash, *The History of Victoria College* (Toronto: Victoria College Press, 1927), 482.
2 See Catherine Gidney, "Dating and Gating: The Moral Regulation of Men and Women at Victoria and University Colleges, University of Toronto, 1920–1960," *Journal of Canadian Studies*, 41, no. 2 (Spring 2007): 138–60; and Catherine Gidney, *The Long Eclipse: The Liberal Protestant Establishment and the Canadian University, 1920–1970* (Montreal and Kingston: McGill-Queen's University Press, 2004).
3 Donald Creighton, "John A. Macdonald, Robert Baldwin, and the University of Toronto," in Donald Creighton, *The Passionate Observer* (Toronto: McClelland and Stewart, 1980), 108. Student dances were not permitted until 1926, the year after Creighton graduated.
4 See Carl Dolmetsch, *The Smart Set: A History and Anthology* (New York: Dial Press, 1966).
5 Isabel Wilson, untitled six-page memoir of her childhood. Original in Ramsay Derry's possession. Author's interview with Cynthia Flood, 3 June 2005.
6 Donald Creighton to Sally Creighton, 25 September 1977. Original in possession of Denis Creighton.
7 Author's interview with Cynthia Flood, 3 June 2005.
8 Ibid.
9 Quotation in Phyllis Airhart, *Serving the Present Age: Revivalism, Progressivism, and the Methodist Tradition in Canada* (Montreal and Kingston: McGill-Queen's, 1992), 84.
10 For example, in his senior year, 1919–20, he received a 35 in first-term algebra; in first- and second-term geometry he failed badly with a 40 and a 17 respectively. I am grateful to Rose Fine, Humberside Collegiate, for this information.
11 Donald Creighton, Student Record Card, Victoria University Archives, Victoria Registrar's Office, fonds 2049, 89.107V, box 3, file 2. Students wrote their examinations under assigned pseudonyms to allow professors to grade them blindly.
12 LAC, MG 31 D 77, Donald Creighton fonds, vol. 28, file General Correspondence 1966, "Donald Grant Creighton: An Autobiographical Sketch." None of his early short stories or novels have survived.

13 Donald Creighton, transcript of TVO interview with Scott Symons, n.d., LAC, R/E 2002-0087, Scott Symons fonds, box 49, Interim box 14, file T.V. Ontario, #5 Creighton.

14 Donald Creighton, "Popular Canadian Fiction," *Acta Victoriana,* 46, no. 6 (June 1922): 268–71. Creighton's essay was similar in content and tone to Douglas Bush, "A Plea for Original Sin," *Canadian Forum* (April 1922). "We are so firmly entrenched behind our rampart of middle-class morality that we are afraid, even in imagination, to look over the top," Bush wrote. "Such an atmosphere, of course, stifles artistic impulse; worse than that, it makes artistic impulse impossible." Had Creighton read Bush's essay and its assertion that "no one reads a Canadian novel unless by mistake"? Probably.

15 Donald Creighton, "Swift on Moralizing," n.d. Original in possession of Cynthia Flood.

16 Donald Creighton, "Romeo and Juliet as Poetry and Drama," n.d. LAC, MG 31 D 77, Donald Creighton fonds, vol. 15, file English Literature Essays.

17 Author's interview with Philip Creighton, 30 September 2004.

18 Donald Creighton, "Newfoundland Verse," *Acta Victoriana,* 48, no. 1 (October 1923): 12–14.

19 See Sandra Campbell, "The Canadian Literary Career of Professor Pelham Edgar" (PhD thesis, University of Ottawa, 1993).

20 Ibid., 204.

21 Donald Creighton, "III English & History," n.d. A paper on Canadian poetry. Original in possession of Cynthia Flood.

22 See Sherwood Anderson, *Winesburg, Ohio* (New York: B.W. Huebsch, 1919).

23 Donald Creighton, "III English & History," n.d. A paper on Canadian poetry. Original in possession of Cynthia Flood.

24 Donald Creighton, "III English & History," n.d. A paper on Jane Austen. Original in possession of Cynthia Flood.

25 Ibid.

26 Campbell, "The Canadian Literary Career of Professor Pelham Edgar," 204.

27 Donald Creighton, "Tendencies in Modern American Poetry," n.d. Original in possession of Cynthia Flood. Defending Walt Whitman against James Harlan, who fired him from his job as a clerk for authoring *Leaves of Grass*, Mencken wrote: "Let us repair once a year, to our accustomed houses of worship and there give thanks to God that one day in 1865 brought together the greatest poet that America has ever produced and the damndest ass." H.L. Mencken, "Three American Immortals," in H.L. Mencken, *Prejudices: A Selection* (Baltimore: Johns Hopkins University Press, 2006), 46.

28 George Wrong, notes prepared at the suggestion of George Smith, 1944, University of Toronto Archives, University of Toronto Press, CHR files, A86-0044, box 5, file CHR, 25th Anniversary Letters, no. 1.

29 Frank Underhill to George Wrong, 2 February 1912, University of Toronto, Thomas Fisher Rare Book Library, MS Coll. 36, Wrong Papers, box 3, file 59; George Wrong to Frank Underhill, 14 March 1912, LAC, MG 30 D 204, Frank Underhill fonds, vol. 2, file G.M. Wrong, 1907–1927.

30 Donald Creighton, "Charles Perry Stacey: Intellectual Independence and the Official Historian," in Creighton, *The Passionate Observer*, 173.

31 "Out of the turmoil comes a new awareness of ourselves: Donald Creighton interviewed by Allan Anderson," *University of Toronto Graduate*, June 1968, 43. George Smith, who had joined the department in 1912, was still in his early thirties. Bart Brebner was just twenty-six when he joined the department in 1920 and Hume Wrong was twenty-seven when he arrived the following year.

32 Campbell, "The Canadian Literary Career of Professor Pelham Edgar," 203–4.

33 Bartlet Brebner to J.M.S. Careless, 21 April 1954, Columbia University Rare Book and Manuscript Library, J. Bartlet Brebner fonds, box 1, file C (1948–1957).

34 Donald Creighton, "A Comparison of Elizabethan and Early Stuart Colonial Policy," n.d. LAC, MG 31 D 77, Donald Creighton fonds, vol. 15, file English Literature Essays.

35 Ibid.

36 Robert Bothwell, *Laying the Foundation: A Century of History at the University of Toronto* (Toronto, 1991), 61; Charles Stacey, *A Date with History* (Ottawa: Deneau, 1982), 14.

37 Donald Creighton, Transcript of TVO interview with Scott Symons, n.d., LAC, R/E 2002–0087, Scott Symons fonds, box 49, Interim box 14, file T.V. Ontario, #5 Creighton.

38 Donald Creighton, "III English & History," n.d. A paper on the Estates General. Original in the possession of Cynthia Flood.

39 Ibid.

40 Ibid.

41 See Russell Kirk, *The Conservative Mind* (London: Faber and Faber, 1954).

42 Donald Creighton, "Editorials," *Acta Victoriana* 49, no. 1 (October 1924): 18.

43 Donald Creighton, "Far Away and Long Ago," *Acta Victoriana* 49, no. 1 (October 1924): 21–4.

44 Douglas Duncan to Norman Endicott, 5 November 1924, Art Gallery of Ontario, E.P. Taylor Research Library and Archives, Douglas Duncan fonds, box 1, file 24.

45 Donald Creighton, "Editorial," *Acta Victoriana* 49, no. 2 (November 1924): 20–1.

46 Glenney F. Bannerman, Letter to the Editor, *Acta Victoriana* 49, no. 4 (January 1925): 21–2.

47 In the Book of Job, Job instructed that "no mention shall be made of coral, or of pearls: for the price of wisdom is above rubies" (Job 28:18). Donald Creighton, "Editorial," *Acta Victoriana* 49, no. 4 (January 1925): 19–20.

48 Creighton, "John A. Macdonald, Robert Baldwin, and the University of Toronto," 108.

49 John Harvie Creighton, "Bargains," *Acta Victoriana* 49, no. 1 (October 1924): 7–12;
Mary Isabel Creighton, "The Victorian Don Quixotes," *Acta Victoriana* 49, no. 2
(November 1924): 16–18; Megalopsychides, "Defence of Intellectual Arrogance,"
Acta Victoriana 49, no. 5 (February 1925): 24.

50 Lester Pearson, "The Cult of Cleverness," *Acta Victoriana* 49, no. 4 (January 1925):
9–13.

51 C.F.C.A., "Non – Sed – ," *Acta Victoriana* 49, 6 (March 1925): 12–14. C.F.C.A. was
actually Lester Pearson. See Douglas Duncan to Norman Endicott, n.d., c. spring
1925, Art Gallery of Ontario, E.P. Taylor Research Library and Archives, Douglas
Duncan fonds, box 1, file 24.

52 "Algy Met the Bear," *Acta Victoriana* 49, no. 6 (March 1925): 21.

53 Norman Endicott to Harold Wilson, 1 March 1925. Original in possession of Philip
Creighton.

54 J.A. Irving, "Editorials," *Acta Victoriana* 50, no. 1 (October 1925): 22–3.

55 Douglas Duncan to Norman Endicott, 24 November 1924, Art Gallery of Ontario,
E.P. Taylor Research Library and Archives, Douglas Duncan fonds, box 1, file 27.
See also Mary Vipond, "Canadian Nationalism and the Plight of Canadian
Magazines in the 1920s," *Canadian Historical Review* 58, no. 1 (1977): 43–63.

56 Douglas Duncan to Norman Endicott, 2 February 1925, Art Gallery of Ontario,
E.P. Taylor Research Library and Archives, Douglas Duncan fonds, box 1, file 27.

57 Lorne Pierce, "The Minister in His Workshop," in Lorne Pierce, *In Conference with
the Best Minds* (Toronto: Ryerson Press, 1927), 232. See Sandra Campbell, *Both
Hands: A Life of Lorne Pierce of Ryerson Press* (Montreal and Kingston: McGill-
Queen's University Press, 2013).

58 "The Will of Cecil Rhodes," in Anthony Kenny, ed., *The History of the Rhodes
Trust, 1902–1999* (Oxford: Oxford University Press, 2001), 571, 573.

59 See Douglas McCalla, "The Rhodes Scholarships in Canada and Newfoundland," in
Kenny ed., *History of the Rhodes Trust*; and David Torrance, "Instructor to Empire:
Canada and the Rhodes Scholarship," in Phillip Buckner and R. Douglas Francis,
eds, *Canada and the British World: Culture, Migration, and Identity* (Vancouver:
UBC Press, 2006).

60 Reverend Richard P. Bowles [to Rhodes Scholarship Committee], 16 October 1924,
Victoria University Archives, fonds 2021, Records of the Victoria University
President's Office, 89.130V, box 13, file 141.

61 Hume Wrong to A.D. Lindsay, 28 December 1924, Balliol College Archives, Student
files, D.G. Creighton.

62 *Acta Victoriana* 49, no. 4 (January 1925): 21.

63 Hume Wrong to A.D. Lindsay, 28 December 1924, Balliol College Archives, Student
files, D.G. Creighton.

64 Ibid., Hume Wrong to Kenneth Bell, 28 December 1924.

65 A.D. Lindsay to Donald Creighton, 5 February 1925. Original in possession of Cynthia Flood.

66 Ramsay Cook, "Kylie, Edward Joseph," *Dictionary of Canadian Biography,* vol. 14.

67 "Eastern Canada Swelters in Tropical Temperatures," *Globe,* 6 June 1925.

68 Douglas Duncan to Norman Endicott, 31 May–7 June 1925, Art Gallery of Ontario, E.P. Taylor Research Library and Archives, Douglas Duncan fonds, box 1, file 27.

69 According to one scholar, puerperal fever was "cruelly democratic": cruel because it meant acute abdominal pain, delirium, and eventual death, and democratic because it claimed the lives of women from all walks and stations. See Gail Pat Parsons, "Puerperal Fever, Anticontagionists, and Miasmatic Infection, 1840–1860: Toward a New History of Puerperal Fever in Antebellum America," *Journal of the History of Medicine and Allied Sciences* 52, no. 4 (1997): 424. Wendy Mitchinson concludes: "Compared with many other Western countries, Canada had a high rate of maternal mortality" in the first half of the twentieth century. Wendy Mitchinson, *Giving Birth in Canada, 1900–1950* (Toronto: University of Toronto Press, 2002), 260.

70 See Carolyn Strange, *Toronto's Girl Problem: The Perils and Pleasures of the City, 1880–1930* (Toronto: University of Toronto Press, 1995); and Ruth Frager and Carmela Patrias, *Discounted Labour: Women Workers in Canada, 1870–1939* (Toronto: University of Toronto Press, 2005).

71 William Lyon Mackenzie King, *Industry and Humanity* (Toronto: University of Toronto Press, 1973), 207–9.

72 University of Waterloo, Doris Lewis Rare Book Room, Luella Creighton fonds, GA 99, series 2, box 1, file 6.

73 Luella Bruce's childhood and adolescence are pieced together from the following sources: Sarah Margaret Bonesteel, "Luella Bruce Creighton: A Writer's Diary" (MA thesis, University of Waterloo, 2001); author's interview with Cynthia Flood, 3 June 2005; and Cynthia Flood, "The Meaning of Marriage," in *My Father Took a Cake to France* (Vancouver: Talon Books, 1992). Her salary figures come from "Memories Recalled by Teachers, Students," *Stouffville Tribune,* 25 June 1986.

74 "Luella S. Bruce," *Torontonensis 1926,* University of Toronto Archives (UTA), University of Toronto Yearbook Collection.

75 "The Monocle," *Acta Victoriana* 49, no. 6 (March 1925): 30.

76 "Locals," *Acta Victoriana* 49, no. 2 (November 1924): 46; and "Locals," *Acta Victoriana* 49, no. 4 (January 1925): 52.

77 See "True, He Was Born a Prince – Better Still, He Proved a Prince," *Globe,* 16 October 1924; and "Prince Is on Time to Gain His Train, but Not Too Early," *Globe,* 17 October 1924.

78 Diary entry, 16 October 1924, University of Waterloo, Doris Lewis Rare Book Room, Luella Creighton fonds, GA 99, series 1, box 1, file 2.

79 "Good Qualities Balance Faults of Modern Girl," n.d., ca 1925 or 1926. A newspaper clipping of an interview with Margaret Addison in Victoria University Archives, Dorothy (Butcher) Bernhardt fonds, accession no. 1999.147v, box 1, scrapbook.

80 Diary entry, 9 October 1924, University of Waterloo, Doris Lewis Rare Book Room, Luella Creighton fonds, GA 99, series 1, box 1, file 2.

81 Luella Bruce, "The Supernatural Element in Poetry," n.d. University of Waterloo, Doris Lewis Rare Book Room, Luella Creighton fonds, GA 99, series 1, box 1, file 1.

82 Luella Creighton, "Prelude," n.d., ca 1968–1970, University of Waterloo, Doris Lewis Rare Book Room, Luella Creighton fonds, GA 99, series 5, box 9, file 86.

83 The details of Donald Creighton's and Luella Bruce's meeting and falling in love come from the following three letters: Donald Creighton to Harold Wilson, 11 December 1925; Donald Creighton to Harold Wilson, 16 December 1925; Donald Creighton to Harold Wilson, 16 January 1926. Originals in possession of Philip Creighton.

4 Oxford and Paris

1 Quotation in Jan Morris, *Oxford* (Oxford: Oxford University Press, 1978), 71.

2 Ibid, 71.

3 Donald Creighton, *John A. Macdonald: The Young Chieftain* (Toronto: Macmillan, 1952), 416–17.

4 Morris, *Oxford*, 5.

5 Donald Creighton to Harold Wilson, 16 January 1926. Original in the possession of Philip Creighton.

6 Eugene Forsey to Florence Forsey, 17 October 1926, LAC, MG 30 A25, Eugene Forsey fonds, vol. 45, file Correspondence, Personal, 1926.

7 Donald Creighton to Harold Wilson, 4 October 1925. Original in the possession of Philip Creighton.

8 Charles Ritchie, *An Appetite for Life: The Education of a Young Diarist, 1924–1927* (Toronto: Macmillan, 1977), 109.

9 Morris, *Oxford*, 138.

10 Quotation in John Jones, *Balliol College: A History* (Oxford: Oxford University Press, 1997), 226.

11 LAC, RG 150, accession no. 1992–93/166, box 6783, file McDougall, Donald James.

12 Donald Creighton to C. Bailey, 11 August 1925, Balliol College Archives, Student files, D.G. Creighton.

13 Eugene Forsey, *A Life on the Fringe* (Toronto: Oxford University Press, 1990), 40.

14 Norman Endicott to Douglas Duncan, 8 November 1926, Art Gallery of Ontario, E.P. Taylor Research Library and Archives, Douglas Duncan fonds, box 2, file 5.

15 Norman Endicott to Douglas Duncan, 8 November 1926, Art Gallery of Ontario, E.P. Taylor Research Library and Archives, Douglas Duncan fonds, box 2, file 5. Gordon Robertson, *Memoirs of A Very Civil Servant: Mackenzie King to Pierre Trudeau* (Toronto: University of Toronto Press, 2000), 19.

16 Raymond Massey, "My Oxford," in Ann Thwaite, ed., *My Oxford* (London: Robson Books, 1977), 40.

17 *Handbook to the University of Oxford* (Oxford: Oxford University Press, 1956), 151; Hugh Whitney Morrison, *Oxford Today and the Canadian Rhodes Scholarships* (Toronto: Gage, 1958), 27; Morris, *Oxford*, 46.

18 Stephen Leacock, *My Discovery of England* (Teddington: Echo Library, 2006; first published 1922), 44.

19 Quotation in W.D. Meikle, "And Gladly Teach: G.M. Wrong and the Department of History at the University of Toronto" (PhD thesis, Michigan State University, 1977), 144.

20 Helen Bott, "The Department of History," *University of Toronto Monthly* 21, no. 8 (May 1921): 354.

21 Norman Sherry, *The Life of Graham Greene*, vol. 1: *1904–1939* (New York: Viking, 1989), 240, 129, 240.

22 Massey, "My Oxford," 42.

23 Forsey, *A Life on the Fringe*, 40.

24 Reba Soffer, "Nation, Duty, Character, and Confidence: History at Oxford, 1850–1914," *Historical Journal* 30, no. 1 (1987): 78–9.

25 See Reba Soffer, *Discipline and Power: The University, History, and the Making of an English Elite, 1870–1930* (Stanford: Stanford University Press, 1994).

26 Kenneth Bell, "History Teaching in Schools," *University of Toronto Monthly* 10, no. 7 (May 1910): 387.

27 Faye Anderson, *An Historian's Life: Max Crawford and the Politics of Academic Freedom* (Melbourne: Melbourne University Press, 2005), 26.

28 Donald Creighton to W.B. Creighton, 22 December 1925. Original in the possession of Philip Creighton.

29 C.G. Stone and F.F. Urquhart reported their comments to K.N. Bell, who, in turn, recorded them in a notebook tracking student progress. N.d., ca Fall 1925, Balliol College Archives, K.N. Bell Papers, box 1, notebook, March 1925.

30 LAC, MG 31 D 77, Donald Creighton fonds, vol. 28, file General Correspondence 1966, "Donald Grant Creighton: An Autobiographical Sketch." On Creighton's use of narrative, see Kenneth Dewar, "Where to Begin and How: Narrative Openings in Donald Creighton's Historiography," *Canadian Historical Review* 72, no. 3 (1991): 348–69.

31 Lawrence Stone, "The Revival of Narrative: Reflections on a New Old History," *Past and Present* 85 (November 1979): 3–4.

32 Edward Gibbon, *The History of the Decline and Fall of the Roman Empire* (London: Chatto and Windus, 1960), 902.

33 LAC, MG 31 D 77, Donald Creighton fonds, vol. 63, file Thomas Babington Macaulay, manuscript, n.d.

34 Thomas Macaulay, "History," in Thomas Macaulay, *The Miscellaneous Writings and Speeches of Lord Macaulay* (London: Longmans, 1873), 155, 157.

35 Peter Gay, *Style in History* (New York: W.W. Norton, 1974), 112–13.

36 LAC, MG 31 D 77, Donald Creighton fonds, vol. 63, file Thomas Babington Macaulay, manuscript, n.d.

37 Quotation in Frederick Brown, *Zola: A Life* (New York: Farrar Straus Giroux, 1995), 190.

38 Philip Walker, "Zola and the Art of Containing the Uncontainable," in Roberts Lethbridge and Terry Keefe, eds, *Zola and the Craft of Fiction* (Leicester: Leicester University Press, 1990), 30.

39 LAC, MG 31 D 77, Donald Creighton fonds, vol. 66, file 4, Diary entry, 12 December 1976.

40 Donald Creighton to W.B. Creighton, 14 February 1926. Original in the possession of Philip Creighton.

41 Donald Creighton to Harold Wilson, 17 November 1925. Original in the possession of Philip Creighton.

42 Donald Creighton to Harold Wilson, 11 December 1925. Original in the possession of Philip Creighton.

43 Ibid.

44 Donald Creighton to W.B. Creighton, 22 December 1925. Original in possession of Philip Creighton.

45 Ibid.

46 See F.W. Beare, "Varsity in Paris," *University of Toronto Monthly*, February 1928.

47 Thomas Fisher Rare Book Library, MS Coll. 324, Robert Finch Papers, box 10, Diary and Journal Extracts, file 3, Diary entry, 31 December 1925. It is not clear why bits and pieces of Douglas Duncan's diary are tucked into Robert Finch's diary.

48 Donald Creighton, "Newfoundland Verse," *Acta Victoriana* 48, no. 1 (October 1923): 12; Heather Robertson, "The Man Who Invented Canada," *Saturday Night*, October 1977, 23.

49 Sherry, *Life of Graham Greene*, 1:119.

50 Ritchie, *Appetite for Life*, 144.

51 On what he called the "the great division" between the Hearties and the Aesthetes at Oxford in the 1920s, see A.J.P. Taylor, *A Personal History* (London: Hamish Hamilton, 1983), 74.

52 See the dinner programs from The Hotbed, 1926–7, in the possession of Cynthia Flood.

53 Author's interview with Carl Berger, 4 May 2006; Robertson, "The Man Who Invented Canada," 23.
54 Donald Creighton to W.B. Creighton, 14 February 1926. Original in the possession of Philip Creighton.
55 University of Waterloo, Doris Lewis Rare Book Room, Luella Creighton fonds, GA 99, series 1, box 1, file 2, Victoria College Graduation Dinner Party, 3 March 1926.
56 Norman Endicott to Harold Wilson, 25 June 1926. Original in possession of Philip Creighton.
57 Donald Creighton to Laura Creighton, 14 November 1926. Original in the possession of Philip Creighton.
58 Donald Creighton to Harold Wilson, 13 July 1926. Original in the possession of Philip Creighton.
59 This quotation comes from Robert Finch's memorial tribute to Donald Creighton. The two men shared many enthusiasms, including French literature. See "Donald Grant Creighton: Tribute to a Scholar," University of Toronto *Bulletin*, 25 February 1980, 4. The lengthy quotation, however, was not included in the printed version. It is contained in the original version in the possession of Ramsay Derry.
60 Donald Creighton, *The Story of Canada* (Toronto: Macmillan, 1959), 11.
61 Luella Creighton, "La Lune de Miel 1926." Original in the possession of Cynthia Flood.
62 Luella Creighton to Harold Wilson, 4 December 1926. Original in the possession of Philip Creighton.
63 Ritchie, *Appetite for Life*, 118.
64 Luella Creighton to Harold Wilson, 4 December 1926. Original in the possession of Philip Creighton.
65 Donald Creighton to Laura Creighton, 14 November 1926. Original in the possession of Philip Creighton.
66 B.H. Sumner reported his comments to K.N. Bell, who, in turn, recorded them in a notebook tracking student progress. N.d., ca Fall 1926, Balliol College Archives, K.N. Bell Papers, box 1, notebook, March 1925.
67 Author's conversation with Ramsay Derry. According to Derry, Creighton liked to talk about Paris and his lost youth. On one occasion, he talked about seeing Luella after a long separation and how they fell into each other's arms in front of the fireplace. Although he didn't say that they made love, the implication was obvious.
68 Donald Creighton to Harold Wilson, 13 July 1926. Original in the possession of Philip Creighton.
69 K.N. Bell, n.d., ca Spring 1927, Balliol College Archives, K.N. Bell Papers, box 1, notebook, March 1925.
70 Donald Creighton to George Smith, n.d., ca March 1927. Original in the possession of Philip Creighton.

71 Frank Underhill to K.N. Bell, 15 April 1927, LAC, MG 30 D 204, Frank Underhill fonds, vol. 1, file K.N. Bell, 1907–27.

72 Ibid., K.N. Bell to Frank Underhill, 7 May 1927.

73 George Smith to Robert Falconer, 1 March 1927; George Smith to Robert Falconer, 16 March 1927, University of Toronto Archives, A67-0007, box 111, file History, Department of.

74 Ibid., George Smith to Robert Falconer, 7 April 1927.

75 Evelyn Waugh, *Brideshead Revisited* (Boston: Little, Brown, 1945), 26.

76 Luella Creighton to Laura Creighton, 14 April 1927. Original in the possession of Philip Creighton.

77 Laura Creighton to Luella Creighton, 7 May 1927. Original in the possession of Cynthia Flood.

78 Luella Creighton to Laura Creighton, 14 April 1927. Original in the possession of Philip Creighton.

79 Lester Pearson, *Mike: The Memoirs of the Rt. Hon. Lester B. Pearson* (Toronto: University of Toronto Press, 1972), 1:49–50.

80 C.P. Champion, "Mike Pearson at Oxford: War, Varsity, and Canadianism," *Canadian Historical Review* 88, no. 2 (June 2007): 285.

81 Ibid.

82 Waugh, *Brideshead Revisited*, 26.

83 Donald Creighton to Laura Creighton, 14 November 1926. Original in the possession of Philip Creighton.

84 R. Douglas Francis, *Frank H. Underhill: Intellectual Provocateur* (Toronto: University of Toronto Press, 1986), 22. See also Champion, "Mike Pearson at Oxford," 276.

85 Vincent Massey, *What's Past Is Prologue* (Toronto: Macmillan, 1963), 26; Lester Pearson, "Oxford – Ancient, Yet Modern," *Christian Guardian*, 16 August 1922; J. Bartlet Brebner, "Oxford, Toronto, Columbia," *Columbia University Quarterly* 23, no. 3 (1931): 234.

86 Champion, "Mike Pearson at Oxford," 277.

87 Eugene Forsey to Florence Forsey, 17 October 1926, LAC, MG 30 A25, Eugene Forsey fonds, vol. 45, file Correspondence, Personal, 1926.

88 Forsey, *A Life on the Fringe*, 44, 48.

89 Brebner, "Oxford, Toronto, Columbia," 234.

90 Donald Creighton to Laura Creighton, 14 November 1926. Original in the possession of Philip Creighton.

91 Creighton, *John A. Macdonald: The Young Chieftain*, 460.

92 Morley Callaghan, *That Summer in Paris: Memories of Tangled Friendships with Hemingway, Fitzgerald, and Some Others* (Toronto: Macmillan, 1963), 115.

93 See the letters of Harcourt Brown to Dorothy Stacey Brown, summer 1928. Originals in the possession of Jennifer Brown, Department of History, University of Winnipeg.

94 See Jacques Godechot, "Mes souvenirs sur Albert Mathiez," *Annales* 31, no. 2 (1959): 97–109. Mathiez wore dark, smoky glasses because he had lost his left eye in a childhood accident.

95 See James Friguglietti, *Albert Mathiez: Historien révolutionnaire* (Paris: Société des Études Robespierristes, 1974), especially chapter 6, "Mathiez à la Sorbonne: la montée au sommet (1924–1928)."

96 W.K. Lamb, "Keeping the Past Up to Date," unpublished manuscript, p. 15, MG 31 D8, W.K. Lamb fonds, vol. 18, file 6.

97 George Iggers, *New Directions in European Historiography* (Middletown, CT: Wesleyan University Press, 1975), 144.

98 Donald Creighton, "Recent Tendencies in French Revolutionary History," n.d., LAC, MG 31 D 77, Donald Creighton fonds, vol. 19, file Recent Tendencies in French Revolutionary History Manuscript. This is the only paper that has survived from Creighton's two years at Oxford.

99 Carl Berger, *The Writing of Canadian History: Aspects of English-Canadian Historical Writing since 1900* (Toronto: University of Toronto Press, 1986), 210.

100 Donald Creighton, "Recent Tendencies in French Revolutionary History."

101 Donald Creighton, Transcript of TVO interview with Scott Symons, n.d., LAC, R/E 2002-0087, Scott Symons fonds, box 49, interim box 14, file T.V. Ontario, #5 Creighton.

102 Harcourt Brown to Dorothy Stacey Brown, 7 July 1928. Original in the possession of Jennifer Brown, Department of History, University of Winnipeg.

103 Ibid.

104 As Florence Bird said, "We were very daring and modern; we went in swimming without suits, men and women." See Molly Ungar, "The Last Ulysseans: Culture and Modernism in Montreal, 1930–1939" (PhD thesis, York University, 2003), 211.

105 See LAC, MG 30, D 163, John Glassco fonds, vol. 1, file Memoirs Chapters II, III and Notes, Manuscript Draft (2 of 2). See also John Glassco, *Memoirs of Montparnasse* (Toronto: Oxford University Press, 1970).

106 Harcourt Brown to Dorothy Stacey Brown, 7 July 1928. Original in the possession of Jennifer Brown, Department of History, University of Winnipeg.

107 For the reference to the deodorant spray, see Ramsay Derry, "Introduction," in Donald Creighton, *The Passionate Observer: Selected Writings* (Toronto: McClelland and Stewart, 1980), x. For Creighton's description of his topic and of his supervisor, see Donald Creighton, Transcript of TVO interview with Scott Symons, n.d., LAC, R/E 2002-0087, Scott Symons fonds, box 49, interim box 14, file T.V. Ontario, #5 Creighton.

108 Donald Creighton, Transcript of TVO interview with Scott Symons, n.d., LAC, R/E 2002-0087, Scott Symons fonds, box 49, interim box 14, file T.V. Ontario, #5 Creighton.

5 Historian

1 Charles Taylor, *Radical Tories: The Conservative Tradition in Canada* (Toronto: Anansi, 1982), 32.

2 Laura Harvie Creighton to Isabel Creighton, 21 May 1929. Original in possession of Philip Creighton.

3 Luella Creighton to Isabel Creighton, 22 May 1929. Original in possession of Philip Creighton. See also Marie Stopes, *Radiant Motherhood* (London: G.P. Putnam, 1920), 232. Actually, although Stopes referred to the full torture of childbirth, she also said that there was nothing to indicate that a woman who delivered by C-section could not love her child as much as as a woman who delivered vaginally.

4 Laura Harvie Creighton to Isabel Creighton, 1 June 1929. Original in possession of Philip Creighton.

5 Luella Creighton to Isabel Creighton, 22 May 1929. Original in possession of Philip Creighton.

6 Laura Harvie Creighton to Isabel Creighton, 26 June 1929. Original in possession of Philip Creighton.

7 Isabel Creighton to Harold Wilson, n.d., ca March 1930. Original in possession of Philip Creighton.

8 Luella Creighton to Harold Wilson, 26 March 1930. Original in possession of Philip Creighton. Sarah Bonesteel, "Luella Bruce Creighton: A Writer's Diary" (MA thesis, University of Waterloo, 2001), 42.

9 Arthur Lower to George Glazebrook, 26 February 1938, Queen's University Archives (QUA), Arthur Lower fonds, Collection 5072, box 1, file A10. See M. Brook Taylor, *Promoters, Patriots, and Partisans: Historiography in Nineteenth-Century English Canada* (Toronto: University of Toronto Press, 1989); and Carl Berger, *The Writing of Canadian History: Aspects of English-Canadian Historical Writing 1900–1970* (Toronto: University of Toronto Press, 1976).

10 Donald Wright, *The Professionalization of History in English Canada* (Toronto: University of Toronto Press, 2005); A.L. Burt to Dorothy Burt, 13 July 1926, LAC, MG 30 D 103, A.L. Burt fonds, vol.1, file 1.

11 Taylor, *Radical Tories*, 28.

12 Donald Creighton to Harold Wilson, 20 June 1930. Original in possession of Philip Creighton.

13 Ramsay Cook, "An Interview with Donald Creighton," in Eleanor Cook, ed., *The Craft of History* (Toronto: CBC, 1973), 133.

14 Taylor, *Radical Tories*, 29.
15 W.L. Morton, "Clio in Canada: The Interpretation of Canadian History," reprinted in Carl Berger, ed., *Approaches to Canadian History* (Toronto: University of Toronto Press, 1967); Gary S. Dunbar, "Harold Innis and Canadian Geography," *Canadian Geographer* 29, no. 2 (1985): 160.
16 Donald Creighton, *Harold Adams Innis: Portrait of a Scholar* (Toronto: University of Toronto Press, 1957), 67.
17 Harold Innis, *The Fur Trade in Canada* (New Haven, CT: Yale University Press, 1930), 391.
18 On the origins of the staples thesis see Berger, *The Writing of Canadian History*.
19 Bartlet Brebner, "Harold Adams Innis as Historian," *Annual Report of the Canadian Historical Association* (1953): 17.
20 Innis, *Fur Trade in Canada*, 393; Donald Creighton, Review of *The Fur Trade in Canada*, *New Outlook*, 8 April 1931.
21 Marion Newbigin, *Canada: The Great River, the Lands, and the Men* (London: Christophers, 1927), 6, 288; Brebner, "Harold Adams Innis as Historian," 17–18; and Donald Creighton to Gary S. Dunbar, 6 July 1979. Original in possession of Gary Dunbar.
22 George Brown, "The St. Lawrence as a Factor in International Trade and Politics, 1783–1854" (PhD thesis, University of Chicago, 1924), 1. Brown also cited the river's importance for getting Canadian staples to their British markets (151). Years later, after Creighton's status as English Canada's leading historian had been conferred, Brown liked to say that Creighton had "stolen" the idea from him (author's interview with Robert Bothwell, 30 September 2005). But if Brown's dissertation and Creighton's book covered similar terrain, they were different in topic, conclusion, and temperament. Brown's thesis was a study in British-Canadian-American relations, not in Canadian commerce and politics or in the ambitions of Montreal's merchant class. And whereas Creighton ended his book in 1849 with the crisis of legitimacy in Lower Canada and the subsequent annexation movement, Brown extended his dissertation to 1854, the Reciprocity Treaty, and the free navigation of the St Lawrence by British and American shipping. He ended, therefore, not on a note of defeat like Creighton but on a note of international cooperation: the annexation crisis of 1849 is overcome, prosperity is enhanced, and the British connection ensured.
23 George Brown, "The St. Lawrence in the Boundary Settlement of 1783," *Canadian Historical Review* 9, no. 3 (1928): 238, 224.
24 Donald Creighton, Review of *Toronto during the French Regime*, *New Outlook*, 14 March 1934.
25 See Donald Creighton, "The Struggle for Financial Control in Lower Canada, 1818–1831," *Canadian Historical Review* 12, no. 2 (June 1931): 120–44; Donald

Creighton, "The Commercial Class in Canadian Politics, 1792–1840," *Papers and Proceedings of the Canadian Political Science Association* 5 (May 1933): 43–58.

26 See LAC, MG 31 D 77, Donald Creighton fonds, vols 12, 13, and 14.

27 Donald Creighton, *Towards the Discovery of Canada* (Toronto: Macmillan, 1972), 2.

28 "Memorandum for Dr. Crane on Canadian-American Relations," 8 April 1932, Columbia University Rare Book and Manuscript Library (CURBML), James Shotwell fonds, box 286, file Can-American Relations, H.A. Innis.

29 Donald Creighton, *Harold Adams Innis: Portrait of a Scholar* (Toronto: University of Toronto Press, 1957), 79. See also Wright, *The Professionalization of History in English Canada*, 121–46.

30 Harold Innis to James Shotwell, 11 August 1932, CURBML, James Shotwell fonds, box 286, file Can-American Relations, H.A. Innis.

31 See Innis's remarks in "Canadian-American Relations Conference on Research," 12 November 1933, CURBML, Carnegie Endowment fonds, box 525.

32 Harold Innis to James Shotwell, 15 November 1933, CURBML, James Shotwell fonds, box 286, file Can-American Relations, H.A. Innis.

33 J. Bartlet Brebner, "Memorandum on the Innis Budget," 23 January 1934, ibid., box 284, file Can-American Relations, J.B. Brebner.

34 James Shotwell to Donald Creighton, 25 April 1934, ibid., box 285, file Can-American Relations, D.G. Creighton.

35 Donald Creighton to James Shotwell, 8 May 1934, ibid.

36 Donald Creighton to James Shotwell, 6 June 1934, ibid.

37 Quotation in Bonesteel, "Luella Bruce Creighton: A Writer's Diary," 13. See Luella Creighton, "Prelude," University of Waterloo, Doris Lewis Rare Book Room, Luella Creighton fonds, GA 99, series 5, box 9, files 86–7.

38 Virginia Woolf, "Professions for Women," in Virginia Woolf, *Selected Essays* (Oxford: Oxford University Press, 2008), 140–5.

39 Luella Creighton, "The Observations of Gutrik the Gargoyle," *New Outlook*, 27 November 1929; Luella Creighton, "The Blue Rabbit," *New Outlook*, 23 March 1932; Luella Creighton, "The Coming of Spuddie," *New Outlook*, 13 June 1934.

40 Luella Creighton, "Miss Kidd," in Bertram Brooker, ed., *Yearbook of the Arts in Canada* (Toronto: Macmillan, 1936), 137–47. The story was first published in the *Canadian Forum*.

41 Luella Creighton, "The Cornfield," *Canadian Forum* (June 1937): 97–9.

42 Earle Birney, *Canadian Forum* (June 1937): 97.

43 See Sally Murphy, "Mr. Justice Denis Murphy," *UBC Alumni Chronicle* (Spring 1928): 16–17, 27.

44 Luella Creighton to Harold Wilson, n.d., ca April 1927. Original in possession of Philip Creighton.

45 Luella Creighton to Laura Creighton, 14 April 1927. Original in possession of Philip Creighton.

46 Author's interview with Cynthia Flood, 6 June 2005.

47 See Sally Creighton, "Some Feminine Followers of a Great Tradition," *New Outlook*, 30 November 1932.

48 Isabel Creighton to Harold Wilson, 27 July 1933. Original in possession of Philip Creighton.

49 Isabel Creighton to Harold Wilson, 27 July 1933. Original in possession of Philip Creighton. Author's interview with Denis Creighton, 6 June 2005.

50 See Mary Quayle Innis, Diary 1931, UTA, B91-0029, Harold Innis Family fonds, box 57, file 5.

51 Author's interview with Anne Innis Daag, 14 January 2005, and author's interview with Mary Innis Cates Rutledge, 22 January 2005.

52 James Shotwell to Harold Innis, 29 April 1937, LAC, MG 31 D 77, Donald Creighton fonds, vol. 14, file The Commercial Empire of the St. Lawrence and The Empire of the St. Lawrence 1937–1956, correspondence, clippings of book reviews.

53 For a wonderful discussion of the tension in the historical profession over who, exactly, historians should write for, for each other or the general reader, see Ian Hesketh, "Writing History in Macaulay's Shadow: J.R. Seeley, E.A. Freeman, and the Audience for Scientific History in Late Victorian Britain," *Journal of the Canadian Historical Association* 22, no. 2 (2011): 30–56.

54 Jean Jules Jusserand et al., *The Writing of History* (New York: Charles Scribner's Sons, 1926); W.S. Wallace, "Some Vices of Clio," *Canadian Historical Review* 7, no. 2 (1926).

55 Bartlet Brebner to Donald Creighton, 15 August 1937, LAC, MG 31 D 77, Donald Creighton fonds, vol. 14, file The Commercial Empire of the St. Lawrence and The Empire of the St. Lawrence 1937–1956, correspondence, clippings of book reviews.

56 See Status Report, "The Relations of Canada and the United States," 17 August 1937, CURBML, J. Bartlet Brebner fonds, box 10, file August 1937–August 1940.

57 My reading of *The Empire of the St. Lawrence* has been influenced by Berger, *The Writing of Canadian History*, 210–17, and by David Tough, "An Agreeable Landscape Filled with Uncertainties: Imagination, Sympathy, and Authority in Donald Creighton's Historical Prose" (unpublished graduate research paper, Carleton University, 2006).

58 Ramsay Cook, "An Interview with Donald Creighton," 134.

59 Gerald Craig, ed., *Lord Durham's Report* (Montreal and Kingston: McGill-Queen's University Press, 2007), 55.

60 Donald Creighton, *The Empire of the St. Lawrence* (Toronto: University of Toronto Press, 2002), 22, 87, 202, 370, 382.

61 On the annexation movement, see S.F. Wise, *God's Peculiar Peoples: Essays on Political Culture in Nineteenth-Century Canada* (Ottawa: Carleton University Press, 1993), 115–47.

62 Christopher Moore, "A River with Attitude: *The Empire of the St. Lawrence*, Donald Creighton, and the History of Canada," in Creighton, *The Empire of the St. Lawrence*, x.

63 Ramsay Cook, ed., *The Voyages of Jacques Cartier* (Toronto: University of Toronto Press, 1993), 38, 110.

64 Creighton, *The Empire of the St. Lawrence*, 4–7.

65 Donald Creighton, "The Colony of Great Britain and the United States," LAC, MG 31 D 77, Donald Creighton fonds, vol. 14, file The Colony of Great Britain and the United States 1932. Donald's brother, Jack, took the manuscript to Sam Gundy, the head of Oxford University Press. Although he didn't want to publish it, he was impressed with the author's verbal dexterity. "I once saw a juggler keeping sixteen glass balls in the air all at one time. It was wonderful, and he knew it." Sam Gundy to John Creighton, 19 January 1932. The paper was never published.

66 See Damien-Claude Bélanger, *Pride and Prejudice: Canadian Intellectuals Confront the United States, 1891–1945* (Toronto: University of Toronto Press, 2011).

67 Creighton, *The Empire of the St. Lawrence*, 70, 357.

68 Cook, "An Interview with Donald Creighton," 134.

69 Simon Schama, *Landscape and Memory* (New York: Alfred A. Knopf, 1995), 363; Herodotus, *The History* (Chicago: University of Chicago Press, 1987), 133.

70 Schama, *Landscape and Memory*, 362; Cook, "An Interview with Donald Creighton," 134.

71 Creighton, *The Empire of the St. Lawrence*, 22, 79.

72 Ibid., 17–18.

73 Taylor, *Radical Tories*, 32.

74 Oswald Spengler, *The Decline of the West* (New York: Knopf, 1926), 1.

75 Creighton, *The Empire of the St. Lawrence*, 7, 384. Creighton also described the river as "fatally defective." Ibid., 71.

76 Taylor, *Radical Tories*, 32.

77 Arthur Lower, review of *The Commercial Empire of the St. Lawrence, Canadian Historical Review* 19 (1938): 209.

78 Taylor, *Radical Tories*, 31.

79 Hayden White, *Metahistory: The Historical Imagination in Nineteenth-Century Europe* (Baltimore: Johns Hopkins University Press, 1973), 9. For a detailed analysis of Creighton's narrative structure, see Kenneth C. Dewar, "Where to Begin and How: Narrative Openings in Donald Creighton's Historiography," *Canadian Historical Review* 72, no. 3 (1991): 348–69.

80 Creighton, *The Empire of the St. Lawrence*, 378, 383.

81 Herbert Heaton, review of *The Commercial Empire of the St. Lawrence, Canadian Journal of Economics and Political Science* 4 (1938): 570; Charles Stacey, review of *The Commercial Empire of the St. Lawrence, Canadian Forum* 18 (1938): 57; Daniel Harvey, review of *The Commercial Empire of the St. Lawrence, Dalhousie Review* 18 (1938): 120; Gilbert Tucker, review of *The Commercial Empire of the St. Lawrence, American Historical Review* 44, no. 4 (1939): 891.

82 Fred Landon to Donald Creighton, 31 January 1938, LAC, MG 31 D 77, Donald Creighton fonds, vol. 14, file The Commercial Empire of the St. Lawrence and The Empire of the St. Lawrence; J.J. Talman to Donald Creighton, 29 April 1938, ibid.; S.D. Clark to Donald Creighton, 17 February 1938, ibid.; A.L. Burt to Donald Creighton, 26 February 1938, ibid.

83 Luella Creighton, Diary entry, 10 November 1938. Original in possession of Cynthia Flood.

84 Charles Stacey, review of *The Commercial Empire of the St. Lawrence, Canadian Forum* 18 (1938): 58; Gilbert Tucker, review of *The Commercial Empire of the St. Lawrence, American Historical Review* 44, no. 4 (1939): 892.

85 Creighton, *The Empire of the St. Lawrence*, 6, 21.

86 Craig, ed., *Lord Durham's Report*, 33, 18, 16, 21; Creighton, *The Empire of the St. Lawrence*, 127, 39, 51, 126, 154, 328, 111, 115, 127, 272.

87 Creighton, "The Struggle for Financial Control in Lower Canada," 121. This theme would be repeated in his next article. See Creighton, "The Commercial Class in Canadian Politics, 1792–1840."

88 Ralph Heintzman, "Political Space and Economic Space: Quebec and the Empire of the St. Lawrence," *Journal of Canadian Studies* 29, no. 2 (1994): 19.

89 Bélanger, *Pride and Prejudice*, 138.

90 Morton, "Clio in Canada," 46–7. Writing some four decades after Morton, another western Canadian academic cut to the chase. The Laurentian thesis, Barry Cooper said, is "patent nonsense." Barry Cooper, "Western Political Consciousness," in Stephen Brooks, ed., *Political Thought in Canada* (Toronto: Irwin, 1984), 215. Lewis G. Thomas believed that Donald Creighton only understood the west as a colony of central Canada, as something to be acquired and exploited. See Ruth Sandwell, Interview with Lewis G. Thomas, 12 May 1999, UBC Archives, Margaret Ormsby Oral History Collection. In his defence, Creighton never said that his book could explain western Canada. Indeed, he freely acknowledged its limitations. "*The Commercial Empire of the St. Lawrence,*" he said, "is intended to serve as an introduction to a theme of enduring significance in Canadian development. It is not meant to provide a final and self-sufficient interpretation of Canadian history." Creighton, *The Empire of the St. Lawrence*, xx.

91 See Fernand Ouellet, *Economic and Social History of Quebec, 1760–1850: Structures and Conjunctures* (Toronto: Gage, 1980; first published in French in 1966). For an

interesting comparison of Creighton and Ouellet, see Nigel Kent-Barber, "La théorie du commerce principal chez MM. Creighton et Ouellet," *Revue d'histoire de l'Amérique française* 22, no. 3 (1968): 401–14. For his part, Allan Greer agreed with Ouellet, who also happened to be his former professor: "Creightonian ideologies to the contrary, there was nothing very revolutionary, heroic, or even progressive" about the intrusion of mercantile capital into the St Lawrence River Valley. See Allan Greer, *Peasant, Lord, and Merchant: Rural Society in Three Quebec Parishes 1740–1840* (Toronto: University of Toronto Press, 1985), xii–xiii.

92 Arthur Lower, *Colony to Nation* (Toronto: Longmans, 1946), 276; R.T. Naylor, "The Rise and Fall of the Third Commercial Empire of the St. Lawrence," in Gary Teeple, ed., *Capitalism and the National Question in Canada* (Toronto: University of Toronto Press, 1972), 4–5. Bill Eccles to Gary Dunbar, 14 May 1980. Original in possession of Gary Dunbar. Bill Eccles said the same thing about Harold Innis, that he began with an answer and selected evidence accordingly. See W.J. Eccles, "A Belated Review of Harold Adams Innis, *The Fur Trade in Canada*," *Canadian Historical Review* 60, no. 4 (1979): 441. Gerry Tulchinsky, *The River Barons: Montreal Businessmen and the Growth of Industry and Transportation, 1837–1853* (Toronto: University of Toronto Press, 1977), 234. Author's interview with Michael Bliss, 7 March 2006. See also Michael Bliss, *Northern Enterprise: Five Centuries of Canadian Business* (Toronto: McClelland and Stewart, 1987), 119. Most recently, Cole Harris has argued that the importance of commercial capital to British North America has been exaggerated. He emphasized instead the family farm. It constituted "the essential dynamic of land and life in the agricultural countrysides." See Cole Harris, *The Reluctant Land: Society, Space, and Environment in Canada before Confederation* (Toronto: UBC Press, 2008), 458.

93 On the failure of the twentieth century to recognize the river's limits, see Daniel Macfarlane, *To the Heart of the Continent: The Creation of the St. Lawrence Seaway and Power Project* (Vancouver: UBC Press, 2014); and Heather M. Cox, Brendan G. DeMelle, Glenn R. Harris, Christopher P. Lee, and Laura K. Montondo, "Drowning Voices and Drowning Shoreline: A Riverside View of the Social and Ecological Impacts of the St. Lawrence Seaway and Power Project," *Rural History* 10, no. 2 (1999): 235–57.

94 Quotation in Hannah Hoag, "A Slippery Slope," *Globe and Mail*, 31 March 2007.

6 Professor

1 Luella Creighton, Diary 1938–1939. Original in possession of Cynthia Flood.

2 *Stouffville Tribune*, 6 May 1937, 5; author's interview with Philip Creighton, 30 September 2004; author's interview with Cynthia Flood, 3 June 2005.

3 Donald Creighton, *John A. Macdonald: The Old Chieftain* (Toronto: Macmillan, 1955), 10.

4 Mackenzie King's Diaries, 21 July 1937; *Report of the Royal Commission on Dominion-Provincial Relations*, Book I (Ottawa: King's Printer, 1940), 9.
5 See Michiel Horn, "Academics and Canadian Social and Economic Policy in the Depression and War Years," *Journal of Canadian Studies* 13, no. 4 (1978–9): 3–10.
6 Donald Creighton, *British North America at Confederation* (Ottawa: King's Printer 1939), 14, 10.
7 Ibid., 48–9, 60.
8 See Paul Romney, *Getting It Wrong: How Canadians Forgot Their Past and Imperiled Confederation* (Toronto: University of Toronto Press, 1999), 161–80.
9 Doug Owram, *The Government Generation: Canadian Intellectuals and the State* (Toronto: University of Toronto Press, 1986), 233.
10 See Corey Slumkoski, "'... a fair show and a square deal': New Brunswick and the Renegotiation of Canadian Federalism," *Journal of New Brunswick Studies* 1, no. 1 (2010).
11 E.R. Forbes, "The 1930s: Depression and Retrenchment," in E.R. Forbes and Del Muise, eds, *The Atlantic Provinces in Confederation* (Toronto: University of Toronto Press, 1993), 302.
12 Mackenzie King's Diaries, 11 December 1935.
13 Alexander P. Patterson, *The True Story of Confederation* (Fredericton: Government of New Brunswick, 1926), 18. See also Kenneth Hector LeBlanc, "A.P. Patterson and New Brunswick's Response to Constitutional Change, 1935–1939" (MA report, University of New Brunswick, 1989).
14 See E.R. Forbes, *The Maritime Rights Movement, 1919–1927: A Study in Canadian Regionalism* (Montreal and Kingston: McGill-Queen's University Press, 1979).
15 *Submission by the Government of the Province of New Brunswick to the Royal Commission on Dominion-Provincial Relations* (April 1938), 113, 118. For a rebuttal of the New Brunswick submission, see J.R. Mallory, "The Compact Theory of Confederation," *Dalhousie Review* 21 (1941): 342–51.
16 Royal Commission on Dominion-Provincial Relations Transcripts of Public Hearings, 1937–1938 (24 November 1938), 10 118.
17 *Supplementary Submission by the Government of the Province of New Brunswick to the Royal Commission on Dominion-Provincial Relations* (November 1938), 26.
18 W.P. Jones, "Confidential Submission by the Province of New Brunswick in Respect of Research Studies Made for the Commission by Professor Creighton and Others," November 1938, Provincial Archives of New Brunswick, Records of the Office of Premier J.B. McNair, RS 414, box 3, file C6b2. For the reference to "sovereign nations," see *Submission by the Government of the Province of New Brunswick to the Royal Commission on Dominion-Provincial Relations* (April 1938), 101.
19 In her diary, Luella wrote: "Don gone to Ottawa to defend his Commission effort against the protests of the lads from New Brunswick." Diary 23 November 1938. Original in possession of Cynthia Flood.

20 Creighton, *British North America at Confederation*, 44.
21 Alex Skelton to Donald Creighton, 10 August 1939, LAC, MG 31 D 77, Donald Creighton fonds, vol. 7, file Correspondence Royal Commission 1937/40. For example, Creighton cited an article by V. Evan Gray, a constitutional lawyer from Ontario who argued that, in fact, the Judicial Committee of the Privy Council had not erred in its decisions. Gray's article represented the only challenge to centralist orthodoxy in the 1930s and 1940s. See Creighton, *British North America at Confederation*, 58. See also V. Evan Gray, "The O'Connor Report on the British North America Act, 1867," *Canadian Bar Review* 17 (May 1939).
22 Creighton, *British North America at Confederation*, 49; Donald Creighton to Joseph Sirois, 31 October 1939, LAC, MG 31 D 77, Donald Creighton fonds, vol. 7, file Correspondence Royal Commission 1937/40.
23 In Book II, the commission addressed the question of Resolution 66 in considerable detail before concluding as follows: "We are thus unable to accept the contention of New Brunswick that Resolution 66 of the London Conference constituted in any sense a contract or agreement with the Maritime Provinces; or that the term 'improvements' used therein implied the means of forcing trade through Maritime ports as New Brunswick contends; or that the term 'seaboard' meant only the seacoast of the Maritime Provinces. But we have examined the submissions of New Brunswick carefully and, we trust, with detachment, in the hope that a complete review may not merely show why we are unable to recommend that this claim be allowed, but may also serve to remove a sense of grievance which has been long standing." *Report of the Royal Commission on Dominion-Provincial Relations, Book II: Recommendations* (Ottawa: King's Printer, 1940), 253.
24 See *Report of the Royal Commission on Dominion-Provincial Relations, Book I* (Ottawa: King's Printer, 1940), 19–46.
25 Romney, *Getting It Wrong*, 170.
26 *Report of the Royal Commission on Dominion-Provincial Relations, Book II* (Ottawa: King's Printer, 1940), 10. As Donald Smiley rightly argued over fifty years ago, the report respected provincial autonomy. See D.V. Smiley, "The Rowell-Sirois Report, Provincial Autonomy, and Post-War Canadian Federalism," *Canadian Journal of Political Science* 28, no. 1 (February 1962).
27 John W. Dafoe to Alex Skelton, 15 December 1938, LAC, MG 30 D 45, John Wesley Dafoe fonds, reel M-78.
28 John W. Dafoe to Alex Skelton, 30 December 1938, ibid. Barry Ferguson and Robert Wardhaugh, "Impossible Conditions of Inequality: John W. Dafoe, the Rowell-Sirois Royal Commission, and the Interpretation of Canadian Federalism," *Canadian Historical Review* 84, no. 4 (2003): 569. Ferguson and Wardhaugh have provided a sophisticated reading of the Rowell-Sirois Commission and, in the process, have shifted our understanding of the commission: it advocated a model of

classical federalism in which the two orders of government are sovereign in their spheres of jurisdiction. On the classical federalism inherent in the Rowell-Sirois Commission, see also T. Stephen Henderson, *Angus L. Macdonald: A Provincial Liberal* (Toronto: University of Toronto Press, 2007), and D.V. Smiley, "The Rowell-Sirois Report, Provincial Autonomy, and Post-War Canadian Federalism," *Canadian Journal of Economics and Political Science*, 28, no. 1 (1962).

29 John W. Dafoe to Alex Skelton, 24 July 1939, LAC, MG 30 D 45, John Wesley Dafoe fonds, reel M-78.

30 Creighton, *British North America at Confederation*, 80.

31 Luella Creighton, Diary entries, 21 October 1938, 29 November 1938, 30 November 1938. Original in possession of Cynthia Flood.

32 Ibid., no date, ca spring 1939.

33 Ibid., 3 July 1939, 5 July 1939.

34 Ibid., 11 April 1939.

35 *Globe and Mail*, 23 May 1939, 1.

36 Luella Creighton, Diary entry, 25 May 1939. Original in possession of Cynthia Flood.

37 Donald Creighton, "Reminiscences of a Historian," n.d., ca 1970s. Original in possession of Ramsay Derry.

38 Desmond Morton, *Fight or Pay: Soldiers' Families in the Great War* (Vancouver: UBC Press, 2004), 240.

39 Donald Creighton, *Harold Adams Innis: Portrait of a Scholar* (Toronto: University of Toronto Press, 1957), 95.

40 Author's interview with Cynthia Flood, 3 June 2005.

41 Creighton, *Harold Adams Innis*, 106. See also Alexander John Watson, *Marginal Man: The Dark Vision of Harold Innis* (Toronto: University of Toronto Press, 2006), 225–34.

42 Henry Allen Moe to Donald Creighton, 9 August 1939, LAC, MG 31 D 77, Donald Creighton fonds, vol. 5, file Correspondence, Guggenheim Fellowship, 1939–1941.

43 Chester Martin to John Simon Guggenheim Memorial Foundation, 16 January 1940; James Shotwell to John Simon Guggenheim Memorial Foundation, 8 February 1940; Robert MacKay to John Simon Guggenheim Memorial Foundation, 1 December 1939. I would like to thank the John Simon Guggenheim Memorial Foundation for making available to me a copy of Donald Creighton's file. All reasonable efforts were taken to contact the estates of Chester Martin, James Shotwell, and Robert MacKay for permission to quote from their letters of recommendation.

44 "Previous Research, Plans for Work," n.d., ca October 1939, ibid.

45 Author's interview with Ramsay Cook, 3 December 2004.

46 Author's interview with Peter Waite, 6 November 2002.

47 John Ayre, *Northrop Frye: A Biography* (Toronto: Random House, 1989), 65.

48 See "Donald Grant Creighton: Tribute to a Scholar," University of Toronto *Bulletin* (25 February 1980): 3.
49 Author's interview with Norman Shefffe, 7 April 2005.
50 Donald Creighton, "Conservatism and National Unity," in Ralph Flenley, ed., *Essays in Canadian History* (Toronto: Macmillan, 1939), 160.
51 Molly Ungar, "When the King and Queen of Canada Came to America: The Royal Visit of 1939," unpublished paper, Association of Canadian Studies in the United States, November 2009.
52 Luella Creighton, Diary entry, 3 February 1939. Original in possession of Cynthia Flood; Henry Allen Moe to Donald Creighton, 27 March 1940, LAC, MG 31 D 77, Donald Creighton fonds, vol. 5, file Correspondence, Guggenheim Fellowship, 1939–1941; Jack Creighton to Donald Creighton, n.d., ca April 1940, ibid.
53 Laura Harvie Creighton to Donald Creighton, 20 October 1940, LAC, MG 31 D 77, Donald Creighton fonds, vol. 1, file General Correspondence 1940.
54 Creighton, *Harold Adams Innis*, 72.
55 Author's interview with Philip Creighton, 30 September 2004.
56 Author's interview with Cynthia Flood, 4 June 2005.
57 Donald Creighton to Gerry Riddell, 30 December 1946, UTA, B86-0002, box 1, file Correspondence 1946–47.
58 Donald Creighton, "Reminiscences of a Historian," n.d., ca 1970s. Original in possession of Ramsay Derry.
59 Jack Creighton to Donald Creighton, 5 March 1941. Original in possession of Denis Creighton. In this one part of the letter, Jack was quoting Donald.
60 Donald Creighton, Interview with Larry Zolf, 29 June 1970, LAC, V1 7905-011.
61 Quotation in Robert Bothwell, Ian Drummond, and John English, *Canada 1900–1945* (Toronto: University of Toronto Press, 1987), 274. Actually, the federal government did not need the Rowell-Sirois Report because the war provided all the justification it needed to invade provincial taxation spheres through a series of tax rental agreements wherein the provinces agreed to "rent," or give up, to the federal government the power to levy direct taxes in return for payments back to the provinces.
62 Edgar McInnis to Donald Creighton, 18 January 1941, LAC, MG 31 D 77, Donald Creighton fonds, vol. 1, file General Correspondence 1940. The McInnis letter is misfiled; it should be in the 1941 file. John Deutsch to Donald Creighton, 17 February 1941, ibid., vol. 1, file General Correspondence 1941.
63 For full accounts of the Underhill affair see R. Douglas Francis, *Frank H. Underhill: Intellectual Provocateur* (Toronto: University of Toronto Press, 1986), and Michiel Horn, *Academic Freedom in Canada: A History* (Toronto: University of Toronto Press, 1999).
64 Quotation in Martin Friedland, *The University of Toronto: A History* (Toronto: University of Toronto Press, 2002), 321.

65 Quotation in Francis, *Frank H. Underhill*, 107.
66 "Toronto Professors Censured in Legislature; Hepburn Demands Curbs," *Globe and Mail*, 14 April 1939.
67 Luella Creighton, Diary entry, 13 April 1939. Original in possession of Cynthia Flood.
68 "University Professors Unite in a Protest," *Globe*, 16 January 1931. Incidentally, the *Globe* sided with the Toronto Police Commission: "The police have taken action to protect the community against the invasion of foreign propaganda, openly promoted to supplant Christianity by atheism." The issue of free speech was nothing but a "red herring." See "The Free Speech Herring," *Globe*, 16 January 1931. See also Michiel Horn, "Free Speech within the Law: The Letter of the Sixty-Eight Toronto Professors, 1931," *Ontario History* 72, no. 1 (1980): 27. See also Horn, *Academic Freedom in Canada*.
69 Luella Creighton, Diary entry, 13 April 1939. Original in possession of Cynthia Flood.
70 Frank Underhill to Bartlet Brebner, 14 September 1940 and 18 September 1940, Columbia University Rare Books and Manuscript Library, J. Bartlet Brebner fonds, box 3, file U.
71 Author's interview with Robert Blackburn, 4 November 2005.
72 Donald Creighton, *Dominion of the North* (Toronto: Macmillan, 1957), 511–12; John T. Saywell, *Just Call Me Mitch: The Life of Mitchell F. Hepburn* (Toronto: University of Toronto Press, 1991), 451.
73 Donald Creighton to Frank Underhill, 3 September 1940, LAC, MG 30 D 204, Frank Underhill fonds, vol. 3, file D.G. Creighton, 1928–1956; Donald Creighton to Frank Underhill, 29 September 1940, ibid.
74 Donald Creighton to Frank Underhill, 9 January 1941, ibid.
75 Donald Creighton to Frank Scott, 10 January 1941, LAC, MG 30 D 211, Francis Reginald Scott fonds, vol. 29, file 16.
76 Donald Creighton, "The Ogdensburg Agreement and F.H. Underhill," in Donald Creighton, *The Passionate Observer: Selected Writings* (Toronto: McClelland and Stewart, 1980), 134.
77 Quotation in Francis, *Frank H. Underhill*, 124; Frank Underhill to Arthur Lower, 17 December 1937, Queen's University Archives, Collection 5072, Arthur Lower Papers, box 1, A9. The Young Communist League also believed that Hepburn had authored the plot against Underhill and it interpreted the affair as "a prelude to a general attack on academic freedom." Really, it "heralded fascist regimentation." "Fight Underhill Ouster, Varsity Students Urged by Young Communists," *Globe and Mail*, 10 January 1941.
78 Creighton, "The Ogdensburg Agreement and F.H. Underhill," 139.
79 Horn, *Academic Freedom in Canada*, 164.
80 Frank Underhill to Donald Creighton, 15 January 1941, LAC, MG 31 D 77, Donald Creighton fonds, vol. 1, file General Correspondence 1941.

81 Donald Creighton to Freya Hahn, 8 April 1941. Original in possession of Katharine Hooke.

7 Mid-Career

1 J.B. Brebner, Review of *British North America at Confederation, Canadian Journal of Economics and Political Science* 7, no. 1 (1941): 73; J.B. Brebner to Donald Creighton, 6 September 1940, LAC, MG 31 D 77, Donald Creighton fonds, vol. 1, file General Correspondence 1940.

2 Quotation in Martin Friedland, *The University of Toronto: A History* (Toronto: University of Toronto Press, 2002), 348.

3 Donald Creighton, "Canada in the English-Speaking World," *Canadian Historical Review* 26 (June 1945): 119.

4 William Cobb to Donald Creighton, 21 October 1941, LAC, MG 31 D 77, Donald Creighton fonds, vol. 5, file General Correspondence, Houghton Mifflin, 1944–46, 1951.

5 Donald Creighton, *Towards the Discovery of Canada* (Toronto: Macmillan, 1972), 2.

6 William Cobb to Donald Creighton, 1 November 1941, LAC, MG 31 D 77, Donald Creighton fonds, vol. 5, file General Correspondence, Houghton Mifflin, 1944–46, 1951.

7 Paul Brooks to Donald Creighton, 24 February 1942, ibid.; Paul Brooks to Donald Creighton, 23 July 1943, ibid.

8 Quotation in Donald Creighton, *The Passionate Observer: Selected Writings* (Toronto: McClelland and Stewart, 1980), 199.

9 Donald Creighton to Paul Brooks, 22 September 1943, ibid.; Donald Creighton to Paul Brooks, 22 October 1943, ibid.; Paul Brooks to Donald Creighton, 22 October 1943, ibid.

10 Creighton used north in the same way that the Canada First movement – that late-nineteenth-century movement of poets, essayists, and nationalists – had used it: Canada was a northern nation simply because it was located to the north of the United States. See Janice Cavell, "The Second Frontier: The North in English-Canadian Historical Writing," *Canadian Historical Review* 83, no. 3 (2002): 368.

11 Laura Creighton to Donald Creighton, 13 January 1941, LAC, MG 31 D 77, Donald Creighton fonds, vol. 1, file General Correspondence 1941.

12 Isabel Wilson to Harold Wilson, n.d., ca January 1944. Original in possession of Philip Creighton.

13 Author's interview with Philip Creighton, 3 December 2004.

14 Author's interview with Cynthia Flood, 3 June 2005.

15 Ibid., 4 June 2005.

16 Ibid., 3 June 2005; author's interview with Philip Creighton, 3 December 2004.

17 Philip Creighton, "Luella Sanders Browning Bruce Creighton," unpublished address delivered to the Toronto Heliconian Club, 25 March 2009. Copy in author's possession.
18 Luella Creighton, *High Bright Buggy Wheels* (Toronto: McClelland and Stewart, 1951), 342.
19 Jack Creighton to Luella Creighton, 23 October 1951, University of Waterloo, Doris Lewis Rare Book Room, Luella Creighton fonds, GA 99, series 4, box 4, file 34.
20 Author's interview with Philip Creighton, 3 December 2004.
21 Terry Craig offers a very different reading of the novel. *HBBW*, he argues, is an example of assimilation in English-Canadian fiction. Having turned their backs on racism, English-Canadian writers now encouraged assimilation into the mainstream. Creighton, he writes, "seems never to have thought that" Tillie's decision to leave her community "might not be a great step forward." As a result, *HBBW* shows the "persistent influence of the English-Canadian attempt to standardize all Canadians after their own image." It also shows, he said, "a lack of sympathy for and an ignorance of her subject matter." Indeed, her depiction of the Mennonite faith as shallow, backwards, and repressive is a caricature. Terrence Craig, *Racial Attitudes in English-Canadian Fiction, 1905–1980* (Waterloo, ON: Wilfrid Laurier University Press, 1987), 109. See also Milda Danyte, "Choosing Self-Hatred: How Canadian Ethnic Minority Novels of the 1950s Reflect Racist Ideas Propagated Earlier by the Dominant Majority," *Transnational Literature* 4, no. 1 (2011). For its part, the *Mennonite Quarterly Review* carried a negative review comparing *HBBW* to Helen R. Martin's 1904 book *Tillie the Mennonite Maid*, which ridiculed Mennonites. Although *HBBW* "does not come to us in the same harsh vein," it suffers "from careless handling of the cultural materials." As a character, Tillie Shantz is "artificial" and "lacks the dynamic, genuine, lively and sprightly girlishness found in the real Mennonite community." John Hosteler, Review of *HBBW*, *Mennonite Quarterly Review* 27, no. 1 (January 1953): 86. A Mennonite bishop in Vineland, Ontario, wrote to Creighton objecting to her "misrepresentation": "The Mennonite people have lived consistent and honourable lives. Some of their doctrines are distinctive but not crude nor ridiculous." S.F. Coffman to Luella Creighton, 18 February 1952, University of Waterloo, Doris Lewis Rare Book Room, Luella Creighton fonds, GA 99, series 4, file 34.
22 "Synopsis of the Book," n.d., LAC, MG 31 D 77, Donald Creighton fonds, vol. 5, file General Correspondence, Houghton Mifflin, 1944–46, 1951.
23 Donald Creighton, "Views on the Writing of History: Aims and Methods as an Historian," n.d., ca early 1970s. LAC, MG 31 D 77, Donald Creighton fonds, vol. 35, file Views on the Writing of History.
24 Donald Creighton, *Dominion of the North* (Boston: Houghton Mifflin, 1944), 1.
25 Diamond Jenness, *The Indians of Canada* (Ottawa: National Museum of Canada, 1932), 248.

26 Donald Creighton, *The Empire of the St. Lawrence* (Toronto: University of Toronto Press, 2002), 201, 144.

27 Creighton, *Dominion of the North*, 7, 30, 40, 46, 47, 64, 82, 92, 138. Creighton's decision to describe in graphic detail the torture of Pierre-Esprit Radisson was an easy and gratuitous hook to titillate the reader. As one scholar noted, "almost all [early] histories allude to Indian torture of prisoners and many feel obliged to satisfy their readers' baser instincts with the goriest of unnecessary details." James W. St G. Walker, "The Indian in Canadian Historical Writing," *Historical Papers* (1971): 22.

28 Creighton, *Dominion of the North*, 113.

29 Ibid., 360, 361, 362.

30 J.R. Miller, *Shingwauk's Vision: A History of Native Residential Schools* (Toronto: University of Toronto Press, 1996), 87–8.

31 See Chad Reimer, *Writing British Columbia History, 1784–1958* (Vancouver: UBC Press, 2009).

32 W.E.H. Stanner, *After the Dreaming: The 1968 Boyer Lectures* (Sydney, 1968).

33 Bruce Trigger, "The Historians' Indian: Native Americans in Canadian Historical Writing from Charlevoix to the Present," *Canadian Historical Review* 67, no. 3 (1986): 325. See also Bruce Trigger, *Natives and Newcomers: Canada's "Heroic Age" Reconsidered* (Montreal and Kingston: McGill-Queen's University Press, 1985), 3–49.

34 Harold Innis, *The Fur Trade in Canada* (New Haven, CT: Yale University Press, 1930), 392.

35 Jenness, *The Indians of Canada*, 250.

36 Alfred Bailey, *The Conflict of European and Eastern Algonkian Cultures, 1504–1700* (Toronto: University of Toronto Press, 1969; first published 1937), 125.

37 Creighton, *Dominion of the North*, 82, 138.

38 Ibid., 5, 21, 69.

39 Ibid., 214–15, 109. On the persistent use of stereotypes to write about French Canada, and their debt to Francis Parkman, see José Igartua, "The Genealogy of Stereotypes: French Canadians in Two English-language Canadian History Textbooks," *Journal of Canadian Studies* 42, no. 3 (Fall 2008): 106–32.

40 John B. O'Reilly, "Canada from a College Window," *Canadian Messenger of the Sacred Heart* (1944): 701, 702.

41 A.L. Burt, *A Short History of Canada for Americans* (Minneapolis: University of Minnesota Press, 1942), 16–17. Séraphin Marion also favourably compared Burt's treatment of French Canada in *A Short History of Canada for Americans* to Creighton's treatment of French Canada in *Dominion of the North*. See Séraphin Marion, *Péchés d'omission d'un historien canadien* (Ottawa, 1966).

42 Creighton, *Dominion of the North*, 58.

43 Creighton, *The Empire of the St. Lawrence*, 196, 351.

44 Francis Parkman, *The Old Regime in Canada* (Boston: Little, Brown, 1880), 104.

45 W.J. Eccles, "The History of New France According to Francis Parkman," *William and Mary Quarterly* 18, no. 2 (1961): 169, 166.

46 Hilda Neatby, review of *Dominion of the North*, *Pacific Northwest Quarterly* 35, no. 3 (1944): 274. In their reviews of *Dominion of the North*, both Fred Soward and Donald Masters criticized Creighton's approach to French Canada. Soward thought that Lord Durham's "blunt condemnation of French Canadian civilization" demanded some kind of comment. It's not an accident, he said, "that Lord Durham's statue does not adorn the lawns of Parliament Hill." Masters felt that Creighton's treatment of nineteenth-century Quebec lacked sympathy, or "patience." Fred Soward, review of *Dominion of the North*, *American Historical Review* 50, no. 1 (1944): 152; D.C. Masters, review of *Dominion of the North*, *Canadian Forum* 24 (June 1944): 65.

47 Creighton, *Dominion of the North*, 122, 127, 125, 325–6.

48 Rev. John B. O'Reilly to A.L. Burt, 14 November 1944, LAC, MG 30 D 103, A.L. Burt fonds, vol.1, file 2.

49 Donald Creighton, *The Empire of the St. Lawrence* (Toronto: University of Toronto Press, 2002), 70.

50 Creighton, *Dominion of the North*, 158.

51 Ibid., 298.

52 Robin Winks, *Canada and the United States: The Civil War Years* (Montreal and Kingston: McGill-Queen's University Press, 1998), 17.

53 Creighton, *Dominion of the North*, 286, 288. See also Vernon Parrington, *Main Currents in American Thought: The Romantic Revolution in America, 1800–1860* (New York: Harcourt Brace Jovanovich, 1927), 473–4.

54 Donald Creighton, "Economic Nationalism and Confederation," *Report of the Annual Meeting of the Canadian Historical Association* 21 (1942): 49.

55 Ibid., 271.

56 J.B. Brebner, review of *Dominion of the North*, *Political Science Quarterly* 59, 3 (1944): 455.

57 See Rohit Aggarwala, "Non-Resident Me: John Bartlet Brebner and the Canadian Historical Profession," *Journal of the Canadian Historical Association* 10 (1999): 237–77; Elizabeth Elliot-Meisel, "John Bartlet Brebner: The Private Man behind the Professional Historian," *American Review of Canadian Studies* 32, no. 4 (2002): 609–38.

58 Creighton, *Dominion of the North*, 435.

59 H. Gordon Skilling to Donald Creighton, 11 January 1945, LAC, Donald Creighton fonds, MG 31 D 77, vol. 1, file General Correspondence 1945. In 1959 Skilling returned to Canada when he received an appointment at Toronto.

60 Donald Creighton, "Synopsis of the Book," n.d., LAC, MG 31 D 77, Donald Creighton fonds, vol. 5, file General Correspondence, Houghton Mifflin, 1944–46, 1951.

61 John Darwin, *The Empire Project: The Rise and Fall of the British World-System, 1830–1970* (Cambridge: Cambridge University Press, 2009), 476.

62 Creighton, *Dominion of the North*, 503.

63 *Saturday Night*, 6 May 1944; *Montreal Gazette*, 21 July 1944; *New York Times*, 23 April 1944; *United Church Observer*, 15 August 1944. A.L. Burt to Donald Creighton, 28 May 1944, LAC, MG 31 D 77, Donald Creighton fonds, vol. 1, file General Correspondence 1944, file 1; Irene Spry to Donald Creighton, 31 August 1945, LAC, MG 31 D 77, Donald Creighton fonds, vol. 1, file General Correspondence 1945, file 1; A.G.B. Claxton to Donald Creighton, 11 October 1944, LAC, MG 31 D 77, Donald Creighton fonds, vol. 1, file General Correspondence 1944, file 1; Jack Creighton to Donald Creighton, 3 May 1945. Original in possession of Philip Creighton.

64 Stefan Berger, "The Power of National Pasts: Writing National History in Nineteenth- and Twentieth-Century Europe," in Stefan Berger, ed., *Writing the Nation: A Global Perspective* (New York: Palgrave Macmillan, 2007), 38.

65 Gita Deneckere and Thomas Welskopp, "The Nation and Class: European National Master Narratives and Their Social Other," in Stefan Berger and Chris Lorenz eds, *The Contested Nation: Ethnicity, Class, Religion and Gender in National Histories* (New York: Palgrave Macmillan, 2008), 135.

66 Herbert Heaton, review of *The Commercial Empire of the St. Lawrence*, *Canadian Journal of Economics and Political Science* 4 (1938): 565; Bartlet Brebner, "Creighton Mss. I," n.d., ca August 1937, Columbia University Rare Book and Manuscript Library, J. Bartlet Brebner fonds, box 10, file March 1937–August 1937; Brebner, review of *British North America at Confederation*, *Canadian Journal of Economics and Political Science* 7, no. 1 (1941): 69; LAC, MG 30 D 211, Frank Scott fonds, vol. 110, file 6.

67 Donald Creighton, "Canada in the World," in G.P. Gilmour, ed., *Canada's Tomorrow* (Toronto: Macmillan, 1954), 241; Stanley Ryerson, *1837: The Birth of Canadian Democracy* (Toronto: Francis White, 1937), 9; Donald Creighton, review of *1837: The Birth of Canadian Democracy*, *Canadian Historical Review* 19, no. 1 (1938): 73.

68 Creighton, *Dominion of the North*, 240–5.

69 For his full treatment of the 1872 printers' strike see Donald Creighton, "George Brown, Sir John Macdonald, and the Workingman," *Canadian Historical Review* 24, no. 4 (1943): 362–76. According to Greg Kealey, the 1872 strike for a nine-hour day was "the most famous of nineteenth-century Canadian labour struggles" and a "benchmark both in the evolution of Canadian working-class consciousness and in the development of mature organizational forms." That Donald Creighton should have missed the significance of the printers' strike was not a surprise. "Traditional

political history has never allowed the unwashed to sully its elegant pages. The biographies of politicians also manage to avoid discussion of those whose votes made their subjects famous and often rich." Gregory Kealey, *Toronto Workers Respond to Industrial Capitalism, 1867–1892* (Toronto: University of Toronto Press, 1980), 90, 128, 366.

70 Creighton, *Dominion of the North*, 423.

71 Benedict Anderson, *Imagined Communities: Reflections on the Origin and Spread of Nationalism* (London: Verso, 1991), 7; Christopher L. Hill, *National History and the World of Nations* (Durham, NC: Duke University Press, 2008), xi; Howard Zinn, *A People's History of the United States* (New York: Harper Collins, 2001), 10; Allan Megill, *Historical Knowledge, Historical Error: A Contemporary Guide to Practice* (Chicago: University of Chicago Press, 2007), 77.

72 R. Douglas Francis, "Historical Perspectives on Britain: The Ideas of Frank H. Underhill and Arthur R.M. Lower," in Phillip Buckner and R. Douglas Francis, eds, *Canada and the British World: Culture, Migration, and Identity* (Vancouver: UBC Press, 2006), 309.

73 Gustave Lanctôt to Arthur Lower, 5 December 1944, Queen's University Archives, collection 5072, Arthur Lower Papers, box 26, B690

74 Donald Creighton to John Marshall, 20 May 1944, Rockefeller Archives Center (RAC), RF, RG 1.2, series 427 R, box 14, file 128.

75 John Marshall, Ontario Visit, 22–27 November 1942, RAC, RG 1.1, series 427 R, box 27, file 264; Internal RF document based on interview between Anne Bezanson and John Marhsall, 16 December 1942, RAC, RF, RG 1.2, series 427 R, box 14, file 128; Interview with Harold Innis, 25 January 1943, RAC, RF, RG 1.2, series 427 R, box 166, file 5; John Marshall to Donald Creighton, 22 April 1943, RAC, RF, RG 1.2, series 427 R, box 14, file 128.

76 See Donald Wright, *The Professionalization of History in English Canada* (Toronto: University of Toronto Press, 2005), 147–70.

77 Donald Creighton to John Marshall, 5 January 1944 and 21 February 1944, RAC, RF, RG 1.2, series 427 R, box 14, file 128.

78 S.D. Clark to Donald Creighton and George Brown, 31 October 1944, University of Toronto Archives, University of Toronto Press, CHR Files, A86-0044, box 5, file CHR, 25th Anniversary Letters, no. 1. See also S.D. Clark, *Church and Sect in Canada* (Toronto: University of Toronto Press, 1948).

79 Carl Berger, *The Writing of Canadian History: Aspects of English Canadian Historical Writing, 1900–1970* (Toronto: Oxford University Press, 1976), 217. See also Donald Creighton, "Some Reminiscences of an Historian," n.d. ca 1970s. Original in possession of Ramsay Derry.

80 Donald Creighton to John Marshall, 21 February 1944, RAC, RF, RG 1.2, series 427 R, box 14, file 128; Donald Creighton to John Marshall, 21 April 1944, ibid.

81 Donald Creighton., "Aims and Methods as an Historian," n.d., ca 1970s, LAC, MG 31 D 77 Donald Creighton fonds, vol. 35, file Aims and Methods as an Historian.
82 Author's interview with Philip Creighton, 3 December 2004; author's interview with Cynthia Flood, 3 June 2005. When Laura and William died in 1946, Isabel and Harold stayed in the apartment.
83 Donald Creighton, "The Writing of History in Canada," UNB Founders' Day Address, 1945. Copy in University of New Brunswick Archives and Special Collections.
84 Michael Jennings, Howard Eiland, Gary Smith, eds, *Walter Benjamin: Selected Writings, 1927–1930* (Cambridge: Harvard University Press, 1999), 238.

8 Macdonald

1 Donald Creighton to John Marshall, 14 July 1945, Rockefeller Archives Center (RAC), RF, RG 1.2, series 427 R, box 14, file 128; Chester Martin to Donald Creighton, 23 July 1945, LAC, MG 31 D 77, Donald Creighton fonds, vol. 1, file General Correspondence 1945.
2 Author's interview with Norman Sheffe, 7 April 2005.
3 See Peter Clarke, *The Last Thousand Days of the British Empire* (London: Allen Lane, 2007).
4 King George VI, "Victory in Europe Address," *New York Times*, 8 May 1945.
5 Quotations in John Darwin, *The Empire Project: The Rise and Fall of the British World-System, 1830–1970* (Cambridge: Cambridge University Press, 2009), 519, 550.
6 George Grant, "The Empire – Yes or No?" in Arthur Davis and Peter Emberly, eds, *Collected Works of George Grant*, vol. 1: *1933–1950* (Toronto: University of Toronto Press, 2000), 114.
7 Alexander John Watson, *Marginal Man: The Dark Vision of Harold Innis* (Toronto: University of Toronto Press, 2006), 380.
8 Harold Innis, "Great Britain, The United States, and Canada," University of Nottingham, Cust Foundation Lecture (21 May 1948), 24, 18, 21, 18, 4.
9 Quotation in Watson, *Marginal Man*, 376.
10 Harold Innis, "The Strategy of Culture," in Harold Innis, *Changing Concepts of Time* (Toronto: University of Toronto Press, 1952), 20.
11 Donald Creighton, "Macdonald and Canadian Historians," in Donald Creighton, *Towards the Discovery of Canada* (Toronto: Macmillan, 1972), 196, 198, 197, 199. In his preface to *The Eminent Victorians*, Strachey referred to "those two fat volumes" used to "commemorate the dead" which have all the style and tone of the "undertaker." Lytton Strachey, *The Eminent Victorians* (London: Continuum, 2002), 4.
12 Virginia Woolf, "The New Biography" and "The Art of Biography" in Virginia Woolf, *Selected Essays* (Oxford: Oxford University Press, 2008), 96, 118.

13 Creighton, "Macdonald and Canadian Historians," 201; Isabel Skelton quotation in Terry Crowley, *Marriage of Minds: Isabel and Oscar Skelton Reinventing Canada* (Toronto: University of Toronto Press, 2003), 258; Creighton, "Macdonald and Canadian Historians," 206

14 Ibid., 209.

15 John Gray, "Publisher's Foreword," in John Moir, ed., *Character and Circumstance: Essays in Honour of Donald Grant Creighton* (Toronto: Macmillan, 1970), vii.

16 John Gray to Daniel Macmillan, 25 October 1948, The William Ready Division of Archives and Research Collection, McMaster University Library (MUL), Macmillan Co. of Canada fonds, box 88, file 8.

17 Gray, "Publisher's Foreword," viii.

18 R.G. Collingwood, *The Idea of History* (Oxford: Oxford University Press, 1946), 245.

19 Donald Creighton, "History and Literature," in Donald Creighton, *Towards the Discovery of Canada* (Toronto: Macmillan, 1972), 19.

20 Donald Creighton, *John A. Macdonald: The Young Politician* (Toronto: Macmillan, 1952), 1.

21 Donald Creighton, *The Empire of the St. Lawrence* (Toronto: University of Toronto Press, 2002), 6.

22 Creighton, *The Young Politician*, 11, 25; Creighton, *The Empire of the St. Lawrence*, 4; Creighton, *The Young Politician*, 34.

23 Creighton, "History and Literature," 21.

24 Ibid.

25 Honoré de Balzac, *Old Goriot* (London: David Campbell, 1991), 5–6; Jane Austen, *Emma* (New York: Dover, 1999), 284; Charles Dickens, *Bleak House* (New York: W.W. Norton, 1977), 5.

26 W.M. Mellor, "Timothy Findley's True Fictions: A Conversation in Stone Orchard," *Studies in Canadian Literature* 19, no. 2 (1994).

27 Donald Creighton to Jim Conacher, 21 September 1956, UTA, Jim Conacher fonds, B2005-0011, box 2, file 1.

28 *High Bright Buggy Wheels*, he said, didn't have "the depth of thought or feeling" or "the final distinction of style" to be considered a great novel. Desmond Pacey, Review of *High Bright Buggy Wheels*, *Fredericton Daily Gleaner*, 12 October 1951; Northrop Frye, Review of *High Bright Buggy Wheels*, "Critically Speaking," CBC Radio, 28 October 1951. Copy in University of Waterloo, Doris Lewis Rare Book Room, Luella Creighton fonds, GA 99, series 4, box 4, file 36.

29 Donald Creighton, Diary entry for 31 January 1952, LAC, Donald Creighton fonds, MG 31 D 77, vol. 65, file 1; Lord Beaverbrook to Donald Creighton, 31 May 1948, ibid., vol. 2, file General Correspondence 1948. Beaverbrook described Creighton's essay as "brilliantly written."

30 See Donald Wright, "Donald Creighton, John Gray, and the Making of Macdonald," Historical Perspectives on Canadian Publishing, http://hpcanpub.mcmaster.ca.

31 Luella Creighton, Diary entry for 29 January 1952, University of Waterloo, Doris Lewis Rare Book Room (UW), Luella Creighton fonds, GA 99, box 1, file 1.

32 Donald Creighton to John Gray, 14 February 1952, MUL, Macmillan Co. of Canada fonds, box 88, file 8.

33 "Editorial Notes," n.d., ca January 1952, MUL, Macmillan Co. of Canada fonds, box 88, file 8.

34 John Gray to Donald Creighton, 22 February 1952, and John Gray to Donald Creighton, 18 March 1952, LAC, Donald Creighton fonds, MG 31 D 77, vol. 6, file Macmillan Co. of Canada, 1951–1952.

35 Creighton, *The Young Politician*, 68.

36 Joseph Pope, *Memoirs of the Right Honourable Sir John Alexander Macdonald First Prime Minister of the Dominion of Canada* (Ottawa, 1894), 1:6. Quotation in Claire Tomalin, *Charles Dickens: A Life* (London: Viking, 2011), 243.

37 Ibid., 260.

38 Donald Creighton to John Gray, 21 March 1952, MUL, Macmillan Co. of Canada fonds, box 88, file 8.

39 Quotation in Margaret Aitken, "Between You and Me," *Toronto Telegram*, 23 February 1956.

40 Norman Flower, ed., *The Journal of Arnold Bennett*, vol. 1: *1896–1910* (London: Cassell, 1932), 19.

41 Creighton, *The Young Politician*, 106, 310, 398, 158, 411, 334, 191. The Charles Dickens character Seth Pecksniff prated on and on about moral obligations and duties but was, in fact, a hypocrite of the worst sort.

42 Ibid., 349, 372–73, 453, 463. Macdonald's reference to Highclere Castle is in J.K. Johnson, ed., *Affectionately Yours: The Letters of Sir John A. Macdonald and His Family* (Toronto: Macmillan, 1969), 139.

43 Creighton, *The Young Politician*, 480, 481. See J.M.S. Careless, "Donald Creighton and Canadian History: Some Reflections," in Moir, ed., *Character and Circumstance*, 11–12.

44 Donald Creighton to John Gray, 14 February 1952, MUL, Macmillan Co. of Canada fonds, box 88, file 8.

45 Donald Creighton to John Gray, 31 March 1952; Donald Creighton to John Gray, 1 April, 1952, ibid.

46 Donald Creighton to John Gray, 30 April 1952, ibid.

47 Donald Creighton to Harold Innis, 26 April 1952, University of Toronto Archives (UTA), Harold Innis fonds, B1972-0003, box 5, R616.

48 Harold Innis to Donald Creighton, 11 May 1952, ibid.; Harold Innis to Donald Creighton, 2 August 1952, LAC, Donald Creighton fonds, MG 31 D 77, vol. 28, General Correspondence 1952.

49 Harold Innis to John Gray, 23 July 1952, MUL, Macmillan Co. of Canada fonds, box 88, file 9.

50 See Mary Quayle Innis, Diary entry for 3 September 1952, UTA, Harold Innis Family fonds, B91-0029, box 58, file 2; and Donald Creighton, Diary entry for 3 September 1952, LAC, MG 31 D 77, vol. 65, file 1.

51 Author's interview with John Moir, 4 July 2003. Dr Moir provided the details about Creighton's visit with Innis, the weather, and the leaves.

52 Donald Creighton, *Harold Adams Innis* (Toronto: University of Toronto Press, 1957), 142. See also Donald Creighton, *Towards the Discovery of Canada* (Toronto: Macmillan, 1972), 8.

53 Robert Teigrob, *Warming Up to the Cold War: Canada and the United States' Coalition of the Willing from Hiroshima to Korea* (Toronto: University of Toronto Press, 2009), 17. In this fascinating study, Teigrob argues that Canadians had been so conditioned by the American interpretation of the Cold War that they forced reluctant policymakers in Ottawa to commit Canadian troops to Korea. In his book *Orienting Canada: Race, Empire, and the Transpacific*, John Price contends that, reluctant or not, policymakers predicated Canadian policy in East Asia "not on the needs of people in the region but, rather, on the belief that Canadian interests required reinforcing US power in the Pacific." See John Price, *Orienting Canada* (Vancouver: UBC Press, 2011), 190.

54 "100 Fought Off 1,000 Reds; Canadian Casualties Heavy," *Globe and Mail*, 29 October 1952.

55 John Gray to Louis St Laurent, 9 October 1952; PMO to John Gray, 16 October 1952, MUL, Macmillan Co. of Canada fonds, box 88, file 9.

56 Donald Creighton, Diary entry for 10 November 1952, LAC, MG 31 D77, vol. 65, file 1; Robert Finch, Diary entry for 10 November 1952, Thomas Fisher Rare Book Library, MS Coll. 324, Robert Finch Papers, box 8, Journals, 1942, 1952–1960, 1970; Donald Creighton, Diary entry for 10 November 1952, LAC, MG 31 D 77, vol. 65, file 1.

57 Donald Creighton to Luella Creighton, 15 November 1952 and 21 November 1952, UW, Luella Creighton fonds, GA 99, series 2, box 1, file 7.

58 *Kingston Whig-Standard*, 13 November 1952; *Winnipeg Free Press*, 29 November 1952; *Saskatoon Star-Phoenix*, 29 November 1952; *New York Times*, 15 November 1952; *Times Literary Supplement*, 20 February 1953; *Manchester Guardian*, 3 February 1953; *Canadian Business*, May 1953; *Saturday Night*, 29 November 1952; *Globe and Mail*, 18 October 1952; Donald Creighton, Diary entry for 18 October 1952, LAC, MG 31 D 77, vol. 65, file 1; Donald Creighton, Diary entry for 24 February 1953, ibid.; *Spectator*, 6 March 1953.

59 See letters in LAC, MG 31 D 77, vol. 6, file Correspondence John A. Macdonald: The Young Politician. Angus MacInnis, *Hansard*, 5 February 1953, p. 1635, 39-1953-1½; M.J. Coldwell, *Hansard*, 17 March 1953, p. 3019, 67-1953-2; Lester

Pearson to Donald Creighton, LAC, MG 31 D 77, vol. 6, file Correspondence John A. Macdonald: The Young Politician.

60 Donald Creighton to Frank Upjohn, 26 July 1953, MUL, Macmillan Co. of Canada fonds, box 88, file 9. By 1964, it had sold 14,053 copies.

61 Arthur Lower, review of *The Young Politician*, *United Church Observer*, 1 December 1952; Hilda Neatby,, "Hilda Neatby," CBC Radio, 23 November 1952; transcript in Saskatchewan Archives Board, Saskatoon, Hilda Neatby fonds, A139, VIII. 202(5); George Stanley, "The Young Macdonald," *Queen's Quarterly* 60 (Spring 1953): 75; C.P. Stacey, review of *The Young Politician*, *Canadian Historical Review* 34 (March 1953): 54–5; Albert Corey, review of *The Young Politician*, *American Historical Review* 59 (October 1953): 171–2; Thomas Peardon, review of *The Young Politician*, *Political Science Quarterly* 68 (December 1953): 635; Creighton, *The Young Politician*, 115, 116, 216; Michel Brunet, review of *The Young Politician*, *Revue d'histoire de l'Amérique française* 6, no. 4 (mars 1953): 579–82.

62 W.L. Morton, review of *The Young Politician*, *International Journal* 8 (Spring 1953): 126.

63 Donald Creighton, Diary entry for 4 February 1953 to 8 May 1953, LAC, Donald Creighton fonds, MG 31 D 77, vol. 65, file 1.

64 Donald Creighton, Diary entry for 17 May 1953 to 5 September 1953, ibid.

65 Donald Creighton, Diary entry for 21 September 1953, ibid.

66 Donald Creighton to John Gray, 25 March 1952, MUL, Macmillan Co. of Canada fonds, box 88, file 8. Emphasis in original.

67 Donald Creighton, Diary entries for 6 May 1954, 13 May 1954, 15 May 1954, LAC, Donald Creighton fonds, MG 31 D 77, vol. 65, file 2.

68 Donald Creighton, *John A. Macdonald: The Old Chieftain* (Toronto: Macmillan, 1955), 10.

69 Ibid., 3, 3, 4, 283, 415, 389, 546, 57. Technically, Creighton did not call Blake fat-faced, but said that he had a "broad, fat, rather babyish face."

70 Creighton, *The Old Chieftain*, 563.

71 Donald Creighton to John Gray, 9 July 1955, MUL, Macmillan Co. of Canada fonds, box 88, file 10.

72 Creighton, *The Young Politician*, 481.

73 Donald Creighton to John Gray, 9 July 1955, MUL, Macmillan Co. of Canada fonds, box 88, file 10.

74 *Globe and Mail*, 17 September 1955; *Victoria Daily Times*, 29 September 1955; *Ottawa Journal*, 28 February 1956; *Manchester Guardian*, 16 December 1955; *New York Times*, 18 March 1956; *Economist*, 7 July 1956; *Times Literary Supplement*, 4 May 1956; *Spectator*, 23 March 1956.

75 Vincent Massey to Donald Creighton, 4 November 1955; Arthur Meighen to Donald Creighton, 7 October 1955; Isabella Gainsford to Donald Creighton, 12 November

1955; Hugh MacLennan to Donald Creighton, 5 February 1956; Mary Innis to Donald Creighton, 15 November 1955, LAC, Donald Creighton fonds, MG 31 D 77, vol. 6, file John A. Macdonald: The Old Chieftain, Correspondence, no. 1.

76 Macmillan Royalty Ledger, 1955–1959, MUL, Macmillan Co. of Canada fonds, box 88, file 10. By 1964, it had sold 13,350 copies.

77 George Stanley, review of *The Old Chieftain, Queen's Quarterly* 62 (Winter 1956): 592–4; C.P. Stacey, review of *The Old Chieftain, Canadian Historical Review* 37 (March 1956): 77–8; Gordon Sinclair, CFRB Radio, 23 September 1955, transcript in LAC, Donald Creighton fonds, MG 31 D 77, vol. 16, file John A. Macdonald: The Old Chieftain, reviews. In the same file see the following reviews: *Regina Leader Post*, 26 November 1955; *Winnipeg Tribune*, 29 October 1955; *Winnipeg Free Press*, n.d., *Time and Tide*, 21 January 1956; *Montreal Star*, n.d.; *The Advertiser*, n.d.; *The Ensign*, n.d., *Canadian Tribune*, n. d. One academic reviewer, however, saluted Creighton's interpretation. Writing in *Saskatchewan History*, Lewis H. Thomas argued that "the exposure of Riel's feet of clay will not be welcome in some circles, but it is a salutary corrective to the emotional and distorted hagiography which has obtained wide circulation in recent years on the prairies." *Saskatchewan History* 9 (Autumn 1956).

78 Creighton, *The Old Chieftain*, 383, 414, 534, 415, 384, 385, 387, 384, 178. In his first book Creighton had described the Métis who lived at Red River as "a mob of restless, reckless half-breeds." Creighton, *The Empire of the St. Lawrence*, 186.

79 John Gray to Donald Creighton, 17 December 1954, MUL, Macmillan Co. of Canada fonds, box 88, file 10.

80 Emphasis mine. Quotation in Peter Waite, "Donald Creighton: Casting the Net of His Macdonald," *The Beaver* (February–March 1998): 34. Waite intimates that Creighton had suppressed the second part of the letter. See also Peter Waite, *Reefs Unsuspected: Historians and Biography in Canada, Australia and Elsewhere* (Sydney: Macquarie University, 1983).

81 Creighton, *The Old Chieftain*, 47.

82 John Gray to Donald Creighton, 8 July 1955, MUL, Macmillan Co. of Canada fonds, box 88, file 10.

83 Creighton, *The Old Chieftain*, 439.

84 See Albert Braz, *The False Traitor: Louis Riel in Canadian Culture* (Toronto: University of Toronto Press, 2003).

85 J.A. Jackson to Donald Creighton, 8 May 1956; Donald Creighton to J.A. Jackson, 16 May 1956, LAC, Donald Creighton fonds, MG 31 D 77, vol. 6, file John A. Macdonald: The Old Chieftain, Correspondence, no. 1.

86 Donald Creighton to Ramsay Cook, 25 July 1963. Original in possession of Ramsay Cook.

87 Creighton, *The Old Chieftain*, 414, 205, 127; Guy Frégault, review of *The Old Chieftain, Revue d'histoire de l'Amérique française* 9, no. 3 (1955): 446.

88 Creighton, *The Old Chieftain*, 163.
89 Michael Bliss, *Right Honourable Men: The Descent of Canadian Politics from Macdonald to Mulroney* (Toronto: HarperCollins, 1994), 24. See also S.J.R. Noel, *Patrons, Clients, and Brokers: Ontario Society and Politics, 1791–1896* (Toronto: University of Toronto Press, 1990).
90 See Ged Martin, *Favourite Son? John A. Macdonald and the Voters of Kingston* (Kingston: Kingston Historical Society, 2008), 154–60, 189–90.
91 Creighton, *The Old Chieftain*, 542–3.
92 Creighton, *The Old Politician*, 15, 39, 68, 171, 401.
93 Arthur Lower, *United Church Observer*, 15 November 1955.
94 Donald Creighton, "History and Literature," in Creighton, *Towards the Discovery of Canada*, 23.
95 Julian Barnes, "The Art of Fiction No. 165," *Paris Review* (Winter 2000).
96 J.A. Froude. Quotation in Michael Holroyd, "What Justifies Biography?" in Michael Holroyd, *Works on Paper: The Craft of Biography and Autobiography* (Washington, DC: Counterpoint, 2002), 24.
97 Woolf, "The Art of Biography," 119.
98 Creighton, *The Old Chieftain*, 575; *The Young Politician*, 2; *The Old Chieftain*, 578.
99 John Gray to Donald Creighton, 8 July 1955, MUL, Macmillan Co. of Canada fonds, box 88, file 10; Donald Creighton to John Gray, 9 July 1955, ibid.

9 Chairman

1 Donald Creighton's disdain for Bertie Wilkinson and George Brown was notorious. Author's interviews with John Cairns, 2 December 2004; Robert Spencer, 25 May 2006; and Willard Piepenburg, 4 May 2005. Donald Creighton, Diary entry for 7 June 1954, Library and Archives Canada (LAC), Donald Creighton fonds, MG 31 D 77, vol. 65, file 2; Donald Creighton to Sidney Smith, 15 June 1952, University of Toronto Archives (UTA), University Historian, A83-0036, box 6, file Dept. of History; Diary entries for 29 April 1952 and 2 June 1952, LAC, Donald Creighton fonds, MG 31 D 77, vol. 65, file 1; Donald Creighton to Harold Innis, 15 June 1952, UTA, Harold Innis fonds, B1972-0003, box 5, R616.
2 Donald Creighton, Diary entry for 8 June 1954, Library and Archives Canada (LAC), Donald Creighton fonds, MG 31 D 77, vol. 65, file 2.
3 Luella Creighton, *Turn East, Turn West* (Toronto: McClelland and Stewart, 1954), 289, 306.
4 Luella Creighton, no title, *The Empire Club of Canada Addresses* (1 April 1954), 279–98.
5 Luella Creighton to Irene Spry, Christmas 1953, LAC, MG 30 C 249, Irene Spry fonds, vol. 23, file Luella Bruce Creighton.

6 Jim Conacher to Frank Underhill, 18 December 1954, LAC, Frank Underhill fonds, MG 30 D 204, vol. 3, file Jim Conacher; author's interview with Robert Spencer, 25 May 2006; Jim Conacher, Manuscript of his memoirs, University of Toronto Archives (UTA), James B. Conacher fonds, B2005-0011, box 17, file 14; Donald McDougall to Jim Conacher, 31 December 1954, ibid., box 1, file 7.

7 Frank Underhill to Kenneth McNaught, 11 September 1955, UTA, Kenneth McNaught fonds, B97-0031, box 1, file 6.

8 Jim Conacher to Frank Underhill, 18 December 1954, LAC, Frank Underhill fonds, MG 30 D 204, vol. 3, file Jim Conacher.

9 Donald Creighton, "The Ogdensburg Agreement and F.H. Underhill," in Donald Creighton, *The Passionate Observer: Selected Writings* (Toronto: McClelland and Stewart, 1980), 130.

10 Author's interview with Margaret Prang, 18 January 2005.

11 Kenneth McNaught, *Conscience and History: A Memoir* (Toronto: University of Toronto Press, 1999), 25. See also R. Douglas Francis, *Frank H. Underhill: Intellectual Provocateur* (Toronto: University of Toronto Press, 1986), 160. For Creighton's reference to Underhill as a pot-bellied little bastard, see Ramsay Cook to Kenneth McNaught, 2 January 1965, UTA, Kenneth McNaught fonds, B97-0031, box 1, file 9.

12 Frank Underhill, "Concerning Mr. King," in Frank Underhill, *In Search of Canadian Liberalism* (Toronto: Macmillan, 1960), 135–6.

13 J.L. Granatstein, *Yankee Go Home? Canadians and Anti-Americanism* (Toronto: HarperCollins, 1996), 225, 6.

14 Herbert Butterfield, *Christianity, Diplomacy and War* (London: Epworth Press, 1953), 17, 26, 43, 18.

15 Donald Creighton, "Canada in the World," in G.P. Gilmour, ed., *Canada's Tomorrow* (Toronto: Macmillan, 1954), 228, 232, 246, 252.

16 Donald Creighton, Diary entry for 15 June 1954, Library and Archives Canada (LAC), Donald Creighton fonds, MG 31 D 77, vol. 65, file 2.

17 Donald Creighton, "Canada in World Affairs: Are We Pulling Our Weight?" 13 August 1954. Reprinted as "Canada and the Cold War" in Creighton, *Towards the Discovery of Canada* (Toronto: Macmillan, 1972), 254–5, 245.

18 Creighton, "Introduction," *Towards the Discovery of Canada*, 9.

19 Creighton, "Canada and the Cold War," *Towards the Discovery of Canada*, 247.

20 Marcus Long, "Canada in World Affairs: Are We Pulling Our Weight? Statement by Marcus Long," LAC, Donald Creighton fonds, MG 31 D 77, vol. 33, file Couchiching Conference Speech.

21 J.F. Boland, letter to the editor, *Globe and Mail*, 20 August 1954.

22 "Professors Get Out of Focus, Too," *Vancouver Province*, 17 August 1954.

23 Name illegible to Donald Creighton, n.d., ca August 1954, LAC, Donald Creighton fonds, MG 31 D 77, vol. 33, file Couchiching Conference Speech.

24 Frank Peers to Donald Creighton, 1 October 1954, ibid.

25 George Stanley to Donald Creighton, 17 August 1954, ibid.

26 Donald Creighton to Ronald MacEachern, 9 September 1954, ibid.; Creighton, "Introduction," *Towards the Discovery of Canada*, 9.

27 Creighton, "Canada and the Cold War," *Towards the Discovery of Canada*, 247.

28 Creighton, "Introduction," *Towards the Discovery of Canada*, 8.

29 Donald Creighton to Moffat Woodside, 21 October 1955, UTA, A67-0008, box 14, file History, Departmental Gen. and Chairmanships.

30 Anne Bezanson to Joseph Willits, 18 November 1952, Rockefeller Archives Center (RAC), RF, RG 1.2, series 427 S, box 16, file 160.

31 Donald Creighton to John Marshall, 7 June 1955, RAC, Rockefeller Foundation Archives, RG 1.1, series 427 S, box 32, file 325; Donald Creighton to Lester Pearson, 7 June 1955, LAC, Donald Creighton fonds, MG 31 D 77, vol. 10, Humanities Research Council, 1954–1955; Donald Creighton to John Marshall, 16 September 1955, RAC, Rockefeller Foundation Archives, RG 1.1, series 427 S, box 32, file 325.

32 LAC, Donald Creighton fonds, MG 31 D 77, vol. 3, file General Correspondence 1956, file 3; George Nowlan to Miriam Nowlan, 22 February 1956. Quotation in Margaret Conrad, "Studies in Canada's Recent History," *Acadiensis* 6, no. 2 (Spring 1977): 120. On the Progressive Conservative Party and Donald Creighton, see Cara Spittal, "The Diefenbaker Moment" (PhD thesis, University of Toronto, 2011).

33 Jack Saywell to Jim Conacher, 10 November 1956, UTA, James B. Conacher fonds, B2005-0011, box 2, file 1.

34 Author's interview with Ramsay Cook, 3 December 2004; author's interview with Margaret Prang, 18 January 2005; author's interview with Father Francis W.P. Bolger, 8 November 2005; Donald Creighton to Bill Morton, 16 October 1956, LAC, MG 31 D 77, Donald Creighton fonds, vol. 3, file General Correspondence 1956, file 3.

35 Author's interview with Willard Piepenburg, 4 May 2005.

36 Willard Piepenburg to Jim Conacher, 6 December 1956, UTA, James B. Conacher fonds, B2005-0011, box 2, file 1; John Cairns to Jim Conacher, 17 December 1956, ibid.; Maurice Careless to Jim Conacher, 17 December 1956, ibid.

37 Author's interview with John Cairns, 2 December 2004.

38 Donald Creighton, *John A. Macdonald: The Young Politician* (Toronto: Macmillan, 1952), 83, 316.

39 Author's interview with Jack Saywell, 8 December 2004; McNaught, *Conscience and History*, 143.

40 Robert Spencer to Jim Conacher, 7 January 1957, UTA, James B. Conacher fonds, B2005-0011, box 2, file 3; Jim Conacher, unpublished memoirs, ibid., box 17, file 14; Robert Spencer to Jim Conacher, 21 April 1957, ibid., box 2, file 3.

41 Arthur Lower, Diary entries for 15 and 20 November 1956. Ellipses in original. Queen's University Archives (QUA), Arthur Lower fonds, Collection 5072, box 57, file E61.

42 Quotation in José Igartua, *The Other Quiet Revolution: National Identities in English Canada, 1945–71* (Vancouver: UBC Press, 2006), 116.

43 Jack Saywell to Jim Conacher, 10 November 1956, UTA, James B. Conacher fonds, B2005-0011, box 2, file 1.

44 Willard Piepenburg to Jim Conacher, 6 December 1956, ibid. Also see author's interview with Willard Piepenburg, 4 May 2005.

45 Robert Spencer to Jim Conacher, 7 January 1957, UTA, James B. Conacher fonds, B2005-0011, box 2, file 3.

46 *Globe and Mail*, 2 November 1956.

47 John Cairns to George A. Foote, 25 November 1956. Copy in possession of John Cairns. Willard Piepenburg to Jim Conacher, 6 December 1956, UTA, James B. Conacher fonds, B2005-0011, box 2, file 1.

48 Jack Saywell to Jim Conacher, 31 January 1957, UTA, James B. Conacher fonds, B2005-0011, box 2, file 3.

49 Howard Norman to Donald Creighton, 28 September 1957, LAC, MG 31 D 77, Donald Creighton fonds, vol. 3, file General Correspondence 1957, file 2; Donald Creighton to Howard Norman, 10 October 1957, ibid.

50 C.P. Stacey, *A Date with History* (Ottawa: Deneau, 1983), 226.

51 Author's interview with John Cairns, 2 December 2004.

52 Eugene Forsey, *A Life on the Fringe* (Toronto: Oxford University Press, 1990), 200.

53 John Cairns to Willard Piepenburg, 26 June 1957. Copy in possession of John Cairns.

54 Quotation in John English, *The Life of Lester Pearson*, vol. 2: *The Worldly Years* (Toronto: Vintage, 1992), 191.

55 Donald Creighton, "Doctrine and the Interpretation of History," in Creighton, *Towards the Discovery of Canada*, 40, 34, 33.

56 Author's interview with John Cairns, 2 December 2004.

57 Author's interview with Margaret Prang, 18 January 2005.

58 Author's interview with John Cairns, 2 December 2004.

59 John Cairns to Robert Spencer, 18 July 1957. Copy in possession of John Cairns.

60 Ibid.

61 Hilda Neatby to Frank Underhill, 25 August 1957, MG 30 D 204, Frank Underhill fonds, vol. 13 file H. Neatby 1957–1971.

62 Mary Innis, Diary entry for 24 April 1956, UTA, Harold Innis Family fonds, B91-0029, box 58, file 3; author's interview with Anne Innis Daag, 14 January 2005.

63 Donald Creighton, *Harold Adams Innis: Portrait of a Scholar* (Toronto: University of Toronto Press, 1978), 3–5.

64 Ibid., 31.

65 Ibid., 135.

66 Ibid., 101.

67 Mary Cates to Donald Creighton, 4 January 1958; Anne Innis to Donald Creighton, 26 November 1957; Hugh Innis to Donald Creighton, 26 November 1957, LAC, MG 31 D 77, Donald Creighton fonds, vol. 16, Harold Adams Innis: Portrait of A Scholar, Correspondence, Memoranda, Reviews. Author's interview with Mary Rutledge, 22 January 2005; author's interview with Anne Innis Daag, 14 January 2005. Gerald Graham to Donald Creighton, 11 March 1958, LAC, MG 31 D 77, Donald Creighton fonds, vol. 4, file General Correspondence 1958, no. 3.

68 See the reviews contained in LAC, MG 31 D 77, Donald Creighton fonds, vol. 16, Harold Adams Innis: Portrait of a Scholar, Correspondence, Memoranda, Reviews.

69 Alexander John Watson, *Marginal Man: The Dark Vision of Harold Innis* (Toronto: University of Toronto Press, 2006), 434.

70 Creighton, *Portrait of a Scholar*, xiii.

71 Ibid., 92–4, 103–4.

72 In response, Frank Underhill rejected Creighton's insistence that Innis "had ceased spiritually to be a North American": "I can think of no one who was more typically North American than Harold Innis, in his personality, his speech, his way of writing, in everything about him. If he ever kidded himself that he had ceased spiritually to be a North American, he was a more naïve individual than I ever saw reason to believe. This kind of writing, however, is mainly significant as revealing the lengths to which anti-Americans in Canada will go just now in their search for a Canadian identity that will have nothing American about it." Frank Underhill, "Canadian and American Ties with Europe," *Queen's Quarterly* 66, no. 3 (1959): 369.

73 Creighton, *Portrait of a Scholar*, 120.

74 Boris Swerling to Donald Creighton, 22 October 1958, LAC, MG 31 D 77, Donald Creighton fonds, vol. 16, Harold Adams Innis: Portrait of A Scholar, Correspondence, Memoranda, Reviews; Tom Easterbrook to Donald Creighton, 6 January 1958, ibid. See also Carman Fish to Donald Creighton, 9 January 1968, ibid., vol. 5, file General Correspondence 1968 no. 2. Fish had been Innis's boyhood friend and, after the war, followed him to the University of Chicago; he even served as the best man at his wedding. Fish very much admired the biography which he had recently come across, but he was "shocked" by his old friend's anti-Americanism: "Harold's statement about U.S. imperialism sounds like the Moscow-Peking line."

75 Creighton, *Portrait of a Scholar*, 146.

76 Donald Creighton to Graham Spry, 20 January 1958, LAC, MG 31 D 77, Donald Creighton fonds, vol. 8, file Canadian Broadcasting League 1.

77 Author's interviews with Cynthia Flood, 5 June 2005 and 6 June 2005.

78 Alfred Knopf to C.D. Howe, 27 October 1952, LAC, C.D. Howe fonds, MG 27 III B 20, vol. 181 file 42; C.D. Howe to Alfred Knopf, 30 October 1952, ibid.

79 Donald Creighton to Alfred Knopf, 24 November 1952, Alfred A. Knopf Inc. fonds, Harvey Ransom Center, University of Texas at Austin, 102.6. On the joint publication of *The Story of Canada* by Knopf, Faber and Faber, and Macmillan, see Alfred Knopf to Peter du Sautoy, 7 February 1958, and Peter du Sautoy to Alfred Knopf, 10 February 1958, Harvey Ransom Center, University of Texas at Austin, Alfred A. Knopf Inc. fonds, 228.6. Alfred Knopf to Donald Creighton, 21 February 1958, LAC, MG 31 D 77, vol. 21, file Story of Canada, Correspondence.

80 Donald Creighton to Alfred Knopf, 3 March 1958, Ibid; Alfred Knopf to Donald Creighton, 21 March 1958, Ibid; Donald Creighton to Alfred Knopf, 24 March 1958, ibid.

81 Graham Spry to Donald Creighton, 11 July 1958, LAC, MG 31 D 77, Donald Creighton fonds, vol. 8, file Canadian Broadcasting League 1.

82 "Delegation of the Canadian Broadcasting League to Meet the Right Honourable John Diefenbaker," ibid.

83 Hon. George C. Nowlan, *House of Commons Debates*, vol. 4, 1958, 18 August 1958, 3749.

84 Jim Conacher to Maurice Careless, 4 July 1958, UTA, James B. Conacher fonds, B2005-0011, box 2, file 5.

85 On anti-Semitism in the historical profession, see Donald Wright, *The Professionalization of History in English Canada* (Toronto: University of Toronto Press, 2005). Author's interview with Cynthia Flood, 3 June 2005.

86 Author's interview with Morris Zaslow, 31 January 2005. Gerry Tulchinsky said very much the same thing. Creighton was "always polite, kind even; he was nothing but professional, thoroughly professional, and helpful even." Author's interview with Gerry Tulchinsky, 24 October 2005.

87 Author's interview with Willard Piepenburg, 4 May 2005.

88 Jim Conacher to Maurice Careless, 4 July 1958, UTA, James B. Conacher fonds, B2005-0011, box 2, file 5.

89 Author's interview with Ramsay Cook, 3 December 2004.

90 Quotation in Claude Bissell, *Halfway up Parnassus: A Personal Account of the University of Toronto, 1932–1971* (Toronto: University of Toronto Press, 1974), 42.

91 Jim Conacher to Maurice Careless, 4 July 1958, UTA, James B. Conacher fonds, B2005-0011, box 2, file 5.

92 Donald Creighton to Claude Bissell, 8 February 1959, LAC, MG 31 D 77, Donald Creighton fonds, vol. 28, file General Correspondence 1953–1960.

93 Donald Creighton to Claude Bissell, 18 November 1957, LAC, MG 31 D 77, Donald Creighton fonds, vol. 3, file General Correspondence 1957, file 1; Claude Bissell to Donald Creighton, 22 November 1957, ibid.

94 Letter to editor, *Globe and Mail*, 12 December 1958.

95 Interview with J.M.S. Careless, 13 July 1983, UTA, B86-0038, tape VI.

96 Jim Conacher to Ken McNaught, 10 May 1959, UTA, B97-0031, box 1, file 7.

97 Interview with J.M.S. Careless, 13 July 1983, UTA, B86-0038, tape VI.

98 See Donald Creighton to Dean Woodside, 14 January 1957, UTA, A67-0008, box 14, file History, Departmental Gen. and Chairmanships.

99 Donald Creighton to Gerry Graham, 28 January 1959, King's College London Archives, Gerald Graham fonds, K/PP043, file Creighton.

100 Donald Creighton to Gerry Graham, 13 June 1959, ibid.

101 Quotation in Heather Robertson, "The Man Who Invented Canada," *Saturday Night*, October 1977, 25. The phrase "storm of weeping" comes from D.H. Lawrence's *Lady Chatterley's Lover*. Creighton loved literary references.

102 Jim Conacher to Gerry Craig, 17 November 1959, UTA, James B. Conacher fonds, B2005-0011, box 2, file 6.

103 After Creighton's dispute with Alfred Knopf, *The Story of Canada* was published in the United States by Houghton-Mifflin in 1960.

104 Donald Creighton, *The Story of Canada* (Toronto: Macmillan, 1959), 14, 18, 155, 159, 191, 218, 272, 273.

105 W.L. Morton, Review of *The Story of Canada*, *Winnipeg Free Press*, 24 October 1959; Walter O'Hearn, CBC Radio, "Critically Speaking," 20 December 1959. Copy in the William Ready Division of Archives and Research Collection, McMaster University Library (MUL), Macmillan Co. of Canada fonds, box 154, file The Story of Canada.

106 Donald Creighton to John Marshall, n.d., 1954, LAC, MG 31 D 77, Donald Creighton fonds, vol. 3, file General Correspondence 1954, file 2; Arthur Lower to Frank Underhill, 18 June 1955 and 1 November 1955, LAC, MG 30, D 204, Frank Underhill fonds, vol. 5, file A.R.M. Lower, 1928–1956.

107 Review of *The Story of Canada*, *Globe and Mail*, 31 October 1959.

108 McNaught, *Conscience and History*, 145.

109 Arthur Lower to Paul Martin, 14 November 1936, QUA, Arthur Lower fonds, Collection 5072, box 1, file A8; Underhill, "Canadian and American Ties with Europe," 376, 366, 368, 370, 372.

110 Ibid., 369.

111 Lester Pearson to Frank Underhill, 22 December 1959, LAC, Frank Underhill fonds, MG 30 D 204, vol. 13, file L.B. Pearson 1957–1971.

10 Decolonization

1 Quotation in Ronald Hyam and William Roger Louis, eds., *The Conservative Government and the End of Empire, 1957–1964 Part I* (London: Institute of Commonwealth Studies, 2000), xxvii.

2 John Darwin, *The Empire Project: The Rise and Fall of the British World-System, 1830–1970* (Cambridge: Cambridge University Press, 2008), 610.

3 Ibid., 616.

4 See Ronald Hyam, "The Geopolitical Origins of the Central African Federation: Britain, Rhodesia, and South Africa, 1948–1953," *Historical Journal* 30 (1987), and Philip Murphy, "Government by Blackmail: The Origins of the Central African Federation Reconsidered," in Martin Lynn, ed., *The British Empire in the 1950s: Retreat or Revival?* (London: Palgrave Macmillan, 2006).

5 John Darwin, "Was There a Fourth British Empire?" in Martin Lynn, ed., *The British Empire in the 1950s: Retreat or Revival* (London: Palgrave Macmillan, 2006), 26.

6 John Darwin, "The Central African Emergency, 1959," *Journal of Imperial and Commonwealth History* 21, no. 3 (1993): 219.

7 "The Federation of Rhodesia and Nyasaland: Note by the Secretary of State for Commonwealth Relations," 12 November 1958, NA, CAB 129 c.58 232; Ian N. Moles, "Race and Politics," *Australian Quarterly* 33, no. 1 (1961): 86.

8 Harold Macmillan, 21 July and 22 July 1959, *Parliamentary Debates Commons, 1958–59*, 609: 1072, 1316–17; Lord Home to Roy Welensky, 13 March 1959, Rhodes House (RH), Roy Welensky Papers, box 202, file 8.

9 "Appointment of Commission: Sequence of Events," 22 July 1959, ibid., box 204, file 2.

10 Roy Welensky to Harold Macmillan, 22 April 1959, RH, Roy Welensky Papers, box 203, file 2; Colonial Office to Roy Welensky, 16 September 1959, National Archives (NA), DO 121/236.

11 High Commission (Ottawa) to Colonial Office, 10 November 1959, NA, PREM 5/253.

12 Ibid.

13 Harold Macmillan, 24 November 1959, *Parliamentary Debates Commons, 1958–59*, 614: 209.

14 Colonial Office to Prime Minister Macmillan, 22 December 1959, NA, PREM 5/254.

15 Joey Power, *Political Culture and Nationalism in Malawi: Building Kwacha* (Rochester: University of Rochester Press, 2010), 146, 149. The Commonwealth Relations Office had prepared an answer for Harold Macmillan should the argument be put forward in the House "that the Africans are stooges and that the Commission generally is weighted against African opinion." The prime minister, the CRO said, might respond that "5 out of 13 is not a bad weightage when viewed against the strong independent and Commonwealth names in the rest of the Commission and the chairmanship of Lord Monckton." Monckton Commission Possible Answers to criticisms by Mr. Hugh Gaitskell, 16 November 1959, NA,

PREM 5/253. Five out of thirteen refers to the thirteen members from the Central African Federation.

16 Colonial Office to High Commission (Salisbury), Press Reaction, 25 November 1959, NA, PREM 5/253.

17 Donald Creighton to High Commission (Ottawa), 21 December 1959. Copy in High Commission to Colonial Office, 21 December 1959, NA, PREM 5/254.

18 Colonial Office to High Commission (Ottawa), 22 December 1959, ibid.

19 High Commission (Ottawa) to Colonial Office, 23 December 1959, ibid.

20 Donald Creighton to John Diefenbaker, 25 November 1959, LAC, Donald Creighton fonds, MG 31 D 77, vol. 22, file The Monckton Advisory Commission, 1959–1960, Correspondence on Creighton's Appointment; "Canada in Central Africa," *Globe and Mail*, 27 November 1959.

21 Donald Creighton, Diary entry for 17 January 1960, LAC, Donald Creighton fonds, MG 31 D 77, vol. 65, file 3.

22 See Preliminary Note on Administrative Arrangements, n.d., ca December 1959, LAC, Donald Creighton fonds, MG 31 D 77, vol. 22, file The Monckton Advisory Commission 1960, Memoranda, Itineraries.

23 Donald Creighton, "The Victorians and the Empire," in Donald Creighton, *Towards the Discovery of Canada* (Toronto: Macmillan, 1972), 152. In my interviews with Donald Creighton's children and his Toronto colleagues, a number of people referenced the teasing Creighton received about being the next David Livingstone.

24 See Wendy Kann's memoir of her Rhodesian childhood, *Casting with a Fragile Thread* (New York: Henry Holt, 2006), 4.

25 Donald Creighton, Diary entry for 5 February 1960, LAC, Donald Creighton fonds, MG 31 D 77, vol. 65, file 3; Vincent Massey, *What's Past Is Prologue* (Toronto: Macmillan, 1963), 29.

26 Harold Macmillan to Lord Monckton, 22 August 1959, Bodleian Library, Department of Special Collections and Western Manuscripts, Dep. Monckton, box 52; *Daily Telegraph,* 12 February 1960. I would like to thank Balliol College for permission to quote from Lord Monckton's papers.

27 "Problems That Lie Ahead in the Area of the Federation of Rhodesia and Nyasaland, Memorandum by the Secretary of State for Commonwealth Relations," 12 November 1958, NA, CAB 129 c.58 232.

28 Elspeth Huxley, Diary entry for 21 February 1960, RH, Mss. Afr. s. 2154, box 11, file 4, 1960 Diary of Travels for Monckton Commission on Central Africa.

29 Elspeth Huxley, Diary entry for 22 February 1960, ibid. See also Government House, Lusaka, Northern Rhodesia to Colonial Office, 22 February 1960, NA, DO 35/7595. Whitehall had always feared that Welensky might undermine the commission's work. See Lord Home to Harold Macmillan, 17 January 1960, in Philip Murphy, ed., *British Documents on the End of Empire: Central Africa, Part II, Crisis*

and Dissolution, 1959–1965 (London: Institute for Commonwealth Studies, 2005), 102.

30 Harold Macmillan, 24 November 1959, *Parliamentary Debates Commons, 1958–59*, 614: 207; Harold Macmillan to Roy Welensky, 24 November 1959, RH, Roy Welensky papers, box 203, file 3.

31 Lord Birkenhead, *Walter Monckton: The Life of Viscount Monckton of Brenchley* (London: Weidenfeld and Nicholson, 1969), 346; High Commission (Salisbury) to Colonial Office, 12 May 1960, NA, DO 35/7595.

32 Birkenhead, *Walter Monckton*, 346. In his memoirs, Commission member Aidan Crawley stressed that his decision to join the commission had been contingent on its being allowed to hear evidence on secession. See Aidan Crawley, *Leap before You Look: A Memoir* (London: Collins, 1988), 375–6.

33 Kann, *Casting with a Fragile Thread*, 143.

34 Chishinga Native Authority, Kawambwa District, Luapula Province, Northern Rhodesia, March 1960, NA, CO 1015/2314; Memorandum from the Federal Standing Committee of the United Federal Party, n.d, ca January 1960, NA, DO 35/7592.

35 W.S.T. Banda, Parliamentary Papers, 1960–1961, Vol. XI, Advisory Commission on the Review of the Constitution of the Federation of Rhodesia and Nyasaland, Report – Appendix VIII, Volume III, Part I, 13; Angus Montrose, Parliamentary Papers, 1960–1961, Vol. XII, Advisory Commission on the Review of the Constitution the Federation of Rhodesia and Nyasaland, Report – Appendix VIII, Volume IV, 416–18.

36 G.L. Lipschild, Parliamentary Papers, 1960–1961, Vol. XI, Advisory Commission on the Review of the Constitution of the Federation of Rhodesia and Nyasaland, Report – Appendix VIII, Volume II, Part I, 112, 117. In *Sexuality and Empire*, Ronald Hyam argued that "the peculiarly emotional hostility towards black men which [racism] has so often engendered requires a sexual explanation." "Sex," he said, "is at the very heart of racism." Ronald Hyam, *Sexuality and Empire: The British Experience* (Manchester: Manchester University Press, 1990), 200.

37 Elspeth Huxley to Gervas Huxley, 17 February 1960, RH, Mss. Afr. s. 2154, box 9, file 5.

38 See Donald Creighton's 1960 diary, LAC, LAC, MG 31 D 77, vol. 65, file 3, and his African diary, ibid., vol. 22, file The Monckton Advisory Commission – D.G. Creighton's Diary 19 February–21 March 1960. See also Lord Monckton's Commission notebooks, Bodleian Library, Department of Special Collections and Western Manuscripts, Dep. Monckton, box 55; and Parliamentary Papers, 1960–1961, Vols. XI and XII.

39 Monckton Commission Possible Answers to criticisms by Mr. Hugh Gaitskell, 16 November 1959, NA, PREM 5/253.

40 Donald Creighton, Diary entry for 8 March 1960, LAC, MG 31 D 77, vol. 65, file 3; Parliamentary Papers, 1960–1961, Vol. XI, Advisory Commission on the Review of the Constitution of the Federation of Rhodesia and Nyasaland, Report – Appendix VIII, Volume I, 267.

41 Parliamentary Papers, 1960–1961, Vol. XI, Advisory Commission on the Review of the Constitution of the Federation of Rhodesia and Nyasaland, Report – Appendix VIII, Volume III, Part I, 99; Donald Creighton Diary entry for 30 March 1960, LAC, MG 31 D 77, vol. 65, file 3. For a discussion of SARAN, see Robin Palmer, "European Resistance to African Majority Rule: The Settlers and Residents Association of Nyasaland, 1960–63," *African Affairs* 72, no. 288 (1973): 256–72.

42 Parliamentary Papers, 1960–1961, Vol. XI, Advisory Commission on the Review of the Constitution of the Federation of Rhodesia and Nyasaland, Report – Appendix VIII, Volume III, Part I, 71; Donald Creighton Diary entry for 29 March 1960, LAC, MG 31 D 77, vol. 65, file 3.

43 Elspeth Huxley recorded Creighton's reaction to Banda's presentation in her diary. Elspeth Huxley, Diary entry for 3 April 1960, RH, Mss. Afr. s. 2154, box 11, file 4, 1960 Diary of Travels for Monckton Commission on Central Africa.

44 Donald Creighton, Diary entry for 30 March 1960, LAC, MG 31 D 77, vol. 65, file 3.

45 Elspeth Huxley to Gervas Huxley, 13 March 1960, RH, Mss. Afr. s. 2154, box 9, file 5.

46 Donald Creighton, Diary entries for 15 and 17 April 1960, LAC, MG 31 D 77, vol. 65, file 3.

47 Donald Creighton, Diary entries for 15 February and 7 March 1960, ibid.

48 Donald Creighton, Diary entries for 4 and 8 March 1960, LAC, MG 31 D 77, vol. 22, file The Monckton Advisory Commission – D.G. Creighton's Diary 19 February–21 March 1960.

49 Elspeth Huxley to Gervas Huxley, 28 February 1960, RH, Mss. Afr. s. 2154, box 9, file 5. See C.S. Nicholls, *Elspeth Huxley: A Biography* (London: HarperCollins, 2002).

50 Donald Creighton, Diary entry for 19 February 1960, LAC, MG 31 D 77, vol. 65, file 3.

51 Donald Creighton, Diary entry for 2–10 March 1960, LAC, MG 31 D 77, vol. 22, file The Monckton Advisory Commission – D.G. Creighton's Diary 19 February–21 March 1960. Cynthia Flood remembers her father "having been quite moved by the landscape, by its beauty. It was new to him. It was different and so unlike anything he had seen before." Author's interview with Cynthia Flood, 3 June 2005.

52 See John Weaver, *The Great Land Rush and the Making of the Modern World, 1650–1900* (Montreal and Kingston: McGill-Queen's University Press, 2003); and Carole Pateman, "The Settler Contract," in Carole Pateman and Charles Mills, *Contract and Domination* (Cambridge: Polity, 2007).

53 I. Kandanda, Parliamentary Papers, 1960–1961, Vol. XI, Advisory Commission on the Review of the Constitution of the Federation of Rhodesia and Nyasaland, Report – Appendix VIII, Volume I, 38; The Chewa Lundazi Native Authority, ibid., 250; Damon Mtonga, ibid., 256; G.S.J. Ngoma, ibid., 254.

54 A.D. (Taffy) Evans, Communique no. 2, 16 February 1960, RH, Roy Welensky Papers, box 208, file 1.

55 A.D. (Taffy) Evans, Communique no. 21, 30 March 1960, ibid., box 208, file 2.

56 A.D. (Taffy) Evans, Communique no. 29, 12 April 1960, ibid., box 208, file 3.

57 Donald Creighton, *John A. Macdonald: The Old Chieftain* (Toronto: Macmillan, 1955), 407–8.

58 Donald Creighton, Diary entries for 11 and 14 July 1960, LAC, MG 31 D 77, vol. 65, file 3.

59 Donald Creighton, Diary entry for 23 July 1960, ibid.

60 Hand-written motion of thanks to Lord Monckton, 2 September 1960, LAC, MG 31 D 77, vol. 22, file The Monckton Advisory Commission, 1959–1960.

61 Elspeth Huxley to Gervas Huxley, 17 February 1960, RH, Mss. Afr. s. 2154, box 9, file 5.

62 Ronald Hyam described the Central African Federation as "the most controversial large-scale imperial exercise in constructive state-building ever undertaken by the British government." Hyam, "The Geopolitical Origins of the Central African Federation," 26. Lord Monckton to Harold Macmillan, 5 September 1960, NA, PREM 5/255.

63 Parliamentary Papers, 1959–1960, Vol. XI, Report of the Advisory Commission on the Review of the Constitution of the Federation of Rhodesia and Nyasaland, 99.

64 Ibid., 16.

65 Donald Creighton, Diary entry for 18 August 1960, LAC, MG 31 D 77, vol. 65, file 3.

66 Donald Creighton, Diary entry for 14 June 1960, LAC, MG 31 D 77, vol. 65, file 3. For the recommendation of a Bill of Rights like the proposed Canadian Bill of Rights, see Report of the Advisory Commission on the Review of the Constitution of the Federation of Rhodesia and Nyasaland, 80.

67 Report of the Advisory Commission on the Review of the Constitution of the Federation of Rhodesia and Nyasaland, 29, 75.

68 See Pateman, "The Settler Contract"; G.M. Craig, ed., *Lord Durham's Report* (Montreal and Kingston: McGill-Queen's University Press, 2007), 7.

69 A.D. (Taffy) Evans to Roy Welensky, 6 September 1960, RH, Roy Welensky Papers, box 209, file 2; Roy Welensky to Harold Macmillan, 14 September 1960, ibid., box 203, file 4.

70 Minute by B. St. J. Trend to Harold Macmillan on the publication of the report and the timing of the review conference, 15 September 1960, in Murphy, ed., *British*

Documents on the End of Empire, 159; Roy Welensky, Statement by the Federal Prime Minister, 11 October 1960, RH, Roy Welensky papers, box 204, file 5.

71 Roy Welensky to Denis Winchester-Gould, (N. Rhodesia) 14 October 1960, ibid. See also Roy Welensky, *Welensky's 4000 Days: The Life and Death of the Federation of Rhodesia and Nyasaland* (London: Collins, 1964); Ian Douglas Smith, *The Great Betrayal: The Memoirs of Ian Douglas Smith* (London: Blake, 1997); Stuart Ward, "Worlds Apart: Three 'British' Prime Ministers at Empire's End," in Phillip Buckner and R. Douglas Francis, eds, *Rediscovering the British World* (Calgary: University of Calgary Press, 2005).

72 Donald Creighton, "Should the Republic of South Africa be re-admitted to the Commonwealth?" 18 February 1961, LAC, MG 31 D 77, vol. 28, file General Correspondence, 1961.

73 Harold Macmillan, Diary entry for 24 March 1961, Bodleian Library, Department of Special Collections and Western Manuscripts, Dep. Macmillan, d. 41. I want to thank the trustees of the Harold Macmillan Book Trust, Copyright and Archives Fund, for permission to quote from the Harold Macmillan papers.

74 Denis Smith, *Rogue Tory: The Life and Legend of John G. Diefenbaker* (Toronto: MacFarlane, Walter, and Ross, 1995), 366. See also John Hilliker and Donald Barry, *Canada's Department of External Affairs*, vol. 2: *Coming of Age, 1946–1968* (Ottawa: Supply and Services, 1995), 163–6.

75 Donald Creighton to Eugene Forsey, 27 April 1961, LAC, MG 31 D 77, vol. 26, file Correspondence with Eugene Forsey, 1944–1964; Eugene Forsey to Donald Creighton, 30 April 1961, ibid. In fairness, Creighton overstated the department's opposition. Within the department there was considerable debate and much hand wringing over the best way to handle the South African problem. See H. Basil Robinson, *Diefenbaker's World: A Populist in Foreign Affairs* (Toronto: University of Toronto Press, 1989), and Robert Bothwell, *Alliance and Illusion: Canada and the World, 1945–1984* (Vancouver: UBC Press, 2007).

76 Darwin, *The Empire Project*, 626.

77 Luella Creighton, "Diary of a Village Woman," 23 May [1962?], University of Waterloo, Doris Lewis Rare Book Room, Luella Creighton fonds, GA 99, series 5, file 106.

78 Donald Creighton to Gerald Graham, 3 July 1961, King's College London Archives, Gerald Graham fonds, K/PP043, file Creighton.

79 Donald Creighton, Diary entry for 15 September 1960, LAC, MG 31 D 77, vol. 65, vol. 3.

80 Luella Creighton, "Diary of a Village Woman," 23 May [1962?], University of Waterloo, Doris Lewis Rare Book Room, Luella Creighton fonds, GA 99, series 5, file 106.

81 Elspeth Huxley, "Phantom Commonwealth," *Weekly Telegraph*, 7 June 1968.

82 On Britain, Canada, and the European Economic Community, see Andrea Benvenuti and Stuart Ward, "Britain, Europe, and the Other Quiet Revolution in Canada," in Phillip Buckner, ed., *Canada and the End of Empire* (Vancouver: UBC Press, 2005). On the Commonwealth, see Philip Murphy, "Britain and the Commonwealth: Confronting the Past – Imagining the Future," *Roundtable* 100, no. 414 (June 2011): 267–83.

83 On Australia's search for "a post-imperial successor myth," see James Curran and Stuart Ward, *The Unknown Nation: Australia after Empire* (Melbourne: Melbourne University Press, 2010).

84 Donald Creighton, *Canada's First Century* (Toronto: Macmillan, 1970), 271; quotation in Louis Fournier, *F.L.Q.: The Anatomy of an Underground Movement* (Toronto: NC Press, 1984), 16. See also Sean Mills, *The Empire Within: Postcolonial Thought and Political Activism in Sixties Montreal* (Montreal and Kingston: McGill-Queen's University Press, 2010).

85 José Igartua, *The Other Quiet Revolution: National Identities in English Canada, 1945–1971* (Vancouver: UBC Press, 2006). See also See A.G. Hopkins, "Rethinking Decolonization," *Past and Present* 200 (August 2008): 211–47.

86 Pierre Trudeau, "New Treason of the Intellectuals," in Pierre Trudeau, *Against the Current: Selected Writings, 1939–1996* (Toronto: McClelland and Stewart, 1996), 178.

87 Luella Creighton, "Hallie Chisolm," unpublished manuscript, University of Waterloo, Doris Lewis Rare Book Room, Luella Creighton fonds, GA 99, series 5, box 11, file 115.

88 Luella Creighton, Diary entry for 14 January 1963, University of Waterloo, Doris Lewis Rare Book Room, Luella Creighton fonds, GA 99, series 3, box 2, file 9.

89 Luella Creighton, *Canada: The Struggle for Empire* (Toronto: Dent, 1960), 235, 370. For a detailed analysis of *The Struggle for Empire* and *Trial and Triumph*, see Igartua, *The Other Quiet Revolution*, 146–8.

90 The phrase "giggling bow-tied bastard" is contained in a letter from Gerald Graham to Donald Creighton, but it is clear that Graham is quoting Creighton. See Gerald Graham to Donald Creighton, 16 April 1974, LAC, MG 31 D 77, vol. 65, file 3.

91 Donald Creighton to Eugene Forsey, 23 January 1963, LAC, MG 31 D 77, vol. 26, file Correspondence with Eugene Forsey, 1944–1964.

92 On a newspaper clipping about Lester Pearson from the *London Times* dated 31 August 1964, Creighton pencilled "Go after the bastard." LAC, MG 31 D 77, vol. 27, file Biculturalism 1964. Charles Taylor, *Radical Tories: The Conservative Tradition in Canada* (Toronto: Anansi, 1982), 23.

93 Quotation in Igartua, *The Other Quiet Revolution*, 197.

94 Donald Creighton to Eugene Forsey, 4 August 1963, LAC, MG 31 D 77, vol. 26, file Correspondence with Eugene Forsey, 1944–1964; Eugene Forsey to Donald Creighton, 31 July 1963, ibid.

95 Ramsay Cook, "A Time to Break Silence," *Canadian Forum* 43 (July 1963): 79.
96 Donald Creighton to Ramsay Cook, 4 August 1963. Original in possession of Ramsay Cook
97 Ramsay Cook to Donald Creighton, 21 August 1963, MG 31 D 77, vol. 28, file General Correspondence 1963.
98 Through brute force, Rhodesia held out for another fifteen years, but in 1980 it became Zimbabwe. On the final collapse of the Central African Federation, see John Darwin, *Britain and Decolonization: The Retreat from Empire in the Post-War World* (London: Macmillan, 1988).
99 Taylor, *Radical Tories*, 24.
100 Gregory A. Johnson, "The Last Gasp of Empire: The 1964 Flag Debate Revisited," in Buckner, ed., *Canada and the End of Empire*, 233.
101 Donald Creighton to W.L. Morton, 26 April 1964, McMaster University Library (MUL), W.L. Morton fonds, box 6, file Creighton D.G., 1962–64; Donald Creighton to Gerald Graham, 8 August 1964, King's College London Archives, Gerald Graham fonds, K/PP043, file Creighton.
102 Donald Creighton, Diary entry for 18 June 1964, LAC, MG 31 D 77, vol. 65, file 5.
103 Luella Creighton, Diary entry for 7 May 1964, University of Waterloo, Doris Lewis Rare Book Room, Luella Creighton fonds, GA 99, series 3, box 2, file 10.
104 Donald Creighton et al. to Lester Pearson, 27 May 1964, LAC, MG 31 D 77, vol. 30, file The New Flag.
105 "Flag Design Opposed by 12 Scholars, Termed Poor Symbol," *Globe and Mail*, 29 May 1964; Lester Pearson, House of Commons, *Debates*, 1 June 1964, 3783–4.
106 Quotation in Johnson, "Last Gasp of Empire," 236; Donald Creighton to Gerald Graham, 8 August 1964, King's College London Archives, Gerald Graham fonds, K/PP043, file Creighton; C.P. Champion, "A Very British Coup: Canadianism, Quebec, and Ethnicity in the Flag Debate, 1964–1965," *Journal of Canadian Studies* 40, no. 3 (2006): 68–99.
107 Philip Buckner, "The Last Great Royal Tour: Queen Elizabeth's 1959 Royal Tour to Canada," in Buckner, ed., *Canada and the End of Empire*, 84
108 Lester Pearson, *Mike: The Memoirs of The Right Honourable Lester B. Pearson*, vol. 3 (Toronto: University of Toronto Press, 1975), 292; "The Queen's Visit," *Globe and Mail*, 17 September 1964.
109 "Quebec Police Club Separatists," *Globe and Mail*, 12 October 1964.
110 Donald Creighton, Diary entry for 10 October 1964, LAC, MG 31 D 77, vol. 65, file 5; Donald Creighton to W. L. Morton, 21 March 1961, MUL, W.L. Morton fonds, box 6, file Creighton, D.G., 1955–1961.
111 Donald Creighton to W.L. Morton, 22 September 1964, ibid., box 6, file Creighton, D.G., 1962–1964.

112 Scott Symons to W.L. Morton, 6 October 1965, MUL, W.L. Morton fonds, box 21, file Symons, S. 1963–1966; author's interview with Scott Symons, 18 November 2005. See also Scott Symons, *Combat Journal for Place d'Armes: A Personal Narrative by Scott Symons* (Toronto: McClelland and Stewart, 1967), 5, 79.

113 Author's interview with Ramsay Cook, 3 December 2004; Donald Creighton, *Canada's First Century* (Toronto: Oxford University Press, 2012), 337.

114 See Johnson, "Last Gasp of Empire."

115 Arthur Lower, "Centennial Ends: Centennial Begins," *Queen's Quarterly* 74, no. 2 (1967): 237.

116 See C.P. Champion, *The Strange Demise of British Canada: The Liberals and Canadian Nationalism, 1964–1968* (Montreal and Kingston: McGill-Queen's University Press, 2010).

11 Confederation

1 *A Preliminary Report of the Royal Commission on Bilingualism and Biculturalism* (Ottawa: Queen's Printer, 1965), 13.

2 Lester Pearson, *Mike: The Memoirs of The Right Honourable Lester B. Pearson*, vol. 3 (Toronto: University of Toronto Press, 1975), 238.

3 Author's interview with John Cairns, 2 December 2004.

4 Donald Creighton, Diary entry for 18 August 1961, LAC, MG 31 D 77, Donald Creighton fonds, vol. 65, file 3.

5 Donald Creighton to Noel Fieldhouse, 19 August 1964, ibid., vol. 4, file General Correspondence 1964.

6 Donald Creighton to Eugene Forsey, 16 August 1964, ibid., vol. 26, file Correspondence with Eugene Forsey, 1944–1964.

7 Donald Creighton to Gerald Graham, 8 August 1964, King's College London Archives, Gerald Graham fonds, K/PP043, file Creighton.

8 Moffatt Woodside to Donald Creighton, 20 July 1965, MG 31 D 77, vol. 35, file The Road to Confederation, Correspondence, Reviews; [Name illegible, Department of Classics] to Donald Creighton, 23 June 1965, ibid.; Jack Creighton to Donald Creighton, 11 November 1964, ibid.

9 Ged Martin prefers the metaphor of logjam over the usual metaphor of deadlock. The former implies the possibility of movement, the latter doesn't. Besides, logjam is better suited to British North America, which, in a way, was a collection of timber colonies. Ged Martin, *Past Futures: The Impossible Necessity of History* (Toronto: University of Toronto Press, 2004), 95.

10 S.R. Mealing, Review of *The Road to Confederation*, *Queen's Quarterly* 72 (Winter 1966): 702; Albert Tucker, "The Ambiguous Middle," *Canadian Literature* 26 (Fall 1965): 64.

11 See Reginald Trotter, *Canadian Federation, Its Origin and Achievement: A Study in Nation Building* (London: J.M. Dent and Sons, 1924); Donald Creighton, *British North America at Confederation* (Ottawa: King's Printer, 1939); Donald Creighton, "The Course of Canadian Democracy," *University of Toronto Quarterly* 11 (1942); Chester Martin, *Foundations of Canadian Nationhood* (Toronto: University of Toronto Press, 1955); Donald Creighton, *John A. Macdonald: The Young Politician* (Toronto: Macmillan, 1952); J.M.S. Careless, *Brown of the Globe: The Statesman of Confederation* (Toronto: Macmillan, 1963); Peter Waite, *The Life and Times of Confederation, 1864–1867* (Toronto: University of Toronto Press, 1962); and W.L. Morton, *The Critical Years: The Union of British North America, 1857–1873* (Toronto: McClelland and Stewart, 1964); F.W.P. Bolger, *Prince Edward Island and Confederation, 1863–1873* (Charlottetown: St Dunstan's University Press, 1964). Technically, Creighton didn't have access to the Morton and Bolger books while he was writing his book. However, he had read Morton's book in manuscript form and had supervised Bolger's doctoral thesis.

12 Donald Creighton, *The Road to Confederation: The Emergence of Canada, 1863–867* (Oxford: Oxford University Press, 2012), 198, 224, 236, 311.

13 Ibid., 103. See also 4, 48, 131, 134, 136, 158, 233, 234, 288, 335, 437–9.

14 George Orwell, "Charles Dickens," in George Orwell, *Collected Essays* (London: Secker & Warburg, 1968), 75.

15 Quotation in John Clive, *Not By Fact Alone* (New York: Knopf, 1989), 199.

16 Creighton, *The Road to Confederation*, 104, 159, 438.

17 Ibid., 147, 159.

18 Ibid., 220, 235, 283. See also Carl Berger, *The Writing of Canadian History: Aspects of English-Canadian Historical Writing since 1900* (Toronto: University of Toronto Press, 1976), 234.

19 Ibid., 270.

20 Donald Creighton to Eugene Forsey, 1 December 1962, LAC, MG 31 D 77, Donald Creighton fonds, vol. 26, file Correspondence with Eugene Forsey, 1944–1964.

21 Creighton, *The Road to Confederation*, 178.

22 Ibid., 166, 164. See also 92, 98, 113, 118, 128, 130, 144–5, 163–8, 216, 398. Creighton's assumption that the Fathers of Confederation intended to create a strong central government was the assumption of his scholarly generation. See Norman McLeod Rogers, "The Compact Theory of Confederation," *Proceedings of the Canadian Political Science Association* (1931); F.R. Scott, "The Development of Canadian Federalism," *Proceedings of the Canadian Political Science Association* (1931); Eugene Forsey, "Disallowance of Provincial Acts, Reservation of Provincial Bills, and Refusal of Assent by Lieutenant-Governors since 1867," *Canadian Journal of Economics and Political Science* 4, no. 1 (1938); W.P.M. Kennedy, "The Terms of the British North America Act," in Ralph Flenley, ed., *Essays in Canadian History*

(Toronto: Macmillan, 1939); Wilfrid Eggleston, *The Road to Nationhood: A Chronicle of Dominion-Provincial Relations* (Toronto: Oxford University Press, 1946); and Arthur Lower, *Colony to Nation: A History of Canada* (Toronto: Longmans, Green, 1947).

23 Creighton, *The Road to Confederation*, 275. See also 7–8, 16–19, 30, 110–11, 194–5, 212–14, 220, 229–30, 243–4, 270–1, 273–5, 282, 303–5. On the limited impact of the Civil War on Confederation see Martin, *Past Futures*, 46–9.

24 Donald Creighton to Eugene Forsey, 1 December 1962, LAC, MG 31 D 77, Donald Creighton fonds, vol. 26, file Correspondence with Eugene Forsey, 1944–1964.

25 Creighton, *The Road to Confederation*, 439.

26 Roger Graham, Review of *The Road to Confederation*, *Canadian Historical Review* 46, no. 3 (1965): 253; W.L. Morton, Review of *The Road to Confederation*, *Winnipeg Tribune*, 1964. Copy in McMaster University Library (MUL), Macmillan Co. of Canada fonds, box 154, file Road to Confederation; Ramsay Cook, Review of *The Road to Confederation*, *Montreal Star*, 24 October 1964; Donald Creighton, Diary entries for 9 December 1964 and 27 October 1964, LAC, MG 31 D 77, Donald Creighton fonds, vol. 65, file 5.

27 Christopher Moore, *1867: How the Fathers Made a Deal* (Toronto: McClelland and Stewart, 1997), 36; author's interview with Peter Russell, 14 October 2005.

28 Arthur Lower, Review of *The Road to Confederation*, *Winnipeg Free Press*, 5 November 1964; Margaret Ormsby, Review of *The Road to Confederation*, *Vancouver Sun*, 20 November 1964; Claude Ryan, "Aux origines de la confédération," *Le Devoir*, 9 January 1965; Michel Brunet, Review of *The Road to Confederation*, CBC Radio, "Critically Speaking," 19 December 1964. Copy in MUL, Macmillan Co. of Canada fonds, box 154, file Road to Confederation; Paul L'Allier, Review of *The Road to Confederation*, *Relations* 25, no. 295 (July 1965): 218.

29 Arthur Silver effectively challenges Creighton's assertion that what was good enough for 1867 was good enough for 1967. He argues that French Canada's idea of Confederation initially centred on separation and independence: separation from Upper Canada and independence for Quebec within its spheres of jurisdiction. In the three decades after 1867, Quebec expanded its idea of Confederation to include both language and religious rights for French-speaking Canadians outside of Quebec. In the same way that a parsimonious Creighton used history to limit bilingualism, a generous Silver used history to make the case for greater bilingualism. A.I. Silver, *The French-Canadian Idea of Confederation 1864–1900*, 2nd ed. (Toronto: University of Toronto Press, 1997). See also Marcel Bellavance, *Le Québec et la confédération: un choix libre? Le clergé et la constitution de 1867* (Sillery: Septentrion, 1992).

30 Creighton, *The Road to Confederation*, 12, 34, 105, 242, 342.

31 Quotation in C.M. Wallace, "Smith, Sir Albert James," *Dictionary of Canadian Biography*.

32 Creighton, *The Road to Confederation*, 248, 5, 356.

33 Ibid., 288, 376. For an excellent analysis of the historiography on the Maritimes and Confederation see Phillip Buckner, "The Maritimes and Confederation: A Reassessment," *Canadian Historical Review* 71, no. 1 (1990): 1–45.

34 See Allan Smith, "Old Ontario and the Emergence of a National Frame of Mind," in Allan Smith, *Canada: An American Nation* (Montreal and Kingston: McGill-Queen's University Press, 1994).

35 Ged Martin, "Introduction to the 2006 Edition," in Peter Waite, ed., *The Confederation Debates in the Province of Canada* (Montreal and Kingston: McGill-Queen's University Press, 2006), xxxii; Peter Waite, "Introduction to the First Edition," ibid., xliv. See also Ged Martin, "The Case against Canadian Confederation," in Ged Martin, ed., *The Causes of Canadian Confederation* (Fredericton: Acadiensis Press, 1990).

36 Waite, ed., *The Confederation Debates*, 9, 24.

37 Creighton, *The Road to Confederation*, 168.

38 Donald Creighton, *The Empire of the St. Lawrence* (Toronto: University of Toronto Press, 2002), 6.

39 Creighton, *The Road to Confederation*, 6, 181, 437, 148.

40 Author's interview with Cynthia Flood, 4 June 2005.

41 Luella Creighton, Diary entries for 14 December 1964, 30 November 1964, 2 December 1964, 3 December 1964, University of Waterloo, Doris Lewis Rare Book Room, Luella Creighton fonds, GA 99, series 3, box 2, file 10.

42 The phrase "hot, breathless" comes from Donald Creighton, "Romeo and Juliet as Poetry and Drama," n.d., LAC, MG 31 D 77, Donald Creighton fonds, vol. 15, file English Literature Essays.

43 When Hugh Macdonald indicated that he hadn't "the smallest intention of altering his decision," Sir John A. "found himself playing" his assigned role in the "romantically banal" stage production of boy meets girl, that of "the heavy father at the expense of two devoted and defiant lovers." Donald Creighton, *John A. Macdonald: The Old Politician* (Toronto: Macmillan, 1955), 201.

44 Luella Creighton, Diary entry for 2 December 1964, University of Waterloo, Doris Lewis Rare Book Room, Luella Creighton fonds, GA 99, series 3, box 2, file 10.

45 Luella Creighton to W.L. Morton, 27 March 1965, MUL, W.L. Morton fonds, box 6, file Creighton D.G., 1965–1969.

46 Donald Creighton, Diary entries for 22 May 1965 and 23 May 1965, LAC, MG 31 D 77, Donald Creighton fonds, vol. 65, file 5; Donald Creighton to W.L. Morton, 28 May 1965 and 14 June 1965, MUL, W.L. Morton fonds, box 6, file Creighton D.G., 1965–1969.

47 "Professor's Daughter Marries," *Globe and Mail*, 24 May 1965; "Amending Plan, Plea to Queen Draw Criticism," *Globe and Mail*, 24 May 1965.

48 Author's interview with John Meisel, 2 November 2004.

49 Author's interview with H. Ian Macdonald, 11 February 2004; Ontario Advisory Committee on Confederation Terms of Reference, 5 January 1965, Archives of Ontario (AO), F1017, MU5311, file Notices and Agendas, 1965–1966.

50 Donald Creighton, Diary entry for 29 November 1964, LAC, MG 31 D 77, Donald Creighton fonds, vol. 65, file 5.

51 Donald Creighton to Eugene Forsey, 14 January 1965, ibid., vol. 26, file Correspondence with Eugene Forsey, 1965–1975.

52 Smith, "Old Ontario," 274.

53 Donald Creighton, *Sir John A. Macdonald: The Old Chieftain* (Toronto: Macmillan, 1955), 220–1.

54 John Meisel recalls that in 1965 he was "an emerging Canadian nationalist" who didn't want "to see the country smashed" and who found "Quebecers *très sympathique.*" John Meisel, *A Life of Learning and Other Pleasures: John Meisel's Tale* (Yarker, ON: Wintergreen Studios Press, 2012), 248.

55 Author's interview with Tom Symons, 26 January 2004. See also T.H.B. Symons, "Proposals for an Ontario Cultural and Educational Exchange Program," in Ontario Advisory Committee on Confederation, *The Confederation Challenge: Background Papers and Reports* (Toronto: Queen's Printer, 1967); and Charles Beer, "Quiet Revolutionary: Tom Symons, National Unity, and Linguistic Rights," in Ralph Heintzman, ed., *Tom Symons: A Canadian Life* (Ottawa: University of Ottawa Press, 2011).

56 Ontario Advisory Committee on Confederation, Verbatim Report of Proceedings, 21–2 April 1967, Trent University Archives, Ontario Advisory Committee on Confederation, Accession no. 86-030, box 5, folder 11.

57 Donald Creighton, "The Dominance of English in Ontario," n.d., ca spring 1966, LAC, MG 31 D 77, Donald Creighton fonds, vol. 15, file 7.

58 Ontario Advisory Committee on Confederation, Verbatim Report of Proceedings, 24 April 1966, Archives of Ontario, F 1017, MU 5326; Gerald Craig, ed., *Lord Durham's Report* (Montreal and Kingston: McGill-Queen's University Press, 2007), 147–8. On the policy of voluntary assimilation, see Chad Gaffield, *Language, Schooling, and Cultural Conflict: The Origins of the French-language Controversy in Ontario* (Montreal and Kingston: McGill-Queen's University Press, 1987), 5–30.

59 Ontario Advisory Committee on Confederation, Verbatim Report, 24 April 1966, Archives of Ontario, F 1017, MU 5326.

60 Donald Creighton to Eugene Forsey, 26 April 1966, LAC, MG 31 D 77, Donald Creighton fonds, vol. 26, file Correspondence with Eugene Forsey, 1965–1975.

61 Ontario Advisory Committee on Confederation, Verbatim Report, 24 April 1966, Archives of Ontario, F 1017, MU 5326.

62 Eugene Forsey to Donald Creighton, 28 April 1966, LAC, MG 31 D 77, Donald Creighton fonds, vol. 26, file Correspondence with Eugene Forsey, 1965–1975; Eugene Forsey to Donald Creighton, 1 March 1966, ibid.

63 Ted McWhinney, 31 July 2007. Personal communication to author.

64 Donald Creighton to Eugene Forsey, 31 August 1964, LAC, MG 31 D 77, Donald Creighton fonds, vol. 26, file Correspondence with Eugene Forsey, 1944–1964.

65 Donald Creighton, Diary entry for 4 June 1966, LAC, MG 31 D 77, Donald Creighton fonds, vol. 65, file 6; Donald Creighton to W.L. Morton, 27 November 1966, MUL, W.L. Morton fonds, box 6, file Creighton, D.G. 1965–1969.

66 Kildare Dobbs to Donald Creighton, 11 July 1966, MUL, Saturday Night fonds, box 9, file 6; Donald Creighton to Kildare Dobbs, 13 July 1966.

67 Donald Creighton, "The Myth of Biculturalism or The Great French-Canadian Sales Campaign," *Saturday Night*, September 1966.

68 Donald Creighton to Joseph Thornson, 13 January 1969, LAC, MG 31 D 77, Donald Creighton fonds, vol. 28, file General Correspondence 1969; Donald Creighton to Ramsay Cook, 4 August 1963. Original in possession of Ramsay Cook.

69 Donald Creighton to Kildare Dobbs, 23 July 1966, MUL, Saturday Night fonds, box 9, file 6; Donald Creighton to Kildare Dobbs, 13 July 1966. A copy of the original manuscript is in this file.

70 Solange Chaput-Rolland, Letter to the Editor, *Saturday Night*, November 1966; John Trent, Letter to the Editor, ibid.

71 K.W. Taylor, Letter to the Editor, *Saturday Night*, December 1966; Peter Hopwood, Letter to the Editor, ibid.

72 Claude Ryan, "Notes sur un article récent (et malheureux) du professeur Donald Creighton," *Le Devoir*, 17 September 1966. See also Gilles Boyer, "Le mythe de M. Creighton," *Le Devoir*, 15 September 1966. Boyer also draws on Ramsay Cook to refute Creighton.

73 Donald Creighton to Eugene Forsey, 12 February 1967, LAC, MG 31 D 77, Donald Creighton fonds, vol. 26, file Correspondence with Eugene Forsey, 1965–1975; Donald Creighton, Diary entry for 11 October 1966, ibid., vol. 65, file 6.

74 Donald Creighton to Eugene Forsey, 17 April 1967, ibid., vol. 26, file Correspondence with Eugene Forsey, 1965–1975.

75 W.L. Morton, Review of H. Blair Neatby, *William Lyon Mackenzie King: The Lonely Heights, 1924–1932, Canadian Historical Review* 45, no. 4 (1964): 320–1.

76 Quotation in Ramsay Cook, "Nation, Identity, Rights: Reflections on W.L. Morton's Canadian Identity," *Journal of Canadian Studies* 29, no. 2 (1994): 10.

77 W.L. Morton, "Foreword," in Solange Chaput-Rolland, *My Country, Canada or Quebec* (Toronto: Macmillan, 1966), xi. For an interesting discussion of Chaput-Rolland, see Pierre Berton, *1967: The Last Good Year* (Toronto: Doubleday, 1997), 325–35.

78 Donald Creighton to W.L. Morton, 19 December 1966, MUL, W.L. Morton fonds, box 6, file Creighton, D.G. 1965–1969; Donald Creighton to John Gray, n.d., ca

December 1966, LAC, MG 31 D 77, Donald Creighton fonds, vol. 28, file General Correspondence 1966; W.L. Morton to Donald Creighton, 23 December 1966, ibid.

79 Donald Creighton, "John A. Macdonald, Confederation and the Canadian West," *Historical and Scientific Society of Manitoba Transactions*, series III, 23 (1966–7): 9, 10, 7.

80 Donald Creighton, Diary entry for 11 January 1967, LAC, MG 31 D 77, Donald Creighton fonds, vol. 65, file 7; "Arpin's Blood Boils at Speech," *Winnipeg Free Press*, 12 January 1967; "Doern Attacks Historian," *Winnipeg Free Press*, 13 January 1967; Cornelius Jaenen, "Professors Clash Over Confederation," *Winnipeg Free Press*, 14 January 1967; "Come Off It Professor," *Ottawa Citizen*, 17 January 1967; Tim Creery, "Historian's Choice Plea for Secession," *Ottawa Citizen*, 18 January 1967. Curiously enough, Doern would later lead a campaign against the extension of French-language services in Manitoba. See Russell Doern, *The Battle over Bilingualism: The Manitoba Language Question, 1983–85* (Winnipeg: Cambridge Publishers, 1985).

81 Donald Creighton to Editor, *Winnipeg Free Press*, 19 January 1967, LAC, MG 31 D 77, Donald Creighton fonds, vol. 30, file Manitoba Historical Society.

82 Donald Creighton to Shane MacKay, 28 February 1967, LAC, MG 31 D 77, Donald Creighton fonds, vol. 5, file General Correspondence 1967 no. 1.

83 See Michel Brunet to Donald Creighton, 10 July 1956, 11 August 1956, and 1 November 1958, LAC, MG 31 D 77, Donald Creighton fonds, vol. 3, file General Correspondence 1956 no. 1 and vol. 4, file General Correspondence 1958 no. 2. For a summary of the fallout from Creighton's Winnipeg address in Quebec see "Creighton Trod Where Angels Fear," *Montreal Gazette*, 8 February 1967.

84 Michel Brunet to Cornelius Jaenen, 26 January 1967. Original in possession of Cornelius Jaenen. Michel Brunet to Donald Creighton, 15 July 1967, LAC, MG 31 D 77, Donald Creighton fonds, vol. 28, file General Correspondence 1967.

85 See Edmund A. Aunger, "Justifying the End of Official Bilingualism: Canada's North-West Assembly and the Dual-Language Question, 1889–1892," *Canadian Journal of Political Science* 34, no. 3 (2001): 451–86.

86 W.L. Morton, "Manitoba Schools and Canadian Nationality, 1890–1923," *Report of the Annual Meeting of the Canadian Historical Association* 30, no. 1 (1951): 51.

87 Donald Creighton to W.D. Smith, 7 March 1967, LAC, MG 31 D 77, Donald Creighton fonds, vol. 5, file General Correspondence 1967.

88 Donald Creighton, Diary entry for 21 September 1960, ibid., vol. 65, file 3.

89 Donald Creighton, Richardson manuscript. Original in possession of Ramsay Derry.

90 This amount was more than was originally agreed to because the stock had increased in value. In today's dollars, $40,747.24 would be over $270,000.

91 Berton, *1967: The Last Good Year*, 39.

92 Michael Bliss, *A Professor's Life* (Toronto: Dundurn, 2011), 114; author's interview with Michael Bliss, 7 March 2005. George Grant believed that Diefenbaker had neglected the university community. "To take one example – it is difficult to believe that the leading contemporary theorist of the conservative view of Canada, Professor D.G. Creighton, should never have been used on the manifold boards, councils, commissions, etc., that formulate our national policies. Not only was he the biographer of Diefenbaker's hero, Sir John A. Macdonald, but Creighton had defined the conservative view of Canada to a whole generation." *Lament for a Nation* (Montreal and Kingston: McGill-Queen's University Press, 2005), 24–5. Actually, Diefenbaker very much admired Creighton's *Macdonald*. See Cara Spittal, "The Diefenbaker Moment" (PhD thesis, University of Toronto, 2011).
93 Donald Creighton to Eugene Forsey, 24 July 1967, LAC, MG 31 D 77, Donald Creighton fonds, vol. 26, file Correspondence with Eugene Forsey, 1965–1975.
94 Quotation in Berton, *1867: The Last Good Year*, 361.
95 I am paraphrasing Myra Rutherdale and J.R. Miller, "'It's our country': First Nations' Participation in the Indian Pavilion at Expo 67," *Journal of the Canadian Historical Association* 17, no. 2 (2006): 173.
96 Quotation in Bryan Palmer, *Canada's 1960s: The Ironies of Identity in a Rebellious Era* (Toronto: University of Toronto Press, 2009), 391.
97 "Indian Pavilion Tries Not to Be Restful," *Globe and Mail*, 1 May 1967.
98 "Queen Silent after Viewing Indians' Demand for Better Deal," *Globe and Mail*, 4 July 1967; "Indians' Sad Story Fails to Mover Her," *Toronto Daily Star*, 3 July 1967.
99 Donald Creighton, Diary entry for 27 September 1967, LAC, MG 31 D 77, Donald Creighton fonds, vol. 65, file 6.
100 Donald Creighton, *Dominion of the North* (Boston: Houghton Mifflin, 1944), 113.
101 Luella Creighton, *The Elegant Canadians* (Toronto: McClelland and Stewart, 1967), 10, 9, 158, 135, 52. For a fuller analysis, see my introduction to Luella Creighton, *The Elegant Canadians* (Toronto: Oxford University Press, 2013).
102 Gordon Sinclair, CBC Radio review of *The Elegant Canadians*, copy in University of Waterloo, Doris Lewis Rare Book Room, Luella Creighton fonds, GA 99, series 4, box 5, file 50.
103 Margaret Prang, "Nationalism in Canada's First Century," *Historical Papers* 3, no. 1 (1968): 123.
104 Donald Creighton, Diary entry for 30 December 1967, LAC, MG 31 D 77, Donald Creighton fonds, vol. 65, file 6.
105 Maurice Careless, "Limited Identities in Canada," *Canadian Historical Review* 50, no. 1 (March 1969): 1.
106 Donald Creighton, Diary entry for 30 December 1967, LAC, MG 31 D 77, Donald Creighton fonds, vol. 65, file 6.

107 Donald Creighton once told Michael Cross that, for the reasons listed, 1883 had been Canada's last good year. Michael Cross, personal communication with author, 26 October 2012.

12 Despair

1 Donald Creighton, Diary entry for 27 May 1969, LAC, MG 31 D 77, Donald Creighton fonds, vol. 65, file 7.
2 Author's interview with Richard Clippingdale, 20 May 2006.
3 Kenneth Dewar, "The Professionalization of History," *This Magazine* 5 (1971): 52.
4 Donald Creighton, "The Decline and Fall of the Empire of the St. Lawrence," *Historical Papers* 4 (1969): 15.
5 Donald Creighton, "Towards the Discovery of Canada," in Donald Creighton, *Towards the Discovery of Canada* (Toronto: Macmillan, 1972), 48.
6 Donald Creighton, "Aims and Methods of an Historian," unpublished talk, ca early 1970s. Original in possession of Ramsay Derry. See also Donald Creighton, "The Reviewers Reviewed," in Donald Creighton, *The Passionate Observer: Selected Writings* (Toronto: McClelland and Stewart, 1980).
7 Creighton, "Decline and Fall," 25.
8 Dewar, "Professionalization of History," 52.
9 Mark Phillips, "The Professionalization of History," *This Magazine* 5 (1971): 36.
10 See Irving Abella, "The CIO, the Communist Party, and the Canadian Congress of Labour, 1936–1941," *Historical Papers* 4 (1969): 112–28.
11 Donald Creighton to Eugene Forsey, 4 July 1969, LAC, MG 31 D 77, Donald Creighton fonds, vol. 26, file Correspondence with Eugene Forsey, 1965–1975.
12 Donald Creighton, Diary entry for 10 October 1969, LAC, MG 31 D 77, Donald Creighton fonds, vol. 65, file 7.
13 Luella Creighton, Diary entries for 25 December 1969 and 16 May 1970, University of Waterloo, Doris Lewis Rare Book Room, Luella Creighton fonds, GA 99, series 3, box 2, files 15 and 16.
14 Quotation in Robert Finch, Diary, 1970, Thomas Fisher Rare Book Library, MS Coll. 324, Robert Finch Papers, box 8, 1970 Notebook.
15 Donald Creighton, Diary entry for 14 February 1962, LAC, MG 31 D 77, Donald Creighton fonds, vol. 65, file 4.
16 Luella Creighton, Diary entry for 12 February 1970, University of Waterloo, Doris Lewis Rare Book Room, Luella Creighton fonds, GA 99, series 3, box 2, file 16.
17 Luella Creighton, *The Hitching Post* (Toronto: McClelland and Stewart, 1969), 16.
18 Luella Creighton, Diary entry for 30 July 1968, University of Waterloo, Doris Lewis Rare Book Room, Luella Creighton fonds, GA 99, series 3, box 2, file 14.

19 Creighton, *The Hitching Post*, 93.
20 Luella Creighton, Untitled speech, n.d., University of Waterloo, Doris Lewis Rare Book Room, Luella Creighton fonds, GA 99, series 5, box 10, file 105.
21 Luella Creighton, "Prelude," ibid., box 9, files 86–7.
22 Author's interview with Cynthia Flood, 3 June 2005.
23 Donald Creighton, *Canada's First Century* (Toronto: Oxford University Press, 2012), 1, 14.
24 Ibid., 13, 8.
25 Ibid., 174, 163, 174.
26 Ibid., 163; Donald Creighton, "Prostitutes Left Out in Account of Mackenzie King's Career," *Globe and Mail*, 28 February 1976.
27 Creighton, *Canada's First Century*, 268.
28 Ibid., 294, 319–20.
29 Ibid., 332.
30 Donald Creighton, *The Empire of the St. Lawrence* (Toronto: University of Toronto Press, 2002), 384; Creighton, *Canada's First Century*, 351, 356.
31 Donald Creighton, "History and Literature," in Creighton, *Towards the Discovery of Canada*, 21.
32 Luella Creighton, Diary entry for 25 November 1963, University of Waterloo, Doris Lewis Rare Book Room, Luella Creighton fonds, GA 99, series 3, box 2, file 9; Donald Creighton to W.L. Morton, 1 October 1961, McMaster University Library (MUL), W.L. Morton fonds, box 6, file Creighton, D.G., 1955–1961; Creighton, *Canada's First Century*, 324, 327; Donald Creighton, Interview with Larry Zolf, 29 June 1970, LAC, V1 7905-011.
33 See Philip Massolin, *Canadian Intellectuals, the Tory Tradition, and the Challenge of Modernity, 1939–1970* (Toronto: University of Toronto Press, 2001).
34 Creighton, *Canada's First Century*, 355, 356, 309, 318–319.
35 See Kenneth Dewar, "Nationalism, Professionalism, and Canadian History," *Canadian Dimension*, December 1970; and William Westfall, "Creighton's Tragic Vision," *Canadian Forum*, September 1970.
36 Michael Gordon, Review of *Canada's First Century*, *Atlantic Advocate*, May 1970; Alan Heisey, Review of *Canada's First Century*, *The Executive*, May 1970; Dale C. Thomson, "Canada through Blue- and Pink-Coloured Glasses," *International Journal* 26 (Winter 1970–1): 180; Michael Barkway, Review of *Canada's First Century*, *Financial Post*, 20 April 1970; Ronald Grantham, Review of *Canada's First Century*, *Ottawa Citizen*, 4 April 1970; Shaun Herron, Review of *Canada's First Century*, *Winnipeg Free Press*, 21 November 1970; Andrew Snaddon, Review of *Canada's First Century*, *Edmonton Journal*, 4 April 1970.
37 George Woodcock, Review of *Canada's First Century*, *Victoria Daily Times*, 18 April 1970.

38 Creighton, *Canada's First Century*, 343. On anti-Americanism in 1960s English Canada see Jack Granatstein, *Yankee Go Home? Canadians and Anti-Americanism* (Toronto: HarperCollins, 1996); and Adam Green, "Images of Americans: The United States in Canadian Newspapers during the 1960s" (PhD thesis, University of Ottawa, 2007).

39 On the intellectual and personal connections between tory nationalism and New Left nationalism see Massolin, 272–85; and Jon Sufrin, "The Canadian Apocalypse: Nationalists and the End of Canada, 1963–1983" (PhD thesis, York University, 2009).

40 Creighton made this statement in his interview with Larry Zolf. Mel Hurtig – who had watched the interview and who "thought it was one of the best things I've ever seen on television" – reported Creighton's statement to Watkins and Watkins's reaction to Creighton. In a short 2002 essay, Larry Zolf wrote that it was Creighton and his passionate defence of Canada that had made him (Zolf) "a real Canadian at last." Mel Hurtig to Donald Creighton, 6 July 1970, LAC, MG 31 D 77, vol. 27, file Canada's First Century 1970; Larry Zolf, "History Lessons," CBC News "Viewpoint," 29 October 2002.

41 T.W. Johannsen, *Winnipeg Free Press*, 12 May 1970.

42 Jack Creighton to Donald Creighton, 15 April 1970, LAC, MG 31 D 77, Donald Creighton fonds, vol. 27, file Canada's First Century 1970; Isabel Wilson to Donald Creighton, 3 April 1970, ibid.

43 On a newspaper clipping about Lester Pearson from the *London Times* dated 31 August 1964, Creighton pencilled "Go after the bastard." LAC, MG 31 D 77, Donald Creighton fonds, vol. 27, file Biculturalism 1964.

44 Both *Lament for a Nation* and *Canada's First Century* conform to a genre of writing that Jon Sufrin labels English-Canadian apocalyptica. See Sufrin, "The Canadian Apocalypse."

45 Referring to Donald Creighton, George Grant wrote that "he had the courage to do this [to define and defend a conservative view of Canada] when a definition of conservatism was not being welcomed by the Liberal establishment." George Grant, *Lament for a Nation*, 40th Anniversary Edition (Montreal and Kingston: McGill-Queen's University Press, 2005), 25. See also Westfall, "Creighton's Tragic Vision."

46 Author's interview with John Cairns, 2 December 2004.

47 Donald Creighton, Diary entry for 6 September 1970, LAC, MG 31 D 77, Donald Creighton fonds, vol. 66, file 1.

48 Robert Finch, Diary, 1970, Thomas Fisher Rare Book Library, MS Coll. 324, Robert Finch Papers, box 8, 1970 Notebook.

49 Quotation in Robert Finch's 1970 Notebook, ibid. In his diary, Creighton said that he had been "much affected" by the memory. Donald Creighton, Diary entry for 3 September 1970, LAC, MG 31 D 77, Donald Creighton fonds, vol. 66, file 1.

50 Cynthia Flood to Donald Creighton, 23 September 1970, LAC, MG 31 D 77, Donald Creighton fonds, vol. 29, file General Correspondence 1970 no. 2; Cynthia Flood to Donald Creighton, 5 October 1970, ibid.

51 Donald Creighton, Diary entry for 7 October 1970, ibid., vol. 66, file 1.

52 Luella Creighton to John Gray, 11 November 1963, MUL, Macmillan Co. of Canada fonds, box 89, file 2.

53 Donald Creighton, Diary entry for 17 July 1961, LAC, MG 31 D 77, Donald Creighton fonds, vol. 65, file 3. In her diary, Luella quoted Donald's phrase "The Cell Block." See Luella Creighton, Diary entry for 16 July 1961, University of Waterloo, Doris Lewis Rare Book Room, Luella Creighton fonds, GA 99, box 1, file 2.

54 Donald Creighton, Diary entries for 20 January 1962, 10 February 1966, 17 May 1966, and 18 May 1966, LAC, MG 31 D 77, Donald Creighton fonds, vol. 65, files 4 and 6. On the curriculum review, see Robert Bothwell, *Laying the Foundation: A Century of History at the University of Toronto* (Toronto: Department of History, 1991), 140–50; and Robert Spencer, *A European Affair: Memoirs* (Ottawa, 2007), 355–6.

55 Because of the department's clumsiness and insensitivity, it fell to Luella Creighton to arrange a gift and to organize a retirement party for Freya Hahn. John Cairns was so bothered by the maladroit handling of Hahn's retirement after nearly four decades of dedicated service that he had flowers sent to her as if from anonymous admirers. He even had his aunt write the card so that Hahn would not recognize his handwriting.

56 Donald Creighton, Diary entries for 31 January 1967 and 12 February 1962, ibid., vol. 65, files 6 and 4. Robert Spencer attributed the phrase "American imports" to Donald Creighton. Author's interview with Robert Spencer, 25 May 2006.

57 A.P. Thornton to Brown, Cairns, Careless, Conacher, Craig, Eccles, McNaught, Moir, H. Nelson, W. Nelson, Powicke, Spencer, Stacey, White, Zacour, 16 February 1971, University of Toronto Archives (UTA), A90-0023, box 7, file 56; W.J. Eccles to A.P. Thornton, 16 February, ibid.

58 Author's interview with W.J. Eccles, 23 April 1996.

59 Luella Creighton, Diary entry for 1 May 1971, University of Waterloo, Doris Lewis Rare Book Room, Luella Creighton fonds, GA 99, box 2, file 17; Donald Creighton, Diary entry for 1 May 1971, LAC, MG 31 D 77, Donald Creighton fonds, vol. 66, file 1.

60 Donald Creighton to Richard Clippingdale, 9 July 1970, Comments on Chapter VIII. Original in possession of Richard Clippingdale.

61 Donald Creighton, Diary entry for 11 January 1974, ibid., vol. 66, file 3.

62 Author's interview with Jim Miller, 26 March 2004. This section is based on interviews with Donald Creighton's former students. Author's interview with Ken

McLaughlin, 8 May 2006; author's interview with Richard Clippingdale, 20 May 2006. See also LAC, MG 31 D 77, Donald Creighton fonds, vol. 6, file Correspondence H.V. Nelles, 1966, 1968–70.

63 Author's interview with Robert Bothwell, 30 September 2005; Donald Creighton, Diary entry for 16 January 1974. See also LAC, MG 31, D 77, Donald Creighton fonds, vol. 5, file Correspondence, A.D. Gilbert, 1966–69, 1972–74. The reference to Bothwell having a knife in both Creighton and Gilbert is in Luella Creighton, Diary entry for 16 January 1974, University of Waterloo, Doris Lewis Rare Book Room, Luella Creighton fonds, GA 99, series 3, box 2, file 19.

64 Author's interview with Jill Ker Conway, 9 June 1998; Jill Ker Conway, *True North* (Toronto: Vintage, 1995), 165.

65 Author's interview with Bernadine Dodge, 26 January 2004.

66 Author's interview with Margaret Banks, 15 October 1997. See Donald Wright, *The Professionalization of History in English Canada* (Toronto: University of Toronto Press, 2005). When Lita-Rose Betcherman inquired about a teaching position at Toronto in the 1960s, she received the following condescending response from a senior professor: "Oh, my dear Mrs. Betcherman, we have no ladies' colleges here as they do at Oxford or Cambridge, no Lady Margaret Hall or Somerville College." Quotation in Judy Stoffman, "Historian, 78, Takes On Noble Endeavour," *Toronto Star*, 21 January 2006.

67 Viv Nelles to Donald Creighton, 16 February 1970, LAC, MG 31 D 77, Donald Creighton fonds, vol. 6, file Correspondence H.V. Nelles, 1966, 1968–70.

68 Donald Creighton to Eugene Forsey, 16 February 1970, LAC, MG 31 D 77, Donald Creighton fonds, vol. 26, file Correspondence with Eugene Forsey, 1965–1975.

69 Donald Creighton to Ralph Heintzman, n.d., LAC, MG 31 D 77, Donald Creighton fonds, vol. 29, file General Correspondence, 1970, no. 2. On the compact thesis as historical myth, see Stéphane Paquin, *L'invention d'un mythe – le pacte entre deux peuples fondateurs* (Montreal: VLB, 1999).

70 W.L. Morton to Ralph Heintzman, 24 November 1970; Ralph Heintzman to W.L. Morton, 2 December 1970, MUL, W.L. Morton fonds, box 10, file Heintzman, R.

71 See Ralph Heintzman, "The Spirit of Confederation: Professor Creighton, Biculturalism, and the Use of History," *Canadian Historical Review* 52, no. 3 (September 1971): 245–75.

72 "I have just got, and am reading, Heintzman's counter-attack," Eugene Forsey wrote. "I suppose you will answer him; but I've a great mind to have a whack my-self. Even in the first few pages there are some notions which outdo any previous 'mug' statements for sheer nonsense. I am especially entertained by the idea that a contracting party's 'impression' of what's in a contract, or his 'expectation' of what he'll get out of it, form *part* of the *contract*." Eugene Forsey to Donald Creighton, 4 October 1971, LAC, MG 31 D 77, Donald Creighton fonds, vol. 26, file

Correspondence with Eugene Forsey, 1965–1975. Two weeks later, Forsey referred to Ralph Heintzman as "Master Heintzman." Eugene Forsey to Donald Creighton, 20 October 1971, ibid. Eugene Forsey to Donald Creighton, 22 March 1974, ibid., vol. 29, file General Correspondence 1974.

73 Donald Creighton to Craig Brown, 11 December 1972, LAC, MG 31 D 77, Donald Creighton fonds, vol. 29, file General Correspondence 1972.
74 Author's interview with Jim Miller, 26 March 2004.
75 Craig Brown to Donald Creighton, 4 December 1972, LAC, MG 31 D 77, Donald Creighton fonds, vol. 29, file General Correspondence 1972.
76 D.J. Hall to Donald Creighton, 8 August 1975, LAC, MG 31 D 77, Donald Creighton fonds, vol. 29, file General Correspondence 1975.
77 Author's interview with D.J. Hall, 28 November 2006.
78 Maurice Careless, undated assessment, UTA, A79-0004, box 2.
79 Michael Cross to Robert Bothwell to D.J. Hall, 30 October 1973. Copy in LAC, MG 31 D 77, Donald Creighton fonds, vol. 29, file General Correspondence 1975.
80 See D.J. Hall, "The Spirit of Confederation: Ralph Heintzman, Professor Creighton, and the Bicultural Compact Theory," *Journal of Canadian Studies* 9, no. 4 (November 1974): 24–42.
81 Donald Creighton, Diary entry for 17 February 1973, LAC, MG 31 D 77, Donald Creighton fonds, vol. 66, file 2.
82 Author's interview with Cynthia Flood, 3 June 2005.
83 Luella Creighton, Diary entry for 10 August 1974, University of Waterloo, Doris Lewis Rare Book Room, Luella Creighton fonds, GA 99, series 3, box 2, file 19; Donald Creighton, Diary entry for 10 August 1974, LAC, MG 31 D 77, Donald Creighton fonds, vol. 66, file 3.
84 Author's interview with Philip Creighton, 30 September 2004.
85 Luella Creighton, Diary entry for 27 September 1973, University of Waterloo, Doris Lewis Rare Book Room, Luella Creighton fonds, GA 99, accrual 2000, box 1, file 3.
86 Author's interview with Cynthia Flood, 3 June 2005.
87 Jack Creighton to Isabel Wilson, 27 September 1972. Original in possession of Denis Creighton.
88 Donald Creighton, Diary entries for 5–9 November 1973, LAC, MG 31 D 77, Donald Creighton fonds, vol. 66, file 2; Luella Creighton, 9 November 1973, University of Waterloo, Doris Lewis Rare Book Room, Luella Creighton fonds, GA 99, accrual 2000, box 1, file 3.
89 Author's interview with Cynthia Flood, 3 June 2005. Although Philip was born by C-section, Luella would have had tenderness in the pelvic region in addition to post-operative abdominal soreness.
90 He had published his tenth book in 1972, a collection of previously published essays called *Towards the Discovery of Canada*.

91 George Robertson to Donald Creighton, 28 January 1972, LAC, MG 31 D 77, Donald Creighton fonds, vol. 27, file CBC Talk Historic Sites; Transcript, Historic Beginnings, n.d., ibid., vol. 33, file CBC Heroic Beginnings.

92 Donald Creighton, Diary entries for 16 March 1973, 6 August 1974, 10 August 1974, 12 September 1974, ibid., vol. 66, files 2 and 3.

93 Donald Creighton, *Canada: The Heroic Beginnings* (Toronto: Macmillan, with Indian and Northern Affairs, Parks Canada, 1974), 7, 140, 162–3.

94 Robert Saunders, "Calling Up the Past," *Winnipeg Free Press*, 22 February 1975; J.R.N., "Reliving Canada's Past," *Saskatoon Star-Phoenix*, 8 February 1975; Helen Gray, Review of *Canada: The Heroic Beginnings*, *BC Library Quarterly* (Spring 1976): 47; James McCook, Review of *Canada: The Heroic Beginnings*, *Canadian Geographical Journal* 93 (December 1976–January 1977): 70; Dillon O'Leary, "Vignettes from a Storied Past," *Ottawa Journal*, 15 February 1975.

95 Creighton, *Heroic Beginnings*, 199.

96 Barbara Roberts, "They Drove Him to Drink: Donald Creighton's Macdonald and His Wives," *Canada: An Historical Magazine* 3, no. 2 (December 1975): 51–64.

97 George Grant, *Lament for a Nation* (Montreal and Kingston: McGill-Queen's University Press, 2005), 55, 56.

98 Donald Creighton, "The Individual and the Welfare State," LAC, MG 31 D 77, Donald Creighton fonds, vol. 63, file The Individual and the Welfare State, 1976, Dunning Trust Lecture.

99 Donald Creighton, "Is Canada More Than We Can Hope For?" *Maclean's*, September 1973. Reprinted as "The Future in Canada" in Creighton, *The Passionate Observer*, 23.

100 Donald Creighton, "We've Been Fat For Too Long and Now It's Too Late," *Maclean's*, April 1975. Reprinted as "Surviving the Post-Keynesian Era," in ibid., 41, 38, 37.

101 Grant, *Lament for a Nation*, 87, 88.

102 Creighton, "The Future in Canada," 31, 29.

103 Ibid., 23, 27, 32.

104 Donald Creighton, "Watching the Sun Quietly Set on Canada," *Maclean's*, November 1971. Reprinted as "Canadian Nationalism and Its Opponents," in Creighton, *Towards the Discovery of Canada*, 280–1.

105 Gerald Graham, Review of *Towards the Discovery of Canada*, *Times Literary Supplement*, 6 September 1974; John K. Elliott, Review of *Towards the Discovery of Canada*, *London Free Press*, 20 May 1972; Phillip Buckner, Review of *Towards the Discovery of Canada*, *Dalhousie Review* 53 (Autumn 1973): 556; Viv Nelles, "A Report on the Laurentian Empire and the Canadian Nationality," February 1971, MUL, Macmillan Co. of Canada fonds, box 246, file Creighton, D. Towards the Discovery of Canada; Ramsay Cook, Review of *Towards the Discovery of Canada*,

Globe and Mail, 13 May 1972; Ramsay Cook, *The Maple Leaf Forever: Essays on Nationalism and Politics in Canada* (Toronto: Macmillan, 1977), 139.

106 See David W. Noble, *Historians against History: The Frontier Thesis and the National Covenant in American Historical Writing since 1830* (Minneapolis: University of Minnesota Press, 1965); Mark McKenna, *An Eye for Eternity: The Life of Manning Clark* (Melbourne: Melbourne University Press, 2011); Eric Hobsbawm, "Socialism Has Failed. Now Capitalism Is Bankrupt. So What Comes Next?" *Guardian*, 10 April 2009. Writing in the *Globe and Mail*, Modris Eksteins compared Hobsbawm to an Old Testament prophet. See Modris Eksteins, "My Favourite Marxist: Remembering Eric Hobsbawm," *Globe and Mail*, 5 October 2012.

107 Phillip Buckner, Review of *Towards the Discovery of Canada*, *Dalhousie Review*, 53 (Autumn 1973): 557.

108 Ramsay Cook, Review of *Towards the Discovery of Canada*, *Globe and Mail*, 13 May 1972.

109 G.M. Craig, ed., *Lord Durham's Report* (Montreal and Kingston: McGill-Queen's University Press, 2007), 114

110 Quotation in Cook, Review of *Towards the Discovery of Canada*, *Globe and Mail*, 13 May 1972.

111 Carl Berger, *The Writing of Canadian History: Aspects of English-Canadian Historical Writing since 1900* (Toronto: University of Toronto Press, 1976), 236.

112 Donald Creighton, Diary entry for 29 March 1975, LAC, MG 31 D 77, Donald Creighton fonds, vol. 66, file 3.

113 Donald Creighton, Diary entry for 28 November 1974, ibid., vol. 66, file 3; Bishop Garnsworthy to Donald Creighton, 10 December 1974, ibid., vol. 29, file General Correspondence 1974.

114 Donald Creighton, Diary entry for 29 February 1976, ibid., vol. 66, file 4.

115 Donald Creighton, Diary entries for 25 May 1976, 16 April 1976, ibid., vol. 66, file 4.

116 Donald Creighton to Bill Morton, 3 September 1976, MUL, W.L. Morton fonds, box 6, file Creighton, D.G. 1970–1978.

117 Donald Creighton to Bill Morton, 25 May 1977, ibid.; Donald Creighton to Bill Morton, 10 January 1961, ibid., box 6, file Creighton, D.G. 1955–1961.

118 Marcel Trudel did not provide any details except to say that he felt rushed by the publisher and that he was "especially unhappy" with his contribution to the Centenary Series. Marcel Trudel, *Memoirs of a Less Travelled Road: A Historian's Life* (Montreal: Véhicule Press, 2002), 230. John Herd Thompson, "Integrating Regional Patterns into a National Canadian History," *Acadiensis* 20, no. 1 (1990): 177. With Allen Seager, Thompson wrote *Decades of Discord: Canada, 1922–1939*. Thompson also noted that in 1957, he was still reading comic books while his co-author "was struggling to learn the alphabet." The nineteenth and final volume was not published until 1988. Both Donald Creighton and Bill Morton were dead

and Ramsay Cook had been named executive editor. For an analysis of the intellectual origins of the series and its conceptual hurdles, see Lyle Dick, "'A Growing Necessity for Canada': W.L. Morton's Centenary Series and the Forms of National History, 1955–80," *Canadian Historical Review* 82, no. 2 (2001): 223–52.

119 Jack McClelland to Donald Creighton, 28 April 1975 and 16 February 1976, MUL, McClelland and Stewart fonds, box 78, file Creighton, Donald and Luella. On King's "verbal flatulence," see Donald Creighton, *The Forked Road: Canada, 1939–1957* (Toronto: McClelland and Stewart, 1976), 2.

120 Jack McClelland to Peter Taylor, 11 August 1976, ibid.

121 Creighton, *The Forked Road*, 131, 262, 30, 163, 168, 205, 175, 89, 174, 7, 262.

122 Frank Underhill, "The Revival of Conservatism in North America," *Transactions of the Royal Society of Canada* 52, series III (June 1958): 17; Marg Conrad, "Studies in Canada's Recent History," *Acadiensis* 6, no. 2 (Spring 1977): 122; Michael Cross, Review of *The Forked Road*, *Books in Canada* (January 1977): 16; Reginald Whitaker, Review of *Forked Road*, *Canadian Historical Review* 59 (March 1978): 106; Jack Granatstein, Review of *Forked Road*, *Queen's Quarterly* 84 (Autumn 1977): 490; Fred Soward, Review of *Forked Road*, *International Journal* 32 (Summer 1977): 672; Fred Soward to Robert Spencer, 28 April 1977, University of British Columbia Archives, Frederick H. Soward fonds, box 1, file 1; Denis Smith, Review of *Forked Road*, *Saturday Night* (November 1976): 55; Paul Fox, Review of *Forked Road*, *Globe and Mail*, 6 November 1976. The newspaper review containing the reference to an M&S flunky is not identified but is located in LAC, MG 31 D 77, Donald Creighton fonds, vol. 33, file The Forked Road, 1976–1977. Davidson Dunton, Review of *Forked Road*, *Ottawa Citizen*, 6 November 1976.

123 Donald Creighton to Lovat Dickson, 23 November 1976 and 24 December 1976, LAC, MG 30 D 237, Lovat Dickson fonds, vol. 19, file Creighton, Donald G. 1971–1979.

124 Creighton, *The Forked Road*, 251.

125 Fernand Braudel, *The Mediterranean and the Mediterranean World in the Age of Philip II* (London: Collins, 1972), 21.

126 Donald Creighton, *The Empire of the St. Lawrence* (Toronto: University of Toronto Press, 2002), 7, 6, 383, 6.

127 Luella Creighton, Diary entry for 16 September 1976, University of Waterloo, Doris Lewis Rare Book Room, Luella Creighton fonds, GA 99, accrual 2000, box 1, file 4.

128 Donald Creighton, Diary entry for 10 February 1977, LAC, MG 31 D 77, Donald Creighton fonds, vol. 66, file 4.

13 Endings

1 Peter Newman, *Sometimes a Great Nation* (Toronto: McClelland and Stewart, 1988), 244, 243, 245.

2 Camille Laurin, *Quebec's Policy on the French Language* (Quebec, 1977), 52.
3 Elspeth Cameron, *Hugh MacLennan: A Writer's Life* (Toronto: University of Toronto Press, 1981), 375.
4 Donald Creighton, Diary entries for 2 April 1977, 3 April 1977, and 6 April 1977, LAC, Donald Creighton fonds, MG 31 D 77, vol. 66, file 4.
5 Donald Creighton, Diary entry for 2 April 1977, ibid.; "The PQ's Language Gamble," *Globe and Mail*, 4 April 1977; "Senator Sees Bid to Get English Out," *Globe and Mail*, 4 April 1977.
6 Donald Creighton, Diary entry for 27 May 1977, LAC, Donald Creighton fonds, MG 31 D 77, vol. 66, file 4.
7 Donald Creighton to Eugene Forsey, 9 May 1971, LAC, MG 31 D 77, Donald Creighton fonds, vol. 26, file Correspondence with Eugene Forsey 1965–1975.
8 Donald Creighton, "Beyond the Referendum," in Donald Creighton, *Passionate Observer: Selected Writings* (Toronto: McClelland and Stewart, 1980). This article was originally published as "No More Concessions," *Maclean's*, 27 June 1977.
9 Newman, *Sometimes a Great Nation*, 244. *Maclean's* magazine informed its readers that the response to this article was the "heaviest" response it had received to a single article since switching to a newsmagazine format a few years earlier. *Maclean's*, 25 July 1977.
10 See Letters to the Editor, *Maclean's*, 25 July 1977.
11 See Mrs – to Donald Creighton, 22 June 1977; Mr – to Donald Creighton, 29 June 1977; Mr – to Donald Creighton, 2 July 1977, LAC, MG 31 D 77, Donald Creighton fonds, vol. 34, file No More Concessions, Maclean's article, 1977.
12 One scholar has referred to it as a "crackpot" outfit. Marc Levine, *The Re-Conquest of Montreal: Language Policy and Social Change in a Bilingual City* (Philadelphia: Temple University Press, 1990), 112. The Preparatory Committee's letter can be found in LAC, MG 31 D 77, Donald Creighton fonds, vol. 34, file No More Concessions, Maclean's article, 1977.
13 J.V. Andrew to Donald Creighton, 27 August 1977, LAC, MG 31 D 77, Donald Creighton fonds, vol. 29, file General Correspondence 1977; Robin Reid, President of the Alliance for the Preservation of English in Canada, to Donald Creighton, 30 January 1978, ibid., vol. 30, file General Correspondence 1978; Donald Creighton, Diary entry for 29 September 1978, LAC, MG 31 D 77, Donald Creighton fonds, vol. 66, file 5; Leonard Jones, "The Bigot." Speech delivered at APEC, 20 November 1978. Copy in author's possession.
14 "Not Rage, Reason," *Globe and Mail*, 1 July 1977; "Crying Havoc," *Winnipeg Free Press*, 30 July 1977; Roger Guay, "A Viewpoint Which Replies to Creighton on Unity," *Regina Leader-Post*, 13 July 1977; "Breaking the Silence," *Hamilton Spectator*, 9 July 1977; John Roberts, quotation in *Calgary Herald*, 4 July 1977; Senator Maurice Lamontagne, quotation in *Globe and Mail*, 1 July 1977; George Grant,

quotation in *Globe and Mail*, 1 July 1977; George Grant to Derek Bedson, 14 August 1977, Provincial Archives of Manitoba, Derek Bedson fonds; George Grant, *Lament for a Nation* (Montreal and Kingston: McGill-Queen's University Press, 2005), 20–1; F.R. Scott to Donald Creighton, 17 July 1977, LAC, MG 31 D 77, Donald Creighton fonds, vol. 34, file No More Concessions, Maclean's article, 1977; Bill Morton to Donald Creighton, 7 July 1977, McMaster University Library (MUL), W.L. Morton fonds, box 6, file Creighton, D.G., 1970–1978; W.L. Morton, "In Defence of Professor Creighton," *Winnipeg Free Press*, 10 August 1977; Eugene Forsey to Donald Creighton, 4 August 1977, LAC, MG 31 D 77, Donald Creighton fonds, vol. 34, file No More Concessions, Maclean's article, 1977.

15 Peter Taylor to Jack McClelland, 14 July 1977, MUL, McClelland and Stewart fonds, box 78, file Creighton, Donald and Luella.

16 Ramsay Cook to Eugene Forsey, 6 July 1977, LAC, MG 30 A 25, Eugene Forsey Fonds, vol. 42, file Cook, Ramsay; Gerald Craig, ed., *Lord Durham's Report* (Montreal and Kingston: McGill-Queen's University Press, 2007), 38, 39; Ramsay Cook to Eugene Forsey, 9 August 1977, ibid.

17 Donald Creighton, "Final Copy Arts and Letters," LAC, MG 31 D 77, Donald Creighton fonds, vol. 32, file Arts and Letters Talk 27 October 1977.

18 Heather Robertson, "The Man Who Invented Canada," *Saturday Night*, October 1977, 19-25. See also Preston Jones, "Towards a Study of the Bible in Canadian Public Life," *Journal of Canadian Studies* 34, no. 1 (1999): 161–72.

19 Donald Creighton, Diary entry for 24 September 1977, LAC, MG 31 D 77, Donald Creighton fonds, vol. 66, file 4.

20 Donald Creighton, Diary entry for 22 September 1977, ibid.; Jack Creighton to Donald Creighton, 4 July 1932, original in possession of Cynthia Flood.

21 Author's interview with Philip Creighton, 30 September 2004; Donald Creighton, Diary entry for 16 February 1964, LAC, MG 31 D 77, Donald Creighton fonds, vol. 65, file 5; Anna Porter to Jack McClelland, 6 January 1978, MUL, McClelland and Stewart fonds, box 78, file Creighton, Donald and Luella; Ellen Seligman to Jack McClelland, 11 January 1978, ibid.

22 Donald Creighton, *Takeover* (Toronto: McClelland and Stewart, 1978), 8.

23 Donald Creighton, *The Empire of the St. Lawrence* (Toronto: University of Toronto Press, 2002), 384.

24 Creighton, *Takeover*, 8–9, 11, 51.

25 Ibid., 82–3, 168, 162, 118, 196.

26 Author's interview with Ramsay Cook, 3 December 2004.

27 William French, Review of *Takeover*, *Globe and Mail*, 14 October 1978; David Cohen, Review of *Takeover*, *Quill & Quire* 44, no. 13 (1978): 11; Michael Bliss, Review of *Takeover*, *Maclean's*, 23 October 1978; Ramsay Cook, Review of *Takeover*, *Saturday Night*, November 1978.

28 I am paraphrasing Ramsay Cook. In his essay "Nationalist Ideologies in Canada" he wrote, "For every Lionel Groulx, a Donald Creighton." See Ramsay Cook, *Canada, Quebec, and the Uses of Nationalism* (Toronto: McClelland and Stewart, 1986), 190. Cook was not the first person to liken Donald Creighton to Lionel Groulx. The Marxist historian Stanley Ryerson argued that the corporatist Groulx misread the Rebellions of 1837 as a "race war" which had "nothing to do" with democracy, while the tory Creighton celebrated the mercantile oligarchy: "The Toronto tory and the Quebec corporatist meet on common ground: hostility to the democratic peoples' movement [and] denial of our democratic heritage." Stanley Ryerson, *1837: The Birth of Canadian Democracy* (Toronto: Francis White, 1937), 52; and Stanley Ryerson, *French Canada: A Study in Canadian Democracy* (Toronto: Progress Books, 1943), 36. For a sustained comparison of Creighton and Groulx, see George Woodcock, "The Servants of Clio: Notes on Creighton and Groulx," *Canadian Literature* 83 (Winter 1979): 131–41.

29 Author's interview with Ramsay Cook, 3 December 2004.

30 Donald Creighton, Manuscript of "The Ogdensburg Agreement and Frank Underhill," n.d., LAC, MG 31 D 77, Donald Creighton fonds, vol. 63, file Frank Underhill Dinner – Manuscript, Photocopies. This essay appeared in Carl Berger and Ramsay Cook, eds, *The West and the Nation: Essays in Honour of W.L. Morton* (Toronto: McClelland and Stewart, 1976). Thankfully, Creighton's better instincts triumphed when he deleted from the published version what was a gratuitous shot against his former graduate student.

31 Donald Creighton, Diary entry for 20 December 1978, LAC, MG 31 D 77, Donald Creighton fonds, vol. 66, file 5.

32 For a fascinating discussion on the past, the present, memory, and identity, see Jocelyn Létourneau, *A History for the Future: Rewriting Memory and Identity in Quebec* (Montreal and Kingston: McGill-Queen's University Press, 2004).

33 Donald Creighton, Diary entries for 8 January 1979, 18 January 1979, 28 January 1979, LAC, MG 31 D 77, Donald Creighton fonds, vol. 66, file 5; Luella Creighton, Diary entry for 28 January 1979, University of Waterloo, Doris Lewis Rare Book Room, Luella Creighton fonds, GA 99, series 3, box 3, file 23.

34 Luella Creighton, Diary entries for 4 February 1979, 6 March 1979, ibid.

35 Author's interview with Cynthia Flood, 5 June 2005. Actually, the *Oxford English Dictionary* states that both pronunciations are correct in both Great Britain and the United States.

36 Luella Creighton, Diary entry for 3 May 1979, ibid.; author's interview with Cynthia Flood, 5 June 2005.

37 Luella Creighton, Diary entry for 28 May 1979, University of Waterloo, Doris Lewis Rare Book Room, Luella Creighton fonds, GA 99, series 3, box 3, file 23. For Donald Creighton's response to Psalm 23, see Luella Creighton, Diary entry for

8 December 1969, ibid., box 2, file 15; and Donald Creighton, Diary entry for 8 December 1969, LAC, MG 31 D 77, Donald Creighton fonds, vol. 65, file 7.

38 Ramsay Cook to Donald Creighton, 14 May 1979, ibid., vol. 30, file General Correspondence 1979 (file 2).

39 Author's interview with Ramsay Cook, 4 December 2004.

40 Scott Symons, "Notes on Visit to Donald Creighton, May 24, 1979," 7 May 1980, LAC, Scott Symons fonds, R/E 2002-0087, box 47; interim box 5, file Items for Diary, Diaryfacts etc. 1981.

41 Charles Taylor, *Radical Tories: The Conservative Tradition in Canada* (Toronto: Anansi, 1982), 24.

42 Luella Creighton, Diary entries for 7 July 1979, 25 August 1979, 19 August 1979, University of Waterloo, Doris Lewis Rare Book Room, Luella Creighton fonds, GA 99, Series 3, box 3, file 23.

43 Author's interview with John Cairns, 2 December 2004.

44 Luella Creighton, Diary entries for 12 November 1979, 19 November 1979, 3 December 1979, 8 December 1979, University of Waterloo, Doris Lewis Rare Book Room, Luella Creighton fonds, GA 99, series 3, box 3, file 23.

45 Author's interview with John Cairns, 2 December 2004.

46 Luella Creighton, Diary entry for 19 December 1979, University of Waterloo, Doris Lewis Rare Book Room, Luella Creighton fonds, GA 99, series 3, box 3, file 23.

47 Luella Creighton, Diary entry for 21 December 1979, ibid.

48 "Noted Historian Donald Creighton Dies of Cancer at 77," *Toronto Star*, 20 December 1979.

49 Luella Creighton, Diary entries for 26 December 1979; 29 December 1979; 23 December 1979, University of Waterloo, Doris Lewis Rare Book Room, Luella Creighton fonds, GA 99, series 3, box 3, file 23.

50 Dennis Duffy, "As Canadian as a Snowflake," *University of Toronto Magazine*, Spring 2002.

51 See J.M.S. Careless, Ramsay Cook, and Robert Finch, "Donald Grant Creighton: Tribute to a Scholar," University of Toronto *Bulletin*, 25 February 1980.

52 Luella Creighton, Diary entry for 30 January 1980, University of Waterloo, Doris Lewis Rare Book Room, Luella Creighton fonds, GA 99, series 3, box 3, file 23; Luella Creighton to Robert Finch, Candlemas Day, 1980, Thomas Fisher Rare Book, Library Robert Finch Papers, MS Collection, 324, box 17, file 10.

53 Author's interview with Philip Creighton, 3 December 2004; Cynthia Flood, *My Father Took a Cake to France* (Vancouver: Talonbooks, 1992); author's interview with Cynthia Flood, 3 June 2005.

54 Luella Creighton, "Leave Me My Roses," n.d., University of Waterloo, Doris Lewis Rare Book Room, Luella Creighton fonds, GA 99, series 5, file 106.

Bibliography

Primary Sources

Archives

Art Gallery of Ontario, E.P. Taylor Research Library and Archives
    Douglas Duncan fonds
Balliol College Archives
    K.N. Bell fonds
    Student files, D.G. Creighton
Bodleian Library, Department of Special Collections and Western Manuscripts
    Harold Macmillan fonds
    Walter Monckton fonds
Columbia University Rare Book and Manuscript Library
    J. Bartlet Brebner fonds
    James Shotwell fonds
    Carnegie Endowment fonds
Library and Archives Canadaw
    A.L. Burt fonds
    Canadian Historical Association fonds
    Donald Creighton fonds
    J.W. Dafoe fonds
    Lovat Dickson fonds
    Eugene Forsey fonds
    John Glassco fonds
    John Gray fonds
    W.K. Lamb fonds

   Arnaud Maggs fonds
   Frank Scott fonds
   Irene Spry fonds
   Scott Symonds fonds
   Neville Thompson fonds
   Frank Underhill fonds
McMaster University, William Ready Division of Archives and Research Collections
   Macmillan fonds
   McClelland and Stewart fonds
   W.L. Morton fonds
   Saturday Night fonds
National Archives, United Kingdom
   Cabinet Office
   Foreign and Commonwealth Office
   Prime Minister's Office
Provincial Archives of New Brunswick
   Records of the Office of Premier J.B. McNair
Queen's University Archives
   Arthur Lower fonds
Rhodes House, Oxford
   Elspeth Huxley fonds
   Albert Robinson fonds
   Roy Welensky fonds
Rockefeller Archives Center
   Rockefeller Foundation fonds
Toronto Public Library
   Long Branch Local History Collection
   Osborne Collection of Early Children's Books
United Church Archives
   Christian Guardian
   Howard Park United Church fonds
University of British Columbia Archives
   Roy Daniells fonds
   Norman Mackenzie fonds
   Frederick H. Soward fonds
   Margaret Ormsby Oral History Collection
University of Saskatchewan Archives
   Hilda Neatby fonds
University of Texas at Austin, Harvey Ransom Center
   Alfred A. Knopf Inc. fonds

Bibliography

University of Toronto Archives
    Michael Bliss fonds
    Alex Brady fonds
    George Brown fonds
    J.M.S. Careless fonds
    James B. Conacher fonds
    Harold Innis fonds
    Kenneth McNaught fonds
    Gerald Riddell fonds
    Charles Stacey fonds
    Canadian Historical Review fonds
    Dean of Arts and Science fonds
    Department of History fonds
    Office of the President fonds
    Torontoensis
    University Historian fonds
    Interview with J.M.S. Careless
    Interview with James B. Conacher
University of Toronto, Thomas Fischer Rare Book Library
    Robert Finch fonds
University of Waterloo, Doris Lewis Rare Book Room
    Luella Creighton fonds
Victoria University, E.J. Pratt Library
    Acta Victoriana
Victoria University Archives
    Records of the Victoria University President's Office
    Registrar's Office fonds

Interviews

Carl Berger, 5 May 2006
Robert Blackburn, 4 November 2005
Michael Bliss, 7 March 2005
Father Francis W.P. Bolger, 8 November 2005
Robert Bothwell, 30 September 2005
John Cairns, 2 December 2004
J.M.S. Careless, 20 September 2001
Ramsay Cook, 3 December 2004
Denis Creighton, 6 June 2005
Philip Creighton, 30 September 2004; 3 December 2004; 14 July 2005

Anne Innis Dagg, 14 January 2005
Bernadine Dodge, 26 January 2004
Cynthia Flood, 3 June 2005; 4 June 2005; 5 June 2005
Paul Fox, 13 November 2003
Lynda Franklin, 8 February 2005 (personal communication)
James A. Gibson, 13 June 2001
Joy Grant, 6 July 2003
Sheila Grant, 31 January 2007
John Grube, 20 October 2005
Lorne Hill, 2 April 2005 (personal communication)
Bill Hull, 13 June 2001
Ian Macdonald, 11 February 2004
Alan W. MacIntosh, 10 November 2005
Stewart Marks, 16 May 2005
Kenneth McRae, 6–7 July 2005
Ted McWhinney, 19 October 2004
John Meisel, 2 November 2004
Diane Mew, 21 October 2004
Jim Miller, 26 March 2004
John Moir, 4 July 2003; 5 March 2005
Willard Piepenberg, 4 May 2006
Margaret Prang, 18 January 2005
Keith Ralston, 23 May 2003
Mary Innis Cates Rutledge, 22 January 2005
Jack Saywell, 8 December 2004
Norman Sheffe, 7 April 2005
Sidney Soban, 16 December 2004 (personal communication)
Robert Spencer, 25 May 2006
Tom Symons, 26 January 2004
Scott Symons, 18 November 2005
Gerry Tulchinsky, 24 October 2005
Wesley Turner, 7 July 2005
Peter Waite, 6 November 2002
Morris Zaslow, 31 January 2005

Published Memoirs

Bliss, Michael. *Writing History: A Professor's Life*. Toronto: Dundurn, 2011.
Callaghan, Morley. *That Summer in Paris: Memories of Tangled Friendships with Hemingway, Fitzgerald, and Some Others*. Toronto: Macmillan, 1963.

Creighton, W.B. *Round 'bout Sun-Up: Some Memories that Live.* Toronto: Ryerson Press, 1946.

Forsey, Eugene. *A Life on the Fringe.* Toronto: Oxford University Press, 1990.

Lower, A.R.M. *My First Seventy-Five Years.* Toronto: Macmillan, 1967.

Massey, Vincent. *What's Past Is Prologue.* Toronto: Macmillan, 1963.

McNaught, Kenneth. *Conscience and History: A Memoir.* Toronto: University of Toronto Press, 1999.

Meisel, John. *A Life of Learning and Other Pleasures: John Meisel's Tale*, Yarker, ON: Wintergreen Studios Press, 2012.

Pearson, Lester. *Mike: The Memoirs of the Rt. Hon. Lester B. Pearson.* Toronto: University of Toronto Press, 1972.

Ritchie, Charles, *An Appetite for Life: The Education of a Young Diarist, 1924–1927.* Toronto: Macmillan, 1977.

Spencer, Robert. *A European Affair: Memoirs.* Ottawa, 2007.

Stacey, C.P. *A Date With History.* Ottawa: Deneau, 1983.

Trudel, Marcel. *Memoirs of a Less Travelled Road: A Historian's Life.* Montreal: Véhicule Press, 2002.

Secondary Sources

Aggarwala, Rohit. "Non-Resident Me: John Bartlet Brebner and the Canadian Historical Profession." *Journal of the Canadian Historical Association* 10 (1999).

Airhart, Phyllis. *Serving the Present Age: Revivalism, Progressivism, and the Methodist Tradition in Canada.* Montreal and Kingston: McGill-Queen's University Press, 1992.

Akenson, Donald. *The Irish in Ontario: A Study in Rural History.* Montreal and Kingston: McGill-Queen's University Press, 1984.

Anderson, Allan. "Out of the Turmoil Comes a New Awareness of Ourselves: Donald Creighton Interviewed." *University of Toronto Graduate*, June 1968.

Beattie, Kim. *48th Highlanders of Canada: 1891–1928.* Toronto: Southam Press, 1932.

Bélanger, Damien-Claude. *Pride and Prejudice: Canadian Intellectuals Confront the United States, 1891–1945.* Toronto: University of Toronto Press, 2011.

Berger, Carl. *The Sense of Power: Studies in the Ideas of Canadian Imperialism, 1867–1914.* Toronto: University of Toronto Press, 1970.

– *The Writing of Canadian History: Aspects of English-Canadian Historical Writing since 1900.* Toronto: University of Toronto Press, 1976.

Berger, Stefan, ed. *Writing the Nation: A Global Perspective.* New York: Palgrave Macmillan, 2007.

Berger, Stefan, and Chris Lorenz, eds. *The Contested Nation: Ethnicity, Class, Religion and Gender in National Histories.* New York: Palgrave Macmillan, 2008.

Bickerstaff, Isaac. "A Caricature Gallery of Literary Masters." *Tamarack Review* 67 (October 1975).

Birkenhead, Lord. *Walter Monckton: The Life of Viscount Monckton of Brenchley.* London: Weidenfeld and Nicholson, 1969.

Bliss, Michael. "Privatizing the Mind: The Sundering of Canadian History, the Sundering of Canada." *Journal of Canadian Studies* 26, no. 4 (Winter 1991–2).

– *Right Honourable Men: The Descent of Canadian Politics from Macdonald to Mulroney.* Toronto: HarperCollins, 1994.

Bonesteel, Sarah. "Luella Bruce Creighton: A Writer's Diary." Unpublished MA thesis, University of Waterloo, 2001.

Bothwell, Robert. *Laying the Foundation: A Century of History at University of Toronto.* Toronto: University of Toronto Department of History, 1991.

Braz, Albert. *The False Traitor: Louis Riel in Canadian Culture.* Toronto: University of Toronto Press, 2003.

Buckner, Phillip. "The Maritimes and Confederation: A Reassessment." *Canadian Historical Review* 71, no. 1 (1990).

Buckner, Phillip, and R. Douglas Francis, eds. *Rediscovering the British World.* Calgary: University of Calgary Press, 2005.

– *Canada and the British World: Culture, Migration, and Identity.* Vancouver: UBC Press, 2006.

Burwash, Nathanael. *The History of Victoria College.* Toronto: Victoria College Press, 1927.

Campbell, Sandra. "The Canadian Literary Career of Professor Pelham Edgar." Unpublished PhD thesis, University of Ottawa, 1993.

– *Both Hands: A Life of Lorne Pierce of Ryerson Press.* Montreal and Kingston: McGill-Queen's University Press, 2013.

Careless, Maurice. "Limited Identities in Canada." *Canadian Historical Review* 50, no. 1 (1969).

Cavell, Janice. "The Second Frontier: The North in English-Canadian Historical Writing." *Canadian Historical Review* 83, no. 3 (2002).

Champion, C.P. "A Very British Coup: Canadianism, Quebec, and Ethnicity in the Flag Debate, 1964–1965." *Journal of Canadian Studies* 40, no. 3 (2006).

– "Mike Pearson at Oxford: War, Varsity, and Canadianism." *Canadian Historical Review* 88, no. 2 (June 2007).

– *The Strange Demise of British Canada: The Liberals and Canadian Nationalism, 1964–1968.* Montreal and Kingston: McGill-Queen's University Press, 2010.

Christie, Nancy, ed. *Households of Faith: Family, Gender, and Community in Canada, 1760–1969.* Montreal and Kingston: McGill-Queen's University Press, 2002.

Collingwood, R.G. *The Idea of History.* Oxford: Oxford University Press, 1946.

Comacchio, Cynthia. *The Infinite Bonds of Family: Domesticity in Canada, 1850–1940.* Toronto: University of Toronto Press, 1999.

Conway, Jill Ker. *True North*. Toronto: Vintage, 1995.

Cook, Eleanor, and Ramsay Cook, eds. *The Craft of History*. Toronto: Canadian Broadcasting Corporation, 1973.

Cook, Ramsay. *The Regenerators: Social Criticism in Late Victorian English Canada*. Toronto: University of Toronto Press, 1985.

– *Canada, Quebec, and the Uses of Nationalism*. Toronto: McClelland and Stewart, 1986.

– "Nation, Identity, Rights: Reflections on W.L. Morton's Canadian Identity." *Journal of Canadian Studies* 29, no. 2 (1994).

Craig, Gerald, ed. *Lord Durham's Report*. Montreal and Kingston: McGill-Queen's University Press, 2007.

Creighton, Philip. "John Harvie." *York Pioneer* 81 (Summer 1986).

– "Creighton, Eliza Jane (Harvie)." *Dictionary of Canadian Biography*. Available online at www.biographi.ca.

– "Harvie (Harvey), John." *Dictionary of Canadian Biography*. Available online at www.biographi.ca.

Crowley, Terry. *Marriage of Minds: Isabel and Oscar Skelton Reinventing Canada* Toronto: University of Toronto Press, 2003.

Curran, James, and Stuart Ward. *The Unknown Nation: Australia after Empire*. Melbourne: Melbourne University Press, 2010.

Darwin, John. *Britain and Decolonization: The Retreat from Empire in the Post-War World*. London: Macmillan, 1988.

– "The Central African Emergency, 1959." *Journal of Imperial and Commonwealth History* 21, no. 3 (1993).

– *The Empire Project: The Rise and Fall of the British World-System, 1830–1970*. Cambridge: Cambridge University Press, 2009.

Darroch, Gordon. "Scanty Fortunes and Rural Middle-Class Formation in Nineteenth-Century Central Ontario." *Canadian Historical Review* 79, no. 4 (December 1998).

Dewar, Kenneth. "Nationalism, Professionalism, and Canadian History." *Canadian Dimension* (December 1970).

– "The Professionalization of History." *This Magazine* 5 (1971).

– "Where to Begin and How: Narrative Openings in Donald Creighton's Historiography." *Canadian Historical Review* 72, no. 3 (1991).

Dick, Lyle. "A Growing Necessity for Canada": W.L. Morton's Centenary Series and the Forms of National History, 1955–80; *Canadian Historical Review* 82, no. 2 (2001).

Dirks, Patricia. "'Getting a Grip on Harry': Canada's Methodists Respond to the 'Big Boy' Problem, 1900–1925." *Canadian Methodist Historical Society Papers* 7 (1990).

Dunae, Patrick. "Boys Literature and the Idea of Empire." *Victorian Studies* (Autumn 1980).

Eccles, W.J. "The History of New France According to Francis Parkman." *William and Mary Quarterly* 18, no. 2 (1961).

Elliot-Meisel, Elizabeth. "John Bartlet Brebner: The Private Man behind the Professional Historian." *American Review of Canadian Studies* 32, no. 4 (2002).

Ferguson, Barry, and Robert Wardhaugh. "Impossible Conditions of Inequality: John W. Dafoe, the Rowell-Sirois Royal Commission, and the Interpretation of Canadian Federalism." *Canadian Historical Review* 84, no. 4 (2003).

Flood, Cynthia. *My Father Took a Cake to France*. Vancouver: Talon Books, 1992.

Forbes, E.R. *The Maritime Rights Movement, 1919–1927: A Study in Canadian Regionalism*. Montreal and Kingston: McGill-Queen's University Press, 1979.

Frager, Ruth, and Carmela Patrias. *Discounted Labour: Women Workers in Canada, 1870–1939*. Toronto: University of Toronto Press, 2005.

Francis, R. Douglas. *Frank H. Underhill: Intellectual Provocateur*. Toronto: University of Toronto Press, 1986.

Friedland, Martin. *The University of Toronto: A History*. Toronto: University of Toronto Press, 2002.

Gidney, Catherine. "Dating and Gating: The Moral Regulation of Men and Women at Victoria and University Colleges, University of Toronto, 1920–1960." *Journal of Canadian Studies*, 41, 2 (Spring 2007).

Gidney, Catherine. *The Long Eclipse: The Liberal Protestant Establishment and the Canadian University, 1920–1970*. Montreal and Kingston: McGill-Queen's, 2004.

Graham, John. "William Lyon Mackenzie King, Elizabeth Harvie, and Edna: A Prostitute Rescuing Initiative in Late Victorian Toronto." *Canadian Journal of Human Sexuality* 81, no. 1 (Spring 1999).

Granatstein, J.L. *Yankee Go Home? Canadians and Anti-Americanism*. Toronto: HarperCollins, 1996.

Grant, George. *Lament for a Nation*. Toronto: McClelland and Stewart, 1965.

– "The Empire – Yes or No?" In Arthur Davis and Peter Emberly, eds, *Collected Works of George Grant*, vol. 1: *1933–1950*. Toronto: University of Toronto Press, 2000.

Green, Adam. "Images of Americans: The United States in Canadian Newspapers during the 1960s." Unpublished PhD thesis, University of Ottawa, 2007.

Green, Martin. *Dreams of Adventure, Deeds of Empire*. New York: Basic Books, 1979.

Hall, D.J. "The Spirit of Confederation: Ralph Heintzman, Professor Creighton, and the Bicultural Compact Theory." *Journal of Canadian Studies* 9, no. 4 (1974).

Heintzman, Ralph. "The Spirit of Confederation: Professor Creighton, Biculturalism, and the Use of History." *Canadian Historical Review* 52, no. 3 (1971).

– "Political Space and Economic Space: Quebec and the Empire of the St. Lawrence." *Journal of Canadian Studies* 29, no. 2 (1994).

Hesketh, Ian. "Writing History in Macaulay's Shadow: J.R. Seeley, E.A. Freeman, and the Audience for Scientific History in Late Victorian Britain." *Journal of the Canadian Historical Association* 22, no. 2 (2011).

Hidas, Kristina, ed. *Humberside: The First Century, 1892–1992*. Toronto: n.p., 1992.

Hill, Christopher L. *National History and the World of Nations*. Durham, NC: Duke University Press, 2008.

Holroyd, Michael. *Works on Paper: The Craft of Biography and Autobiography*. Washington: Counterpoint, 2002.

Hopkins, A.G. "Rethinking Decolonization." *Past and Present* 200 (August 2008).

Horn, Michiel. "Academics and Canadian Social and Economic Policy in the Depression and War Years." *Journal of Canadian Studies* 13, no. 4 (1978–9).

– "Free Speech within the Law: The Letter of the Sixty-Eight Toronto Professors, 1931." *Ontario History*, 72, 1 (1980).

– *Academic Freedom in Canada: A History*. Toronto: University of Toronto Press, 1999.

Houston, Cecil, and William Smyth. *Irish Emigration and Canadian Settlement: Patterns, Links, and Letters*. Toronto: University of Toronto Press, 1990.

Hyam, Ronald. "The Geopolitical Origins of the Central African Federation: Britain, Rhodesia, and South Africa, 1948–1953." *Historical Journal* 30 (1987).

– *Sexuality and Empire: The British Experience*. Manchester: Manchester University Press, 1990.

Igartua, José. *The Other Quiet Revolution: National Identities in English Canada, 1945–71*. Vancouver: UBC Press, 2006.

– "The Genealogy of Stereotypes: French Canadians in Two English-language Canadian History Textbooks." *Journal of Canadian Studies* 42, no. 3 (Fall 2008).

Innis, Harold. *The Fur Trade in Canada*. New Haven, CT: Yale University Press, 1930.

– *Changing Concepts of Time*. Toronto: University of Toronto Press, 1952.

Jasen, Patricia. *Wild Things: Nature, Culture, and Tourism in Ontario, 1790–1914*. Toronto: University of Toronto Press, 1995.

Jones, John. *Balliol College: A History*. Oxford: Oxford University Press, 1997.

Jones, Preston. "Towards a Study of the Bible in Canadian Public Life." *Journal of Canadian Studies* 34, no. 1 (1999).

Kent-Barber, Nigel. "La théorie du commerce principal chez MM. Creighton et Ouellet." *Revue d'histoire de l'Amérique française* 22, no. 3 (1968).

Létourneau, Jocelyn. *A History for the Future: Rewriting Memory and Identity in Quebec*. Montreal and Kingston: McGill-Queen's University Press, 2004.

Martin, Ged, ed. *The Causes of Canadian Confederation*. Fredericton: Acadiensis Press, 1990.

– *Past Futures: The Impossible Necessity of History*. Toronto: University of Toronto Press, 2004.

– *Favourite Son? John A. Macdonald and the Voters of Kingston*. Kingston: Kingston Historical Society, 2008.

– *John A. Macdonald: Canada's First Prime Minister*. Toronto: Dundurn, 2013.

Massolin, Philip. *Canadian Intellectuals, The Tory Tradition, and the Challenge of Modernity, 1939–1970*. Toronto: University of Toronto Press, 2001.

McCalla, Douglas. "The Rhodes Scholarships in Canada and Newfoundland." In Anthony Kenny, ed., *The History of the Rhodes Trust, 1902–1999*. Oxford: Oxford University Press, 2001.

McKellar, Hugh D. *Our Cloud of Witnesses: The Centennial History of Emmanuel–Howard Park United Church*. Toronto: n.p., 1990.

Megill, Allan. *Historical Knowledge, Historical Error: A Contemporary Guide to Practice*. Chicago: University of Chicago Press, 2007.

Meikle, W.D. "And Gladly Teach: G.M. Wrong and the Department of History at the University of Toronto." Unpublished PhD thesis, Michigan State, 1977.

Mellor, W.M. "Timothy Findley's True Fictions: A Conversation in Stone Orchard." *Studies in Canadian Literature* 19, no. 2 (1994).

Miller, J.R. *Shingwauk's Vision: A History of Native Residential Schools*. Toronto: University of Toronto Press, 1996.

Mills, Sean. *The Empire Within: Postcolonial Thought and Political Activism in Sixties Montreal*. Montreal and Kingston: McGill-Queen's University Press, 2010.

Moir, John. ed. *Character and Circumstance: Essays in Honour of Donald Grant Creighton*. Toronto: Macmillan, 1970.

Morris, Jan. *Oxford*. Oxford: Oxford University Press, 1978.

Morton, W.L. "Foreword." In Solange Chaput-Rolland, *My Country, Canada or Quebec*. Toronto: Macmillan, 1966.

– "Clio in Canada: The Interpretation of Canadian History." In Carl Berger, ed., *Approaches to Canadian History*. Toronto: University of Toronto Press, 1967.

Munro, Doug. "Biographies of Historians – or, The Cliographer's Craft." *Australian Historical Studies* 43, no. 1 (2012).

Murphy, Philip. "Government by Blackmail: The Origins of the Central African Federation Reconsidered." In Martin Lynn, ed., *The British Empire in the 1950s: Retreat or Revival?* London: Palgrave Macmillan, 2006.

Nicholls, C.S. *Elspeth Huxley: A Biography*. London: HarperCollins, 2002.

Owram, Doug. *The Government Generation: Canadian Intellectuals and the State* Toronto: University of Toronto Press, 1986.

Palmer, Bryan. *Canada's 1960s: The Ironies of Identity in a Rebellious Era*. Toronto: University of Toronto Press, 2009.

Palmer, Robin. "European Resistance to African Majority Rule: The Settlers and Residents Association of Nyasaland, 1960–63." *African Affairs* 72, no. 288 (1973).

Paquin, Stéphane. *L'invention d'un mythe – le pacte entre deux peuples fondateurs*. Montreal: VLB, 1999.

Phillips, Mark. "The Professionalization of History." *This Magazine* 5 (1971).

Prang, Margaret. "Nationalism in Canada's First Century." *Historical Papers* 3, no. 1 (1968).

– "The Girl God Would Have Me Be: The Canadian Girls in Training, 1915–1939." *Canadian Historical Review* 62, no. 1 (1985).

Reimer, Chad. *Writing British Columbia History, 1784–1958*. Vancouver: UBC Press, 2009.

Roberts, Barbara. "They Drove Him to Drink: Donald Creighton's Macdonald and his Wives." *Canada: An Historical Magazine* 3, no. 2 (1975).

Robertson, Heather. "The Man Who Invented Canada." *Saturday Night*, October 1977.

Romney, Paul. *Getting It Wrong: How Canadians Forgot Their Past and Imperiled Confederation*. Toronto: University of Toronto Press, 1999.

Selles, Johanna. *Methodists and Women's Education in Ontario, 1836–1925*. Montreal and Kingston: McGill-Queen's University Press, 1996.

Semple, Neil. *The Lord's Dominion: The History of Canadian Methodism*. Montreal and Kingston: McGill-Queen's University Press, 1996.

– *Faithful Intellect: Samuel S. Nelles and Victoria University*. Montreal and Kingston: McGill-Queen's University Press, 2005.

Silver, A.I. *The French-Canadian Idea of Confederation 1864–1900*. 2nd ed. Toronto: University of Toronto Press, 1997.

Slumkoski, Corey. "… a fair show and a square deal: New Brunswick and the Renegotiation of Canadian Federalism." *Journal of New Brunswick Studies* 1, no. 1 (2010).

Smith, Denis. *Rogue Tory: The Life and Legend of John G. Diefenbaker*. Toronto: MacFarlane, Walter, and Ross, 1995.

Soffer, Reba. "Nation, Duty, Character, and Confidence: History at Oxford, 1850–1914." *Historical Journal* 30, no. 1 (1987).

– *Discipline and Power: The University, History, and the Making of an English Elite, 1870–1930*. Stanford, CA: Stanford University Press, 1994.

Spengler, Oswald. *The Decline of the West*. New York: Knopf, 1926.

Spittal, Cara. "The Diefenbaker Moment." Unpublished PhD thesis, University of Toronto, 2011.

Strachey, Lytton. *The Eminent Victorians*. London: Continuum, 2002.

Strange, Carolyn. *Toronto's Girl Problem: The Perils and Pleasures of the City, 1880–1930*. Toronto: University of Toronto Press, 1995.

Strong-Boag, Veronica. "Contested Space: The Politics of Canadian Memory." *Journal of the Canadian Historical Association* 5 (1994).

Suffrin, Jon. "The Canadian Apocalypse: Nationalists and The End of Canada, 1963–1983." Unpublished PhD thesis, York University, 2009.

Taylor, Charles. *Radical Tories: The Conservative Tradition in Canada*. Toronto: Anansi, 1982.

Taylor, M. Brook. *Promoters, Patriots, and Partisans: Historiography in Nineteenth-Century English Canada*. Toronto: University of Toronto Press, 1989.

Trigger, Bruce. "The Historians' Indian: Native Americans in Canadian Historical Writing from Charlevoix to the Present." *Canadian Historical Review* 67, no. 3 (1986).

Underhill, Frank. *In Search of Canadian Liberalism*. Toronto: Macmillan, 1960.

Vipond, Mary. "Canadian Nationalism and the Plight of Canadian Magazines in the 1920s." *Canadian Historical Review* 58, no. 1 (1977).

Waite, Peter. *Reefs Unsuspected: Historians and Biography in Canada, Australia and Elsewhere* Sydney: Macquarie University, 1983.

– "Donald Creighton: Casting the Net of His *Macdonald*." *The Beaver* (February/March 1998).

Walker, James W. St. G. "The Indian in Canadian Historical Writing." *Historical Papers* (1971).

Watson, Alexander John. *Marginal Man: The Dark Vision of Harold Innis*. Toronto: University of Toronto Press, 2006.

Weaver, John. *The Great Land Rush and the Making of the Modern World, 1650–1900*. Montreal and Kingston: McGill-Queen's University Press, 2003.

Welensky, Roy. *Welensky's 4000 Days: The Life and Death of the Federation of Rhodesia and Nyasaland*. London: Collins, 1964.

Westfall, William. "Creighton's Tragic Vision." *Canadian Forum* (September 1970).

– *Two Worlds: The Protestant Culture of Nineteenth-Century Ontario*. Montreal and Kingston: McGill-Queen's University Press, 1989.

White, Hayden. *Metahistory: The Historical Imagination in Nineteenth-Century Europe*. Baltimore: Johns Hopkins University Press, 1973.

Whitely, Marilyn Färdig. *Canadian Methodist Women, 1766–1925: Marys, Marthas, Mothers in Israel*. Waterloo, ON: Wilfrid Laurier University Press, 2005.

Wilson, Catharine Anne. *Tenants in Time: Family Strategies, Land, and Liberalism in Upper Canada, 1799–1871*. Montreal and Kingston: McGill-Queen's University Press, 2009.

Woodcock, George. "The Servants of Clio: Notes on Creighton and Groulx." *Canadian Literature* 83 (1979).

Woolf, Virginia. *Selected Essays*. Oxford: Oxford University Press, 2008.

Wright, Donald. "Donald Creighton and the French Fact, 1920s to 1970s." *Journal of the Canadian Historical Association* 6 (1995).

– *The Professionalization of History in English Canada*. Toronto: University of Toronto Press, 2005.

Illustration Credits

Donald Creighton's desk. Photograph by Thomas Cheney.

Creighton Family Tree. Prepared by Marc F. Gagnon.

Map of Dorchester North Township, Middlesex County. *Illustrated Historical Atlas of the County of Middlesex, Ont.* Toronto: H.R. Page, 1878. Reproduced with the permission of McGill University Library.

Kennedy Creighton. Original in possession of Philip Creighton.

Eliza (Lizzie) Jane Creighton Harvie. Original in possession of Philip Creighton.

Hillside, c. 1905. Original in possession of Amy Humphreys, Colorado, USA.

William Black Creighton. Original in possession of Philip Creighton.

Laura Creighton Harvie. Original in possession of Philip Creighton.

Donald Creighton and Jack Creighton. Original in possession of Philip Creighton.

Donald Creighton and Isabel Creighton. Original in possession of Cynthia Flood.

Canadian Nature Journal, two images. Originals in possession of Philip Creighton.

Jack Creighton at Niagara-on-the-Lake, 1918. Original in possession of Denis Creighton.

Donald Creighton, graduation photo, 1925. Original in possession of Philip Creighton.

Sarah Luella Sanders, ca 1900. Original in possession of Cynthia Flood.

William Bruce and Luella Bruce, ca 1906. Original in possession of Cynthia Flood.

Luella Bruce in CGIT. Original in possession of Cynthia Flood.

Luella Bruce, graduation photo, 1926. Original in possession of Philip Creighton.

Somerset Cottage. Original in possession of Philip Creighton.

Donald Creighton and kitten in Somerset. Original in possession of Philip Creighton.

William and Laura Creighton, Muskoka, ca 1930s. Original in possession of Cynthia Flood.

Donald Creighton's writing hut, Muskoka. Photograph by Donald Wright.

Portrait of Donald Creighton, n.d., ca 1940. Original in possession of Cynthia Flood.

Promoting *High Bright Buggy Wheels*, 1951. University of Waterloo, Dana Porter Library, Special Collections and Archives, Luella Creighton fonds, GA 99 121.

Donald Creighton, Luella Creighton, and Cynthia Creighton on the *Empress of France*, 1953. Original in possession of Cynthia Flood.

Donald Creighton on his porch at Muskoka, n.d. Original in possession of Cynthia Flood.

Donald Creighton and Claude Bissell, 1961, by Jack Marshall. University of Toronto Archives, A1978–0041/005 (2).

Donald Creighton leading a 1959 seminar, by Ken Bell. University of Toronto Archives, A1978–0041/005 (2).

Map of Central African Federation, 1960. Government of the Federation of Rhodesia and Nyasaland.

Norman Mansbridge, *Punch*, 16 December 1959. Reproduced with the permission of Punch Limited.

Three photographs of the Monckton Commission. Library and Archives Canada, Donald Creighton fonds, MG 31 D 77. All reasonable steps were taken to determine copyright holder.

Lionel Groulx, 1965. John Daggett, The Montreal Star fonds, The Montreal Gazette photo archives.

Ontario Advisory Committee on Confederation. Library and Archives Canada, Donald Creighton fonds, MG 31 D 77. Copyright Queen's Printer for Ontario, 2014. Reproduced with permission.

Prime Minister John Diefenbaker, E.J. Pratt, and Margaret Ray, librarian, at the opening of the E.J. Pratt Library. 1961. Victoria University Archives, Photograph Collection. Reproduced with the permission of Bob Lansdale, photographer.

Luella Creighton and her cat, ca mid-1960s. University of Waterloo, Dana Porter Library, Special Collections and Archives, Luella Creighton fonds, GA 99 199.

Donald Creighton and John Gray, 1970. Library and Archives Canada, Donald Creighton fonds, MG 31 D 77. Reproduced with the permission of Pete Paterson, photographer.

Donald Creighton: The Old Chieftain by Isaac Bickerstaff, 1975. Isaac Bickerstaff fonds, Special Collections, Libraries and Cultural Resources, University of Calgary. Reproduced with the permission of Don Evans.

Donald Creighton and George Robertson, July 1972. Original in possession of Cynthia Flood.

Donald Creighton in his backyard, 1970. Library and Archives Canada, Donald Creighton fonds, MG 31 D 77. Reproduced with the permission of Alain Masson, photographer.

Donald Creighton in his study, Brooklin, Ontario, 1977. Library and Archives Canada, Arnaud Maggs fonds, R7959, vol. 811, envelope 3247. Reproduced with the permission of the Arnaud Maggs estate.

Jack Creighton, ca 1918. Original in possession of Denis Creighton.

Donald Creighton at home, Brooklin, Ontario, 1977. Library and Archives Canada, Arnaud Maggs fonds, R7959, vol. 811, envelope 3247. Reproduced with the permission of the Arnaud Maggs estate.

Gravestones of Donald Creighton and Luella Creighton. Photograph by David Calverley.

Index

15 Princess Street, Brooklin, ON, 258, 259, 287
32 Hewitt Avenue, Toronto, 49, 59, 63, 82, 135, 157, 267, 288, 336
48th Highlanders, 55, 287, 336

Abbott, Douglas, 241
Abella, Irving, 296
Aboriginal handicrafts: John Diefenbaker gives as gifts, 289; Queen Elizabeth comments on, 290
Aboriginal peoples: collect frozen apples on Creighton farm, 32; dispossession of, 21; in Donald Creighton's historical writing, 159–61, 235, 274, 318, 325; in Luella Creighton's *The Elegant Canadians*, 290; Kennedy Creighton serves as minister to, 23–4; Lizzie Harvie tours Presbyterian missions and schools in Manitoba and the northwest, 26–7, 160. *See also* Big Bear; Indians of Canada Pavilion; Poundmaker; Riel, Louis
Acheson, Dean, 325
Acta Victoriana, 44, 64, 65–6, 70–4, 75, 81
Addison, Margaret, 81

Alliance for the Preservation of English in Canada, 333
American Historical Association, 291
Anderson, Sherwood, 67, 73, 74
Anglican Church of Canada, 322
Anglicanism, 22
Arpin, Maurice, 284–5
Arts and Letters Club, 334
Atwood, Margaret, 71
Austen, Jane, 67, 68, 179

Bailey, Alfred, 66, 160
Baker, Josephine, 105
Baldwin House, 105, 116, 218, 345
Balliol College, 5, 9, 76, 85–9, 94, 95, 103, 104, 106, 179, 180, 187, 193, 245, 246, 260
Balzac, Honoré de, 62, 179
Banda, Hastings, 239, 242
Banda, T.D.T., 250
Beame, Ed, 232, 233
Beard, Charles, 321
Beaverbrook, Lord, 180–1, 186, 214, 215
Bell, Kenneth, 75, 89, 101
Beloff, Max, 191, 198
Bennett, Arnold, 9, 183, 202
Bennett, R.B., 136, 214

Berger, Carl, 10
Bernard, Agnes (John A. Macdonald's second wife), 26, 197, 201–2, 203, 318–19
Bevan, Nye, 244
Big Bear, 160, 318
Bilingual Today, French Tomorrow: Trudeau's Master Plan and How It Can Be Stopped, 333
Birney, Earle, 66, 120
Bissell, Claude, 232, 234
Bladen, Vincent, 257
Blake, Edward, 197, 210, 233
Bliss, Michael, 133, 288
Borden, Robert Laird, 63, 190, 214, 265
Bothwell, Robert, 311–12, 314
Bourassa, Henri, 282
Bowles, Reverend Richard P., 75
Boy's Own Paper, 50, 51, 245
Brady, Alexander, 215, 226
Braudel, Fernand, 327
Brebner, Bartlet, 69, 104, 114, 115, 117, 124, 152–3, 165, 167
British connection, 192, 221, 236, 260, 282. *See also* imperial connection
British North America at Confederation, 7, 137–8, 140–1, 146, 152, 167; New Brunswick objects to, 139–40, 392n23
Brock, General Isaac, 113, 200, 318, 340
Brooker, Bertram, 120
Brown, Craig, 275, 312–13
Brown, George (historian), 115, 116, 207, 209, 217, 233, 234, 385n22
Brown, George (nineteenth-century politician), 168, 184, 191, 218, 268, 269, 281, 287
Brown, Harcourt, 107, 108
Bruce, James Walter, 77, 79, 95, 112
Brunet, Michel, 191, 271, 285–6
Buckner, Phillip, 321

Burt, A.L., 113–14, 130, 152, 162, 163, 166
Butterfield, Herbert, 210, 213, 319

Cairns, John, xiii, 217, 218, 220, 224, 344, 435n55
Callaghan, Morley, 105, 107, 120
Canada: The Struggle for Empire, 259–60, 298
Canada: Trial and Triumph, 259–60, 298
Canada's First Century, 8, 9, 10, 235, 296–7, 301–6, 312, 318, 336
Canadian Broadcasting League, 228, 230, 234
Canadian Forum, 120, 136, 148, 149, 187, 210, 261
Canadian Girls in Training, 83
Canadian Historical Association, 113, 216, 221–4, 291, 295–6, 320
Canadian Historical Review, 113, 116, 124, 312, 313, 314
Careless, J.M.S., 145, 214, 217, 233, 291, 310, 314, 319, 346
Carleton University, 222, 232
Carlyle, Thomas, 202
Carman, Bliss, 42, 67
Carnegie Endowment for International Peace, 117, 118, 143, 210
Cartier, Jacques, 97, 125, 134, 160, 161, 164, 269, 318
Cartier, George-Étienne, 268, 269, 272, 290
Central African Federation of Rhodesia and Nyasaland, 4, 237, 239–57, 258, 345
Centenary Series, 8, 216, 323–4, 329
Chapais, Thomas, 282
Chapel of St James-the-Less, Toronto, 345
Chaput-Rolland, Solange, 282, 283, 288
Charron, Claude, 8–9, 361n22

Christian Guardian, 5, 24, 34, 36, 40, 43–4, 54, 56, 74, 171, 335

Churchill, Winston, 104, 186, 215, 326, 332

Clark, Isabella (John A. Macdonald's first wife), 183, 318–19

Clark, Joe, 332, 333, 345

Clark, Manning, 321

Clark, S.D., 170, 215, 226

Clarkson, Stephen, 8

Claxton, A.G.B., 166

Claxton, Brooke, 166, 325

Clippingdale, Richard, 311

Cod Fisheries, The, 228

Cody, Henry J., 148–50, 170

Coldwell, M.J., 191

Collingwood, R.G., 177

Colony to Nation, 169

Commercial Empire of the St. Lawrence, The, 6, 7, 8, 9, 124–34, 135, 137, 144, 146, 152, 154, 155, 159, 161, 162, 163, 165, 167, 171, 178, 182, 190, 267, 274, 295, 301, 312, 318, 334, 343, 346

Commonweath, 154, 166, 174, 212, 219, 234, 237–8, 239, 242, 243, 256–7, 258, 260, 303, 324, 325, 326

Conacher, Jim, 233, 235, 236

Conlogue, Ray, 8–9

Conrad, Joseph, 62

Conrad, Margaret, 325

continentalism, 124, 127, 133, 163, 165, 175, 235, 260, 270, 271, 301, 304, 316, 340

Conway, John, 276–7

Cook, Ramsay, xiii, 9, 261–2, 271, 275, 281, 282, 285, 316, 321, 326, 334, 335, 340–1, 342–3, 346

Co-operative Commonweath Federation, 167, 227

Corey, Albert, 191

Creary, Tim, 285

Creighton, Angus, 315

Creighton, Ann (English), 20, 28–9, 30, 31

Creighton, Denis, xiii, 121

Creighton, Donald: academic freedom, 233; address to Manitoba Historical Society, 284–6; anger, 9, 63, 94, 220, 227, 229, 260, 264, 306, 316, 321, 324, 336; anti-Americanism, 51, 74, 126, 137, 146, 163–5, 174–5, 191, 200, 210–13, 219–20, 221, 222, 227, 229–30, 233, 237, 270–1, 277, 301, 303–5, 321–2, 325; anti-Catholicism, 162–3, 275; anti-Semitism, 231; appointment to Monckton Commission, 241–3; appointment to Ontario Advisory Committee on Confederation, 276–7; Authorized Version/Grit Historical Enterprises, 193, 222–3, 227, 237, 311, 340; begins PhD at the Sorbonne, 105–8; birth, 39; British children's magazines, 50–3; "Canadian Nature Journal," 52–3; cancer, 326–7, 341–2; childhood illness, 47–8; class as a category of analysis, 167–9; collapses from exhaustion, 195; death, 344–5; Dunning Trust Lecture, 319–20; early love of reading, 40–2; editor of *Acta Victoriana*, 71–4; falls in love, 5–6, 77, 82–3; as father and husband, 147; feud with Underhill, 209–11; First World War, 54–60; French Canada, 4–5, 7–9, 131–2, 161–3, 191–2, 235, 260–1, 266–7, 270, 272, 278–85, 297, 330–5; French history, 6, 70, 105–8, 295, 325; as grandfather, 315; gradu-ates from Vic, 76; hired at Toronto, 101; history as literature, 3, 10, 90, 111, 144, 172, 177, 178–9, 201–2,

345; influence of Charles Dickens, 162, 179, 269–70, 325; influence of Oxford, 104–5; influence of Richard Wagner, 93, 128–9, 301–2; instinctive conservatism, 70; instinctive need for attention and recognition, 73, 207, 216, 288, 317, 344; instinctive pessimism, 49; joins Anglican church, 322–3; keynote address to the Canadian Historical Association, 295–6; *The Last English Canadian*, 314; love of details in historical writing, 91, 179, 224, 269–70, 302; love of Lake Muskoka, xi, 121, 134, 195–6, 267; love of opera, 9, 93, 121, 157, 185, 245, 254, 311, 322, 343; love of words, 5; loses Rhodes Scholarship, 75; narrative history, 12, 90–1, 131, 158, 178–9, 185, 192–3, 226, 267, 311, 321; nation as a category of analysis, 166–9; offered position at McGill, 173; offered position at Trent, 280; opposition to apartheid, 256–7, 264; opposition to Maple Leaf flag, 262–5; opposition to Royal Commission on Bilingualism and Biculturalism, 260–1; origins of *Macdonald*, 171–2; origins of *The Commercial Empire of the St. Lawrence*, 114–16; Paris, 86, 93, 97, 99, 100, 105–8, 114, 308, 335, 346; as PhD supervisor, 311–12; physical health, 216, 220, 228–9, 245, 253, 257, 323; presidential address to Canadian Historical Association, 222–4; reacts angrily to criticism, 181–2, 190, 236, 326, 340–1; relationship with Cynthia, 147, 229, 274–6, 308–9, 311, 315–16, 328, 336, 342; resigns chairmanship, 232; retirement, 234–5, 257, 309–10; Second World War, 142–3; sells papers to Public Archives, 3–4; sex, 100, 157, 189–90, 298, 316; studies modern history at Balliol, 88–90; summers at Long Branch, 45–7; switch from English to history, 69; Underhill affair, 148–51; as university teacher, 4, 145, 236; wedding and honeymoon, 94–9; wins Edward Kylie Award, 76; wins Governor General's Award, 191, 198; wins Molson Prize, 3. *See also British North America at Confederation*; *Canada's First Century*; *Commercial Empire of the St. Lawrence*; *Dominion of the North*; *Forked Road*; *Harold Adams Innis: Portrait of a Scholar*; "James Richardson & Sons"; *Road to Confederation*; *Story of Canada*; *Sir John A. Macdonald*; *Takeover*

Creighton, Isabella, 16, 18
Creighton, Jack, 5, 35, 40, 42, 43, 45, 50, 54, 55–6, 57–9, 60, 63, 73, 120, 121, 135, 143, 147, 158, 166, 171, 190, 195, 268, 275, 306, 335–6, 338
Creighton, James, 18–20, 28–31, 37
Creighton, John, 15–18, 20, 23, 37, 321
Creighton, Kennedy, 16, 18, 23–4, 26, 27, 31, 37, 335, 365n39
Creighton, Laura, 5, 31, 35, 36, 39 , 40, 41, 42, 43, 45, 46, 47, 49, 50, 57, 58, 94, 100, 102; 112, 120, 121–2, 135, 147, 156, 171, 188, 195, 275, 306, 343
Creighton, Laura (Hart), 23, 24, 31
Creighton, Luella Bruce: admires "My Father Took a Cake to France," 348; anti-Semitism, 231; begins writing fiction, 118–20; burns love letters, 341; childhood, adolescence, and university, 77–84, 209; death, 348; Donald's final illness and death,

342–5; Donald's funeral and memorial service, 345–6; first novel, 157–8; graduates from Vic, 95; as grandmother, 315; her heroines as herself, 209; history department politics, 217; Kinsail, fictional town of, 157–8, 180, 208, 209, 259, 300; London, 185–6, 253–5; manages Donald's health, 228–9, 243, 245, 257, 267; mother's death, 77, 298–301; moves to Brooklin, 257–8; Oxford, 179–80; Paimpol, 97, 99, 308; Paris, 86, 92, 99–100, 105–8, 119; pregnant with Cynthia, 146–7; pregnant with Philip, 111–12; relationship with Cynthia, 274–6, 300–1, 315, 323, 342; resumes writing fiction, 141–2; room of her own, 157, 258, 298; second novel, 208–9; sells real estate, 136; sex, 157, 189–90; social history of Confederation, 290–1, 298; stepmother, 77, 79, 80, 82, 97, 120, 141, 157, 322; turns to writing history, 259–60; wedding and honeymoon, 94–99, 112; worries about her weight, 297, 310; on writers, 298; on writing, 5–6, 209, 300. *See also Canada: The Struggle for Empire*; *Canada: Trial and Triumph*; *Elegant Canadians*; *High Bright Buggy Wheels*; *Hitching Post*; "Music in the Park"; "Prelude"; *Turn East, Turn West*

Creighton, Margaret, 18

Creighton, Mary (English), 20, 28

Creighton, Nancy, 18

Creighton, Philip, xi, xiii, 46, 48, 65, 112, 120, 135, 136, 142, 156, 158, 164, 179, 187, 192, 195, 234, 245, 275, 309, 315, 316, 336, 345, 346

Creighton, Sally, 120, 121, 338

Creighton, William Black, 5, 31–7, 39, 40, 42, 43–6, 48, 49–50, 54, 58, 59, 63, 64, 74, 112, 115, 120, 121–2, 135, 156, 171, 188, 190, 195, 322, 335

Cross, Michael, 314, 325, 326

Crowe, Harry, 233

Daag, Anne Innis, 224, 226

Dafoe, J.W., 140–1, 143, 211

Daniells, Ray, 66

Davies, Robertson, 176

Deacon, William Arthur, 190, 191, 198

de Gaulle, Charles, 288

Department of History, University of Toronto, 6, 68–9, 73, 76, 89, 100–1, 105, 113, 115–16, 152, 190, 207–8, 209, 214, 216–18, 231–4, 344

Dickens, Charles, 9, 40, 41, 50, 63, 87, 147, 162, 179, 183, 186, 195, 269, 306, 311, 325, 343

Dickson, Lovat, 334

Diefenbaker, John, 7, 190, 212, 213, 221–2, 230, 235, 241, 243, 256–7, 258, 260, 263, 264, 265, 287, 288, 289, 296

Disraeli, Benjamin, 180, 258

Dobbs, Kildare, 280, 281

Dodge, Bernadine, 312

Doern, Russell, 285

Dominion of the North, 154, 158–69, 190, 229, 271, 291

Dorion, Antoine-Aimé, 272

Doyle, Arthur Conan, 64

Duncan, Douglas, 72, 74, 75, 93, 107

Dunton, Davidson, 326

Duplessis, Maurice, 325

Durham, Lord, 17, 125, 132, 243, 253, 255, 279, 321, 330, 334, 399n46

Easterbrook, Tom, 228

Eccles, W.J., 133, 310, 311

Eden, Anthony, 218–19, 220

Edgar, Pelham, 66, 67, 69, 82
Edward, Prince of Wales, 81
Edward VII, King, 42, 306
Edward VIII, King, 245–6
Eisenhower, Dwight, 219
El Dominio del Norte, 166
Elegant Canadians, The, 290–1, 298
Eliot, T.S., 62, 63, 65, 68, 71, 75, 346
Elizabeth II, Queen, 186, 235, 254, 258,
    263–4, 267, 280–1, 290
Elliott, John K., 321
Ely Cathedral, 306
emptiness, language of, 21, 32, 199, 235,
    251
end of empire, 4, 238, 262, 265, 270
Endicott, James, 56–7
Endicott, Norman, 57, 71, 72, 73, 77, 88,
    336
Evans, A.D. (Taffy), 251, 255
Expo 67, 7, 288–90

Fairclough, Ellen, 216
Fairley, Barker, 334
Falconer, Robert, 101
Faulkner, William, 10
Fetherling, George, 8
Flenley, Ralph, 207
Finch, Robert, 9, 308–9, 344, 346
flag debate, 262–5, 283. *See also* Maple
    Leaf flag; Red Ensign
Flavelle House, 188, 216, 217, 218
Flood, Cynthia, xiii, 48, 49, 147, 179,
    180, 187, 192, 193, 195, 229, 231, 234,
    245, 257, 274–6, 288, 300–1, 308–9,
    311, 315–16, 323, 327–8, 336, 342,
    343, 345, 346–8
Flood, Isabel, 315
Flood, Margaret, 328
Flood, Maurice, 275–6, 288, 300, 309,
    315

Ford, Ford Madox, 62, 105
Forked Road, The: Canada, 1939–1957,
    324–6, 336, 346
Forsey, Eugene, 7, 86, 88, 89, 104, 155,
    222, 223, 256–7, 261, 262, 263, 267,
    270, 271, 276, 279–80, 285, 312, 313,
    330, 333, 334, 435n72
Fox, Paul, 276, 278, 279, 326
Frégault, Guy, 200
Frost, Leslie, 287
Frye, Northrop, 10–11, 16, 41, 66, 71,
    145, 180, 310, 319
Fulton, Davie, 190, 216
Fur Trade in Canada, The, 109, 115, 130,
    226

Gaitskell, Hugh, 244
Galbraith, John Kenneth, 226, 319
Galt, Alexander, 268, 269
Garneau, François-Xavier, 6
Garnsworthy, Bishop Lewis, 322–3
George VI, King, 142, 146, 174, 186, 246,
    254
Gibbon, Edward, 90–1, 267
Gilbert, Angus, 311–12
Glassco, John, 105, 107
Gordon, Charles W., 64
Graham, Gerald, 226, 321
Granatstein, Jack, 326
Grant, George, 10, 13 174, 190, 226, 304,
    306, 319, 320, 322, 333
Grant, George Munro, 265
Gray, John, 9, 176–7, 181–2, 187, 188,
    199, 203, 267, 282, 283, 297, 302, 324,
    334
great land rush, 20, 251
Green, Howard, 219
Greene, Graham, 89
Groulx, Lionel, 131, 163, 271–2, 273,
    333, 340, 341, 442n28

Guggenheim Memorial Foundation, 143, 144, 147, 151, 152, 210

Hahn, Freya, 116, 152, 218, 309, 310, 435n55
Hall, D.J., 313–14
Hancock, Keith, 226
Hardy, Thomas, 9, 62, 68, 75, 85
Harold Adams Innis: Portrait of a Scholar, 216, 218, 224–8
Harvey, Daniel, 130
Harvie, John, 25–6, 33
Harvie, Lizzie, 25–8, 31, 37, 46, 82, 160, 303, 335
Heaton, Herbert, 130, 167
Heeney, Arnold, 103
Heintzman, Ralph, 312–14, 435n72
Hemingway, Ernest, 86, 103, 105, 107
Hepburn, Mitch, 148–9, 150, 151
Heroic Beginnings, 316–19
High Bright Buggy Wheels, 157–8, 179, 180, 181, 208, 397n21
Hilliard, Marion, 147
Historic Sites and Monuments Board, 288
Historical Club (University of Toronto), 74
history wars, 284, 289
Hitching Post, The, 298–301
Hobsbawm, Eric, 321
Howard Park Methodist Church, Toronto, 49, 50, 53
Howe, C.D., 222, 229
Humanities Research Council, 215, 216
Humberside Collegiate, 5, 59, 111
Hutchison, Bruce, 190
Huxley, Aldous, 73
Huxley, Elspeth, 246, 250–1, 252, 258
Hysterical Club (Victoria College), 74, 126, 222

Idea of History, The, 177
imperial connection, 7, 39, 104, 124, 126, 127, 129, 132, 169, 176, 268, 301, 324. *See also* British connection
improvement, doctrine of, 17, 20, 21, 23, 132, 159, 161, 241, 247, 251, 321
Indians of Canada Pavilion, Expo 67, 289–90
Innis, Harold, 10, 105, 107, 109, 114, 115, 116, 117, 118, 121, 122, 124, 143, 149, 160, 170, 171, 174–5, 186–9, 192, 198, 213–14, 215, 220, 227, 230, 231, 232, 304, 336, 412n72, 412n74. *See also Harold Adams Innis: Portrait of a Scholar*
Innis, Mary Quayle, 121, 122, 149, 186, 189, 192, 198, 215, 224–5, 336
Irish emigration, 15–17, 21

Jaenen, Cornelius, 285–6
"James Richardson & Sons" (unpublished manuscript), 214–15, 216, 234, 235, 245, 257, 286–7
Jenness, Diamond, 159, 160
Johnson, Daniel, 276, 288
Johnston, Wayne, 205
Jones, Leonard, 333
Jones, Peter, 23
Jones, W.P., 138
Journal of Canadian Studies, 280, 314
Joyce, James, 105

Keenleyside, Hugh, 8
Kennedy, John F., 304, 305
Kennedy, Joseph, 148, 304, 305
Kennedy, W.P.M., 113
Keynes, John Maynard, 174
King, Mackenzie, 27, 28, 63, 80, 136, 138, 166, 193, 210–11, 213, 235, 241, 282, 302–3, 318, 324, 325

Knister, Raymond, 66
Knopf, Alfred, 229–30
Korean War, 188, 192, 219, 220, 227, 405n53
Krevor, Horace, 285
Kylie, Edward, 75, 87, 221

L'Allier, Paul, 271
Lamb, W.K., 106
Lament for a Nation, 8, 13, 306, 319, 322, 333
Lamontagne, Maurice, 333
Lanctôt, Gustave, 169
Laskin, Bora, 285
Laurendeau, André, 282
Laurentian Shield, xi, 21, 77, 121, 134, 178, 182, 185, 196, 198, 251, 268
Laurentian thesis, xi, 6, 114, 115, 132, 154, 174, 178, 184, 195, 197, 199, 200, 201, 203, 215, 230, 268, 272, 287, 296, 301, 304, 324, 347, 389n90
Laurentide Ice Sheet, 225, 265
Laurier, Wilfrid, 42, 43, 63, 175, 176, 265, 303
Laurier House, 209, 223
Laval, Bishop, 162–3
Lawrence, D.H., 62
Leacock, Stephen, 88, 265
League for Social Reconstruction, 149, 210, 227
Lee, Dennis, 71
Lesage, Jean, 276, 280
Lévesque, René, 280, 328, 329, 330, 332, 333, 345
Lighthall, W.D., 41–2
limited identities, 291, 319
Lindsay, A.D., 75
Little Folks, 51, 52, 53, 245, 306
Livingstone, David, 245, 246, 251
Locke, George H., 68

Locke, John, 20, 21, 32, 168
Long, Marcus, 212, 213
Long Branch, 45–8, 50, 56, 67
Loos, Battle of, 55
Loti, Pierre, 97
Lower, Arthur, 8, 113, 129, 133, 169, 191, 202, 214, 219, 235–6, 264, 271, 272

MacArthur, General Douglas, 325
Macaulay, Thomas Babington, 90–1, 93, 268, 269
Macdonald, Ian, 276
Macdonald, Sir John A., 26, 31, 37, 42, 85, 105, 137, 146, 168, 171, 172, 189, 191, 195, 199, 217–18, 224, 230, 232, 235, 238, 258, 259, 260, 266, 268, 269, 274, 275, 277, 281, 284, 285, 287, 288, 290, 291, 301, 303, 307, 318, 333, 339, 345. *See also Sir John A. Macdonald*
MacKay, Louis, 75, 107
MacKay, Robert, 143–4
MacKenzie, Alexander, 260
MacKenzie, Larry, 150
Mackintosh, W.A., 114
MacLennan, Hugh, 176, 198, 330
Macmillan, Daniel, 177
Macmillan, Harold, 7, 238–9, 241, 242, 243, 246, 254, 255, 256, 258, 289
Macpherson, C.B., 10
Maggs, Arnaud, 347
Maheux, Abbé Arthur, 163
Maple Leaf flag, 7, 260, 326, 330. *See also* flag debate; Red Ensign
Marion, Séraphin, 8, 398n41
Marshall, John, 170
Martin, Chester, 143–4, 145, 207, 231
Massey, Raymond, 88, 89
Massey, Vincent, 76, 88, 103, 104, 198, 246
Mathiez, Albert, 106, 108
Matté, Lucien, 276

Mau Mau, 245, 248
McCall, Christina, 8
McClelland, Jack, 181, 215, 323, 324, 334
McDougall, Donald, 88, 209
McGill University, 167, 173
McInnis, Edgar, 214
McLaughlin, Ken, 311
McLuhan, Marshall, 10
McNaught, Ken, 210, 233
McWhinney, Ted, 276, 278, 280
Mealing, Stan, 268
Meighen, Arthur, 150, 190, 198
Meisel, John, 276, 278, 279
Mencken, H.L., 63, 68, 71, 74, 374n27
Methodism, 22–26, 32–3, 43–5, 63, 86, 94–5
Methodist Church of Canada, 5, 23, 32, 33, 36, 37, 43–5, 49, 55, 56, 221
Middlesex County, ON, 17–18
Miller, J.R., 311, 312, 313
Mitchell, W.O., 176
Moe, Henry Allen, 143
Monckton, Walter, 245–6, 247, 248, 254, 255
Monckton Commission, 4, 239–256, 258, 262, 264, 288
Moore, Christopher, 271
Morton, Desmond, 8
Morton, W.L., 114, 132, 192, 216, 235, 263, 264, 271, 276, 282–3, 285, 286, 304, 313, 314, 324, 333
Mowat, Oliver, 184, 197, 218
"Music in the Park," 259
Muskoka, Lake, xi, 53, 54, 56, 77, 82, 121, 122, 134, 195, 196, 215, 226, 234, 239, 261, 267, 287, 309, 315, 336
"My Father Took a Cake to France," 348

Nasser, Gamal Abdel, 218, 220, 221
Neatby, Hilda, 162, 191, 202, 224, 304

Nelles, Samuel, 32, 33
Nelles, Viv, 311, 312, 321
Newbigin, Marion, 115
Newman, Peter, 329, 330, 332, 343
Nora, Pierre, 321
Norman, Herbert, 220–1, 222
Norman, Howard, 221
North Dorchester, Township of, ON, 18–19, 28
Nowlan, George, 216, 230
Nuffield Foundation, 179

Olivier, Louis Auguste, 274
Ontario Advisory Committee on Confederation, 276–80, 285
Ormsby, Margaret, 271
Orwell, George, 269
Other Quiet Revolution, 4, 259, 263, 270
Oxford University, 7, 44, 68, 69, 75, 76, 77, 84, 85, 86, 87, 88, 89, 90, 91, 92, 94, 100, 101, 102, 103–5, 111, 177, 179, 186, 193, 232, 260, 296, 336, 346

Pacey, Desmond, 66, 180
Page, Donald, 311
Parkman, Francis, 123, 131, 162, 171
Passchendaele, 54, 55, 57–8, 60, 143, 149
Patterson, A.P., 138
Pearson, Lester, 73, 103, 104, 190, 212, 215, 219, 220, 221, 227, 237, 260, 262, 263, 264, 265, 266, 284, 288, 302–3, 306, 336, 341
Pickersgill, Jack, 325
Piepenberg, Willard, 217, 218, 220
Pierce, Lorne, 74, 190
Porter, Anna, 336
Pound, Ezra, 62, 68, 71, 75, 105
Poundmaker, 160, 318
Prang, Margaret, 223, 231, 232, 291, 312
Pratt, E.J., 65, 66, 71, 289

"Prelude," 118, 300–1
Preparatory Committee for an Eleventh
    Province, 332
Priestly, J.B., 189
printers' strike, 1872, 168, 400n69
Prison Gate Mission and Haven, 27, 28
professionalization of history, 89, 113,
    124, 133, 167, 232
Proust, Marcel, 9, 62
Purdy, Al, 71

Queen Mother, 142, 146, 254
Queen's University, 236, 282, 319
Quiet Revolution, 4, 258, 263, 266, 268,
    270, 330

Rassemblement pour l'Indépendence
    Nationale, 258, 264
Ray, Man, 105
Ray, Margaret, 289
Red Ensign, 262, 263, 265, 326. *See also*
    flag debate; Maple Leaf flag
Rhodes House, 193
Rhodes Scholarship, 71, 75, 76, 86, 88
Rice, Elmer, 74, 75
Richardson, James, 286, 287
Richardson, Mrs James A., 214–15
Riel, Louis, 160, 197, 198–200, 284–5,
    318, 330, 407n77
Ring Cycle, 9, 128–9, 301–3, 311. *See
    also* Wagner, Richard
Ritchie, Charles, 87, 94, 100, 104
Road to Confederation, The, 9, 10, 235,
    257, 267–74, 277, 288, 301, 343
Robarts, John, 276, 278
Roberts, Barbara, 318–19
Roberts, Charles G.D., 42
Roberts, John, 333
Robertson, George, 316–17
Robertson, Gordon, 88

Robertson, Heather, 335
Rockefeller Foundation, 143, 169–70,
    192, 210, 215, 235
Ross, George W., 279
Rowell, Newton, 137
Royal Commission on Bilingualism and
    Biculturalism, 260, 266, 333
Royal Commission on Dominion-
    Provincial Relations, 7, 135, 137, 139,
    148, 152, 334
royal tour (1939), 142, 146
royal tour (1959), 263
royal visit (1964), 263–4, 267, 280–1
Rusk, Dean, 215
Russell, Peter, 271
Rutherford, Paul, 311
Rutledge, Mary, 226
Ryan, Claude, 271, 281, 282
Ryerson, Stanley, 167, 168, 442n28
Ryerson Press, 74, 118, 124, 190

Sanders, Sarah Luella, 77, 79, 298, 348
Sassoon, Sigfried, 57
Saunders, Dick, 310
Saywell, Jack, 216, 218, 219–20, 224, 233–4
Scott, F.R., 103, 167, 333, 341
Séguin, Roger, 276, 278, 279
Seligman, Ellen, 336
settler contract, 255, 256
Shakespeare, William: *Julius Caesar*, 343;
    King Lear, 4, 193; *Richard III*, 193;
    Romeo and Juliet, 65, 82, 84
Shelley, Percy Bysshe, 67
Shotwell, James, 117, 118, 123, 124,
    143–4
Sidney Smith Hall, 309–10
Simpson, Napier, 287, 337
Sinclair, Gordon, 198
Sir John A. Macdonald, 7, 9, 10, 172,
    175–6, 178–9, 182–5, 187, 188, 190–2,

195–203, 211, 216, 221, 222, 225, 228, 229, 253, 267, 277, 288, 308, 318, 325, 343, 346; John Diefenbaker gives as a gift, 7, 289. *See also* Macdonald, Sir John A.
Sirois, Joseph, 137, 140
Skelton, Alex, 135, 137, 138, 140
Skelton, O.D., 176, 211, 256, 265
Skilling, Gordon, 165
Smart Set, The, 63
Smith, Albert J., 272
Smith, Denis, 263, 326
Smith, George, 65, 100, 101, 102
Smith, Goldwin, 265
Smith, Sidney, 207, 208, 214
Soldiers of the Soil, 59
Sorbonne, 6, 100, 105, 106, 111, 346
South Africa, 39, 42, 165, 237, 238, 239, 243, 255, 256–7
Soward, Fred, 326
Spencer, Robert, 218
Spengler, Oswald, 11, 42, 128, 320
Spring, David, 231
Spry, Graham, 228, 230
Spry, Irene, 166
St Francis Xavier University, 288
St Laurent, Louis, 188, 219, 221, 235, 241, 302–3, 325
St Lawrence River, xi, 97, 114, 115, 116, 134, 137, 140, 146, 161, 164, 178, 182, 184, 185, 193, 197, 199, 203, 230, 235, 237, 263, 268–9, 302, 327, 339, 345
St Paul's Anglican Cemetery, Brooklin, ON, 348–9
St Thomas' Anglican Church, Brooklin, ON, 322, 342
Stacey, C.P., 8, 130, 191, 198, 200, 221–2
Stanley, G.F.G., 191, 198, 199, 213
Statten, Taylor, 59
Stein, Gertrude, 105

Stouffer, Mary Ann, 80
Stone, C.G., 90
Stopes, Marie, 112, 384n3
Story of Canada, The, 234, 235–6, 264
Strachey, Lytton, 62, 175, 202, 203
Strong-Boag, Veronica, 8
Student Christian Movement, 71, 72, 84
Suez Crisis, 218–21, 222, 238, 241
Sumner, B.H., 100
Swerling, Boris, 228
Swift, Jonathan, 64
Symons, Scott, 262, 264, 343
Symons, T.H.B., 232, 263, 276, 278, 280

Takeover, 328, 336–41, 346
Tamlaght O'Crilly, Northern Ireland, 15, 16, 18, 37, 363n4
Taylor, Charles, 343
Tennyson, Alfred, 41, 50, 104, 306, 343
terra nullius, 251
Thompson, John Herd, 324
Thomson, Tom, 6, 267
Thornton, Archie, 310
Thucydides, 267
Tilley, Leonard, 155, 268
Trent, John, 282
Trent University, 167, 173
Trevelyan, G.M., 12
Trudeau, Pierre, 7, 259, 262, 283, 332, 334, 345
Trudel, Marcel, 324
Tucker, Albert, 268
Tucker, Gilbert, 130, 131
Tulchinsky, Gerald, 133
Tupper, Charles, 268
Turn East, Turn West, 180, 208–9
Turner, Frederick Jackson, 321

Underhill, Frank, 10, 69, 101, 103, 104, 105, 114, 130, 145, 148–51, 152, 154,

165, 176, 209–11, 214, 216, 217, 218, 223–4, 227, 231, 233, 236–7, 238, 261, 325, 336, 340–1
United College, 233, 285, 325
University of British Columbia, 120, 135
University of Cambridge, 179, 186, 193, 296
University of New Brunswick, 150, 172
University of Ottawa, 221, 223
University of Saskatchewan, 101, 156, 171, 313
University of Toronto, 4, 5, 27, 28, 69, 76, 86, 88, 89, 90, 91, 100, 101, 104, 105, 106, 107, 111, 117, 120, 144, 148, 149, 150, 170, 173, 179, 175, 186, 190, 207, 212, 215, 231, 232, 233, 234, 235, 267, 276, 285, 296, 309, 336, 345
University of Victoria, 288
Urquhart, F.F., 90

Vallières, Pierre, 259
Vancouver Women's Caucus, 300
Victoria, Queen, 24, 41, 185, 203, 258, 287
Victoria College, 5, 6, 32, 33, 34, 55, 62, 72, 75, 78, 81, 84, 96, 147, 221, 222, 289, 336
Victoria Falls Hotel, 246, 248
Vimy Ridge, 55, 143, 225

Wagner, Richard, 9, 93, 121, 128–9, 301, 302, 311, 322, 343. *See also* Ring Cycle

Watkins, Mel, 306
Waugh, Evelyn, 94, 102
Welensky, Roy, 239, 241, 246, 247, 251, 255
Wesley, Charles, 86
Wesley, John, 22, 86, 95
Wesley's Chapel, London, England, 95
Whitaker, Reg, 325
White Niggers of America, 259
Wilkinson, 207, 209, 217
Wilson, Alan, 231, 232
Wilson, Harold, 82, 92, 114, 135, 155, 172, 245, 275, 336
Wilson, Isabel, 5, 35, 40, 42, 43, 45, 50, 52, 58, 63, 73, 82, 112, 120, 121, 135, 155, 171–2, 195, 245, 275, 306, 315, 336, 345
Wise, S.F., 293
Wodehouse, P.G., 64
Women's Foreign Missionary Society, 26–7
Woodcock, George, 11, 305
Woodside, Moffat, 209, 214, 233
Woolf, Virginia, xi, 118, 121, 175, 203, 300
Wrong, George, 68, 69, 70, 74, 75, 89, 100, 146
Wrong, Hume, 69, 70, 76, 101

Zaslow, Morris, 231
Zola, Émile, 9, 10, 62, 66, 91, 93, 97